MAGIC IN H

CW00538917

The Bathhouse at Midnight

AN HISTORICAL SURVEY OF MAGIC AND DIVINATION IN RUSSIA

W.F. RYAN

SUTTON PUBLISHING

First published in the United Kingdom in 1999 by
Sutton Publishing Limited · Phoenix Mill
Thrupp · Stroud · Gloucestershire · GL5 2BU

British Library Cataloguing in Publication Data
A catalogue record for this book is available from the British Library.

ISBN 0-7509-2110-2 (hb)
ISBN 0-7509-2111-0 (pb)

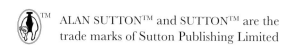

ALAN SUTTON™ and SUTTON™ are the
trade marks of Sutton Publishing Limited

Typeset in 10/12pt Baskerville.
Typesetting and origination by
Sutton Publishing Limited.
Printed in Great Britain by
Redwood Books, Trowbridge, Wiltshire.

CONTENTS

ACKNOWLEDGEMENTS

This book has been compiled over some thirty years and I should like to express my thanks to the following who, either in discussion or by correspondence, have helped me in one way or another, great or small, to complete it: the late Anne Pennington, Charles Schmitt and Boris Unbegaun; Adelina Angusheva-Tihanova, Florentina Badalanova, Charles Burnett, A. V. Chernetsov, Charles Drage, Simon Franklin, Georgette Donchin, Lindsey Hughes, Linda Ivanits, Edward Kasinec, Francis Knowles, Lauren Leighton, Christopher Ligota, Mahmoud Manzalaoui, Caroline Oates, A. B. Ostrovskii, Isabel de Madariaga, Ihor Ševčenko, John Simmons, Jeffrey Spier, Amitai Spitzer, Yuri Stoyanov, Moshe Taube, Boris Uspenskii, Faith Wigzell; the contributors to the 'Magic and Divination' seminar at the Warburg Institute, and, not least, my wife Janet Hartley for historical advice, proof-reading, and adamantly insisting on a completion date. They are, of course, in no way responsible for any failures of concept or defects and infelicities of text. I must also thank the editors of the *Oxford Slavonic Papers* and the *Slavonic and East European Review* and the Council of the Society for the History of Alchemy and Chemistry, which publishes *Ambix*, for permission to include material which appeared in an earlier form in their journals. The book could not have been completed without the generous financial assistance of the Leverhulme Trust, which enabled me to take a year of sabbatical leave in 1997–8 as a Leverhulme Research Fellow, and the forbearance of my colleagues at the Warburg Institute, in particular the Deputy Librarian John Perkins, who have shouldered whatever burdens my absence has caused.

W.F. Ryan
Warburg Institute
School of Advanced Study
University of London
September 1998

LIST OF ILLUSTRATIONS

INTRODUCTION

This book has grown out of material which I collected for my Oxford doctoral dissertation on Old Russian astrological and astronomical terminology,[1] and for a series of articles on the history of science and magic texts in Russia. I had originally intended producing a study of the tradition of divinatory and 'occult' texts and their language in Old Russian literature, and this philological approach will still be evident in much of the book. It soon became clear, however, that a study of the written tradition alone would produce a distorted picture, in view of the constant interaction of the oral and written traditions in magic and divination.[2] It was also urged on me that non-russophone and non-specialist readers would be interested and that a more general historical survey might be welcomed, the more so in that no such general survey has so far been attempted,[3] and Western scholarship on post-classical magic, witchcraft and divination in Europe, apart from a few specialized monographs, has little to say about Russia.

The decision to write a general historical survey for an English readership in turn made it necessary to include where possible a comparative element and bibliographical references to material in English and other Western European languages, as well as translations and summaries of some texts. Some comparative element in any case became desirable since the banal truth soon became obvious, that there are few magical texts, practices, beliefs or objects which are exclusive to Russia or even the Slavs, or for that matter anywhere else: after allowing for elements of natural selection as a result of local climate, flora, fauna, language and historical circumstance,[4] most things can be seen either to derive from, or have an analogue or cognate in other cultures. For Russia the sources and analogues must usually be sought in late antiquity by way of Byzantium, and at a later date medieval Western Europe, with some Jewish influence. Finno-Ugrian, Central Asian, and direct Arabic influence are less apparent (with some local exceptions). For popular magic and divination the comparatively well researched areas of Balkan, Greek, Scandinavian, German, Anglo-Saxon and English beliefs and practices offered many useful points of comparison. In finding analogies I have not disdained the older antiquarian literature, although I have usually made some reference to the reliability or otherwise of such sources. At the same time, I am very aware of the fact, cogently expressed by Richard Kieckhefer,[5] that while analogues may help to illustrate the history of an idea, they do not necessarily contribute to the analysis of a particular historical text, practice, event or setting.

Insofar as there are elements of recorded folklore (here taken broadly to mean popular belief and practice, and oral literature) in the book, I have tried to bear in mind the strictures of the folklorist Alan Dundes, who has drawn attention to two 'erroneous assumptions' which may be made about any given item of folklore: the first, that it may be peculiar to one culture, he ascribes to some schools of anthropology; the second, that it is universal, he ascribes typically to the literary or psychologically oriented student.[6] I hope that this book will not go to either of these two extremes, although it may fall into the third error castigated by Dundes, that of being too descriptive and insufficiently analytical. I have tried also to keep before me the warning of my teacher and dissertation supervisor the late Boris Unbegaun (to a large extent the instigator of the research which led to this book, which he approvingly described as 'academic depravity'): 'La folklore toutefois, en tant que manifestation mouvante et instable de la vie populaire, ne peut être utilisée qu'avec une extrême prudence.'[7]

I must also enter the caveat that it is not the purpose of this book to attempt any kind of anthropological analysis of the magic and divination of Russia, the fieldwork for which, for a foreigner, has been almost impossible for the last seventy years, and for which in any case I have no specialist training.[8] Nor will the book offer any new solution to the old and vexed question of what magic is, and if, or how, it differs from religion, beyond perhaps remarking that the goals of Russian magic, as of magic anywhere else, are in the vast majority of cases the expression of personal desires for sex, power, wealth, revenge, relief from sickness or protection from harm or someone else's magic, while religions, even at their most unlovely, usually have social, ethical, spiritual and numinous aspects which transcend individual aspirations. In general the many attempts to define and classify magic and religion can be put into two categories. The first is the belligerently rationalist, paradoxically allied in this with the eclectic 'New Age', and the views of some anthropologists, in which magic and religion are regarded as essentially the same phenomenon – a good proportion of Soviet writing fell into this category, as do many 'New Age' effusions, albeit with a different emphasis. The second is the more common binary approach in which magic as seen as 'alternative religion', the 'other side of the coin' of religion, or as a corruption of it, or as parasitic to it, or as a deviation from a spiritual or social norm, or as a semiotic system of oppositions. A recent thoughtful attempt to defend a qualified binary approach remarks ruefully: 'Scholars in earlier decades of this century were luckier: they knew both what magic was and how to find it. They simply opposed its characteristics to those of either science or religion, which they knew as well'.[9]

David Aune reviewed the extensive Western debate on this subject in his 'Magic in Early Christianity' (1980) and offered his own working definition: 'Magic is defined as that form of religious deviance whereby individual or social goals are sought by means alternate to those normally sanctioned by the dominant religious institution.'[10] Most attempts to come to terms with the sameness or distinctness of concepts of magic and religion suffer to some extent from ethno- or culturocentricity, perhaps inevitably so: almost all can be made to fit the evidence at most points, and almost all break down at some points in specific cases. The semiotics of belief systems (and this taxonomically useful term also begs questions) and the comparative semantics of the magical terminology of different languages may look similar in outline but can be crucially different in detail (for illustration of this point see Ch. 3.1). It is a convenience for anyone looking at magic and religion in the Russian context that the cultural semioticians Lotman and Uspenskii and others associated with the so-called Moscow-Tartu School and the Institute of Slavonic and Balkan Studies in Moscow have dealt on several occasions with the kind of material which is surveyed in several of the chapters in this book.[11] The approach to cultural analysis ('secondary modelling systems') of these Russian scholars is also binary, being derived primarily from linguistic models,[12] and is very seductive in one respect: it can be used to organize evidence without the use of culturally or morally loaded terminology, even if one feels that cultural history must surely be more complicated than binary models, and suspects that the search for an objective and culturally neutral standpoint is ultimately a waste of time. Unfortunately, the emphasis on 'ethnogenesis' and 'ethnolinguistics', which is evident in some Russian writing in this field, tends to deprive it of the insights which a more broadly based comparative method might have offered.

It must also be said that convenient but risky binary oppositions such as high/low, written/oral widely used in literary and historical scholarship both within and outside Russia, run into particular difficulties in this area of Russian cultural history, as Faith Wigzell has pointed out in her study of Russian fortune-telling books.[13] Certain distinctive features of Russian cultural history are relevant here. One is the fact that printing, introduced into Muscovy in the sixteenth century, remained in official (Church or State) hands, or was subject to censorship for most of the time until very recently. Perhaps as a result of this there has always been a flourishing manuscript (later typescript) culture in Russia. This was a vehicle for heterodox texts of all kinds, including imported literature (it has been calculated that there were more manuscript than printed copies of works of Voltaire in eighteenth-century Russia); in particular it was the chief method of publication of the various millenarian Old Believer sects, whose scriptoria survive to this day. In consequence there are curious examples of ideas and texts moving from the oral tradition into the manuscript tradition, then into the world of printed books, then back again.[14] A good deal of the considerable quantity of catchpenny popular folk magic and medicine being published in Russia at present may indeed have been collected *viva voce*, but much of the detail is recognizably that of nineteenth-century printed books which is being more or less cynically recycled. The eclecticism and constant cultural repositioning possible in this situation, even without commercial exploitation, can defy tidy analysis, as, for example, when one reaches the tertiary level of the oral-to-written tradition which can be discerned in the case of omens from itches, sneezes, etc. The history of modern-period occultism and the printing and dissemination of modern-period fortune-telling books is not examined in detail in this book.[15]

To return to the religion–magic distinction, Aune's broad definition of magic and religion in the period of early Christianity, quoted above, is sometimes apt when applied to the material under discussion in this book, but more often the notion of 'deviance' immediately causes further problems of definition. The practitioners and consumers of many kinds of magic throughout Europe, and certainly in Russia, have frequently been in fact the clergy of the 'dominant religious institution'; and it is often impossible to draw a generally acceptable dividing line with regard to either form or function between, say, an 'orthodox' prayer and a 'magic' prayer, or an icon and an amulet. Moreover, divination falls only partly into the field of magic thus defined. Kieckhefer in his book *Magic in the Middle Ages* has a thoughtful and detailed discussion of definitions of magic and settles for a series of perspectives, of which he prefers, for the purpose of his own subject area, the old distinction of natural and demonic, as understood by the intellectuals of the late medieval period, as a starting point for a more nuanced treatment of particular points. I would not dissent from this approach to the subject. The same kind of problem of definition arises with the definition of witchcraft – as Gábor Klaniczay has put it: 'The wide array of theoretical explanatory tools and comparative sets stands in puzzling contrast to the ease with which each general proposition can be contradicted'.[16]

When in doubt as to what should be included in this survey and what left out, I have usually erred on the side of inclusiveness – I have not, for example, excluded astrology and alchemy – and in general I have emphasized description at the expense of theory and classification; when faced with everyday objects or texts used as amulets, and ritual objects used as mere decoration, with any number of subjective gradations in between, it seems to be the most practical approach. I have also tried to emphasize cultural perspective and terminology. One must feel great sympathy for the eighteenth-century Russian peasant who, when accused in court, like Apuleius before him, of trying to win the love of a widow by magic (in this case whispering over a bottle and then giving her a drink from it), protested in his defence that he did not know that this was magic (see p. 422 below). This was, of course, a poor defence, and I, like the court, have duly recorded the incident as an example of the use of magic – but it also illustrates clearly the problem of cultural perspectives and semantics in this area.

The decision to include at least an outline of popular magic, magic medicine, and witchcraft presented particular difficulties. The whole area of 'witchcraft studies', which has developed and matured remarkably, mostly in Western Europe, in the last few decades, has largely ignored Russia and has had little influence in Russian scholarship.[17] The material for popular magic has often to be culled from accounts in works which are outdated in approach or not of a scholarly nature, most of it in Russian, and much of it difficult of access. Moreover, the commonest official view during most of the Soviet period – that magic and religion were either part of the old order and not worth discussing, or superstitious relics of that order which had to be extirpated – discouraged or distorted research into what people actually believe and do, so that new contributions to the subject were sparse. This is not to say that the subject was ignored – simply that much scholarship has, until quite recently, been unable to separate analysis from political propaganda and social re-education.[18]

One solution for some Soviet scholars was a kind of hearty slavophil neo-paganism, a *fol'kloristika* which would please the authorities by being scornful of official religion in the approved manner, but defend the intrinsic interest of the subject by emphasizing the robust poetry of indigenous pagan mythology and the earthy wisdom and patriotism of the Russian peasant.[19] The self-congratulating nationalism of this approach (which had little to do with Marxism and a great deal to do with nineteenth-century populist thought, pre-revolutionary official Holy Russia propaganda, and early twentieth-century esotericism) together with the enforced cultural isolation of Soviet scholarship in the Stalin period and its aftermath, meant that few scholars knew what was happening outside the Soviet Union, and even fewer risked referring to foreign research except to condemn it. Much of the more valuable Soviet writing on the subject of magic was in fact produced under the headings of archaeology, literature, semiotics, and folk medicine or folklore. I have not thought it appropriate here to go into the history of Russian theoretical scholarship on the subject to any large extent: the successive and often overlapping schools, from all-embracing mythologism, to the historical, comparative historical, semiotic, and ethnolinguistic, are a subject in themselves and have an internal dynamic which has developed within a distinguished academic and intellectual tradition which has nevertheless only occasionally impinged on schools of thought which have developed in other parts of the world.[20]

With divination the problem is not so much of concept as of classification, although even here difficulties arise. Although it is fairly easy to see that most divination is an attempt to predict an outcome or reach a correct decision rather than to produce a result, the means of achieving a prediction may differ little from the magic employed to obtain a result or prevent a prediction from being realized. At another level, it is frequently difficult to distinguish between divination and games, or popular pastimes and seasonal festivities; and to what extent are weather and crop predictions divination or prognosis based on past observation; and is physiognomy a form of divination or a protoscience? Here too I have been inclusive, even discursive. Most recent classifications of divination have been conceptual;[21] while in no way dissenting from this approach and having no wish to go to the other extreme of Rabelais's preposterous list of 'mancies, I have, as with magic, allowed the availability of evidence and the convenience of composition to guide my presentation of the material.

And the last difficulty is perhaps the greatest: what do I mean by Russia? Even the area inhabited by speakers of Great Russian in modern times is not a single cultural entity, and Russia viewed historically is even more difficult to pin down. In fact I have taken as my cultural area the Orthodox East Slavs of Kiev Rus' and their descendants, roughly speaking the Great Russians (including the Russian population of Siberia), Ukrainians and Belorussians, with a heavy emphasis on Muscovite and Imperial Russia.

What is attempted here then is a fairly detailed account of the magical and divinatory texts in the East Slavonic languages and Church Slavonic (up to the eighteenth century for the most part) and a more general overview of popular magic, divination and witchcraft. This in turn has prompted a structure which offers first a general historical survey, then chapters devoted to different areas of magic and divination. The division by chapter is largely determined by the nature and quantity of the material available and is not to be regarded as a classification; some subjects could easily be treated under more than one of the chapter headings chosen and a considerable amount of cross-referencing has been necessary to avoid undue repetition.

It is told that St Leo, when writing a treatise against the heretic Nestorius, left his manuscript overnight lying on a relic of St Peter, and in the morning found that his text had been corrected.[22] I am not sure whether this should be classified as religion, magic, or experimental science, but I have to say that no such saintly assistance has been available to me (apart, of course, from the much-tested patience of my wife and children), and I can only apologize for any inaccuracies in this book and attribute them to a malignant *bannik* resentful of this foreign intrusion into his world.

Notes

1. Ryan, 'Astronomical and Astrological Terminology in Old Russian Literature'.

2. Valerie Flint, in her *The Rise of Magic in Early Modern Europe*, pp. 37–8, has made this point convincingly for Western Europe.

3. At the level of oral literature, folklore and custom the pioneering work of the eighteenth century was that of the industrious M. Chulkov, who published periodicals, tales, songs, a guide to Russian provincial fairs, a history of Russian trade, a medical and veterinary handbook for country folk, Petrarch translations, legal and mythological dictionaries, and, most importantly, the dictionary of Russian folk customs, superstitions, magic and divination, the *Slovar' russkikh sueverii, idolopoklonnicheskikh zhertvoprinoshenii, svadebnykh prostonarodnykh obriadov, koldovstva, shemanstva, i proch.* (Moscow, 1772; the second edition appeared as *Abevega ruskikh sueverii, idolopoklonnicheskikh zhertvoprinoshenii, svadebnykh prostonarodnykh obriadov, koldovstva, shemanstva, i proch.*, Moscow, 1786). This was utilized by the authors of many later popular works, and may well have been one of the sources for chapter 5 of Pushkin's *Eugene Onegin* (see Ch. 4.3 below). Works of a more scholarly kind were to follow in the nineteenth century: Snegirev, *Russkie prostonarodnye prazdniki i suevernye obriady* (1837–9); Sakharov, *Skazaniia russkogo naroda* (1885 and later editions); Tereshchenko, *Byt russkogo naroda* (1847–8). These were conservative antiquarian works. The first attempt at a theoretical synthesis, and the major work of the Russian mythological school, was Afanas'ev's, *Poeticheskie vozzreniia slavian na prirodu* (1866–9) (this provided much of the material for Ralston's misleadingly titled *The Songs of the Russian People* (2nd edn, 1872), the only published survey in English before Ivanits (see below)). Two detailed works with strong comparative elements by Mansikka are also important, although not much less dated, and were much criticized at one time on theoretical grounds: *Über russische Zauberformeln* (1909) and *Der Religion der Ostslaven* (1921). The mythological approach has never quite disappeared, and has at present some distinguished exponents, but more ethnographic approaches fitted Marxist ideology better in the Soviet period – for example, the 'history of labour' approach of Chicherov,

Zimnii period russkogo narodnogo zemledel'cheskogo kalendaria XVI–XIX vekov (1957). Bogatyrev's, *Actes magiques, rites et croyances en Russie Subcarpathique* (1929), is a survey of popular magic in an area on the westernmost edge of East Slav territory. It offers many analogies with Great Russian practices and contains bibliographies of magic arranged by type at pp. 84–91; 99–101; 110–1; 126–8. Later Soviet work tended to be more specialized and narrower in scope and will be referred to as the occasion demands. Since the end of the Soviet regime there has been an upsurge in interest in magic characterized by a spate of catchpenny fortune-telling books, reprints of nineteenth-century classics such as Afanas'ev, publications of important rare or hitherto unavailable works by Zelenin and Eleonskaia from the early part of this century, and a number of serious new contributions to the general field of folk belief. A modern survey in English of Great Russian folk beliefs with a rather condensed but very useful discussion of sorcery, witchcraft and divination is Ivanits, *Russian Folk Belief* (1989). For popular fortune-telling books of the modern period (eighteenth century onwards) and their social significance see Wigzell, *Reading Russian Fortunes*.

On the text-historical aspects of the subject the main authorities are still the pre-Revolutionary scholars A. N. Veselovskii (who also wrote extensively on comparative folklore with a strong textual bias), A. N. Pypin, A. I. Sobolevskii, N. Tikhonravov, dated though they may be. Recent surveys of Old Russian texts in English are Ryan, 'Magic and Divination' and Mathiesen, 'Magic in Slavia Orthodoxa'. An increase of interest recently has produced a series of journal articles which will be mentioned in their place. On the history of science aspects of the subject Soviet scholars were more active: see in particular the entries in the bibliography for Peretts, Rainov, Raikov, and more recently Chernetsov, Simonov and Turilov.

4. By this I mean simply that, for example, the interpretation of a stove as an omen of grief depends on a Slavonic pun (*pech'/pechal'*) not duplicated elsewhere, that predictions relating to camels should not be expected in north Russia, while divinations involving holes in the ice will be found in both Scandinavia and Russia and are unlikely to be borrowings from Greek. But even these expectations can be confounded.

5. Kieckhefer, *Forbidden Rites*, p. 11.

6. Dundes, ed., *The Evil Eye. A Folklore Casebook*, pp. v–vi.

7. B.O. Unbegaun, 'La Religion des anciens slavs', p. 390.

8. After reading the intimidating review by Morton Smith of D. L. O'Keefe's *Stolen Lightning: The Social Theory of Magic* (New York, 1982) in the *Jewish Quarterly Review* (LXXIV, 3, 1984, pp. 301–12) I decided that one needs a more powerful talisman than I have discovered to risk crossing the boundaries of academic tribal territories in this matter.

9. Versnel, 'Some Reflections on the Relationship Magic – Religion', p. 178.

10. Aune, 'Magic in Early Christianity', p. 1515.

11. See in particular Lotman and Uspenskii, 'The Role of Dual Model in the Dynamics of Russian Culture (up to the end of the Eighteenth Century)' and *idem*, 'New Aspects in the Study of Early Russian Culture' (an assessment of Bakhtin's notion of 'carnivalization' and 'laughter culture' as applied to medieval Russia by Likhachev and Panchenko) in *idem*, *The Semeiotics of Russian Culture*, pp. 3–35, 36–52. For an account of Lotman's semiotics and its historical context see Ann Shukman, *Literature and Semeiotics*.

12. Without the synchronic-diachronic opposition but against a historical background which includes Marxist dialectic, Soviet Formalism, structuralism, the work of Propp in the field of folklore, and Bakhtin with his notions of dialogic text and the cultural role of carnival.

13. Wigzell, *Russian Fortune Telling*, introduction and *passim*. The point has been made more generally with regard to West European medieval culture by Valerie Flint: *The Rise of Magic in Early Modern Europe*, pp. 37–9.

14. The so-called 'urban myths' of the contemporary world may exhibit this characteristic. For a good nineteenth-century example of the confusion of written and oral traditions, and how this can be misconstrued in academic writing on the subject, see Ch. 6.6.

15. On the subject of eighteenth- and nineteenth-century urban fortune-telling, and the publishing history of divinatory compendia and chapbooks in Russia see the detailed study by Wigzell, *Reading Russian Fortunes*. For a wide-ranging collection of papers on Russian occultism, mostly of the twentieth century, see Rosenthal, ed., *The Occult in Russian and Soviet Culture*.

16. Klaniczay, 'Witch-hunting in Hungary', p. 67.

17. A good survey of the development of witchcraft studies up to 1987 may be found in the introductory chapter of Behringer, *Witchcraft Persecutions in Bavaria* (German original 1987, English version 1997). There is little general discussion in English of witchcraft in Russia, apart from a short section in Ralston and more recently in Ivanits. On Russian witchcraft trials see Russell Zguta, 'Witchcraft Trials in Seventeenth-Century Russia', now amplified by Kivelson, 'Through the Prism of Witchcraft'. This question has been further examined in a wider historical context by the author in Ryan, 'The Witchcraft Hysteria'. See also Worobec, 'Witchcraft Beliefs and Practices' for Russia and the Ukraine in the nineteenth century (this includes details of cases of persecution for witchcraft, with a tendency towards the 'battle of the sexes' interpretation, and information on alleged demonic possession and *klikushestvo*).

18. The works of Min'ko, for example, contain a good deal of interesting material on Belorussian folk beliefs and practices, mixed with ridicule of the gullible folk who accept them, demands for renewed educational efforts to eradicate them, and condemnation of Western bourgeois ruling cliques who allegedly promote magic, religion and alternative medicine as a palliative to the wretched lot of the working class.

19. A striking example of this genre from the 1980s is Rybakov, *Iazychestvo drevnykh slavian*.

20. Propp and Bakhtin, for example, are still in vogue in some circles in Western Europe and America, although their reception has been skewed by the limited availability of their work in translation.

21. I have in mind in particular the article on divination by Evan Zuesse in the *Encylopedia of Religion*, ed. M. Eliade, and Hullkrantz, 'Divinationsformer: en klassifikation'.

22. Recorded in Brewer, *A Dictionary of Miracles*, p. 465 and ascribed to Damasus, *Lives of the Popes* (presumably the *Liber pontificalis*, formerly attributed to Damasus, although I can find no such story there).

1
AN OUTLINE HISTORY

1. *Kiev Rus' and the 'Byzantine Heritage'*

The political history of the East Slavs (the Great Russians, Ukrainians, and Belorussians) can be crudely outlined in geographical and chronological terms without much difficulty, if not without argument. Their cultural history is a much more complicated thing. To borrow from the felicitous titles of two influential books, Kiev Rus' was part of the 'Byzantine Commonwealth' and Muscovite Russia was in some measure also a 'Byzance après Byzance'.[1] But what did this Byzantine connection mean? After the conversion of Rus' to Christianity it could have meant access to a cultural and literary tradition going back to classical antiquity, but this possibility was not realized to any significant extent. In fact the Russians were unfortunate in that the Byzantine cultural influence in Kiev Rus' did not extend much beyond the monastic sphere. And while Kiev's northern successor, Muscovite Russia, could eventually aspire, as the only major free Orthodox state after the fall of Byzantium in 1453, to the leadership of the Orthodox world and imperial status, it did not acquire many of the benefits of Byzantine high culture.

This was partly because, unlike the Western Church which, following the collapse of the Western Roman Empire, developed into a supra-national church with a supra-national language, offering any number of useful cultural by-products, the Eastern Orthodox Churches, despite the enormous pretensions and prestige of Byzantium, did not, and could not in the quite different historical circumstances, impose a common liturgical, ecclesiastical or canon law language. Greek did not become the ecclesiastical, cultural and administrative *lingua franca* of the Orthodox world to anything like the extent to which Latin dominated the West. Although Greek was for a time the liturgical language of the Bulgarians, Old Church Slavonic, a stylized form of a Macedonian dialect of Bulgarian, very soon became the liturgical and literary language of the South and East Slavs, with the result that Slav contact with Byzantine written culture had after a while to be maintained almost exclusively through the medium of translation.[2] Since the translators, and arbiters of what was proper to be translated, were clergy, it is perhaps not surprising that the fluctuating secular culture of Byzantium, and in particular the more sophisticated literary, philosophical or scientific texts in Greek, should not have been high in their scale of priorities.[3]

What Lemerle called the 'First Byzantine Humanism' of the ninth and tenth centuries left little mark on the Slavs,[4] and as Ihor Ševčenko has pointed out, the Orthodox Slavs translated fewer of the scientific and philosophical works available in Byzantium than did the Syrians, Arabs or Latins, and indeed no complete major work of Greek antique philosophy or science was translated, and no sophisticated ancient Greek or Byzantine work of history or literature (apart from works of Josephus and George of Pisidia) was available in Slavonic until comparatively modern times.[5] In Kiev Rus' knowledge of the culture, scholarship, philosophy and science of classical antiquity and Byzantium was available only through the medium of unscholarly works, mostly translated in Bulgaria in the tenth century. These were works such the *Physiologus*, or the *Christian Topography* of Cosmas Indicopleustes. Other fragments of knowledge were transmitted incidentally in translations of the Byzantine popular chronicles of John Malalas (sixth century) and George Hamartolos (ninth century), or the popular historical romance about Alexander the Great by pseudo-Callisthenes, or, more seriously, the *De bello judaico* of Flavius Josephus. Other sources were hagiographic and homilectic texts and exegetical literature (in particular in the exegesis of Genesis in several *Hexaemera*, i.e. commentaries on the six days of creation), and fragments, often simplified or garbled, of patristic writing gathered together in florilegia such as the two *Izborniki Sviatoslava* of 1073 and 1076.

It is entirely possible that this situation might have improved had it not been for the Mongol-Tatar invasion in the thirteenth century which completed the disintegration of the Kievan state of dynastically linked principalities after a decline which had begun in the twelfth century. Although there was some subsequent infusion of new translated literature from Bulgaria in the fourteenth century and from Serbia in the fourteenth and early fifteenth centuries,[6] the literary sources of scientific and pseudo-scientific ideas[7] were still for the most part low-brow Byzantine until the late fifteenth century,[8] and Russian culture can still be characterized as medieval (with some oriental elements) up to the end of the seventeenth century. Indeed, as a major contributor to the history of this subject has put it: 'Pour la littérature scientifique slave, le moyen âge ne prend fin en réalité qu'au debut du XVIII siècle'.[9]

Neither Kievan nor Muscovite Russia had an equivalent of scholasticism or Renaissance; there were no universities, only occasional schools, and no learned professions; there was little knowledge of Greek,[10] effectively none of Latin. Richard Kieckhefer, in his *Magic in the Middle Ages*, states that: 'One of the clearest distinctions between high and popular culture in medieval [Western] Europe is that intellectuals derived many of their conceptions of magic from their reading of classical literature'.[11] This was not so in Russia, and the situation was not much different among the Orthodox South Slavs. This makes an enormous difference at the level of major texts, which did not reach the Slavs, but as we shall see, the differences between Orthodox and Latin Europe at more popular levels, and at the level of ecclesiastical condemnation, are much smaller.

2. *After Kiev Rus'*

The successor states to Kiev Rus' after the Mongol period were Muscovy and the Grand Duchy of Lithuania. Moscow between the fourteenth and sixteenth centuries freed itself from Mongol overlordship and by degrees established control over Novgorod and the old principalities of central and northern Russia. By the middle of the fifteenth century Byzantium had fallen; the end of the seventh, and, if you followed the widespread chiliastic belief, last millennium was approaching, and in the minds and writings of some the notion of the *translatio imperii* to Moscow, the 'Third Rome' in the words of one polemical writer, had begun.[12] The 'Third Rome' was a politico-ecclesiastical, partly millenarian notion (it was also to be the *last* Rome); it has become something of a catchphrase for historians and organizers of conferences and exhibitions, but one should perhaps not exaggerate its importance as a coherent political or ecclesiastical doctrine. A marginally related and rather imprecise concept, the 'Second South Slavonic Influence', has been widely used in linguistic and literary scholarship. This implies a movement of people and ideas from the old world of Byzantium and the Balkans in the last days of the Byzantine empire to Russia in the north. (In fact it was generally the Orthodox zealots who looked to the north while the scholars found employment with humanist patrons in Italy.) Insofar as it affects the subject of this book, the 'Second South Slavonic Influence' meant an influx of popular divinatory texts and an intensification of apocalyptic modes of thought.

The remaining areas of Kiev Rus', the old south-western principalities in what is now the Ukraine and Belarus,[13] fell to the Grand Duchy of Lithuania, which brought them into the Polish sphere of cultural influence (this included not only Catholic but to some extent Protestant, Jewish, and Islamic elements) and thus into closer contact with Western Europe and its alternative classical, and classicizing, tradition. At the same time the closeness of this area to Muscovy in terms of a common religious, literary, and linguistic heritage made it an important link to the West. Indeed the 'Russia' of this book can at many points be thought of as a cultural continuum embracing the whole of the East Slav territory, or the greater part of what Riccardo Picchio has called *Slavia orthodoxa*.[14]

3. *Magic and the Orthodox Slavs*

The *Third Pskovian Chronicle*, *sub anno* 1570, states that Russians are 'deceivers and prone to witchcraft'.[15] And 'In no other quarter of Europe has magic, in all the various forms assumed by it from the dawn of history to the present day, exercised so great a sway as in the Balto-Slavic countries', wrote Schrader in the *Encyclopedia of Religion and Ethics*.[16] The value of such categorical statements is questionable, and with regard to 'learned' magic certainly untrue, but it does at least suggest that the perceived extent of the subject of this book is considerable.

The kind of magic which existed among the East Slavs before the coming of Christianity was, as far as one can tell, the shamanism of the *volkhvy*, with whom the Church and state authorities in Kiev Rus' struggled for a long time, and traces of which undoubtedly survived (see in particular Chs 2, 3, and 16), and still survive, in popular beliefs and practices.[17] In some cases these were simply reshaped into a 'Christian' model, a process well-known in other parts of Christendom. We have no record for the East Slavs of the kind of divination which is recorded for the Baltic Slavs by Saxo Grammaticus,[18] but perhaps some kind of numerical omen, as well as an apprehension of possible technical superiority, is in the mind of the author of the *Russian Primary Chronicle* when he reports the dismay of the Khazar elders, who had single-edged swords, when they saw the 'evil tribute' of two-edged swords offered by Polianian Slavs.[19]

The *Russian Primary Chronicle*, as well as subsequent Russian chronicles (almost all written in a monastic milieu), tells several more specific stories of magic. The most famous perhaps is found in the entry for the year 912 in which a magician foretold that the death of Prince Oleg of Kiev would be caused by his horse.[20] The horse died and Oleg laughed at the magician, but shortly afterwards he was bitten, with fatal consequences, by a snake which crawled out of the horse's skull.[21] This story is interesting in that it appears to justify the claims of magic and is in fact the occasion for a long and confused digression in the chronicle on the powers of Apollonius of Tyana, endorsed by St Anastasius, and on the magicians and seers mentioned in the Bible (Balaam, Saul, Caiaphas, Jude, the sons of Sceva, Nebuchadnezzar, Simon Magus, Menander) who are seen as bearing witness to the power of God. The conclusion, 'Of such men it has truly been said, "be not deceived by miracles"', is hardly consonant with what has gone before and the whole digression is a good example of the difficulties which religious writers and translators experienced in interpreting magical and divinatory episodes in scripture and early church history.[22]

A similar ambivalence about the powers of pagan magicians can be seen in the *Russian Primary Chronicle* entry for 1024 in which it is reported that magicians came to Suzdal', killed old people by the power of Satan and caused a famine by blighting the crops. Prince Iaroslav dispersed the magicians and punished some of them, saying 'In proportion to its sin, God inflicts upon every land hunger, pest, drought or some other chastisement, and man has no understanding thereof'.[23] In the entry for 1071 there is a further substantial section on magicians.[24] First there was one who foretold that the Dnieper would flow backwards and that countries, in particular Rus' and Greece, would change places. Next we are told of a number of magicians who stated that they worshipped the Antichrist and who were killing women on a large scale and claiming to be able to produce grain and fish from their bodies; these were executed by the Grand Prince's lieutenant with the comment that they were false prophets because they did not foresee their own fate – a motif not confined to Russia.[25] Then there was a Novgorodian who approached a Chud'[26] magician to have his fortune told but had to leave his cross outside the house because the magician's demons could not operate in its presence. Historical examples for the performance of magical marvels are quoted: Simon Magus,[27] Kynops,[28] Jannes and Jambres.[29] All these involve magical contests in which the ungodly magicians failed. We may note that in almost all cases the power of the magicians is described as demonic. The final example quoted, however, is once again an illustration of the inability of a magician to foretell his own death at the hands of his questioner: Prince Gleb killed him with an axe, thus falsifying the magician's prediction.[30]

The *Russian Primary Chronicle* entry for 1044, on the other hand, suggests that the princes of Kiev Rus' were not necessarily, or always, at odds with magicians. It states that Prince Vseslav of Polotsk was conceived by enchantment and born with a caul, and his mother was instructed by magicians to bind the caul to his head so that he might wear it for the rest of his life. This he did, says the chronicle, which is why he was so pitiless in bloodshed.[31] The chronicle does not comment on this blatant employment of pagan magicians by the wife of a ruling prince, nor on the lifelong wearing of an amulet by her son, nor on this apparent early manifestation of the Slavonic vampire tradition.[32] Moreover, in the *Tale of Prince Igor* (authenticity not universally accepted) Vseslav is described as being able to turn into a wolf or other wild beast, a characteristic of witches and magicians in later folk belief in Russia and elsewhere.

In applying what would nowadays be thought to be a double standard to magic the Kievan princes in no way differed from their Byzantine mentors: three examples from many possible are: (1) the emperor Constantine Porphyrogenitus, who showed no embarrassment in recommending that Byzantine emperors should take various divinatory books on their campaigns (see Ch. 14); (2) the early ninth-century Nikephoras who recorded as fact in his *Breviarium* that the monk Paul, who was an expert astrologer, foretold that Leontios would become emperor (in 695);[33] and (3) an episode in the autobiography of Nikephoras Blemmydes, the thirteenth-century ecclesiastic and scholar. In the last case Blemmydes described in his autobiography an incident in which a member of the empress's retinue tried to kill him but was unable to remove his sword from its scabbard. The courtier accused Blemmydes of witchcraft; Blemmydes for his part attributed the sticking sword to divine intervention.[34] Both, in other words, accepted as a fact that the sword had indeed been immobilized and that this was a supernatural occurrence. This example demonstrates neatly that the distinction between magic and religion may depend on a very slight shift in point of view.

The newer kinds of magic and divination which came to Russia as part of its Byzantine heritage were not, as I have indicated above, the learned treatises or mathematically complicated horoscopes of the Greek world. Nor, except in chance fragments, did the neo-Platonic tradition impinge on Russian consciousness. What Christianity did bring, through the Bible and patristic literature, was a familiarity at least with the popular notions of magic and divination prevalent in the ancient East and classical antiquity. Christians could read about sorcery and sorcerers in the Old and New Testaments, about Balaam, the Witch of Endor, Simon Magus; in hagiographic literature they could read about a wizard who became a bishop and a saint, in the person of St Cyprian of Antioch (c. 300), a magician who was thwarted by the sign of the cross while attempting to seduce a Christian virgin called Justina by demonic magic,[35] or the young man in the very popular pseudo-Amphilochian *Life of St Basil* who followed the advice of a magician and made a written pact with the Devil so that he could by magic entice into marriage a young woman intended for the cloister.[36]

The new Slav Christians also became familiar with the portent lore of the ancient world. The entry for the year 1064 in the *Russian Primary Chronicle* contains a substantial digression on portents: the appearance of a comet, described as a 'bloody star', a monstrously deformed child caught in nets by some fishermen, and a pallor on the sun, were followed by much strife and bloodshed. These are compared with the comets, visions of warriors in the sky, monstrous births, earthquakes, prophetic mules, the behaviour of birds, etc., which the author had gleaned from Josephus and the Byzantine chronographs, and which he firmly states to be presages of war, famine and death.

The 'Byzantine heritage' also brought on the back of Christianity a host of other un-Christian superstitious practices of the more popular kind: amulets, divination from thunder and lightning, animal auguries, predictions from involuntary movements, the belief in 'good and bad days', bibliomancy, pagan and quasi-Christian magic spells, and dice divination. And most of these, to judge from extant texts, are fairly late importations by way of the South Slavs and one must conclude that the colporteurs were the clergy, who until quite recent times continued to be practitioners in magic and divination among the East and South Slavs, both Orthodox and Catholic.[37]

Russian historians frequently characterize popular religion in Russia as part of *dvoeverie*, literally 'double belief', as if this was somehow exclusive to the region.[38] Sometimes this is defined as the coexistence of two separate belief systems, Christian and pagan, sometimes as the deliberate and simultaneous acceptance by communities of Christianity and paganism, sometimes as syncretism. Certainly the archaeological evidence from the first two or three centuries of Christianity in Russia shows a preponderance of pagan over Christian cult artefacts (e.g. amulets) at village level.[39] This is a complicated issue, but the evidence from other societies shows that Russia as a whole differs little from the rest of Christendom, Eastern or Western, in the matter.[40] It is worth making here an observation which, even if it will be obvious to some, it will be necessary to repeat at several points in this book: although it will be seen fairly clearly that much of the magic and divination of Russia, when viewed from the standpoint of extant texts and artefacts, can be traced back to late antiquity by way of Byzantium, it is also true that exactly the same kind of evidence from the same source can be found all over Europe, Catholic and Protestant, intermingled in the same way with official canonical religion. At the same time, as far as Muscovite Russia is concerned, it is also worth bearing in mind an apt comment made by Paul Bushkovitch in his *Religion and Society in Russia*: 'No presently known sources exist that could unambiguously reveal the beliefs and values of the greater part of the rural population'.[41] In other words, we cannot know how far the picture we can paint for ourselves from the fairly meagre historical records available to us corresponds with what people of different kinds, in different places, and at different times actually believed and did.

4. *The Written Tradition*

The various Russian chronicles and ecclesiastical texts such as lists of banned books and episcopal letters and penitentials give evidence of magical practice in early Russia, but this evidence is unreliable and misleading. The chronicle references have usually a polemic intent, and the canon law texts are for the most part translations from Greek which only occasionally give a clue to contemporary local practices among the Slavs. And while they do at least offer us the basic vocabulary of the subject, they do not provide magical or divinatory texts. For this we must look to the encyclopedic, or more exactly florilegistic tradition, which begins in Kiev Rus' in the eleventh century with the two *Izborniki* of Sviatoslav already mentioned, and continued to provide the main vehicle in post-Kiev Rus' for fragments of ancient scientific and pseudo-scientific information.

The most important manifestation of this tradition was the series of florilegia produced at the end of the fourteenth and in the first quarter of the fifteenth centuries by Kiril Belozerskii and his followers in the monastery founded by Kiril at Belozero in Novgorodian territory north-east of present-day St Petersburg.

One example is a manuscript which contains calendrical and eschatological information about the end of the millennium and the coming of the Antichrist, and the first medical text of any substance to appear in Russian ('Galen on Hippocrates' and 'Alexander' on conception and embryology, possibly derived either from the *Dioptra* of Philippos Monotropos or from a common source – this offers in dialogue form the doctrines of the four elements and the four humours, the macrocosm and microcosm, parts of the body, a definition of the role of the physician and medical and dietary advice for the four seasons; human conception and embryology); this is followed by a kind of lunar almanac giving the times of waxing and waning and eclipses, and a list of the hours in each day on which planting and sowing, pruning, tree-felling, slaughtering of cattle, bloodletting, haircutting, etc. may be done with advantage, with a list of days on which this should not be attempted. The manuscript also contains articles on the length and breadth of the earth, on the distance of the sky from the earth, on clouds, thunder and lightning, the four seas, the river which surrounds the earth, meteors.[42]

The Belozero tradition continues in the later part of the fifteenth century when the extensive florilegia of Efrosin provide us with a snapshot of the literature available in the monastic libraries of the north in that period. Efrosin was a monk and scribe (and, for a while in 1477, abbot) of the Kirillo-Belozerskii monastery.[43] He has been described, with careful accuracy, as 'a Russian contemporary of the Renaissance', a description he shares with the diplomat and state official Fedor Kuritsyn.[44] Of the two, Kuritsyn, author of the *Tale of Dracula*, is the more recognizable quasi-Renaissance figure and Efrosin is the monkish medieval encyclopedist, albeit with an eye for the exotic. Efrosin's miscellanies include whole texts or extracts from a very wide range of literature, orthodox biblical, patristic, hagiographic, homilectic and historical on the one hand, and on the other, notwithstanding the inclusion of indexes of banned books, a profusion of profane literature such as the *Alexander Romance, The Tale of Dracula, Solomon and Kitovras, Stefanit and Ikhnilat, Varlaam and Ioasaf, Physiologus,* 'Galen on Hippocrates' (as in the Kiril miscellany described above), and of apocryphal works such as the *Gospel of Nicodemus, The Twelve Dreams of Shakhaisha, The Twelve Fridays, The Sunday Letter* (the last two are later used as amulets – see Ch. 10), and of divinatory works such as the 'Good and Bad Days' and the *Koliadnik* (the Greek *Kalendologion,*which makes predictions based on the day of the week on which Christmas, or the New Year falls), which is actually listed as a banned book in the same manuscript.[45]

5. *Jewish and Oriental Influences*

In the late fifteenth and early sixteenth centuries this Byzantine encyclopedic tradition was supplemented by other texts from non-Byzantine sources. The greater part of this new material comes from the corpus of translations from Hebrew which was apparently made in the Grand Duchy of Lithuania, most probably in its Belorussian territory, and which has often been associated with the sect of Judaizers which flourished in Novgorod and Moscow at the turn of the fifteenth and sixteenth centuries.[46] This included two tracts on logic (one of which contains also a section on metaphysics), together with the *De sphera* of Sacrobosco and the *Six Wings* of Emmanuel Bonfils, the first concerned with astronomy and cosmography, and the second with calendar computation. The most important of these texts from the point of view of both science and magic and the extent of its dissemination and influence, was the pseudo-Aristotelian *Secretum secretorum*. To avoid repetition in later chapters, and since several different kinds of magic and divination are involved in this compendium, I shall go into some detail here.

The original *Secretum secretorum* was an Arabic 'Mirror of Princes' of the ninth or tenth century, an encyclopedia of advice on a variety of subjects ranging from statecraft to medicine and esoteric knowledge, purporting to have been written for Alexander the Great by Aristotle.[47] The Old Russian (or more properly Belorussian/Ukrainian) version was published by M.N. Speranskii in an often incomprehensible form in 1908.[48] This version was translated from a Hebrew version[49] of the so-called Short Form of the text,[50] probably at the end of the fifteenth century in the Grand Duchy of Lithuania, and was even more encyclopedic than the original in that it contained extensive interpolations, including three additional medical texts by Maimonides (*On Poisons, On Sexual Intercourse, On Asthma*),[51] the physiognomy from Rhazes's *Liber ad Almansorem*, a cure for Alexander's horse Dutsifal (Bucephalas),[52] and a 'Life of Aristotle' which is an epitome of the life by Diogenes Laertius.[53] All these interpolations except the last are to be found in all the complete manuscripts of the Old Russian text of the *Secretum*, usually in the same order, and may be assumed on linguistic grounds also to be part of the Hebrew text from which the Old Russian version was made. Since the medical interpolations are from Hebrew translations from the Arabic by members of the ibn Tibbon family and are consistent in terminology and style with their host text, the *Secretum*, it seems probable that this text too is a Tibbonid translation and not the work of al-Harizi as was assumed until comparatively recently.[54] From a chain of evidence which I have summarized elsewhere, it is not unreasonable to assume that the Old Russian translation was made before 1489; the circumstances of the translation, its possible connection with the so-called Judaizer heresy, and its links with other texts of the same period also apparently translated from Hebrew are still a matter for debate and further research.[55] The *Secretum* is notable in that it is not only a work which would appeal to Russians because of its association with the popular Alexander stories, but also because of its advocacy of astrology, and the fact that it contained an onomantic table for predicting the outcome of battles, the first alchemical text in Old Russian, a description of the magical properties of precious stones and magical talismans, and two separate works of physiognomy. It could, moreover, lay slightly more claim to intellectual respectability on a European scale – the only other derivative of the Hebrew version of the *Secretum* is a Latin translation published by Alessandro Achillini (in four editions: 1501, 1516, 1520, 1528) which in turn was utilized by Francesco Storella in his annotated 'critical' edition of 1555, the last to appear in Latin before the work was finally excluded from the Renaissance Aristotelian canon and banished to the less philosophically demanding world of vernacular literature.[56]

One should note in passing that there has been considerable controversy about all these translations from Hebrew, which Sobolevskii in 1903 had labelled as 'Judaizer literature',[57] ever since the appearance in 1955 of Kazakova and Lur'e's *Antifeodal'nye ereticheskie dvizheniia* which disputed (in Ch. 4) the existence of any such heretical corpus and talked rather of 'humanist circles in South-West Russia'. (This used to be the politically correct description of the Belorussian and Ukrainian parts of the Grand Duchy of Lithuania.) Lur'e summarized this controversy and restated his position in 1984, reaffirming that though those who were accused of the judaizing heresy may have used some of these works there is no evidence that they were actually translated by the alleged heretics, or that they necessarily have anything in common with each other.[58] It should perhaps be said in this connection that an interest in esoteric learning is by no means an exclusive badge of humanism – all the 'Judaizer' texts would undoubtedly have been scorned as medieval by West European humanists. Regrettably, the most recent Russian general study of Russian medieval philosophy blandly ignores the subtleties of this controversy and, without a scrap of new evidence or argument, once again ascribes the works to the Judaizers, sanitized under the new name of the 'Moscow Anti-trinitarians', who allegedly used them to propagate their 'rationalist', 'sceptical', 'humanist', 'freethinking' views.[59]

It is certainly true that the evidence linking these texts is largely inferential but it is surely perverse to deny the strong probability that there is indeed a connection between translations from Hebrew, some of which can definitely be dated to the late fifteenth century,[60] which are all apparently of Sephardic origin, share a common technical vocabulary, are of an intellectual character consistent with a common source, and appear suddenly with no predecessors and no successors in a milieu not otherwise demonstrating any strong Jewish cultural influence. This is not to say that there were not considerable Jewish communities in the Grand Duchy, simply that there is little other evidence of Jewish influence in the literature of Muscovy, Belorussia or the Ukraine.[61]

It is not, of course, necessary to support exclusively either the 'Judaizing heretics' view or the 'humanist circles' view. It has been observed that manuscripts of the Hebrew *Secretum* often belonged to Jewish doctors, and frequently also contained other texts of a medical and ethical character.[62] The *Secretum* itself has medical and magico-medical elements including a physiognomy, a 'regimen of health' with seasonal diets, and a section on the curative and talismanic properties of precious stones. The Old Russian version also contains an extra interpolated physiognomy[63] taken from the second tractate of Rhazes's *Liber ad Almansorem* (which in the Latin West also is textually linked with Maimonides's medical aphorisms)[64] and it is clear that both these and the Maimonides texts were interpolated into the seventh book of the eight-book Short Form of the *Secretum*[65] in a Hebrew version and constituted a kind of medical compendium.[66] Such a compendium does not require either the old 'Judaizer' or the more recent 'humanist, rationalist, antifeudal' explanation for its existence: it probably belonged to an ordinary Jewish physician. On the other hand the Russian *Secretum* is the closest that Muscovy came to the hermetic revival and neo-Platonism of West European Renaissance 'high magic'.

While there were probably very few Jews in Novgorod or Muscovy at the end of the fifteenth century, there is not much difficulty in accounting for the appearance of these works, albeit of Sephardic origin, in the Jewish communities of the Grand Duchy and Poland. These were places of refuge to which Jewish doctors and apothecaries from Spain were coming, via Italy, in this period;[67] and the growing awareness both there and in Muscovy that foreign scientific and medical knowledge and expertise might be cheaply imported by employing religious and political refugees is perhaps a good enough reason for their translation.

A second compendium of magic and divination recently discovered, which, to judge from part of the content and some names (e.g. Shmoil), could well have some Jewish sources, is the work of a certain priest or official in sixteenth-century Pskov, Ivan Rykov. Though not found in more than one copy and thus of less continuing influence that the *Secretum*, its importance as evidence of the level of interest in esoteric learning in Muscovy is immense. Since it is primarily a geomantic text it is discussed in detail in Ch. 12.

6. *The* Stoglav *and* Domostroi

While some of the condemnations of magical practices and texts in penitentials and lists of 'good and bad books' can be shown to be *topoi* or simply textual survivals from earlier periods of Greek Christianity, this is not always the case.

Some idea of the extent and nature of magical texts and practices in sixteenth-century Muscovy, or at least of ecclesiastical concern with them, can be gleaned from two works, the *Stoglav* and the *Domostroi*.[68]

The first of these was the account of the deliberations of the Church Council in Moscow in 1551. This was headed by Metropolitan Makarii but apparently actually summoned at the insistence of the Tsar, Ivan IV (the Terrible). The text, usually called *Stoglav* ('Hundred Chapters'), consists of questions from the Tsar on the subject of superstitions, irreligious practices, and innovations and abuses within the Church, and the formal collective answers and decisions of the senior churchmen who made up the Council. The text is something of an oddity; it is unlike any other Russian ecclesiastical document and it is rather chaotic in its presentation. Nevertheless, there is no serious question of its authenticity.[69] It was relied on heavily by the Old Believer sectarians from the seventeenth century onwards as supporting their view on such matters as the correct form of the cross and the shaving of beards.

Among the questions and answers of the *Stoglav* are several which touch on magic. They are, in the order in which they appear in the text:

Chapter 5, Question 11. This concerns the women who bake the communion bread. They are alleged to have been in the habit of selling the bread to credulous people who wish to pray for the dead or for their own health; they made spells over the bread with the names of the beneficiary 'like the Chud' magicians'(see n. 26 above). The answer of the Council (Chapter 8) is that the women who prepare the communion bread should make only a cross on the bread and say only the Jesus Prayer. Everything else is strictly forbidden, and they should have no access to the altar. Chapter 12 repeats this and insists that nothing should be placed on the altar except the cross, Gospels, and consecrated vessels and other appropriate consecrated objects.

Chapter 36. The Council's advice on the instruction of children quotes St Paul, 1 Corinthians VI:10 on those who will not enter the kingdom of Heaven. The list is expanded from the original catalogue of sexual deviants, drunkards and thieves to include magicians (*charodei*).

Chapter 41, Question and answer 2. Some of the common people bring cauls of newborn infants to the priest and ask that they be allowed to lie on the altar for six weeks. The priest is forbidden to do this under pain of ecclesiastical ban.

Chapter 41, Question and answer 3. People bring soap to the consecration of a church and ask for it to be left on the altar for six weeks. (The magical power of soap as an antidote to malefic magic, and in particular soap which has been used in the pre-wedding bath or to wash a corpse is described elsewhere in this book see Chs 7, 8, and 9.)

Chapter 41, Question and answer 17. 'In our kingdom Orthodox Christians are in conflict and kiss the cross or icons in false witness, and resort to judicial combat, and at these times wizards and sorcerers (*volkhvy, charodei*) aid them with magic, and consult the *Gates of Aristotle* and the *Rafli*,[70] and observe the stars and planets, and the days and hours.[71] They rely on these magical aids and as a result do not become reconciled but meet in combat and kill each other'. The fathers of the Council reply that these devilish Hellene (i.e. pagan Greek) practices and heresies must be totally condemned and stamped out, and the Tsar must proclaim this as law in all the towns of his realm and punish transgressors severely, while the Church must excommunicate them. This juridical objection to magic gives an unusual twist to the anti-magic argument but evidently it was a matter of concern to Ivan; in fact judicial combat by rival litigants or their hired surrogates was normal in Muscovite Russia of this period. This accusation by Ivan is, if it has any substance, the only evidence we have of the application of these divinatory texts in real life, and the first evidence of the employment of astrology.

Chapter 41, Question 22. This lists as 'evil heresies' a number of magical or divinatory works and practices: *Rafli*,[72] *Shestokryl*, Crow-Cawing,[73] Astronomy, Signs of the Zodiac, Almanac, Stargazer, *Gates of Aristotle*[74] and other works and heretical wisdoms and devilish prognostications. The fathers of the Council reply again that the Tsar must condemn and punish these in all parts of his realm and that the Church must apply its severest condemnation.

Once again the association of heresy, magic, paganism, and the Devil is explicit. It relies on patristic authority. Neither here nor in the other articles is the death penalty mentioned.

Chapter 41, Question and answer 23. On Trinity Saturday people gather at cemeteries and lament, and entertainers dance and sing satanic songs. This is condemned.

Chapter 41, Question and answer 24. On the eves of St John, Christmas Day and the Epiphany people gather at night and dance and sing satanic songs and bathe in the river. The fathers of the Council recommend that the Tsar should send an order to all priests in every town and village to instruct their flocks to desist from these ancient Hellenic devilries.

Chapter 41, Question and answer 26. On Thursday of Passion Week people burn straw and call up the dead, and on this day ignorant priests put salt under the altar, which they then keep until the seventh Thursday after Easter, when it becomes a cure for sick men or beasts. The Council replies that this is a Hellene seduction and heresy and any priest involved in this is to be excluded from the priesthood.

In fact this problem of people wishing to place non-liturgical objects on the altar for magical purposes, mentioned in three questions in the *Stoglav*, is one which goes back to the early Church: it is forbidden in the fourth-century *Apostolic Canons*, 3.

Chapter 63. The text, more or less, of the law code of Grand Prince Vladimir (end of the tenth century), which establishes the area of jurisdiction of ecclesiastical courts to be marriage law and domestic disputes, sexual deviance, magical practices, blasphemy, sacrilege, offences against the Church. It also defines the classes of people and institutions subject to ecclesiastical jurisdiction: all clergy and employees of the Church, freed serfs, widows, pilgrims, the blind and lame; monasteries, hospitals, hermitages, pilgrim hostels.

Chapter 93. Refers to Rules 61 and 62 of the Sixth Ecumenical Council (III Constantinople, AD 680–81) forbidding the consultation of magicians and condemning the pagan customs of the Greeks. The commentary extends this to condemn bear-leading, horoscopes, and games in general. The chapter finishes with the statement that all sorcery is forbidden by God because it entails serving the Devil.

The *Domostroi* is a manual of family and domestic governance and proper behaviour, apparently designed for the lesser nobility and prosperous merchant families. Its authorship is not definite but in its earliest form it probably goes back to the late fifteenth century, and its later sixteenth-century form was perhaps the work of Sil'vestr, an influential priest in the Annunciation Cathedral in the Moscow Kremlin. The author was familiar with trade and running a large and prosperous household with many servants. The work, which exists in several distinct versions, and incorporates passages from other works, includes advice on keeping the women of the house away from village magicians of both sexes,[75] and gives a list of the sins of the godless man. The latter includes gluttony, illicit sexual practices, and magical texts and practices. The list of magical texts and practices is similar to that given in the *Stoglav*:[76] casting spells and sorcery, amulets (*nauzy*), astrology, *Rafli*,[77] almanacs,[78] black magic (*chernoknizhie*), crow-cawing,[79] *Six Wings*,[80] thunder arrows, axeheads,[81] *usovniki*,[82] *dnakamenie*,[83] magic bones.[84] The *Domostroi* also recommends suffering with humility the illness and misfortunes which are God's punishment for sin, rather than calling in magicians, of which it lists five kinds: *charodei, kudesniki, volkhvy, mechetniki, zeleiniki*.[85] Like the *Stoglav*, which it is probably quoting, the *Domostroi* refers to specific points in canon law in condemning magicians: canon 61 of the Sixth Ecumenical Council (681–2); 24 of the Synod of Ancyra (314–15); 61 and 11 of the Trullan Synod (which was in effect a continuation of the Sixth Ecumenical Council); 72 of St Basil the Great. The *Domostroi* at several points is concerned that the women of the household should not become acquainted with magicians or themselves practise magic, but, like the early Russian law codes, it recommends that a wife who errs in this way should be punished privately by her husband.

It will be seen that some of the condemnations in these texts relate to popular magic or pagan survivals, some to magical objects, some to learned magic or texts of Greek, Hebrew and Arabic, and Latin origin. The confused manner of their presentation suggests that not all these items were familiar to the fathers of the Stoglav Council or the author of the *Domostroi*. This is also largely true of the various lists of 'good and bad books' which occur in Russia from the Kievan period up to comparatively recent times.[86] The association of magic with sexual misdemeanours is also usual in Western penitentials.

7. *Western Influences*

The Jewish influence discussed earlier could be described as being at the same time Eastern and Western in that all the texts of Hebrew origin, whether they be part of a judaizing movement or not, appear to come from the Sephardic community in Spain.

But there was also, of course, a more unambiguously West European influence with texts translated from Latin and later from Western vernaculars; and if in Kiev Rus' it was the clergy which appears to have been the main importer of Byzantine magical texts and practices, the prime movers in importing occult sciences from the West into Muscovy were its rulers. No doubt the interest in magic shown by most of them to some extent encouraged prudence on the part of all but the most censorious – there were few laymen who were as bold and learned as Prince Kurbskii who denounced Ivan the Terrible in the sixteenth century, or priests as intransigent or outspoken as Avvakum, one of the leaders of the seventeenth-century Old Believer schism.[87]

In the fifteenth century the Grand Princes of Moscow began to import court physicians from Western Europe. One of these, variously known as Nicolaus Bülow, Nicolaus of Lübeck, or Nicolaus the German, was also skilled in astronomy and astrology, and seems to have been involved in the new calendar computations required at the end of the fifteenth century. He is also credited with introducing the new popular medical text, the *Hortus sanitatis*, which contained information on the magical properties of stones and some astrological medicine, and in its Russian version was to include parts of the *Secretum secretorum*. His astrological interests were probably responsible for the Russian version of the *Almanach nova* of Johannes Stöffler, from the introduction to which the Russians became acquainted with the astrology of Alchabitius.[88]

From Ivan III, who employed Nicolaus Bülow, all the rulers of Muscovy for the next two centuries up to Peter the Great seem to have had, or were accused of having, some interest in magic, alchemy or astrology, or all three.[89] Most of the physicians who came to Moscow in this period were expected to be expert in alchemy and astrology, and despite the unpleasant end which many of them suffered, either at the hands of their disappointed employers or from mobs convinced that they were magicians, they continued to come, often no more than adventurers but sometimes scientists of some note. This subject is examined in more detail in Chs 2.4, 13.4 and 15.5. Sometimes noted alchemists and astronomers who were not physicians were invited to serve the Tsar. Perhaps the most famous were Dr John Dee, the Elizabethan magus, who turned down the invitation and the offer of an enormous salary, and Adam Olearius, the learned diplomat in the service of Holstein who spent much time in Moscow between 1634 and 1643. The latter observed that the Muscovites regarded astronomy and astrology as witchcraft, and, on hearing rumours that a magician was coming to court, realized that he himself was meant, and refused the invitation to become court astronomer. Among other things he had injudiciously set up a dark room as a *camera obscura*; the image with its moving figures which this produced was thought by the Russian chancellor to be the work of sorcery, the more so because it was, of course, upside down![90]

The new interest of Muscovite sovereigns in Western magical arts together

with their continuing interest in, and fear of, indigenous magic shows that
cultural divisions which were to culminate in the eighteenth century was already
beginning. On the one hand there were texts, practices and beliefs which were
imported, exotic, occasionally blended with serious scientific ideas and largely
restricted to court and high official circles these could be classified as 'high'
culture, whatever their status in Western Europe where they originated. And on
the other hand there was the 'low' culture of popular magic and medicine, mixed
with the older Byzantine textual tradition of minor divinatory texts, surviving in
monastic and Old Believer florilegia.[91] The latter was the common property of
all classes – Tsar Aleksei Mikhailovich sent an official to the house of an old witch
who had just died to search for 'roots, herbs, stones and written spells which she
used to help guard sick people from bewitchments'.[92] And, like many of their
Western counterparts, the tsars were quite capable of legislating against, and
savagely repressing, the very practices in which they themselves indulged.

But this cultural split was only a beginning: most of Europe in the seventeenth
century could combine religion, superstition, science and magic, however these
categories are defined, often with no apparent sense of incongruity, if not always
without protest, and certainly at every social level. Muscovy was no exception: in
the later part of the century Tsar Aleksei Mikhailovich ordered the collection of
magic herbs at midsummer and at the same time had an astronomical ceiling
painted in his palace at Kolomenskoe,[93] and an armillary sphere on the roof, and
was certainly interested in astrology to the extent of ordering foreign almanachs
to be translated. These continued in the regency of Sofia (1682–9), when there
was considerable upsurge in interest at court in magic and astrology, perhaps
exacerbated by the precarious nature of the regime.

The increasing influence of Western Europe on Muscovy culminated in the
reign of Peter the Great (1682–1725), who had a robust enthusiasm for almost
anything Western, in particular in the areas of technology, both civil and military,
administration and manners. Peter's practicality belonged more to the
Enlightenment than to the seventeenth century and there are few traces in him
or his court of the occult interests of his father Tsar Aleksei and his sister Sofia,
despite the alleged magical plot against his life. It is true that Peter, like most of
the rulers of Russia after him, felt obliged to legislate against witchcraft and
magic (see Ch. 16), but there is no evidence that these subjects interested him as
anything more than offences against good order and manifestations of discontent.
Although the parodies of religion indulged in by Peter do raise some questions
(see Ch. 2), his 'occult' interests probably did not extend beyond the Freemasonry
which was coming into fashion and even for that the evidence is tenuous and may
point to little more than a liking for hell-fire clubs.[94] After Peter no other ruler of
Russia displayed any particular interest in magic and the occult (although
Catherine II felt obliged to legislate against both, and Alexander I toyed with
some fashionable varieties of Western mysticism), until Nicholas II. The last tsar
was for a while a Martinist and welcomed occultists at his court (most notably
Papus (Gérard d'Encausse)).[95] He and his wife eventually fell under the fatal spell

of Rasputin, a man who fits closely the traditional description of the *koldun* or Russian magician.

Indeed, leaving aside the occasional fashions for occultism, the wilder varieties of alternative medicine, and atavistic or exotic cults, all of which which affect European and American society from time to time, Russia since Peter the Great has followed Western Europe in a pattern of cultural development in which 'high' culture has rejected magic (the exceptions are the Freemasons, Rosicrucians and Martinists of the eighteenth and nineteenth centuries, and would-be 'magi' such as Gurdzhiev and Mme Blavatsky and associated occultist circles at the end of the nineteenth century and beginning of the twentieth) and most of the forms of magic and divination described in this book became the 'low' culture of the uneducated, amusements for the bourgeois, or simply games for children. In conclusion, it should be noted that the terms 'high' and 'low' have been used here and henceforth as very loose conventional labels. Binary distinctions of 'high' and 'low', 'learned' and 'popular', are always risky, and can easily mislead anyone looking at Russian cultural history from a modern West European perspective.[96]

Notes

1. See Iorga, *Byzance après Byzance*, and Obolensky, *The Byzantine Commonwealth*. Iorga was in fact writing about Moldavia and Wallachia.

2. For what this meant in practice see Thomson, '*Sensus* or *proprietas verborum*'.

3. Eremin, *Literatura drevnei Rusi*, p. 12, points out that almost all translations from Greek were of religious texts written between the fourth and sixth centuries. Francis Thomson has further demonstrated that even these were of a very limited nature: see Thomson, 'The Nature of the Reception'.

4. Lemerle, *Le Premier Humanisme byzantin*, and review by Ihor Ševčenko in *The American Historical Review*, 79, 1974, pp. 1531–5.

5. For an authoritative survey of the subject and the secondary literature see Ševčenko, 'Remarks on the Diffusion'. For the Old Church Slavonic texts available in Bulgaria see Kristanov and Duichev, *Estestvoznanieto*; for a recent study of this material see Cholova, *Estestvenonauchnite znaniia*.

6. Obolensky draws attention to the fact that there was in the fourteenth century a considerable intermingling of Greeks, South Slavs and Russians in the monastic centres of Mt Athos, Constantinople, Thessalonica and the north Balkan centres of Paroria and Kilifarevo: see Obolensky, 'Late Byzantine Culture and the Slavs', pp. 8–9.

7. In using terms such as 'scientific', 'sub-scientific', 'pseudo-scientific' I am, of course, guilty of crude anachronism, both in language and in the historical taxonomy of knowledge. I use the terms for convenience wherever suitable alternatives are not available.

8. These are outlined by K. Vogel in the *Cambridge Medieval History*, IV, II, ch. XXVIII, and more recently in Samodurova, 'K voprosu', with a sequel to follow.

9. Grmek, *Les Sciences*, p. 6.

10. For a judicious discussion of the evidence and arguments about the extent of the use of Greek in Kiev Rus' see Franklin, 'Greek in Kievan Rus''.

11. Kieckhefer, *Magic in the Middle Ages*, p. 17.

12. For a concise description in English see Obolensky, *The Byzantine Commonwealth*, pp. 466–73. For recent research see *Da Roma alla Terza Roma: Studi e documenti* (series of conference papers published irregularly under various imprints from about 1983) and Uspenskii, 'Vospriiatie istorii' (this very fully annotated).

13. Although Belarus is the current name of the state, in historical and linguistic contexts I have used Belorussia and Belorussian as being more appropriate.

14. Picchio, 'A proposito della Slavia ortodossa', pp. 105–27.

15. *Pskovskie letopisi*, p. 262. The context is the influence of Eliseus Bomel at the court of Ivan the Terrible: see Ch. 13.4.

16. *ERE*, III, col. 465a.

17. The broadest survey of the history of magic among the East Slavs is the inevitably dated Mansikka, *Der Religion der Ostslaven*. More convenient, but also dated, is the *Encyclopedia of Religion and Ethics*, s.vv. *Demons and Spirits (Slavic)* (V. J. Mansikka); *Divination (Litu-Slavic)* (O. Schrader); *Charms and Amulets (Slavic)* (O. Schrader); *Magic (Slavic)* (L. A. Magnus) (the last listed is brief and not very helpful). See also Chap. 2, nn. 1 and 2. Specialized studies are quoted elsewhere as appropriate.

18. See Ch. 11.10.1.

19. For text see the *Russian Primary Chronicle*, p. 58.

20. The *Russian Primary Chronicle*, pp. 69–71.

21. This motif has parallels elsewhere and both Scandinavian and Turkish-Byzantine origins are claimed for it: see the *Russian Primary Chronicle*, p. 224, n. 40, and the summary of opinions in Oinas, 'Folklore and History', pp. 31–47 (32–3).

22. The route by which this story passed, with exegetical adjustment, from the chronicle of John Malalas to that of George the Monk (Hamartolos), and there via a bad Slavonic translation to the *Primary Chronicle*, where it has a quite different message from the original version of John Malalas, is decribed in Franklin, 'The Reception of Byzantine Culture', pp. 386–8.

23. The *Russian Primary Chronicle*, pp. 134–5.

24. For a detailed discussion of this section of the Chronicle and its significance in early Russian religious history see Faccani, 'Jan' Vyšatič e l'«anno dei maghi»'.

25. It is found as an *exemplum* in Western medieval literature: see Tubach, *Index Exemplorum*, no. 404. Maxim the Greek in the sixteenth century used the same argument in an epigram on the astrologer Nicolaus Bülow – see p. 22 below.

26. Chud' is the general name given to the Finnic (mostly) peoples of northern European Russia, and later also the legendary people who built the burial mounds of Siberia. Although there is probably no etymological link with Russian *chudo*, 'miracle; something strange and wonderful', there can be no doubt that folk etymology saw a connection between this meaning and the widespread European reputation of the Finns for possessing magic powers.

27. The eponym of simony: Simon is supposed to have attempted to buy the spiritual power of the apostles and died trying to fly in order to demonstrate the superiority of his magic over the powers of St Peter. See *Acta Petri* in James, *Apocryphal New Testament*, pp. 331–2.

28. A wizard on Patmos exposed by St John and turned by him into stone: see *Acta Ioannis*, p. 90ff.

29. The priests of the pharaoh who competed in magic with Moses: the event is recounted in Exodus 7, but the priests are named only in 2 Timothy 3,8. Jannes is also named in a list of magicians in the *Apologia* of Apuleius: Apuleius, *Works*, p. 336, and in Pliny, *Naturalis historia*, XXX,ii,11. Interestingly enough, in view of his probable interest in magic, Ivan IV refers to these two wizards in

one of his letters to Prince Kurbskii: see Fennell, *The Correspondence between Prince A. M. Kurbsky and Tsar Ivan IV*, pp. 44–5.

30. The *Russian Primary Chronicle*, pp. 150–4. On this and the concept of 'combat by prophecy' see Franklin, 'The Reception of Byzantine Culture', p. 391.

31. The *Russian Primary Chronicle*, p. 139. The Russian has *iazveno*; Cross's translation 'caul' is plausible and generally accepted but not certain.

32. For some discussion of the association of cauls and vampirism see Barber, *Vampires*, p. 31.

33. Nikephoras, *Breviarium*, ed. C. Mango, p. 95. Mango translates Greek *astronomos* as 'astronomer', but in fact it more commonly means 'astrologer', if indeed the distinction can usefully be made at this period.

34. See Munitiz, *Nikephoras Blemmydes*, p. 84.

35. See *Velikie chet'i minei* for 2 October. He became a bishop and she an abbess, and their dubious story was well known in both the East and the West. They were supposed in some accounts to have been martyred together in the persecution of Diocletian; a fourteenth-century fresco in the church of Sartheim in the south Tirol shows them being boiled together naked in a large pot (see Gruber, *Südtiroler Heilgenhimmel*, p. 83, pl. 148.) They were united in a single feastday (26 September): see the *Catholic Encyclopedia* (1907), s.v. They were removed from the list of saints by the Vatican in 1968. For an extended erotic spell ostensibly by Cyprian see *Ancient Christian Magic*, pp. 153–8. The *De nigromancia* ascribed to Roger Bacon includes an elaborate method of consecrating a magic circle which among other things involves getting a priest to say a mass in honour of St Cyprian: see *De Nigromancia of Roger Bacon*, ii. 4–6, pp. 13–26.

36. Extant in Church Slavonic from the twelfth century, perhaps known in the eleventh century – for the history and literary influence of this text in Russia see Cleminson, 'The Miracle *De juvene qui Christum negaverat*'.

37. Priests and monks are several times accused of magical practices or fortune-telling in legal cases of the seventeenth and eighteenth centuries in Russia. Dubasov, 'Ocherki Tambovskogo byta', p. 663, even states that some *volkhvy* in the seventeenth century were members of the clergy. See Smilianskaia, '"Suevernaia" knizhitsa' for the role of the parish clergy in copying magic recipe books. Russia was not unique in this respect. In Croatia in the eighteenth century it was observed that priests used to sell amulet scrolls to cure or ward off disease: see Fortis, *Travels in Dalmatia*, p. 63. Vukanovič is probably recording the same thing in stating that in the Dubrovnik area priests used to give 'blessings in a sealed booklet' as a protection against witches: Vukanovič, 'Witchcraft, II', p. 226. For clerical involvement in demonic magic in the West in the Middle Ages see Kieckhefer, *Forbidden Rites*, p. 4 ('particularly on the fringes of the clerical elite') and idem, *Magic in the Middle Ages*, pp. 153–6. Keith Thomas quotes many English examples from the fifteenth to the seventeenth century of Catholic and Anglican clergy engaging in magic and astrology, even publishing almanacs: *Religion and the Decline of Magic*, esp. at pp. 274, 379ff. For accusations against the clergy in Germany in the sixteenth and seventeenth century see Schwillus, *Kleriker im Hexenprozeß*.

38. A good and timely reexamination of the concept is the article by Levin, '*Dvoeverie* and Popular Religion'.

39. See Krianev and Pavlova, 'Dvoeverie na Rusi', pp. 364–5.

40. The very similar situation in Greece, for example, was commented upon by Lawson, *Modern Greek Folklore and Ancient Greek Religion*, p. 47. More recent studies of Greece and the Balkans in

particular reveal patterns of belief very like that of Russia, and sometimes identical: see Stewart, *Demons*; Vukanovič, 'Witchcraft'.

41. Bushkovitch, *Religion and Society*, pp. 212–13.

42. MS St Petersburg, GPB, Kir. Bel. sobr. XII, ff. 311–2v. See Prokhorov, 'Knigi Kirilla Belozerskogo'. For the text see Tikhonravov, *Pamiatniki*, II, pp. 405–21 (a sixteenth-century version); for the greater part of the text with a modern Russian translation see *Pamiatniki literatury Drevnei Rusi. Vtoraia polovina* XV veka, pp. 192–215.

43. See *Slovar' knizhnikov i knizhnosti*, 2, 1, s.v.

44. See Lur'e, *Russkie sovremenniki Vozrozhdeniia*.

45. The contents of Efrosin's miscellanies are given in Kagan, Ponyrko, and Rozhdestvenskaia, 'Opisanie sbornikov', pp. 3–300. An index of banned books appears at f 42 of MS St Petersburg, GPB, Kirillo-Belozersoe sobr. 22/1099 and the *Koliadnik* ascribed to the Prophet Esdras appears at ff. 109r–v.

46. Notwithstanding the fact that these texts have many linguistic features in common and appear roughly at the same time as the sect, not all scholars accept that there must be a connection. Ia. S. Lur'e in particular prefers to speak of 'humanist circles' – see p. 17 below.

47. For a succinct description see Manzalaoui, 'Secretum Secretorum' in *Dictionary of the Middle Ages*, 11, p. 135; for a survey of research on the *Secretum* and the fairly extensive literature on the subject see *Pseudo-Aristotle: The Secret of Secrets: Sources and Influences*, pp. 124–31.

48. Speranskii, *Iz istorii otrechennykh knig. IV*. The greater part of the *Secretum* text, but without Book 8 (which contains the alchemy) or the Maimonides and Rhazes interpolations, has been republished by Bulanin in *Pamiatniki literatury Drevnei Rusi. Konets XV – pervaia polovina XVI veka*, pp. 534–91, 750–4, with a modern Russian translation. Speranskii's basic text was Belorussian/Ukrainian but all the other twenty or so manuscripts of the text are probably Muscovite. For a comparison of the Old Russian text with Gaster's Hebrew text (see next note) see Ryan, 'The Old Russian Version'.

49. The only published Hebrew version is Gaster, 'The Hebrew Version'. This includes an English translation; it was a pioneer study of difficult manuscripts but must now be considered unsatisfactory: see Spitzer, 'The Hebrew Translation'. For other considerations of the underlying Hebrew text see Grignaschi, 'L'Origine' and 'Remarques'. On this text and Alexander in the wider context of Hebrew literature see Van Bekkum, 'Alexander the Great'.

50. The classification is that of Manzalaoui, 'The Pseudo-Aristotelian *Kitāb Sirr al-Asrār*'. The structure of the Old Russian *Secretum*, using Manzalaoui's sigla, is: 1A 2Bab 3C 4DabcEG 5F 6H 7Iac [interpolations] Bdc 8GJaf, compared with the standard structure of the eight-book Short Form: 7Iabc 8Jaf Bdc.

51. See Ryan, 'Maimonides'.

52. See Ryan, 'Aristotle and Pseudo-Aristotle in Kievan and Muscovite Russia'.

53. See Ryan, 'Drevnerusskii perevod'.

54. See Spitzer, 'The Hebrew Translation', pp. 35–6. Spitzer points out that some but not all of the terminology is Tibbonic and gives a date for the Hebrew translation of late thirteenth–early fourteenth century.

55. For a summary see Ryan, 'Maimonides'. This has been updated by Moshe Taube in a series of articles which also throw light on other aspects of this and other 'Judaizer' texts: M. Taube, 'The Kievan Jew Zacharia and the Astronomical Works of the Judaizers'; 'The "Poem on the Soul" in the Laodicean Epistle and the Literature of the Judaizers'; 'The Spiritual Circle in the Secret of Secrets

and the Poem on the Soul'; 'Poslеslovie k «Logicheskim terminam» Maimonida i eres' zhidovstvuiushchikh'. See also, for a slightly different approach (in 1989): Turilov and Chernetsov, 'K kul'turno-istoricheskoi kharakteristike'.

56. See Schmitt, 'Francesco Storella'.

57. Sobolevskii, *Perevodnaia literatura*, pp. 409–28.

58. Luria [Lur'e], 'Unresolved Issues', pp. 151–7.

59. See Zamaleev, *Filosofskaia mysl'*, pp. 192–6. This misleading label has also recently been used by Bushkovich, *Religion and Society in Russia*.

60. Gennadii's letter appears to give the latest date for the translation of the *Logic*, and the *Logic* in its turn contains an apparent reference to the *Secretum* which in any case is quoted in another text of the late fifteenth century 'Budi vedomo ezhe prezhe vsego sotvoril bog samovlastie dukhovnoe . . .' ('Be it known that first of all God created autonomy[?] of the spirit'). This is discussed in Klibanov, *Reformatsionnye dvizheniia,* p. 348 n. 43. Klibanov regards the passage as evidence of a humanistic statement on intellectual freedom, albeit distantly derived from 'Platonic-Plotinian' ideas, but it is in fact simply a terse exposition of Plotinian emanationary theory in a text (the *Secretum secretorum*) which was very quickly rejected by the humanists. Klibanov's 'humanistic' interpretation of this passage has been regularly repeated, most recently in *Filosofskaia mysl' v Kieve*, p. 94.

61. Meshcherskii has offered some evidence (which is not widely accepted) for translation from Hebrew at an earlier period, including perhaps the whole of the *Josippon*: Meshcherskii, *Istochniki*, pp. 30–1. For a criticism of Meshcherskii's theory see Lunt and Taube, 'Early East Slavonic Translations from Hebrew?'. See also Arkhipov, 'O proiskhozhdenii', pp. 79–81, arguing the Hebrew and cabbalistic origin of the names and possibly techniques of types of Slavonic cryptography.

62. See Spitzer, 'The Hebrew Translation', pp. 36–7.

63. Although the *Secretum* contains the most extensive physiognomical information in Old Russian literature, it is not the first work on the subject – some elements may be found in the works of John the Exarch of Bulgaria which were well known to the Orthodox Slavs.

64. See for example *Liber Rasis ad Almansorem*, Venice, 1487, and later editions: these are in fact miscellanies and contain *Aphorismi Rabi Moysis* as well as aphorisms of John Damascene and Hippocrates.

65. Within book seven the 'gate' numbering begins with the onomantic section and continue through the Rhazes interpolation; then follows a series of four chapter ('glavizna') numbers running through the first two Maimonidean texts (on poisons and sex); the treatise on asthma then reverts to 'gate' numbers in a series running from 1 to 16. See Manzalaoui, 'The Pseudo-Aristotelian *Kitāb sirr al-asrār*', pp. 166–9.

66. This contention is supported by the fact that there are no copies of the Old Russian *Secretum* lacking the interpolations, all the texts share a common vocabulary, and a continuous system of text division by the names of the days of the week runs through all the texts, beginning with Sunday. This is considered by Speranskii to be the Jewish system of daily readings but see Arkhipov, *Drevnerusskaia Kniga Proroka Daniila*, p. 13 n. 26, who disputes this and leaves open the question of the purpose of the day-name divisions.

67. See Balaban, 'Evrei-vrachi', p. 38. One such doctor became royal physician. In Muscovy a Jewish doctor from Italy, Leon, was court physician to Grand Prince Ivan III and was executed for failing to effect a cure; in this he followed a German doctor put to death in 1485 for the same reason: see Florinskii, *Russkie prostonarodnye travniki*, p. v. More generally on Jews and Slavs in this period see Baron, *Social and Religious History*, pp. 264–72, and Birnbaum, 'On Some Evidence'.

68. This is an overview of these two textual sources. For bibliography and current state of research on the two texts see *Slovar' knizhnikov*, vyp. 2, ch. 2, s.v. *Sil'vestr*, pp. 323–33 (D.M. Bulanin, V.V. Kolesov) and s.v. *Stoglav*, pp. 423–7 (D.M. Bulanin). For discussion elsewhere in this book of the individual practices, objects and texts mentioned, refer to the index.

69. See the introduction to *Le Stoglav*, ed. Duchesne, pp. ix–xvi.

70. See Ch. 12.

71. See Ch. 14.

72. See Ch. 12.

73. See Ch. 5.

74. See Ch. 12.

75. *Domostroi*, ed. Pouncy, pp. 107–10.

76. This section is largely misunderstood in the Pouncy translation.

77. Geomancy – see Ch. 12.

78. See Chs 14 and 15.

79. See Ch. 5.7.

80. See previous section and Ch. 15.7.

81. On thunder arrows and axeheads as amulets see Ch. 8.

82. The editor of *Domostroi*, 1990, *ad indicem*, suggests that these are recipes for curing illnesses (*usov'e*), but the context suggests rather amulets for the same purpose.

83. The meaning of this word is not clear, but perhaps it is connected with the enigmatic *dna* for which see Ch. 8.6.6.1.

84. Perhaps dice. See Ch. 11.

85. For discussion of these and other names for magicians see Ch. 3.

86. For more discussion see Ch. 5.7.

87. See Ch. 15, p. 393, in particular, and Index.

88. For further information on the activities of Nicolaus see Chs 13.4 and 15.2 and 4.

89. For a useful survey see Simonov, 'Russkie pridvornye «matematiki»'.

90. Cited from the English translation of Olearius in Cross, *Russia under Western Eyes*, p. 91.

91. For a lively and learned discussion of this cultural division in the context of the schism in the Church see Uspensky, 'Schism and Cultural Conflict in the Seventeenth Century'.

92. Longworth, *Alexis*, p. 198.

93. The second point is, of course, flimsy evidence – astronomy and astrology were hardly to be distinguished, and ceilings like this could be found from Renaissance palaces in Italy to the Minor Schools lecture hall in the University of Salamanca.

94. For a convenient overview see Cross, 'The Bung College or British Monastery in Petrine Russia'.

95. For an outline of the occult interests of Russian court and society in the late nineteenth and early twentieth century see Carlson, '*No Religion Higher than Truth*', ch. 1.

96. This is not to dismiss these concepts entirely: see the extremely interesting semiotic analysis of the dualism of eighteenth-century Russian culture in Lotman and Uspenskii, 'K semioticheskoi tipologii', which offers a compound structure of oppositions such as 'own – other', 'old – new', 'Russia – West', 'high – low', 'Church Slavonic – Russian'. Much of what Lotman and Uspenskii say here is also pertinent to Russia both before and after the eighteenth century.

2

POPULAR MAGIC

1. *Introduction*

This chapter will survey those areas of popular belief which are connected with magic and divination. Practitioners of magic and divination will be described in Ch. 3, and specific types of popular divination will be described in Ch. 4.

As has been remarked elsewhere in this book, the detailed literature of the subject is quite extensive, but its quality is uneven, often out of date and usually unverifiable.[1] Broad surveys are rare.[2] Insofar as much of the material in this chapter is derived from these sources it must to some extent share their inadequacies, the commonest of which are a lack of place, date or context.

A frequent difficulty is that of distinguishing beliefs and practices of literary origin (many of which, as we shall see in later chapters, can be traced back to classical or oriental antiquity), from those of 'popular' origin (which often means simply that their origin is not known). Moreover, magical beliefs and practices do appear to be remarkably contagious, and infinitely and speedily adaptable. The recent popularity in the West of the so-called 'Chinese zodiac' is a fine example of how part of one culture can be torn out of its context, reinterpreted in another culture, and cheerfully exploited by purveyors of the 'wisdom of the East'. For an early Russian manifestation of this see the 'Uighur cycle' in Ch. 15.

In Russia, as in the West, many heterodox ideas, religious, magical or political, were probably spread from area to area and from the learned to the unlearned by the very condemnations of Church and State which attempted to combat them. Such condemnations give them, to use a once popular political phrase, 'the oxygen of publicity'. The list of practices, magical and sexual, about which Russian parish priests from the earliest times up to at least the eighteenth century were supposed to interrogate those going to confession, must surely have put ideas into perhaps innocent minds, and binary systems of analysis which look for high or learned versus low or popular culture run into difficulties of definition in this kind of situation.

The close identification of Church and State in Muscovite Russia is well illustrated by the content of a memorandum from the governor (*voevoda*) of Verkhotur'e to the town commissioner (*prikazchik*) of Irbitskaia sloboda in 1649 instructing him to stop people talking in church, getting drunk, listening to travelling entertainers (*skomorokhi*), summoning witches and wizards to cure illnesses, fortune-telling from the first day of the new moon or by pouring wax and tin [see marital prospects divination in Ch. 4], playing dice, cards, chess [see Ch. 11.10–12], knuckle-bones (*lodygi*), leading bears,[3] singing devilish songs, dancing, clapping hands, playing on swings. Those engaging in these reprehensible activities were to be beaten with rods.[4] A similar list of proscriptions was sent by Tsar Aleksei Mikhailovich to the other provincial governors. One seventeenth-century Moscow patriarch even banned church burial for anyone drowned while bathing or killed by falling from a swing, regarding such misadventures as self-inflicted and therefore the equivalent of suicide.[5] Such prohibitions continued locally into modern times.[6]

This puritanical attitude to sinful frivolities persisted into the eighteenth century and beyond. As an example of what was thought unacceptable for a good Orthodox Russian in the eighteenth century I quote (with some abbreviation) a manuscript penitential listing 'accursed' practices for which a penance was to be imposed:

– burying gold [i.e. the Yuletide game with an element of divination. See Ch. 4]
– playing blind man's buff,
– listening at thresholds and windows [i.e. a popular form of marital prospect divination – see Ch. 4],
– smearing one's face with soot [i.e. engaging in the Christmas season masquerades],
– wetting one's head with cloths,
– beating with cloth twists [i.e. a game],
– playing musical instruments,
– playing chess, dice or cards [see Ch. 11],
– looking at hands or letting a magician look at your own or your children's hands [i.e. chiromancy – not a practice recorded in Russia before the eighteenth century; see Ch. 6.3],
– rubbing with salt or ointment or turpentine or oil or mercury or human blood or human or animal milk or honey or dew or tar or hops [various medical or magical procedures with or without magical spells attached],
– listening to thunder [for divination by the *Gromnik* see Ch. 14.4; here more probably the direction from which the thunder came was used to make prediction, or perhaps the magical practice of seeking to bathe during a thunderstorm is being referred to],
– rolling in the snow [a marital prospects divination – see below],
– carrying water in a sieve [sieves are commonly used in divination: see below. Carrying water in a sieve in a number of sayings means trying to do something absurdly impossible: see Dal', *Tolkovyi slovar'*, s.v. *reshetka*. Cf. Pliny, *Naturalis historia*, XXVII.iii.ii–iv.12. The task of carrying water in a sieve is given to simpleton heroes or devils in a number of folk stories],
– listening to dogs or cats or geese or ducks or horses or oxen [for animal oracles see Chs 4 and 5], . . .

(believing in the following omens:)

– a mouse eats your trousers (clothes) [this distinctive omen alerts us to the fact that a good number of the omens here are taken from the *Volkhovnik* or 'Book of the Wizard' – see Ch. 5.7],

- a moth spoils your clothes,
- a mouse builds its nest high in the corn [an omen that corn prices will be high – see Dal', *Tolkovyi slovar'*, s.v. *mysh'*],
- the bones aching and the back of the knee itching means a journey,
- the palms itching means money,
- the eyes itching means tears to come [see also Ch. 6.6],
- meeting various animals and birds [see Ch. 5.2],
- the hut creaks, the fire crackles, the forest murmurs and tree scrapes against tree, squirrels jump [see the omens in the *Volkhovnik*, Ch. 5.7],
- performing magic over livestock with stones and iron and frying pans and icons,
- going to wizards and heretics and impious old women and witches who perform magic on St John's Night [i.e. one of the most magical times of the year – see below, section 8],
- bathing with herbs in the bathhouse [a practice associated in particular with magic midsummer herbs gathered on the feast of Agrafena-Kupal'nitsa (23 June) – see 2.6 below, and 9.4],
- cutting off the first hair of children [in fact this seems to have been a common practice in churches. Giles Fletcher, writing about Russia in 1591, declares: 'After the baptisme the manner is to cut of the haire from the childes head, and having wrapped it within a piece of wax, to lay it up, as a relique, or monument in a secret place of the church'],[7]
- pregnant women giving bread to a bear: if it growls she will have a girl; if it is silent, a boy [for a variant see Ch. 13.6],
- divining with a key in a psalter [see Ch. 11.4].

The documents quoted above give a fair idea of the extent and kind of popular domestic magic and divination practised in Russia in the Muscovite period (although, interestingly enough, they give little indication of the extensive fertility beliefs and rituals of the Russian countryside, perhaps because these were not thought to be 'magical').[8] They have in most cases analogies with beliefs and practices in other parts of Europe in the same period.

2. The Evil Eye

Belief in the Evil Eye is found in very many parts of the world. Its ramifications, including some Russian, Ukrainian and Belorussian details, were exhaustively charted by Seligmann.[9] The earliest specific reference to Russian belief in the Evil Eye appears to be in Reginald Scot's *Discovery of Witchcraft* (1584)[10] where the belief is imputed to the Irish, Muscovites and West Indians. The earliest Russian textual reference to the Evil Eye, as far as I can discover, is in a sixteenth-century prayer against 'zlo sretenie i lukavo oko' ('evil meeting and evil eye').[11] The notion of the Evil Eye probably first came to the Slavs from Byzantium; certainly types of amulet used against the Evil Eye in Byzantium can be found also in the Balkans and in Russia and it is hard to resist a diffusionist interpretation of the evidence.[12] Dal' (s.v. *glaz*) lists *glazit'*, *sglazit'*, *(iz)urochit'*, *ozevat'*, *isportit' glazom*, *oprizorit'* as verbs meaning 'to put the Evil Eye on', and as nouns *sglaz*, *khudoi glaz*, *durnoi glaz*, *nekhoroshii glaz*, *nechistyi glaz*, *ozeva*, *porcha*, *prikos*, *pritka s glazu* (*pritka* is normally a sudden misfortune or illness), *prizor*, *urok*. It should be noted that *porcha*, literally 'spoiling', although often the effect of an Evil Eye, can also be the result of any kind of malefic magic.

Reputed possessors of the Evil Eye in Russia, as in most other places, were any witch or wizard; anyone with black, deepset, protruding, crossed or in some other way distinctive eyes or otherwise of peculiar appearance,[13] foreigners; priests.[14] The use of the word *eretun* (from *eretik* 'heretic'; coll. 'wizard') in Karelia to mean 'man with a squint' and the more general use of words with the primary meaning of 'squint' in the sense of 'Evil Eye' demonstrates clearly the association of magic with ocular peculiarity.[15] As late as 1881 a Russian newspaper ran a story that a prisoner who had been condemned to death had been handed over to the Academy of Sciences for an experiment to test the power of the Evil Eye. He was starved for three days in the presence of a loaf of bread. At the end of this period analysis showed that the bread contained a poisonous substance![16]

The Evil Eye can also be cast inadvertently: there is a still common practice in Russia of spitting three times, crossing oneself, and saying 'ne sglazi' ('don't put the Evil Eye on me') if anyone makes a remark which tempts fate (rather as in England people say and do 'touch wood'), or is guilty of a slip of the tongue, or yawns or laughs at an inappropriate moment.[17] The practice of apotropaeic expectoration in such circumstances has ancient antecedents and many analogues.[18] Spitting may also be used in spells: see Ch. 7. Triple spitting even penetrated Orthodox ritual: Captain John Perry records in 1716 the ceremony of re-baptism of foreigners wishing to join the Russian Orthodox Church. This required the man to spit three times over his left shoulder and then repeat after the priest: 'Cursed are my parents that brought me up in the religion that I have been taught, I spit upon them.'[19] Another form of protection still employed is the fig gesture.

The close association of the Evil Eye *stricto sensu* with incurring misfortune by other means, such as tempting fate by expressing a hope or intention or by injudicious praising, is very common.[20] Aksakov in his memoirs of provincial life in late eighteenth-century Russia recalls the terror of a Russian midwife that a German doctor would put the Evil Eye on a newborn infant by praising it. This was particularly frightening because of the combination of the foreignness of the doctor and the fate-tempting praise.[21] Zabylin records, 'with shame', that in his time (i.e. the late nineteenth century), even in families of the higher merchant class, it was common for nurses to keep new-born infants locked away for six weeks from the gaze of all but the closest members of the family, and that the praise of a stranger was particularly feared.[22] Zabylin might have been surprised, and even more shamed, had he known that this belief persists to the present day.

In March 1998 a baby was stolen from a pram left outside a Moscow clinic. It was only twenty-three days old and its mother would not take it in, fearing the Evil Eye if it were to be seen by anyone before forty days had elapsed.[23] Even the use of the name of a child in the presence of strangers could, it was thought, have dire consequences – Robert Pinkerton wrote in 1833: '… after such an inauspicious encounter, they spit several times on the ground, repeating, at the same time, prayers against the effects of the evil eye and all satanic influences'.[24]

3. Malefic Magic

Possessors of the Evil Eye may, as has been shown above, be simply inadvertent blighters of babies, crops, weddings, etc., indeed of anything in which hopes are invested and the possibility of misfortune high. Equally they may be witches or wizards for whom the Evil Eye is a manifestation of their power. Here the notion of the Evil Eye is assimilated into the wider concept of malefic magic in general, for which the word *porcha*, 'spoiling' is most commonly used. But if the effect of the Evil Eye is one form of *porcha* it is not the only one. Almost any misfortune can be ascribed to *porcha*, so accusations of its use are far more common than evidence for its actual use. Moreover, practitioners of malefic magic and their clients are more likely to wish to preserve secrecy, if only for their own safety, than are the employers of the various kinds of protective magic which often rely on being self-evident for their effect.

Instances of various kinds of malefic magic have been discussed elsewhere in this book. They may be summarized as:

3.1. *Malefic verbal magic, zagovory.* This may include spells to bring illness on an enemy, or hiccups, to bring marital discord, destroy love, harm the crops or cattle of an enemy, make weapons misfire, etc. These *zagovory* may be accompanied by ritual movements or be required to be performed a particular number of times (often three), in a particular manner (often by whispering), at particular times or places, or to employ magical objects. They may also sometimes be written. This kind of magic may have specific demonic elements. *Zagovory* are discussed in detail in Ch. 7. The common word for a curse in the sense of an invocation of divine punishment, or the punishment itself, is *prokliatie*. This seems to require a Christian context and not to be used in the sense of magical spell.

3.2. *'Sending on the wind'.*[25] A distinctive subdivision of the above is the practice of sending 'spells on the wind'. *Nasylat' po vetru* 'to send on the wind' means to bewitch from a distance and a *naslan'* or *naslyshche* is an illness or other misfortune caused by a spell.[26] In Kaluga a variant of this was called *steklo*, a version of the word for glass – it involved sending ground glass 'on the wind' so that it entered the victim's body.[27]

There are references to wind-borne magic in Russia from the sixteenth century onwards: Prince Kurbskii describes the Tatars of Kazan' as trying to bewitch the besieging Russian army in this way,[28] and the servitors of Tsars Boris Godunov and Vassily Shuiskii had to swear not to 'send spells on the wind'. In 1689 in aftermath of one of the protest riots of the *strel'tsy*, the peculiar semi-professional militia regiments of Moscow who resisted the Petrine reforms and were eventually put down with great ferocity, one of the prisoners, 'the wizard Doroshka' (Dorofeika) from Nizhnii Novgorod and his associates were accused of 'sending spells on the wind' against the young Tsar Peter and his mother.[29] As late as the 1850s in the Tiumen' province of Siberia a tailor was seized during an epidemic and accused of sending the cholera 'on the wind'.[30]

A description of how spells are 'sent on the wind' in popular magic is given by Sakharov and Zabylin: the *koldun* waits until there is a wind blowing in the direction of his victim, asks his client for a handful of earth, snow, or dust, throws this in the wind in the direction of the victim and pronounces 'Kulla, Kulla! Blind N., black, blue, brown, white, red eyes. Blow up his belly larger than a charcoal pit, dry up his body thinner than the meadow grass, kill him quicker than a viper'.[31] It is worth noting in this connection that the common Russian word for 'epidemic', especially plague, is *povetrie*, which means 'something carried on the wind'; an earlier term *vetrennaia nechist'* 'wind uncleanness' includes both the wind element and the 'unclean' which was a common term for an evil spirit as well as skin and venereal diseases. In one twentieth-century report an informant states that at one time *porcha* was sent on the wind but now the wind is replaced by the telephone.[32]

For other examples of the wind in spells see Ch. 7 on love spells; for other beliefs about whirlwinds and witches see below.

3.3. *The use of magical herbs and roots.* These, having an objective existence, often feature as evidence in the witchcraft trials of the sixteenth, seventeenth and eighteenth centuries. Their purpose is the same as that of spoken spells, with which they were sometimes accompanied. In some cases they were no doubt simply poisons, but in many court cases the accused would defend himself or herself by claiming that the herbs or roots in question were kept for benign purposes of self-protection. This seems never to have been accepted as a defence. The actual method of use of magical herbs and roots in malefic magic, as also other kinds of magical object listed below, varied, but a common method was *podmet*, which means roughly in this context 'something insinuated into the clothing or belongings or surreptitiously strewn in the path of someone'. It is also worth recalling that in Old Russian *zel'e* could mean 'herb; medicine; magic potion; poison' and even 'gunpowder' (see Ch. 9.2). For further discussion of herbs and roots and other *materia magica* such as graveyard earth or dust, bones, coffin nails, parts of corpses, human fat, fingernail parings, hair clippings, both in malefic magic and in magic generally, see Chs 7 and 9.

3.4. *Personal possessions.* Items which have been in close contact with the body of an intended victim, e.g. clothing, especially underwear, are particularly useful to wizards when casting evil or love spells. Spells cast on them are transferred to the victim by renewed contact. This universal notion is known to have been one of the concerns of the Russian tsars in the sixteenth and seventeenth centuries (see Ch. 16) and continues to the present time in popular magic.

3.5. *Magical artefacts.* This category includes certain types of amulets. Knots and knotted cords, usually a protective amulet, may be used in malefic magic (see Ch. 8.4).[33] The piercing, destruction, casting into water, or burial, of dolls representing victims, or for other ritual purposes (see also Ch. 8.5) is also known in Russia, and the word for doll, *kukla*, can be used for a knotted figure made in corn which will bring harm to the one who gathers it.[34] Piercing a doll representing a victim is a fairly widespread magical practice, and in Russia the notion was reinforced by translated literature: the 'Tale of the Merchant Grigorii' reworked from a Polish version of a story in the *Gesta Romanorum*, tells of a Jewish wizard who tried to kill Grigorii in this way – he escaped by watching the wizard in a magic mirror and ducking just as the wizard shot the fatal arrow (which then killed the wizard instead).[35]

3.6. *Footprints.* Like nail parings or underclothes, a man's footprint was thought be so personal to him that it could be used in hostile magic. This is a very widespread notion,[36] and was common in Russia. It featured in the oaths of loyalty to the tsar and in evidence at witchcraft trials. A detailed description of the procedure in Russian popular magic in the last century is given by Zabylin: when you find a well-defined foot- or bootprint in sand, dust, mud, dew, or snow, particularly if it contains a human or animal hair, cover it carefully to protect it, then get the *koldun* to cut or dig up the print, preferably with a broad knife bloodied by a whirlwind. (Whirlwinds are thought to be transformed witches who can be stopped by stabbing the whirlwind with a knife.) A spell is muttered over the print which is then placed under a beam of the house of the victim to cause him grief, or burned in the bathhouse if his death is required. An antidote for a spell of this kind is for a friendly *koldun* or *znakhar'* to throw another print down wind. If a print cannot be found, then the victim must burn his underclothes on the feast of the Annunciation in order to be free of the spell.[37] A simpler method of footprint cursing is to measure the footprint of the victim with a thread and then burn the thread.[38]

4. *Ancient Gods, Evil Spirits and Magic*

Various kinds of supernatural being are very common in Russian belief. The ancient deities of the Slavs, in particular Perun and Veles, have been much written about, often with more imagination than evidence, and at times when the possession of a native pantheon and a national epic was a matter of some importance for the self-respect of nation-states. A readiness to associate popular magic, the demons of popular imagination and folklore, and the supposed pagan religion of the pre-Christian Slavs, can be seen in most schools of thought in Russia from the eighteenth-century to the present day. The assumption of such an association should be treated with some caution – comparison of Russian beliefs and practices with those of other peoples in Europe, and consideration of the ability of magic to cross cultural and linguistic boundaries, and the power of folkloric adaptation, can often point to different conclusions.[39] Since the survival of ancient deities in the folk memory is sparse and fragmentary (and indeed may well be no more than the survival of names),[40] they impinge little on the subject of this book, except insofar as the magicians of early Russian literature are often presumed to have been their devotees.[41]

On the other hand the various goblins of Russian folk belief, a fairy belief system of presumably later date, are still real in some parts of Russia and have often been assimilated to the evil spirits of the Judaeo-Christian tradition.[42] According to popular tradition in the Olonets region of northern Russia, when Michael the Archangel drove the rebellious angels from heaven some fell into hell and became devils, others fell into the forest and became wood sprites, others fell into water and became water sprites, while others fell into barns, bathhouses and dwelling houses and became their resident goblins.[43] This is analogous to Irish and other north European beliefs about the origins of fairies.[44] An alternative legend is that they are the children of Adam and Eve, conceived after the Fall, and hidden out of shame in barns, bathhouses, etc.[45] In fact throughout East Slav territory the hut or house, and often the various parts of it, not to mention the bathhouse, the barn, the well, river, forest, and most places where people live and work, have their spritely 'owners' who may have many names and manifest themselves in a variety of forms. Other supernatural beings may be associated with natural phenomena such as whirlwinds.[46] The history of belief in such beings before the early modern period is not well documented in scholarly literature, mainly for lack of evidence, but the roots of such belief are no doubt ancient. The names of these sprites, usually indicating their haunts but sometimes euphemisms, are for the most part not attested before the seventeenth century, but we may note that in the sixteenth century Fedor Syrkov, a noble of Novgorod, threatened Ivan the Terrible with the demons who lived in the River Volkhov.[47]

In local traditions some of these sprites may be thought of as good, friendly, or at least as having benign moods, but most are by reputation capricious or downright hostile and may have to be propitiated.[48] Attitudes can also be seen to vary according to whether the sprite is 'own' or 'other'[49] – a *domovoi* or house-sprite for example, if treated correctly, could protect the household but be hostile to intruders or new owners of the house. This ambivalence of attitude is probably ascribable to the survival of pre-Christian beliefs, but is complicated by the fact, already mentioned, that some of the names of these sprites may be euphemisms (e.g. *khoziain* 'owner, head of the household', or *dedushka* 'grandfather', for both the house-sprite and the wood-sprite). They are a part of the magic described in this book only insofar as their magical assistance may occasionally be invoked and because sometimes they must be guarded against by magical means.

4.1. *Demonic magic and the fear of witchcraft.* Several historians of the European witch hunts of the sixteenth and seventeenth centuries have mentioned Russia as not conforming to the general pattern of European witch persecution.[50] This opinion seems first to have been voiced by a nineteenth-century Russian scholar who remarked that in South Russia and the Ukraine the connection between the Devil and witchcraft was made only in the eighteenth century, and then only by the literate classes influenced by Western books.[51] One Western historian ascribes the non-occurrence in Russia of a witch-hunt on the scale seen in some other parts of Europe to an alleged lack a demonic theory of witchcraft and quite wrongly asserts that in Russia witches were not thought to fly, have sabbaths or kill children;[52] another states that in Russia the notion of the 'demonic pact' did not exist, and that there was little reference to conspiracy in witch trials.[53]

The situation among the Orthodox East Slavs is not in fact so simple. The reference in Isaiah 28;15 to a 'pact with hell' was often quoted by Latin theologians and writers and was no doubt familiar to Orthodox writers also; the references to Simon Magus in Luke and Acts, and their expansion in the apocryphal *Acta Petri*, and to how Simon practised magic with the aid of evil spirits was certainly known to them; the *volkhvy*, the pagan wizards with whom the priests and princes of early Russia had to contend, were certainly thought of as practising demonic magic (e.g. the *Laurentian Chronicle* talks of *besovskaia volshven'ia* 'devilish sorceries').[54] In the early sixteenth century Maxim the Greek introduced Russians to the Faust legend in his letter to Fedor Karpov on astrology and in a short tract 'An Explanation of the Blasphemous Pact'.[55] Magical practices and popular amusements are regularly described in the sixteenth century as 'devilish' (*besovskii*) and 'Hellenic' (*ellinskii*) in texts such as the *Domostroi* and *Stoglav* – i.e. anything not specifically Christian is the province of the Devil.[56] Indeed, almost all references in Russian ecclesiastical and annalistic texts before the eighteenth century to anything which could be described as magic condemn these practices as demonic and pagan ('Hellenic'), and this is the sole reason for their condemnation. Prince Andrei Kurbskii, in one of his diatribes against Ivan the Terrible, the *History of the Grand Prince of Muscovy*, denounces Ivan as having been conceived by the magic of Karelian witches summoned by his father, and of himself employing them, and various types of *charovnik* and *sheptun* who commune with the Devil. He states specifically: 'Magic, as everyone knows, cannot be performed without renouncing God and making a pact with the Devil'.[57] He also claimed that the Devil had corrupted the rulers of Russia through their sorcerous wives (i.e. Sofia Palaeologa and Elena Glinskaia, the wives of Ivan III and Vassilii III, the grandfather and father of Ivan IV), and that Ivan drank toasts to the Devil and danced in masks.[58] As evidence of knowledge of the demonic nature of magic, and of the demonic pact, in sixteenth-century Russia this would seem to be compelling. We cannot, however be sure that Kurbskii was as familiar with it before he left Muscovy as he appears to be in this text: he was fond of sneering at Ivan's alleged provincial ignorance from the safe distance of the Grand Duchy of Lithuania. On the other hand, in the view of at least one scholar, the text may be a seventeenth-century forgery; in either case we are still left with stronger evidence of a much earlier acquaintance with the demonic pact than has hitherto been admitted.

The early seventeenth century also offers a contemporary chronicle of unquestioned authenticity which accuses the usurper of the throne, the False Dmitrii, of practising 'magic with devils'.[59] Another account of the death of Dmitrii makes it clear that he was buried as if he had been a *koldun* (see Ch. 16), and the reputation of Dmitrii as a wizard, with or without specific demonic associations, was well known outside Russia. One more or less contemporary history claims that the Muscovites regarded Dmitrii as a sorcerer who kept a devil in a fearful war machine, which was eventually burned with his corpse; also that the Muscovites thought that Dmitrii adored as gods the masks which he had prepared for a court entertainment.[60] To Russians masks were associated primarily with pagan, usually midwinter, rituals which were regularly condemned by the Russian Church as satanic, a 'soul-destroying sin' as Patriarch Ioakim described them in an *ukaz* of 1684. (The most frequently quoted theological authority for this was the acts of the Trullan Synod held in Constantinople in 692: among other things this regulated marriage and sexual behaviour; forbade association with Jews; forbade mixed bathing, going to horse-races, mimes, animal shows, theatrical dancing, consulting diviners, sorcerers, cloud-chasers, purveyors of amulets; forbade celebrating the Calends, Vota and Brumalia, and forbade wearing comic, satyric or tragic masks, or jumping over fires at the beginning of the month.)

In a slightly later English account of 1654 we read:

> The 29 of May, Demetrius his body, was disinterned, and drawne out of the Citie, it being there burnt, and consumed to ashes, and the multitude said, they would have it thus performed: alleadging, how it was to prevent the charmes of that dead Enchaunter . . . the night after his body was burnt, it was yet a far greater frost, so that these barbarous, and infidell people beleeve, that in his lifetime he was a great Nigromancer.[61]

Variations on this story, which is also recorded by Karamzin,[62] continued to crop up in travel accounts in the eighteenth and nineteenth century: the Reverend William Coxe, in his famous itinerary of northern Europe, states that among the accounts of the death of Dmitrii is a story that music was heard at night and spectres seen at the place of his death, for which reason his remains were dug up, burned, the ashes mixed with gunpowder and fired from a cannon in the direction of Poland.[63] This may be seen either as one of several incidents of burning witches, a punishment often stated not to have been practised in Russia, or as the fairly common practice of exhuming dead wizards who were thought to be polluting the earth and thus causing misfortunes.[64]

At a more popular level, and without such textual precision, demonic associations were certainly attributed to witches in parts of Russia and Siberia, and even more so in the Ukraine and Belorussia where more Western influence can be detected; witches could be thought to be in league with the Devil; whirlwinds, particularly at crossroads, one of the magic places haunted by demons and sprites, were thought to be the Devil mating with witches.[65] This seems to be a relatively modern idea; the specific Western belief that the copulation of witches and the Devil sealed the demonic pact, as expressed in the *Malleus maleficarum*, is not commonly found in Russia.

When devils are mentioned, what kind or kinds of devil are involved? A modern writer on magic and the demonic in Luke's Gospel and Acts states: 'For many ancient Jewish and Christian authors, to talk about magic was at one and the same time to talk about the Devil'.[66] This is a useful corrective to the view, sometimes expressed in modern literature on witchcraft, despite abundant ancient and medieval evidence to the contrary, that the association of the demonic with magic is an invention of the Renaissance period. But one must add that the Russian Church was no different from the Western Church in the imprecise nature and history of its demonology and its ambivalence about personifications of evil.

There is no definite or indefinite article in Russian so that one cannot always know whether a text is speaking of *a* devil, i.e. any kind of demonic force, or *the* Devil, i.e. Lucifer the fallen angel, the promoter of evil, tempter of mankind, and ruler of hell and lesser imps, and just as often there will be references to other evil forces under a variety of names.[67] Church Slavonic and Russian *bes* regularly translates Greek *daimōn*, the term used in patristic texts for all pagan gods and supernatural beings; *diiavol* is found for Greek *diabolos* from the earliest translations of the Gospels onwards; *sotona* (Russian *satana*) is found for both *satanas* and *diabolos* in Greek; and *chert, chort* is probably the commonest name in colloquial Russian, and in popular belief the Devil's own preferred name for himself.[68]

These and other words may be distinguished in fixed locutions or by preponderance of stylistic context but the Russian sayings 'Net ni chorta ni d'iavola' (= 'there is no one/nothing there') and 'The Devil is nice only to Satan'[69] demonstrate that there is some semantic confusion. Moreover the Devil, or devils, of the Bible and Christian literature, as visualized by medieval Christian writers and artists, were regularly identified with the spirits of Slavonic folklore mentioned above. Indeed, as Cherepanova has shown in her study of north Russian beliefs and terminology of the supernatural,[70] there can be an almost complete coalescence of the Christian and pagan traditions, to the extent of creating names for evil spirits which are compounds of names drawn from what were originally separate belief systems. A whole series of ambivalent creatures is thus created: *lesnoi bes* 'forest devil', *vodianoi chert* 'water devil', *chert podpolnyi* 'the devil under the floor' and so on. In northern Russia these creatures may even turn up in hagiographic literature.[71] The evidence for a close association in Russian folklore between Christian and non-Christian *nechistaia sila* (lit. 'unclean power'), and the use of the word *eretik* 'heretic' to mean also 'wizard', 'demon' and 'vampire', has

been brought together by Felix Oinas in a valuable series of essays.[72] We may add
to these meanings a further one – 'revenant spirit of a dead atheist' in northern
Siberia; this explains what otherwise would have been a puzzling local expression
'Why are you wandering round at night like a heretic?'[73] One of the problems of
interpreting this information is that most of it is folkloric and was not recorded
before the nineteenth century. When, how, and where this syncretistic process
developed cannot be established with any certainty, although references to hostile
revenants, *upyr'* (= vampire, later also used for evil magicians) are recorded from
early times (e.g. the *Russian Primary Chronicle*) and are a persistent feature in
Slavonic folk belief.

In popular belief evil spirits share with witches and sorcerers the ability to
change shape and appear in the guise of animals. Maksimov reports that these
animals are usually black cats or dogs, whereas witches and sorcerers take the
form of white or grey creatures. Devils never take the shape of cocks, doves, or
asses, because of their New Testament associations, and can usually be detected
by their loud hoarse voices which they cannot disguise, or their tails, which they
usually manage to hide.[74] Loud laughter was also regarded as the sign of a
disguised devil.

Demonic possession was, as in most places, a common alternative to magic
spells as an explanation of mental disorder – *beshennyi* 'mad' meant 'possessed'
originally – and exorcism or some other kind of spiritual healing was its orthodox
cure.[75] Whether resorting to the state religion in such cases is the same as, or an
alternative to hiring your own witch to counter the spells of a hostile witch, must
depend on which view you take of the witchcraft and religion debate.

4.2. *The demonic pact.* Beside the evidence mentioned above, even such literary
notions as selling one's soul to the Devil can be encountered in Russia quite
early.[76] The Greek *Life of St Basil*, once attributed to St Amphilochius but now
thought to originate in a Greek community in North Italy *c.* 800, contains an
episode in which a young man approaches a magician who helps him to draw up
a pact with the Devil by which he will renounce Christ in order to win the
affection of a young lady who had vowed to enter a convent. Eventually he is
taken to a church by St Basil and the prayers of the congregation defeat the wiles
and torments of the Devil; the pact comes floating through the air into the saint's
hands. The last part of the story is represented pictorially in a sixteenth-century
fresco in the Cathedral of the Annunciation in the Moscow Kremlin. This story
was extremely widely known and copied in Russia and the Balkans from at least
the twelfth century; it was translated three times and was included in the *Menaia*
and *Synaxarion*. It was the main source of later purely Russian works,[77] in
particular the seventeenth-century *Tale of Savva Grudtsyn*.[78] A similar theme can be
found in the *Tale of the Poor Man made Tsar by the Devil*.[79]

Nor is the demonic pact in Russia confined to literature; the contract for one
such bargain, signed in blood, was even produced in evidence at the trial of a
colonel's servant Iliia Chovpilo in 1744.[80]

There also is certainly plenty of documentary evidence from the seventeenth century onwards for a popular belief in the connection between magic and evil spirits as the agents of the *koldun*, be they the Christian Devil or indigenous sprites or an amalgam of the two; some spells specifically call on spirits, others are 'anti-prayers' which negate the usual prayer formulas, some spells and forms of divination involve removing crosses or covering icons, and sometimes the use of demons for magical purposes in spells culminated in a rejection of Christ and placing the cross under one's (left) heel.[81] Afanas'ev quotes two methods of summoning a wood sprite which well illustrate the conflation of traditions in Russia: you could cut down some birch saplings and make a circle of them, stand in the middle, remove your cross and shout 'Grandfather!' (one of the euphemisms for the *leshii*, the *khoziain* or master of the forest, whose real name was a taboo word);[82] or, on St John's Eve you could cut down an aspen so that it fell to the east, stand on the stump, look between your legs and say 'Uncle Leshii, appear, not as a grey wolf, not as a black crow or a fir tree, but in the same shape as I am!' There will be a rustle and the *leshii* will appear; you may then exchange your soul for success in hunting and for the protection of your cattle.[83] Similar 'anti-prayers' were employed by the *kolduns* in the northern region of Zaonezh'e to find lost cattle: at the crossroads at night they would recite 'anti-prayers' and make three times nine bows 'not to the east'.[84]

Another method of entering into such pacts, attested by a peasant from the Altai region in the eighteenth century, was to wrap your written promise to the Devil round a stone and throw it into a millpond, which was where demons lived, according to popular imagination.[85] Here too the Devil seems to have become confused with the various demons of Russian folk belief.

The general association of sex, magic, and the Devil was, of course, nothing new to the Russians, who shared the common Judaeo-Christian tradition in this matter, through scripture and those parts of patristic literature available to them (although this was very limited; Augustine, the only father of the Church to have developed a theory of magic,[86] was hardly known in Russia). It should, however, be stated that the literary evidence for explicit or implicit demonic pacts in Russia involving sexual congress is available only from the seventeenth century onwards in works such as the *Tale of the Possessed Woman Solomoniia*.[87] Moreover, the *legal* distinction between demonic and non-demonic magic first entered Russian law in Peter the Great's code of military law at the beginning of the eighteenth century: the practice of the first was a capital offence, the second a misdemeanor (see Ch. 16). It should perhaps also be stated here that the 'satanism' of the Russian literary world of the eighteenth and nineteenth centuries was primarily an import from the West, even if it then filtered down to less intellectual levels.[88]

5. *Protection from Magic, Witchcraft, and Evil Spirits*

This has to a large extent been dealt with in Ch. 4.2 on protection during divination, Ch. 7 on spells and magic prayers, and Ch. 8 on amulets and talismans. The forms of protection are common to most of Europe: religious objects such as crosses, relics, blessed water, incense, talismans, the wearing of amulets, and the use of magic prayers and spells, even the use of Church Slavonic, are the main defences against sorcery as well as sickness and misfortune or evil spirits, the latter sometimes personifying the former. Inversion is a common element.

5.1 *Protection from witchcraft*. There were many beliefs about this, both general and local. A simple protection from a *koldun* was to press your ring finger against a twig or knot in a piece of wood and spit in the magician's face; this causes him to lose his power for a while, either from sheer astonishment or from the apotropaic quality of spittle.[89] Certain plants could also protect one from witchcraft (see Ch. 9.4): the *neodolim-trava* ('unconquerable herb'), for example, would safeguard your cattle from witches,[90] and heather and thistles gathered on Holy Thursday would protect a house from a hostile *koldun* if placed under the house or burned in the stove.[91] Protection from witches on January 18, reputed to be their holiday, could be obtained by hiring a *znakhar'* to come at midnight, put a spell on the chimney, drive a spike into the topmost roof-beam, and sprinkle the stove area with ash from seven stoves.[92] Protection from witches on St John's Eve, when they were most active, could be achieved by placing nettles in the window, hanging a dead squirrel in the doorway, or lighting a candle from the feast of the Presentation of Christ (2 February).[93] In the trans-Baikal region on St John's day the priest would read a prayer at each fence-post and make a cross of fresh tar on the gates as a protection against the witches who were liable to go around in the shape of dogs and steal the milk from the cows.[94] Moreover, as mentioned above, one could always employ one's own magician to foil the spells of a hostile magician.

5.2 *Protection from demons*. Certain types of demon in popular belief could be placated or foiled. The *domovoi* or house-sprite,[95] for example, who was usually invisible or a shadow, but was responsible for nightmares and noisily throwing household objects about at night,[96] had to be given food and drink, in particular on the feast of St Ephraem the Syrian (28 January) (see also below, p. 143). One kind of malicious house-sprite, the *kikimora*, was particularly to be found in empty houses, and could in fact be introduced into a new house by the carpenters if the owner was insufficiently generous with the vodka.[97] This could be done by placing a small wooden doll in the foundations; as a protection a new house had to be incensed and sprinkled with holy water.[98] Alternatively a disgruntled builder might reverse the ritual prayer said at the foundation of a new house.[99] There was a belief that if you thought you heard someone calling your name, this was probably the *domovoi* preparing to trick you in some way; a defence was to repeat silently the slightly surreal febrifuge spell: 'Mary, daughter of Herod, come yesterday'.[100]

The more hostile and fearsome *leshii* (wood-sprite),[101] who could appear in the form of a man, a giant, a horse or a whirlwind, was capable of all kinds of harm such as leading travellers astray, kidnapping maidens, etc. He could be foiled by wearing one's clothes inside out,[102] a magical deception also sometimes mentioned as being necessary when performing certain types of magic, or by wearing one's shoes and clothes back to front.[103] Both of these methods are variants of the very common notion of magic by reversal.

Hunters could ensure the *leshii*'s aid by offering a piece of bread with salt, the traditional gesture of hospitality.[104] In far northern Siberia the *leshii* was thought to be fond of playing cards, but without the clubs suit (which resembled crosses and were therefore demonifuges); local magicians, it was said, would play cards with the *leshii* and beat him by suddenly producing a club and saying 'clubs are trumps!'. In this region one was advised to make the sign of the cross and draw a circle if a *leshii* was encountered unexpectedly.[105]

Dr Matthew Guthrie, in his *Noctes Rossicae* (late eighteenth century) records that on St George's Day, when by tradition in north Russia the cows were first taken out to the spring pasture, a priest would perform a ceremony to protect the livestock from malicious wood sprites:

> A branch of Palm preserved for the purpose from Palm Sunday, with a lighted Taper, a Pot of Barsly and two Eggs (one for the Cowherd, the other for a Beggar) are placed before the family image or Saint, and then carried thrice around the Group of Cattle, together with a Cross, sprinkling them each time with the Palm dipt in holy Water, after which they are driven over a hatchet buried under the threshold, by the same consecrated Palm, and from thence to pasture; after which they may defy, in the opinion of the Rustics, all the Spells and Witchery of Satan and his Imps, but to secure the matter still more the holy Palm must be either thrown into running Water, or stuck into an anthill, and the Barsly sown on the field.[106]

5.3 *Protection when using magic or divination.* Extra protection is required against evil spirits if you are yourself engaged in magic or divination. This has been mentioned in several other chapters. As in other parts of the Christian and Islamic world it usually involved saying a prayer before embarking on the divination; the further common requirements of bathing and fasting which are mentioned in literary texts are sometimes also specified for popular divination.[107] Further necessary conditions such as particular times, places, directions etc. are discussed below. Even if the diviner has removed his cross, etc., in the knowledge that it is spirits who perform his magic, he nevertheless usually protects himself with a magic circle, as is demonstrated by some of the practices described below, or uses the magic exclamation 'Chur!' or 'Chur, nashe mesto sviato!' (see Ch. 11.2).

5.4 *Magic circles.* One of the most widespread methods of protection against evil spirits is the magic circle.[108] Magic circles in Russia, as in the West, may have several functions:[109] they may protect from demonic forces; they may focus demonic forces (in practice this may amount to the same thing); they may be a demonifuge, or a talisman. The earliest example I have found in Russia is in the account of the founding of Kazan' in the *Kazanskaia istoriia* (1560s), a work written to celebrate to capture of Kazan', the centre of the Tatar khanate, by Ivan the Terrible's army in 1552. In this text 'Tsar Sain the Bulgarian' wishes to build a new town but is prevented by a nest of serpents, led by a giant two-headed serpent which devoured men and horses. A cunning wizard (*volkhv, oboialnik*) came to him and promised to destroy the serpents; by magic he gathered them all together and inscribed a circle round them so that none could escape, and then, by a 'devilish act', he killed them all.[110]

The protective role of the circle is to be found in several accounts of magical and divinatory practices, as, for example, in the magic fern ritual for finding treasure (see Ch. 7.5.8), in the New Year mirror divination described below, and in Nikolai Gogol''s story *Vii* in which a student in the Ukraine is protected from the fatal embrace of a sprite in the form of a living corpse by drawing a circle about him and reciting prayers and curses which he had learned from a monk 'who all his life had been seeing witches and unclean spirits'. The student eventually dies of terror because he is unable to prevent himself from looking at the giant sprite, the *Vii*. An erstwhile companion at the end of the story remarks that he had died needlessly – all he had to do was to make the sign of the cross and spit on the tail of the witch who had embroiled him in all this supernatural unpleasantness.[111] This is, of course, a literary work and Gogol' had a Hoffmannesque imagination, but he also had an extensive knowledge of the popular beliefs and superstitions of the Ukraine of his time.[112] Ralston had apparently forgotten the Gogol' story when he described similar giant beings with a destructive gaze in Russian (evidently variants of the folk beliefs about St Cassian – see below, pp. 48–9) and West Slav folklore, and a Serbian one also called Vii.[113] In one part of Belorussia the *rusalka* (a creature which in the various parts of East Slav territory may be a water-sprite, the soul of an unbaptized child, the soul of a drowned person, or an evil spirit who tickles victims to death)[114] was thought to be the spirit of a suicide, who would hang from trees, play in fields of rye, and attack travellers unless they protected themselves by drawing a magic circle.[115]

Sometimes it is specified that magic circles should be made with a burning spill or a lighted church candle; in the Kostroma region other items having a connection with fire, such as charcoal or a frying pan, are also recorded as being used to make magic circles, and the circle may be anything from a line drawn round an inflamed area of the body to stop the inflammation spreading, to a line drawn round a house at the time of an epidemic,[116] or an icon carried round a farm to protect it from magic or pestilence. The most spectacular example of the last-mentioned type of magic circle is that which is ploughed round a village by women, often naked, at midnight to keep out plague – see Ch. 7.5.

It is recorded that Siberian Russians believed that the Devil fears circles, as well as crosses (*chortogon* 'expeller of devils' in popular Russian),[117] blessings, incense, the name of God, and cock-crow.[118] The same belief could probably be found in most areas (cock-crow is particularly common in folk tales as the banisher of devils and revenants)[119] and is matched by similar beliefs in many other parts of Europe. One curious use of the magic circle is found in the belief that a mother who overlaid her child had to perform a penance by going on three successive nights to the church, where she had to pray standing in a circle drawn by the hand of the priest.[120] How far the clergy co-operated in this practice is not recorded.

Magic circles could themselves be invoked as magic oracles; one practice in the Old Believer communities of the trans-Baikal region was to draw a circle on the ground and then say 'Circle, circle, tell me the real truth, what is my fate?'[121]

6. Magical Times

Ancient ideas of 'good and bad days', and predictions based on the day on which Christmas falls, which are literary borrowings from Byzantium, are discussed in Ch. 14.8, because they normally occur in the manuscripts in company with astrological texts. The favourability of the individual days of the week is also discussed there. We are here concerned more with the times and places at which popular magic and divination is practised, and at which vulnerability to magic or hostile forces is greatest. Typically these are times of transition: birth, marriage, death, moving house, midsummer, midwinter, the equinoxes, dawn (but rarely dusk), midday (rarely, except for the 'midday demon'), midnight (very common).

Dal' in his great collection of Russian sayings gives a large number of prognostications by date.[122] Often the origin of these is fairly obvious from the saint whose day it is. In Russia as in many other parts of Europe the time around Christmas and Midsummer were particularly suitable for magic and divination. The practices varied a little locally but the period from Christmas Eve to Twelfth Night was a time of festivity which included all kinds of *gadaniia* or divination, sometimes to find out what the new year would bring with regard to weather and harvest, often to discover a future husband. Of the days in this period the commonest for divination were New Year's Eve and the eve of the Epiphany, and the most characteristic form of popular divination was a kind of musical lottery, the *podbliudnye pesni* ('under-the-bowl songs') for details of which see Ch. 4.4.

Yuletide was also the time of various kinds of mumming, cross-dressing, dressing as animals,[123] wearing masks, wearing clothes inside out or upside down, and dramatized rites such as 'playing at corpses' in which a feigned, or even real corpse is brought into the house in a parody of the burial rites of the Church. This practice survived in the Vladimir area up to the Second World War with the extra element of inversion that the role of the priest was played by a woman.[124] Its survival in modern times is also recorded in Vologda.[125] Propp draws attention to a bizarre development of this ceremony, a folk comedy *Mavrukh* (i.e. a corruption of Marlborough via the form 'Mal'bruk' derived from the French popular song about the Duke of Marlborough which became widely known in

Europe: 'Malbrouck s'en va en guerre') in which the dead 'Marlborough' is brought on, seated on a bench, to be the central figure in a kind of wake in which indecent songs were sung to liturgical music.[126] Parody of religious rites may be seen as carnival or as the inversion typical of demonic magic, but the essentially unchristian nature of all this mumming and divination was often the target of ecclesiastical disapprobation, and was recognized by the peasants themselves in the custom of sweeping out devils with brooms after the last divination games of the season,[127] and for those who had engaged in mumming to bathe in the 'Jordan', the place on the river (or hole in the ice) where the 'Blessing of the Water' took place on the feast of the Epiphany.[128] (The most important celebration of this was in fact a court ritual in Moscow, conducted in the presence of the Patriarch and Tsar on the Moscow river – it is known from the sixteenth century onwards from foreign accounts.)[129] In parts of northern Russia and Siberia the one word *shilikun* may denote either a masked mummer or a demon (often a water spirit who appears out of a hole in the ice, especially the Epiphany 'Jordan').[130]

For further marital divination at midwinter see Ch. 4.4; this was also the time when the *sonnik* ('dream book') and *Krug Solomona* ('Circle of Solomon' oracle: see Ch. 11.11) would be brought out, and other types of popular fortune-telling, such as pouring molten wax or tin into water, would be indulged in (see Ch. 4.5.1)

The period of Midsummer, about the feast of St John (Ivan Kupala) and its eve, was a very magical time, especially for witches, were-animals, and domestic goblins such as the *domovoi*. It was the time for gathering magical and medicinal herbs (often it is specified that a particular non-iron implement should be used and that the herbs should still have the morning dew on them), for indulging in various kinds of divination,[131] and for young men to look for wives.[132] This is why in parts of Siberia, and possibly elsewhere, the popular name of St John's Day is Ivan Travnik (John the Herbal) or Ivan Koldovnik (John the Magician).[133] The abbot of the Eleazarov Monastery at the beginning of the sixteenth century wrote:

> When the great feast of the birth of the Precursor comes, indeed before this great feast, men and women witches and wizards come out into the fields and marshes and open lands and forests seeking for fatal herbs and poisonous plants for the destruction of men and beasts and dig up strange roots for women to give men as aphrodisiacs.[134]

The belief in this as a magical time in the seventeenth century was not simply rural quaintness; it was evidently held by Tsar Aleksei Mikhailovich (1629–76), who gave instructions for the gathering of herbs on St John's Day.[135] This was an old custom which was still observed at the beginning of this century; Makarenko records that the young women of the Enisei region of Siberia would go out to collect 'twelve different herbs' on St John's Eve. These were to be placed under the pillow and any dream that night would be prophetic. In the Tver' region of

European Russia much the same custom was known: after gathering the herbs a girl had to return home without speaking, place the herbs under her pillow, and say 'John and Mary herb, head herb, and all twelve herbs, tell me who my husband will be' – she would then see her future husband in a dream.[136] A similar practice with nine flowers gathered on Midsummer Eve and placed under the pillow to induce a prophetic dream is known in Swedish-speaking Finland.[137] The names of the twelve St John's herbs vary from region to region; many of them are described in Ch. 8.

The healing properties of curative herbs were considered to be greatly enhanced if gathered on St John's Eve or the morning of St John's Day, and there was a ritual and spell to be observed on this occasion: they were to be gathered between matins and mass on St John's Day; the gatherer was to be alone, naked, seen by none, and not afraid of any of the manifestations he or she might see; before plucking the herbs the gatherer was to ask Mother Earth (*mat' syraia zemlia* – a folklore formula) for her blessing. An alternative was to bow to the earth six times at home before setting out on the herb-gathering expedition, and again six times when reaching the place where the herbs were growing.[138] The dew collected that night was a specific for eye complaints;[139] in Siberia a cloth would be drawn over the dewy grass and the dew thus collected would be used to wash the hands and face to prevent illnesses and protect the face from pimples.[140] Dew gathered on St George's day was also a protection against the Evil Eye,[141] as was rain collected on Elijah's day.[142] The herb Ivan-da-Mar'ia (lit. 'John and Mary' – either cow wheat or heart's ease) plucked at this time would protect your home from thieves.[143] The importance of St John's Eve for the dangerous magic fern ritual is described in Ch. 7.5.8.

Although the Church was theoretically against such practices, and indeed often banned them and preached against them, this did not prevent the invention of a Church ceremony, a kind of harvest festival in which the herbs gathered on this day were blessed. They were called 'St John's herbs' and were kept for the whole year as medicine or as a charm against witchcraft.[144] Midsummer and the feast of St John have similar magical connotations in most parts of Europe, although nine rather than twelve seems to be the more common number of herbs.[145]

The feast day of St Cassian (29 February, i.e. the intercalary day) was generally a very unlucky day, and by extension leap year was also thought to be full of misfortune (or perhaps *vice versa*).[146] John Cassian, the fourth–fifth-century churchman generally considered the originator of semi-Pelagianism, is a saint in the Eastern but not in the Western Church. There seems to be nothing in his life to give rise to his unpleasant image and reputation in Russian folk tradition, where he is described as a demonic creature rather like Gogol's *Vii*. One of his conventional epithets is *nemilostivyi*, the opposite of *milostivyi* 'good, kind', the epithet of St Nicholas.[147] One must assume that it is the curious nature of the intercalary day, and the reputation both Byzantine and Western of the leap year as unlucky, which prompted the development of the magical belief, and that this was transferred to the saint of the day and then embellished. One Russian legend accounts for the three-year gaps in the celebration of St Cassian's day as a punishment by God: in the legend SS. Nicholas and Cassian were out walking when they saw a peasant with a cart which had stuck in the mud; St Nicholas helped him but St Cassian would not; God therefore gave St Cassian a feastday only once in every four years, but to St Nicholas he gave two feastdays in every year.[148] To some extent the similarity of sound with the adjective *kosoi*, 'crooked' has contributed to the legend: Cassian 'looks crookedly', i.e. squints and puts the Evil Eye on everything. He is reputed to sit with downcast eyes but on his feast day he looks up and withers anything he sees. He is also supposed to control the winds. In church his icon hangs on the back wall over the doorway.[149]

One of the most detailed Russian descriptions of folk divination was published by V. Smirnov in 1927.[150] He lists the following days in Kostroma when divination was practised (I have added the generalized detail in parentheses – practices in fact vary from place to place): New Year's Eve (general divination, but especially marital), Annunciation (25 March), Ivan Kupala (24 June – general divination, gathering of magic plants, etc.), Pokrov (1 October – a women's feast day, marital divination), St Paraskeva (28 October – a women's feast day), the Presentation of the Virgin (22 November – a womens' feast day), SS Merkurii and Catherine (24 November – a women's feast day), Znameniia (27 November – a women's feast day), St Andrew (30 November – a feast day for young people: a piece of clothing from a member of the opposite sex is placed under the pillow with an invocation to induce a dream of one's eventual spouse),[151] St Barbara (4 December – a women's feast day, in particular for pregnant women), St Nicholas (6 December, 9 May), SS Ananii, Azarii, Misail (17 December); St Samson (27 June – 'Samson days' were thought to be wet and were a time for young people to relax)[152] and the Thursdays before Easter and Trinity. More generally Friday, or the night before, in some places on Monday, preferably at midnight.

Makarenko's survey of Siberian calendar customs (some already mentioned) offers the following, most of which have similar practices attached to them in other parts of Russia: Agrafena Kupal'nitsa (23 June – a women's feast day; for prophetic dreams and divination with plants); Thursday of Holy Week (day for practising magic and collecting curative herbs); Semik (Thursday before Trinity – feast day of unmarried girls; marital divination, collection of curative and magical herbs); Trinity Sunday (marital divination); Easter Sunday (wizards could be made visible; when the priest sang 'Christ is risen' in the liturgy if bold hunters and card-players shouted out 'I have a bullet!' or 'I have an ace!' respectively, they would be successful in their avocations for the whole year; a candle successfully carried home alight from church would have magical properties). Days which were thought to be particularly helpful in childbirth were: SS. Joachim and Anne (9 September); Anne (9 December); the apocryphal Solomonida (1 August and 27 December); Barbara (4 December); Catherine (24 November); Epiphany (6 January); Mary Magdalene (22 July); Paraskeva (14 October).[153]

The time of day most commonly prescribed for magic and divination is midnight, as can be seen from the examples quoted, although dawn was often specified in *zagovory* spell formulas ('I shall arise at dawn…'). Midnight is the time of demons and revenants, as in Western Europe, and not a safe time to be out alone.[154] As has been mentioned elsewhere, and as everyone anywhere in Europe still knows, these spectres are banished by the crowing of a cock, perhaps because it heralds the dawn.

7. Magical Places and Directions

As the examples quoted in this chapter and elsewhere in the book will demonstrate, the places associated with popular magic and divination are bathhouses and crossroads (these are the most common),[155] churches, cemeteries, barns, thresholds, boundaries, holes in the ice on a lake or river, hopfields.[156] Most of these are either the reputed haunts of demonic forces or can clearly be seen to be liminal areas at which a magical other world begins. As elsewhere in Europe holy springs and wells were also common, but their curative powers were sometimes restricted to particular times such as St John's Day.[157] Maksimov states that magical springs and wells were all under the patronage of St Paraskeva (Piatnitsa), and that her icon placed near a spring or well was considered to have thaumaturgic qualities.[158] Peter the Great's *Spiritual Regulation* required bishops to seek out tricksters who made money out of 'false miracles, connected with icons, wells, springs, etc.'[159]

7.1. *The bathhouse.* A modern book of popular magic has a chapter on becoming a *koldun* which asks the question 'where should one begin to learn to be a *koldun*?'. The answer given is 'Anywhere you like. But best is a bathhouse . . . at midnight'.[160] The communal village bathhouse and midnight represent the conditions *par excellence* for popular magic and divination in Russia – hence the title of this book.[161] The bathhouse has an ancient history among the Slavs; according to the *Russian Primary Chronicle* the Apostle Andrew reported to Rome on the strange Slavonic bathing customs, and its place in a dualist view of religion is recorded for 1071 in the same chronicle when two magicians claim that man was created after a quarrel between God and Satan when God was bathing in a bathhouse. When questioned the magicians said that the name of their God was Antichrist.[162] Lotman and Uspenskii have suggested that in a binary model of sacred locations, places such as bathhouses demonstrate the fate of pagan temples in a Christian world where they become the reputed focus of evil forces.[163]

The Russian wizard, not noted for cleanliness, was nevertheless reputed to go off to the bathhouse when everyone else goes to church.[164] When he did this he was not necessarily going to bathe; indeed the Russian village bathhouse, a fairly hot steam bath, is only heated when people are going to use it. His use of the bathhouse, according to popular belief, was more likely to be magical: the casting of spells, praying to demons or practising malefic magic such as the burning of footprint traces mentioned above. For the same reason anyone who did not bathe at the usual times (e.g. St John's Day or any Friday or Saturday) could well be suspected of being a *koldun*.[165] In 1691 part of the evidence against Prince Vasilii Vasil'evich Golitsyn in a treason trial was that he kept a *koldun* in his bathhouse to make magic love spells to attract the Regent Sofia;[166] this suggests that some of the more elaborate procedures for conjuring up the image of a future spouse in more recent popular divination go back a long way.

Most villages had a bathhouse, usually some way off from the rest of the houses in the village, where possible near water. It was usually a dilapidated building. It was thought to be a dangerous place with its own resident sprite, the *bannik*, the most hostile of the Russian domestic goblins, and was not a place to visit alone.[167] The *bannik* or *baennik* (there are many variants of his name) was variously envisaged as a naked dwarf or a little old man; occasionally the demon was female (*baennitsa, bannaia babushka*)[168] with only one eye, and a danger to women in labour if they were left alone in the bathhouse. After midnight the bathhouse was the haunt of evil spirits. The proper time for people to use it was the five (or seven) hours before midday. Only three (in some areas two) bathing sessions were safe; after that it was the Devil's turn and no peasant would go in after the third session, or after sundown.[169] The demonic guardians of the bathhouse in Russia have close parallels in the world of early Christianity, where several works attest to the belief that bathhouses are haunted by malign demons. Even the belief, recorded in the apocryphal *Acta Ioannis* with reference to the bath of Dioscorides, that human sacrifices were made in the foundations of bathhouses has a Russian parallel in the burial of a black hen under the threshhold or bench when building a new *bania*.[170]

The reputation of the bathhouse as a fearful and magic place was no doubt reinforced by the fact that, for purely practical reasons, it was here that bathers removed their primary magical protection: the cross from around their necks and the belt from around their waists,[171] not to mention any other amulets they may have had. A *banishche* (site of a former bathhouse) was unlucky, even evil (*nechistii* 'unclean'), and new houses were not built there.[172] This superstition also applied in Belorussia to places which were the site of any misfortune, especially if blood had been spilled, or which were near an uprooted or blasted tree; to be quite sure a *koldun* or *znakhar'* would often be employed when selecting a place to build a house.[173]

Going to the bathhouse was, and is, often regarded as a way of getting rid of illnesses. In one Russian legend the wonder-working St Nicholas is wandering with a priest and the two let it be known that they are *znakhari* (practitioners of folk medicine); they are asked to cure various people and on each occasion they take the patient to the bathhouse to be treated. (The treatment consists in cutting up the patient and washing each part before reassembling and revivifying him or her!)[174]

The close relationship of popular medicine with magic, and the association of the notions of physical cleanliness and ritual purification, reinforced the magical role of the bathhouse. As we have seen elsewhere the bathhouse was the site of a good many rituals designed to ascertain marital prospects. There is surely a link here with the use of the bathhouse as a place for the ritual pre-marriage bath and for the delivery of babies, recorded in a number of sources as a practice in Russia, Belorussia and the Baltic region. The Russian expression 'The bathhouse is your (second) mother', and the dreadful curse on newborn babies, 'Out of the bathhouse into the pit!', illustrate this connection.[175] Dal' suggests that the use of the bathhouse for the delivery of babies was simply because there was not much room in a peasant house.[176] This may well have been an important consideration, but it fails to account for the fact that historically women of all rank would follow this practice – Grigorii Kotoshikhin, the renegade senior functionary of Tsar Aleksei Mikhailovich who described so unflatteringly the intimate details of life at the court of the seventeenth-century tsars, mentions that even the tsaritsa, when she goes into labour, is taken off to the bathhouse, where she remains with only her midwife and female attendants until her child is born.[177] The last detail is consonant with another belief mentioned by Dal', that the bathhouse sprite did not like women in labour and for this reason they were never to be left there alone.

These childbirth practices are not necessarily an indication of the magical status of the bathhouse – the practical considerations, as Dal' suggests, are no doubt important – but they must surely have contributed to it. And one further, and definitely magical, practice linking the bathhouse with childbirth was the custom, recorded by Dal', of having the naked midwife carry a newborn baby round the bathhouse chanting an invocation to the dawn, or Morning Star, to keep the child from crying.[178] Dal' did not say where this custom was observed but one must assume from purely practical considerations that it was uncommon in the north and in winter.

With regard to the ritual bath of a bride, a component part of the village marriage ceremonies, which in many parts of Russia were protracted and fairly elaborate, at least one source states that in the Pskov region the village *koldun* or wizard was in charge of this,[179] just as he was often in charge of other parts of the marriage ceremony (see the discussion of the *koldun* in 14.2 above).

The common association of bathhouses with evil is not necessarily part of a typology of cult places. It has also a basis in ecclesiastical history: in late antiquity the public baths were all too often the centre of vice and promiscuity and both civil and ecclesiastical authorities found it necessary to attempt to regulate them. They were centres of prostitution, male and female, and, as in Russia, seem to have been thought suitable places for malefic magic. No doubt it was for this reason that St John Chrysostom in the fourth century thought it appropriate for Christians to make the sign of the cross before entering;[180] and in St Basil's prayer of exorcism the bathhouse is the only building given in the list of places from which the unclean spirit is to depart.[181] Justinian in the sixth century laid down strict penalties for misbehaviour at the bathhouse, and condemnations of mixed bathing as an occasion of sin appear often in the records of councils and synods, and in patristic and later Christian literature.[182] Since the canons of the Council of Laodicea in the year 320 and the decrees of the Trullan synod of 692 which dealt with this matter were known to the Russians (and indeed the prohibition on mixed bathing, especially for the clergy, is included in the twelfth-century code of canon law, the *Kormchaia Efremovskaia*, and repeated in later codes of canon law,[183] and is mentioned in Ch. 41 of the *Stoglav* Council of 1551 as an evil practised in Pskov),[184] one might have expected bathing to have been more of an issue in the Russian Church, but in fact in Russia and Finland bathing in communal, sometimes mixed, bathhouses was normal, and many a foreign visitor to Muscovy was shocked by scenes of mixed nude bathing in Russian bathhouses.

In fact communal, even mixed communal bathing, was known in England and France from the time of the Crusades to the sixteenth century when the public stews were closed, partly because they were associated with prostitution; the same was true of spa baths in Renaissance Italy.[185] In eighteenth-century England mixed bathing for therapeutic purposes was the rule in the spa at Bath, and even though this was performed clothed the opportunities for indecorous behaviour were commented upon by several writers.[186]

It would seem that Western views on Russian baths are therefore coloured by the reputation which public baths had acquired in the West. Several accounts of Russia describe in pious indignation, and sometimes also illustrate in detail, the depravity which was supposed to ensue from mixed communal bathing.[187] Indeed, where would modern anthropology be without the pioneer work of salacious travel writers?[188]

One of the most notorious of these accounts was the Abbé Chappe d'Auteroche's derogatory description of Russia and its morals and manners in his *Voyage en Sibérie* (4 vols, Paris, 1768) which contained engravings of drawings by Le Prince, a pioneer illustrator of the customs and dress of the Russian Empire.[189] Although the greater part of the book is concerned with ethnography, climatology and geology, the abbé also showed a lively interest in marriage and bathing customs. (The reason for Chappe d'Auteroche's visit to Russia was, perhaps appropriately, to observe the transit of Venus.) He wrote an amusingly wry account of his visit to a public bathhouse and this description was duly illustrated by Le Prince in an engraving. As with most of Le Prince's engravings there is some artistic licence in the scene and it may well have seemed salacious to many contemporary eyes, but it does show familiarity with the details of the Russian method of bathing.[190] The book and its illustrations provoked the ire of no less a person than the Empress Catherine II, who had almost certainly never visited a public bathhouse but, jealous of the reputation of her empire, described the engraving as 'most indecent' in her *Antidote* (1770), an anonymously published refutation of the abbé's book. The engraving was certainly a good deal less indecent than some of the notorious erotic 'works of art' in Catherine's collections, but she nevertheless found it expedient to reinforce earlier condemnations of mixed public bathing in her Police Statute of 1782.

7.2. *Crossroads*. Crossroads were magic and 'unclean' places (the Russian adjective *nechistyi* 'unclean', can mean ritually unclean of animals and lepers for example, and often refers to evil spirits; as a noun it means the Devil), as examples above will also have shown. Suicides and unidentified corpses were buried there,[191] and as will have become clear earlier in this chapter and in Ch. 7, it was one of the favourite places for casting magic spells and practising various kinds of divination. Witches met there, evil spirits lived there, like the djinns of the Muslim world, and it was the haunt of the *vstrechnyi*, a goblin who liked to lead travellers astray. Practising divination at crossroads and in deserted huts was a dangerous pursuit and could send the would-be diviner mad.[192] Perhaps because of the sacrilegious, if necessary, nature of the process, icons which had to be disposed of were burned at the crossroads (see Ch. 8.6.2). Given this reputation it is not surprising that crossroads and cemeteries were among the places which had to be avoided by wedding processions, which, as we have seen elsewhere, were particularly vulnerable to evil influences.[193] On the other hand shrines, usually crude statues, to the rather ambivalent St Paraskeva (or Piatnitsa, i.e. Friday), the saint of women and provider of husbands, were also often situated at crossroads.[194]

7.3. *Thresholds*. Thresholds were also places of magical significance. It was the place to hide spells and magical objects, both protective and malefic, and it was, and still is, thought to be unlucky to greet a visitor over the threshold, stand on the threshold or accept anything over it,[195] or to go back over the threshold once one had set out on a journey.[196]

7.4. *Cemeteries*. In the Pskov and Tver' regions cemeteries are used as a place of Yuletide divination; in this capacity they may be known as *bui* or *buivishche*, as may be the divination itself.[197] They are also mentioned occasionally in other accounts of divination and as a place from which the earth has magical properties, and from which one might for magical purposes extract parts of corpses or grave goods such as 'dead crosses' (see Ch. 7.5.6 and 9.2). They were to be avoided by wedding processions (see Crossroads above).

7.5. *Magical directions*. The magical significance of actual locations is supplemented by the significance attached to directions. The requirement to face east in a number of spells is mentioned in Ch. 7 (west was the 'Devil's side'), and the divination of the direction from which a future spouse will come (i.e. in most cases from which part of the village, or from which neighbouring village) is found above in this chapter. To this we should add the Russian variants of the ubiquitous superstitions and practices relating to left and right.

The Russian word for 'right' (*pravyi*), as in most European languages, means both 'on the right hand' and 'good, correct, true, just'; and as in many other cultures the left in Russia is unlucky, unjust, bad,[198] secret, demonic, and the Revolution can only have reinforced this in the minds of many, as well as adding illicit, black market connotations (to sell something 'on the left'). Although this belief is not restricted to Christian cultures, and indeed lefthandedness probably has a physiological basis,[199] it must certainly have received regular reinforcement for Christians from the biblical emphasis on the right hand as the place of honour and from Matthew's account of the Last Judgement when the good sheep will be placed on the Lord's right hand and the bad goats will be placed on the left, after which those on the left were to be thrown into eternal fire (Matthew, 25: 33, 41). Perhaps for this reason one of the euphemisms for the Devil in some parts of Russia is simply *levyi* 'the left one'.[200] It is also noteworthy that the demonic *leshii* or woodsprite reputedly brushed his hair to the left and fastened his kaftan to the right (i.e. opposite to normal practice); to foil him one had to wear one's clothes inside out.[201] In the 1850s in Siberia a tailor was thought to be a magician who had caused a cholera epidemic; he narrowly missed being beaten to death because he cast his fishing line from the left and threw his beer dregs to the left.[202] There was a common dualist belief in Russia that a child at its birth was allocated not only a guardian angel, who always hovered on the right, but also an attendant devil, who took up his position on the left. Consequently many Russians would never spit to the right and would always sleep on their left side so as to be facing the angel and not see the Devil in nightmares.[203] This belief in a good and bad guardian spirit has analogues in Greek and Jewish popular belief.[204] For other examples of the evil, magical, or inverse significance of the left in this book see the Index.

It will be seen in some of the divinations described above in this chapter that the left hand or foot may be involved in the process. Moreover, in popular omens the left is invariably unlucky: getting out of bed with the left foot means you will have a bad day; putting your left shoe on first is sinful, but will cure toothache;[205] itches and twitches on the left side are bad omens (see Ch. 6.6).

Associated with popular notions of left and right is the widespread belief, found also in Russia, in the magical significance of clockwise and anti-clockwise circles or movements (which many people in fact see in terms of left and right).[206] Several examples of this have been quoted in this book and no doubt similar considerations entered into the debate in the Russian Church about the direction to be taken when processing around the church, sunwise (*posolon'*, lit. 'according to the sun'), or widdershins. This came to be one of the issues in the seventeenth century between the official Russian Orthodox Church and the anti-reform Old Believers, for whom the *posolon'* became an article of faith, and its opposite a devilish practice of the Antichrist, although in fact the argument had begun much earlier, in the fifteenth century, and in different circumstances.[207] The heterodoxy of anti-clockwise movement is also a feature of popular belief among the Orthodox of Bulgaria where witches are reputed to go in anti-clockwise procession around churches.[208]

Walking backwards also has a significance in magical beliefs, in particular when dealing with the demons of popular belief such as the bathhouse sprite, to whom one should never turn one's back. (Alternatively, if fleeing from a magical encounter, it was imperative not to look back – this is also specified for the performance of many divinatory rituals as we have seen elsewhere.) Walking backwards, or returning over one's own footprints, was supposedly one of the ways of deceiving the demons of sickness into leaving their intended victim.[209]

Turning somersaults (usually over a knife-blade) was sometimes specified as part of the procedure for becoming a were-animal or magician. This may be seen both as reversal and as crossing a boundary into an alternative magical world. A similar way of seeing that alternative world was to look at it upside down from between your legs.[210]

8. *Parodies of Religion*

Associated with inversion and reversal as indications of magical otherness is religious parody. Although parodies of orthodox religion are perhaps not quite so well-known a feature of Russian magic as they are in the West, there are some examples of blasphemous parody which may have had some magical element. Ivan the Terrible in the sixteenth century set up a strange alternative state, the *oprichnina* (lit. the 'outside' or 'other place') in which his officers dressed in quasi-monastic uniform. He is also reputed to have danced with young monks to the music of the Creed.[211] In the seventeenth century a text entitled *The Tavern Service* (*Sluzhba kabaku*) was current – this was a satirical work probably taking its origin in West European 'Services for Drunkards' which are known from the thirteenth century onwards.[212] Blasphemous parody of the burial service has been mentioned above (in 2.6 *Magical times*), and Gorelkina has pointed out that the instructions on how to become a *koldun* given in a magic manual cited in a court case in 1730 in fact amounts to an inversion of the ceremony of baptism.[213] In the eighteenth century Peter the Great had his 'All-Jesting Synod' or 'Most Holy Synod of Drunkards and Fools' with similar dressing-up and a blasphemous mock marriage ceremony, as well as ordinations and 'papal investitures' in which vows were taken to Bacchus (whose name in Russian is very similar in pronunciation to the Russian for God), anointings with vodka, and 'Gospels' which were imitation books containing bottles of vodka and drinking vessels.[214] The Cross itself was not spared: a blasphemous 'blessing' of a pleasure palace of Peter's close associate François Lefort involved the use of a cross made of two tobacco pipes.[215] The tradition was continued later in the century by the Empress Anna who punished Prince M.A. Golitsyn for his conversion to Catholicism by making him court jester, a fate shared by Count A.P. Apraksin for the same reason. Golitsyn was made to sit on eggs and cluck like a hen while Anna was in chapel – this has been recently interpreted as a reference to the 'chicken god', the pagan cunniform amulet widely used in Russia, and mentioned in Ch. 8.3.[216] The wretched prince was also forced to undergo a mock marriage in a house of ice with a bathhouse and marriage bed of ice on the river Neva.[217]

At a more humble level the period from Christmas to Epiphany was, as mentioned above, a time both of magic and divination and of a variety of carnival practices of pagan origin including dressing as animals, the wearing of 'devilish' masks, cross-dressing, and mock burials complete with 'priests', 'deacons', etc. All these practices were regularly condemned, but tacitly condoned by the Church. To what degree these practices should be seen as carnivalesque and to what degree as the inversion which is typical of magic, and especially demonic magic, is debatable. Certainly there was a feeling that there was something unholy about them which required ritual cleansing at the Epiphany Blessing of the Water ceremony.

It is noticeable that the *koldun* does not normally seem to include parody of religion in his repertoire; indeed in village weddings in some accounts he appears to act in effect as a surrogate or colleague of the priest; and those accused of witchcraft only rarely have any kind of parodic practice mentioned in their trial records. Indeed, in a rare example of parody of this kind in 1729 the perpetrator was not a *koldun*, but a monk who was found to be in possession of parodies of the Lord's Prayer (see p. 421). Most of the magic prayers discussed in Ch. 7 are not so much parodies as extensions of orthodox prayer, although those which are addressed to the Devil may be seen as parodic inversion. Practices such as wearing your cross back to front, or turning the icon to the wall, or placing a candle upside down and reciting a memorial prayer in order to cause the death of an enemy, are certainly inversions with magical intent, as are the wearing of clothes inside out, or back to front, or writing a petition to the 'tsar of the forest' from right to left, reading prayers backwards, or the Lord's Prayer with each verb negated, or counting with the negative particle 'ne' before each number.[218] There was a belief from the Novgorod region that reading the prayer 'Da voskresnet Bog' three times was protection against witchcraft; the same thing done twelve times in the morning would reveal a murderer.[219] Desecration of religious objects, such as trampling on a cross or an icon, or abusing communion bread, practices which are occasionally attributed to *kolduny* and those accused of witchcraft, or of wishing to become a *koldun*, and may be specified in some types of *zagovor*, are a related but different kind of magical 'anti-behaviour'.

Notes

1. Articles in journals such as *Zhivaia starina*, *Ètnograficheskoe obozrenie*, and the many local studies journals; these are quoted below as appropriate. Most will be found listed in the appropriate sections of the various volumes of *Russkii fol'klor: Bibliograficheskii ukazatel'*.

2. In English the now dated Ralston is still worth reading, as is the relatively recent Ivanits, *Russia Folk Belief*, which gives a good succinct account of many subjects discussed here. In German Mansikka's work and Felix Haase, *Volksglaube und Brauchtum der Ostslaven*, are dated but still useful, as is the Polish Moszyński, *Kultura ludowa słowian. Cz. II, Kultura duchowa*. In Russian the classic is Afanas'ev, *Poèticheskie vozzreniia slavian na prirodu*, 1865, but this suffers from under-documentation, a confusion of information and interpretation, and a marked determination to make the material fit a preconceived mythological model; recent studies which are valuable in covering considerable areas are Uspenskii, *Filogicheskie razyskaniia*, and Cherepanova, *Mifologicheskaia leksika russkogo severa*. Other works are quoted where appropriate.

3. On bears in popular seasonal entertainment and beliefs connected with them see Nekrylova, *Russkie narodnye gorodskie prazdniki*, pp. 35–53: 'Medvezh'ia komediia'.

4. Popov, *Sud i nakazaniia*, pp. 98, 162.

5. Koshel', *Istoriia nakazaniia v Rossii*, p. 17.

6. For some Siberian examples see *Kalendarno-obriadovaia poèziia sibiriakov*, p. 184.

7. *Of the Russe Common Wealth*, London, 1591, p. 94. For similar superstitions in Britain see Opie and Tatem, *Dictionary of Superstitions, s.v. nails and hair, cutting: baby's*. For similar beliefs among the Volga Germans see Koch, *The Volga Germans*, p. 166.

8. For an detailed survey of such beliefs, in particular as they relate to livestock, see Zhuravlev, *Domashnii skot*; for a detailed study of such beliefs and rituals associated with cereals and bread see Strakhov, *Kul't khleba u vostochnykh slavian*.

9. Seligmann wrote extensively on the subject. His *Der Bose Blick* is still the most wide-ranging assessment of the subject and his *Die Zauberkraft des Auges und das Berufen*, has a short section on Russia at pp. 44–6 as well as scattered references elsewhere. For English material on the subject in general see Elworthy, *The Evil Eye* and his article in *ERE*, V, cols. 608a–615b, and more recently Opie and Tatem, *Dictionary of Superstitions*, s.v. *Eyes, peculiar*. See also the anthology of papers edited by Dundes, *The Evil Eye: A Folklore Casebook*, and the conference papers edited by Clarence Maloney, *The Evil Eye*.

10. Reginald Scot, *Discovery of Witchcraft*, p. 37.

11. *Slovar' drevnerusskogo iazyka (XI–XIV vv), s.v. oko*. There is also a seventeenth-century entry under the later Russian word for eye: *glaz*.

12. E.g. small bells and *zmeeviki* (see Ch. 6.5 and 6.6): see Russell, 'The Evil Eye in Early Byzantine Society', pp. 540–41, 543.

13. Afanas'ev, *Poèticheskie vozzreniia*, p. 173.

14. This list is also applicable in other parts of Europe. In the case of priests even Pope Pius IX (d. 1878) was thought by superstitious Italians to possess the *mal'occhio*.

15. See *Ètnokul'turnye protsessy v Karelii*, p. 44; Afanas'ev, *Poèticheskie vozzreniia*, p. 173.

16. A story cited at several removes by Benjamin Gordon, 'Oculus fascinus', p. 306.

17. Popov, *Russkaia narodno-bytovaia meditsina*, p. 36.

18. E.g. Pliny, *Naturalis historia*, XXVIII.iv.36–9; Persius, in his *Satires* (ii, 31–4) notes the use of spittle to avert the Evil Eye, Theocritus (*Idylls*, VI) spits three times on his breast to ward off magic charms, and Petronius in his *Satyricon* (131) describes the use of coloured threads and spitting three times for the same purpose. Spitting three times as a precaution against the Evil Eye is described in Elworthy, *The Evil Eye*, p. 417, and Brewer, *Dictionary of Phrase and Fable*, s.v. *magpie* notes the practice in Devon of spitting three times if you see a magpie. The magical significance of spittle was enhanced for Christian communities by the accounts in the Gospels in which Jesus cured the blind and dumb (John 15:6–7; Mark 7:32–5, and 8:22–4). For a detailed discussion of the magical and therapeutic power of spitting and spittle in ancient Egypt see ch. 3 of Ritner, *Mechanics*. For other examples of classical and English practices of spitting for luck, to avert evil, or to cure, see Opie and Tatem, *Dictionary*, s.v. *spitting*; Hazlitt, *Dictionary*, s.v. *spitting*. For Greek beliefs and practices similar to the Russian see Stewart, *Demons and the Devil*, pp. 208, 233.

19. Perry, *The State of Russia*, pp. 152-3.

20. For a general survey of this belief in ancient and modern cultures see McCartney, 'Praise and Dispraise'.

21. Aksakov, *Chronicles of a Russian Family*, pp. 224–5. For another, fictional, example from 'the time

when Russians were Russians' see N.M. Karamzin's short story *Natal'ia the Boyar's Daughter*. For British parallels see Opie and Tatem, *Dictionary, s.v. Praising*.

22. Zabylin, *Russkii narod*, p. 261. Cf. Pliny, *Naturalis historia*, XXVIII.vii.3–9.

23. Report by Phil Reeves in the *Independent*, 18 March, 1998, p. 8.

24. Pinkerton, *Russia*, p. 155.

25. See Vlasova, *Novaia abevega*, s.v. *veter*, for a general account of wind and magically caused illness, and ibid., s.v. *vikhr* for whirlwinds as demonic forces.

26. Dal', *Tolkovyi slovar'*, s.v. *nasylat'*.

27. Dal', *Tolkovyi slovar'*, s.v. *steklo*.

28. Fennell, *Kurbsky's History of Ivan IV*, pp. 52–3.

29. *Polnoe sobranie zakonov*, III, p. 49. See also Truvorov, 'Volkhvy i vorozhei', esp. p. 703.

30. Minenko, *Russkaia krest'ianskaia obshchina*, p. 152.

31. Zabylin, *Russkii narod*, p. 394.

32. Adon'eva, Ovchinnikova, *Traditsionnaia russkaia magiia*, no. 574.

33. From the classical world onwards, and throughout Europe knots tied by a magician have been thought capable of preventing conception or childbirth. See Frazer, *Golden Bough*, abridged edn, p. 240. For Anglo-Saxon, English and Scottish beliefs see Opie and Tatem, *Dictionary*, s.v. *knots hinder conception*.

34. Dal', *Tolkovyi slovar'*, s.v. *kukla*.

35. Text in *Zvezdochtets*, pp. 46–8.

36. See Frazer, *Golden Bough*, abridged edn, pp. 44–5. For condemnation in the West see the *Corrector* of Burchard of Worms in McNeill and Gamer, *Medieval Handbooks of Penance* (reprint 1965), p. 339.

37. Zabylin, *Russkii narod*, pp. 397–8; Popov, *Russkaia narodno-bytovaia meditsina*, p. 24.

38. Zabylin, *Russkii narod*, p. 408.

39. Strakhov, 'Na sviatogo Nikolu . . .', makes some interesting and valid observations on this matter in his criticism of the methodology of B.A. Uspenskii in the latter's book on St Nicholas (although the same criticism could have been levelled at any number of other books, and the value of Uspenkii's work is still enormous even if some of Strakhov's points are accepted).

40. Just as an Englishman employing the expression 'By Jove' may convey thereby several pieces of information about himself, a belief in, or even awareness of, the religion of ancient Rome is probably not among them. De-etymologization and folk etymology can be very rapid processes, and significant ones in the subject area of this book.

41. An old but still useful account is Maksimov, *Nechistaia, nevedomaia i krestnaia sila*. This is rather popular in style and rarely gives sources or locations. An English-language account from an Orthodox position is Fedotov, *The Russian Religious Mind*, ch. 12: 'Paganism and Christianity'. More recent is Rybakov, *Iazychestvo*, which is fanciful and leaves much to be desired; his views on the supposed deity Rod have been convincingly dismissed by Klein, 'Pamiati iazycheskogo boga Roda', pp. 13–26. Uspenskii in his *Filologicheskie razyskaniia* makes an enormously learned attempt to demonstrate a continuity of the cult of the god Veles in the cult of St Nicholas. Ivanov and Toporov, *Issledovaniia v oblasti slavianskikh drevnostei*, is a serious attempt at a semeiotic assessment of alleged underlying elements of pagan religion in Slav Christianity and folklore, using linguistic evidence in particular. (Ch. 10 offers a list of oppositional pairs of concepts.) A useful list of much of the literature on ancient Slav religion, although thin on survival aspects, is Kulikowski, *A Bibliography of Slavic Mythology*.

42. The devils who possess Solomoniia in the seventeenth-century *Tale of the Possessed Woman Solomoniia* are water-devils from the Russian folk tale tradition. See Pigin, *Iz istorii russkoi demonologii*, p. 102 (an eighteenth-century MS illustration is reproduced at p. 73).

43. Rybnikov, *Pesni*, 1991 edn, III, p. 314, s.v. *baennik*.

44. See Dando, 'The Neutral Angels', pp. 265–7.

45. See Vlasova, *Novaia abevega*, s.v. *Adamovy deti*.

46. As among the South Slavs: Pócs, *Fairies and Witches at the Boundary of South Eastern and Central Europe*, p. 16.

47. Graham, 'A Brief Account', p. 236.

48. See Afanas'ev, *Poèticheskie vozzreniia*, *ad indicem* for considerable amounts of information on these. Good recent surveys are to be found in Pomerantseva, *Mifologicheskie personazhi*; Cherepanova, *Mifologicheskaia leksika*; Tolstoi, 'Iz zametok po slavianskoi demonologii' I and II (this discusses what the various Russian sprites are supposed to look like); Vlasova, *Novaia abevega* (a good distillation in dictionary form of earlier work in the field). For English discussions see Ralston, *Songs of the Russian People*, and Ivanits, *Russian Folk Belief*.

49. Vlasova, *Novaia abevega*, p. 18 emphasizes the 'own'/'other' duality of the Russian peasant world.

50. For a more elaborate discussion of this point see my 'The Witchcraft Hysteria in Early Modern Europe: Was Russia an Exception?'.

51. Antonovich, *Koldovstvo*, p. 8.

52. Levack, *The Witch Hunt in Early Modern Europe*, pp. 200–201. It should, however, be noted that in Scotland, where witch hunts were some of the worst in Europe, and in northern England, witches were often accused of traffic with fairies rather than with Lucifer: see Briggs, *A Dictionary of Fairies*, s.v. *traffic with fairies*.

53. Larner, *Enemies of God*, p. 11, 197.

54. The linking of *volkhv* and its derivatives with the word *bes* 'devil' or its derivatives can be seen in many of the examples quoted in *SRIa XI–XVII*. The *Russian Primary Chronicle* for 1071, quoted above, is unequivocal in its definition of magic as having an infernal origin.

55. See Haney, *From Italy to Muscovy*, pp. 155–7.

56. See Cherepanova, 'Nabliudeniia nad leksikoi Stoglava', pp. 17–25.

57. Fennell, *Kurbsky's History of Ivan IV*, pp. 202–3

58. Fennell, *Kurbsky's History of Ivan IV*, pp. 2–3, 180–1.

59. *Chronograph of 1617, PLDR XVI–XVII*, pp. 328, 332.

60. Massa, *A Short History*, pp. 118, 138, 147.

61. J. F., *A Brief Historical account of the Empire of Russia*, London, 1654, quoted in Cross, *Russia under Western Eyes*, p. 88. See also the account of Jacques Margeret: Dunning (ed.), *The Russian Empire*, p. 73.

62. Karamzin, *Istoriia*, IX, p. 308.

63. Coxe, *Travels in Poland, Russia, Sweden, and Denmark*, II, p. 15.

64. See Ch. 4.3.

65. Dal', *Poslovitsy*, p. 185. The notion is referred to in Pushkin's poem 'Besy' ('The Devils'), stanza 6.

66. Garrett, *The Demise of the Devil*, p. ix. This book has useful contributions to make to the debate on the relation between 'magic' and 'religion'.

67. Dal', *Tolkovyi slovar'*, s.v. *bes* gives an extensive list of names and euphemisms. Maksimov, *Nechistaia*, p. 4, repeats this list and gives a few more, to a total of over forty. Some are a little

unexpected: 'Hagarene' (this usually means a Muslim), 'not-one-of-us' (evidently a Thatcherite devil), 'joker', and 'the unwashed one'.

68. Uspenskii, 'Language Situation', p. 384. For *chert* in general in folk belief see Vlasova, *Novaia abevega*, pp. 430–58, s.v. *chert*.

69. Dal', *Poslovitsy*, p. 19.

70. Cherepanova, *Mifologicheskaia leksika russkogo severa*, esp. pp. 41–4. For individual sprites see also Vlasova, *Novaia abevega*, s.v. *leshii, vodianoi*, etc.

71. See Pigin, 'Narodnaia mifologiia'.

72. See Oinas, *Essays on Russian Folklore and Mythology*, 1985.

73. Chikachev, *Russkie na Indigirke*, p. 130.

74. Maksimov, *Nechistaia*, pp. 11–12.

75. For a survey of this subject see Dewey, 'Some Perceptions of Mental Disorder in Pre-Petrine Russia'.

76. The history of the idea of the pact with the Devil is traced in Radermacher, *Griechische Quellen zur Faustsage*; this, although it deals with the Byzantine aspects of the subject, does not mention Slavonic literature. See also Pietersma, *The Apocryphon of Jannes and Jambres*, pp. 64–70, 182–3, for a ?first-century AD pact involving the Devil and the magicians who fought with Moses. The Faust story, including the detail of soul-selling, probably first became known to Russians through a puppet play of German origin performed in Moscow in 1761: Peretts, *Kukol'nyi teatr*, pp. 31–42.

77. For the history and literary influence of this text in Russia see Cleminson, 'The Miracle *De juvene qui Christum negaverat*'.

78. See text edited with commentary by Iu. K. Begunov, in *Izbornik*, pp. 609–25. See also Skripil', 'Povest' o Savve Grudtsyne (teksty)', pp. 228–33. Savva writes his pact on parchment with ink.

79. See Demkova and Droblenkova, 'Povest' o ubogom cheloveke'.

80. See *Opisanie dokumentov*, XIV, p. 529. For some discussion of this and other cases of 'selling one's soul to the Devil' and 'letters to the Devil' in eighteenth-century Russia, with bibliography, see Gorelkina, 'K voprosu o magicheskikh predstavleniiakh'.

81. Four cases are quoted by Cherepnin, 'Iz istorii drevnerusskogo koldovstva', pp. 101–2.

82. Vasmer, *Ètimologicheskii slovar'*, s.v.

83. Afanas'ev, *Poèticheskie vozzreniia*, II, pp. 345–6.

84. Loginov, *Material'naia kul'tura i proizvodstvenno-bytovaia magiia russkikh Zaonezh'ia*, p. 33.

85. Pokrovskii, 'Ispoved' altaiskogo krestianina', p. 53.

86. This is argued persuasively by Markus, 'Augustine on Magic'. Maxim the Greek refers to Augustine in his tract on Vives's commentary on Augustine's *City of God* (see Bulanin, *Perevody i poslaniia Maksima Greka*, pp. 23–4), but since Augustine or Vives can have been known to few if any of his Russian readers, and Maxim was a former humanist who had worked in Italy, this can hardly be considered evidence of Russian familiarity with Augustine. A Greek manuscript translation of some works of Augustine (341 folios) by Maximos Planudes and Prokhoros Cydones was in Moscow in the later sixteenth century – it was copied by Hierotheos of Monembasia for the Jerusalem archimandrite Damaskinos who lived in Moscow from 1590 to 1604: see Fonkich, *Grechesko-russkie kulturnye sviazi*, pp. 51–2.

87. For a detailed discussion of the assimilation of folklore themes such as the serpent lover with stories of demonic possession see Pigin, *Iz istorii russkoi demonologii*, pp. 105–9. Pigin considers Western influence improbable here.

88. For a detailed and entertaining account see Boss, *Milton*.

89. Popov, *Russkaia narodno-bytovaia meditsina*, p. 35.

90. Matveeva, *Mifologicheskie rasskazy*, p. 315. Zabylin, *Russkii narod*, p. 241 observes that wormwood, nettle, *plakun* ('weeper-herb'), Adam's Head and Peter's Cross, all anti-witch herbs, were currently (in 1880) on sale in Moscow at a good price.

91. Zabylin, *Russkii narod*, p. 51.

92. Zabylin, *Russkii narod*, p. 241.

93. Zabylin, *Russkii narod*, p. 240.

94. Bolonev, *Narodnyi kalendar' semeiskikh Zabaikal'ia*, p. 83.

95. For a recent good study of the *domovoi* with particular reference to Yuletide divination in northern Russia see Krinichnaia, *Domashnyi dukh*. See also Vlasova, *Novaia abevega*, pp. 125–39, s.v. *domovoi*.

96. Especially on the feastday of St John Climacus. Dal', *Tolkovyi slovar'*, s.v. *domovoi*, lists various types, and mentions the beliefs that he was hairy (like many of the depictions of devils in Byzantine and Russian icons), that he could be seen on Easter Sunday eve, that to see him was a sign of impending ill fortune or death. See also Vlasova, *Novaia abevega*, s.v. *domovoi*.

97. Kondrat'eva, *Metamorfozy sobstvennogo imeni*, s.v. *kikimora*. The *kikimora* was a female goblin often thought of as the wife of a house-goblin (*domovoi*) or a wood-sprite (*leshii*); in the popular calendar she had a feast day on 17 February: see Iudin, *Dni velichal'nye*, pp. 61–2.

98. Chikachev, *Russkie na Indigirke*, p. 130. On dolls in Russian magic see Ch. 8.5.

99. Miloradovich, 'Zhit'e-byt'e lubenskogo krestianina', (reprint p. 172). This article contains a very detailed account of all the rituals and beliefs associated with building a new house in one area of the Ukraine.

100. Kondrat'eva, *Metamorfozy sobstvennogo imeni*, s.v. *Irod*.

101. For a good recent study of the *leshii*, modestly produced in Petrozavodsk and therefore not widely available, see Krinichnaia, *Lesnye navazhdeniia*.

102. Dal', *Tolkovyi slovar'*, s.v. *les*; Zinov'eva, *Ukazatel'*, motif no. AI 8b. Exactly the same precaution against being 'pixy-led' was employed in England: see Briggs, *Dictionary*, s.v. *protection against fairies*; for similar beliefs in Kentucky see Thomas, *Kentucky Superstitions*, no. 3036 and 3822. The other forms of protection mentioned by Briggs are also common in Russia.

103. Afanas'ev, *Poèticheskie vozzreniia*, II, p. 342; Romanov, *Belorusskii sbornik*, V, p. 3. Romanov adds that the Belorussian practice also required the sign of the cross and the recitation of the Lord's Prayer. See also Uspenskii, 'Dualisticheskii kharakter'.

104. Afanas'ev, *Poèticheskie vozzreniia*, II, p. 343.

105. Chikachev, *Russkie na Indigirke*, p. 129.

106. Guthrie, *Noctes Rossicae*, f. 80v.

107. Common in many societies: cf. the English case of William Barckseale, a Southampton wizard, who would pray and fast for three days before trying to detect stolen goods – Thomas, *Religion and the Decline of Magic*, pp. 271–2.

108. For a (dated) general account of magic circles see *ERE*, VIII, cols 321a–324b; for a good modern discussion see Kieckhefer, *Forbidden Rites*, pp. 172–6. The use of magic circles by necromancers to protect themselves from the demons they had summoned, and the dire consequences of letting even a limb protrude beyond the circle, are described graphically in the *Dialogue on Miracles*, an early thirteenth-century Latin text by Caesarius of Heisterbach: see *The Dialogue on Miracles*, V, ch. 2.

109. Kieckhefer (see previous note) observes that the precise role of the magic circle can be ambiguous.

110. *Kazanskaia istoriia*, p. 47.

111. Spitting is an ancient safeguard against magic: see Evil Eye above. On the tails of witches see also Ch. 3, under Witches.

112. Gogol', *Vii*, first published in 1835 in the *Mirgorod* collection.

113. Ralston, *Songs of the Russian People*, p. 100. On the *Vii* see Abaev, 'Obraz Viia v poveste N. V. Gogolia'. Abaev thinks that the *Vii* is not in fact known in Russian and Ukrainian folklore, does not mention any Serbian analogue, and claims that the word is derived from the Indo-Iranian god Vaya. In fact the characteristics of the *Vii* correspond closely to those of St Cassian in popular belief – see below, pp. 18–9.

114. Dal', *Tolkovyi slovar'*, s.v. For a detailed exposition of *rusalka* lore see Zelenin, *Izbrannye trudy*, ch. 5. He lists crosses, circles, garlic and iron implements as protection against *rusalki*, i.e. the same kind of protection as is required against other kinds of demon. See also Vlasova, *Novaia abevega*, pp. 298–312, s.v. *rusalka*.

115. Bulgakovskii, 'Pinchuki', p. 190.

116. See Afanas'ev, *Poèticheskie vozzreniia*, ii, p. 92; Smirnov, 'Narodnye gadan'ia Kostromskogo kraia', p. 27.

117. Dal', *Tolkovyi slovar'*, s.v. *chert*; Efimenko, *Materialy*, p. 163.

118. Matveeva, *Mifologicheskie rasskazy*, p. 311.

119. See for example Afanas'ev, *Narodnye russkie skazki*, 1984–5 edn, nos 364, 367, 371, 373, 564, 577.

120. Zabylin, *Russkii narod*, p. 242.

121. Bolonev, *Narodnyi kalendar' semeiskikh Zabaikal'ia*, p. 58.

122. Dal', *Poslovitsy russkogo naroda* (1994 reprint), pp. 546–62. Dal' gives no sources or regions.

123. This is no doubt the same practice as was condemned in the medieval Western penitentials: see for example the early eleventh-century *Corrector* of Burchard of Worms in McNeill and Gamer, *Medieval Handbooks of Penance* (reprint 1965), p. 334.

124. See *Traditsionnyi fol'klor vladimirskoi derevni*, p. 128.

125. Mazo, '"We don't summon Spring in the Summer"', pp. 81–2.

126. Propp, *Russkie agrarnye prazdniki*, pp. 70–71. For more detail see *Fol'klornyi teatr*, pp. 48–57, and Warner, *Russian Folk Theatre*, pp. 74–6.

127. Noted in Dal', *Tolkovyi slovar'*, s.v. *gadat'*.

128. Dal', *Tolkovyi slovar'*, s.v. *iordan'*.

129. For some description and discussion see Flier, 'Court Ceremony', p. 76.

130. Dal', *Tolkovyi slovar'*, s.v. On this word and its various meanings see Tolstoi, 'Shilikuny'; Vlasova, *Novaia abevega'*, s.v.

131. See Dal', *Tolkovyi slovar'*, s.v. *kupat'* and Dal', *Poslovitsy*, s.v.

132. See Graham, *Undiscovered Russia*, p. 38.

133. Bolonev, *Narodnyi kalendar' semeiskikh Zabaikal'ia*, p. 79.

134. Mansikka, *Religion*, p. 224.

135. See Longworth, *Alexis*, p. 135. He also ordered a Siberian wizard to send a report on plants and their virtues: *ERE, III*, p. 465b.

136. Quoted in Ivanov, 'Narodnye obychai, pover'ia i gadaniia'. Ivanov notes that all the midsummer divinations then surviving in this area are concerned with future husbands.

137. Wikman, 'Popular Divination', p. 176. 'Nine herb' spells are also known in Anglo-Saxon and German magic.

138. Maikov, 'Velikorusskie zaklinaniia', nos. 253–4.

139. Makarenko, *Sibirskii narodnyi kalendar'*, pp. 85–6.

140. Maksimov, *Nechistaia sila*, p. 474. The same beliefs in Britain are attached to Mayday: see Opie and Tatem, *Dictionary of Superstitions*, s.v. *May Dew*.

141. Dal', *Poslovitsy russkogo naroda* (1994 reprint), p. 550.

142. Afanas'ev, *Poèticheskie vozzreniia*, p. 364.

143. Makarenko, *Sibirskii narodnyi kalendar'*, pp. 85–6.

144. A. Kirkor, 'Ètnograficheskie vzgliady na Vilenskuiu guberniiu', p. 158.

145. On the herbs used for divination at the feast of St John in various countries see Frazer, *Golden Bough*, II, p. 129. See Storms, *Anglo-Saxon Magic*, pp. 9, 187 for the Anglo-Saxon practice and 'Nine Herbs Spell'. For Germany and general remarks see *Handwörterbuch des deutschen Aberglaubens*, s.v. *Johannes der Täufer*. For the ancient world see Delatte, *Herbarius*.

146. Makarenko, *Sibirskii narodnyi kalendar'*, pp. 58–60.

147. See Dal', *Tolkovyi slovar'*, s.v. *visokos* for a list of epithets and popular sayings.

148. Afanas'ev, *Russkie narodnye legendy*, p. 78.

149. See Cherepanova, *Mifologicheskaia leksika russkogo severa*, pp. 72, 80; Kondrat'eva, *Metamorfozy sobstvennogo imeni*, s.v. *Kas'ian*. For a detailed study of the unlucky St Cassian from Karelia to Siberia and in the Balkans see Loorits, *Der Heilige Kassian und der Schaltjahrlegende*.

150. Smirnov, 'Narodnye gadan'ia Kostromskogo kraia'.

151. Makarenko, *Sibirskii narodnyi kalendar'*, p. 123.

152. Kondrat'eva, *Metamorfozy*, s.v.

153. Makarenko, *Sibirskii narodnyi kalendar'*, passim.

154. See Dal', *Tolkovyi slovar'*, s.v. *pola (polnoch')*.

155. For brief but well annotated survey with particular emphasis on boundaries see Hand, *Boundaries, Portals and Other Magical Spots*. For a comparable belief in bathhouses and crossroads as the abode of djinns in the Islamic world see Hughes, *Dictionary of Islam*, p. 136.

156. The hopfield variant is in the Volga region: Shapovalova and Lavrent'eva, *Traditsionnye obriady*, p. 16.

157. Popov, *Russkaia narodno-bytovaia meditsina*, p. 196.

158. Maksimov, *Nechistaia sila* (1993), I, pp. 230–31.

159. Muller, *The Spiritual Regulation*, p. 29.

160. Stepanova, *Chernaia magiia*, p. 295.

161. For an extensive monograph on the history of the Russian bathhouse (which is similar to a sauna), with emphasis on folklore aspects, and in particular the ritual bride bath, see Vahros, *Zur Geschichte und Folklor der grossrussischen Sauna*.

162. *Russian Primary Chronicle*, pp. 54, 151–2.

163. Lotman and Uspenskij, 'The Role of Dual Models of Russian Culture', p. 9.

164. Ibid.

165. Popov, *Russkaia narodno-bytovaia meditsina*, p. 197.

166. See Hughes, *Russia and the West*, p. 88.

167. For a brief survey of beliefs about the bathhouse demon see Maksimov, *Nechistaia sila*, IV; Novichkova, *Russkii demonologicheskii slovar'*, pp. 35–40; Vlasova, *Novaia abevega*, s.vv. *bannik, bainikha*.

168. The *bannaia babushka* could also be a midwife with magical powers: see Vlasova, *Novaia abevega*, s.v. *bannaia babushka*.

169. Maksimov, *Nechistaia*, pp. 49–50. For a more recent report of the last-mentioned belief in Karelia see *Ètnokul'turnye protsessy v Karelii*, p. 48 and Loginov, *Material'naia kul'tura i proizvodstvenno-bytovaia magiia russkikh Zaonezh'ia*, p. 96; for the same in Siberian stories see Zinov'eva, 'Ukazatel'', motif no. B5a, B5e.

170. Bonner, 'Demons of the Bath', pp. 204–5, 208; Vlasova, *Novaia abevega*, p. 51. An alternative to the cock in the northern region of Zaonezh'e is a drop of mercury: Loginov, *Material'naia kul'tura i proizvodstvenno-bytovaia magiia russkikh Zaonezh'ia*, p. 96.

171. The evidence for this varies: Nikitina, 'K voprosu o russkikh koldunakh', pp. 319–20, states that a belt was worn at all times next to the body as a protection against magic and was not removed even in the bathhouse. For an interesting survey of belts in Russian folk customs and magic see Lebedeva, 'Znachenie poiasa'; she remarks that there is no general study of this subject (p. 229). See also Tolstoi, 'Opolzanie i opoiasivanie khrama', primarily on rituals of circling churches among the Slavs but with some interesting observations on the magic of belts.

172. Dal', *Tolkovyi slovar'*, s.v. *bania*; Maksimov, *Nechistaia sila*, p. 55.

173. Min'ko, *Sueveriia*, p. 150.

174. Afanas'ev, *Narodnye russkie legendy*, pp. 49–52.

175. Dal', *Tolkovyi slovar'*, s.v. *bania*. Levin, 'Childbirth', p. 51, notes that even women who killed their illegitimate offspring went to the bathhouse for delivery first.

176. Dal', *Tolkovyi slovar'*, s.v. *banit'*.

177. *Pamiatniki literatury Drevnei Rusi XVII vek*, kn. 2, p. 265.

178. Dal', *Tolkovyi slovar'*, s.v. *zaria* (= both 'dawn' and 'Morning Star'). The word *babka* in this reference is a diminutive of one of the words meaning woman, and is commonly used, as I have assumed it does here, to mean a midwife or a 'wise woman'.

179. Kozyrev, 'Svadebnye obriady i obychai', pp. 79–80.

180. See Nielsen, *Thermae et Balnea*, pp. 145–8. Nielsen particularly emphasizes that there was no break in the tradition of trying to regulate the baths. The Church essentially continued the policy of the pre-Christian emperors, and the opinion of Christian writers often echoed that of pagan writers. See also Ward, 'Women in Roman Baths'. On the other hand it should be noted that St John Chrysostom also appropriates the bath as a symbol of purification at baptism and as the actual place of baptism: Harkins, *St John Chrysostom*, pp. 135–8, 170.

181. See Migne, *Patrologia graeca*, 31, col. 1682.

182. For an extensive survey see *DACL*, II, s.v. *bain*. For Byzantine attitudes and practices see more recently Berger, *Das Bad in der Byzantinischen Zeit*, and for a detailed account of ecclesiastical attitudes to the bath in medieval Constaninople see Magdalino, 'Church, Bath and *Diakonia*'. On the bath as a magical and erotic element in later Byzantine romances see Agapitos, 'The Erotic Bath'.

183. *SDIa*, s.v. *bania*; Smirnov, *Materialy*, p. 43.

184. *Stoglav*, p. 137. The reference to Pskov is tendentious: the many references in the *Stoglav* to Pskov and Novgorod as the home of various aberrant practices may be explained by the fact that these two towns had been independent city-states until comparatively recently and were often guilty of anti-Muscovite behaviour. Ivan the Terrible dealt with the problem by massacring most of the population of Novgorod in 1570.

185. Richard Palmer, '"In this our lightye and learned tyme": Italian Baths in the Era of the Renaissance', p. 19.

186. For the Russian bathhouse in the social history of washing see Giedion, *Mechanization Takes Command*, pp. 646–50, and Wright, *Clean and Decent*, pp. 60–61, 82–3.

187. For example Struys, *Les Voyages de Jean Struys en Muscovie . . .*, 1681, p. 134, states that mixed bathing for all ages was the norm. Richardson, *Anecdotes of the Russian Empire*, 1784, pp. 213–4, states that mixed bathing once a week was the usual custom.

188. For an illustrated survey of the genre see Cross, 'The Russian *Banya*'.

189. See most recently Rorschach, *Drawings by Jean-Baptiste Le Prince*.

190. It was no doubt the *succès de scandale* of Le Prince's bathhouse scene which began the vogue for similar pictures of more or less artistic merit: see Cross, 'The Russian *Banya*'.

191. Dal', *Tolkovyi slovar'*, s.v. *perekreshchivat'*.

192. Smirnov, 'Narodnye gadaniia v Kostromskom krae', p. 18.

193. See Warner and Kustovski, *Russian Traditional Folksong*, p. 42.

194. Dal', *Tolkovyi slovar'*, s.v. *piat'*; Kondrat'eva, *Metamorfozy sobstvennogo imeni*, s.v. *piatnitsa*; Maksimov, *Nechistaia sila* (1993), I, p. 230–31.

195. Dal', *Tolkovyi slovar'*, s.v. *porog*.

196. In general for taboos on leaving a house see Frazer, *Golden Bough*, III, pp. 122–6.

197. Kondrat'eva, *Metamorfozy sobstvennogo imeni*, s.v. *bui*.

198. See Dal', *Tolkovyi slovar'*, s.v. *lèvyi, shuitsa*. *Slovar' XI–XVII vv.*, s.v. *levyi* shows that this meaning is known in Russia from at least the thirteenth century. See Uspenskii, 'Antipovedenie' for many aspects of this belief; also Tolstoi, 'O prirode sviazei binarnykh protivopostavlenii tipa pravyi–levyi'. (This gives primarily Serbo-Croatian examples but is of wider application.)

199. This is argued on the basis of extensive evidence in Coren, *The Left-Hander Syndrome*. Coren also outlines the history of the unlucky and demonic significance of the left in the Jewish, Christian and Islamic traditions.

200. Maksimov, *Nechistaia sila*, p. 4.

201. Dal', *Tolkovyi slovar'*, s.v. *les*; Chikachev, *Russkie na Indigirke*, p. 128. But Herberstein noted in the 16th century that Christians in Russia buttoned on the right side whereas Tatars buttoned on the left: Herberstein, *Notes upon Russia*, I, p. 100.

202. Minenko, *Russkaia krest'ianskaia obshchina*, p. 152.

203. Maksimov, *Nechistaia*, p. 28.

204. For similar Greek beliefs see Stewart, *Demons*, p. 178. For Jewish beliefs see Coren, *The Left-Hander Syndrome*, pp. 12, 13.

205. Dal', *Tolkovyi slovar'*, s.v. *noga*.

206. See Opie and Tatem, *Dictionary*, s.v. *Sunwise* for British, mostly Celtic, examples. For early Scandinavian examples see Boyer, *Le Monde du double*, pp. 164–5.

207. For a convenient summary of the history of *posolon'* in Russia see *Polnyi pravoslavnyi bogoslovskii entsiklopedicheskii slovar*, s.v.

208. Pócs, *Fairies and Witches at the Boundary of South Eastern and Central Europe*, p. 86.

209. See Usacheva, 'Ritual'nyi obman'.

210. See Uspenskii, 'Antipovedenie' for an example in the *Tale of Peter and Fevroniia*.

211. For some discussion see Panchenko, *Russkaia kul'tura v kanun petrovskikh reform*, p. 84. Birnbaum, 'Laughter, Play, and Carnival in Old Rus'', pp. 21–39; also on Ivan the Terrible and more generally

on parody see Likhachev and Panchenko, *"Smekhovoi mir" Drevnei Rusi*.

212. Uspenskii, 'The Language Situation', p. 371. Uspenskii has a number of interesting things to say about parody and demonic aspects of language use in Russia, in particular the use of Church Slavonic as a demonifuge.

213. Gorelkina, 'K voprosu o magicheskikh predstavleniiakh', p. 298.

214. Uspenskii, 'The Language Situation', p. 377. For a fairly detailed account of these activities of Peter see Semonova, *Ocherki istorii byta i kul'turnoi zhizni Rossii*, pp. 174–199; for the same activities viewed as 'the sense of humour of Peter the Great' see Semevskii, *Slovo i delo*, pp. 279–334.

215. As witnessed by Korb, *Diary*, pp. 257–8.

216. Uspenskii and Shishkin, *Trediakovskii i iansenisty*, p. 170.

217. Ibid., pp. 171–3. Note 201 adds the information that ice-houses figure in some Russian spells against chills.

218. See Uspenskii, 'Religiozno-mifologicheskii aspekt', p. 210; Tolstoi, 'Ne – ne "ne"'. Dragomanov, *Malorusskie narodnie predaniia*, p. 30, gives a spell against serpents which was also effective for horses if read backwards. Writing backwards for magical effect is not uncommon; an example from Roman Britain is quoted in Tomlin, *Tabellae Sulis*, p. 112.

219. Vlasova, *Novaia abevega*, p. 26.

WIZARDS AND WITCHES

1. *Introduction*

The magic and divination of the recognized or professional practitioner overlaps to some extent the beliefs and procedures outlined in the previous chapter, but some characterization of these practitioners and what they do or did, or are believed to do or to have done, is now necessary. Robert Rowland, in a comparative study of European witch-beliefs, has stated that: 'The witches' attributes and behaviour mark them off from normal society, and the world of witches often constitutes a systematized structure of negation, an inversion of the world in which people who hold these beliefs live'.[1] Rowland did not consider the Russian evidence, but his statement comes close to the semeiotic model of the Russian scholar B.A. Uspenskii, with the difference that while Rowland is speaking of behaviour merely imputed to witches, Uspenskii is describing not only beliefs about magicians, but also known behaviour (or more often, in his terminology, 'anti-behaviour') of actual magicians.[2]

An immediate difficulty in characterizing the attributes and behaviour of magical practitioners is that the description or reputation of a particular local witch or wizard as a known and necessary member of a particular local community may be quite different from the popular perception of the *koldun* or *ved'ma* in general as reported by informants, or described in folk literature, where they can be credited with fantastic and demonic powers and extraordinary malignancy. This is perhaps not so important if one is trying to achieve a synchronic description of the beliefs and practices of a single community, where 'own wizard' versus 'other wizard' makes a convenient binary distinction, but it is a problem for the scholar attempting a diachronic cultural history of magic from the evidence available.

In the appendix to this chapter most of the terms which may be found in Russian and Old Russian to describe magic and its practitioners are listed. The nature of the persons designated by these terms at different times in the various parts of Russia, Belorussia and the Ukraine, and the powers attributed to them, can vary considerably, and the sources from which the information about them is obtained also vary a great deal in reliability. In fact, of course, it is usually impossible to know with any degree of clarity what lies behind the various terms used for magical practices and their devotees, especially when words surviving from a pre-Christian belief-system are used in a later Christian context, for example to translate Greek words in patristic literature. Moreover, the terminological distinctions about 'magic', 'sorcery', or 'witchcraft' and their practitioners, made confidently by anglophone scholars using the English words available to them, run into difficulties in Russian contexts.[3] For example, a remark by Valerie Kivelson, in an invaluable article about a seventeenth-century witchcraft panic, to the effect that there was no distinction between black and white magic in Russia is literally true but semantically anachronistic: the terms did not exist in Old Russian and the underlying concepts had different resonances and were expressed differently.[4] Kivelson is nevertheless in good company: by the nineteenth century the Western distinction of 'black' and 'white' magic had influenced educated, and perhaps uneducated, Russians – even the great Russian lexicographer and collector of folk wisdom Vladimir Dal' stated in his dictionary, in the entry for *magiia* (a late and fairly learned lexical import into Russian), that magic is regarded as being either white or black. He went on to say that black magic includes *chernoknizhie*, *volkhovstvo*, *koldovstvo*, *volshebstvo* (i.e. the usual words used in accusations of enchantment, witchcraft or sorcery) and involves the intervention of the spirit world, while *znakharstvo* may be either. In other words, Dal' knew exactly what words and concepts Russians actually had in earlier periods, but tried to force them into a taxonomy which, though imported, was probably more familiar to the educated users of his late nineteenth-century dictionary.

There was a rich vocabulary of words in Church Slavonic, Old Russian and Russian dialect used to denote practices which can be loosely grouped under the headings of magic, *maleficium*, and divination, and for those who practise magical arts either habitually or as a profession. A fair number of them survive in modern Russian, especially at dialect level, and although they are etymologically distinct, in practice they often function as synonyms, or near-synonyms, with semantic distinctions which may be very local (or even specific to an informant). With one or two individual exceptions, in medieval Russia there was little more than hearsay knowledge of astrology or alchemy, no 'learned' magic, no learned theological discussion of licit and illicit practices, and effectively no way of distinguishing terminologically between magic, sorcery and witchcraft as occasionally defined in modern literature, if indeed the concepts were separable at all. The first clue that we have to the importation into Russia of the distinction between 'natural' and 'demonic' magic is a mention of natural magic in the charter of the foundation of the Slavonic-Greek-Latin Academy in Moscow in 1682 under Tsar Fedor Alekseevich, which forbids both natural and demonic magic, together with divination, under pain of death by burning.[5]

When discussing the terminology and semantics of magic and witchcraft it has also to be borne in mind that there was in Russia no equivalent of the scholastic theological and legal discussion of demonology, or of types of magic and divination and their relationship to heresy, such as was found in the West.

The Russian archaeologist Rybakov has discerned a whole hierarchy of magical specialists among the early East Slavs. This includes many of the names given in the appendix to this book, but adds also *oblakoprogoniteli* ('cloud-dispersers'), *zhretsy* (usually this means 'pagan priest'), *khranil'niki* ('maker of talismans'), *potvorniki* ('maker of potions'), *koshchunniki* (?'teller of fables' but later used in the sense of mocker of religion, blasphemer, sacrilegious person'), and *baiany* ('performer of incantations').[6] In fact, of course, it is usually impossible to know what lies behind appellations of this kind at such a distance in time and with such scanty evidence, most of it ecclesiastical and hostile. Equally it is not always easy to tell which practices and beliefs recorded in more modern times have a long local history, and which are imported from other areas. Indeed, in literary contexts the multiple terms for magicians which can occasionally be found may well be no more than reduplication for rhetorical effect. For example, in the *vita* of St Stefan of Perm' by Epifanii Premudryi (fourteenth-fifteenth century), the chief of the Permian wizards Pam is described as a *volkhv, charodeevyi starets, kudesnik, obavnik*, and poisoner.[7] It is unlikely that the author, the best known exponent of the elaborate style known as 'word-weaving', was actually making distinctions here: the idea that there was an organized hierarchy of priest-magicians in early Russia, with clearly labelled specialist subgroups, must be treated with great scepticism. Moreover, any suggestion of a definable corpus of *exclusively* Slavonic or Russian magic must be generally discounted; as one work on Anglo-Saxon magic has it: 'Of all cultural expressions, magic passes most rapidly from people to people'.[8]

It must at the same time be admitted that the history and status of the magical practitioner in Russia has peculiar aspects which are sometimes difficult to define. While one may state positively with regard to Russia that astrological and divinatory texts and some amulets are cultural imports, the origins of beliefs and practices recorded in modern times are more difficult to assess. For example, the belief in the ability of witches to fly after using a magic ointment, and foregathering for Witches' Sabbaths, must surely be a late borrowing from the West, probably via Belorussia and the Ukraine (Bald Mountain, near Kiev, is the commonly reported venue),[9] but is the belief that witches can turn into birds part of the same tradition or part of an older stratum of Slavonic belief in were-animals?[10]

Bearing in mind these difficulties we can nevertheless attempt a rough characterization of the main categories of magical practitioner as defined by the commonest names for them.

2. *The Volkhv*

As has already been mentioned in Ch. 1, *volkhv* is the term used in the earliest Church Slavonic and Old Russian texts, including the Chronicles, for wizards, and in particular the pagan sorcerers or shamans of the pre-Christian Slavs and their Finnic neighbours.[11] In texts translated from Greek it is often used for the Greek *pharmakos*; its etymology is a matter of dispute but many consider the word to be Finnic in origin.[12] The word continued to be used of magicians in general, but the contexts can be ambiguous. In the *Third Pskov Chronicle, sub anno* 1570, Eliseus Bomel, the disgraced ex-Cambridge German court physician and astrologer of Ivan the Terrible, was described as a 'ferocious *volkhv*',[13] and in one

Old Believer manuscript miniature of the seventeenth-eighteenth century the
damned are depicted with labels above listing fornicators, adulterers, brigands,
charodei and *volkhv*, drunkards, slanderers, heretics and Arians.[14] Here the
archaizing tendency of the Old Believers and the fact that the text is in Church
Slavonic may well have influenced the choice of terms (the association of
magicians with fornicators, adulterers, etc. is from Revelations 25:15). In the *vita*
version of the *Tale of the Possessed Woman Solomoniia* (late seventeenth century) there
is mention of a *potvornik volkhv* who sends a devil to torment the woman.[15] This
text too is essentially in Russian Church Slavonic. The same is true of the *Tale of
Savva Grudtsyn*, another seventeenth-century work, in which an urban *volkhv* who
possesses magic books is consulted as a seer.[16] In learned literature from the
eighteenth century onwards, *volkhv* could often be used for the oracles and priests
of pagan cults. The word has also a feminine form *volkhva* and a number of
derivatives, of which the adjective *volshebnyi* is in common modern use in the
sense of 'magical'.

    At least one instance in folk literature suggests that at a popular level a *volkhv*
was not distinguished from a medical doctor: in the verse about the merchant
Terentysh in the Kirsha Danilov collection assembled in the eighteenth century,
the young wife of the merchant begs him to fetch doctors and to invite *volkhvy* to
treat her feigned illness.[17] The word was used to describe Nectanebus in the
Slavonic *Alexander Romance*, and for the Three Kings in the Church Slavonic and
Russian translations of the Gospel of Matthew (Matt. 2). In this respect it is worth
noting that while 'Three Kings' or 'Wise Men', even the Latin 'Magi', and their
equivalents in other West European languages, are relatively innocuous to a West
European ear, they were in fact oriental magicians (in the tradition of Zoroaster
according to many early sources) and their purpose in the Gospel Nativity story is
to demonstrate that the ancient religion of the East was accepting the superior
truth of the new dispensation. The Gospel does not imply that they were bad or
that their magic was bogus; indeed they were granted a prophetic dream and
their astrology in fact brought them to Bethlehem, which might suggest that God
works through astrology.[18] Since the image of the *volkhv* for Russians was entirely
that of a pagan magician within their own cultural experience, their
understanding of the Gospel of Matthew at this point must have differed
somewhat from the West European understanding. In this connection it is
interesting that the *Kazanskaia istoriia*, written to celebrate and legitimate the
capture the Tatar city of Kazan' in 1552 by Ivan the Terrible, records that the
Tatar *volkhvy* prophesied that the city would fall to the Christians, 'just as the
Hellene *volkhvy* had foretold the coming of Christ'.[19] This is a curious extension of
the meaning of *volkhv* to include Plato and Aristotle and presumably is an echo of
the tradition that places the pagan philosophers among the prophets in some
texts and church frescoes.[20]

    It seems best to regard the *volkhv* as a shaman-like figure of pre-Christian and
Kievan Russia and a person of some social, even political, significance. It is
noteworthy that, if the Chronicles are to be believed in this matter, it was the Slav

volkhvy who led uprisings against the new religion of Christianity, and the Varangian princes, not Christian priests, who broke their power. (For more circumstantial detail see Ch. 1.) Saxo Grammaticus in his history of the Danes tells of one encounter between invading Norsemen and Slavs in which a Slav, 'a man of outstanding appearance, a wizard by occupation' challenged and killed the Danish champion.[21] This role of tribal leader inevitably disappeared in time.

Some of the other characteristics of the *volkhv* were inherited by the *koldun*, and indeed the latter was occasionally called a *volkhv* (in 1689 a horse-doctor (*konoval*) called Doroshka, designated a *volkhv* in the documents, who had learned magic from another horse-doctor, was accused of 'sending a spell on the wind' to harm the young Tsar Peter, and also whispering spells, reading palms, and bean divination),[22] but essentially the *koldun* belongs to a different, and later, belief system. In the various Russian penitentials the words *volkhv* and *kudesnik* are found quite commonly, even in late texts, but rarely the Russian word *koldun*. This is no doubt because most of the prohibitions in Russian canon law texts have ancient models and are essentially Church Slavonic in terminology.

3. *The Koldun*

The word *koldun* is attested mainly from the seventeenth century onwards, although the kind of village magician to which it is usually applied is certainly older.[23] One rare earlier example of the use of the word is in an episcopal instruction, known in a mid-sixteenth-century copy, which states that 'women fortune-tellers and *kolduny*' are to be driven out of the parish by parish priests and handed over to the secular law.[24] Several classifications of *koldun* have been proposed by writers on the subject. Zabylin, for example, proposed a rather unsatisfactory classification of (1) the simple *koldun*, who has some physical distinguishing mark (a parallel perhaps with the 'Devil's mark' which was looked for on the body of suspected witches in Western Europe) or is eccentric (e.g. he goes to bed when others are rising – a satisfying example of otherness for the Moscow-Tartu school of semeiotics); (2) the involuntary *koldun* (a story is quoted in which a miller acquires a magical reputation by chance); (3) the *koldun* by conviction; the malignant *koldun*.[25] But the variety of beliefs at different times and places makes any useful taxonomy difficult to achieve.

The *koldun* (fem. *koldun'ia*) usually has the knowledge and expertise in folk medicine of the *znakhar'* (see below) but may also be a more sinister figure who can cast evil spells with demonic assistance,[26] sometimes just for the hell of it, is strong, gloomy, dirty, has the Evil Eye, and lives alone. Some *kolduny* were thought to be so powerful that they could wither or send mad with a glance.[27] It seems to have been fairly generally believed that the powers of a *koldun* or a *ved'ma* were either innate or acquired by a pact with the Devil, and that they could be transmitted, sometimes within a family (see *Ved'ma* below). A born *koldun* or *ved'ma* was thought to have a small tail,[28] or to have been born with two teeth,[29] and to be the product of three generations of illegitimacy[30] (or in the case of the *ved'ma*, tenth or thirteenth daughter) [31] A modern popular book of magic spells states that anyone may learn to be a *koldun*, and that the best place to do it is in the bathhouse at midnight (see Ch. 2.7.1 below). One northern account of a magical initiation says that the *koldun* goes to a bathhouse at dawn where he summons a frog which has to be swallowed by the aspiring new *koldun*.[32] The *koldun* is strong and healthy; if he bleeds or loses his teeth or any part of his body, this diminishes his magical power.[33]

A tradition found in Russia and Belorussia has it that a *koldun* went to considerable lengths to pass on to a willing or unwilling heir the burden of his knowledge before his death, which was usually agonizing (because his soul has horns which impede its departure from the body). He was obliged to do this by his pact with the Devil, which he has signed with blood from his left little finger. His usual stratagem was to crawl under the stove and lie there groaning with one hand stretched out for help. Anyone who took his hand to help him would immediately assume his role whether they liked it or not. At this point the house would shake and a small black animal would be seen scurrying away: this was the wizard's soul, and it had to be immediately speared with an aspen stake, the usual implement for magical impalements.[34] A further belief was that the Devil enters the body of the dead *koldun* through his mouth, flays him and eats his flesh before donning his skin.[35] The demon in the body of a dead magician was sometimes thought to haunt bell-towers.[36]

Another way of becoming a *koldun* in Belorussia was to enter into a pact with the Devil by grinding a cross under your heel (a common element in demonic magic) and shooting a piece of communion bread.[37] Alternatively one could place an icon face down on the ground, preferably at midnight at a crossroads or in a bathhouse and, while standing on it, revile God. The demon who would then appear would expect the would-be magician to sign a pact in blood, or, if he was illiterate, to do twelve somersaults between knives stuck into the ground.[38]

In one version of that curious seventeenth-century compendium of popular cosmological and eschatological beliefs in the form of a 'spiritual verse', the *Golubinnaia kniga*, 'Tsar Votolomon' (Solomon) declares that magicians of this type ('*veduny i charodei*') go straight to hell and do not even have their cases reviewed at the Last Judgement.[39]

Hell did, however, allow the *koldun* considerable mobility as a revenant, for it was commonly thought that the earth would not accept such corpses and the *koldun* was liable to rise from the grave as a ghost or vampire or were-animal, particularly if he had not succeeded in passing on his powers before death, if he was not prevented by a stake through his heart (struck with a single blow – a second would revive him!) or by hamstringing or having his heels cut off.[40] If the ghost of his Belorussian variant walked he had to be dug up, his head cut off and placed between his legs and then reburied and the place sprinkled with wild poppy seed.[41] In a variant of this from Subcarpathian Ruthenia an informant stated that a sorcerer was dug up and found to be covered in blood (i.e. he was a vampire); his head was therefore cut off and placed between his legs and he was then cut up into little pieces. This treatment allegedly caused the dead *koldun* to scream: 'Why are you torturing me?'[42] A less violent Belorussian method of dealing with the walking dead (usually the corpses of wizards, drowned persons or rich men, who went about killing babies) was to sprinkle blessed wild poppy seed about their graves and between the house and the churchyard.[43] Once again the cooperation of the clergy, in this area probably Catholic, appears to be called for. Belorussian revenants could also be frightened off by firing blessed salt through a window at midnight.[44] In the Ukraine it was believed that vampires were the result of sexual encounters between witches and werewolves.[45] The connection between vampires, were-animals and magicians is also clear in the usage in some places of *upyr* (normally vampire) in the sense of *koldun*, and *ved'mak* in the sense of were-animal or vampire.[46]

The *koldun* could also be called *eretik* ('heretic'),[47] particularly if he was an practitioner in malefic magic or one of the walking dead (who could also be spirits of suicides or anyone who had suffered an unnatural death)[48] just mentioned, or *charovnik* ('spell-caster') or, in some regions *ved'mar* or *ved'mak* ('a knower').[49] Magicians, suicides, and those who had suffered a violent death, or died of a surfeit of alcohol, tended to be grouped together in Russian beliefs and superstitious practices. In many parts of Russia they were supposed to be buried at the place of their death, although they were often dug up again and thrown into a bog or river since it was thought that this offence to the earth would lead to misfortune, especially if they were buried in consecrated ground. The latter belief is recorded as early as 1273 in a sermon of Serapion, bishop of Vladimir and also mentioned by Maxim the Greek in the early sixteenth century.[50]

The *koldun* was thought to be particularly apt to put the Evil Eye on weddings, and there are several cases of peasants burning or otherwise killing them for this in the nineteenth century.[51] For this reason he was part of the wedding procession and was given the place of honour at weddings and other family or village festivities so as to protect them from the Evil Eye and other hostile witches or magicians who might turn them into wild animals, indeed the *koldun* may even be the *druzhka* (a kind of 'best man' and master of ceremonies: the role has no exact English equivalent). In the Perm' region the magician's duties included casting straw beneath the feet of the bride to protect her from spells and the Evil Eye, giving the bride water to wash her face in, and even washing her himself, going round all the vehicles of the wedding procession to make sure that no evil spells had been cast, accompanying the bride and groom after the wedding meal to their bridal chamber, putting them to bed, then circling them whispering a protective spell; he was also responsible for waking them the following morning.[52] The *koldun* was also reputed to be very rude and sit at table with his hat on, and this is why his euphemistic name was *vezhlivets*, 'the polite one'.[53] One writer on Russian customs in Siberia described the *vezhlivets* as a person of standing in the village who knew the weddings rituals well, and, in a rather ambiguous phrase 'played the part of the *koldun*'.[54] Another states that *vezhlivets*, *druzhka* and *storozh* are synonyms, and that their task was to ensure the magical protection of the wedding procession, mainly by impressing on all present wax pellets taken from the church candles of the previous Easter.[55] Dal' notes that the Siberian *bol'shak* was present at all weddings to protect the ceremony and its participants from the Evil Eye.[56]

The Abbé Chappe d'Auteroche, in his account of the Russian Empire in the second half of the eighteenth century, described what was evidently a fairly large urban wedding in Tobol'sk at which the *koldun* was in attendance to counteract any possible hostile magic from other magicians, and led the procession to the nuptial chamber.[57]

In several regions the *koldun* was also responsible for supervising the ritual bath of the bride.[58] As recently as 1971 in the Vologda region it is recorded that the magician (called *storozh* 'guard' in this case) was to lead the bride to the ritual bath with a fishnet round his waist; then he was to beat her with birch twigs (the normal procedure in north Russian bathhouses) and recite the spell: 'On this birch besom the leaves will never go away. The same will happen to God's servant Ekaterina, the husband will never go away from her. Amen.' The sweat was wiped from her body with a whole raw fish which was then to be cooked and given to the groom to eat.[59] The significance of both fish and sweat in sex magic is discussed in Ch. 9.3.1.

Zabylin, whose book on Russian popular beliefs and customs shares with most Russian and Soviet books on the subject a pedagogical urge to instruct the simple in the error of their ways, explains that the reputed ability of hostile magicians to harm the marriage procession is achieved by spreading the blood of a wolf or bear on the road where the horses will have to pass, thus terrifying them and bringing chaos to the proceedings.[60]

Besides employing a *koldun* one can even today in some regions take simple measures against the Evil Eye at weddings by putting into the bride's clothing needles from which the eyes have been broken, or winding a charmed thread round her body during her ritual bath, or simply by reciting your own *zagovor* spell.[61] This would counteract, for example, the truly cruel magic recorded in the Vologda region which made a bride break wind every time she bowed during her wedding feast. In this region the evil *koldun* would put a bear's paw or fur on the road so that the horses of the wedding procession would refuse to pass, or throw a pea-pod with nine peas into the straw in the sledge so that, once again, the horses would not move.[62]

The source of hostile magic at weddings could also be a female witch – see *Ved'ma* below.

The *koldun* (and *znakhar'* according to Dal')[63] may also put destructive spells on crops by a *zakrut(ka)* or *zalom*, that is by twisting over the top of a plant and tying it down,[64] or putting a spell on a wedding procession by bending over a twig on a tree. One account from the Minsk region of Belorussia describes how this could be done: the evil magician was to go to a field of rye at midday or midnight, strip naked, seize in his hand a bunch of rye stalks and twist them into a circle or cup shape, and then walk round the twisted stems three times while uttering certain secret words. Then he was to lie down and roll round the twisted stems three times, whispering the secret spell again. Finally he was to dig a hole with his hands, sprinkle salt, charcoal, and a few other unspecified things into it, and carefully cover it over. This would bring misfortune to the owner of the field, his wife, children or livestock.[65] This kind of malefic magic could only be countered by another wizard, who had to break off the *zalom* and burn it,[66] or pronounce a counter-spell. One account of this belief in Siberia states that in this way the *koldun* sends the crop underground to his own barns and that a *zalom* of twelve stalks twisted together is particularly to be feared.[67] Popov, in his 1903 survey of folk medicine, remarks that the *zalom* is a talisman made of the tops of cereal crops, usually rye. Sometimes it was tied with a hair from a horse or a woman, and sprinkled with charcoal, stove ash, earth from a cemetery, etc. It could affect a whole field, and no one would touch bread made from a field blighted in this way. Only a stronger wizard or a priest could remove the spell.[68]

Matveeva lists among the powers attributed to the *koldun* in Siberia the ability to change into an animal (this is in fact a widespread belief in Russia and in many other cultures) and to foresee the future (this reputed ability he shares with Siberian shamans).[69] A spell for turning into a werewolf is quoted by Ralston – it runs:

> In the ocean sea, on the island of Buian, in the open plain, shines the moon upon an aspen stump, into the green wood, into the spreading vale. Around the stump goes a shaggy wolf; under his teeth are all the horned cattle; but into the wood the wolf goes not, in the vale the wolf does not roam. Moon, moon! golden horns! Melt the bullet, blunt the knife, rot the cudgel, strike fear into man, beast, and reptile, so that they may not seize the grey wolf, nor tear from him his warm hide. My word is firm, firmer than sleep or the strength of heroes.[70]

Another method given by Dal' in his dictionary (in the entry *volk*, 'wolf') is to find a smoothly cut tree stump in the forest, stick a knife in it, and somersault over it; to reverse the process, come back to the stump from the other direction and somersault over it again to turn back into a man – if in the meantime the knife has been removed then the man will be a wolf for ever. Witches could turn into animals in the same way by jumping over twelve knives or by applying the twelve St John's Eve herbs; if these were-animals were struck with an ash rod they would revert to their proper form and renounce witchcraft.[71] Number 81 in Tikhonravov's list of works banned by the Church in indexes of 'good and bad books' is the *Charovnik* (book of spells). This is not extant but is described as having twelve chapters giving instruction on how to leave your body as if dead and fly like an eagle or a hawk or a crow or a magpie or an owl, or run like a panther, a savage beast, a wild beast, a wolf or a bear, or fly like a serpent.[72] Most of the banned books in Russian indexes are of Byzantine origin, but the details of this one sound Russian and shamanistic.

Involuntary werewolves could be members of a wedding procession cursed by a *koldun*. In the Vologda region it was believed that these could be restored to human form by walking round them three times and pulling off their hides.[73] Another account of changing wedding parties into werewolves noted that the party had to be twelve in number, and that the change was not for life or for an even number of years. The *koldun* in this case had to take a pea from a pod containing twelve and stretch a thread across the road in front of the wedding procession. Werewolves created in this manner were usually supposed to be vegetarian or eat only scraps from meals left by normal humans. They could be killed only by firearms, and clothing would be found under the wolfskin. The *koldun* could not himself undo the spell but it could be counteracted by someone tearing his shirt or trousers apart at a single rip and throwing them over the werewolf.[74]

Siberian Russians believed the *koldun* to be vulnerable to a bullet made from a melted-down metal cross.[75] A *koldun* was often buried together with a *gromovaia strela* ('thunderbolt'), a type of talisman described in Ch. 8.4.2 Any profession, because of its special, perhaps secret, skills, could popularly be thought to have magical connections, but two in particular were regularly associated with magic in many parts of Europe: that of the blacksmith and that of the miller. In Russia the blacksmith could often be involved in magical operations in folk tales or invoked in spells, but was not himself a *koldun* whereas the miller could well be; Zabylin published an autobiographical account of a miller who acquired the reputation of being a *koldun* by accident and was thereafter obliged to continue in the role.[76] In Ablesimov's comic opera, *The Miller – Wizard, Deceiver and Matchmaker*, first performed in 1779, the miller of the title explains in his first speech that every mill is supposed have its *koldun*, and a later remark in the opera makes it clear that wizards were still thought of as being able to change into were-animals. In Karelia all millers are reputed to be wizards.[77] In 1689, in the so-called Shaklovitii plot to harm the young Tsar Peter, the professions of those accused of malefic magic were: miller, horse-doctor (who had learned his magic from another horse-doctor), tailor. Other professions whose members could well be *kolduny* are the solitary callings of hunter, fisherman, woodsman, beekeeper, shepherd.[78]

Although the regular village *kolduns* were self-professed, the malevolent ones who peopled the fears of superstitious Russians could only be detected by magical means. These varied from region to region: a field in which a green or yellow circle appears was a venue for witches and wizards, and its owner was probably a *koldun*;[79] a Palm Sunday candle showed witches and wizards upside down; if aspen logs were put into the stove on Holy Thursday all the wizards and witches would come to ask for the embers; a rowan twig would detect people standing with their backs to the iconostasis; if one took the very first egg of a young pullet to church, the horns on the head of a *koldun* would become visible.[80] Here as elsewhere the *koldun* was confused with the Devil and in any case the *koldun* was commonly supposed not to go to church!

This confusion conceals two distinct attitudes to witches and wizards in the popular mind: there were those whom you knew, who had a particular professional role in village life, and those whom you did not know but feared, who went about disguising their real nature and doing harm and against whom measures had to be taken. The *koldun* appears as a professional and more or less positive figure in the account of a self-confessed *koldun* to the Synodal court in 1744:[81] he was employed by many in the Viatka region, even by the Governor's wife, to predict marriages, find lost livestock and similar tasks.

By the late nineteenth century the *koldun* was generally regarded as a person who had sold his soul to the Devil and had imps at his command.[82] He was by no means an endangered species: N.A. Nikitina noted in 1926 that the *koldun* was known to all the East Slavs and still had enormous power (she was writing in particular about the Nizhnii Novgorod region): they could kill birds in flight with their gaze, bring plague on cattle, and change wedding parties into wolves.[83] Min'ko in 1975 was still complaining of the influence of witchcraft and popular magic medicine in Soviet Belorussia.[84]

By the early twentieth century the country *koldun* had a town cousin, an urban professional with a telephone: Maurice Baring told a story of an English colleague in pre-Revolutionary St Petersburg who suffered a severe toothache on a holiday when no dentists were working; a Russian recommended a *koldun* in Moscow called Kozlov who duly cured the toothache by telephone for a fee of ten roubles.[85] Today the profession of *koldun* appears to be as flourishing in Russia as that of astrologers and their kind in the West. On Moscow television in October 1989 a *koldun* was interviewed and shown calming a woman possessed by demons. He said: '*Kolduns* are much needed in these times and I intend starting our own trade union'.[86] This would not be new; the *kolduny* of earlier times appear to have had professional collectives.[87]

4. *The Ved'ma*

Literally a 'knower', and sometimes called *koldun'ia* or *vedun'ia*. The word is common to all the Slavonic languages and seems to have been used in the sense both of a demonic personage and of a witch.[88] In popular belief the *ved'ma* was usually the female equivalent of a *koldun* and could be credited with any of his characteristics. Dal' (s.v. *vĕdat'*) quotes a saying that a learned witch (i.e. one who has learned her craft) is worse than a born one; this confirms that, as with the *koldun*, a witch could have either innate or acquired magic power.

Female practitioners in magic are known in Russia from the earliest historical times. The *Russian Primary Chronicle*, in the entry for 1071, which is a compendium of stories of pagan demonic witchcraft, the chronicler observes:

> Magic is performed through infernal instigation. Particularly through the agency of woman are infernal enchantments brought to pass, for in the beginning the devil deceived woman and she in turn deceived man. Thus even

down to the present day women perform magic by black arts, poison and other devilish deceits.[89]

Note once again the characteristic association of black magic with poison (see Ch. 9.2), together with a fairly common Christian emphasis on women as practitioners of magic, although in fact men have played a very large role in Russian magic. While the *koldun* may be both a real figure of village life and a fantastic figure of folklore, the *ved'ma* was more common in folklore and popular fear, perhaps, than in real life, and was maybe more prevalent in Belorussia and the Ukraine, which were under Polish, and thus German and Western, influence in general.[90] The confusion of witches as real-life practitioners in magic, with malevolent female demons of mythology and folklore is most evident in the figure of the *baba iaga* or *iagaia baba* who has an ancient lineage as a child-stealing and child-eating demon.[91] She is often the magical enemy, but sometimes the magical friend, of the hero of the story. One series of *byliny* popular in Siberia tells of the hero Dobrynia and a beautiful young witch Marinka, who entices young men to become her lovers, then kills them, or turns them into wild animals, sometimes even eats them.[92] In folk tales both the *ved'ma* and the *baba-iaga* can change their form, may catch and eat children,[93] either cooked or raw. One folk story recorded in the Vladimir region in the 1960s tells of a witch who carries off a child by imitating its mother's voice after she has had it remodelled from its natural witch-like harshness by a blacksmith. She tries to roast and eat the child.[94] Both the *baba-iaga* and the *ved'ma* in folk tales may supplant a real princess or wife by taking on her appearance.[95] Indeed, in popular prints of the eighteenth century Catherine the Great is portrayed in the guise of a *baba-iaga*.[96]

According to Samuel Collins, personal physician to Tsar Aleksei Mikhailovich in the seventeenth century, witches were also thought at that time to be the source of hostile magic at weddings and the cause of impotence. He writes:

> Seldom a wedding passes without some witch-craft (if people of quality marry), chiefly acted, as 'tis thought by nuns, whose prime devotion tends that way. I saw a fellow coming out of the bride-chamber, tearing his hair as though he had been mad, and being demanded the reason why he did so, he cry'd out: I am undone: I am bewitched. The remedy they use is to address themselves to a white witch, who for money will unravel the charm, and untie the codpiece point, which was this young man's case; it seems some old woman had tyed up his codpiece point.[97]

The detail of the knot causing impotence is convincing since it is an ancient and widespread magical belief;[98] the allegation about the preoccupation of Russian nuns is supported by relatively little evidence (but see below, p. 82), but in general, as we have seen elsewhere, the lesser members of the Orthodox Church were often involved in popular magic, and the presence of both monks and nuns at weddings was thought to be unlucky.[99] No doubt celibacy is associated with infertility in these beliefs, and since Russian monasteries and convents were often used as places of incarceration and punishment, popular imagination might very well impute to the involuntarily celibate a desire to gain his or her revenge by rendering others impotent or sterile. It is worth noting, when considering how far models of 'high' and 'low' culture can be applied to pre-Petrine Russia, that Collins moved only in court circles during his eight years in Russia, and says himself that his observations apply to the weddings of 'people of quality'.

Even at the beginning of the twentieth century impotence and sterility were commonly attributed to *porcha* or maleficium. Newly-wed couples were particularly vulnerable: a pin stuck in the bridal bed would cause impotence and an oak leaf thrown on the bride would make her sterile.[100]

In the recorded popular beliefs of Belorussia and the Ukraine and some parts of Russia the witch could fly up chimneys, naked and covered with ointment, on broomsticks or pokers and off to a Shabash (Witches' Sabbath) on Bald Mountain near Kiev on St John's day (24 June). She was assisted in flying by sprinkling herself with water which had been boiled with the embers of the mid-summer Kupala bonfire or by an ointment made from gentian.[101] In the Ukraine the witch was commonly thought to dress in a long shift and to have her hair unbound (a commonly required condition for practising magic and also a demonic attribute); she could assume any shape, and could be driven away by the herb *plakun*.[102] The belief that witches use a 'flying ointment' is old: it occurs as an episode in the second-century novel *The Golden Ass* or *Metamorphoses* of Apuleius, and was well known in Western Europe and also among the Balkan Slavs.[103] A fictional example of the use of 'flying ointment' in Soviet Moscow occurs in Bulgakov's novel *The Master and Margarita* (written 1928–40, published 1966–7); Bulgakov's magic and religion are, however, of a highly eclectic nature and this episode cannot be regarded as evidence of a native Russian tradition.

Witches, like *kolduny*, were reputed to be able to turn themselves and others into animals and even inanimate objects, and, as in other parts of Europe, were commonly accused of milking someone else's cows.[104] Dal', *Tolkovyi slovar'*, s.v. *gadit'* recorded the name *gadunitsa* for witches in Archangel province who both stole milk and could turn into magpies. In the trans-Baikal they would steal the milk while in the shape of dogs.[105] One way of dealing with milk-stealing witches in Belorussia was to put a strainer in a pot, pour in holy water, bring to the boil, stirring all the time with a blessed willow twig – as the heat increased so would the heat in the breast of the witch and she would come running begging for forgiveness.[106]

Sometimes witches were reputedly young and beautiful but in Great Russia they were more often thought to be old and ugly. They could well be married and have children; in Smolensk, on the border of Russia and Belorussia, witches incompetent enough to die in childbirth were supposed to come back from the grave to feed their child for six weeks after their death. Only exorcism by a priest could prevent this.[107] In Eastern Siberian stories witches were supposed to steal and eat embryos, commonly took the shape of magpies or other birds, would fly up chimneys after applying magic ointment, and make off to their Sabbath.[108] Witches were commonly held to be able to control rain, and in particular to cause drought by stealing it.[109]

In the Ukraine and some parts of Russia witches were supposed to have tails, catch falling stars, and keep them in jugs.[110] In both the Ukraine and North Russia, as elsewhere in the world, witches were thought to steal the moon at the time of eclipses.[111]

Another name for a witch is *veshchitsa* (*veshchun'ia*, *veshchuika*); in the Balkans this is the name of a child-stealing demon but in Russia, asserts Dal' (s.v. *věshchat'*), it was a witch who would leave her body under a mortar and fly up the chimney as a magpie. The association of witches with magpies is common elsewhere (hence the occasional name of witches *soroka-veshchitsa*, 'magpie-witch'); in Siberia a witch could become any kind of bird or animal but most commonly a magpie. (She also had the Evil Eye, could cause suicide or death, harm crops, livestock and guns, steal unborn children, control serpents, fly up chimneys, foretell the future; she would die painfully and walk after death unless staked down.)[112] In one popular story Ivan the Terrible gathered all the witches of Russia in Red Square to burn them, at which they turned into magpies and flew away.[113] The wife of the seventeenth-century usurper called the False Dimitrii is supposed to have escaped from Moscow as a magpie; magpies were never seen in Moscow because they were under a curse for stealing a lenten pancake from a fasting man, or because they betrayed the boyar Kuchka,[114] or because they were banned by Metropolitan Aleksei to get rid of witches,[115] and magpies are often hung on peasant barns to frighten off witches.[116]

Like the *koldun*, certainly by the late nineteenth century and probably long before, the *ved'ma* was normally considered to be in league with the Devil. Also like the *koldun* she was reputed to die in agony and make every attempt to pass on her powers to another, willing or unwilling.[117] Pomerantseva records a story from the Kaluga region of a witch dying in agony and passing on her powers to her unsuspecting daughter; the latter only realized what had happened when three devils appeared asking for instructions, and could only be got rid of by calling in a *vorozheika* (another kind of magical practitioner – see below).[118]

It is noteworthy that it is the female *ved'ma* rather than the male *koldun* whose image seems to have been most influenced by Western witch hysteria; indeed since in most of the West, and crucially in Poland and Germany, it was predominantly women who were accused of witchcraft, one may say that there is a strong likelihood that the whole notion of witchcraft took a new direction among the Russians as a result of greater contact with the more Westernized populations of Belorussia and the Ukraine, as those territories were acquired by Muscovy and Imperial Russia from the seventeenth century onwards.

This must inevitably have been strengthened by the great surge in literary translation from Western languages which began in the eighteenth century. It is not without interest that when Pushkin and Gogol' introduced occult elements into their work, they still had, for the most part, a recognizable Russian or

Ukrainian quality, while the much more recent satanic and witchcraft themes in Bulgakov's *Master and Margarita* are entirely Western and literary (*Faust* mostly, with more of Gounod than Goethe).

A small sub-category of female practitioners of magic may have been nuns, although the evidence is limited. Samuel Collins at the end of the seventeenth century stated that nuns' 'prime devotion tends that way' (see n. 97 above), nuns at Smolensk allegedly used to perform a ceremony with a doll to aid childless mothers (see Ch. 8.5), and a mid-nineteenth-century manuscript of magical notes by Brice de Beauregard describes the use of globes filled with water for fortune-telling as a religious act performed mostly by *religieuses* who are *voyantes*.[119] This information, he says, came from a Dr Rosch who had spent fourteen years in Russia.

5. *The Znakhar'*

The *znakhar'* (fem. *znakharka*), literally 'one who knows' (cf. English 'cunning-man') is usually a person who engages in folk medicine, interprets dreams, may use magic prayers and benign spells, does not invoke spirits, but can on occasion cast malefic spells. He was, and in some areas still is, an important element in popular medicine.[120] A favoured method of making a spell, and one which goes back at least to classical antiquity,[121] was to whisper it over the agent used – water, butter, bread, salt, tea.[122] This is why another name for a *znakhar'* is *sheptun* (see above), and the verb *sheptat'* 'to whisper' can mean 'to cast a spell'. This practice was mentioned by Prince Kurbskii in the sixteenth century,[123] and 'whispering over paper, herbs and drink' was among the magical practices listed as criminal offences under Catherine the Great in the later eighteenth century.[124] The *znakhar'* could also be employed to detect poison or witchcraft (the two are regularly linked as we see elsewhere in this book), find out thieves and enemies, and counteract an evil spell or the Evil Eye. On St Athanasius's day (18 January) the *znakhari* were supposed to drive out witches.[125] The *znakhar'*, like the *koldun*, could by repute have exceptional abilities such as the power to hear over long distances.[126] Another name for the *znakhar'* is *zeleinik*, f. *zeleinitsa* (from *zel'e* 'herb; medicine; magic potion; poison').

The female of this species, the *znakharka*, who may well have been more numerous than the male,[127] could also be the village midwife; indeed the usual words for a midwife *baba*, *babka* can be found with both senses. *Baba* historically may mean simply a woman, usually married, or a grandmother, but frequently also means a midwife or a practitioner of some kind of magic. In the last sense the word *baba* may also be reinforced by an adjective or another noun in apposition making the magical connotation quite clear.[128]

6. *The Vorozhei (vorozheia, vorozheika)*

Etymologically *vorozhei, vorozheia, vorozheika* appear to derive from Church Slavonic *vrag* 'enemy; devil' (and in later Russian 'wood-sprite'); 'magician', and in view of the cognates found in other Slavonic languages these associations of meaning may well go back to Common Slavonic, i.e. well before Christian contact with the Slavs. The verb *vrazhiti* meant 'to practise magic; to practise augury'. The Russian *vorozhei* and *vorozhets* are given in Dal' as regional words, but dictionaries of Old Russian do not attest these forms. The word *vorozhil'nik* in 1689, coupled with *vorozheia*, seems to be the only pre-eighteenth-century attested masculine form.[129] In the middle of the eighteenth century the form *vorozheia* could be either masculine or feminine and denote magicians of either sex: in a court document of 1754 a village magician called Maksim Markov was referred to as *vorozheia*, and *vrazheia* (a Church Slavonic form) and only once as *vorozhei*.[130] Both the masculine and feminine forms may be used for almost any kind of magical practitioner; the *vorozheia* Markov was in fact employed to kill a land-owner by magic. More commonly, however, *vorozheia* means a fortune-teller, possibly a foreigner such as a Gypsy, Finn or Tatar. He or she might use dice, cards, palmistry, tea leaves, coals, salt; or stare into water in which a cross is immersed.[131] In folk tales, and no doubt in real life, fortune-tellers of this kind may also be called upon to locate lost or stolen objects.[132]

The female *vorozheia* seems to crop up more commonly than her male counterpart both in folklore and in historical texts. In an official document of 1551 a list of undesirable persons who should be expelled from the region included thieves, brigands, *volkhvy* (wizards), *skomorokhi* (itinerant entertainers), and *baby vorozheii* (fortune-telling women).[133] These were the only women included, and the context suggests that they were thought of as a professional group on the fringes of society. As mentioned above the term originally seems to have designated a person able to offer a wider range of magical services than simply fortune-telling. In a court case in 1635 a woman in the entourage of the tsaritsa confessed under torture that the root called *obratim* (see Ch. 9.4), which she had dropped in the palace, was not intended to harm the royal family but to restore her husband's affection. It had been supplied to her by the wife of a *strelets* (a member of the train-band militia of Moscow, i.e. probably a substantial citizen) who is described in the record as a *vorozheia*. This serves to identify, though clearly not exclusively, both the kind of person who could at that time be called a *vorozheia* and the nature of her activity.[134] The fact that in this case the alleged *vorozheia* was obviously not an itinerant or a member of the criminal underworld is worth noting; words used with pejorative intent in criminal cases, as in Western witchcraft trials, have to be treated with caution. It is not impossible that more was involved in this case: both the woman and her husband were exiled to Siberia although the original case had not been directed against them.

In the eighteenth century women described as *vorozheia* seem to be more commonly thought of as professional fortune-tellers and evidently had a sufficiently distinct social or professional role to be recognized by dress. Fig. 1 is taken from a plate of ethnographic illustrations of Russian peasant dress and is labelled 'Fortune-teller'. (This appeared in an English book but must surely be of Russian origin.) As evidence that male fortune-tellers also existed, and indeed could make a living from the practice, one may quote the anonymous eighteenth-century novel *Neschastnyi Nikanor* ('The Unfortunate Nikanor; or the Life Adventure of a Russian Nobleman'), in which the hero travels from St Petersburg to Moscow, supporting himself *en route* by telling fortunes, although 'it pained my conscience greatly to deceive inquisitive women'.[135] It should also be noted that while this identification of women as the main consumers of fortune-telling in the eighteenth and nineteenth centuries is borne out by the evidence presented in the previous chapter, there was also no lack of men in all stations of life who also had recourse to it.

7. *The Iconography of Magic and Magicians*

Word pictures of magicians and what they do are common enough, and are quoted above and elsewhere where appropriate. Graphic representations are less common. Pagan priests and magicians are occasionally depicted in Russian medieval art. One such, described as an *obavnik*, appears in the *Kiev Psalter* (1397) to illustrate Psalm 58 (4–5: 'they are like the deaf-adder that stoppeth her ear; which will not hearken to the voice of the charmers') and in the *Uglich Psalter* (end of the fifteenth century): in both cases he is a snake-charmer with a high conical hat, playing a pipe.[136] The context, unfortunately, does not allow us to assume that the artists had Russian realia in mind. The *Radziwiłł Chronicle* (late fifteenth century), on the other hand, contains several pictures of *volkhvy* in a Russian context, but only one is in distinctive clothing, in fact in Western dress, presumably to express his otherness.[137] The same chronicle shows a Novgorodian asking for divination from a Chud' shaman with a drum.[138] The *Illuminated Chronicle* (sixteenth century) contains a version of the *Alexander Romance* which has representations of Nectanebus with a ram's head and wand performing magic rites.[139] Two incidents involving magicians, described as *kudesniki* are illustrated in the sixteenth/seventeenth-century *Tale of Zosima and Savvatii of Solovki* from the Solovetskii monastery in the far north of Russia in Novgorodian territory; the magicians have no particular distinguishing marks or clothing, perhaps because they were perceived to be Russians rather than exotic foreigners.[140]

APPENDIX
TYPES OF MAGIC AND MAGICIAN

1. *What magic is called*

There are many words that have been and may still be used in Russian to denote magic of one kind or another, and to judge from Russian dictionaries, many of these words lost their etymological meaning long ago and may be used interchangeably (see also for further discussion 3.1 above, and for words in particular contexts see Index). Some of the words for magic are recorded only in certain regions, some vary in meaning according to region. Examples are: *baianie* (from *baiati* 'to speak'; S. Slav cognates also mean magic), *balovanie, bal'stvo* (cf. *balii*, 'doctor; magician'),[141] *chary, charovanie, charodeianie, charodeistvo* (Vasmer indicates Indo-European cognates with the sense of 'to do, make'), *chernoknizhie, chernoknizhestvo* (these two mean literally '[art of] black books' – the etymology is not clear; the term has existed since the sixteenth century: see Ch. 8.5.4), *gadanie* (divination, from a verb which probably originally meant 'to think, talk'), *kob', kobenie, koblenie, kobovanie* (this group means in particular augury from bird movements and cries, or from chance meetings; the first may also mean fate or fortune, or in classical contexts Fortuna), *koldovanie, koldovstvo, kud (kudes, kudeshenie, kudeshestvo, kudesnichanie) (kud* also means an evil spirit; cognate with *chudo*, 'a wonder, miracle'),[142] *magiia* (a learned borrowing, probably from Latin, perhaps via German, not current before the eighteenth century), *obaianie, obavanie, obavnichestvo, obavy* (from *baiati* 'to speak'), *potvor* (from *tvoriti* 'to make, create', and also having the meanings of 'potion, herb, poison'; attested at least from the thirteenth, perhaps from the eleventh century in Church Slavonic and Old Russian), *vědovstvo, vědunstvo (vědati* 'to know'; attested from thirteenth century), *volkhvovanie (volkhovanie, volchba, volshba, volshebstvo, volshenie, volshestvie, volshestvo, volshevstvo, volshvenie)* (attested from the twelfth century; from *volkhv), vorozhba, vorozha* (attested from the thirteenth–fourteenth century), *vorozhka, vorozhenie)* (the most likely derivation is from *vorog* [*vrag*] 'enemy; the Devil; wood sprite; magician' see Dal', *Tolkovyi slovar'*, s.v. *vorog* – these all tend to be used in the sense of 'fortune-telling'), *znakharstvo* (from *znati* 'to know'; now primarily benign folk medicine). To these one might add *porcha* (lit. 'spoiling, damage'), malefic magic (usually in the form of sickness of man, beast, or crops) and *sglaz, nechistyi glaz, durnoi glaz*, etc., the Evil Eye (see Ch. 2.2).

The practice of magic, witchcraft, divination and fortune-telling has a corresponding number of verbs, some of which can also mean to consult a person who practises these arts: *charovat' (charodeistvovat', charodeiat'), gadat' (otgadyvat', razgadyvat', ugadyvat'), koldovat', kudesit', obavat' (obavit', obavliat'), portit', potvorit', prizorit', sheptat', smyvat'* (to cure or remove the Evil Eye magically by sprinkling magic water), *uznavat', volkhvovat', volshebnichat' (volshebstvovat'), vorozhbit' (vorozhit', vrazhit'), zagovarivat', znakharit'*, and a good many more.

2. *What magicians are called*

There is an equally large number of words to denote practitioners in magic, many of them, of course, derived from the words for magic listed above. Men may be: *akudnik (okudnik)*,[143] *akundin, akindin* (usually a folktale figure),[144] *arbui* (attested only in sixteenth-century sources, e.g. *Stoglav*, where it refers to Chud' magicians; from Finnish *arpoja*, 'magician'), *ared* ('old wizard; devil', probably derived from *Herod*),[145] *baanik* (recorded only in one text, the translation of the chronicle of George Hamartolos),[146] *baia*,[147] *baian, bakhar', baal'nik, baial'nik* (originally 'a storyteller' <*baiat'* 'to speak', *bakhorit'* 'to chatter'),[147] *balii* (a Church Slavonic word for physician or prophet, attested in the seventeenth century in the sense of magician),[148] *basarog* (male or female),[149] *bol'shak* (usually 'head of household, leader' from *bol'shoi* 'big'), *charodei* (*charodeets*,[150] *charovatel', charovnik*), *chernoknizhnik, doka, eretik* (*eretnik, eretun*) (lit. 'heretic' but also 'reptile, snake, frog'), *gad* (this word may be perceived as the root of *gadati*, the main verb meaning 'to divine', but inevitably is coloured by the negative connotations of its homonym meaning 'reptile; repulsive person') *gadatel', gadala, gadal'shchik* (all from *gadati* 'to divine', *glavnoi* (lit. 'the chief person'),[151] *kashchei* (more usually a folktale figure),[152] *kletnik* (Dal', *Tolkovyi slovar'*, s.v. *klet'* gives this as a north Russian term for a *znakhar'* at a wedding who protects the couple from the Evil Eye; it can also mean a house goblin), *kobil'nik, kobnik, koldun, kudesnik, nauznik* (lit. 'a maker of amulets'), *mag, mechetnik*,[153] *morokun*,[154] *obadnik, obaiatel', obavannik, obavatel', obavnik, opasnoi* (lit. 'the dangerous one' in modern Russian but probably originally 'the one who protects', cf. *opasnaia ladonka*, an amulet to ward off illness and the Evil Eye),[155] *portezhnik, porchel'nik, portel'shchik* (from *portit'* 'to spoil'; one who spoils, i.e. puts the Evil Eye on something, a hostile *koldun*), *prikosnik, sheptun* (from *sheptat'* 'to whisper'), *potvornik, storozh*,[156] *ugadatel', vedun, ved'mak* (esp. in Belorussia and the Ukraine; can be both wizard and were-animal or revenant: from *vedati*, 'to know'), *veshchun, veshchets, veshchel'*) (cf. *veshchat'* 'to speak, foretell', *veshchii*, 'wise, all-knowing'), *vezhlivets, vezhlivoi* (lit. 'the polite one'; Dal', *Tolkovyi slovar'*, s.v. *vezha*, says that this is a euphemism for a *koldun* or *znakhar'*), *viritnik*,[157] *volkhv, volkhvun, volkhovnik, volsvinik, volshebnik* (probably derived from Finnish *velho*, 'magician'; in early texts *volkhv* translates Greek *magos* and *mantis*), *vorozhei, vorozhil'nik, vrazhnoi* (from *vrag*, 'enemy, devil, etc.'), *zberezhatyi* (lit. 'protector'),[158] *zeleinik, zeleishchik* ('a user of *zelie* herbs; potions'; see Ch. 9.2 3), *znakhar', znatok, znatnik* (from *znati* 'to know').

Women practitioners of magic have names which are often the etymological equivalents of names for male magicians, although a few are distinctively female only. They may be *baba, baba-belogolovka*,[159] *baba-iaga, baba-nerascheska* (*prostovoloska*) (woman with unbound hair – a characteristic state for performing magic),[160] *baial'nitsa, baliia, bilitsa*,[161] *besovka, besikha* (witch; devil),[162] *charovnitsa, chernoknizhnitsa, chertovka, chertikha*,[163] *gadalka, gadal'nitsa, gadal'shchitsa, gadunitsa, koldun'ia, koldunikha, koldunitsa, kudesnitsa, mara*,[164] *morokun'ia morokusha; obavatel'nitsa, portezhnitsa, potvornitsa, sheptukha, sheptun'ia, vedun'ia, vedema, ved'ma* (especially in Belorussia and the Ukraine and in folktales),[165] *veshchitsa* (*aveshchitsa, soroka-veshchitsa*),[166] *volkhva, volkhvitka*,[167] *volshebnitsa, volshnitsa, vorozheia, vorozheika, znakharka*.[168]

Notes

1. Rowland, 'Fantasticall and Devilishe Persons', p. 169.
2. See Uspenskii, 'The Role of Dual Models'.
3. The terminological difficulty also arises when one compares English, French, German, and

Latin: for some discussion see Edward Peters, *The Magician, the Witch and the Law*, Philadelphia, 1978, pp. xvi–xvii.

4. Kivelson, 'Through the Prism of Witchcraft'. Kivelson amended this statement in a later paper: 'Patrolling the Boundaries', p. 310, where she correctly states that neither Orthodoxy nor Muscovite law made the distinction.

5. Nikolai Novikov, *Drevniaia russkaia vivliofika*, 6, 2nd edn, Moscow, 1788, pp. 415–7.

6. Rybakov, *Iazychestvo*, p. 298.

7. *Pamiatniki starinnoi russkoi literatury*, IV, p. 138.

8. Grattan and Singer, *Anglo-Saxon Magic and Medicine*, p. 9.

9. See, for example, Dal', *Slovar'*, s.v. *lysii*.

10. Bethencourt, 'Portugal', p. 421, claims, against much evidence to the contrary, that the ability of witches to change into birds is a peculiarity of Portuguese belief, and that this was a survival of the *strix* myth from antiquity.

11. For a convenient recent account see Sorlin, 'Femmes et sorciers. Note sur la permanence des rituels païens en Russie, XIe–XIXe siècle', pp. 459–75. Despite its title this is concerned primarily with the accounts of *volkhvy* in the earliest period of Russian Christianity, on which see also Franklin, 'The Empire of the *Rhomaioi*', pp. 508–37 (on *volkhvy*, p. 523) and Russell Zguta, 'The Pagan Priests of Early Russia', pp. 259–66 (in fact largely concerned with Mordvinian practices). For more modern folk usage see Vlasova, *Novaia abevega*, s.v. *volkhv*.

12. See Shanskii, *Ètimologicheskii slovar'*, s.v.

13. *Pskovskie letopisi*, p. 262.

14. Reproduced in Levin, *Sex and Society*, p. 48.

15. Pigin, *Iz istorii russkoi demonologii*, p. 178.

16. See *Izbornik*, p. 612.

17. Danilov, *Drevnie rossiiskie stikhotvoreniia*, ll. 41–2.

18. The explanation of this point by Tertullian and Isidore is not, as far as I can tell, known in Orthodox theology: see Ch. 14, n. 11.

19. *Kazanskaia istoriia*, pp. 89–90.

20. For some references see Ryan, 'Aristotle and Pseudo-Aristotle', p. 100 and n. 18.

21. Saxo Grammaticus, *History*, 1, p. 80.

22. Truvorov, 'Volkhvi i vorozhei', pp. 704–5.

23. In general on the *koldun* see Vlasova, *Novaia abevega*, pp. 180–87, s.v. *koldun*.

24. Beneshevich, *Pamiatniki*, col. 919. Quoted from the *Velikie chetii minei* of Makarii.

25. Zabylin, *Russkii narod*, pp. 206–12.

26. This appears to have been a general opinion at the end of the nineteenth century: see *Byt velikorusskikh krest'ian-zemlepashtsev*, pp. 129–32, for the evidence from Vladimir province collected by the Tenishev bureau. In the Pinsk region of Belorussia the *charovnik* would put on a horsecollar to commune with the Devil: Bulgakovskii, 'Pinchuki', p. 190. Horsecollars also feature in divination in some areas – see Index.

27. Popov, *Russkaia narodno-bytovaia meditsina*, pp. 35–6.

28. Popov, *Russkaia narodno-bytovaia meditsina*, p. 33; Weideger, *History's Mistress*, p. 241.

29. Mazalova, 'Zhiznennaia sila', p. 26; Dal', *Tolkovyi slovar'*, s.v. *dvoe*.

30. Maksimov, *Nechistaia*, p. 111.

31. Kolchin, 'Verovaniia krest'ian Tul'skoi gubernii', p. 35.

32. Mazalova, 'Zhiznennaia sila', p. 26.

33. Mazalova, 'Zhiznennaia sila'. Mazalova is discussing north Russian magicians.

34. Nikiforovskii, *Prostonarodnye primety i pover'ia*, pp. 282–3. See also Min'ko, *Sueveriia*, p. 32.

35. Zelenin, *Izbrannye trudy*, p. 62.

36. Novichkova, *Russkii demonologicheskii slovar'*, s.v. *kolokol'nyi mertvets*, p. 271.

37. Min'ko, *Sueveriia*, p. 32.

38. Maksimov, *Nechistaia*, p. 112.

39. Text of MS Leningrad IMLI 7, ff. 31–43, published in Malyshev, *Drevnerusskie rukopisi Pushkinskogo Doma*, p. 182.

40. Dal', *Tolkovyi slovar'*, s.v. *kol*, notes that this belief applies to witches and wizards among all the Slav peoples. Olaus Magnus (*Description of the Northern Peoples*, bk 3, ch. 4) records a very similar incident among the Goths in which the corpse of a wizard was dug up and impaled to prevent it from doing mischief. The practice of hamstringing bodies to prevent their ghosts walking is known in several cultures: Frazer, *Golden Bough*, VIII, pp. 272–3. According to Maksimov, *Nechistaia*, p. 108, the hamstringing has to be performed *before* death. See also Zabylin, *Russkii narod*, pp. 217–8. The propensity of magicians to become revenants is referred to in Barber, *Vampires*, p. 30. On the other hand in the Indigirka region of northern Siberia *all* corpses were transfixed by a stake if their relatives did not wish them to return; if their reappearance in the guise of a new child was required then a small hole was left in the top of the coffin: Chikachev, *Russkie na Indigirke*, p. 117. Further examples of beliefs relating to the death of a *koldun* are given in Zelenin, *Izbrannye trudy*, pp. 61–3.

41. Nikiforovskii, *Prostonarodnye primety i pover'ia*, no. 2259; Min'ko, *Sueveriia*, p. 36. This is a common method of dealing with vampires among the Slavs: see Perkowski, *The Darkling*, p. 122. It is part of a tradition not confined to the Slavs; the late twelfth-century Saxo Grammaticus tells the tale of how a cannibalistic walking corpse is subdued, its head cut off, and a stake driven through it: see *Saxo Grammaticus: The History of the Danes*, p. 88 n. 128. On this use of poppy seed, see Barber, *Vampires*, p. 49; Abbot, *Macedonian Folklore*, pp. 218–19, mentions the scattering of millet in similar circumstances so that the vampire would waste time picking up the seed and be overtaken by the dawn.

42. Bogatyrev, *Actes magiques*, p. 124. The idea that the corpse utters a sound when staked is typical of beliefs about vampirism, as is the remedy of decapitation: see Barber, *Vampires*, pp. 19, 25, 73.

43. Bulgakovskii, 'Pinchuki', p. 191.

44. Nikiforovskii, *Prostonarodnye primety i pover'ia*, no. 2260. In Greece, where werewolves and vampires (*vourkolakos*) were also a part of popular belief, a formal office of exorcism by a priest is recorded in an Athonite manuscript: see Delatte, 'Un Office byzantin d'exorcisme', pp. 95–7, 111–13. The Greek, and Serbian, vampire had to be exorcized on a Saturday, the only day when he was confined to the grave. See also Barber, *Vampires*, pp. 58, 67.

45. Markevich, *Obychai* (reprint, p. 113).

46. Dal', *Tolkovyi slovar'*, s.v. *vědat'* (*věd'mak*).

47. See Vlasova, *Novaia abevega*, pp. 143–7, s.v. *eretik*.

48. See Zelenin, *Izbrannye trudy*, chs 1 and 2.

49. Min'ko, *Sueveriia*, p. 24, distinguishes a lesser kind of *koldun* who stops short of magical murder.

50. See Zelenin, *Izbrannye trudy*, ch. 3.

51. Levenstim, 'Sueverie', pp. 157–219; also Matveeva, *Mifologicheskie rasskazy*, p. 316, for current belief in Siberia.

52. Zabylin, *Russkii narod*, pp. 145, 154.

53. See Dal', *Slovar'*, s.v. *vězha*.

54. Lebedeva, 'Material'nye komponenty', p. 203.

55. Minenko, *Russkaia krest'ianskaia sem'ia*, p. 247.

56. Dal', *Slovar'*, s.v. *bol'shoi*.

57. Chappe d'Auteroche, *Voyage en Sibérie*, p. 163.

58. For Pskov see Kozyrev, 'Svadebnye obriady', pp. 79–80.

59. Mazo, '"We don't summon Spring in the Summer"', p. 74.

60. Zabylin, *Russkii narod*, p. 209.

61. A Siberian specimen is quoted in full in Bolonev, 'O nekotorykh arkhaicheskikh elementakh v zagovorakh', p. 68: 'I, servant of God X arise, I bless myself, I shall set out crossing myself, I shall wash in cold spring water, dry myself with a thin towel; I shall cover myself with clouds, gird myself with the red dawn, protect myself with the bright moon, shoe myself with the teeming stars, light myself with the red sun. I shall build round myself and my company an iron fence with a steel floor, and wrought steel sky, so that none may shoot from the east, west, north or south, neither heretic nor female heretic, koldun nor female koldun, good or bad, whoever in the wide world eats bread. My head is a basket, my tongue is a lock.'

62. Balashov, Marchenko, and Kalmykova, *Russkaia svad'ba*, pp. 289–90. In England a pod with nine peas was lucky and was widely used in marital divination: see Opie and Tatem, *Dictionary of Superstitions*, s.v. *peas*.

63. Dal', *Slovar'*, s.v. *zakruchivat'*.

64. See also Afanas'ev, *Poeticheskie vozzreniia*, III, p. 516; Eleonskaia, *Sel'sko-khoziaistvennaia magiia*, p. 173. For this kind of magic and measures taken against it in Belorussia see Romanov, *Belorusskii sbornik*, V, pp. 11–12. For an account of the removal of a *zakrutka* in the Kiev region of the Ukraine see Markevich, *Obychai* (reprint, pp. 121–2).

65. Shein, *Materialy*, p. 528. Shein also gives several counter-spells, including one invoking St Nicholas.

66. Dal', *Tolkovyi slovar'*, s.v. *zalamlivat'*.

67. Bolonev, *Narodnyi kalendar' semeiskikh Zabaikal'ia*, p. 100.

68. Popov, *Russkaia narodno-bytovaia meditsina*, pp. 31–2.

69. Matveeva, *Mifologicheskie rasskazy*, p. 316. Olaus Magnus in the sixteenth century recorded it as a belief among the peoples of the north: Olaus Magnus, *Description of the Northern Peoples*, bk 3, ch. 15.

70. Ralston, p. 405, quoting Sakharov, *Skazaniia*, I, ii, 28.

71. Zabylin, *Russkii narod*, p. 240.

72. Tikhonravov, *Pamiatniki*, p. viii.

73. Balashov, Marchenko and Kalmykova, *Russkaia svad'ba*, p. 290.

74. Nikiforovskii, *Prostonarodnye primety i pover'ia*, pp. 53–70.

75. Matveeva, *Mifologicheskie rasskazy*, p. 316. In the Zaonezh'e region a silver bullet or a bullet with a cross on it would kill a wood demon: Loginov, *Material'naia kul'tura i proizvodstvenno-bytovaia magiia russkikh Zaonezh'ia*, p. 49. Cf. the silver bullet in England and Scotland against which no one is proof and which will kill witches: Opie and Tatem, *A Dictionary of Superstitions*, s.v. *Silver bullet*. Also in America: Thomas, *Kentucky Superstitions*, no. 3832 and 3881 (the latter for killing (*sic*) ghosts). In 1815 the Polish Count Jean Potocki, writer, orientalist, traveller and diplomatist of Tsar Alexander I, shot himself with a silver bullet made from a melted-down samovar, having become convinced that he was a werewolf: Robert Irwin, *The Arabian Nights: A Companion*, London, 1994, p. 257.

76. Zabylin, *Russkii narod*, pp. 206–8.

77. *Ètnokul'turnye protsessy v Karelii*, pp. 40–41.

78. Nikiforovskii, *Prostonarodnye primety i pover'ia*, pp. 282–3.

79. Zabylin, *Russkii narod*, p. 243. In England in recent years the same phenomenon has excited much discussion in the press and has been attributed by some to 'flying saucers'.

80. Maksimov, *Nechistaia*, p. 113.

81. Golikova, 'Derevenskii koldun'. He described how at the age of 43 he had stayed at the house of a Votiak (Udmurt), and together with several others had been instructed in magic by him. He acquired a book of spells (*tetradka*) and a silver copeck which when immersed in water enabled him to make predictions.

82. Pomerantseva, *Mifologicheskie personazhi*, p. 141.

83. Nikitina, 'K voprosu o russkikh koldunakh', p. 299. This includes a bibliography of *koldovstvo*. The reputed ability to kill with a glance and to know what is happening at a distance are powers which the Russian *koldun* shares with the Indian yogi, according to Ibn Battuta: see *The Travels of Ibn Battuta, A.D. 1325–1354*, ed. H.A.R. Gibb and C.F. Beckingham, London, IV, 1994, pp. 788–9.

84. Min'ko, *Sueveriia*, *passim*.

85. Recounted in Graham, *Part of the Wonderful Scene*, p. 42.

86. Reported by John Mitchell in the *Independent Magazine*, 23 December 1989, p. 18.

87. Kostomarov, *Ocherk*, p. 188.

88. For a detailed discussion of local names and characteristics in different Slav areas see Vinogradova, 'Obshchee i spetsificheskoe'.

89. *Russian Primary Chronicle*, s.a. 1071.

90. For detail on Ukrainian beliefs about witches (and vampires) see Ivanov, 'Narodnye rasskazy o ved'makh i upyriakh'.

91. See Vlasova, *Novaia abevega*, s.v. *iaga*; also for some example Novichkova, *Russkii demonologicheskii slovar'*, s.v. *baba-iaga*.

92. For texts see *Russkaia èpicheskaia poèziia Sibiri*, nos 148–50, notes at pp. 415–16; Rybnikov, *Pesni*, sobrannye P.N. Rybnikovym (Petrozavodsk edn), 2, nos 144, 188, 192, for bibliography see notes at p. 551.

93. See Afanas'ev, *Narodnye russkie skazki*, 1984–5 edn, nos. 108–10, 112, 558.

94. *Traditsionnyi fol'klor vladimirskoi derevni*, pp. 213–4.

95. See Afanas'ev, *Narodnye russkie skazki*, 1984–5 edn, nos. 260, 261, 264–6; Kondrat'eva *Metamorfozy sobstvennogo imeni*, s.v. Kondrat'eva also notes that *baba-iaga* may be a synonym for *leshii* or wood-demon.

96. Kondrat'eva, *Metamorfozy sobstvennogo imeni*, s.v. *baba-iaga*.

97. Samuel Collins, *The Present State of Russia*, quoted from Cross, *Russia under Western Eyes*, p. 114.

98. See Frazer, *Golden Bough*, III, pp. 299–301. For Anglo-Saxon, English and Scottish belief see Opie and Tatem, *Dictionary*, s.v. *Knots hinder conception*.

99. Dal', *Tolkovyi slovar'*, s.v. *monastyr'*.

100. Popov, *Russkaia narodno-bytovaia meditsina*, p. 33.

101. Ralston, *Songs of the Russian People*, pp. 384–5.

102. Markevich, *Obychai* (reprint, p. 116). On *plakun* see Ch. 9.4.

103. Vukanović, 'Witchcraft in the Central Balkans. I. Characteristics of Witches', p. 12.

104. See Ralston, *Songs of the Russian People*, pp. 390–2 for variants on this theme. See Frazer, *Golden Bough*, index, for the milk-stealing accusation in other areas.

105. Bolonev, *Narodnyi kalendar' semeiskikh Zabaikal'ia*, p. 83.

106. Min'ko, *Sueveriia*, p. 141.

107. Paul Bartels in *Das Weib* (quoted in Weideger, *History's Mistress*, p. 264). The theme of revenant mothers feeding their babies also occurs in a folk tale: see Afanas'ev, *Narodnye russkie skazki*, 1984–5 edn, III, no. 361.

108. Zinov'eva, *Ukazatel'*, motifs under GI.

109. Ralston, *Songs of the Russian People*, pp. 382–3; Afanas'ev, *Poeticheskie vozzreniia slavian na prirodu*, III, p. 450.

110. Artsikhovskaia, *O koldovstve, porche, i klikushestve*. Witches also have tails in Moldavia, Bukovina and Transylvania: see Éva Pócs, *Fairies and Witches at the Boundary of South Eastern and Central Europe*, p 73 n. 98. There was considerable cultural interaction between these areas and the Ukraine, especially in the seventeenth century.

111. Dal', *Poslovitsy*, IV, p. 185.

112. See Matveeva, *Mifologicheskie rasskazy*, p. 313–14; Minenko, *Russkaia krest'ianskaia sem'ia*, p. 253, adds the detail that the witch-magpie is tailless (SW Siberia).

113. See Perrie, *The Image of Ivan the Terrible in Russian Folklore*, pp. 178–9.

114. Dal', *Tolkovyi slovar'*, s.v. *soroka*.

115. H. Sutherland Edwards, a nineteenth-century writer on Russia and one-time correspondent of *The Times* in that country tells this story in his *The Russians at Home* (p. 299) as if it had recently happened: according to him the Metropolitan was laying the foundation stone of a new church with a golden trowel when it disappeared; a workman was knouted and sent to Siberia for the theft but the trowel was later found in a magpie nest at the top of the Ivan Velikii bell-tower in the Kremlin, upon which the Metropolitan anathematized the magpies of Moscow.

116. Ralston, *Songs of the Russian People*, p. 405. Dal', *Tolkovyi slovar'*, s.v. *soroka*, says it protects a stable from the *domovoi* or house sprite. The Russian beliefs about magpies would appear to be part of a wider European tradition: in England the magpie was thought of as the Devil's own bird (see Elworthy, *The Evil Eye*, p. 91) and Brewer, *Dictionary of Phrase and Fable*, s.v. *magpie*, notes an association with witchcraft in Sweden, and with presages of death in Scotland. Shakespeare observes that magpies are used in augury (*Macbeth*, iii, 4).

117. Zinov'eva, *Ukazatel'*, motif GI 17. Bethencourt, 'Portugal', p. 414, notes the belief in Portugal that dying witches could pass on their powers.

118. Pomerantseva, *Mifologicheskie personazhi*, p. 140.

119. London, Wellcome Institute, MS 1355.

120. A useful recent account of the *znakhar'* with some discussion of medical magic is Ramer 'Traditional Healers and Peasant Culture in Russia', pp. 207–34.

121. Both *susurrus* and *murmur* are found in Latin in the sense of magic spell. The *Lex Cornelia de sicoriis* mentions 'artibus odiosis tam venenis vel susurris magices homines occiderunt': see *Apulei Apologia*, commentary, p. 3, n. 15. In his *Metamorphoses* Apuleius also has the phrase 'omnia … ferali murmure in aliam effigiam translata' (2,1,3), rendered in the English translation as 'Everything had been transformed into another shape by some deadly mumbo-jumbo' (Apuleius, *Metamorphoses*, II, p. 59). On *murmur* see also L. Baldini Moscadi, 'Murmur nella terminologia magica', *Studi italiani di filologia classica*, 48, 1976, pp. 254–62.

122. Matveeva, *Mifologicheskie rasskazy*, p. 316.

123. Fennell, *Kurbsky's History of Ivan IV*, pp. 202–3.

124. See Popov, *Sud i nakazaniia*, p. 381. 1

25. Dal', *Poslovitsy*, IV, s.v.

126. Matveeva, *Mifologicheskie rasskazy*, p. 316.

127. This is asserted, and with some evidence, by Rose Glickman in a well-informed and useful study of *znakharki* (mostly in the nineteenth and twentieth centuries): Glickman, 'The Peasant Woman', p. 149.

128. See Dal', *Tolkovyi slovar'*, s.v.; Sreznevskii, *Materialy*, s.v.; *Polnyi slovar' sibirskogo govora*, s.v. This sense of the word is not recorded in *Slovar' XI–XVII vv.*

129. *Slovar' XI–XVII*, s.v.

130. Beliaev, 'Bytovye ocherki', p. 850n.

131. See Dal', *Tolkovyi slovar'*, s.v. *vorog*. For the last two in the seventeenth century see Cherepnin, 'Iz istorii drevnerusskogo koldovstva', pp. 104–5.

132. See Afanas'ev, *Narodnye russkie skazki*, 1984–5 edn, III, no. 379–81. In no. 379 an old lady predicts the location of lost horses by consulting cards. We may note that in these stories there is trickery involved in the 'divination'.

133. *Slovar' XI–XVII vv.*, s.v.

134. Zabelin, *Domashnii byt russkikh tsarits*, p. 538.

135. *Neschastnyi Nikanor, ili prikliuchenie zhizni rossiiskogo dvorianina*, St Petersburg, 1775 (pt. 1 only) and 1787–9. See Drage, *Russian Literature in the Eighteenth Century*, p. 187.

136. See Chernetsov, 'Medieval Russian Pictorial Materials on Paganism and Superstitions'.

137. Ibid., and Vzdornov, *Issledovaniia*, p. 121 and f. 77v.

138. Ibid., p. 102. On the *Chud'* see Ch. 1, n. 26.

139. Ibid., pp. 101–2.

140. *Povest' o Zosime i Savvatii*, text vol., p. 138, no.137 and p. 141, no. 137; plates vol. ff. 133, 137v.

141. D'iachenko, *Polnyi tserkovno-slavianskii slovar'*, s.vv.

142. Zabylin notes that in the Tikhvin, Novgorod and Vologda regions costumed mummers were also called *kudesy*: Zabylin, *Russkii narod*, p. 12; Dal', *Tolkovyi slovar'*, s.v. *kud*, notes that *kudesa*, more usually 'magic' or 'magic spells', may also mean the popular entertainments of the Christmas period, and the verb *kudesit'sia* may mean dressing up in costume for the Yuletide entertainment. This is direct linguistic evidence of the relationship of magic with seasonal festivals and popular entertainments.

143. Dal', *Slovar'*, s.v. Listed as a term in the Riazan' province.

144. Kondrat'eva, *Metamorfozy sobstvennogo imeni*, s.v., possibly a variant of the preceding term.

145. See Vlasova, *Novaia abevega*, s.v. *ared*.

146. *Slovar' XI–XVII vv.*, s.v.

147. D'iachenko, *Polnyi tserkovno-slavianskii slovar'*, s.v.

148. See Vasmer, s.v.; *Slovar' XI–XVII*, s.v., D'iachenko, *Polnyi tserkovno-slavianskii slovar'*, s.v.

149. Kondrat'eva, *Metamorfozy sobstvennogo imeni*, s.v.

150. This form is found in the Old Russian translation of the *History of the Jewish War* of Josephus, a twelfth-century translation extant in manuscripts from the fifteenth century onwards: Meshcherskii, *Istoriia iudeiskoi voiny*, p. 325.

151. Mentioned in Zelenin, *Russische (ostslavische) Volkskunde*, p. 315.

152. Kondrat'eva, *Metamorfozy sobstvennogo imeni*, s.v. *kashchei*, defined in many senses including 'wizard and were-animal; a hostile warrior in *byliny* and folk tales; miser'.

153. *Slovar' XI–XVII*, s.v.; specifically 'one who foretells the future' but recorded only twice, in the *vita* of Stefan of Perm', and in the *Domostroi*, both in lists of words for magician.

154. See Dal', s.v. *moroka* 'darkness, fog, illusion'.

155. Mentioned in Zelenin, *Russische (ostslavische) Volkskunde*, p. 315. Dal', *Tolkovyi slovar'*, s.v. *opasat'*, quotes this as a Vologda usage and particularly mentions that the *opasnyi* was invited to weddings to ward off the Evil Eye.

156. Mentioned in Zelenin, *Russische (ostslavische) Volkskunde*, p. 315. Not given in Dal'.

157. Popov, *Russkaia narodno-bytovaia meditsina*, p. 35. A name in the Orlov province for magicians who could blight or send mad with a glance.

158. Mentioned in Zelenin, *Russische (ostslavische) Volkskunde*, p. 315. Not in Dal'.

159. In particular as a hostile witch against whom help is invoked in a spell: see Kondrat'eva *Metamorfozy sobstvennogo imeni*, s.v. *Baba* could also occasionally designate a male magician.

160. See Vlasova, *Novaia abevega*, s.v. *baba (devka)-nerascheska (prostovoloska, pustovoloska)*.

161. In the Olonets province: Rybnikov, *Pesni*, 1991 edn, p. 599, s.v.

162. From *bes*, a common word for the Devil: see Vlasova, *Novaia abevega*, s.v. *besikha*.

163. From the commonest word for devil; listed in Dal', s.v. *chert*.

164. Zabylin, *Russkii narod*, p. 239, gives this term for witches in the Voronezh region. See also Kondrat'eva, *Metamorfozy sobstvennogo imeni*, s.v. for the Poles'e region and wider mythological uses. Dal', s.v. lists the meanings of 'deception, spectre, illusion; a kind of *domovoi* or house goblin; in the Ukraine a doll used in spring rituals'.

165. See Vlasova, *Novaia abevega*, pp. 69–78, s.v. *ved'ma*.

166. Kondrat'eva, *Metamorfozy sobstvennogo imeni*, s.v.

167. Bolonev, *Narodnyi kalendar' semeiskikh Zabaikal'ia*, p. 79.

168. For further information see Maksimov, *Nechistaia, nevedomaia i krestnaia sila*; Tokarev, *Religioznye verovaniia vostochnoslavianskikh narodov* (this has an extensive bibliography); Dal', *Tolkovyi slovar'*, s.vv.; *Slovar'*, s.vv. In English consult Min'ko, 'Magical Curing' (this study deals primarily with Belorussia and is partially intended as a contribution to the campaign against religion) and the still useful Ralston, *Songs of the Russian People*. For a long list of names of witches among the South Slavs, some of which are the same as the Russian names, see Vukanović, 'Witchcraft in the Central Balkans. I. Characteristics of Witches', also Kemp, *Healing Ritual*, p. 183.

4
POPULAR DIVINATION

1. *Introduction*

In addition to the forms of divination described in detail in other chapters of this book, of which bibliomancy, and in particular psalmomancy, was probably the oldest and most widespread, there were many kinds of popular divination which did not require a text or the services of a specialist. These have been described by ethnographers, folklorists, and local antiquarians, mostly of the last century, and into the 1920s of the Soviet period, with a revival of interest since the 1980s. The earlier descriptions are not always in a form which inspires great confidence as to their accuracy of detail, but they have enough in common to make comparison possible. One cannot often say much about how old practices are, what their origin might be, how widespread they were when recorded, how much they change with time, how seriously they were taken and by whom, or how far they survive now, although literary evidence and comparison with evidence from other culture areas can give some clue.[1]

The number of methods of prediction to be found is very large, with an even larger number of local variations; what follows below is a selection, but one which should demonstrate the main characteristics of Russian popular divination.

2. *Protection during Divination*

Popular divination may involve elements of magic such as spells or the use of magic objects or rituals, and like magic often required rituals to protect the user from evil spirits. These are described in more detail elsewhere in the book where appropriate, but typically involve praying, bathing, fasting, common requirements for magic in many cultures. The alternative tradition was an acceptance by the would-be diviner that divination was only possible with the help of the 'unclean' spirits which were thought to be abroad in particular at the magical times of midwinter and midsummer. To avoid frightening these spirits away the diviner had to *negate* his normal religious observances, i.e. not pray (but perhaps use a spell), remove the pectoral cross, turn icons to the wall, and ensure that only an odd number of persons was present.[2] Descriptions of this kind of divination may stress that it is dangerous or frightening, and/or that it must be performed within a protective circle. The same method of divination may be described in different sources as being performed either in the orthodox religious mode or the magical, often demonic mode.

3. *Popular Divination in Literature*

Popular divination of one kind or another is referred to or described in many classical Russian works of literature: Zhukovskii, Pushkin, Gogol', Goncharov, Tolstoi, all have passages devoted to it. The two most famous heroines of Russian fiction, Tat'iana in Pushkin's *Eugene Onegin* and Natasha in Tolstoi's *War and Peace* both tried it; in fact an account of popular divination or magic became almost *de rigeur* in nineteenth-century literary descriptions of life in rural Russia. The practices described in Russian fiction generally conform to the descriptions of practices in non-fictional accounts, and indeed may often be derived from them, and in their turn reinforce popular tradition. The particular value of the literary accounts is in identifying the level of social acceptance of these practices, and their male or female orientation, since historians and collectors of folk wisdom in the nineteenth century did not for the most part search for their material in the urban homes of the aristocracy. This is also why the memoirs and travel notes of curious foreign visitors can be so useful, provided that their frequent assumptions of superiority are allowed for.

Perhaps the most famous list of Russian popular divinatory practices occurs in Ch. 5 of Pushkin's *Eugene Onegin* in which he describes how at Christmas young girls seek to know the name, appearance, etc. of their future husbands (5,4); the heroine, Tat'iana, defends ancient popular lore, knows what is foretold by cards and dreams and the moon, the cat on the stove (5.5), or shooting stars, and that a monk or a hare crossing the path is an ill omen (5.6); she knows that pouring molten wax, or consulting the oracle of rings in a bowl can tell her fate (5.8), as can the mirror which she puts under her pillow at night (5.10), that the name of her future husband will be that of the first man she whose name she asks (5.9), and that his image will appear if she sets a table for two in a bathhouse (5.10); most of all she relies on her favourite book, the dream book of Martin Zadek, which she bought from a pedlar (5.22–4).[3]

A little less famous is the ballad *Svetlana* by Pushkin's contemporary Zhukovskii. This was written in 1808–12 and a quotation from it at the head of Ch. 5 of *Eugene Onegin* alerts us to the fact that Pushkin was to an extent parodying Zhukovskii.

In *Svetlana* the village girls are engaged in their Christmastide fortune-telling: they throw shoes, give grain to a hen, melt wax, place rings and earrings into a bowl of water while singing their *podbliudnye pesni*. The love-sick Svetlana is urged to take a gold ring from the bowl and sing the verse:

Smith, forge me a new and golden crown,
Forge me a golden ring,
That I may marry with this crown,
Be betrothed with this ring,
Before the holy altar.

She explains her grief and is then persuaded to sit with a mirror and candle at a table set for two; at midnight her lover will come and sit at his place. She does so but the lover who comes to drive her to their wedding, as he promises, in fact is a demon who carries her off to Gothick horrors. Fortunately, it transpires that she had fallen asleep and the whole thing was a dream; she wakes, her real lover arrives and they live happily ever after. A banal *envoi* assures us that the sense of the ballad is that unhappiness is but a deceiving dream and happiness is waking up.

These two poems contain, as we shall see below, a fairly representative selection of popular fortune-telling devices, and we may note that while Svetlana is of indeterminate social status, Tat'iana is a provincial land-owner's daughter, not at the top but a very long way from the bottom of the Russian social ladder. The same is true of the Oblomov family in Goncharov's novel,[4] or the middling and upper reaches of the aristocracy in the description of the Christmas mumming and divination at the Meliukovs' country estate in Tolstoi's *War and Peace* (IV, ch. 2). Here the young ladies of the house pour wax and project the shadows of the resulting shapes onto the wall. They listen to an old lady's story of the fearful practice of divining in the bathhouse: a young lady took a cock and two sets of plates and cutlery and took her place in the bathhouse in the prescribed manner; after a while she heard the sound of sledge bells approaching, and in came the figure of an officer; she was supposed to keep him talking until cockcrow, but she lost her nerve and covered her eyes whereupon the figure seized her, and she was only rescued by the servant girls who were keeping watch. The same old lady describes how to interpret the noises you hear if you listen at the barn. After the festivities, back in their own bedroom Natasha, daughter of Count Rostov, and her cousin Sonia, try the 'two mirrors with candles' method of conjuring the image of a lover.

These literary descriptions represent with a fair degree of accuracy one of the most popular categories of popular fortune-telling, that of discovering something about one's future spouse. Although most accounts show this to be largely restricted to young women, some, such as Makarenko's description of Siberian practices,[5] and Gromyko's account below, demonstrate that both sexes could be involved.

4. *Yuletide Divination*

Most of the divination described in the previous section took place in the period from Christmas to the Epiphany, thought in Russia to be one of the most magical times of the year (see Ch. 2.6). This time is called *sviatki* ('the holy days') and is divided into the *sviatye* ('holy', also *zolotye* 'golden') and *strashnye* ('fearful') days, the former preceding the New Year, the latter following it. During the *strashnye* nights evil spirits were active and played mischievous tricks; one did not enter the forest or cemetery at this time. Divination was usually performed during the *strashnye* evenings,[6] most effectively between midnight and three in the morning. Marital prospects, life and death, harvest prospects and the detection of thieves were the most common purposes of fortune-telling and popular divination.

One of the most widespread divinatory practices at this season is the *podbliudnye pesni* or 'under-the-bowl-songs', the ring oracle mentioned in *Eugene Onegin* and *Svetlana* above. In this divinatory game, the details of which vary quite widely from region to region, rings or other personal objects were put into a covered bowl, or under an upturned bowl, at a table with a specified number of places and retrieved one by one after each verse, the owner's fortune (riches, poverty, marriage, spinsterhood, journey, parting, being a widow, marrying a widower etc.) being interpreted from the words of the verse.[7]

For the Kaluga province the following elaborate version has been recorded. On New Year's Eve girls astride a poker would set out to fetch water from the well. As they draw water with their pitchers they speak the name of the man they want to marry and say 'Go into the pitcher'. They bring home the water, pour it into a bowl, sprinkle it with oats, place in it a cross, rings, and charcoal, cover it and ask a woman, usually a widow, to stir it with her little finger and take out a ring at the end of each song.[8] As an example, here is a song which foretells death:

Death is walking down the street,
He carries a pancake on a plate,
To the one whose ring is taken out,
It will happen,
It will happen soon,
It can't be escaped.[9]

Even without the death symbol of the pancake (served at both funerals and weddings), this song needs little interpretation. A recording of a New Year performance of *podbliudnye pesni* in the same region in 1991 adds the detail that formerly the water in which the rings, coins, etc. were immersed could not be allowed to remain in the house but had to be taken to the crossroads by the girl in whose hut the session had taken place; she had to face east and pour out the water into the snow.[10]

The divinatory practice of the *podbliudnye pesni* is almost identical to the Midsummer divination called *ho klēdonas* in the Greek world, which must surely be its origin.[11]

A similar Yuletide game with a divinatory element is 'Bury the gold'. This was described by Matthew Guthrie (1743–1807), the British doctor at the Russian court, as follows: the girls form a ring; the leader goes round and hides a gold ring in the clothes of one of them; the others then take turns to guess where it is; the one who guesses is crowned with flowers and then must go out and ask the name of a passer-by; this will then be interpreted by the others.[12]

Much of the Christmas and New Year or Epiphany divination (*sviatochnye gadaniia*) was devoted to the determination of marriage prospects. This kind of divination was not, however, exclusively a Yuletide occupation and the next section will offer a survey of the different methods employed in trying to discover something about one's future spouse regardless of the time of year.

5. *Marital Prospects Divination*

This is certainly the most common kind of divination in modern times and it survives in many parts of Russia. It was used mainly by girls to discover whom they would marry, his name, his wealth, marital status and physical appearance, or the direction from which he would come. The lot of unmarried peasant women was unenviable since they were regarded as a social and economic burden, and the last consideration (direction) was particularly important in rural communities. It could point to a particular person or to another village or town, which in a country as large as Russia could be far distant and a matter of some concern.[13] The most important time for this kind of divination was the *sviatki* or twelve days of Christmas described above. Another important time was Trinity week, called variously *rusal'naia nedelia*, *semikskaia nedelia*, *zelenye sviatki* (week of the rosalia, Semik week, green holy days), for which see 'Plant Oracles' below. St John's Eve (midsummer) and the feasts of the *Pokrov* (1 October) and St Andrew (30 November) were also popular. These divinations could be frustrated, and a rival's chances of marriage spoiled, if girls from one yuletide *vecherinka* (an evening gathering of girls, often ostensibly to sew or spin together, but also to facilitate courtship) went out and threw a besom broom or churn stick onto the roof of a house where another *vecherinka* was taking place. This would ensure that no one in the second house would marry that year, thus enhancing the chances of the girls in the first house.[14]

Dal' gives a long, if not very circumstantial list of girlish fortune-telling,[15] most of which is also recorded in one form or another by other writers interested in folklore and local customs: I have used here mainly Balov for the Iaroslavl' region,[16] Zelenin for the Novgorod region,[17] Zimin[18] and Smirnov[19] for the Kostroma region,[20] Efimenko for the Arkhangel region,[21] Ivanov for the Tver' region, Shapovalova and Lavrent'eva for the Volga region,[22] Makarenko[23] and Matveeva for Siberia,[24] Sumtsov[25] for the Ukraine, Min'ko for Belorussia,[26] and more generally Afanas'ev, Burtsev, Dal', Zabylin, Sakharov, and, in English, Ralston. These writers are by no means equivalent in detail, reliability or scholarship, and wrote at different times.

5.1. *By interpreting shapes in liquid.* On St Basil's Eve tin, lead, wax or egg-white were poured into water (blessed water is sometimes specified) and predictions made from the shapes formed.[27] This is a practice which seems to have been popular at all social levels, from peasant girl to tsarevna,[28] although one must suspect that it was for many no more than a parlour game. John Parkinson, an Oxford don who visited Russian in 1792–4, observed:

> At Count Golofkin's they were casting lead for the purpose of telling fortunes, a piece of superstition constantly practised on the eve of the new year. They also make use of wax for the same purpose. On this night they have also several other superstitious practices which among us are observed on St Mark's Eve.[29]

This scholarly impartiality, it must be said, is a little uncommon among foreign travellers writing about Russia – all too often they describe with scorn or amusement practices which were in fact widespread in their own country.

Several Russian writers have given lists of significant shapes for their areas of Russia, usually as a Christmas period divination. Sakharov gives: a church means marriage for a young woman but death for an old one; a ship with sails means the return of a husband for an older woman, a marriage away from her home village for a young girl; if all the egg-white goes to the bottom this means death, fire or other disaster; in the case of the metals the side on which steam is given off indicates the direction of your future married home.[30] Zimin gives: a church means marriage, a particular church will be that of the parish of your future husband, a cross means a hard life; a stove means grief (by a pun: *pech'* is a stove, *pechal'* is grief).[31] Balov gives: a crown means marriage, a coffin death, a vehicle travel.[32]

Words for this practice and its practitioners are listed in Dal' variously as *voskolitie* 'wax-pouring' (s.v. *vosk*) and *olovolei, olovoliiatel'* 'tin-pourer' or *olovogadatel'* 'tin-diviner' s.v. *olovo*. Nabokov quotes a 1639 *Potrebnik* (book of prayers and services for special occasions) as giving *voskolei* and *olovolei* as two kinds of sorcerer.[33] These methods were thought to be even more effective if performed in a bathhouse at midnight, the most commonly cited combination of time and place for the performance of serious divination in Russia – hence the title of this book. The practice was very widespread all over Europe.[34] A sophisticated variant of tin pouring requires the resulting shape to be held up to a light source to see what kind of predictive shadow it casts.[35] This conveniently takes us on to the next category.

5.2. *By interpreting shadows, smoke or fire*. Divination of this kind is found in many variants all over the world. I list here some particular methods recorded in Russia. Fan-fold a piece of thin paper, stand it upright and set light to it – the shadow cast by the twisted charred remains will tell the future.[36] The direction from which your husband will come can be predicted from the direction in which the smoke from a burning shaving goes.[37] Afanas'ev describes several methods involving fire: hold a splinter to a coal and blow on it – if it takes a long time to catch fire your husband will have a difficult character; observe which way the ash from a splinter falls – this will be the direction from which your future husband will come (Tambov region);[38] pour water into a frying pan and float a piece of cotton flock – if it burns with a crackle your husband will be grumpy, if it soaks up water he will be a drunkard; fill walnut shells, one for each girl present, with pieces of candle, light them and let them float in a bowl of water – the first to go out will marry first, and so on, but if one sinks that girl will remain unmarried. An alternative is to give the nutshells names of the girls and lads present – if two nuts float together this is a sign of their future marriage.

5.3. *By conjuring the image of the future spouse*. The widespread use of mirror divination for this purpose, especially in a bathhouse at midnight, was commonly regarded as the most reliable form of marital divination.[39] Surprisingly it is omitted by Dal' in his *Poslovitsy*; in his dictionary, however, he quotes the saying: 'ei by pered zerkal'tsem pogadat'' ('she ought to ask her fortune in front of the mirror') in the sense 'it is time for her to get married'.[40]

Matveeva mentions that future husbands in Siberia could be seen in mirrors, dreams, or through rings.[41] Bolonev gives another Siberian Old Believer variant in which the ring was looked at through the mirror in a cellar until the groom's image appeared.[42] Balov gives several variants, including one in which the mirror was so positioned that the moon could be seen – if there was only one image then your husband would be an only child, if several then that would be the number of his family (a matter of some importance for expectations of inheritance). He adds the detail that you must never blink while looking in the mirror.[43]

One recent account of this kind of divination, untypically employed by a man (although both sexes are recorded as performing it together in bathhouses in the Pomor'e region in the far north),[44] is found, improbably, in the memoirs of Andrei Gromyko. He records that during his childhood in Belorussia the young people had magical ways of foretelling the future; if you wanted to discover your marriage prospects you had to go to a deserted hut or bathhouse outside the village on a dark night with a torch and mirror. The mirror was to be placed opposite the open door and at midnight the image of your spouse would appear. Young Andrei tried it but confesses that his nerve failed.[45] A similar method is listed in Sakharov.[46]

Another method with a single mirror was for the girl to look into the mirror and recite the formula 'Intended one, betrothed, come and dine with me'; the mirror would cloud over and when she wiped it she would see the face of her future husband looking over her shoulder; this, however, would be the Devil in disguise and she was immediately to shout 'Away, our place is sacred' (a common protective phrase), upon which he would disappear.[47] In some areas it was believed that the image seen was that of the *bezymen* 'the nameless one' who could also be the ghost of a suicide or victim of a violent death.[48] (This invitation of a demon to dine should perhaps be associated with a number of other Yuletide ritual invitations, in particular in parts of Belorussia and the Ukraine, which could be addressed to demons, ghosts, elements of nature, or wild animals or birds, as well as to God or the Virgin Mary, and were intended to ensure good luck, harvests, etc. in the coming year).[49]

In Kostroma this was a practice performed in a group: the village girls would go at night to the summer bathhouse outside the village, take off their girdles and crosses, loosen their hair and unfasten all their buttons;[50] then one girl would be placed in the middle and a circle drawn round her; the others would then in turn look in the mirror and say 'Come forty devils with your imps from under the tree stumps and roots and other places'; if the Devil appeared down to the waist he had to be banished immediately; if he appeared at full length then there was danger because he would follow the girl home.[51] A similar method using two mirrors was to place the mirrors with a candle on either side and sit between them until the face of your Intended appeared.[52] This was elaborated in another version by requiring the diviner to close the shutters, take off her cross and put it under her heel, and sit in nothing more than her shift until midnight when she would see either her future husband or a coffin.[53] A Novgorod version involved placing a horse collar on the stove as a support for the mirror. The young woman then had to say 'Intended one, come and look in the mirror'. She would immediately see members of the family of her future husband moving about in the hut. As soon as she had recognized her future husband she was to say: 'Away, until it is done, Amen.[54]

Two popular prints (Figs. 2 and 3) show variants of mirror divination. The text of Fig. 2 is given below under *Animal oracles*; the text to Fig. 3 is in verse and reads:

The New Year is coming.
How many new cares will it bring?
The girl gets up at midnight,
and with a fearful hand she takes
her mirror
and alone with candles
tries to discern in it
who will possess her.
Not fearing in the least the sin,
she wishes to see her husband-to-be.
And heedless of the fact
that meetings with a husband-to-be
before the proper time and hour
are forbidden by the heavens,
she waits for her husband-to-be.
What happens? Not the bridal crown,
this is a vision of death.
But let us leave these
and look at the others
(incomplete)

Water could be used instead of a mirror. Older ladies could sit beside a hole in the ice of a frozen river; if they were to be married within the year they would see the face of their intended reflected in the water; if they heard a thump beneath the ice, this meant they would remain unmarried.[55] In Belorussia girls would go on Maundy Thursday to the river before dawn, look into the river and say: 'Where this water goes so may my thought go', and spit three times. They would then see the image of their intended husbands.[56] Glasses or bowls of water would also provide a suitable divining medium, especially if a ring was immersed in the liquid.[57]

A similar method, but without a mirror, was to prepare a table as for a meal but without knife or fork, lock the door and summon the future husband to dinner. When he arrived the girl was to sit quietly until he sat down, then ask his name. He would give it and take something out of his pocket. Then the girl had to pronounce certain words, upon which the phantom would vanish, leaving the 'something' behind.[58] The omission of the knife and fork is presumably because iron is inimical to magic.

These methods were evidently recognized as being of a demonic nature and were sometimes described as being dangerous; this may be connected with the belief of the schismatic Old Believers, reported in an eighteenth-century book,[59] that mirrors are the invention of the Devil.

This kind of divination is well known outside Russia. It is recorded, for example, in Macedonia (as a midsummer practice),[60] in Scotland (as a Halloween practice),[61] in England,[62] in Germany,[63] and a photograph of 1900 showing a Finnish girl performing a mirror divination was published by Hullkrantz.[64] A curious twist to this custom is recorded by Belousov, who states that schoolchildren, mostly girls, in present-day Russia use mirrors in the belief that they can conjure up spirits who will answer their questions or help them in examinations. The spirits include the Queen of Spades (from Pushkin's story of the same name), Gnome, Baba-Iaga and Golden Fish (from folklore), and 'Grandfather Lenin'.[65] The specific theme of the Queen of Spades in this role is examined in the same volume in a remarkable ground-breaking piece by Toporkov.[66]

(For a combination of divination by a cock and a mirror see below under *Animal oracles*. For further discussion of mirrors in magic see Ch. 8.5)

5.4. *Conjuring up images in dreams and visions*. There are many ways in which it was thought that a prophetic dream could be induced. Often it was thought that the necessary preconditions were to remove your belt and cross and refrain from praying, i.e. it was recognized that this was divination with a demonic element which would not work if the normal 'Christian' protective measures had been taken. The procedure very commonly required the girl to place some object under her pillow; the symbolism is usually erotic and fairly obvious. She also normally had to recite some magic invocation addressed to the future bridegroom, or less commonly to the object under the pillow. An alternative spell formula often found begins: 'I lie on the hills of Sion, three angels at my bedhead; one hears, one sees, and the third tells [whatever is the subject of the divination]'.

Another method was to hang up a comb in the barn – the future husband would comb his hair and leave some behind as an indication of his colouring.[67] The Novgorod version described by Zelenin adds that the young lady must say: 'Intended one come to me tonight and comb my hair'.[68] A version in use in the Volga region simply requires you to put a comb under your pillow.[69] A hair colour divination not involving dreams was to take a handful of snow and let it melt; if there was a hair left then it would be the colour of the hair of your future husband.[70]

Another Siberian method was for a young lady to place a ring on the little toe of her right foot, which she then dipped in the water at a hole in the ice; she would place one stick, called 'the lock', across the hole and then push another stick, called 'the key', into the hole and stir anticlockwise three times. She would then go home, saying the spell 'Intended one, come to me to ask for the key to the lock on the hole in the ice, so that you will be able to water your horse and ask for the ring'. She would then see her future husband in a dream. Makarenko adds that young men may also employ this method.[71] Smirnov discusses lock and well symbolism in some detail and observes that the phrase 'to drink at someone's well' is a euphemism for having sexual relations. He adds the detail that if the horse is offered moss and eats it, the dreamer will marry in the current year.[72] A further method literally involving a lock was to put a padlock through the plait (i.e. the symbol of virginity which is cut off at marriage) before going to bed, saying: 'Intended husband, come to me and ask for the key'.[73]

Other ways of inducing prophetic dreams were to place bread and scissors, or the kings of all four suits of cards, beneath your pillow (method of interpretation not given but presumably a dream).[74] A single king is quoted for the Volga region, again without indication of how to interpret the dream.[75]

Novgorodian practices recorded by Zelenin are similar to the preceding. The young man or woman would take off his or her cross, go out into the yard, splash a bucket of water over his or her left shoulder on to the middle support of the roof, saying 'Intended one, come to me today for your underwear'. He or she then hurried back into the house without looking back and went to bed without praying, but with some underwear of the opposite sex's under the pillow.[76] Another method was to make a model of a well frame, take off your cross and go to bed without praying, having placed the well frame model on your pillow, and say 'Intended one, come to me to draw water'; he would then appear in a dream.[77]

Similarly suggestive nocturnal invitations require the girl to sprinkle herself with oats and, as she went to bed, say 'Intended one, come to tend your garden' or 'Intended one, come to reap your oats' – she would then see her intended husband in a dream;[78] or she could put the first bite of supper under her pillow – her intended would appear in a dream;[79] A variant from the Volga region was to leave the last mouthful uneaten and put it under the pillow.[80] Or turn a key in a lock under water and say 'Come, my intended and ask for a drink' – the intended would appear in a dream[81] (in another variant the girl would eat some salt before going to bed, and the invocation then invites the young man to bring *her* a drink);[82] or you could thread a needle upside down, stick it into your shift and go to bed – a dream would tell you your marital fortune.[83] Similar to the last but for men, was a spell to be said three times over a new needle which had never been used, with an unbleached thread in its the eye, which had to be passed through the clothing of the woman desired, near the heart.[84]

A dream vision of a future husband could also be induced by removing the belt at night (this was thought by some to be sinful and certainly can be interpreted as lowering your magical defences),[85] and reciting the punning spell: 'Belt, my belt (*poias*), show me my bridegroom and wedding procession (*poezd*)'.[86]

(For further discussion of dream divination see Ch. 6.1.)

5.5. *Divination by sounds and overheard words.* This was a very common method ranging from simply listening to listening in specified places and circumstances. The interpretation of what you heard and the direction from which the sound came is usually obvious.

If you listened at the crossroads (this was often done by placing the ear to the ground) – a little bell meant marriage, a big bell meant death.[87] A variant of the same divination, with a little bell meaning marriage, was performed in the Volga region in a hop field.[88] Zelenin gives a detailed description: because the Devil does not like even numbers, the girls would gather on odd-numbered days in odd-numbered parties; they would take a splinter (once used for lighting in poorer Russian peasant homes) and light one end over their left shoulder, the other over the right; they would take off their crosses and go to the crossroads; then, in the very centre, they would draw a circle with the splinter while saying '*Chur*' ('Keep away from me'); each in turn would lie down in the circle and listen; if there was the sound of a bell or a dog barking the girl would marry in that year; if the cry of a child was heard, this meant she would not marry but would have a child; if a funeral prayer or the sound of wood-cutting was heard, this meant death.[89] Balov adds that on a bright night the girls would cry out also 'Moon, bright Moon, show us our future husbands' and that a variant was to shout out 'a-u' and if there was a loud echo this meant that the 'unclean spirit' would give her a husband.[90] A similar practice in the Volga region required the services of an older woman to recite a spell before listening; here bells meant a wedding, the sound of a sledge would indicate where your husband would come from, a dog barking would indicate the direction in which you would go to be married, the sound of wood on wood meant a coffin and death.[91]

Another belief was that your future husband would come from the direction from which you could hear a dog howling;[92] Burtsev adds the interpretation that a deep bark meant an old husband, a thin yap a young one.[93] Alternatively you could knock at the gate with a spoon and say: 'Bark, bark, dog where is my future husband?'.[94] A variant recorded in Belorussia required a young man to cook a pancake and put it on his head while he listened at the crossroads for a dog barking. The direction would tell him where his bride would come from.[95] If he approved of the prediction he had to throw the pancake in the direction of the barking, if not then he would throw it in the opposite direction. The pancake on the head may also be a feature of divination by stopping a passer-by at random; as a dish pancakes are common in the Russian cuisine and may be part of several seasonal festivals, as well as death and burial rituals, and therefore available for practices of this sort.

If a girl stood by the 'Jordan' (a place by the river, or a hole in the ice for the Blessing of the Water ceremony at the Epiphany) blindfolded she could tell her future from what she heard (cf. similar hole-in-the-ice beliefs below).[96] Straw strewn in the path of the procession to the 'Jordan' could later be gathered and used as magical protection for your cattle.[97]

If a girl listened at night by the church door – a little bell would mean marriage, a thud would mean the grave.[98] If she listened at the threshing barn – many blows would mean marrying into a large family, single blows would mean marrying a man who lives alone.[99]

The stable was also a place for listening: taking off their crosses and without blessing themselves the young women of the Novgorod region went to the stables; they would stand one at a time with their backs to the door and kick the door three times with their left heel, saying 'If I am to be married then put on your bridle'; if the horses came running up, jangling their bits, this meant the girl would marry in that year.[100]

If a girl eavesdropped outside a window, the conversation would tell her about her future husband and her fate in general.[101] Mention of a shirt meant death, a horse collar that her horse would be stolen;[102] the sound of quarrelling meant she would marry into a bad house, laughter meant a good one.[103] Words for mountain, forest, water, going, and flying were good signs; bottom, marsh, sitting and lying down were bad.[104]

5.6. *Rough and smooth.* This is one of several essentially binary selection methods of divination (see also 'Odd and Even', 'Right and Left' below). Girls would put their hand into a barn window at night – if no-one touched it she would be an old maid, if a smooth hand stroked it she would marry a poor man,[105] if a rough hand then a rich man. Makarenko describes this practice in the Enisei region, where it was thought that it was the bathhouse or barn goblin which touched the bare flesh. He adds that 'tragicomic scenes' often ensued because of pranksters.[106] He does not say what these might have been, but the description of the practice given by Maksimov allows room for speculation: he says that maidens engaged in this divination do it by standing with their back to the window and lifting the back of their skirts over their heads.[107] The same custom was observed by the Old Believers of the trans-Baikal region.[108] Another nineteenth-century writer on popular customs, Zabylin, notes that this was a widespread practice, observing tartly that it was just an excuse for licentiousness which could be blamed on a lack of proper parental control.[109] A more detailed account reveals that the girls had to make indelicate suggestions inviting the sprite to fondle their bare buttocks.[110] A variant in the Volga region was to sit naked on a shelf in the barn: if it felt rough you would have a rich life, if smooth a poor one.[111] A similar if less exciting practice was to tug a log out from a stack – a smooth one meant a poor (or handsome) husband, a rough one meant a rich (or ugly) one.[112] In the Volga region a nice regular log meant a good young husband, a crooked knotted one meant an old widower.[113] Zabylin adds that a thick log meant a strong or fat husband, if it also had a good bark this meant a rich husband; no bark meant a poor husband; a twisted log meant a deformed husband.[114] An identical Advent divination in England is described by the sixteenth-century English poet Barnabe Googe:

> In these same dayes yong wanton gyrles
> that meete for marriage bee,
> Doe search to know the names of them
> that shall their husbands bee.
> . . .
> Unto some woodstacke do they go
> and while they there do stande
> Eche one draws out a faggot sticke,
> the next that commes to hande,
> Which if it streight and even be,
> and have no knots at all,
> A gentle husband then they thinke
> shall surely to them fall.
> But if it fowle and crooked be,
> and knottie here and theare,
> A crabbed churlish husband then,
> they earnestly do feare.[115]

A Siberian Old Believer practice was to soak a sleeve by dipping it through a hole in the ice; if it then froze smooth your husband would be poor, if covered with hoarfrost then he would be rich.[116] A similar binary method was to hang out a towel from the window: if it was wet in the morning you would marry; if it was dry you would not.[117]

5.7. *Odd and even.* The significance of odd and even numbers in magic and divination in general is mentioned in several parts of this book. Here we are concerned only with their use in marital prospect divination. Examples are common. If you counted an even number of posts in a fence or load of logs this meant you would marry, uneven meant you would be an old maid; or you could use a repeating list to count the posts in a fence: rich man, poor man, widower, bachelor (cf. the English 'Tinker, tailor, etc.').[118] In a Novgorod version the girl counted only the number of posts which she could span with her arms: if it was an even number she would marry that year.[119] As well as counting the posts and guessing, as described, in the Iaroslavl' region she could also measure the fence with outstretched arms, counting with each measure 'young man', 'widower' – the one she finishes with would be the status of her future husband.[120] Even and odd numbers of posts in a fence could also simply indicate that one's wish would or would not come true.[121] Both the fence method and a version with sacks and partitions in the barn were recorded in the Volga region.[122] A different kind of either/or divination could be achieved by rolling over and over in the snow in the yard until coming up against the wall or gate – if you ended up facing the door you would marry, if with your back to the door you would not.[123]

5.8. *Right and left.* Left is generally associated with 'otherness' or evil, and several magical practices involved throwing something over the left shoulder or stamping on a cross with the left heel. One divination clearly showing this was the practice of going to a hole in the ice at midnight (i.e. a magical place at a magical time) wearing stockings, then return home to bed – if in the remainder of the night the Devil pulled off one of the stockings the right one would mean a good husband, the left a bad one.[124] (See also *Magic Places* below.)

5.9. *Chance meetings.* There are many forms of this. For example, a girl could go out into the street with the first mouthful of dinner in her mouth and ask the first passer-by his name – this would be the name of her husband.[125] The same practice was recorded in the Volga region with the difference that the mouthful had to be of holy water.[126]

Alternatively the girl could ask the first person met what his name was, and this would be the name of her husband.[127] This has a variant in which the diviner took the first pancake cooked for the festival and put it on her (or his) head before going out to ask the question.[128] An alternative was to lock the window and recite the formula 'Intended one, betrothed, walk past my window' – if the next passer-by whistled you would have a gay life, if not, then a dull one.[129]

Chance meetings could also interpreted as omens quite separately from marital divination. These are described in Ch. 5.2.1.

5.10. *Traces.* This involved the fairly obvious interpretation of marks left on an easily marked surface such as sprinkled cinders or snow. Girls would sprinkle cinders and say 'Rich husband step with a boot, poor husband step with a bast shoe' – the next day they would know what kind of husband they would have.[130] A Siberian Old Believer variant was to sprinkle cinders on the snow – if the patch was smooth in the morning the husband would be kind, if lumpy he would be a blacksmith, if churned up he would be quarrelsome.[131] Alternatively girls could lie flat in the snow at night and then make predictions from the impression surviving the following morning: a smooth impression meant a nice husband, a disturbed one meant a quarrelsome husband.[132]

5.11. *Animal oracles.* These involved actively seeking answers to questions from the behaviour of animals in deliberately contrived circumstances. The rather different practice of interpretating as an omen the meeting of animals by chance, or fortuitously observed animal behaviour, is discussed in Ch. 5.2.2.

5.11.1. *Chickens.* There are very many kinds of chicken oracle (*alectryomancy*), some of which are of ancient origin.[133] Essentially the chicken, usually a cock, was offered a choice, literally a pecking order, usually of grain, sometimes of direction, and that choice, which had usually a predetermined meaning, was regarded as a prediction. Within Russia there is variety of local ingenious variants of this method of divination. Girls sprinkled grain on the floor; the girl would marry whose feed was pecked first by the chicken.[134] Or they could put various possessions on the floor – the object pecked at first gave the same prediction.[135] They could sprinkle grain on the floor of a hut, place beside it a saucer of water and a piece of clay, then bring in a cock – if it pecked the grain this meant a rich husband and a good life in the coming year; if it drank the water this meant a poor husband and a poor life; if it pecked the clay this means death.[136] A variant of this: on the floor were placed a ring as a symbol of marriage, bread as a symbol of riches, charcoal as a symbol of poverty, and chalk as a symbol of the grave (this instead of the clay of the previous version – evidently the local subsoils are significant)   whichever the chicken pecked first would be your fate.[137] Afanas'ev has another variant in which the objects are bread, water, and gold, silver and copper rings (the metal of the ring indicating the wealth of the future husband), with the complication that if the chicken flies clucking around the room this is a sign of a bad-tempered future husband. Afanas'ev also describes tying a cock and hen together to see which would pull the most strongly – this predicted who would rule the roost in the marital home.[138] In the Volga region oats had to be stolen from the village priest and sprinkled on the floor; a ring was also placed on the floor, and when the chicken tossed it aside the nearest girl was the one who would marry next.[139] The symbolism of these methods is very clear. In Kostroma the method was to put a chicken feet uppermost in the middle of a room, draw three anticlockwise circles round it, place a handful each of oats, rye, wheat and breadcrumbs and an earring in the middle – whichever direction the chicken would then toss the earring would be the direction from which the future husband would come.[140] Another way was to place a cockerel and a mirror together – if the cockerel looked in the mirror then your husband would be a vain dandy.[141] A combination of this with the methods mentioned in the last paragraph is demonstrated in Fig. 2, for which the text reads:

> The girls, having taken a mirror, some water in a bowl and some barley grains put all this on the floor and let loose chickens. If a chicken goes to the mirror and looks into it the husband will be a dandy; if it drinks the water this portends a drunken husband; if it pecks the grains this means a rich husband. While doing this the girls sing:
>> What will my fated husband be,
>> Rich or vain or ill-tempered,
>> Will he care for me,
>> Or fall for someone else?

This is one of several methods of divination involving cockerels (less commonly chickens), some of which have been mentioned in other contexts elsewhere. In his dictionary Dal' lists also *kuroklik* ('cock-crow') as a method; presumably this is a variant of listening at the crossroads.[142]

The prevalence of the cock in marital divination is hardly fortuitous; the sexual symbolism of the cock is ancient,[143] and in Russian, as in other languages, words for cock (*petukh*, *kur*) may also have the meaning of penis. Afanas'ev observes that a cock used to be carried in Russian wedding processions and eaten at the marriage feast.[144] In fact, since the vulva may be called *kuritsa* 'hen' a kind of symbolic terminological coitus is achieved.[145]

5.11.2. *Horses*. The involvement of horses in divination is mentioned elsewhere in this chapter and in Ch. 5.2.2. A horse oracle among the ancient Slavs is described by Saxo Grammaticus.[146] A more modern popular horse oracle was to blindfold a horse and seat a girl on it – if it went beyond the gate she would marry; the horse was turned round three times, and young men could also join in to discover whence their bride would come.[147] Another horse oracle was to lead the horse over a shaft – if it caught its hoof this meant a bad-tempered husband and an unhappy married life; if it stepped over cleanly all would be well.[148]

5.11.3. *Cows*. A Ukrainian method was for a young woman to go into the cowshed – if the first animal she met was a bull then this meant marriage, a cow meant spinsterhood.[149]

5.11.4. *Pigs*. Pig oracles also existed but were primarily used to predict life and death (see below).

5.11.5. *Other*. The sound of dogs barking has been mentioned in several methods of divination above. A recorded method in the Volga region was to take a cockroach from a neighbour, put it under your pillow, saying: 'Cockroach, take me to the door of my future husband's house'. Then you would see the door in your dream.[150] The same source recommended putting porridge by a well – if a raven came to eat it you would have a useless husband, if a magpie then a lively one.[151]

5.12. *Plant oracles*. These are very varied. A girl could lie face down in a field and plait three bunches of grass – if the grass had untied itself by the morning she would be married the same year. This was a summer custom in the Tver' region.[152] Balov records a similar practice for the Iaroslavl' region: on Thursday before Trinity the girls used to plait wreaths on a birch tree without breaking the twigs and tie them with ribbons; after Mass on the feast of the Trinity they would go to examine the wreaths – a fresh wreath means you would live out that year, or get married, but if it had dried up you would die. Then the wreaths were broken off and floated on a pond; the one whose wreath sank first would die first.[153] In Belorussia girls used to throw wreaths into the Kupala bonfire at midsummer – the first to burn indicated the first to marry.[154]

In the Tver' region after gathering the 'twelve magic herbs'[155] a girl had to return home without speaking, place the herbs under her pillow, and say 'John

and Mary herb, head herb, and all twelve herbs, tell me who my husband will be'
– she will then see her future husband in a dream.[156]

Zabylin quotes a practice in which girls took an onion each and waited for
them to sprout – the one whose onion sprouted first would marry that year.[157]

5.13. *Shoe-throwing*. Throwing a shoe through the door was supposed to indicate
by the direction in which the toe pointed when it came to rest the direction from
which your future husband would come. It is listed by Dal',[158] and the extra
detail that if the shoe pointed back into the yard the thrower would not marry
that year is offered by Zabylin.[159] The Iaroslavl' New Year's Eve practice in
which the shoe was to be thrown over a well is given in Balov.[160] A Siberian
variant was to throw a cushion out of the door to see if it fell into the sledge of
someone from another village. This would mean that the thrower would marry
into that village.[161] Less widely attested variants are throwing a poker, or a rolled
up belt. In the case of the belt,[162] the extent to which it unrolled when it fell
indicated how far off your future husband lived.

5.14. *Other omens*. On New Year's Eve girls swept under the table – a bread crumb
indicated marriage. Or they baked a needle in a loaf – if it pricked a girl's tongue
she would marry.[163] You could spin a bucket – the direction in which it flew off
would indicate where you would marry.[164] You could roll a ring on the floor – if it
turned towards the door this meant marriage for a girl or departure for a man.[165]
You could balance an axe with both hands – it would rock at the name of any girl
to be married in the course of the year.[166] You could spin round at the crossroads
until you were giddy – when you fell down the direction of your head would
indicate where you would marry.[167] You would marry a man from the direction in
which a shooting star falls at Christmastide.[168] You could walk to the wood pile
backwards and take out a log: the number of knotty projections would tell you the
number of children you were to have.[169] You could grease needles and float them
on water – if they moved apart or sank this was a marriage prediction (this
divination was not to be performed by the girl herself but by an older woman or
fortune-teller).[170] A girl could wait for the new moon, spin round on the heel of
her right foot and say: 'New moon, twist a young man about me as I twist about
you'.[171] Or she could put a piece of headgear, a piece of bread and a piece of
wood into a pot and then draw out blindfold: a hat meant marriage, bread meant
no marriage, wood meant a coffin and death.[172] And most directly of all, but
involving a pun, on the feast of the Protection of the Virgin (*Pokrov*, literally
'covering') a girl could go to the church and say as she stepped over the threshold:
'Holy Virgin Mother, cover the earth with snow and me with a husband'.[173]

6. *Popular Divination for Other Purposes*

6.1. *Life and death*. Some of the methods listed above for finding a husband (in
particular the pouring of wax or lead) were also used to foretell length of life. A

practice recorded for Novgorod and Viatka was to put out in the frost a spoon filled with water for each member of the family – if the ice froze with a hole, the owner of that spoon would die that year; if it froze in a hump, this meant a very long life.[174]

Again from Novgorod: if you went to a shed where a slaughtered hog was hanging, drew a circle, sat in it and said: 'Hog, tell me my fate', you would discover what was to befall you. Zelenin reports the story of an old woman who had tried this but, because she had run away when she heard the voice of the boar instead of saying 'Amen', she was followed home by a white figure, who seized the pot which she had put on her head as protection, smashed it to bits, and then disappeared into the earth with a loud laugh.[175] The consultation of pig oracles is known also in Swedish-speaking Finland.[176]

6.2. *To detect a thief.* Levenstim mentions the practice of a 'wise woman' (*vorozheia*) going through the Psalter with a knife – if she names a thief he has to declare himself innocent by swearing an oath in front of the icon of Ivan the Warrior.[177] Other procedures using sieves, keys, and Bibles were common to Russia and other parts of Europe.[178] The best sieve was one that had been covered with snow which was then shaken off by moonlight; it was then to be balanced on a finger while the names of the possible thief were read out – if it turned this indicated the name of the thief. This form of divination was to be performed only by married women. An alternative was to tie a pair of scissors to the top of the sieve and get two witnesses to hold the handles on their middle fingers while questions were asked (e.g. 'was it a fair-haired man?'). Another method of using the sieve was to place a loaf on the table with an icon on top of it; hold a sieve or scissors – they will tilt towards or away from a suspect depending on whether he is guilty or not.[179] If it turned then the answer was yes.[180] This method has a variant in which the names of all the icons of the Virgin (a considerable number!) were recited and asked to find the thief, before the list of the names of potential thieves is recited.[181] Guthrie records a method in which the sieve was rotated on a fork: it would point to a thief or anyone mentioning his name.[182]

A similar method was to place a key in a book with the ring end projecting, bind the book tightly, tie a string to the projecting top of the key and with it suspend the book from the ceiling; then observe which way it swung when names were mentioned – this method could also detect future husbands or girls who will marry within the year (see also Ch. 11.3–4 on Psalter and Bible divination).[183] Thieves could also be caught by putting black chickens covered with soot into a darkened room – only the guilty person would remain untouched.[184] Yet another method was to write the names of suspects on pieces of paper and throw them into a bowl of water – the name of the thief would fall out. This was a practice of *vodogadatel'nitsy* (lit. 'diviners by water') who had to buy their secrets from a *koldun* or wizard.[185] A variant of this recorded in 1843 was, in cases of domestic theft, for the *vorozheia* to be sent for. She would make balls of bread to the number of those present and throw them one by one into a bowl of water, saying as she uttered each name in turn 'If you are guilty this ball will fall to the bottom of the bowl just as your soul will plunge to hell'.[186]

6.3. *To Discover the Sex of an Unborn Child*. Russia has a few local methods to add to the large number known around the world. The pregnant women had to give bread, honey and vodka to a tame bear; if it roared this meant a girl, if it growled it would be a boy.[187] A similar method, except that a boy was indicated by silence, is included in an eighteenth-century manuscript list of games, entertainments, superstitions and omens which are 'accursed' and for which penance must be done.[188] The association of bears and pregancy is perhaps linked with the fact that bears are referred to in wedding rituals in many parts of Russia and Belorussia, even to the extent of calling the groom and bride a bear and she-bear.[189] Bears were important in Russia in popular entertainment (up to the 1930s), in seasonal festivities, and in a variety of magical contexts other than predicting the sex of a child: they could cure illnesses; if led round a house that house would be protected from fire; if you allowed a bear to step over you this would bring good fortune, as would bear's droppings in your barn; bears' heads and claws were common amulets (see Ch. 8, p. 234, and n. 209). Bear-leading was regularly condemned in the sixteenth and seventeenth centuries.[190]

If the bear oracle was too frightening, an expectant mother could opt for the less hazardous expedient of breaking open a fertilized egg before it had hatched: the sex of the chick would be that of her child.[191] Another Slavic practice was to examine the fat on the carcase of a hog killed for Christmas in order to predict the sex of a child; if the fat was lumpy it would be a boy, if soft, a girl.[192]

One method of prediction shares a symbolism found in other kinds of sex magic: the putative mother had to wash a garment stained with menstrual blood, pour the washing water into a hole near the house, then cover the hole with a pot. After three months she was to look under the pot: if there was a flower she would have a child; a blue one meant a boy.[193]

Other signs of the sex of the unborn child were that a male foetus would begin to move earlier than a female, and if a woman dreamt of a fountain or spring she would have a girl, if of a knife or axe then she would have a boy, and if a stone fell from a ring this was an omen that she would have a boy but that he will soon die.[194]

The line to be drawn between prediction and prescription can be fine: an axe also appears in a small magical practice which was employed, unsuccessfully, by the current Russian president Boris Yeltsin, on the advice of 'experts in such matters', to ensure that his wife would have a boy.[195] He had to place an axe and a man's peaked cap under the pillow (presumably at the time of intercourse, although this is delicately left unclear).[196] Another belief hovering between prediction and prescription is that if the husband mounts his wife from the left a girl will be born, if from the right a boy (the 'missionary position' in Russian is *na kone* 'on a horse'), which derives from the right-left/favourable-unfavourable belief and the economic preference in most traditional societies, and certainly in

Russia, for a boy. Russian beliefs of this kind, together with the Soviet bureaucracy, were mocked simultaneously by Iulii Daniel' in his *Chelovek iz Minapa* (1961), a story of politically correct magic in which a young man was found to be able to provide the wives of the *nomenklatura* with the child of their choice by thinking of Karl Marx or Clara Zetkin, depending on the sex required, at the orgasmic moment.

6.4. *General, divination from coffee grounds, beans.*[197] At the beginning of the nineteenth century Alexander I's Greek (but Italian-educated) Foreign Minister Capodistria consulted a ninety-five-year old Finnish fortune-teller to have his fate told from cards and coffee-cups.[198] Sakharov notes that telling fortunes by coffee grounds was an urban not rural practice, and that it was avoided by many because of a belief that such predictions always came true.[199] In any case coffee was not widely available to the Russian peasantry, any more than it is now. Coffee-divining was evidently a practice confined to women: Dal' in his dictionary mentions only *kofeinitsa*, a word which cannot be applied to a man,[200] and the other term found, *chashkogadatel'nitsa* ('cup-diviner'), is also recorded only in the feminine form.[201] Sakharov observes that these women were usually elderly, garrulous, and often drunk. One such fortune-teller, and the practice of coffee-divining, is satirized in a comic opera called *Kofeinitsa* written in 1783 by the Russian fabulist Krylov, although not published until 1869. This appears to have been a popular subject: there are at least two other comic operas in which popular divination is part of the plot: A.O. Ablesimov's *Mel'nik, koldun, obmanshchik i svat* (The Miller, Magician, Deceiver and Matchmaker) (1779) and the anonymous *Koldun, vorozheia i svakha* (The Magician, the Fortune-Teller and the Matchmaker), published in 1791.[202]

Coffee-divining was (and still is) performed in the following manner: a saucer is placed over a cup containing coffee grounds, and the two are then shaken to spread the grounds. The saucer is then removed and the cup is placed at a distance while water is placed in the saucer. The cup is dipped into the water in the saucer three times while the words 'fidelity, friendship, harmony' are pronounced. Then the cup is taken up again and the divination from the pattern of the grounds begins: a man means an assignation if the client is a lover, permanent loss if the client is looking for lost property; buildings mean good fortune for the rich, bad luck for the poor, sudden riches for the generous; shapes of lands and plants mean bad luck, grief, disharmony, the end of relationships; animal shapes mean danger from evil men, an unlucky journey, a letter of bad news, danger for loved ones.

A common method of fortune-telling known at least from the seventeenth century was bean divination (*razvodit'* or *vorozhat' bobami*). Evidence brought against accused persons, both men, in two treason trials in 1650 and 1680 includes references to bean divination.[203] In the next century, as late as 1770, again in a treason case, the evidence against a male peasant included the statement that he practised bean divination.[204] By the eighteenth century, however, this practice was more usually attributed to women. It seems unlikely that this method of divination is native to Russia – it has too many similarities to geomancy, but the route by which it came to Russia, and when this might have happened, is not known.[205] There appears to be no English equivalent, although both peas and beans appear here in other kinds of divination.

The method employed forty-one beans: they are distributed (*razvodit'*) by a fairly complicated method of casting out fours, into three rows of three. Of the groups eventually formed, the middle heap in the first row is called called 'head', which gives predictions about the mind or character; the third group in the first row is called 'hand', which gives predictions about possessions and prosperity; the middle heap in the second row is called 'heart', and gives predictions about feelings and love; 'foot on the road', which gives predictions about journeys, letters, etc. is the third heap in the third row. The fortune-teller when dealing out the beans has to think the words 'I wish, I hope, it will happen' and predictions in answer to questions will be favourable if the number of beans is uneven, unfavourable if the number is even. Sakharov notes that there is remarkable unanimity in the predictions given by fortune-tellers using this method.[206]

Instruction in this kind of divination, as well as coffee-cup divination, has recently (Moscow, 1989) become available again in Russia with the reprint of a dream book first published in 1896.[207] Divination of this type is very similar in its procedure to geomancy and dice divination (see Ch. 11.10 and 12). There is a very similar system in Iran, in which fifty-three peas are employed.[208]

Notes

1. Propp in his *Russkie agrarnye prazdniki* (p. 107), remarked that the classification of popular divination (*gadanie*) is very difficult, and also suggested, perhaps as a result of some ideological discomfort, that it should be regarded more as an amusement than a ritual. Smirnov, 'Narodnye gadaniia', lists 556 different *gadaniia* according to method. A fairly full bibliography will be found in the appropriate sections of the various volumes of *Russkii fol'klor. Bibliographicheskii ukazatel'*. It is not without interest that the beliefs and practices of Finland Swedes outlined briefly in Wikman, 'Popular Divination' correspond very closely with those of Russia.

2. Ivanova, 'Gadaniia na zimnie sviatki', p. 4.

3. The best discussion of this passage appears in Lotman, *Roman A. S. Pushkina 'Evgenii Onegin'*, pp. 260–5. For discussion of the individual practices see the appropriate chapters in this book. For a more detailed discussion of the popular divination in Pushkin and Zhukovskii's poems see Ryan and Wigzell, 'Gullible Girls and Dreadful Dreams', and for some aspects see also Wigzell, *Reading Russian Fortunes*.

4. See Ch. 6 below, n. 87.

5. Makarenko, *Sibirskii narodnyi kalendar'*, pp. 41–6.

6. In the Volga region any day in the period of *sviatki* can be used, but the favoured times are the eves of Christmas, New Year, and Epiphany: Shapovalova and Lavrent'eva, *Traditsionnye obriady*, p. 11. The authors note that this is the only kind of divination which survives in the region.

7. For a modern study of this practice and its symbolism see Kruglov's study of Russian ritual folksongs *Russkie obriadovye pesni*, pp. 52–62 (specimen songs are quoted at pp. 187–9). This is another

of the practices mentioned in Pushkin's *Eugene Onegin*. The ten songs sung for this purpose in the Enisei region of Siberia are given in Makarenko, *Sibirskii narodnyi kalendar'*, pp. 42–5, where the various kinds of divination and folk belief relating to this time are also described. More Siberian songs are given in the anthology *Kalendarno-obriadovaia poèziia sibiriakov*, pp. 108–33. Songs used in the Kaluga region are recorded in Eleonskaia, *Skazka, zagovor i koldovstvo*, pp. 188–90.

8. Eleonskaia, 'Gadanie pod Novyi god v Kozel'skom uezde', p. 74.

9. Kruglov, *Russkie obriadovye pesni*, p. 189.

10. Minenok, 'Podbliudnye gadaniia', p. 242.

11. See Abbott, *Macedonian Folklore*, pp. 53–7. The Greek divination is for both young women and young men and also involves symbolic locks and keys, as does the Rumanian version: see Beza, *Paganism in Rumanian Folklore*, pp. 55–9.

12. Guthrie, *Noctes Rossicae*, ff. 99v–100.

13. This concern with the direction from which a lover or husband will come, or where a girl is to go to be married, is not confined to Russia. For English versions see Opie and Tatem, *Dictionary of Superstitions*, s.v. *ladybird*.

14. Bernshtam, 'Devushka-nevesta', p. 63. This practice is recorded in the Pomor'e region in the far north. The broom as a marital hindrance also features in the belief that to step over a broom would cause difficulties in childbirth.

15. Dal', *Poslovitsy*, IV, pp. 16–18.

16. Balov, 'Ocherk Poshekhon'ia', p. 69.

17. Zelenin, 'Iz byta i poèzii krest'ian', pp. 1–76.

18. Zimin, *Koverninskii krai*.

19. Smirnov, 'Narodnye gadaniia'.

20. Efimenko, *Materialy po ètnografii*.

21. Ivanov, 'Narodnye obychai, pover'ia i gadaniia', pp. 15–16. Ivanov notes that all the midsummer divinations then surviving in this area are concerned with future husbands.

22. Shapovalova and Lavrent'eva, *Traditsionnye obriady*, pp. 10–25. This gives an extensive list of divinatory practices recorded in the 1960s. The authors also state that marital prospect divination is the only form of divination surviving in this area.

23. Makarenko, *Sibirskii narodnyi kalendar'*.

24. Matveeva, *Mifologicheskie rasskazy*, pp. 313–14.

25. Sumtsov, 'Kul'turnye perezhivaniia', p. 78.

26. Min'ko, *Sueveriia*, and Min'ko, 'Magical Curing'. These studies deal primarily with Belorussia and are partially intended as a polemic against religion and superstition and their alleged deliberate propagation by the 'ruling class' in the West.

27. Dal', *Poslovitsy*, IV, pp. 16–18.

28. See Wigzell, *Reading Russian Fortunes*, pp. 51–3 for some examples.

29. Parkinson, *Tour*, p. 75.

30. Sakharov, *Skazaniia russkogo naroda*, pp. 120–1.

31. Zimin, *Koverninskii krai*, p. 30.

32. Balov, 'Ocherk Poshekhon'ia', pp. 69–70. See also Efimenko, *Materialy po ètnografii*, p. 168.

33. Pushkin, *Eugene Onegin*, II, p. 496.

34. Frazer notes that this kind of divination is also found in Lithuania, Sweden, Scotland, Ireland and Spain: Frazer, *Folklore in the Old Testament*, II, p. 433; the variant using egg is found in Spain:

Frazer, *Golden Bough*, X, p. 208; for Greek analogues see Abbott, *Macedonian Folklore*, pp. 51–2; for Swedish-speaking Finns see Wikman, 'Popular Divination', p. 179; for English analogues see Wright and Liones, *British Calendar Customs*, p. 44; Opie and Tatem, *Dictionary*, s.vv. *Eggs, Lead*. The practice is referred to in the *Malleus maleficarum* (see Kramer and Sprenger, p. 87) as being admissible in Canon Law but condemned by theologians.

35. Smirnov, 'Narodnye gadaniia', p. 47. Interpreting the shadow cast by wax shapes was the method mentioned by Tolstoi in *War and Peace*, IV, ch. 11.

36. Efimenko, *Materialy po ètnografii*, p. 169; also in the Iaroslavl' region: Balov, 'Ocherk Poshekhon'ia', p. 69.

37. Balov, 'Ocherk Poshekhon'ia', p. 75.

38. Afanas'ev, *Poèticheskie vozzreniia*, I, p. 458. For an identical belief in Kentucky see Thomas and Thomas, *Kentucky Superstitions*, no. 415.

39. *Russkie narodnye prazdniki i obriady*, p. 9.

40. Dal', *Tolkovyi slovar'*, s.v. *zerkalo*.

41. Matveeva, *Mifologicheskie rasskazy*, p. 320.

42. Bolonev, *Narodnyi kalendar' semeiskikh Zabaikal'ia*, p. 59

43. Balov, 'Ocherk Poshekhon'ia', p. 76. The same practice is recorded for the Volga region: Shapovalova and Lavrent'eva, *Traditsionnye obriady*, p. 22, no. 86.

44. Bernshtam, 'Devushka – nevesta', p. 63.

45. Gromyko, *Memories*, pp. 6–7. Gromyko was a notable Soviet diplomat in the period following the Second World War. He became minister of foreign affairs and eventually first deputy prime minister.

46. Sakharov, *Skazaniia russkogo naroda*, pp. 121–2.

47. Burtsev, *Obzor*, p. 4

48. Novichkova, *Russkii demonologicheskii slovar'*, s.v. *bezymen'*.

49. Vinogradova, Tolstaia, 'Ritual'nye priglasheniia'.

50. As many examples have shown, belts, crosses and buttons are all protections against evil spirits and would therefore have inhibited this kind of spirit-assisted divination. On the necessity for loosened hair and bare feet in the performance of magic see Frazer, *Golden Bough*, III, p. 311. In Russian and South Slav iconography loose hair was also a sign of licentiousness: see Levin, *Sex and Society*, pp. 46–51. On the magical significance of belts and girdles in Russia see Lebedeva, 'Znachenie poiasa'; on religious penalties attaching to the non-wearing of belts by priests see Smirnov, *Materialy*, p. 88.

51. Zimin, *Koverninskii krai*, p. 30.

52. Zabylin, *Russkii narod*, p. 23; Burtsev, *Obzor*, p. 9; Smirnov, 'Narodnye gadaniia', no. 339 adds that if the cock does not crow while the intended groom is 'visiting' the girl may be tormented to death.

53. Efimenko, *Materialy po ètnografii*, p. 169. Ritual nakedness, or at least partial undressing, for divination is widespread. For the Macedonian custom see Abbott, *Macedonian Folklore*, p. 50, and for the Finnish see Wikman, 'Popular Divination', pp. 174–5, 177. The similar English custom may also involve eating an apple: see Opie and Tatem, *Dictionary*, s.v. *Mirror*.

54. Zelenin, 'Iz byta i poèzii krest'ian', p. 8.

55. Ralston, *Songs of the Russian People*, pp. 196–7. See also Balov, 'Ocherk Poshekhon'ia', p. 75 6.

56. Min'ko, *Sueveriia*, p. 49.

57. Shapovalova and Lavrent'eva, *Traditsionnye obriady*, p. 25, no. 140. Cf. also the Russian expression 'kak v vodu gliadel' (lit. 'as if he had looked into water' = 'as if he had foreseen it'). For similar Finnish practice see Wikman, 'Popular Divination' (p. 177) and for American mirror divinations of almost exactly the same kind from Kentucky see Thomas and Thomas, *Kentucky Superstitions*, no. 379, 380 (Hallowe'en), 418–421, 425 (May Day), 433.

58. Ralston, *Songs of the Russian People*, pp. 196–7; Zabylin, *Russkii narod*, p. 26. A similar practice is recorded by Balov, 'Ocherk Poshekhon'ia', p. 77, and is known in Swedish-speaking Finland (Wikman, 'Popular Divination', p. 175) and America (Kentucky – see Thomas and Thomas, *Kentucky Superstitions*, no. 563).

59. Chulkov, *Abevega*, p. 199. See also Zabylin, *Russkii narod*, pp. 265–6.

60. Abbot, *Macedonian Folklore*, pp. 50–51.

61. Described by Robert Burns in a note to his poem 'Hallow E'en': Burns, *Poems, chiefly in the Scottish Dialect*, 1787.

62. See Opie and Tatem, *Dictionary of Superstitions*, s.v. *mirror: divination: to see future spouse*. Both the English and Scottish variants require the girl to be combing her hair, presumably another form of the requirement that hair be unbound for magic.

63. *Handwörterbuch des deutschen Aberglaubens*, s.v. *Spiegel*.

64. Hullkrantz, 'Divinationsformer: en klassifikation'. See also Wikman, 'Popular Divination', p. 174.

65. *Russkii shkol'nyi fol'klor*, p. 13.

66. Toporkov, 'Pikovaia dama'.

67. Dal', *Poslovitsy*, IV, pp. 16–18.

68. Zelenin, 'Iz byta i poèzii krest'ian', p. 8.

69. Shapovalova and Lavrent'eva, *Traditsionnye obriady*, p. 19, no. 53.

70. Balov, 'Ocherk Poshekhon'ia', p. 73.

71. Makarenko, *Sibirskii narodnyi kalendar'*, pp. 45–6.

72. Smirnov, 'Narodnye gadaniia', p. 29. A similar method from Kostroma and the Volga region are described in Zimin, *Koverninskii krai*, p. 30, and Shapovalova and Lavrent'eva, *Traditsionnye obriady*, p. 19, nos 57, 90.

73. Afanas'ev, *Poèticheskie vozzreniia*, I, p. 459.

74. Dal', *Poslovitsy*, IV, pp. 16–18; playing cards and scissors are methods also mentioned for the Kostroma region by Smirnov, 'Narodnye gadaniia', pp. 59–60.

75. Shapovalova and Lavrent'eva, *Traditsionnye obriady*, p. 24, no. 125.

76. Zelenin, 'Iz byta i poèzii krest'ian', p. 8. Zelenin says that his informant did not say what was to happen next and surmised that it was the usual appearance of the future bride or bridegroom in a dream. Sleeping with garments under the pillow to conjure up a dream image is also known in Finland: Wikman, 'Popular Divination', p. 176.

77. This is also recorded by Balov, 'Ocherk Poshekhon'ia', pp. 77–8, and Shapovalova and Lavrent'eva, *Traditsionnye obriady*, p. 16.

78. Smirnov, 'Narodnye gadaniia', no. 262. Also in Balov, 'Ocherk Poshekhon'ia', p. 78.

79. Dal', *Poslovitsy*, IV, pp. 16–18.

80. Shapovalova and Lavrent'eva, *Traditsionnye obriady*, p. 17.

81. Dal', *Poslovitsy*, IV, pp. 16–18.

82. Zabylin, *Russkii narod*, p. 28.

83. Dal', *Poslovitsy*, IV, pp. 16–18.

84. Maikov, 'Velikorusskie zaklinaniia', no. 28.

85. In one Russian penitential of the fifteenth–sixteenth century priests are forbidden to sleep without a belt, under penalty of ten days' fasting : Smirnov, *Materialy*, p. 88.

86. Smirnov, 'Narodnye gadaniia', p. 32.

87. Dal', *Poslovitsy*, IV, pp. 16–18. See also Efimenko, *Materialy po ètnografii*, p. 169; Balov, 'Ocherk Poshekhon'ia', p. 70.

88. Shapovalova and Lavrent'eva, *Traditsionnye obriady*, p. 16, no. 25.

89. Zelenin, 'Iz byta i poèzii krest'ian', p. 7

90. Balov, 'Ocherk Poshekhon'ia', p. 71.

91. Shapovalova and Lavrent'eva, *Traditsionnye obriady*, pp. 19–27, no. 61. For this practice in Swedish-speaking Finland see Wikman, 'Popular Divination', p. 174. For the almost universal magical significance of crossroads see most recently Puhvel, *The Crossroads in Folklore and Myth*. Unfortunately there is only one reference to Russian practice – an ash stake at the crossroads to get rid of plague. This is no doubt a variant of the Suffolk cure for ague by nailing it to the crossroads where it will be transferred to the next passer-by: see Frazer, *Golden Bough*, IX, p. 68. *ERE*, IV, cols 330b–331a notes that burial at a crossroads was a Slavic custom, and that crossroads are generally regarded as the home of evil spirits and thus dangerous or unlucky places. It quotes the *Clavicula Salomonis*: 'For magical operations a secret, remote, deserted and uninhabited place is necessary, but best of all is the crossroads'. It also quotes other examples of listening at the crossroads at midnight to foretell the fortune of the year, and in particular one's marital fortune (col. 334a).

92. Dal', *Poslovitsy*, IV, pp. 16–18; recorded also in Balov, 'Ocherk Poshekhon'ia', p. 70. and in Swedish-speaking Finland by Wikman, 'Popular Divination', p. 178.

93. Burtsev, *Obzor*, p. 7.

94. Dal', *Tolkovyi slovar'* s.v. *sobaka*; Zabylin, *Russkii narod*, p. 18, quotes the spell as: 'Bark, bark dog, howl grey wolf, where the dog barks there lives my intended one'.

95. Nikiforovskii, *Prostonarodnye primety i pover'ia*, p. 51; Min'ko, *Sueveriia*, p. 48.

96. Dal', *Poslovitsy*, IV, pp. 16–18.

97. Makarenko, *Sibirskii narodnyi kalendar'*, p. 51

98. Dal', *Poslovitsy*, IV, pp. 16–18. See also Efimenko, *Materialy po ètnografii*, p. 169; Burtsev, *Obzor*, p. 10; Balov, 'Ocherk Poshekhon'ia', p. 70: the part of the liturgy which you overhear will tell your fortune.

99. Dal', *Poslovitsy*, IV, pp. 16–18.

100. Zelenin, 'Iz byta i poèzii krest'ian', p. 7

101. Dal', *Poslovitsy*, IV, pp. 16–18. See also Ralston, *The Songs of the Russian People*, pp. 196–7; Efimenko, *Materialy po ètnografii*, p. 169; Burtsev, *Obzor*, p. 5; Zimin, *Koverninskii krai*, p. 31; Zelenin, 'Iz byta i poèzii krest'ian', pp. 7–8.)

102. Balov, 'Ocherk Poshekhon'ia', p. 70

103. Shapovalova and Lavrent'eva, *Traditsionnye obriady*, p. 17.

104. Nikiforovskii, *Prostonarodnye primety i pover'ia*, p. 52, no. 331.

105. Dal', *Poslovitsy*, IV, pp. 16–18.

106. Makarenko, *Sibirskii narodnyi kalendar'*, p. 46.

107. Maksimov, *Nechistaia*, p. 60.

108. Bolonev, *Narodnyi kalendar' semeiskikh Zabaikal'ia*, p. 60.

109. Zabylin, *Russkii narod*, p. 27.

110. *Èntsiklopediia obriadov i obychaev*, p. 28. This may be related to the ritual use by women of language normally regarded as obscene, in certain types of fertility magic, a known phenomenon among the Slavs.

111. Shapovalova and Lavrent'eva, *Traditsionnye obriady*, p. 16 no. 23.

112. Dal', *Poslovitsy*, IV, pp. 16–18. Cf. Balov, 'Ocherk Poshekhon'ia', p. 72, and Efimenko, *Materialy po ètnografii*, p. 170.

113. Shapovalova and Lavrent'eva, *Traditsionnye obriady*, p. 24, no. 151.

114. Zabylin, *Russkii narod*, p. 19.

115. As quoted in Hone, *The Every-Day Book*, I, col. 1552.

116. Bolonev, *Narodnyi kalendar' semeiskikh Zabaikal'ia*, p. 58.

117. Zabylin, *Russkii narod*, p. 26.

118. Dal', *Poslovitsy*, IV, pp. 16–18.

119. Zelenin, 'Iz byta i poèzii krest'ian', p. 9.

120. Balov, 'Ocherk Poshekhon'ia', p. 72; Min'ko, *Sueveriia*, p. 48.

121. *Russkie narodnye prazdniki i obriady*, p. 15.

122. Shapovalova and Lavrent'eva, *Traditsionnye obriady*, p. 16, nos. 26, 46.

123. Zimin, *Koverninskii krai*, p. 29.

124. Efimenko, *Materialy po ètnografii*, p. 169.

125. Burtsev, *Obzor*, p. 5. The same custom is reported in the Azores: Frazer, *Golden Bough*, X, p. 209. For the very similar British beliefs see Opie and Tatem, *Dictionary*, s.v. *First-foot*.

126. Shapovalova and Lavrent'eva, *Traditsionnye obriady*, p. 23, no. 113.

127. Ralston, *Songs of the Russian People*, pp. 196–7; Pushkin, *Eugene Onegin* – see above.

128. Balov, 'Ocherk Poshekhon'ia', p. 74; Zabylin, *Russkii narod*, p. 16, records this as a practice in the Iaroslavl' region.

129. Burtsev, *Obzor*, p. 10.

130. Dal', *Poslovitsy*, IV, pp. 16–18. For similar beliefs in Britain see Opie and Tatem, *Dictionary*, s.v. *ashes*.

131. Bolonev, *Narodnyi kalendar' semeiskikh Zabaikal'ia*, p. 58.

132. Balov, 'Ocherk Poshekhon'ia', p. 70; Bolonev, *Narodnyi kalendar' semeiskikh Zabaikal'ia*, p. 59.

133. Opie and Tatem, *Dictionary*, s.v. *Cock crows*, give examples from Petronius Arbiter (first century) and St John Chrysostom (fourth century), as well as English and Irish examples.

134. Dal', *Poslovitsy*, IV, pp. 16–18. An American variant from Kentucky is quoted in Thomas, *Kentucky Superstitions*, no. 295. See also Zelenin (p. 9); Efimenko (p. 169). Afanas'ev, *Poèticheskie vozzreniia*, I, p. 467 describes a variant for girls and lads together.

135. Burtsev, *Obzor*, p. 16.

136. Kruglov, *Russkie obriadovye pesni*, pp. 56–7.

137. Smirnov, 'Narodnye gadaniia', nos. 25–6.

138. Afanas'ev, *Poèticheskie vozzreniia*, I, p. 467; this is recorded for Siberia in Zabylin, *Russkii narod*, p. 17.

139. Shapovalova and Lavrent'eva, *Traditsionnye obriady*, pp. 20–21, no. 70.

140. Zimin, *Koverninskii krai*, p. 75.

141. Dal', *Poslovitsy*, IV, pp. 16–18.

142. Dal', *Tolkovyi slovar'*, s.v. *kur*.

143. For some discussion of its medieval ramifications see Jones, 'Folklore Motifs in Late Medieval Art', pp. 192–5.

144. Afanas'ev, *Poèticheskie vozzreniia*, I, p. 467.

145. See Uspenskii, *Filologicheskie razyskaniia*, p. 153.

146. Saxo Grammaticus, *Gesta Danorum*, XIV, p. 567.

147. Dal', *Poslovitsy*, IV, pp. 16–18; recorded for Kostroma and Iaroslavl' by Zabylin, *Russkii narod*, p. 18.

148. Shapovalova and Lavrent'eva, *Traditsionnye obriady*, p. 21, no. 75; Matveeva *Mifologicheskie rasskazy*, p. 320, and Makarenko, *Sibirskii narodnyi kalendar'*, p. 46. See also Zabylin, *Russkii narod*, p. 17; and Sumtsov, 'Kul'turnye perezhivaniia', p. 78, for the same practice in the Ukraine.

149. Sumtsov, 'Kul'turnye perezhivaniia', p. 78.

150. Shapovalova and Lavrent'eva, *Traditsionnye obriady*, p. 18, no. 52, also nos. 114, 143 which mention the detail that the cockroach should be first put into a box.

151. Shapovalova and Lavrent'eva, *Traditsionnye obriady*, p. 24, no. 122.

152. Ivanov, 'Narodnye obychai, pover'ia i gadaniia', p. 16.

153. Balov, 'Ocherk Poshekhon'ia', pp. 78–9. This is a custom in many parts of Russia.

154. Min'ko, *Sueveriia*, p. 71.

155. For more detail see Ch. 15. The identity of these varies from region to region; many are listed and their alleged properties described in Ch. 8.

156. Ivanov, 'Narodnye obychai, pover'ia i gadaniia'.

157. Zabylin, *Russkii narod*, p. 19.

158. Dal', *Poslovitsy russkogo naroda*, pp. 16–18; a similar Siberian practice is mentioned in Matveeva, *Mifologicheskie rasskazy*, p. 320.

159. Zabylin, *Russkii narod*, p. 18.

160. Balov, 'Ocherk Poshekhon'ia', p. 75. The same practice is found in Swedish-speaking Finland: Wikman, 'Popular Divination', p. 178, and similar forms of shoe-throwing divination can be found in England and Scotland: Opie and Tatem, *Dictionary of Superstitions*, s.v. *Shoes, old*.

161. Makarenko, *Sibirskii narodnyi kalendar'*, p. 43.

162. *Russkie narodnye prazdniki i obriady*, p. 19.

163. Dal', *Poslovitsy*, IV, pp. 16–18.

164. Shapovalova and Lavrent'eva, *Traditsionnye obriady*, pp. 17–18, no. 38.

165. Zabylin, *Russkii narod*, p. 14.

166. Zabylin, *Russkii narod*, p. 18. Zabylin correctly notes that axe divination is an ancient method of detecting guilty persons. Similar methods for detecting thieves are given below.

167. Shapovalova and Lavrent'eva, *Traditsionnye obriady*, p. 18, no. 44.

168. Dal', *Poslovitsy*, IV, pp. 16–18.

169. Shapovalova and Lavrent'eva, *Traditsionnye obriady*, p. 23, no. 108.

170. Sakharov, *Skazaniia russkogo naroda*, p. 127.

171. Maikov, 'Velikorusskie zaklinaniia', no. 34. Viatka region.

172. Zabylin, *Russkii narod*, p. 19.

173. Maikov, 'Velikorusskie zaklinaniia', no. 37. Viatka region. Also noted in Bolonev, *Narodnyi kalendar' semeiskikh Zabaikal'ia*, p. 102–3. Here other spells may involve the same pun.

174. Zelenin, 'Iz byta i poèzii krest'ian', p. 9

175. Zelenin, 'Iz byta i poèzii krest'ian', p. 7. A loud laugh is commonly thought to be an attribute

of the Devil. The authors of the *Malleus maleficarum* quote St Augustine to the effect that Ham 'laughed aloud when he was born and thus showed he was a servant of the Devil': Kramer and Sprenger, *Malleus maleficarum*, pt 1, quest. 2.

176. Wikman, 'Popular Divination', p. 172.

177. Levenstim, 'Sueverie v ego otnoshenie k ugolovnomu pravu', p. 207.

178. Levenstim, 'Sueverie v ego otnoshenie k ugolovnomu pravu', p. 207. Moszyński, *Kultura ludowa słowian*, p. 379, describes this type of divination as common among the Slavs, Finns and Hungarians. For the use of both sieves and books and keys for detecting thieves in England see Thomas, pp. 213–4; Opie and Tatem, *Dictionary*, s.v. *Sieve and shears*; Hazlitt, *Dictionary*, s.vv. *agues* and *coscinomantia*. For the wider use of koskinomancy see the *ERE*, XI, col. 506b.

179. Efimenko, *Materialy po ètnografii*, p. 167.

180. Sakharov, *Skazaniia russkogo naroda*, loc.cit.

181. Smirnov, 'Narodnye gadaniia', p. 72

182. Guthrie, *Noctes Rossicae*, f. 84.

183. Burtsev, *Obzor*, p. 10; Zabylin, *Russkii narod*, pp. 22–3.

184. Sakharov, *Skazaniia russkogo naroda*, pp. 122–3. Cf. other uses of chickens in divination above. A curious modern example can be seen in the Chinese community in America where a chicken was trained to operate a machine which told fortunes by playing-cards: see Richard M. Swiderski, 'Clara the Fortune-Telling Chicken or Pop-Pavlovism in Chinatown', *Journal of Popular Culture*, VIII, 1, 1974, pp. 10–14.

185. Sakharov, *Skazaniia russkogo naroda*, pp. 123–4.

186. Harthausen, *Studies on the Interior of Russia*, p. 111. The author was in Russia in 1843.

187. Zabylin, *Russkii narod*, p. 184; Kostomarov, *Ocherk*, p. 186.

188. Vostokov, *Opisanie*, pp. 549–52: no. 374, *sbornik*, 1754. This list was quoted in full in Ch. 2.1.

189. See Uspenskii, *Filologicheskie razyskaniia*, pp. 163–6.

190. See Nekrylova, *Russkie narodnye gorodskie prazdniki*, pp. 35–53: 'Medvezh'ia komediia' esp. p. 37.

191. Sakharov, *Skazaniia russkogo naroda,*, p. 40; Chulkov, *Abevega*, pp. 147–8.

192. Forbes, *The Midwife and the Witch*, p. 59.

193. Minenko, *Russkaia krest'ianskaia sem'ia*, p. 254. Cf. Storms, *Anglo-Saxon Magic*, p. 203, for an Anglo-Saxon flower oracle to predict the sex of a child (a lily for a boy, a rose for a girl).

194. Russian examples quoted among many similar beliefs from all over Europe in Forbes, *The Midwife and the Witch*, pp. 55–6.

195. Yeltsin, *Against the Grain*, 1990, pp. 79–80.

196. For these beliefs elsewhere see Shumov and Chernykh, 'Beremennost' i rody', p. 177.

197. In general on popular divination of this kind in the eighteenth and nineteenth century, and in particular on social aspects, see now Wigzell, *Reading Russian Fortunes*.

198. See Woodhouse, *Capodistria*, p. 71. Coffee-cup reading is a form of divination widely practised by women in Greece.

199. Sakharov, *Skazaniia russkogo naroda*, pp. 116–17.

200. Dal', *Tolkovyi slovar'*, s.v. *kofe*.

201. Hüttl-Worth, *Die Bereichung des russischen Wortschatzes im XVIII. Jahrhundert*, s.v.

202. Drage, *Russian Literature*, pp. 240–1.

203. *SRIa XI–XVII vv.*, s.v. *bob*.

204. See Ch. 16, p. 423.

205. *The Geomancie of Maister Christopher Cattan*, London, 1591 (translated from French), mentions in ch. 3 that beans or grains are used to produce a geomantic figure in Bologna.

206. The method is described in Zabylin, *Russkii narod*, pp. 21–2.

207. *Odin million 500,000 snov*, Moscow, 1896. Reprinted as *Sonnik*. The bean and coffee divination appears as an appendix.

208. Donaldson, *Wild Rue*, p. 197.

5

SIGNS, OMENS, AUGURIES, CALENDAR PREDICTIONS

1. *Introduction*

The first part of this chapter will discuss popular beliefs relating to the prognostic significance of things observed, things or people met, natural phenomena, especially if unusual, the behaviour of animals, seasonal and calendrical predictions, and predictions based on the examination of animal bones and entrails. Calendrical predictions and prognostications from natural phenomena may often be interlaced with fertility beliefs and rituals of a more magical kind.[1] The second half of the chapter will discuss three texts which exemplify divination and omen interpretation of this kind in Muscovite Russia: the *Lopatochnik* (scapulimancy), the *Trepetnik* (palmomancy), and the *Volkhovnik* (the 'Book of the Wizard').

2. *Omens in General*

As with dreams and other ancient forms of prognostication, the Orthodox Slavs of the Balkans and Kiev Rus' had inherited with Christianity an ambivalence of attitude towards omens. On the one hand the Bible and a good deal of subsequent Christian writing were full of instances of apparently justified belief in omens, and these were reinforced by popular beliefs from many sources which were current in Byzantium. On the other hand the Church regularly condemned such things as false, pagan, and of diabolical origin.

In Kiev Rus' this ambivalence is neatly illustrated by the juxtaposition in the *Russian Primary Chronicle* for the year 1064 of a long and entirely credulous digression on contemporary and historical portents of disaster (celestial phenomena, monstrous births, earthquakes, behaviour of birds, etc.) and a sermon under the year 1068 condemning as pagan the belief in divination by chance meetings, ill-omened encounters with a monk or a pig, or sneezing (all of which continued to be omens into modern times).[2]

It is worth remembering that most natural signs and omens recorded for Russia have exact counterparts in other parts of Europe, and many can be shown to have been known in classical antiquity, from which, by devious routes, they are probably derived.

2.1. *Chance Meetings.* This kind of omen is of great antiquity. It is condemned in the Russian lists of banned books, usually under the title *Putnik* ('Book of the

Road'), which may well be the Greek *Biblion sunantēmatikon*.[3] If a book called *Putnik* ever actually existed in Russia it seems not to have survived, although any number of popular superstitions falling into this category do still exist.

In the sixteenth century Tsar Ivan the Terrible believed that it was an evil omen if anyone crossed his path as he was setting out, and, it is alleged, went so far as to kill anyone who did so.[4] The earliest Russian textual reference to 'evil meetings' ('*zlo sretenie*') appears to be in a sixteenth-century prayer calling for protection from such meetings and from the Evil Eye.[5] In more modern folk belief the *vstrechnyi* or *streshnyi* (lit. 'person met') is a demon who frequented roads and crossroads, led travellers astray and lamed horses.[6]

Hares, foxes, pigs, wolves, bears, squirrels and dogs crossing one's path are mentioned below. It was lucky to meet a Jew or a girl with full pails or a corpse;[7] it was unlucky to meet a blind man,[8] a priest or a monk (the latter was also unlucky at weddings), or a girl with empty pails, a bachelor, a nun, a widow, a widower.[9] It was unlucky to meet anyone in such transitional places as threshold, porch, or bridge.[10] The ominous nature of meeting a priest or a monk was widely recognized. In England it was recorded as early as 1159 in the *Policraticus* of John of Salisbury and frequently thereafter;[11] Olaus Magnus records the belief in sixteenth-century Scandinavia,[12] and the same superstition appears at the other end of Europe in Macedonia.[13] The interpretation of these omens has some similarities with the interpretation of people and animals seen in dreams, for which see Ch. 6. No more flattering to the clergy in Russia was the omen of a priest's girdle becoming untied, which was thought, possibly by ribald association, to presage a birth in the village.[14]

Divination involving the name of the first person met in variously specified circumstances is discussed in Ch. 4.5.9.

2.2. *Animal behaviour*. Divination from animal behaviour is an endless subject. A major category of weather prediction in Russia, as elsewhere, is based on animal behaviour. In many cases this has a rational basis in the observation of animal or bird reactions to particular weather conditions or seasonal changes. In many more, however, the animal simply serves as a random selection device, usually binary, for divination. What follows is necessarily only a selection, much of which is recorded in the great nineteenth-century dictionary of Dal', who was particularly assiduous in noting popular beliefs of this kind.

2.2.1. *Birds*. Prediction from the behaviour of birds is of great antiquity, and the Slavs, even if they did not have indigenous beliefs about birds, which is unlikely, would, at least at the level of the more scholarly clergy, have been aware of references to bird divination in historical writing and the regular condemnation of bird divination in lists of banned books under the titles of *Ptichnik* ('Book of Birds') or *Ptichie charove* ('Bird Charms').[15]

In fact the word *kob'*, used to translate Greek *oionoskopía* in Old Church Slavonic and Old Russian, although also used to mean divination by other types of omen, or magic in general and fate, seems to have meant primarily divination from bird cries and movements.[16] Dal' lists several other words for bird divination and those who practise it, but gives no context and does not say what they involve: *ptitsevolkhovanie, ptitsegadanie, ptitsevolshebstvovatel'*, etc.[17]

Both *kob'* and *voronograi* (crow-cawing) are listed in the proceedings of the *Stoglav* Council of 1551 as 'evil heresies', and in the roughly contemporary *Domostroi*, and 'crow-cawing' also appears in the *Volkhovnik*, together with references to divination from woodpeckers and magpies. One sixteenth-century Russian penitential condemns *kobi* in a list of 'Hellenic' practices such as belief in stars, meetings, sneezing, horoscopes, leap year, good and bad days, *rusalii*, indictions, the Jewish Sabbath, astrology, wizards.[18]

Crows and ravens have been an unfavourable omen since classical antiquity,[19] and continued to be a omen in Russian popular belief: if you sang in the forest and saw a crow, then you would stumble on a wolf; a raven meant death, a crow meant bad weather;[20] a crow cawing on a church cupola or bell tower meant there would soon be a funeral; if on a roof, then there would be a death in that house.[21]

The cry of an eagle owl or a woodpecker pecking at a hut meant death also;[22] other kinds of owl could likewise bring misfortune,[23] although if a *sova* (the general word for owl) called near to the house, this could mean a new child.[24] In Belorussia the note of the owl's call could also predict the outcome of a confinement.[25] The evil reputation of the screech-owl, and the connection with babies is ancient: the *strix* in Roman times was thought to be an old witch woman transformed who preyed on infants by sucking their blood.[26]

The chatter of magpies betokened the arrival of visitors,[27] a common belief in Britain also at least as far back as John of Salisbury in 1159.[28]

The cuckoo in general was a bird of ill omen, especially if you heard it on an empty stomach; the number of times it called was the number of years you had left to live.[29] If it flew through the village there would be a fire; an early cuckoo meant famine, but on the other hand signalled failure to thieves; a cuckoo calling on a dead tree meant frost. If you jingled coins in your pocket at the first sound of a cuckoo you would have more money.[30]

A pigeon flying in at the window was also usually a bad omen, of a fire or death, but sometimes presaged the arrival of news.[31]

The crowing of cocks is another omen listed in the *Volkhovnik* below, and indeed the behaviour or sound of fowls was very common in popular divination, especially those practices designed to discover something about one's future spouse. These are described in some detail in Ch. 4.5.11.1. Chickens' eggs also had their magical and divinatory uses: the first egg from a black pullet would save livestock from wolves; the weight of the first egg of a chicken in spring would reveal the size of the harvest that year; an egg used for the first Easter greeting at matins would put out a fire if thrown over it.[32] It was a sin, however to put out a fire started by lightning (*bozhii ogon'*, lit. 'God's fire').[33]

Perhaps the oddest bird-related belief was that anyone who discarded his shirt at the sound of the first nightingale would be safe from the bite of fleas.[34]

Nightingales had also an oblique connection with witchcraft. They were much prized as singing cage birds by Moscow merchants, who would pay high prices for them. The novelist Turgenev in 1854 recorded the reminiscences of an old serf huntsman who specialized in catching nightingales and swore that witchcraft was sometimes employed against him to lead him away from his quarry or to frighten him off.[35]

The swallow was thought to be protected by God, because it had taken away the nails from the Cross, and it was a sin to kill it or destroy its nest; it brought good fortune to any house where it built a nest, it heralded the spring, and anyone washing with milk at the time of its appearance would have a white complexion. A swallow flying under a cow meant that it would have blood-tinged milk, and anyone killing a swallow would have bad luck with his cattle. If it flew in at the window there would be a death.[36]

The sparrow was popularly thought to hop because it was shackled as a punishment for returning the nails for the Crucifixion which had been removed by the swallows. Alternative legends are that when all the birds, and especially the swallow, tried to lead Christ's Jewish persecutors away from his hiding place, the sparrows chirruped and revealed the place; they then chirruped 'zhiv, zhiv' ('alive, alive') when he was being tormented, which egged on his torturers to new efforts. Sparrows were therefore cursed and could not be used as food, and if they flew into a house this was a sign of great misfortune to come.[37]

A more local form of bird divination is recorded in the eighteenth century among the people of Archangel who used to foretell the flood level from the height at which the gulls were flying.[38] The appearance of gulls meant spring was coming but many gulls in the water at the same time meant bad weather.[39] Farther south it was thought that if cranes were flying high the weather would be bad.[40] Bad weather was also foretold by sparrows twittering.[41] On 15 September, the feast of Nikita-guseprolet (St Nicholas-gooseflight), a swan flying past meant snow, a goose meant rain.[42]

2.2.2. *Cats.* From ancient times cats have served as dream omens and some cat predictions are to be found in the *Volkhovnik* described below. Others are: if the cat settled in the opening of the stove flue (*pechura*) there would be frost (the cat on the stove was one of the omens believed in by Tat'iana in Pushkin's *Evgenii Onegin* (5, 5.)); if the cat was sleeping soundly it would be hot; if the cat covered its nose there would be frost or bad weather; if the cat scratched the floor there would be wind; if the cat scratched the wall there would be bad weather; if the cat lay belly upwards it would be hot; if the cat licked its paws there would be good weather; if it licked its body there would be bad weather; if anyone slept with a cat he would get frogs in his head; if the cat washed itself there would be guests;[43] to kill a (male) cat was to incur seven years bad luck.[44]

2.2.3. *Cows.* Cows were thought to be the victims of witches, who often milked them at night (a widespread belief in many parts of Europe), and sometimes milked them to death, especially on the feast of St Malakhii (possibly because of a similarity of sound with *moloko* 'milk').[45] An extra pair of eyes at milking would also spoil the yield; if the river unfroze on a fast day this would have the same effect. If a black or brindled cow was at the head of the herd this meant bad weather; a white or red cow meant good weather. If a cow gave birth to twin calves of the same colour, this meant good luck, if of different colours, bad luck. To make a cow give birth to a female rather than a male calf the milkmaid had to milk her for the last time sitting on a frying pan; if the udders of a cow in calf swelled up at the rear first she would have a bull calf, if at the front, a heifer.[46]

2.2.4. *Dogs.* Divination from dogs barking was common (see Ch. 4.5.5 for its use in marital prospects divination). Other beliefs were that if a dog swayed on its feet its master would lose his way; if a dog howled with its head down this meant a death, if it howled with its head lifted there would be a fire; if a dog dug up the ground this meant a death; if it rolled on the ground there would be bad weather; if you ate after the dog your throat would swell; if a dog ate grass there would be rain; if a dog pressed up against its master this meant bad luck, and if it ate little and slept a lot this meant bad weather; if the dog would not eat after a sick man then that man would die; if a dog crossed your path this did not mean bad luck but it did mean you would have no great success; black dogs, cats and chickens in the house would preserve it from lightning and thieves, or, alternatively, were dangerous to have in the house during thunderstorms.[47]

2.2.5. *Hares.* Hares are associated with magic and witchcraft in several parts of Europe.[48] In Russia hares came under the protection of the wood-sprite, the *leshii*, who played cards for them with neighbouring wood-sprites (this was held to be an explanation of the lack of game in a particular section of forest),[49] and were in several respects magical animals. A hare running through a village meant a fire (also an English belief).[50] A hare crossing your path is bad luck, as Tat'iana in *Evgenii Onegin* (5, 6) knew. If this happened you had to say the rhymed spell: 'Tree stump and log for you, the path and the road for us'.[51] This is a very widespread superstition;[52] Min'ko, writing of Belorussia, quotes the case of a pilot in the Second World War who aborted a take-off because a hare had run across the runway.[53]

2.2.6. *Horses.* If a horse snorted on the road, this meant a happy meeting; if it just snorted there would be rain; if it shook its head and threw it up the weather would be bad; if a horse lay down in winter it would be warm.[54] The occasional use of horses in marital prospects divination is mentioned in Ch. 4.5.11.2.

2.2.7. *Mice.* There were many beliefs, predictions and practices associated with mice: if mice squeaked it meant famine; if mice left a house it meant a fire; if mice nibbled a loaf on top then bread prices would be high, if on the bottom, low, if on the side, then average; if a mouse got inside your clothing this meant a great misfortune; if mice nibbled your clothes, this meant death (cf. the prediction in the *Volkhovnik* below); if mice made a nest in the flax then there would be heavy snow in the winter; if mice ate up the remains of a meal left on the table then the master of the house would have a toothache; eating what mice have left would strengthen your teeth; spells were to be put on mice on St Trifon's day (1 February);[55] when a child lost a milk tooth the child or its nurse would throw the tooth behind the stove and say: 'Mouse, mouse, here is a radish tooth, forge me an iron one'.[56]

2.2.8. *Pigs.* A pig tugging at straw meant a storm; if pigs and mice ate hay this meant a poor reaping; meeting a pig meant good luck; a pig scratching meant hot weather, squealing meant bad weather.[57] Divination from a pig's entrails is described below in 5.6.

2.2.9. *Others.* A cricket coming into a house meant death or a fire;[58] flies in the house in winter meant death; a fly in your food or drink meant you would be given a present; ants in the house meant good luck; cockroaches in the house meant profit or luck; when they left there would be a fire;[59] when placed under a pillow they would induce dreams of your future husband (see Ch. 4.5.4.); fleas and lice may have also meant luck or prosperity: Martha Wilmot noted in 1807 'I know a very charming young girl (a Russian with the title of her Excellency), who is in the utmost delight whenever a Washerwoman sends her one, amongst her clean linen',[60] and Dal' gives the proverb 'If you have a louse, you will soon have money'.[61] A wolf or bear crossing your path meant good luck, a fox or squirrel meant bad luck;[62] if a ruff was your first catch your fishing trip would be unsuccessful.[63]

2.3. *Plants and Trees.* Prognostications can also be made from plants and trees. Some of these may be ancient and transmitted textually as in the case of certain of the predictions in the *Volkhovnik* (see next section), others may be of undetermined origin, part of 'folk knowledge'. Examples are: when a tree (especially oak and birch) was not stripped clean of its leaves in autumn then there would be a severe winter; when the oak put out leaves it was time for catching pike; if leaves fell with the shiny side uppermost there would be a bad harvest, and vice versa;[64] if the birch came into leaf before the alder there would be a dry summer, and vice versa;[65] an extra petal in a flower meant good luck.[66]

2.4. *Domestic, Culinary.* A great many of the omens and methods of divination listed in in this and other chapters of this book are, of course, linked to domestic objects, events or routines. I give here only a few which are not classified elsewhere.

Kasha is a general term for porridges made from a variety of cereals, and supplies a number of omens: if it darkened in the stove in the summer it meant rain, in winter – snow; if it boiled over into the stove this meant bad luck, outside the stove meant good luck.[67] This kind of divination is practised in particular on the feast of St Barbara (4 December), probably because of the phonetic association of 'Varvara' and *varit'* 'to boil, cook'.[68] If someone sitting at table eating the Christmas *kutiia* (a special kind of porridge like the old English frumenty eaten at the same season) was be observed not to have a shadow, this meant he would soon die.[69] If salt was spilled friends would fall out.[70]

The behaviour of smoke from a chimney was also used to predict weather, as it is in other countries.[71]

3. *Calendar Predictions*

The association of particular times of the year with particular tasks or climatic expectations is probably universal. In the ancient Greek world *parapēgmata* gave weather predictions based on the rising times of particular stars and their dates in the civil calendar, and this continued in the textual tradition of the later Byzantine and medieval Islamic and Latin worlds.[72] The paucity of texts of this kind in Russia does not mean, however, that Russia did not share the very similar, if simpler, common European practice of associating weather changes, or the beginning of agricultural or other avocational seasons, with dates in the Christian calendar. Every day of the Russian Church calendar had a double name, of which the first part was usually its Christian calendar name and the second usually something to do with weather or the proper date to start or finish some agricultural task, or some other important point in the annual domestic or agricultural cycle.[73] We may assume that Goncharov in his famous novel *Oblomov* (1859) was recording something he had observed in Russian provincial life when he wrote that 'they reckoned the time by holy-days, by the seasons of the years, by different family and domestic occurrences, and never referred to dates or months'.[74] Naturally enough in a country as large and climatically varied as Russia these names are often regional.

As examples one may offer:

Spiridon solntse-povorot – 'St Spiridon's day sun turn-around': 12 December (i.e. the winter solstice).

Vasilii solnovorot – 'St Basil's day sun turn-around': 1 January (an imprecise version of the preceding). A personification of this day can be seen in *Moroz Vasil'evich* 'Frost, son of Basil' who was called to eat the New Year *kasha* to persuade him not to come in summer.[75]

Aksiniia-polukhlebnitsa – 'St Aksinia half-corn': 24 January, when half the winter store of grain had been used up.

Aleksei-s-gor-voda, Aleksei-prolei-kuvshin – 'St Aleksei water from the hills', 'St Aleksei pour out the pitcher' and other variants: 17 March.

Lukerii-komarnitsy – 'St Lukerii-mosquito day' when the mosquitoes came out: 13 May.[76]

Luk'ian-vetrenik – 'St Lucian-wind day'. The day on which wind divination and rain spells were practised: 3 June. An allegedly unlucky day.[77]

Paraskeva-l'nianitsa – 'St Paraskeva the flaxen': 28 October, the day when work began on the flax.

These day names are not so much predictions as popular mnemonics based on experience, which provide a commonly understood structure to the year in a largely agricultural community. Where communal work is involved, a generally accepted date for harvesting, for example, has obvious social advantages. But elements of divination may be interwoven with these day names. Weather predictions in Russia, as elsewhere, are frequently encapsulated in proverbs and sayings such as: If the ice sinks in spring it will be a hard year without bread;[78] if it rains as you set out on a journey, this means good luck;[79] if the paths show black on Christmas Eve there will be a good grain harvest.[80] These predictions are often a kind of verse, in two halves with two ictuses per half and sometimes in rhyme or near-rhyme, and may also be associated with predictions based on the date. Sometimes a pun, suggestive rhyme or folk etymology (what N.I. Tolstoi has called 'etymological magic')[81] is involved: '*Boris i Gleb seiut khleb*', lit. 'SS. Boris and Gleb sow the corn' is an agricultural rhyming mnemonic; '*Fedor Studit zemliu studit*' (Theodore the Studite freezes the earth) for 3 November relies on the fact that *Studit* 'the Studite' is a homonym of *studit* 'it freezes', while '*Vasilii Pariiskii zemliu parit*' (St Basil of Parium heats the earth) for 12 April is a similar play on words. The same principle explains why St Cassian (29 February) 'looks crookedly (*koso*)' (i.e. causes misfortune – for more on St Cassian see Ch. 2.5) and blacksmiths (*kuznets*) must not work on the feast of St Kuz'ma (Cosmas), why the wind blows on St Theodulos's day (*dul* means 'he blew'), why on the feast of St Simon the Zealot you gather herbs from the marsh ('*Na Simona-Zilota sobirai zel'ia iz bolota*'), why St Luke is invoked (on 7 September) in hunting spells and for trading in onions (*luk* is both a bow and an onion), and why St Tikhon is invoked in medical spells to soothe pain (*tikhii* means quiet, calm).[82] A similar association of ideas can be seen in the belief that the weather on the feast of the Forty Martyrs (9 March) would last for forty days.[83]

In most cases the prediction takes the form of foretelling the weather of the whole season, or crop prospects, from the weather on a particular day (e.g. St Eudoxia (Avdot'ia) (4 August), Aksinia (24 January), the Annunciation (25 March), as with the commonest prediction of this kind in Britain (rain on St Swithun's Day). A typical rhyming example is: '*Platon da Roman kazhut zimu nam*' ('Platon and Roman [i.e. the calendar saints for December 1] show us the winter'). Dal' in his great collection of Russian sayings gives a large number of prognostications by date (pp. 129–65), by agricultural signs (pp. 166–74), seasonal and weather predictions (pp. 175–85).[84] Ermolov in his comparative study of the popular calendar also lists very many beliefs and predictions associated with particular days.[85]

The literature on local calendar predictions is considerable, and given the great range of climatic conditions and geographical zones in a country which stretches from the White Sea to the Black Sea and from the Baltic to the Pacific, the predictions themselves vary a great deal from region to region. One of the most extensive and useful studies, in that the calendar is related to other aspects of local rural life, is the survey of the folk calendar of the Enisei region of Siberia by Makarenko.[86]

The more important feasts tended to attract a larger number of predictions: what follows is only a sample of a vast range of calendrical predictions, signs and methods of divination:

Christmas: Christmas had a whole series of predictions depending on which day of the week it occurred. These are to be found in a popular text of ancient origin called the *Koliadnik* (see Ch. 14.7). Simpler unsystematized predictions are: clear weather during the Christmas fast means a good harvest; hoar frost at Christmas means a good corn harvest and a starry sky means a good crop of peas; a snowstorm means the bees would swarm well; good roads at Christmas are a sign of a good buckwheat harvest; do not put on a fresh shirt or there would be a bad harvest.[87] Do not engage in sewing at Christmas or else a blind child would be born, and if you weave bast shoes at this time your child would be born crooked.[88] From Christmas to the Epiphany (the period known as *sviatki*, the main period for divination of marital prospects – see Ch. 4.4–5) you must not do curved work such as barrel hoops, or else your cattle would be barren; dark days in this period mean cows would give plenty of milk, and light days mean that hens would lay well.[89]

New Year: New Year's Eve was another favourite time for divination, especially marital prospect divination (see Ch. 4.4–5). The situation is complicated by the fact that before Peter the Great's reforms in 1700 the new year began on 1 September. Most of the recorded beliefs relating to the New Year are either not specific with regard to date or are clearly post-1700. Predictions on this day are fairly obvious: if New Year's Day (St Basil's Day) was happy so would be the rest of the year;[90] do not work on New Year's Day, or else the whole year would be spent in hard work.[91] Weather conditions, especially a starry night, on St Basil's Eve in many parts of Russia was an indication of the quality of the harvest in the following year (the actual crop depends on the region);[92] this was also the night when owners of orchards would shake their trees to ensure a good crop, and when witches would go out to steal the moon.[93]

Epiphany: The Eve of the Epiphany was the third popular day of the *sviatki* for divination (see Ch. 4.4). If the dogs bark a lot at the Epiphany, game would be plentiful; melted Epiphany snow (also March snow) is good as a bleach and a medicine for a variety of ills, as Tat'iana knew in *Eugene Onegin* (see Ch. 4.3); heaven opens at the Epiphany and whatever you pray for then would come true; if the Epiphany Blessing of the Water ceremony takes place in fog then corn would be plentiful, and if there is a full moon, or the hole in the ice at the 'Jordan' is full of water, then there would be floods; clouds at midday at the

Epiphany mean a good harvest; a starry night means a good harvest of peas and berries and mushrooms and a good year for lambs.[94]

The Annunciation (25 March): Dal' states that among the peasants this was the most important religious festival. On this day and at Easter the souls in hell are not tormented. You may not spin or weave on this day,[95] nor plait your hair, nor heat the stove, nor cook hot meals. Moles are blind because they dug on this day, and cuckoos have no nest because they made nests on this day. Whatever happens on this day would set the pattern for the whole year, which is why thieves always try to steal something in the hope of being successful for the rest of the year. Whatever day of the week the Annunciation falls on should be observed for the rest of the year as a day on which nothing is undertaken. If it rains on this day there would be a good rye harvest; and many more similar predictions.[96]

Gabriel's Day (26 March): An unlucky day. If you were to work at spinning on (or after) this day the work would be spoiled (presumably a carry-over from the previous day).[97] Children or livestock born on this day were expected to be defective in some way.[98]

St George's Day (23 April): This is known as 'Warm George', as distinct from 'Cold George' (26 November). This had many weather and agricultural predictions, and the early dew on this day would protect you from the Evil Eye and seven sicknesses but could also be used by magicians for malefic magic.[99]

Easter: Thunder at Easter meant a good harvest. The bones of whatever animal was eaten for the Easter dinner were buried in cornfields to protect the crops from hailstones.

SS. Boris and Gleb (2 May): Tradesmen had to make a good deal on this day to guarantee good business for the rest of the year.

St John's Eve and Day (23–24 June): Roughly the summer solstice and, together with the winter *sviatki*, the most magical time of the year, especially for the gathering and use of magical herbs and roots (see Ch. 2.6). Predictions include: a starry night means many mushrooms; a heavy dew means a good cucumber crop; in the Ukraine (and Poland) if there is a thunderstorm on St John's Day the nut harvest would fail.[100]

St Peter and Paul's Day (29 June): On this day the sun 'played' (see Sun and Moon predictions below); if it rained on this day, there would be a good harvest.[101]

The day of Elijah the Prophet (20 July): In many areas this was the beginning of the harvest season and there are many weather and crop predictions linked with this day.

Elijah is associated with the Slavonic thunder-god Perun and rain and thunder often form part of the predictions. E. Zamiatin in his story *A Provincial Tale* (1913) mentioned the belief that if you are late for church on this day you will cry for a whole year. On this day there was no work in the fields and cattle were not taken out to pasture for fear of lightning and snakes (it is their feast day). It was a day for cleaning bee hives and hunting wolves. Rain which fell on that day had therapeutic qualities and gave protection from the Evil Eye and malefic magic.[102]

Pokrov (1 October): The first day of winter. A day for divination by wind – a north wind meant a cold winter, a south wind a mild one, a strong wind meant a snowy winter, no wind meant no snow. Also a day of marital prospects divination – see Ch. 4.5.[103]

St Andrew's Day (30 November): One had to listen to the flow of water at night: if it was quiet there would be a good winter, if noisy then frosts and storms.[104] As in other parts of Europe, this was also a day for marital divination by placing clothes under the pillow to induce dreams of one's future spouse.[105]

St Spiridon's Day (12 December): The winter solstice, concerning which there were many popular beliefs. Each of the twelve days following would indicate the weather for each of the ensuing twelve months.[106]

4. Celestial Phenomena

4.1. *Sun and moon predictions.* The interpretation of rings round the sun and moon is one of the most ancient recorded forms of divination. Together with omens of the moon on the first day of the month, thunder, earthquakes, etc. they were employed by the court astrologers of ancient Mesopotamia,[107] and continue to occur thereafter in books of omens and portents such as the *Liber de ostentis*, the Byzantine anthology of such material which was compiled by Johannes Lydus in the sixth century.[108] A rich variety of moon horn and sun and moon halo predictions is recorded by Olaus Magnus among the northern peoples adjacent to Russia.[109] Russian predictions of this kind include the belief that if the horns were sharp and clear the weather would be fine, if blunt there would be frost; and the direction of the horns of the moon on the feast of St Evlampii (10 October) would show the direction from which the wind would blow.[110]

A ring round the moon may simply be a countryman's sign of a change for the worse in the weather.[111] Dal' quotes beliefs that a ring round the sun meant bad weather (but rings round the sun on the feast of St Basil (22 March) meant a good harvest – s.v. *vasilek*), while a ring round the moon meant wind; alternatively a short-lived red ring around the moon presaged fine weather but if there were two such rings, or one faint one, there would be frost, if red then wind, if broken then snow.[112] In some cases, however, this was elaborated into a whole system and recorded in manuscripts.

One such is an eighteenth-century manuscript, of a text probably much older, in which the predictions are arranged by month. It reads:

> If the moon has a halo in March great tsars and princes will do battle from east to west.
> If the moon has a halo in April there will be much fruit.
> If the moon has a halo in May great hailstorms will destroy.
> If the moon has a halo in June there will be war.
> If the moon has a halo in July there will be death to animals.
> If the moon has a halo in August fish and honey will be plentiful.
> If the moon has a halo in September there will be little rain.
> If the moon has a halo in October the summer will be dry.
> If the moon has a halo in November there will be war.
> If the moon has a halo in December there will be famine.
> If the moon has a halo in January there will be great rains.
> (February missing.)[113]

The moon could also have other kinds of predictive value. Tat'iana in Pushkin's *Eugene Onegin* sought the moons image in a mirror (5.9), and shivered and went pale when she saw the horned moon on the left (5.5) – see Ch. 4.3. The horns of a crescent moon when sharp and bright meant a hot summer;[114] to be born at the new moon meant you would have a long life.[115]

Parhelia, or multiple suns as a result of abnormal weather conditions (*pasolntse* in Russian), have been recorded on a number of occasions in Russia. Richard James, the English chaplain to the Muscovy Company factory near Archangel described one such phenomenon and two local interpretations of it in 1614 (see Ch. 15.2). The *pasolntse* in general betokened calm weather; in summer it meant heat and drought, in winter severe frost. An alternative Russian expression, 'sun with ears' or 'sun in gloves' is also listed as a portent of frost.[116]

Another solar phenomenon is known in Russia as the 'playing of the sun' (*igranie solntsa, solntse igraet*). This can mean a variety of visual effects such as flickering or emitting fiery or coloured rays, usually at sunrise. This was supposed to happen in particular at Easter, Christmas, Epiphany, Annunciation, the feast of the birth of St John.[117] In the Tula region, on the eve of St Peter and Paul's Day, a whole ceremony of 'seeing in' the playing of the sun was observed by singing and playing games all night.[118] If the moon 'played' at moonrise on the feast of St Athanasius of Athos (5 July) this meant a good harvest. The phenomena of 'three suns' and fiery rays and other 'celestial signs' were certainly seen as omens by the authors of the various Russian chronicles, and indeed appear prominently with rays of influence issuing from them in the illustrations of the historical events which they were thought to mark in the *Radziwiłł Chronicle* of the late fifteenth century and the *Illuminated Chronicle* (*Litsevoi letopisnyi svod*) of the second half of the sixteenth century.[119]

A high rainbow meant fine weather, a low flat one foretold bad weather.[120]

4.2. *Stars*. Stars could figure in popular calendar predictions in ways quite different from astrology. Dal' (s.v. *zvězda*) gives the feast of St Andronicus (12 October) as the day on which to make star prognostications about the weather and the harvest; and a starry night of St Trifon (1 February) meant a late spring while the same thing on St James's night (30 April) meant a good harvest. A starry St Basil's night promised a good berry crop.[121] In the Pinega region of north Russia, stars on Christmas Eve were a sign of a wealth of mushrooms and berries the following year; if there were no stars on New Year's Eve then there would be no mushrooms.[122]

4.3. *Shooting Stars*. Both comets and meteors were often thought of as fiery serpents. An eighteenth-century dictionary of Russian superstitions states that comets foretell bad luck, plague, famine, war, etc., and that shooting stars are demons who come out at night to have intercourse with women, in particular virgins and recent widows. This leaves the women emaciated. To prevent evil effects of this kind you must immediately say: '*Amen, Amen, rassyp'sia!*' (Amen, Amen, disperse!).[123] This belief is evidently a local development of incubus-lore and probably an importation from the West. Witches in the Ukraine were reputed to catch falling stars and keep them in jars, perhaps for this very purpose. The sexual connotation may also be seen in the belief that a girl's future husband would come from the direction in which she saw a shooting star.[124] This was perhaps the belief to which Tat'iana subscribed in Pushkin's *Evgenii Onegin* (5, 6) when she made a wish on seeing a shooting star. Other prognostications from falling stars are that they foretell wind, and that if you fall ill on the feast of St Leo (20 February) and see a falling star, then you would die.[125]

4.4. *Thunder and lightning*. Belief in thunder and lightning as omens is ancient, and its occurrence in systematic divination in Russian texts is discussed in Ch. 14.4. In popular belief thunder was associated in earlier times with the pagan god Perun, and later with Elijah the Prophet – his feast day, 30 July, was called Thunder Day.[126] 'Thunder arrows' were well known as amulets in Russia as elsewhere, and thunderstorms could endow objects with magic power (see Ch. 8.4.2). The first thunder of the season provided seasonal predictions: if it thundered in a north wind there would be a cold spring; if in an east wind a dry and warm spring; if in a west wind the spring would be wet, if in a south wind it would be warm but with many worms and insects.[127]

5. *Haruspicy*

There are no obvious references in the various Russian lists of banned books and practices (most of which were derived from Greek lists of a very much earlier date) to divination from animal entrails, but the practice has existed among all the Slav peoples.[128] Dal' observes that the *sviatki*, the period from Christmas to the Epiphany which is one of the main 'magical' periods in the Russian year, was the time when predictions about the severity of the winter were made from inspecting the liver and spleen, but does not indicate the method or locality; in his entry for *Anis'i-Zheludochnitsy* (i.e. St Anisia-entrails – 30 December – a name which in itself draws attention to the practice) he notes that the belly, liver and spleen were boiled and used to predict the harshness of the forthcoming winter; and in his entry for *pech'* he also quotes a belief that if the liver of a pike is thicker at the head end, then it would be better to sow crops early, and if at the tail end, then later.[129] One account of Ukrainian popular divination notes a similar practice of divination from the thickness of a hog's spleen (if the back is thick the winter would be severe, if thin, then it would be mild),[130] a method of divination which has also survived in parts of Greece.[131] I have been unable to find any record in primary sources of how the interpretation of entrails, liver or spleen was to be carried out.

6. *Scapulimancy*

The practice of scapulimancy, or divination from markings on a sheep's shoulder blade, is known in many different cultures: the various peoples of Central Asia, North Africa, the Chinese and Japanese, North American Indians, and is also known in many parts of Europe.[132] In the British Isles Gerald of Wales records a twelfth-century Flemish community in Wales as practising scapulimancy – apparently the earliest European textual reference – and the practice is further recorded from the seventeenth century to the nineteenth in England and Scotland.[133] Four Latin treatises exist: two by Hugo of Santalla, who was also responsible for the translation of other divinatory texts, including geomancy. Two are from same Arabic work attributed to Alkindi. All have much the same detail and explanation of method, although the actual composition of the texts varies considerably. Note that all Arabic and Latin texts suggest boiling the bone (the 'non-calcinating' method). Mongol, Chinese, and Japanese, as well as American Indian, methods all involve baking, as does the Russian and the presumably Byzantine method described in a text attributed to Psellus:

> Gathering together to make the divination they choose from the flock a sheep or ram having in advance thought or spoken the object of the divination; then killing the ram they extract from the carcass the shoulder blade as the instrument of their prediction and roast it on coals and cleaning away the meat they receive indications of the answers to their questions.[134]

The cultures in which scapulimancy survives, at least until recent times, include the West and South Slavs, and the adjacent Greeks.[135] Moszyński and Eisenberger note the practice in Poland, Jugoslavia and Bulgaria.[136]

There is no record of the practice of scapulimancy among the East Slavs, unless one is prepared to include the mad White Russian general Baron Roman

Fedorovich von Ungern-Sternberg who had local soothsayers to read the omens from cracks in sheep's shoulder blades to assist him in his attempted liberation of Mongolia in 1921.[137] There is, however, a text, which exists in only one copy.[138] This is the important sixteenth-century miscellany of divinatory texts which includes the earliest known copy of the Old Russian *Secretum secretorum* (see Ch. 1.5). The manuscript containing the text was described by Dobrianskii in his catalogue of the Vilnius Public Library collection, but he does not mention this particular part of it.[139] The text was published with introductory notes by Speranskii in 1900,[140] and was described by Sobolevskii a few years later,[141] but nothing of significance has been added to our knowledge of it since. Speranskii notes that the text is first referred to in a list of banned books in the seventeenth century in later versions of the *Kirillova kniga* (a collection of religious polemic texts, 1644) together with the *Trepetnik* (divination by involuntary body movements) under the general category of *Volkhovnik* ('Book of the Magician'), but attributes its translation (for no convincing reason) to not later than the middle of the fourteenth century, a period of renewed interest in divinatory and magic literature in Byzantium and Bulgaria. We may note, however, that in Iatsimirskii's analysis of indexes of banned books the *Lopatochnik* ('Book of the Shoulder Blade') is listed only in the later indexes together with various kinds of augury from the behaviour of animals and natural omens.[142] Speranskii draws attention to the existence of the practice in modern Greece, among the Lapps and Kirghiz, Kalmuks, Mongols, Serbs and Bulgars. He considers the text to be translated from Greek and to be probably of South Slav immediate origin: the rather thin argument for this is that it is ascribed to 'Peter the Egyptian', which would be a typical late Byzantine ascription to an oriental source, and the argument from silence, that the practice of scapulimancy, although attested for the Greeks, South Slavs, Lapps, Central Asians, Poles, Germans (i.e. practically all the peoples surrounding Russia) is not known in Russia itself. At the same time the language of the text, Russian Church Slavonic, unlike that of its manuscript neighbour the *Secretum secretorum*, gives no hint at all of Greek, Latin, or Hebrew provenance.

The language of the fairly short text was by no means clear even to Sobolevskii, and the text appears to be incomplete and defective (for example, the contents do not correspond entirely with the statement of contents at the beginning). The text may be tentatively summarized as follows:

The Book of Peter the Egyptian.

The shoulder blade shows defeat, victory, illness or health, death or long life, trade, weather, how to know your enemy or conquer your adversary. Take a sheep or lamb. Keep in mind what you want to know. Bake the chosen shoulder blade on coals, scrape it, examine it to see how wide the upper and lower ends are. Place it rib uppermost. If the middle part is wider and the right narrower it will show the length of life of man and beast; if it is dark it shows a short life . . .

If you want to make love to a beautiful wife or mistress and know the beauty of women, do as the signs say: if the right side is clean and the left discoloured (*mutnyi*) then embrace.

Of marriage and sexual intercourse: if you see a red circle like a hair and discoloured on the left side with long black fibres then the couple will have long life and much wealth, but if you see this sign on both sides this is bad.

Poverty: if you wish to know whether there will be relief or if you will die in want, look to see if there are straight red fibres. If they lie across the blade this means relief but if along the blade this means death.

Of tsars and armies and seiges and routs: if you wish to know how long or short his reign will be, whether he will be deposed by by relatives or others, look on the right side of the blade. If it is clean this means a short reign; if the left side is dark it means war and great bloodshed; if there is a blue place on the left side in the middle then he will be deposed by a relative . . .

Of wars and bloodshed and victory: if you want to know who will win or lose, see if on the right side there is a red spot – this means a great war and great bloodshed . . . a blue spot means death to horses . . .

If you want to know what is happening in Poland and who will take power . . . red fibres above and in the middle on the upper side of the blade and on the right hand side then he will take power without war, but if there are three blue lines on the left side in this place and two horizontal fibres then he will take power but by bloodshed, and if he sees this sign on the left side in the middle it means his death . . .

On the conduct of war: when facing battle slaughter a white ram; look on the right side of the shoulder blade above the middle – if it bends to the right this will aid your army; then look at the spine of the shoulder blade – if the top twists to the right this means the destruction of your enemy . . .

Riches and poverty. . . .

The main characteristics of the system of divination described here are:
1. The animal is a sheep or lamb, or, at one point, a white ram.
2. The preparation involves baking and scraping.
3. The significant areas are right or left, upper or lower, the spine, the curvature of the top.
4. The signs depend on area, darkness or lightness, presence of fibres and spots which may be red, blue, or black. Note that although the preparation indicates the calcinating method there is no mention here of cracks. The reading *polskiia strany* ('Polish land') in the text is curiously specific. An alternative reading of the superscript 'l' would give *ploskiia strany* 'flat land'. The first makes better sense but inexplicably neither Speranskii nor Sobolevskii comment on this point. If it is not a misreading, then notwithstanding Speranskii's remarks about the Great Russian characteristics of the language of the text, it strengthens the case for the probable area of translation (or at least of reworking) being the same as that of the *Secretum*, i.e. the Grand Duchy of

Lithuania. Speranskii's belief in an underlying Greek text is probably well founded – the thirteenth-century Greek text published by Delatte[143] claims that it is a book of the Turks and Barbarians and offers prognostications about the weather, victory or defeat in war, going on journeys, the outcome of illnesses, love, number of children, etc. in much the same terms as the Russian text and with the same kind of reference to the parts of the blade and black and red spots. It differs in detail but is clearly in the same tradition as the Russian text. Whether or not both texts derive from a 'Turkish or Barbarian' source has yet to be established but one can certainly say that the Arabic text from Spain given by Burnett is totally different.[144]

7. *The Volkhovnik or 'Book of the Wizard'*

The conversion of the East and South Slavs to Orthodox Christianity brought with it not only a limited selection of texts translated from Greek but also a ready-made censorship in the form of lists of 'good and bad books'.[145] Although sometimes compared with the Latin *Index librorum prohibitorum*, and indeed recent Russian work uses the term *indeks* for the genre,[146] that institution was in fact a sixteenth-century Counter-Reformation measure designed for a printed-book milieu and different in scope, if less so in purpose, from the relatively brief Greek and Slavonic lists. These were culled from patristic literature and the acts of Church councils and synods and were intended partly as warnings against uncanonical and heretical books (the first part of the 'index' usually gives a list of apocryphal and heretical works), and partly to identify forbidden magic and divinatory texts (this is the most variable part of the list and in Russia may relate to a specifically Russian context).

It is reasonable to assume that when a new item occurs in a Russian list, as happened increasingly in the sixteenth and seventeenth centuries, then it does refer to something specific which has only recently become a source of worry to the authorities. A prime example is the 'Gates of Aristotle', a work of geomancy which is listed in the acts of the Stoglav Council in 1551. A more mysterious work is that given in several manuscript lists of 'false books' as *Volkhovnik*, perhaps best translated as 'The Book of the Wizard'.[147]

By the sixteenth century a full list of such omens had appeared.[148] The five manuscript versions given by Iatsimirskii all begin: 'The Book of the Wizard, performing bird magic with birds and beasts, that is . . .' and are then followed by the lists as given below [the roman numerals indicate the version number given by Iatsimirskii].

XI	XII	XIII	XIV	XV
1. the house creaks	1. the house creaks	1. wall-crack	1. the house creaks	1. the house creaks
2. ear-ringing	2. the ear rings	2. ear-ringing	2. ear-ringing	2. ear-ringing
3. crow-cawing	3. a crow caws	3. crow-cawing	3. crow-cawing	3. crow-cawing
4. cock-crow	4. a cock crows	4. cock-crow	4. cock-crow	4. a cock crows
5. eye-blink	5. a dog howls	5. eye-blink	5. eye-blink	5. eye-blink
6. the fire roars	6. the fire roars	6. the fire roars	6. the fire roars	6. the fire roars
7. a dog howls	7. an eye twitches	7. a dog howls	7. a dog howls	7. a dog howls
8. mouse-squeak	8. an arm [?] twitches	8. mouse-squeak	8. a mouse squeaks	8. mouse squeak
9. a mouse gnaws clothes		9. a mouse gnaws clothes	9. a mouse gnaws clothes	9. a mouse gnaws clothes
10. a toad croaks			10. a toad croaks[149]	10. a toad croaks
11. a cat in a dream			11. a cat in the window	11. a cat miaows
12. a muscle twitches		12. a muscle twitches	12. a muscle twitches	12. a muscle twitches
13. a fearful dream		13. a fearful dream	13. a fearful dream	13. a dream fightens
14. meeting a blind man		14. meeting a blind man	14. meeting a blind man[150]	14. meeting a blind man
15. something catches fire		15. something catches fire	15. something catches fire	15. something catches fire
16. the fire squeaks		16. the fire squeaks	16. the fire squeaks	16. the fire squeaks
17. a spark from the fire		17. a spark from the fire	17. sparks from the fire	17. a spark from the fire flares up
18. a cat miaows		18. a cat miaows	18. a cat miaows	18. a man falls
19. a man falls		19. a man falls	19. a man falls	19. a candle goes out
20. a candle goes out		20. a candle goes out	20. a candle goes out	20. a horse neighs
21. a horse neighs		21. a horse neighs	21. a horse neighs	21. ox mounts ox
22. ox on ox.		22. ox on ox	22. ox on ox	

A further list in all versions except **XII** adds: 'Bird book of various birds:

XI		XIII	XIV	XV
23. bee, fish and grass rustle		23. bee, fish and grass rustle	23. birds, fish and grass rustle	23 a bee sings
24. a magpie chatters		24. tree [rubs?] against tree	24.tree [rubs ?] against tree	24. a fish flounders
25. a woodpecker		25. a leaf rustles	25. a leaf rustles	25. grass rustles
26. a large woodpecker		26. a magpie chatters	26. a magpie chatters	26. tree scrapes on tree
27. a wolf howls		27. a woodpecker	27. a woodpecker	27. a leaf rustles
28. a guest arrives.		28. a large woodpecker	28. a large woodpecker	28. a magpie chatters
29.		29. a wolf howls	29. a wolf howls	29. a woodpecker
30.		30. a guest arrives	30. a guest arrives[151]	30. a large woodpecker
31.		31.	31.	31. a wolf howls
32.		32.	32.	32. grief comes[152]

All the lists except XII then mention, apparently as separate texts *Stenoshchelk* ('wall-crack') and *Lopatochnik* '[the book of the] shoulder blade' and 'various other kinds of magic'.

Pypin, in an article on the history of 'false books',[153] seems to have been the first to draw attention to this work but was confused by the fact that several of the omens listed are the same as those in another divinatory work, the *Trepetnik* ('Book of Tremblings'), in which predictions are made from itches and twitches in various parts of the body (palmomancy, a method of divination evidently borrowed from Greece). This confusion was taken further by M.N. Speranskii in the introduction to his edition of the *Trepetnik*,[154] where he concludes that the *Volkhovnik* was the title of a compendium or cycle of texts, also known separately, comprising the *Ptichnik* (divination from birds); *Trepetnik* (palmomancy); *Putnik* ('Book of the Road' – see pp. 123–4 above), but also says that in some copies the various omens appearing in the book seem to have replaced the title, *Volkhovnik*, in what is otherwise a list of books and practices.

This does indeed appear to be the case. Charles Burnett has drawn attention to two Latin manuscripts of the eleventh and thirteenth centuries containing prognostication tables entitled *Tabula prenostica Salomonis*.[155] The horizontal axis of this table gives the names of the twelve signs of the zodiac while the vertical axis gives twenty-four 'unexpected events'. The same system of prognostication with some extra 'unexpected events' was published in the sixteenth century by the German alchemist Heinrich Khunrath under the title *Liber Zebelis*. Most of the 'unexpected events' in these works correspond almost exactly with the list of omens given in the Russian lists of banned books, as the Latin list below will show:

1. De sonitu domus	(the creaking of the house)
2. De tinitu aurium	(ringing in the ears)
3. De voce corvi	(the cawing of a crow)
4. De voce galli	(the crowing of a cock)
5. De motu oculorum	(a tic in the eyes)
6. De sonitu ignis	(the hissing of the fire)
7. De ululatu canis	(the howling of a dog)
8. De voce soricis	(the squeak of a shrew-mouse)
9. De incensis vestibus	(clothing on fire)
10. De terremotu	(an earth-tremor)
11. De clamore gatte	(caterwauling)
12. De inquinata veste femore [?fetore]	(clothing stained with [?filth])
13. De casu avis iuxta te in via	(a bird falling in your path)
14. De subito candela extincta	(a candle suddenly extinguished)
15. De intuitu gatte in foramine	(on seeing a cat through a hole)
16. De pulsu brachii	(a spasm in the arm)
17. De pavore somnii	(a night terror)
18. De occursu fere	(on meeting a wild animal)
19. Si sorex vestimentum roserit	(if a shrew-mouse has bitten a hole in garment)
20. De eo si vestimentum lanerit	(if it has torn it)
21. De subito incursu bestie in curte	(the sudden entry of a beast into a courtyard)

22. De crepitu ignis	(the crackling of the fire)
23. Si ignis sintillat	(if the fire gives off sparks)
24. Si vestimentum inquinatum sangui(ne)	(if a garment is stained in blood)

The variations in the Slavonic lists are mostly explicable by simple misreading: the 'cat in the dream' (*koshka vo sne*) is clearly a mistake for 'cat in the window' (*koshka v okne*), an error easily made if you know that cats invariably occur in dream books;[156] *gost'* 'guest' and *gorest'* 'grief' in 30 are also easily confused.

The Latin and Slavonic lists correspond to such a degree that they must have common origin. There are some differences: Latin 9 'clothing' becomes 'something' in Russian 15; Latin 10, 12 and 24 are missing in the Russian; Latin 13 'bird falling' becomes 'man falling' in Russian 19; 'wild animal' in Latin 18 becomes 'blind man' in Russian 14; the beast entering the courtyard in Latin 21 becomes the even more unexpected sodomitic oxen in Russian 22. These all suggest simple errors of translation, or perhaps no more than copying, at some stage in the transmission of the Russian text. The subjoined lists in the Slavonic versions do not correspond with anything in the Latin text, nor, despite their ostensible title, are all the omens birds. These elements are listed as separate items in Tikhonravov's list: '90. Bird book of various birds: crow croak, cockcrow, magpie chatter, woodpecker; 91. The book of tremblings: a muscle twitches, scapulimancy, various kinds of magic; 92. The book of the road in which is written various kinds of meeting, meeting a blind man; 93. Dream book.

The 'Book of Tremblings' or *Trepetnik*, and the scapulimancy or *Lopatochnik*, did in fact exist as complete texts in their own right, the latter being extant only in one copy (see below). No text for the *Sonnik* ('Dream Book') or the *Putnik* is extant in Russian but their equivalents existed in Greek.

The Russian lists of true and false books contain a good deal of garbled information and it seems highly probable that a confused description of the *Tabula prenostica Salomonis*, or a closely related text, does lie behind the entry for *Volkhovnik* and was subsequently confused with elements of descriptions of other texts. There is no suggestion in the Russian descriptions of the *Volkhovnik* that this series of omens was ever linked with the zodiac, and it is possible either that the *Tabula* is a elaboration of what might originally have been a simple set of prognostications, or that the Russian text was a simplification of the more elaborate *Tabula*.

There are, of course, any number of popular sayings and superstitions in Russia (with parallels in many other cultures) which are similar to the omens in the *Volkhovnik*, indeed there seems to have been hardly anything in rural life anywhere which was not an omen of something.[157]

A few examples will suffice: many omens relating to ringing in the ears or tics in the eyes or muscles exist, and some are given in the *Trepetnik* mentioned above; a crow cawing means death;[158] a mouse squeaking means famine, a mouse eating a hole in one's clothes means death;[159] a candle going out suddenly means guests;[160] the creaking of a house and a coal jumping from a fire are popular omens,[161] and omens from chicken behaviour, or the direction in which a dog is howling or a horse neighing, are a common part of the various divinatory practices (usually on New Year's Eve) to foretell whom you will marry; the cat on the stove was an omen recognized by Tat'iana in Pushkin's *Eugene Onegin* (5, 5).

It is possible that these popular omens have their origin in the *Volkhovnik* but alas, there is no extant Russian text on which we might test such a hypothesis – and the sheer volume of popular superstitions of this kind makes coincidences almost inevitable. Indeed, one eighteenth-century manuscript which contains a list of games, entertainments, superstitions and omens which are 'accursed' and for which penance must be done (see Ch. 2, 1), includes most of the omens listed above mixed in with palmomantic omens from the *Trepetnik*, many other popular superstitions and methods of divination (such as feeding a bear to discover the sex of an unborn child), and the playing of musical instruments, chess, dice and cards.[162]

The difficulty of separating the 'popular' from the 'learned' tradition, or charting the interaction of the two traditions, if indeed there is such an interaction, is demonstrated by Speranskii's conclusion, in his edition of the *Trepetnik*, that many of the omens published by Dal' were not in fact collected by Dal' from live informants as he claimed, but were taken by him from manuscript *Trepetniki*. Dal' took this dishonest short cut because he assumed that the omens were of 'popular' origin, unaware that they had a literary history which could be traced back to antique models.[163]

Burnett suggests that a Greek, rather than Arabic, original lies behind the Latin of his divinatory text. In the case of the Russian descriptions of the *Volkhovnik*, which are very much later than the Latin texts, if the source of the information was translated before the end of the fifteenth century then in all probability it was translated from Greek, if in the late fifteenth or sixteenth century then Greek, Latin, Polish, German, or even Hebrew are possibilities, given the origin of divinatory material in Russia at that period. A direct Arabic source would be most unlikely, a Byzantine one quite probable.

Iatsimirskii draws attention to a number of early translated works in Slavonic, including the Chronicle of George the Monk, the preface to the *Vita* of St John Chrysostom, and works of SS Cyprian and Ephraem, etc., in which belief in certain portents such as walls creaking, crows cawing, and the squeaking of mice is condemned. And these three omens are specifically mentioned in the first of John Chrysostom's *Baptismal Instructions* as 'foolish practices of the Greeks' and appear to be something of a topos; Chrysostom refers again in his eleventh instruction to 'portents, oracles, omens, observances of times, tokens, amulets, and incantations' as being among the 'pomps of the Devil' to be renounced at baptism. He refers yet again in his twelfth instruction to omens such as seeing a man with one eye or one leg (bad omens), meeting a virgin (sign of an unlucky day), meeting a prostitute (sign of a lucky day), tying coins of Alexander the Great to one's hands or feet as amulets, incantations chanted by old hags.[164] The subject was evidently one which appealed to him – he has another list of omens popular with the Greeks of his time in his commentary on Ephesians. These include a cock crowing as decisive in a business deal, putting on a left shoe first as unlucky, stepping out of the house with the left foot first as unlucky, a tic in the eye, a mule braying, someone sneezing, the sounds of a loom.[165] Most of these were well known in Russia even in recent times.

What seems to have happened in Russia is that the sequence of omens from the source text of the *Tabula prenostica Salomonis* was quoted in a list of 'false books', that the list then lost its textual integrity and was no longer recognized as a text either by compilers of lists of banned books or by later scholars commenting on them. The last stage was for the omens contained in the text to be mingled indiscriminately with omens from other sources. Notwithstanding Speranskii's accusation that Dal' cheated (see p. 143 above and n. 163), the coincidence of some of the omens in the text with omens found in popular beliefs and sayings does not necessarily demonstrate that the latter are of literary origin. At the same time, in the very eclectic world of magic and divination the disintegration of the original textual identity of the omens and their subsequent association with known popular practices makes the rebirth of these 'literary' omens as 'popular' omens entirely possible.

Notes

1. For examples see in particular Zhuravlev, *Domashnii skot*, ideographic index.

2. *Russian Primary Chronicle*, pp. 144–7.

3. An emperor as sophisticated as Constantine Porphyrogenitus in the tenth century recommends in his *De cerimoniis aulae Byzantinae* (see ed. Reiskii, Bonn, 1829, p. 467) that emperors should always take with them on their campaigns most of the popular divination texts including the *Biblion sunantē-matikon* ('Book of Meetings'). This may be the *Putnik* of Russian indexes of banned books – see Granstrem, 'Grecheskii original otrechennoi knigi «Putnik»'. Kobiak appears to concur with this: Kobiak, 'Indeksy otrechennykh i zapreshchennykh knig', p. 50 n. 18.

4. Graham, 'A Brief Account', p. 266.

5. *SRIaXI–XIV vv*, s.v. *oko*.

6. Dal', *Tolkovyi slovar'*, s.v. *vstrechat'*.

7. Dal', *Tolkovyi slovar'*, s.vv. *volk, vstrechat'*. Chulkov, *Abevega*, p. 79, says it is *unlucky* to meet a corpse.

8. Afanas'ev, *Poèticheskie vozzreniia*, p. 174.

9. Dal', *Tolkovyi slovar'*, s.vv. *monakh, pop, volk*.

10. Dal', *Tolkovyi slovar'*, s.v. *vstrechat'*.

11. Opie and Tatem, *Dictionary*, s.v. *clergymen*.

12. Olaus Magnus, *Description of the Northern Peoples*, bk 3, ch. 26.

13. See Abbott, *Macedonian Folklore*, p. 104.

14. Dal', *Tolkovyi slovar'*, s.v. *pop*.

15. Iatsimirskii, *Bibliograficheskii obzor*, pp. 68–9.

16. Vasmer, *Ètimologicheskii slovar*, s.v.; *SRIa XI–XVII vv.*, s.v.; Dal', *Tolkovyi slovar'*, s.v.

17. Dal', *Tolkovyi slovar'*, s.v. *ptakh*. These words are probably learned coinings of the modern period.

18. Smirnov, *Materialy*, p. 124.

19. Opie and Tatem, *Dictionary*, s.vv. *crow, raven.*

20. Dal', *Tolkovyi slovar'*, s.vv. *les, voron.*

21. Zabylin, *Russkii narod*, p. 262. The explanation that the crow as an eater of carrion can scent death is given in the Pinsk region of Belorussia: Bulgakovskii, 'Pinchuki', p. 189.

22. Dal', *Tolkovyi slovar'*, s.vv. *filin, diatel.*

23. For similar beliefs in England see Opie and Tatem, *Dictionary*, s.vv. *owl; owl seen in daytime.*

24. Dal', *Tolkovyi slovar'*, s.v. *sova.*

25. Nikiforovskii, *Prostonarodnye primety i pover'ia*, p. 1. For classical and British beliefs see Opie and Tatem, *Dictionary*, s.v. *owl.*

26. Weyer noted the connection with Lilith: *De praestigiis daemonum*, p. 165.

27. Dal', *Tolkovyi slovar'*, s.v. *soroka.*

28. Opie and Tatem, *Dictionary*, s.v. *magpie.* Also Hazlitt, *Dictionary*, s.v.

29. Smirnov, 'Narodnye gadaniia', p. 50.

30. Dal', *Tolkovyi slovar'*, s.v. *kukushka.* The details of the empty stomach and the coins are also found in Scottish and English cuckoo beliefs: Opie and Tatem, *Dictionary*, s.v. *cuckoo.*

31. Zabylin, *Russkii narod*, p. 262.

32. Dal', *Tolkovyi slovar'*, s.v. *iaitse.* For similar British first egg beliefs see Opie and Tatem, *Dictionary*, s.v. *egg.*

33. Dal', *Tolkovyi slovar'*, s.v. *ogn'.*

34. Dal', *Tolkovyi slovar'*, s.v. *solovei.*

35. *Turgenev's Literary Reminiscences and Autobiographical Fragments*, transl. D. Magarshack, London, 1958, p. 237.

36. Dal', *Tolkovyi slovar'*, s.v. *lastitsa*; Zabylin, *Russkii narod*, pp. 268–9; Afanas'ev, *Narodnye russkie legendy*, Moscow, 1859, p. 13. For similar beliefs in England, including the detail of blood-tinged milk see Opie and Tatem, *Dictionary*, s.vv. *Swallow and Martin, harming nests of; Robin,/Wren/Martin/Swallow sacred.*

37. Zabylin, *Russkii narod*, p. 262. Afanas'ev, *Narodnye russkie legendy*, Moscow, 1859, p. 13.

38. *Slovar' XI–XVII vv.*, s.v. *veshchun.*

39. Dal', *Tolkovyi slovar'*, s.v. *chaika.*

40. Dal', *Tolkovyi slovar'*, s.v. *zhuravl'.*

41. Dal', *Tolkovyi slovar'*, s.v. *vorobei.*

42. Kondrat'eva, *Metamorfozy sobstvennogo imeni*, s.v. *Nikita-guseprolet.*

43. All these in Dal', *Tolkovyi slovar'*, s.v. *koshka.* For several identical beliefs in Great Britain and Ireland see Opie and Tatem, *Dictionary*, s.v. *cat.*

44. Dal', *Tolkovyi slovar'*, s.v. *kot.* For the same belief in Britain see Opie and Tatem, *Dictionary*, s.v. *cat.*

45. Dal', *Tolkovyi slovar'*, s.vv. *korova, gadunitsa, vèdat'.*

46. All from Dal', *Tolkovyi slovar'*, s.v. *korova.*

47. Dal', *Tolkovyi slovar'*, s.v. *sobaka.* For comparable English beliefs in the howling of dogs as an evil omen see Opie and Tatem, *Dictionary*, s.v. *dog howling.*

48. For articles on witches as hares in Ireland and Scandinavia see *Folklore*, 104, 1–2, 1993. See also Opie and Tatem, *Dictionary*, s.v. *hare = witch.*

49. Dal', *Tolkovyi slovar'*, s.v. *les*; Zinov'eva, *Ukazatel'*, motif no. AI 38.

50. Dal', *Tolkovyi slovar'*, s.v. *zaiats.* For the identical belief in Britain see Opie and Tatem, *Dictionary*, s.v. *hare portend fire.*

51. Dal', *Tolkovyi slovar'*, loc. cit.

52. For Macedonia see Abbot, *Macedonian Folklore*, p. 106; for Britain and Ireland see Opie and Tatem, *Dictionary*, s.v. *hare or rabbit, meeting*.

53. Min'ko, *Sueveriia*, p. 38.

54. Dal', *Tolkovyi slovar'*, s.v. *loshad'*.

55. All these in Dal', *Tolkovyi slovar'*, s.v. *mysh'*. Cf. an English belief that a dead mouse will cure toothache: Opie and Tatem, *Dictionary*, s.v. *mouse, other cures using*.

56. Dal', *Tolkovyi slovar'*, s.vv. *repa, skovyvat'*.

57. Dal', *Tolkovyi slovar'*, s.v. *svin'ia*. Nikiforovskii, *Prostonarodnye primety i pover'ia*, p. 120, says it means *bad* luck.

58. Beliefs about ominous crickets are as least as old as Pliny. Svetlana in Zhukovskii's poem of the same name believed in them. For the same belief about the cricket in Britain see Opie and Tatem, *Dictionary*, s.v. *cricket*.

59. Dal', *Tolkovyi slovar'*, s.vv. *sverchok, mukha, muravei, tarakan*.

60. Quoted in Cross, *Anglo-Russica*, p. 161.

61. Dal', *Tolkovyi slovar'*, s.v. *vosh'*.

62. Dal', *Tolkovyi slovar'*, s.v. *volk*.

63. Dal', *Tolkovyi slovar'*, s.v. *ersh*.

64. Dal', *Tolkovyi slovar'*, s.v. *list*.

65. Dal', *Tolkovyi slovar'*, s.v. *bereza*.

66. Dal', *Tolkovyi slovar'*, s.v. *lepen'*.

67. Dal', *Tolkovyi slovar'*, s.v. *kasha*.

68. Kondrat'eva, *Metamorfozy sobstvennogo imeni*, s.v. *Varvara*.

69. Dal', *Tolkovyi slovar'*, s.v. *kutiia*. For similar shadow omens in Britain see Opie and Tatem, *Dictionary*, s.v. *shadow*.

70. Dal', *Tolkovyi slovar'*, s.v. *sol'*. For the same superstition in Britain see Opie and Tatem, *Dictionary*, s.v. *salt*.

71. For a selection see Dal', *Tolkovyi slovar'*, s.v. *dym*.

72. For a useful overview see Burnett, 'An Unknown Latin Version of an Ancient Parapēgma'.

73. Cherepanova, *Mifologocheskaia leksika*, pp. 38–40, sees in this the survival of a system of ancient Slav protective deities – but the fact that the saints' days are not Russian in origin and the rhyming mnemonics are opportunistic must mean that any such survival is minimal. Moreover, the association of saints and saints' days with particular activities or weather phenomena is common in western Europe also.

74. Goncharov, *Oblomov*, pt.1, ch. 9.

75. Kondrat'eva, *Metamorfoza sobstvennogo imeni*, s.v. *Vasil'-vecher*.

76. Dal', *Slovar'*, s.v. *komar*.

77. Kondrat'eva, *Metamorfozy*, s.v.

78. Dal', *Tolkovyi slovar'*, s.v. *led*.

79. Chulkov, *Abevega*, p. 189.

80. Dal', *Tolkovyi slovar'*, s.v. *kutiia*.

81. Tolstoi, 'Narodnaia ètimologiia'.

82. See Cherepanova, *Mifologicheskaia leksika russkogo severa*, p. 72, and Kondrat'eva, *Metamorfoza*, s.vv.

83. Bolonev, *Narodnyi kalendar'*, p. 69.

84. V. Dal', *Poslovitsy russkogo naroda*, 3rd edn, IV, St Petersburg–Moscow, 1904.

85. Ermolov, *Narodnaia sel'skokhoziaistvennaia mudrost'*. See also Zabylin, *Russkii narod*, pp. 282–7. A recent popular book in this field is Khrenov, *Narodnye primety i kalendar'*.

86. Makarenko, *Sibirskii narodnyi kalendar'*. For a more recent account of the calendar in the Pinega region of north Russia see Simina, 'Narodnye primety i pover'ia Pinezh'ia'.

87. Dal', *Tolkovyi slovar'*, s.v. *razhdat'*.

88. Dal', *Tolkovyi slovar'*, s.v. *sviatoi*.

89. Dal', *Tolkovyi slovar'*, s.v. *sviatoi*.

90. Dal', *Poslovitsy russkogo naroda* (1994 reprint), p. 546.

91. Iudin, *Dni velichal'nye*, p. 10.

92. Ermolov, *Narodnaia sel'skokhoziaistvennaia mudrost'*, I, p. 27–30.

93. Dal', *Tolkovyi slovar'*, s.v. *vasilek*.

94. Dal', *Tolkovyi slovar'*, s.v. *krest*, *bogoblagodatnyi* (*Bogoiavlenie*); Ermolov, 'Narodnaia sel'skokhoziaistvennaia mudrost', I, pp. 32–3; Kondrat'eva, *Metamorfozy sobstvennogo imeni*, s.v. *iordan'*.

95. An obscure belief perhaps connected with the fact that in the account of the Annunciation in the popular apocryphal *Protoevangelium of James* the Virgin was spinning when Gabriel approached her.

96. Dal', *Tolkovyi slovar'*, s.v. *blagovelichie*.

97. Dal', *Tolkovyi slovar'*, s.v. *priast'*.

98. Kondrat'eva, *Metamorfozy sobstvennogo imeni*, s.v. *Gavriil-blagovestnik*.

99. Dal', *Tolkovyi slovar'*, s.v. *Iurii-teplyi*.

100. Ermolov, *Narodnaia sel'skokhoziaistvennaia mudrost'*, I, p. 344–9.

101. Dal', *Tolkovyi slovar'*, s.v. *Petrov-den'*.

102. Dal', *Tolkovyi slovar'*, s.v. *Il'in-den'*.

103. Kondrat'eva, *Metamorfozy sobstvennogo imeni*, s.v.

104. Dal', *Tolkovyi slovar'*, s.v. *Andreia-nalivi*. Kondrat'eva, *Metamorfozy*, attributes this divination to another feast of St Andrew, 4 July.

105. Kondrat'eva, *Metamorfozy sobstvennogo imeni*, s.v. *Andrei*; Brand, *Observations on Popular Antiquities*, p. 224.

106. Kondrat'eva, *Metamorfozy sobstvennogo imeni*, s.v. *Spiridon*.

107. See Thomson, *The Reports of the Magicians*, II, pp. xxxiii–lxv.

108. See Lydus, *Liber de ostentis*, ed. C. Wachsmuth, Leipzig, 1887.

109. Olaus Magnus, *Description of the Northern Peoples*, bk. 1. ch. 14.

110. Dal', *Tolkovyi slovar'*, s.vv. *rog*, *veter*. For almost identical beliefs in Britain see Brand, *Observations on Popular Antiquities*, p. 659.

11. See for example Simina, 'Narodnye primety i pover'ia Pinezh'ia', p. 104.

112. Dal', *Tolkovyi slovar'*, s.vv. *kol'tso*, *luna*. Ermolov, *Narodnaia sel'skokhoziaistvennaia mudrost'*, IV, p. 233, gives a number of sun halo predictions.

113. Tikhonravov, *Pamiatniki*, II, p. 397. A similar text with differently arranged predictions is given on p. 396.

114. Dal', *Tolkovyi slovar'*, s.v. *rog*.

115. Dal', *Tolkovyi slovar'*, s.v. *novyi*.

116. Dal', *Tolkovyi slovar'*, s.vv. *pasolntse*, *ukho*.

117. Dal', *Tolkovyi slovar'*, s.v. *razhdati*.

118. Dal', *Tolkovyi slovar'*, s.v. *petrov-den'*; Zabylin, *Russkii narod*, pp. 85–6. For similar English beliefs see Hazlitt, *Dictionary*, s.v. *sun, dancing of the, on Easter Day*.

119. For some discussion and reproductions see Podobedova, *Miniatiury*, pp. 206–14.

120. Dal', *Tolkovyi slovar'*, s.v. *radost'* (*raduga*).

121. Dal', *Tolkovyi slovar'*, s.v. *vasilek*.

122. Simina, 'Narodnye primety i pover'ia Pinezh'ia', p. 101.

123. Chulkov, *Abevega*, pp. 202, 225; see also Zabylin, *Russkii narod*, p. 266.

124. Dal', *Tolkovyi slovar'*, s.v. *zvězda*.

125. Dal', *Tolkovyi slovar'*, s.v. *zvězda*.

126. Dal', *Tolkovyi slovar'*, s.v. *Perun* notes that this god survives in folk belief more in Belorussia than in Great Russia. He is believed to drive across the sky in a chariot shooting bolts of lightning from a bow.

127. Dal', *Tolkovyi slovar'*, s.v. *gromit'*. Dal' notes surprisingly little under thunder and lightning.

128. See Moszyński, *Kultura ludowa słowian*, pp. 403–4.

129. Dal', *Tolkovyi slovar'*, s.vv. *Anis'i-Zheludochnitsy; sviatoi; pech'*. See also Smirnov, *Narodnye gadaniia*, p. 31, for this practice in the Kostroma region.

130. Sumtsov, 'K ob"iasneniiu malorusskikh gadanii'.

131. See Lawson, *Modern Greek Folklore*, p. 325.

132. The best anthropological account is Eisenberger, 'Die Wahrsagen aus dem Schulterblatt'.

133. For this and a good deal more information on scapulimancy see Burnett, 'Arabic Divinatory Texts and Celtic Folklore', pp. 31–42, and *idem*, 'Divination from Sheep's Shoulder Blades', pp. 29–45. See also Opie and Tatem, *Dictionary*, s.v. *blade-bone*.

134. Edited by R. Hercher, in *Philologus*, VIII, 1853, pp. 165–8. Another version is given by N. Polites in *Parthénon*, 1872, pp. 1093 ff., see also Krumbacher, *Geschichte der Byzantinische Litteratur*, p. 442.

135. For a description of Greek scapulimancy at the beginning of this century see Abbott, *Macedonian Folklore*, pp. 96–8; Lawson, *Modern Greek Folklore*, p. 324; for reference to contemporary scapulimancy as a male occupation see Hart, *Time, Religion*, p.164; for the South Slavs see Kemp, *Healing Ritual*, p. 129.

136. Moszyński, *Kultura ludowa słowian*, p. 407.

137. Fitzroy Maclean, *To the Back of Beyond*, pp. 121–4, quoted in Burnett, 'Divination'.

138. MS Vilnius, Public Library 222–272 (now in the Library of the Lithuanian Academy of Sciences), ff. 81v–83v.

139. Dobrianskii, *Opisanie rukopisei*. The full contents of the manuscript are listed only in Lastoŭski, *Hystoriia belaruskaǐ (kryǔskaǐ) knig.*

140. Speranskii, *Iz istorii otrechennykh knig. III. Lopatochnik*.

141. Sobolevskii, *Perevodnaia literatura*, pp. 423–4.

142. Iatsimirskii, *Bibliograficheskii obzor apokrifov*, I, p. 69.

143. Delatte, *Anecdota atheniensia*, pp. 206–9. MS Paris, BN 1493, ff. 155v–159.

144. Burnett, 'Divination from Sheep's Shoulder Blades'.

145. The main anthologies of such 'false' books, often lumped together indiscriminately in the Russian literature as 'apocrypha', are: Pypin, *Lozhnye i otrechennye knigi*; Tikhonravov, *Pamiatniki otrechennoi literatury*, and Porfir'ev, *Apokrificheskie skazaniia o vetkhozavetnykh litsakh* and *idem*, *Apokrificheskie skazaniia o novozavetnykh litsakh i sobytiiakh*; Franko, *Apokrifi i legendy*. Tikhonravov in the introduction to

his book gives a list of all the titles or descriptions of works which have ever been on such an 'index' – in all, one hundred. A bibliographical guide to many of the individual works can be found in de Santos Otero, *Die handschriftliche Überlieferung*. The subject of the lists of false books was analysed most completely by Iatsimirskii, *Bibliograficheskii obzor* (only volume 1 appeared) but even this was a very preliminary survey. Some corrections to Iatsimirskii as well as useful new material has recently been presented by Kobiak: Kobiak, 'Indeksy otrechennykh i zapreshchennykh knig' and *idem*, 'Indeks lozhnykh knig i drevnerusskii chitatel''. In the 1984 article Kobiak states that in Moscow and Leningrad libraries there are some one hundred and seventy specimens of lists of banned books with the bulk coming from the sixteenth and seventeenth centuries (although this is not necessarily significant statistically since most manuscripts in Russia date from this period anyway). The majority of these are in general manuscript miscellanies, with a second large group in canon law codices.

146. See Kobiak's articles in the preceding note.

147. This is numbered 89 in Tikhonravov's composite list (Tikhonravov, *Pamiatniki*, pp. viii–ix) and 101–109 in Iatsimirskii's (Iatsimirskii, *Bibliograficheskii obzor*, pp. 68–9) – see note 1 above.

148. Kobiak, 'Indeksy otrechennykh i zapreshchennykh knig', p. 18, notes that out of sixteen manuscripts examined in Moscow and Leningrad collections, some thirty-two manuscripts of the fifteenth to seventeenth centuries mention the *Volkhovnik*.

149. var. 'jumps into the window'.

150. var. 'a blind man shoots'.

151. var. 'grief'.

152. I have translated all verbs as being in the present tense; in fact many of them are perfective verbs, which in Modern Russian would give a future sense, and are used in the sense of an if-clause.

153. Pypin, 'Dlia istorii lozhnikh knig', pp. 15–27.

154. Speranskii, *Iz istorii otrechennoi literatury. II*, pp. 4–6, 42.

155. Burnett, 'A Note on Two Astrological Fortune-Telling Tables'.

156. To judge from Greek, West European, and later Russian dream books – there seem to be no extant versions in Russian before the eighteenth century, although translations of Polish dream books are found in Sub-Carpathian Ruthenia in the seventeenth century.

157. For example, most of the omens can be found individually in British and American beliefs: see Opie and Tatem, *Dictionary* and Thomas and Thomas, *Kentucky Superstitions*.

158. Dal', *Tolkovyi slovar'*, s.v. *voron*.

159. Ibid., s.v. *mysh'*. Also Sakharov, *Skazaniia*, p. 40. This is an ancient belief mentioned by St Augustine and well known in Britain: see Opie and Tatem, *Dictionary*, s.v. *rats and mice gnawing*. John of Salisbury mentions it as a Spanish belief: John of Salisbury, *Policraticus*, bk. 1, p. 45. It is quoted in English popular fortune-telling books; my copy of *The Popular Fortune Teller . . . by Sibly the Great Astrologer* (London, n.d. but twentieth century) says: 'In the beginning of any work, if rats have been gnawing at your clothes, then desist from your undertakings'. An American example from Kentucky is quoted in Thomas and Thomas, *Kentucky Superstitions*, no. 3977.

160. Dal', *Tolkovyi slovar'*, s.v. *svět*. This is one of the omens mentioned in Goncharov's *Oblomov*. In America this omen means death: see Thomas and Thomas, *Kentucky Superstitions*, no. 1743.

161. Nikiforovskii, *Prostonarodnye primety i pover'ia*, nos 1026 (falling coal means death of a guest) and 1032 (creaking means serious illness); Chikachev, *Russkie na Indigirke*, p. 136 (falling coal means a guest – recorded in 1973).

162. See Vostokov, *Opisanie russkikh i slovenskikh rukopisei*, pp. 549–52: no. 374, *sbornik* 1754.

163. Speranskii, *Trepetnik*, pp. 84–93.

164. I quote the English version: Harkins, *St John Chrysostom: Baptismal Instructions*, pp. 39, 168, 189–91.

165. Harkins, *St John Chrysostom: Baptismal Instructions*, p. 337.

6

PREDICTIONS FROM DREAMS AND THE HUMAN BODY

1. *Dreams and Dream Books*

The interpretation of dreams is probably one of the oldest and most widespread forms of divination. We do not know what form dream divination might have taken among the Slavs before they became Christian, but certainly the introduction of Christianity brought with it both scriptural, iconic,[1] and literary examples of prophetic dreams and their interpretation and, occasionally, ecclesiastical condemnation of them.[2] The Russian indexes of banned books from the earliest times contain references to dream books such as the *Snosudets* (a calque of the Greek *Oneirocriticon*, the name of Greek dream books); sometimes this is called *Tsarevi snosudtsy* or 'Dream interpreters of kings', and sometimes it is attributed to Daniel, presumably because of the statement in the Book of Daniel, 18, that 'Daniel had understanding in all visions and dreams' and the prominence of dream predictions in that book.[3] Dreambooks are also called *Snovidets* (lit. 'dream-seer, dreamer'), or *Sonnik*,[4] and more modern versions *Snotolkovatel'* or *Snotolkovnik* (both lit. 'dream interpreter').[5] These texts are not extant.

One may find in the literature available to the Orthodox Slavs, be it biblical, hagiographic or secular, as well as in folk tales and *byliny*, any number of accounts of dream portents, allegorical dreams and divine warnings or instructions communicated in dreams.[6] Indeed, the biblical mode of dream interpretation may be specifically reinforced in folklore: in one verse collected in the Olonets region of north-west Russia King David is made to interpret the dream of 'Tsar Antoloman'.[7] Further antique authority came from Josephus, who was a respected witness in Orthodox Slavonic literature at least from the twelfth century and certainly reported prophetic dreams and regarded himself as an interpreter of them.[8] The prophetic dream is used to good effect in the propagandistic *Kazanskaia istoriia* (1560s), which was written to celebrate the capture of the Tatar capital of Kazan' in 1552. In this the khan's dreams are interpreted by his wizards and foretell the triumph of the Russian Christians.[9] In more recent times the prime example of a 'biblical' dream is the apocryphal *Dream of the Virgin*, the commonest amuletic text in Russia and the Balkans from the seventeenth century to the present day (for details see Chapter 10.5).

On the other hand one finds relatively little in Old Russia literature, apart from the indexes of banned books and some penitentials, which condemns belief in dreams.[10] V. N. Peretts, discussing Sviatoslav's dream in the *Tale of Prince Igor's*

Campaign, notes that in Old Russian literature only the *Ladder* of John Climacus and an ambivalent passage from St Antiochus in the *Prolog* (*Synaxarion*) actually warned the Orthodox faithful against believing in dreams.[11] Iavorskii, however, has pointed out that a further important condemnation of belief in dreams occurs in Ecclesiasticus (The Wisdom of Jesus, son of Sirach). 34, 1–7,[12] to which he might have added the condemnations of Jeremiah 25–32 and Zechariah 10, 2, not to mention Deuteronomy 18: 9–12 where the Chosen People are warned against the abominations of other nations, including wizards, fortune-tellers, soothsayers, omens and dreams, all of which the Lord abhorreth.

Beside the various biblical and other references to dream portents, both for and against, there is one major text which clearly promotes the belief in the interpretation of prophetic dreams. This is the *Dreams of Shakhaishi* (or *Dreams of Mamer*), a translated eschatological work of Iranian origin which may have arrived in Russia by way of the Balkans perhaps as early as the twelfth or thirteenth century. Its textual history is still rather obscure but it had a resurgence of popularity in Old Believer communities in the eighteenth and nineteenth centuries, probably because of its gloomy prognostications.[13]

Despite this apparent interest in dreams and condemnation of dream books, and notwithstanding the widespread belief in dream interpretation from the eighteenth century to the present day, there seems to be not a single Old Russian text of a *Sonnik* before the late seventeenth century, the first being an alphabetical *sonnik* translated from Polish.[14] Further Polish influence is probably to be seen in a seventeenth-century Carpatho-Ruthenian manuscript, the 'Rakoshinskii sbornik', which contains several apocryphal texts including the Twelve Fridays text and a *Sonnik* ascribed to Daniel which contains 128 dreams in Polish alphabetical order.[15] Although it is likely that this is in fact of Polish origin, we may note the existence of an alphabetically arranged Byzantine dream book ascribed to Daniel and dedicated to Nebuchadnezzar.[16] Iavorskii has also published a seventeenth-century Carpathian text which distinguishes six types of dream according to Gregory Dialogus (Pope Gregory I): 1. Dreams caused by over-eating and drunkenness; 2. Dreams caused by fasting; 3. Dreams caused by transient thoughts and grief; 4. Dreams caused by the Devil and by human thought; 5. Dreams revealed by God; 6. Dreams deriving from human thought and divine revelation. It lists as good dreams those of Joseph, the Pharaoh, Nebuchadnezzar, Mordecai, Daniel, Judas Maccabaeus, Joseph spouse of the Virgin, the three Magi, Pilate's wife and St Paul.[17] I am not aware of any other East Slavonic text which offers any kind of theoretical analysis of dreams.

Popular dream interpretation in this area follows another ancient practice, that of reading dreams by 'opposites', or, as an old English proverb has it 'Dreams prove contrary':[18] thus in Russia a priest in a dream means the Devil, a Jew means a saint (an 'opposition' which says much about local prejudices).[19]

The fact that, notwithstanding the condemnations of dream books in lists of banned books mentioned above, there are no actual Russian dream books extant before the seventeenth century, does not mean that dreams did not feature in divinatory literature. In a lunar divination text deriving from classical antiquity found in several Russian versions from at least as early as the sixteenth century, the prediction for each of the days of the lunar month includes an indication of whether your dream will come true, and when (see Chapter 14.5.2). It does not, however, offer interpretations of specific dreams.

The early eighteenth century has no printed dream books, but manuscript dream books continue from the seventeenth century. The statesman of Peter the Great's time Prince D.M. Golitsyn possessed a very varied library which included a dream book, a fortune-telling book called *Fortuna*, a work of Albertus Magnus (probably pseudo-Albertus *De secretis mulierum*), a cosmography by Vincenzo Coronelli, the *Selenographia* of Hevelius, and a translation of an unspecified work by Ramon Lull.[20] Peter the Great himself, as well as his wife Catherine who became Empress after his death, recorded their dreams over several years, but it is not known whether they attached any revelatory significance to them.[21]

A new tradition of dream books begins in the later eighteenth century, when considerable quantities of them appear. This was part of the influx of Western popular fortune-telling books which is so noticeable in this period.[22] In the reign of Catherine the Great (1762–96) dream interpretation was made a criminal offence, together with various kinds of magical practices and witchcraft.[23] This seems to have had little effect – apart from a few fortune-telling books published at the very end of the century in the reign of Paul 1, all the fortune-telling books, including dream books, which appeared in eighteenth-century Russia were in fact published in the reign of Catherine, by printing houses with official or semi-official status.[24] This is no doubt, at least in part, a result of the great increase in this period of translated literature in general, the larger reading public, in particular for popular literature, and the popularity of all kinds of almanacs, calendars and journals.[25] This literate public had to be primarily the gentry and merchant class, and to judge from references in literary works of the early nineteenth century comprised both women and men.

Besides dream prognostications appearing in some of the more general fortune-telling books, at least eleven editions of actual dream books were published in Russia in the later eighteenth century: a 'lunar interpretation of dreams' translated from Polish and printed in the Moscow University printing house, published in 1768, 1772, and 1788;[26] an alphabetically arranged astrological dream book translated from 'various languages' published in St Petersburg in 1784 and Kaluga in 1787;[27] a dream book printed in St Petersburg in 1799 by the St Petersburg provincial (*guberniia*) administration's printing house;[28] an astrological dream book in verse called 'A Pastime at Morning Tea' printed in 1791 at the Moscow University printing house;[29] a dream book called *The Gipsy; who Interprets Dreams* . . . the 'work of an unknown author' published in Moscow in 1789;[30] a dream book, including a physiognomy and forty-five historical dreams and their outcome explained by a hundred-year-old Greek, published in St Petersburg in 1791.[31]

Perhaps most interesting is a book of predictions of Martin Zadek (or Zadeka).

This is not a fact a dream book. It is a curious work which claims to be translation from a German-language book of predictions published in 1770 in Basle,[32] with the name of the supposed author taken from Voltaire's *Zadig*, according to one hypothesis.[33] The first Russian edition appeared in 1770 (it was printed at the printing house of the Infantry Cadet Corps and tells us that Zadek lived near Solothurn and vouchsafed his secrets to his friends on his deathbed in 1769), with later editions in 1785 and 1798.[34] It retained its fascination and continued to be printed right up to the 1917 Revolution – Sytin, the great purveyor of chapbooks in Russia, produced no fewer than eight editions between 1900 and 1915.

Zadek's book of prognostications was to leave more of a mark on Russian literature that its rivals, if only in the same way that 'Erra Pater' was immortalized in *Hudibras*. It is referred to in Pushkin's *Eugene Onegin* (ch. 5, 25) as one of the many forms of popular divination known to the young heroine Tatiana. Here Martin Zadek is referred to as:

> Chief of the Chaldean wizards,
> diviner and interpreter of dreams.

Either Pushkin was employing a little poetic licence here or he had access only to the 1821 Moscow edition, the title of which omits the reference to Solothurn and the death of Zadek in 1769. In translation it reads: *The ancient and new perpetual divinatory oracle, found after the death of a certain hundred-and-six-year-old man Martin Zadek, by means of which he learned the fate of every man through the circles of good and ill fortune; together with the Magic Mirror or interpretations of dreams, also the rules of physiognomy and chiromancy or the sciences of knowing the character and fortune of men and women from their physical constitution and the arrangement and lines of their hands; with the addition of Zadek's predictions of the most curious happenings in Europe, confirmed by eventualities together with Hocus Pocus and humourous riddles with their answers.*[35]

Pushkin was not the only author to refer to Zadek. In 1913 Evgenii Zamiatin published his first successful tale, *Uezdnoe (A Provincial Tale)*.[36] In this a provincial merchant's widow and her ne'er-do-well young lover would sit relaxing after a meal and conduct a conversation suitable for the digestion: 'about dreams, about the dream book, about Martin Zadek, about signs and spells and portents'. Zamiatin, though best known in the West for his futuristic dystopia *We*, in fact wrote a great deal in that Russian tradition which derives much of its material from folk life and oral literature. Zamiatin would, of course, have remembered Pushkin's use of Zadek but in all probability was also quite familiar with the Zadek text in one of Sytin's editions. Indeed, in an interesting twist of intertextuality, it seems likely that he knew Zadek better: at least he appears to distinguish the Zadek prognostications from dream books.

The compilers of books of magic and divination have always been eclectic in their sources and cavalier in their attributions. Martin Zadek in his turn was pillaged, with or without acknowledgment. A fine example is the *Magazin vsekh uveselenii*, printed in the Moscow University printing house in 1836. Its full title in translation is: 'The shop of all pastimes, or a full and most detailed oracle and book of magic of the famous astronomers and sages: Ptolemy, Tycho Brahe, Bruce,[37] Albert,[38] Joseph Moult, Martin Zadeka, Zoroaster'.

The tradition of dream books in Russia is no more dead than it is in English. A curious Russian fortune-telling book including dream predictions was published in Washington in 1977[39] and since 1989, in the climate of first *glasnost'* and entrepreneurial *perestroika*, then the restoration of the market economy, it has been possible to buy on the streets of Moscow crudely duplicated sheets of dream predictions. These publications are remarkable for their inclusion of modern realia such as motor cars, and as has been remarked in an English newspaper, an evident lack of exposure to popular Freudianism.[40] At the same there has been a vogue for reprinting old fortune-telling books such as the 1989 reprint of a dream-book of 1896 entitled *Odin million 500,000 snov* ('One and a Half Million Dreams') and allegedly drawn from the works of 'famous Indian and Egyptian sages and astronomers', Apollonius, Albumasar, Soncius, Tycho Brahe, Plato, Ptolemy, the 'famous French dream interpreter Mme Lenorman'[41] and, once again, the persistent Martin Zadek.

Dream lore is not, of course, restricted to the interpretation of dreams from dream books. Both dream books and other forms of divination involving dreams were a common part of the Christmas and New Year holiday pastimes, when a clue to the fortunes of the coming year was sought, in varying degrees of jest and earnest.[42] A good many popular magical practices, in particular for discovering one's future marriage partner, have as their final stage the placing of some magical object (key, mirror, etc.) or article belonging to the object of desire (e.g. underwear) under the pillow in order to induce a dream prognostication. These, and the same method applied to the prediction of the sex of an unborn child, are described in Chapter 4.5.4. and 4.6.3. A similar practice is that of Karelian Russians who put a handful of earth from under their new house into a cloth and place this under their pillow so that they shall see in a dream how successful life in the new house will be.[43]

Popular dream predictions may also be handed down in the oral tradition by means of proverbs, rather like the weather predictions of the Russian folk calendar. This usually follows the formula 'if A, then B', which are rhythmically distinctive, normally having two ictuses to each half, sometimes with the two halves roughly rhyming or in assonance like the English 'Rain before seven, gone before eleven'. A recent book on popular superstitions in Belorussia includes a list of dream interpretations such as: sheep = guests; lice = money; dirt = gossip, misfortune; a frog = bad weather; a black horse = something bad; a red-haired person = something good; cutting off a plait = shame; pulling out a tooth = a relative will die; drinking milk = illness; praying = a serious matter; falling down = great misfortune; crying = rejoicing; a pig = meeting an enemy; having a dream within your dream = the worst misfortune, going mad.[44] An equally recent list from northern Siberia (Indigirka) has: dog = visit of a friend; lice =

money; eating meat = unpleasantnesses; blood = meeting relations; a gunshot = news; white string = a pleasant journey; black string = an unpleasant journey.[45]

Dreams may also have a medical application; one *zagovor* by Maikov (no. 252, from the Simbirsk region) is intended to induce a revelatory dream in which you will discover what medicine to take to effect a cure. It runs:

> I, [name], will lie down on the hills of Sion in the holy church. I shall place three angels at the bedhead, one to look, one to listen, one to tell. Let me know, merciful Nikola, what medicine is needed. For ever and ever, Amen.

The three angels are a commonplace of the genre.

The interpretation of dreams also occurs in folk literature, as two differing examples will demonstrate. In the Vologda region the pre-wedding ritual includes a bride-song in which the bride tells a dream, to which the girls in the bride's party respond with another song.[46] Popular belief in dreams and omens such as sneezes and bird calls is further attested in a *bylina* of Novgorodian origin in which the hero scorns such practices and declares that he will rely instead on his cudgel. This is evidently a *topos* and is found elsewhere as a popular saying.[47]

2. *Physiognomy*

Physiognomy is a subject which in the ancient and medieval worlds inhabited a grey area between natural philosophy and divination. It is certainly true that, medically speaking, conditions can be deduced from physical appearances; and semeioticians can demonstrate the systematic nature of body language. Less scientifically, people all the time make conscious or unconscious character assessments based largely on external appearances. It is when appearances are associated with the Evil Eye that magic comes in, and when appearances are linked systematically to an ineluctable destiny one is entering the realm of divination.

The earliest physiognomy text is the *Physiognomonica*, long thought to be by Aristotle but eventually expelled from the corpus of his writings. This gave rise to a series of physiognomic texts in Arabic in the eight–ninth centuries and in the medieval Latin West. The scientific aspects of the subject finished up in areas such as anthropometry, and the mildly divinatory aspect ensured that physiognomy kept a place in popular chapbook compendia of 'wisdom of the ancients' such as the *Grand Albert* and *Aristotle's Masterpiece*. It still survives in the flourishing trade of fortune-telling books.

The literature of Kievan Russia is ignorant of physiognomy, apart from some elements in the florilegia of Ioann the Exarch of Bulgaria, which were known in Russia.[48]

The arrival of full treatises on the subject comes in the fifteenth–sixteenth centuries with the translation in the Grand Duchy of Lithuania of the Hebrew version of the pseudo-Aristotelian *Secretum secretorum* (for full details see Chapter 1.5) and its subsequent dissemination in Muscovy. The Hebrew version used by the translator was special in that it had interpolated within it most of the medical works of Maimonides, and the physiognomy of Rhazes, of which a Hebrew version had been made by Shem Tov ben Isaak. The Rhazes text immediately follows the physiognomical text of the *Secretum* proper, so that the reader had before him almost the whole of Arabic teaching on the subject.[49]

In fact these two physiognomical texts are not magical or divinatory in a direct sense, apart perhaps from warnings to avoid dwarfs and men with blue eyes, which smack rather of popular superstition. They are rather medical treatises designed to enable the ostensible recipient of the text, Alexander and Mansur respectively, to make intelligent judgements in their choice of the men who served them, and in diplomacy. Nevertheless, at the level of learned magic they were an important innovation in Russia; they occur immediately after the onomantic section of the *Secretum*, and taken together with the astrological and alchemical sections they represented a deterministic view of life quite at odds with the Church's teaching on divine omnipotence and individual free will. They are, moreover, part of a new notion of esoteric wisdom recorded in secret books for the eyes of the elect only. Ivan the Terrible, who has been shown elsewhere to have had occult interests, is apparently quoting the physiognomy in the *Secretum* when he warns against trusting men with blue eyes.[50]

Like the Maimonidean interpolations, the physiognomic sections of the Russian *Secretum* can be found separated from their parent text.[51] These ostensibly 'Aristotelian' texts were joined in the seventeenth century by a translation of Michael Scot's *Liber phisionomiae*,[52] and in the eighteenth several manuscript physiognomies of various origins, one with the title of *Personnik* published by the Arkheograficheskaia komissiia.[53] An extended physiognomical text of the first half of the eighteenth century, probably translated, has been found in a *tetradka*, or book of spells.[54] This serves to place physiognomy, at least in popular level perception at that time, clearly in the field of magic and divination. The physiognomy in *Le Grand Albert* (bk. 4) may well be the source of the physiognomical portions of the fortune-telling books discussed in the preceding section on dreams; but the source of the *Complete Physiognomist and Chiromancer*, which also includes some astrology and was published in Moscow in 1795, was presumably not the posthumous papers of 'a certain celebrated Indian sage' as is claimed on the title-page.[55]

3. *Palmistry*

This practice, known in Russia by its learned name of *khiromantiia* and more popularly by a calque of that word *rukogadanie*, does not seem to have been a widespread method of fortune-telling in Russia and it is rarely mentioned in the older literature. One historian of popular superstitions describes it as a bourgeois practice, imported in the seventeeth and eighteenth centuries, which was little known among the common people.[56] In 1630 a Tatar woman is recorded as having engaged in palmistry,[57] and in 1685 a peasant of Kostroma, Romashko

Averkiev, gave an undertaking not to leave the monastery territory, not to do fortune-telling with dice or to look at hands. He failed to keep his promise and in 1692 was tried for the same practices.[58] A painting by Jean-Baptiste Le Prince of 1774 entitled 'The Necromancer' shows an elderly wizard, complete with a globe and an alembic, apparently reading the palm of a young lady.[59] Le Prince was one of the first artists seriously to depict costumes and customs of the Russian Empire but the 'Russian' detail of this picture is so tenuous and unlikely (especially the alembic) that one must wonder whether Le Prince had ever actually seen a Russian wizard reading palms. In fact palmistry, like reading coffee cups, is popularly supposed to be a form of divination restricted to women, and in the case of palm-reading Gypsy and Tatar women are usually thought to be the real specialists. Gypsies in Russia still accost passers-by with offers to read palms if you will give them a 'silver' coin.

The earliest texts dealing with palmistry, as far as I am aware, date from the eighteenth century and are translations from Western books.[60] The first published chiromantic text appears to be the 1795 Moscow *Complete Physiognomist and Chiromancer* mentioned above in the section on physiognomy, followed by the 1821 oracles of Martin Zadek, discussed above in the section on dreams.

4. *Urinoscopy*

This too was not much known in Russia. Probably the first text is in the group of *Hortus* texts deriving from the translation in 1534 by Nicolaus Bülow, e.g. the *Blagoprokhladnyi tsvetnik ili travnik* written in 1616, which also contains articles on the zodiac and propitious days for bloodletting.[61] One seventeenth-century medical miscellany of astrological medicine by season contains an *Epistle to the Egyptian Tsar Ptolemy* which includes a magical urinoscopy: a man sitting in the clouds means the illness will continue but not be fatal, if near the bottom he will soon recover, if in a lying position near the top or bottom, beware that day.[62]

5. *Sneezing and Yawning*

The interpretation of sneezing as a form of divination is ancient,[63] and is referred to in Russia at least as early as the twelfth century, in a sermon of Cyril of Turov,[64] and survives in modern Russian in the saying 'not believing in sneezing or dreams or bird calls', which means 'not to be superstitious'.[65] As in the West sneezing evokes a blessing from those nearby, and a few examples of sneeze interpretation survive: what is said at the time of a sneeze is true; a sneeze on a Monday means a profitable week,[66] the number of times you sneeze on your name day is the number of years you have left to live.[67] There is also a sequence of predictions for each day of the week: sneezing on an empty stomach on Monday means a gift, on a Tuesday – visitors, on a Wednesday – news, on a Thursday – praise, on a Friday – a meeting, on a Saturday – wishes will come true, on a Sunday – guests.[68] This would appear to be a form of divination of some antiquity since very similar English and American sneeze divination rhymes by days of the week also exist.[69]

To yawn at someone is the same as to put the Evil Eye on them; if you do not cross yourself when you yawn your mouth will go awry.[70]

6. *Twitches and Itches – the* Trepetnik

Divination from signs found on one's own body is common in Russia. A simple example is the belief that if you have a birthmark it is bad luck if you can see it and good if you cannot.[71] More elaborate is palmomancy, or divination from twitches and itches in various parts of the body, an ancient and apparently universal method of divination. At the level of Russian popular sayings and beliefs any number of examples of this lore can be found, some of which are familiar in other languages, including English.[72] A noise in the left ear means bad news, in the right ear good news; an itch in the left eye means you will cry, in the right means you will rejoice (for the more general significance of left and right see Chapter 2.7.5);[73] if your ears itch it means that there will be news, or rain, or that friends will have a child, and if they burn it means that someone is talking about you;[74] if your hands, feet, head, fingers or corns hurt it means bad weather;[75] if your head itches someone is abusing you;[76] an itch in the nose means a corpse;[77] if your feet burn you will go on a journey; if your right foot gets cold before the left it is a good sign.[78] Another omen connected with the feet is stumbling, which has been considered an ill omen since antiquity.[79] In Russia it is a less common superstition, but Dal' does record one example of a Russian belief that if you stumble on your way home there will be a quarrel when you get there.[80]

At the textual level palmomancy was studied by Speranskii,[81] and his research was placed in a wider context by Hermann Diels, who also provided German translations of European (including Slavonic) and oriental *Zuchungsbücher*.[82] A Byzantine version is given in Delatte.[83] It should be said that Speranskii, in his study of the *Trepetnik*,[84] claims that Dal' in fact obtained some of his prognostications (many of which are quoted above) not from live informants as he had stated, but from manuscript lists which he thought to be of popular origin, being unaware of the earlier Greek and West European texts from which they were derived.[85] Dal' can perhaps be forgiven for assuming a popular rather than literary origin for palmomantic omens: if the novelist Ivan Goncharov is to be trusted, the Russian provincial population, gentry and peasantry, male and female, of the nineteenth century believed implicitly in omens of this kind, even if they did not necessarily agree on their meaning – the hero of Goncharov's most famous novel *Oblomov* spent his childhood in family surroundings largely dominated by such superstitions.[86]

Notes

1 For the subject of dreams in Orthodox iconography see Dagron, 'Sviashchennye obrazy', pp. 31–4.

2. For some discussion of the ambivalent attitudes of early medieval writers in the West see Bitel, '*In Visu Noctis*'.

3. For a general survey of medieval dream theory and literature see Kruger, *Dreaming in the Middle Ages*. For discussion of late antique and early and patristic Christian attitudes to dreams see Miller, *Dreams in Late Antiquity*. With regard to Daniel it is to be noted that the best known Western dream book is called the *Somniale Danielis*.

4. See Iatsimirskii, *Bibliograficheskii obzor apokrifov*, pp. 66–7; Sreznevskii, *Materialy*, s.v *s"novid'ts'*, *s"nosud'ts'*.

5. Dal', *Tolkovyi slovar'*, s.v. *snotvornyi*.

6. For a list of these see Peretts, *Slovo*, pp. 238–46.

7. Rybnikov, *Pesni*, 1991 edn, p. 335; see also the index to Rybnikov which lists a number of prophetic dreams in *byliny*, and for northern Russian legends involving prophetic dreams see Krinichnaia, *Predaniia russkogo severa*, nos 153, 156, 167, 169–73, 178, 267, 354, 381.

8. See *De bello judaico*, III, 352 in the Loeb edition. For a study of Josephus as a dream interpreter see Gnuse, *Dreams and Dream Reports*.

9. *Kazanskaia istoriia*, pp. 130–1.

10. For one such condemnation in a Russian penitential see Smirnov, *Materialy*, p. 47.

11. Peretts, *Slovo*, pp. 243–4; see also the text printed in *Pamiatniki starinnoi russkoi literatury*, IV, pp. 214–5, 'Slovo o snekh noshchnykh', quoted without further detail from MS Kir. Bibl. 22/1099. For a further discussion and survey of scholarly opinion of the prophetic dream of Sviatoslav in the *Slovo*, see the article by L.V. Sokolova in *Entsiklopediia «Slova o Polku Igoreve»*, V, pp. 30–9.

12. Iavorskii, 'Karpatorusskoe pouchenie o snakh'.

13. For bibliography see *Slovar' knizhnikov*, I, pp. 408–10 and Makhnovets', *Ukrains'ki pis'menniki*, pp. 860–3. For Balkan versions see Gaster, 'The Twelve Dreams of Sehachi'.

14. See Sobolevskii, *Perevodnaia literatura*, p. 226.

15. Iavorskii, *Novye rukopisnye nakhodki*, p. 97 (text at pp. 127–31).

16. It is published in translation in Lewis, *The Interpretation of Dreams and Portents*, pp. 87–9. (This is stated to have been taken from a sixteenth-century Berlin manuscript but is not further identified by the editor.)

17. Iavorskii, 'Karpatorusskoe pouchenie o snakh'.

18. Reginald Scot, *Discovery of Witchcraft* (1584), p.104.

19. Bogatyrev, p. 57. For examples of dream interpretation by contraries from Apuleius' *Golden Ass* to modern Britain see Opie and Tatem, *Dictionary*, s.v. *dreams*.

20. Gradov, *Kloss*, and Koretskii, 'K istorii arkhangel'skoi biblioteki D.M. Golitsyna', nos 19, 51, 88, 182, 222, 259. The Lull translation was probably one of the Old Believer texts referred to in Ch. 13.

21. For text and discussion see Semevskii, 'Petr velikii v ego snakh', and *idem, Slovo i delo*, pp. 271–6. For a good discussion in English which suggests how the dreams could have influenced Peter, but without engaging with the divinatory issue, see Cracraft, 'Some Dreams of Peter the Great'.

22. The *Svodnyi katalog* lists over fifty titles or editions of such works.

23. *Polnoe sobranie zakonov*, XX, no. 14392; XXI, no. 1539. See also Ardalion Popov, *Sud i nakazaniia*, p. 381.

24. The university press in Oxford was also gainfully employed in the production of almanacs in the seventeenth and eighteenth centuries. The tradition persists in Russia: I have a book of spells,

apparently intended for use rather than scholarly study, which was published by the Novosibirsk State Pedagogical Institute in 1992 under the title *Liubovnye, tselitel'nye i okhranit'nye zagovory.*

25. The whole subject of popular fortune-telling books, their publishers and the context of urban fortune-telling in the eighteenth and nineteenth centuries is examined in detail in Wigzell, *Reading Russian Fortunes.*

26. *Svodnyi katalog,* nos 2685–7.

27. *Svodnyi katalog,* nos 6700, 6701.

28. *Svodnyi katalog,* no. 6702.

29. *Svodnyi katalog,* no. 7626.

30. *Svodnyi katalog,* no. 8128.

31. *Svodnyi katalog, dop.,* no. 198.

32. *Wunderbäre und merkwürdige Profezeyung des berühmten Martin Zadecks . . .,* Basle, 1770

33. On the Zadek text see Ryan and Wigzell, 'Gullible Girls and Dreadful Dreams'; Wigzell, 'Dream Books and Lady Macbeth's Cat'; Iskrin, 'Kto takoi Martyn Zadeka?'; Rovinskii, *Russkie narodnye kartinki,* II, pp. 467–72 (this gives the text, and notes that some versions give a 'portrait' of Martin). A recent more literary interpretation of this chapter in *Eugene Onegin* which pays little attention to folklore and, surprisingly, none to Zadek, but finds parallels in *Childe Harold, Melmoth,* and *Faust,* is Erofeeva, 'Son Tat'iany'. See also Wigzell, *Reading Russian Fortunes,* pp. 17–30 on eighteenth- and nineteenth-century dream books in general, and Zadek in particular.

34. See *Svodnyi katalog,* nos 4092, 5677, 5678.

35. The 'Magic Mirror' mentioned here may well be connected with Lev Prokhorov, *The Magic Mirror, Disclosing the Secrets of the Great Albertus, and other Famous Egyptian Sages (!) and Astronomers … together with the Arabian Cabbala which Gives Answers and Foretells the Fate of Every Man,* Moscow, 1794 (*Svodnyi katalog,* no. 8840).

36. See the English translation in Yevgenii Zamyatin, *The Dragon, and other tales,* London, 1972, p. 13. This story of contemporary life, written in 1912, is also remarkable for a scene in which a monk commissions a death spell from a professional sorceress. The spell is given in full.

37. I.e. James Bruce, general, astronomer and scientific advisor to Peter the Great, supposititious author of the original version of the almanac known as *Briusov kalendar'* – see Ch. 15.

38. I.e. Albertus Magnus, the philosopher to whom later works of popular magic, divination, alchemy and medicine were often attributed.

39. *Sonnik, goroskop, gadanie,* Washington, 1977. Seen in the Slavonic Library, Helsinki.

40. See Wigzell, 'Russians who find comfort in their dreams', *The Independent,* 7 June, 1989.

41. The famous French clairvoyant and fortune-teller Mlle Marie-Anne Le Normand. For a good account see ch. 6 of Decker, Depulis and Dummett, *A Wicked Pack of Cards,* and for the Russian context Wigzell, *Reading Russian Fortunes.*

42. Zabylin, *Russkii narod,* p. 27.

43. *Ètnokul'turnye protsessy v Karelii,* p. 46.

44. Min'ko, *Sueveriia,* p. 167.

45. Chikachev, *Russkie na Indigirke,* pp. 136–7.

46. See *Vologodskii fol'klor,* pp. 35–7. This is followed by the setting of a riddle which has to be solved by the bridegroom. Riddles were an important genre in Russian folklore and their association with dreams, *podbliudnye pesni,* etc. is self-evident.

47. See below, n. 66.

48. For some discussion see Sokolov, *Ocherki*, pp. 65–8.

49. The physiognomical section of the *Secretum* is at pp. 175–9, the Rhazes text at pp. 179–20 of Speranskii, *Iz istorii otrechennykh knig. IV.*

50. See Ryan, 'The Secretum secretorum and the Muscovite Autocracy', p. 119. The same passage appears in a mid-sixteenth-century version of the encyclopedic florilegium called *Zlataia tsep'*: see M.S. Krutova, *Metodicheskie rekomendatsii po opisaniu slavianorusskikh rukopisei dlia Svodnogo kataloga rukopisei, khraniashchikhsia v SSSR*, Novosibirsk, 1990, p. 67, no. 15.

51. One example was recorded comparatively recently in *Zapiski Otdela rukopisei*, 19, 1957, p. 150: no. 168 (Moscow, Russian State Library, fond 218, no. 617), a late seventeenth-century *sbornik* including *Shestodnev* passages on cosmology from John Chrysostom, the *Besedy trekh sviatitelei*, and the physiognomy from the *Secretum* at ff. 76–100.

52. Moscow, Russian State Library, MS Rumiantsev 2955, parts published in Buslaev, *Istoricheskaia khristomatiia.*

53. *Letopis' zaniatii Arkheograficheskoi komissii, 1862–3*, St Petersburg, 1862, 2, pp. 98–125.

54. Smilianskaia, '"Suevernaia" knizhitsa', pp. 34–6, text at pp. 35–6.

55. *Svodnyi katalog*, no. 6651.

56. Min'ko, *Sueveriia*, p. 160.

57. Cherepnin, 'Iz istorii drevnerusskogo koldovstva', p. 103.

58. Mordovina and Stanislavskii, 'Gadatel'naia kniga', p. 322.

59. See Rorschach, *Drawings by Jean-Baptiste Le Prince*, p. 35 no. 39.

60. Two such are MSS Uvar. 22241(957) and 2242(317).

61. MSS Moscow, GIM, Uvar. 2191; Leningrad, PB, Q.VI.II. See Zmeev, *Russkie vrachebniki.*

62. See Bychkov, *Opisanie*, MS Pog. 1570.

63. See Opie and Tatem, *Dictionary*, s.v. *sneezing*. This gives a list of writers who attest the belief, beginning with Homer.

64. See Sreznevskii, *Materialy, s.v. ch'kh''* for a number of examples up to the sixteenth century. See also *Russian Primary Chronicle*, p. 147.

65. *SSRLIa*, s.vv. *son, chikhat'*. A reference not later than the eighteenth century occurs in a *bylina* in which the hero, Vasilii Buslaev, declares that he does not believe in dreams or sneezes but relies on a stout red cudgel: Danilov, *Drevnie rossiiskie stikhotvoreniia*, p. 119.

66. Dal', *Tolkovyi slovar'*, s.v. *chikhat'*.

67. Dal', *Poslovitsy*, 1989, I, p. 255.

68. Dal', *Tolkovyi slovar'*, s.v. *ponedèl'nyi*.

69. Opie and Tatem, *Dictionary*, s.v. *sneezing: divination: 'days' rhyme*; Thomas and Thomas, *Kentucky Superstitions*, no. 1035: the two versions quoted are both of the nineteenth century. The predictions coincide with the Russian only for Wednesday.

70. Dal', *Tolkovyi slovar'*, s.v. *zèvat'*. For similar English superstitions see Opie and Tatem, *Dictionary*, s.v. *yawning*.

71. Dal', *Tolkovyi slovar'*, s.v. *razhdati*.

72. For some classical and British beliefs often identical with the Russian see Opie and Tatem, *Dictionary*, s.vv. *ear, elbow, eye, foot, hand*.

73. Min'ko, *Sueveriia*, p. 175; Dal', *Tolkovyi slovar'*, s.v. *chesat'*.

74. Dal', *Tolkovyi slovar'*, s.v. *ukho*.

75. Dal', *Tolkovyi slovar'*, s.v. *ruka*.

76. Dal', *Tolkovyi slovar'*, s.v. *sverbet'*.

77. Dal', *Tolkovyi slovar'*, s.v. *zudit'*.

78. Dal', *Tolkovyi slovar'*, s.v. *noga*.

79. See Opie and Tatem, *Dictionary*, s.v. *stumbling*.

80. Dal', *Tolkovyi slovar'*, s.v. *spotkat'*.

81. See Speranskii, *Iz istorii otrechennoi literatury. II.*

82. Diels, 'Beiträge zur Zuckungsliteratur'.

83. Delatte, *Anecdota*, I, p. 207.

84. *Iz istorii otrechennoi literatury. II.*, pp. 84–93.

85. The phenomenon of a secondary oral tradition in Russian fortune-telling in the eighteenth and nineteenth centuries is emphasized in Wigzell, *Reading Russian Fortunes*, see p. 3 and *passim*.

86. Goncharov, *Oblomov* (1859), in pt.1, ch. 9 'Oblomov's dream' Oblomov's father had 'the latest dreambook', and the whole family believed in omens: if the bridge of the nose itches someone will die, if eyebrows itch it means tears; if ears itch it will rain, and so on; they practised divination at Christmas, protected their children from the Evil Eye, and if anyone was injured in the village he was treated with holy water or whispered spells.

7

SPELLS, CURSES
AND MAGIC PRAYERS

1. *Introduction*

Russian magical utterances, most commonly called *zagovory*, could equally well be discussed under the heading of folk magic in Ch. 2, or with amulets in Ch. 8, since they are often written down and worn as amulets (especially by the illiterate who could not read written spells),[1] or are used in association with rituals, amulets or magical objects,[2] as with the St Sisinnius text given in Ch. 8.6.6.1., or with herbal cures not ostensibly magical. The extent of the subject, however, makes it appropriate to deal with them in a separate chapter, and even then it will be possible only to give an outline with some illustrative specimens. Since non-verbal procedures (rituals) and the use of magical objects or substances often accompany spoken or written spells and curses, or are expected to produce the same result, they are also described here when appropriate.

There are many kinds of Russian spell in the form of Christian prayers but with magical, folkloric, or at least distinctly uncanonical elements in them. As in Western Europe or Greece, such prayers may often differ little in terminology, or even content, from ecclesiastically acceptable prayers, and may be found interspersed with them.[3] Indeed, the difference may in many cases depend simply on who was uttering the prayer/spell or in what circumstances it was uttered. For example, the *Bol'shoi trebnik* (a book of special services and prayers) of the seventeenth-century Metropolitan of Kiev Peter Mogila, published in 1641, contains many prayers which, if uttered by a 'wise woman', would be classed as *zagovory*; and in this he was only following a long established manuscript tradition.[4] These prayers are usually classified in Russian as *lozhnye molitvy* ('false prayers')[5] or *zagovory* (most often translated as 'spell' or sometimes as 'incantation' because, with the exception of the special category of whispered spells, they were often intoned like ecclesiastical chant[6] – Russian peasants are reported to have usually prayed aloud), although the latter term also encompasses spells with no Christian content and indeed could well come from pagan areas in contact with Russia,[7] or from the Latin West.[8]

The very fine line between canonically acceptable prayers and magical invocations is, as in the Catholic West, frequently blurred at popular level by the fact that certain saints are regularly invoked in certain circumstances or illnesses, and this association is constantly reinforced by the attributes or other iconographic characteristics of these saints in religious art. In the case of Russia the following saints or their icons, for example, are invoked: the icon of the Virgin in almost any circumstance, but in the medical context for protection against epidemics and plagues recourse is often specifically to versions of the Bogoliubskii icon (see Ch. 8.6.2); St Antipii in the case of toothache; St John the Warrior against thieves and oppressors; for success in learning and literacy SS. Cosmas and Damian;[9] for headache St John the Baptist; for horses SS. Florus and Laurus; for sheep and difficult births St Anastasius; in matters of sleep and dreams the Nine Martyrs; in marital matters the Evangelists; for women St Paraskeva (Piatnitsa, i.e. Friday); for the cure of the sick the icon of the Virgin of All who Grieve; in time of storms at sea St Nicholas the Wonderworker; for successful fishing St Peter; for cows St Blasius; for cattle in general St George; for rain the Prophet Elijah; for pigs St Basil the Great; for bees SS. Zosima and Savvatii; for chickens St Sergius; for geese St Nicholas the Martyr; to calm anger King David.[10]

As *aide-memoires* icons and popular prints were produced in the nineteenth century which listed the various saints and icons to which one could have recourse in case of illness or misfortune. These could be used as general-purpose thaumaturgic icons (for an example see Fig. 4, a nineteenth-century Palekh icon which groups the figures according to their intercessionary role, and includes St John the Theologian for students of icon-painting, seven archangels, four famous types of Virgin, SS. Nikita, Konon and Simeon for childhood ailments, St Justina for protection againt evil enchantment,[11] St Florus for avoiding drunkenness). From these one may add to the above list, for example the icon of the Virgin of Kazan', or the martyr Mina, or Longinus the Centurion for the recovery of sight; St Martha for curing fevers; the icon of the Virgin of Tikhvin for the health of infants; the Virgin of the Unburning Bush and St Nikita of Novgorod for protection from fires and lightning; St Romanos the Wonderworker for infertility; St Theodore Tiro or St John the Warrior for recovering stolen goods and runaway serfs; SS. Barbara, Charlampios and Onouphrios for preservation from sudden death; SS. Gurios, Samonos and Abibos against family discord; SS. Niphontos and Marophos for protection from evil spirits; St Martimianos against impure passion; SS. Cyprian and Justina against avarice.[12] (See also Ch. 8.6 on wonder-working icons.)

Indeed many saints in their role as protector or patron have specific popular names which indicate their area of activity and sometimes enter into the popular name of their feast day in the folk calendar, in particular when their feast day is taken as a starting point for some agricultural activity (see also Ch. 5.3).[13]

2. *Russian Spells: The* Zagovor

The word *zagovor*, like some of its near synonyms (e.g. *nagovor*, *ogovor*, *prigovor*, *nashepti*)[14] and like the English 'spell' and occasionally the Latin *murmur*, involves the notion of speech (although very many spells also describe accompanying actions). The alternative meaning of *zagovor*, 'conspiracy', is perhaps not entirely fortuitous in view of the frequent association in all ages of magic and sedition – magic as treason is discussed more fully in Ch. 16. The verb form, *zagovorit'*, and the verbs corresponding to the other nouns mentioned above, means 'to cast a spell, to bewitch', and its reflexive form *zagovorit'sia* means 'to be bewitched' or 'to protect oneself by means of a spell'.[15]

A semantically close but more ambiguous synonym of *zagovor*, perhaps with an element of euphemism, is *slovo* 'word'. Dal', s.v. *slovo*, gives as examples 'on takoe slovo znaet' (lit. 'he knows just the right word') and 'klad so slovom kladut' ('treasure is hidden with a word' – the popular belief is that treasure is often placed under a spell when hidden). One north Russian folk story includes an episode in which it is said:

> The robbers had a strong dark word. And they spoke this word on the wind, and the wind took this dark word to its appointed place, and the warrior's horse stopped as if rooted to the ground.[16]

This combines both the use of 'word' in its magical sense and the notion of curses being 'sent on the wind' (see Ch. 2.3.2). Probably analogous with this is *dumu podumat'* 'to think a thought', recorded in northern Siberia in the sense of 'to bewitch or put the Evil Eye on'.[17]

Zaklinanie, and *zakliatie* are also sometimes used as synonyms for *zagovor* although their proper meaning is perhaps better restricted to that of 'curse, magic ban, exorcism, incantation'. The verb from which they derive means, in this context, 'to place under a spell, to forbid by a curse, exorcize, conjure, endow with magical powers, enchant'. A *zaklinatel'* can mean 'conjuror of spirits' and a *zaklinatel' zmeev* is a snake-charmer.[18]

Other words for spells are: *oberegi* (protective spells, rituals or talismans); *privoroty*, *prisushki* (spells to attract affection), *otvoroty*, *otsushki* (spells to destroy affection), *urok* (this can mean a malefic spell, the Evil Eye, the injury caused, or a demonic personification of these).[19]

A little-used term for spell, *chertovshchinnye* (lit. 'devilish things', ultimately from *chert*, also spelt *chort*, 'devil'), emphasizes the diabolical nature of some spells,[20] and it will be seen from some of the examples given below that some spells may be 'anti-prayers' in that they negate or replace with demonic equivalents all the pious practices and invocations of 'good' spells. Uspenskii has pointed out in his study of the magical use of foul language that praying and cursing are in fact functional equivalents in situations where magical assistance is being sought, just as the priest and magician may equally well be consulted by someone who thinks himself to be the victim of magic.[21]

There are several published collections of *zagovory*, of which the most substantial is that of Maikov,[22] and a number of uncanonical prayers has been published by Tikhonravov,[23] Pypin,[24] and Iatsimirskii.[25]

3. *The History of the* Zagovor

The *zagovor* is essentially a magic formula the aim of which is to fulfil the wish of the person employing it, to afford protection, or to exorcize an evil spirit (which may be identified as, or personify an illness), or to harm an enemy or rival. The use of *zagovory* was condemned by the Church very early, and in Grand Prince Vladimir's *Ustav* (Church statute) in the later eleventh century it is listed with witchcraft as one of the crimes which an ecclesiastical court could try. Moisei, Archbishop of Novgorod in the middle of the fourteenth century, listed among reprehensible practices 'bringing sacrifices to devils, curing illnesses with charms and amulets, driving out the devil called "the shaker", writing the names of cursed devils and Greek words on apples and placing them on the altar during mass' and various magical practices employed by those about to go fishing or hunting, or seeking audience with the prince.[26] (The placing of items on the altar so that they might acquire magical power was evidently a widespread practice and was still incurring episcopal condemnation in the sixteenth century at the *Stoglav* Council (see Ch. 1.6); magic to ensure success in hunting was one of the responsibilities of shamans in the non-Russian tribes of the north and Siberia).

In fact it is quite clear that it was often the clergy who were practitioners in spells, and some scholars have even maintained that *zagovory* are essentially of Byzantine clerical origin, and only acquired local pagan colouring later. The general pattern of magic practices and texts in Russia and their parallels and cognates in Byzantium and Western Europe make this an almost tenable thesis.[27]

The discussion of *zagovory* is complicated several factors. The first is that those which have been collected and published have probably been filtered through the exectations or interests of the collector and may well emphasize the exotic, poetic, pagan or other elements of the collected material. Second, the *zagovor* exists in two interactive domains, that of popular oral literature in which a large number of stock elements can be arranged in a variety of traditional structures at the choice of the appellant or performer, and that of the written spell-book, in which the spell assumes a fixed form and may be transmitted, or collected, in this form. Like many other aspects of magic and witchcraft, *zagovory* appear to be at their most popular in Russia in the seventeenth century at all levels of society, although it is quite possible that heightened political and religious sensitivity, higher levels of literacy, and the better documentation of the period make this only appear to be the case. They were still widely used thereafter, and in most Russian houses at one time books of *zagovory* were kept, rather as recipe books or books of domestic medicine (from which they often differed only in detail).[28] This was probably the case in most of Europe – the fifteenth-century Wolfsthurn handbook described by Kieckhefer contains a mixture of domestic and magic recipes,[29] and the tradition survives into the modern world in the form of printed compilations such as *Aristotle's Masterpiece* or the various compendia ascribed to Albertus Magnus (*Le Grand Albert, Le Petit Albert,* etc.).

These books of *zagovory* are not so common in the manuscript collections of Russia as might be expected. This is no doubt because they were domestic items of everyday use and were kept at home until, like cookbooks, they fell apart, and also because, as mentioned above, from the time of Peter the Great onwards possession of such books was technically illegal. When found they, and any other magical items, were supposed to be burned.[30] Moreover, when they were part of the stock in trade of a *koldun* or *znakhar'* they were jealously guarded as professional secrets. One such eighteenth-century *tetradka* (as such booklets were usually described in court cases) which was evidently the property of a *znakhar'* who had gone to some lengths to protect it from profane eyes. It contained a herbal including many magic plants and was written partly in cipher (of the type called *tarabarshchina*), partly in Latin alphabet transcription, and partly in plain text leaving out the vowels.[31] Another, dating from about 1730, but in quite archaic language, includes spells against various illnesses, spells for use in court or confrontation with powerful people, weapon spells, a spell for fishing, for easing childbirth, psalms to be used as charms for various purposes and occasions, various ancient divination texts such as the *Gromnik*, *Lunnik*, *Koliadnik*, the star Chigir, 'good and bad days', 'good and bad hours' (for which see Chs 14 and 15), and two physiognomies.[32]

Although the antique analogues of Russian spells were discussed by a number of scholars, such as Veselovskii, Mansikka, and Vsevolod Miller, at the end of the nineteenth and beginning of the twentieth century,[33] claims have occasionally been made in Soviet literature of the nationalistic kind about the exclusively Russian poetic imagination displayed in *zagovory*. In assessing such claims note should be taken of the very similar nature of spells in other societies, for example the Anglo-Saxon and later English, Scandinavian, German, Balkan Slav, Greek. An American spell to cure a burn, recorded in Kentucky, reads: 'You look east, you look west, you look south, you look north. I saw three angels coming. One had fire; one had frost. Blow out, Fire. Blow in, Frost. Father, Son and Holy Ghost.'[34] If this were translated into Russian it would pass as a Russian *zagovor* without difficulty. This said, it is nevertheless true that some of the more elaborate Russian spells are indeed outstanding for their poetic imagery.

4. *The Structure and Character of the* Zagovor

Zagovory and 'false prayers' may be of any length from a sentence to several pages of text, and can be astonishingly varied and imaginative in content. They do nevertheless tend to follow certain structural patterns, although not all elements are necessarily present in each spell, or always in the same order.[35]

Zagovory frequently begin with an prayer-like invocation which may be addressed to God, a saint, forces of nature (sun, moon, stars, wind, fire, etc.), a demon (either as agent or by way of exorcism, especially where the demon personifies an illness), the person to be bewitched (in love spells or malefic spells), or the object to be bewitched (e.g. a weapon, a talisman). These may be liturgical or quasi-liturgical, such as: 'In the name of the Father and of the Son and of the Holy Spirit . . .' or 'Lord, I beseech you . . .' or 'I, servant of God (name), do hereby . . .'.[36] The appellant may then say that he or she will rise (i.e. it is probably early morning), go out into the open country (*chistoe pole*) and will stand facing the east (alternatively, in some *zagovory* addressed to an evil spirit, or implying demonic aid, the appellant says he will *not* pray or make the sign of the cross; that he will face west (the 'Devil's side'), and he may even state that he is removing his cross and belt). This formula, which suggests the involvement of the rising sun, is found in spells and magic rituals in other culture areas.[37] It seems likely that this performative formula in many cases is supposed to describe what the appellant is actually doing, as well as serving the psychological purpose of marking the transition from the everyday to the magical world with its mythic geography of islands, magic trees, magic stones, biblical mountains and rivers. Unfortunately, only a few of the recorded spells were described by earlier collectors with details of how they were performed. The characteristic use in this formula, but not in other parts of the spell, of the perfective form of the verb, which can be used as a kind of graphic present in folk literature, but is normally employed in Modern Russian as a perfective future, is curiously reminiscent of a special use of the future in some Hellenistic incantations.[38] This formula may then be followed by an invocation to an element of nature (often personified as 'tsar fire', 'tsar of the forest', etc.),[39] or a saint or list of saints, for help or intercession. Most *zagovory* may be pronounced by anyone, but some are part of the professional magic of the *koldun*, while others may have to be pronounced by some other person considered to have magic powers, such as a priest, miller, blacksmith, or midwife. They may be couched in the first person, in which case the appellant often describes his accompanying ritual actions, as described above, or in the form of a comparison or a narrative, usually with symbolic elements, followed by an imperative.

The next element, which may also be an alternative first element, is narrative,[40] usually folkloric (or epic, in Mansikka's definition), and often invoking some distant exotic location. A common example is the rhymed folktale opening 'On the sea, on the ocean, on the great island of Buian, there stands a rock . . . (often 'the hot white stone Alatyr')'.[41] The 'white-hot stone' also occurs frequently in the type of Russian folk epic known as *bylina* – in one version of the Vasilii Buslaev *bylina* the stone stands on Mount Tabor.[42] Several mountains known in religious literature, and a few invented ones, may be used: Mount Athos, Sion, Tabor, Arkhan,[43] Rakhman.[44] On the rock may stand, for example, a tree, a church, three brothers, three angels or a saint. This opening does not necessarily have any perceivable relevance to the spell which follows but has that exotic and incantatory quality which links story-telling and magic. One may note also rhyme and assonance, stock epithets, triple repetition, 'tri-deviat' (three nines), and references to the sun, moon, and stars, the dawn (often personified with a number of names), Mother Earth, or rivers, together with perfectly orthodox invocations to saints. The *zagovory* may also mix their orthodox saints with the names of demons, as in the Sisinnius story in the next chapter. In the case of the invocation of stars, as often as not it is the Morning or Evening Star which is invoked, frequently with the addition of a woman's name – e.g. Mariia, Marem'iana, Anastasiia, Katerina, etc.[45]

There may then follow an episode from Bible lore or the life of a saint, usually linked to the purpose of the *zagovor* by details of the narrative such as an event in the life of a prophet or saint (St Paul bitten by a snake; St John beheaded; St Peter compared to a rock, etc.), or miracles performed by a saint. This is the element often referred to as a *historiola* in studies of ancient-world spells; it supplies a mythic paradigm for the action of the spell, and many West European spells use the same formula.[46] Often the narrative involves an encounter between the saint, or Christ, and a sufferer from the illness against which the spell is directed, or the personified illness or misfortune itself. The encounter is often in the form of questions and answers, and in the case of the personified illness or misfortune it is asked where it is going and what it intends to do. After it reveals its evil intentions it is duly banished by some formula of exorcism.[47] This is the end of the introductory part of the spell, which may be much truncated or even omitted.

The next element is the expression of the purpose of the spell. It may often take the form of sympathetic parallelism, a *similia similibus* formula such as 'As the fire burns so may his/her heart be inflamed with love' or 'As the teeth of the corpse do not ache so may my teeth not ache'.

The spell often ends with a prayer formula ('In the name of the Father, etc.' or 'Now and for ever, Amen) or a binding formula sealing the spell, often with some phrase such as 'My word is firm' and involving keys and locks, or glue, or binding fast, or some other metaphor for its indissoluble and absolute nature.

It is often asserted in the literature of popular magic that spells have to be repeated with absolute accuracy. This is an ancient idea; at the beginning of the third century AD the theologian Origen in his *Contra Celsum* stressed the essential importance of the correct use of names in magic (a point made by Pliny before him)[48] and observed that that if a charm is translated it loses its force.[49] I have to say that while there is evidence for this in other cultures I can find only occasional evidence to prove the contention with regard to Russian spells. Nevertheless, it is unlikely that the Russians differ from other peoples in this respect, and the very pronounced concern in Russian Orthodoxy for the exact performance of the liturgy and the exact wording of prayers, etc., which was so evident in the seventeenth-century schism of the Old Believers, lends credibility to the idea. And certainly there is evidence in the various types of popular story that failure to perform non-verbal magic rituals correctly may lead to disaster – a few examples will be found elsewhere in this book. At the same time a glance at any of the larger collections of spells will immediately demonstrate the great variety of formulation of essentially similar spells, and the freedom with which elements of religious texts, the various genres of folk literature, and even names from serious literature, may be imported into them.

It is worth remembering that, at least in the period when most spells were collected, they could be not only jealously guarded family secrets, but also the stock-in-trade of professional or semi-professional magicians and folk-healers who would have felt the need to impress their clients with something which was not only stylistically recognizable as a spell, but also something which was not simply the mixture as before, or as offered by a rival. It was also a common belief that to communicate a spell was to destroy its power; in Belorussia it is recorded that spells were often communicated only on the owner's deathbed, and then only to next-of-kin.[50]

Like other magical practices, spells have often to be cast in particular circumstances and accompanied by particular acts. Some of these, as mentioned above, may be actually indicated in the spell. They most commonly include performance on particular Church feasts, or their vigils, bathing, fasting and praying beforehand, waiting at the crossroads or on a threshold, in the bathhouse at midnight, or on three successive dawns.[51] It may be required that spells be pronounced facing east, with or without a cross or icon, with hair or clothing loosened, and in a particular manner, for example by singing, whispering or breathing over the subject, or the agent, often food or drink, to be employed in the magic.[52] Commonly it is also required that the appellant should not be seen and should leave the place where the spell or divination was performed without looking back. Some of the more dangerous spells also require the drawing of a magic circle about the performer as a protection from the demons invoked to perform the magical task. *Zagovor* spells among the East Slavs, although they may include invocations to the sun, moon, and stars, have never, as far as I can discover, required astrologically propitious times to secure their efficacy, as is sometimes required in the magical texts of other cultures. This is no doubt a reflection of the relatively primitive level of astrological texts available in Russia and the absence, as far as one can tell, of astrology in folk magic and divination. (For further discussion of astrology see Chs 14 and 15 and for more on magic times, places, and directions see Ch. 2.6–7.)

5. *Categories of* Zagovor

Zagovory exist for almost every aspect of life but I have grouped them roughly as follows:[53]

5.1. *Medical, both prophylactic and curative.*[54] This is, of course, one of the commonest areas of magic. A general spell for health, associated, as spells often are, with a magical object, is referred to in chapter 5 of the acts of the *Stoglav* Council (Moscow, 1551) where the women entrusted with baking the communion bread are accused of accepting money to put a name spell on the bread, 'like Chud' [Finnic] magicians', to protect the health of the named person.[55]

Most commonly general protection against illness is ensured by the wearing of amulets (see Ch. 8 in particular). But more elaborate procedures are known. One example is *opakhivanie* (*opashka*), or 'ploughing round'. This was most common in central and southern provinces and was performed at times of plague or other epidemics and typically involved the women of the village (virgins were usually specified) going out with unbound hair and without belts, in white shifts or even completely naked, at midnight (sometimes dawn) to drag a plough round the village anticlockwise so that the furrow would keep out the epidemic; a pregnant woman had to walk between the handles and an old maid had to steer the plough, and the widows had to sprinkle sand in the furrow, crying out: 'When our sand sprouts, then only may the plague come to us!' All participants had to shout ('Come yesterday!' according to one source),[56] sing, curse, and make loud noises; if any living creature was met it was considered to be the plague personified and killed. In some cases this killing of a small animal was a ritual requirement.[57] Dal' reports that there were even cases of humans being killed on these occasions.[58] The details of this practice vary from place to place;[59] one variant requires that the women be nine widows and three virgins in their shifts.[60]

Another version recorded in 1925–6 in the Mozhaisk region of the Moscow province appears to have been an annual event to protect livestock. At midnight before the feast of the Trinity (a women's feastday) the girls of the village would gather in white clothing (formerly specially made for the occasion), with loosened hair, barefoot, accompanied by a few lads with shepherds' sticks. They would take a plough and go out of the village. The girls were hitched to the plough and would start pulling it; the boys would walk alongside and the procession was headed by one of the girls or a widow carrying an icon; the procession was completely silent; the earth turned over by the plough had to face away from the village. When a crossroads was encountered a cross was ploughed, incense was put in the middle, together with pieces of bread and birch branches. The lads then beat the ground with their sticks, and the procession continued until it returned to its starting point. Then ploughs, sledges, etc., were heaped up in the middle of the village: this was called 'building a new village'. After the ploughing the girls would engage in marriage divination.[61]

In the far northern region of Zaonezh'e there were two variants: the first involved two naked widows who had to circle the village three times holding in either hand a cock and a black cat, which they buried alive on the outskirts of the village; the second variant employed three widows who circled the village at dawn with icons and sickles.[62]

The Russian practice of *opakhivanie* would appear to be part of a wider tradition: a similar practice of ploughing round a village, to protect it from bubonic plague (but without the striking involvement of the women), is recorded in the Peloponnese;[63] a Serbian version involves twin brothers driving twin black oxen; a Bulgarian version adds the detail that the wooden parts of the plough must be made by the twins from the wood of twin trees; a Croatian version requires the ploughing to be done seven times by twelve naked virgins of each sex, who must not look at each other during the ceremony.[64] Both ploughing by naked women (in rain-making magic) and encircling to exclude disease seem to be ancient and widely distributed notions.[65]

Illnesses, even drunkenness and hangovers (*gospodi khmel'*), are often personified in spells, as in the case of the *triasavitsy*, the fevers or daughters of Herod described in Ch. 8.6.6.1, for which there are several spells. The spells recorded by Maikov as nos 103–115 show that the 'daughter of Herod' fevers may be from seven to thirteen in number, and the spells may be addressed to King David, who sealed Herod's daughters in a stony mountain (no. 113), to St Tikhon, or St Pafnutii, or the Evening Star. More recent analysis by Iudin shows more than forty addresses.[66] Maikov's no. 104 specifies three ways in which the spell can be applied: (1) if the patient is literate he must learn the spell by heart and repeat it secretly thirteen times a day and swear never to reveal it; (2) if the patient is illiterate then the magician must repeat the spell several times a day and swear the patient to secrecy; (3) the magician can write the spell on paper, fold it up and tell the patient to wear it round his neck and never unwrap it. It has to be returned to the magician at the end of the treatment. Another way of dealing with *triasavitsy* is to bake twelve pies and leave them wrapped in a napkin at the crossroads, saying: 'Here you are, twelve sisters, here is bread and salt, you have tormented me enough, now leave me', then leave, taking care not to be seen.

In other spells too the personification of the illness is feminine, as in the ancient Solomon amulets, and the words mother, sister, aunt, old woman, friend, even 'welcome guest' may all be employed in addressing the spirit of the illness. The element of euphemism or taboo in these names may even extend to personification by the deferential form of personal names (i.e. with patronymics): measles may be Tsarevna Vasil'evna, smallpox may be Ospa (i.e. pox) Ivanovna, or Afanas'evna.[67] Frequently the illness is disposed of by the apparently universal method of banishing it to another place or into an object or animal.[68]

Toothache was evidently one of the commonest ailments for which other remedies were inadequate. The many spells against toothache frequently involve comparison with stones, corpses, the moon and the wood of the Cross. St Antipii (Antipas of Pergamon) is often invoked, as is the testimony of corpses who are questioned in many spells as to whether their teeth ached! Other prayers against toothache are addressed to John the Baptist (a favourite for complaints of the head because of the nature of his death by beheading).[69] One typical spell has to be repeated at dusk on three successive evenings at dusk – it runs: 'On the ocean sea on the island of Buian lie thirty-three corpses; their teeth have not ached for ages, so may the teeth of servant of God N. not ache'.[70] Another runs: 'On the sea, on the ocean, on the great isle of Buian there stand three tall trees, the first is Petrii, the second is Khitrii, the third is Cypress. Beneath them lies a hare. You toothache, go into the hare'.[71] This spell is remarkable in that such a short statement should contain the fairy tale formula, a reference to the apocryphal story of the three trees that went to make the Cross, another folktale element, the hare, and personified toothache. As evidence that spells recorded in the nineteenth century may have a long history, one spell involving St Antipas was quoted in the evidence against a magician accused in the so-called Shaklovitii case (1689) of trying to harm the young Tsar Peter. It runs:

Lord Jesus Christ, Son of God, have mercy on us. You created, O Lord, heaven and earth. You created them, O Lord, with one word. I charm away aches and pains, I pray to St Antipii and St Nicholas the Wonderworker. I send St Antipii to a corpse: just as the corpse's teeth do not ache, so may your servant X's teeth suffer no aches nor pains nor swellings nor illness for ever and ever, Amen.[72]

Another spell for toothache describes St Peter sitting on a marble rock; Christ approaches him and asks why he is sad; he replies that he has toothache, whereupon Christ drives out the toothache spirit.[73] This exists in many places,[74] including Anglo-Saxon England,[75] and has been traced by Barb to the apocryphal *Gospel of Bartholomew*.[76] The association of St Peter with toothache undoubtedly derives from the quality of rock hardness and marble whiteness which is sought for the tooth, and the renaming of Simon as Peter in the 'Tu es Petrus' episode in the Gospel of Matthew 16, 18. The only other dental association of Peter appears to be the discovery of a tooth of St Peter by the seventh-century St Longis.[77]

The prayer of St Paul against snake-bite (inspired by the incident of St Paul and the viper in Acts 28, 1–8) is also an apocryphal text shared by several cultures.[78] The Russian prayer appears to be, like many other apocryphal and minor magical texts, of Greek origin mediated by South Slavonic (in this case Serbian) versions. Russian versions may expand on the South Slavonic originals and may include *voces magicae* and instructions to write the prayer on water or bread, these to be consumed by the afflicted person. The *historiola* section of the prayer transfers Paul's adventure from Malta to Sicily.[79] A more recent, and more specifically Russian spell against snake-bite is found written inside the cover of a late nineteenth-century manuscript miscellany of apocryphal texts (including the *Dream of the Virgin*, *Twelve Fridays* and the *Jerusalem Letter*). It calls on 'Tsar Kover [lit. carpet!] and Tsaritsa Kovron'ia' to take away their serpent.[80] A large number of spells against snakes was recorded in Belorussia by Romanov.[81] A characteristic feature is that 'tsars' and 'tsaritsas' of the serpent world are often invoked by name. One nineteenth-century collector of Belorussian spells records that one of her informants would only repeat spells in a whisper in a remote clearing in a wood, and all the time looked around fearfully in case the serpent tsar Ir and his tsaritsa Iritsa were listening.[82] A Ukrainian spell of the same type runs: 'I conjure you, serpents, in the name of Our Lord Jesus Christ, the holy megalomartyr and conqueror and all the heavenly hosts. I adjure the three Tsaritsas Kufiia, Neviia and Poliia not to harm X by a hair (colour of hair)'; then read the prayer 'Holy Trinity' five times and 'Our Father' seven times; in the case of a very poisonous snake repeat the spell three times.[83] The serpent name Neviia in this spell occurs in several magic contexts: she is one of the *triasovitsy*, the fevers personified as the daughters of Herod (see Ch. 8.6.6.1). A spell against snake-bite from the Russian Far East recorded in this century runs:

On the sea, on the bay there stands an apple-tree on twelve roots; on the apple-tree there are three wooden beds, and on these beds are three feather pillows. On these pillows lie three elder snakes: the first is Shkurapeia, the second is

Poliukha, the third is Liukha. I beg you Liukha, with great beseechings and deep bows, take away your servants, the poisonous ones, the mossy ones, the ones under the fence, the ones under the log, the ones in the marsh, and all the forgotten ones, and the fisher worm. If you don't take them away the Lord will send Archangel Michael and Cosmas-Damian. Archangel Michael will burn you with fire and Cosmas-Damian will scatter your ashes over the field. The most pure Mother came and blessed this wound with a cross and gave her help.[84]

Iatsimirskii quoted some typical medical spells: for example, to staunch the flow of blood from nose or mouth, inscriptions (in the form of a series of probably random letters) were written on a piece of paper and placed on the breast or forehead of a patient, in one case written in blood. This is followed by the formula: 'If you don't believe this, write the spell on a knife and plunge it into an animal and it will not bleed'. South Slavonic versions of this are found from the fourteenth century, with later Russian versions.[85] Other spells and prayers are also given, e.g. prayers and spells for inability to pass water. These are read over the patient: 'Three angels (or virgins) stand on the other side of the Jordan,[86] one binds, one resolves, the third cries Holy Holy Holy, Lord God of hosts. Khinen egin mantis' (or other Greek words or names of rivers, usually the Four Rivers of Paradise).[87] Other spells include letters written on the finger nails of the sufferer.

One curious spell with no Christian element whatsoever involves going into the forest, finding a rowan tree, performing various rituals and writing a petition to Tsar Musaila, the chief forest goblin, demanding to know why servant of God (name), had become ill, and threatening him with archers from Moscow and Novgorod and Cossacks from Azov, who would cut him down to a stump if he did not answer.[88]

A particular sub-category of medical spells which is very common is that of spells for wounds. The most persistent motif in these is an appeal to the Virgin to sew up the wound. A typical example is: 'Amen. In the sea in the ocean, on the isle of Buian sat the most holy Virgin. She held a golden needle in her hand, she threaded a silk thread, she sewed up the bloody wound. You wound, do not hurt, you blood, do not flow. Amen.'[89]

A seventeenth-century spell against drunkenness requires the afflicted person to go to the grave of an unknown person, open the grave, push a needle through the shroud, then strain water through the shroud and the eye of the needle, and recite the spell:

Just as you, O corpse, have lain for so long without drinking intoxicating liquor, so may I not drink intoxicating liquor, nor wish to, nor see it, nor hear of it, nor think of it until my wooden coffin.

Then drink the water and rebury the corpse.[90] This beneficent use of a corpse contrasts with the necromantic use described elsewhere, and has parallels in English beliefs.[91]

5.2. *For childbirth and new-born children.* Various objects which had been worn by the mother as a bride during her wedding, or a priest's girdle were regarded as a great help in childbirth.[92] Prayers offered in church for a mother approaching childbirth in some parts of Russia were brought home to the mother 'in a hat', a practice which suggests that the prayer was thought of as a spell.[93] It was at any rate recognized as superstitious and condemned in Peter the Great's *Spiritual Regulation* of 1721. Childbirth itself often took place in the bathhouse and could be accompanied by a number of magical practices (for which see Ch. 2.7.1). In Siberia birth precautions included untying all knots, buttons, etc., and unbinding hair, asking for the altar doors in the church to be opened, crawling under the table or under the father's legs,[94] and stepping over an axe; swallowing an egg and saying: 'Just as a chicken lays an egg quickly,[95] so may I, servant of God X, give birth quickly.' These practices, also found in other areas,[96] require no interpretation.

Not surprisingly spells for childbirth are often addressed to the Virgin, for example the icon of the Fedorovskaia Virgin in Kostroma, and sometimes to the womb personified. Less obvious a patron is St Anastasius. Spells to be used for a difficult delivery may ask the Virgin to take her golden keys and unlock the 'fleshy gates' to let out the child.[97] The element of gold (*zoloto, zolotoi*) frequently occurs in these spells, no doubt by association with *zolotnik*, one of the words for womb. It is of interest that these spells may often require the womb to go back to its proper place, which may be a golden chair,[98] just as in the spells against the *dna* (womb-demon) discussed in connection with *zmeeviki* in Ch. 8.6.6.

A curious childbirth practice recorded in the Smolensk and Mogilev provinces, condemned as magical in an early nineteenth-century Old Believer manuscript, appears to be a variety of *couvade*. In it the husband of a woman in labour had to lie on a shelf above the woman, with a thread tied round his penis. The midwife would jerk the thread to coincide with the woman's birth pangs, thus producing sympathetic cries from above.[99]

Spells may also be pronounced over the newborn child to protect it.[100] For a difficult birth a common practice at several levels of society was to light candles which had been preserved from the parents' wedding,[101] or from church services on three days: Friday, Saturday, Sunday.[102] The herb *Adamova golova* (for which see Ch. 7) was prescribed for the same purpose in the Ukraine.[103]

In most parts of Russia there were thought to be particular demons which preyed upon children, such as the *polunoshnik*, the midnight demon which kept babies awake, or the *poludennitsa* or midday demon which could kill them or steal them (see also Ch. 8.6.6). Others personified childish ailments, and have names such as the *revun, vopun,* or *kriksy* (all meaning 'wailer'). There was also a strange being called a *tiren'kii* which could possess a child. Its presence could be detected if the baby laughed after its birth;[104] such children had to be looked after very carefully and never shown to anyone outside the family or else they would become deformed.[105] This is a variation on Evil Eye beliefs (for which see in particular Ch. 2.2). Specific protection from the Evil Eye for babies in Siberia is to wash three corners of a table, three spoons, a doorbolt, throw into the washbowl three matches and blow, then wash the baby in the water; or wash the baby with soap which the mother kept in her bosom during the wedding ceremony.[106] It was important never to show the baby a mirror,[107] lift it above eye-level, talk to it during washing, or cut its nails or hair before its first birthday.[108]

One remarkable and elaborate protective spell for a slightly older child manages to quote a large number of Russian magical themes:

> I have gone into the open land, I have taken the wedding bowl, I have taken out the betrothal candle, I have taken the wedding kerchief, I have drawn water from a mountain spring, I have stood in the deep forest, I have drawn a transparent line around me, and I have cried out in a great voice. I charm my adorable child over the wedding bowl, over the fresh water, over the wedding kerchief, over the betrothal candle.
>
> I wash my child till his face is clean, with my wedding kerchief I dry his sweet lips, his clear eyes, his thoughtful brow, his red cheeks; with my betrothal candle I light up his close-fitting kaftan, his sable form, his patterned girdle, his embroidered boots, his light-brown curls, his eager face, his swift step. Oh my adorable child may you be brighter than the sun, sweeter than a spring day, brighter than spring water, whiter than bright wax, stronger than the burning Alatyr' stone.
>
> I banish from you the fearful devil, I drive away the stormy whirlwind, I take you away from the one-eyed wood-goblin, from the alien house-goblin, from the evil water-sprite, from the Kievan witch and her sister from Murom,[109] from twitchy-eyed mermaids, from the thrice-cursed Baba-Yaga, from the flying fiery serpent; I wave away the fateful raven, the cawing crow, I protect you from the cannibal wizard (*koshchei*), from the cunning black magician (*chernoknizhnik*), from the spell-casting warlock (*kudesnik*), from the savage shaman (*volkhv*), from the blind cunning-man (*znakhar'*), from the old witch woman (*vedun'ia*).
>
> And may you be, my child, protected by my strong word (i.e. spell) in the night and at midnight, every hour and half-hour, on the road and on the path, sleeping and waking, from the evil force, from unclean spirits; may you be kept safe from sudden death, from grief and misfortune; may you be saved on the water from drowning, guarded from burning in fire. And when the hour of your death comes, my child, remember our tender love, our rich hospitality; come back to your wonderful homeland, strike it with your forehead seven by seven times, say farewell to your family and relations, fall to the damp earth and fall asleep with a sweet and unwaking sleep.[110]

Maikov records a variety of spells to make babies sleep or stop crying (nos 56–61). One such, a kind of diminishing spell, is found with minor variants in many areas; evidently it is for use with particularly troublesome infants because it is performed by the village wise woman or *znakharka*. She has first to put her clothes on back to front, a form of magical deception also recommended as protection from the wood-sprite, then takes the sick child in her arms, goes out of the village, faces the dawn and says three times, taking a step back each time and spitting over her left shoulder: 'Dawn, dawn, beautiful maiden, take away from servant of God N. the crying and weeping, day and half-day, hour and half-hour, minute and half-minute'. Then, after three more bows from the waist, she says: 'Dawn, dawn, beautiful maiden, your child is crying and wants to eat and drink but my child is crying and wants to sleep. Take away your sleeplessness and give us your sleep . . . (etc.).[111] Popov in his study of folk medicine observed that spells of this kind are often addressed to the dawn, or to chickens (presumably as proclaimers of dawn). He also quotes two more *zagovory* for this purpose: 1. Go with the child and a 'wise woman' to the bathhouse. Here the 'wise woman' takes the child inside while the mother waits in the entrance. The 'wise woman' says: 'I am steaming, I am steaming'; the mother says, 'Who are you steaming?'; the 'wise woman' replies, 'The *polunoshnik* (midnight demon)'; the mother says, 'Steam him well so that he goes away and never returns'; 2. Recite the spell: 'Evening Star Mariia, Morning Star Marem'iana, give sleep to your servant X and take away sleeplessness'.[112] In an almost identical Siberian *zagovor* the 'wise woman' in her reply identifies herself as Solomonida, the apocryphal midwife at the birth of Jesus, who also appears in some versions of the *Dream of the Virgin*.[113] The same Solomonida was invoked in *zagovory* to encourage babies to grow.[114] Another method of dealing with a crying baby is to wash it in water in which ash from three stoves (the hut, the smithy, the bathhouse) has been placed.[115] A variety of Belorussian spells to banish the *kriksa*, the crying demon,[116] and *noshnitsa*, the demon of wakefulness, is given in Romanov.[117]

Babies which were obviously weak at birth, or suffered from rickets or hernia, in many regions were subjected to the ritual usually called *perepekanie* (lit 're-baking'). This typically involved putting the baby on a bread shovel and inserting it three times into a warm oven. A Ukrainian variant required the oven to have been used first to bake bread which had been mixed by the local *znakharka* with water freshly drawn from three wells.[118] Variants on this practice are known in England from medieval Latin penitentials.[119] Another way in which a sick baby could be 'reborn' was to pass it through the neck of the mother's shift, from top to bottom, three times.[120]

Magic measures for contraception are not well attested, although at least one sixteenth-century Russian 'list of sins' condemns both conception and abortion by means of potions (*zelie*).[121] An alleged abortifacient appearing in one account (seventeenth-eighteenth century) was the 'magical' root *molodilo* (see Chap. 9, pp. 275–6). Locks and keys were known as amulets for this purpose, as was the practice of burying a bottle of water obtained by washing clothes stained with menstrual blood or giving such stained clothes to a *koldun* who would make a contraceptive spell. The use of menstrual blood for contraceptive magic is reported as being popular with unmarried women, widows and soldiers' wives, i.e. women for whom a pregnancy would most probably arise only from illicit relationships.[122] Menstrual blood, which is believed to have harmful properties in many cultures, could also be used for malefic magic (*porcha*) by introducing it into the victim's food or drink.[123] The same concoction could be used in a positive way with a husband or lover to ensure his fidelity.[124] It could also be used to predict the sex of unborn children (see p. 112) and in folk medicine could be drunk as an infusion to remove warts and birthmarks.[125] A practice which was variously thought either to prevent or encourage conception was to eat placenta.[126]

For the more fastidious Galanga held under the tongue by a woman was also supposed to prevent conception,[127] and a slightly confused Siberian spell alleged to be contraceptive runs:

> [Saints] Peter and Paul went by. Where did you spend the night Peter and Paul? In the town of Jerusalem, in the church of God on the throne; we dropped the keys and lock and had nothing to let the sinful soul through: the sinful soul had sinned, it killed the child in the womb; it had eaten every kind of herb and drunk every kind of potion; it fell into the heat, into the burning fire, into the boiling pitch.[128]

At the other end of the scale of reproductive problems, general procedures to encourage fertility are common enough, but, as with modern medicine, specific aids for childless couples are harder to find. The last feather in an eagle's wing was one remedy;[129] another is the herb *kupal'nitsa*.[130] A visit by the childless woman to a wonder-working doll in a convent in Smolensk could also help (see Ch. 8.5).[131]

For methods of foretelling, even predetermining, the sex of an unborn child, see Ch. 4.6.3.

5.3. *Love spells.* This is one of the commonest categories of spell.[132] Many examples survive from the ancient Near East and classical antiquity which differ little from erotic spells found in modern times in Russia. *Prigovory*, *prisushki* or enticement spells were very common at all levels of Russian society. They were employed by both men and women either to attract a lover or coerce someone into sexual relations, or to increase or restore marital affection. A general rule, with a good many exceptions, is that the spells and practices designed to find or keep a marriage partner were used by women, while men were more concerned with their immediate desires.

The making of love potions (variously known as (*liubovnoe*) *zel'e*, *privorot*, *privorotnoe sredstvo*, *liubzha*) was one of the practices which priests were instructed to ask penitents about in confession.[133] This is perhaps not surprising in view of the fact that a significant number of love spells are in fact addressed to the Devil (Satanail Satanailovich in one spell).[134] In fact love magic in general was a frequent concern of both Eastern and Western Churches. A thirteenth-century Western example to compare with the Russian examples below is the improving story in the *Dialogue on Miracles* of Caesarius of Heisterbach concerning the fate of an otherwise pious and respectable matron who suffered agonies in purgatory for the secret sin of using magic to secure her husband's love.[135]

Love spells commonly involve triple repetition, often at dawn, contact with items of clothing, and most characteristically of all, the ingestion of bewitched food or drink, as for example food or drink containing menstrual blood mentioned above. Fire, smoke, and wind are the most commonly recurring symbolic elements.

The earliest surviving Russian love spell of which I am aware is found in a birchbark manuscript of the second half of the fourteenth century from Novgorod. It runs: 'may your heart and your body and your soul be inflamed for me and my body and the sight of me'.[136] But early written examples of love magic are rare before the seventeenth century when details of court cases throw some light on the subject. In 1635 one of the servants of the tsaritsa dropped a handkerchief with a root in it. Under interrogation she admitted it was a charm to make her husband love her: she would put it on a mirror and then look into it. She was tortured and exiled as a punishment.[137] (Kostomarov mentions this practice, naming the 'root' as *obratim*, and adding the spell: 'As I look on the mirror and cannot stop looking, so may N. look on me'.)[138] Three years later a court sempstress was accused of throwing sand and ashes on the footsteps of the tsaritsa: under torture she admitted that beside this treasonable activity she had also used magic salt and soap to increase her husband's affection.[139] In another case of the same period several people were sent to Siberia for engaging in 'love magic'. One woman admitted under torture that she had told women to give their husbands salt and soap and say the spell: 'As people look in the river, so may the husband look on his wife and never tire of looking, and as quickly as the soap washes off so may the husband come to love his wife, and as white as may be the shirt on his body so may the husband be bright.' Another spell, to be whispered over bread and salt, mentioned at the same trial, was: 'Just as people love salt, so may the husband love his wife'.[140]

In a treason case (*slovo i delo* – see Ch. 16, p.) referred to an ecclesiastical court in 1727, a certain Roman Krasnolpolskii gave evidence that, wishing to have women other than his wife, he had copied down a spell from the words of the peasant Moisei Churin. He was to read this letter over salt, put the salt in kvas or food, and give it to girls and women.[141] He swore he had never used it, talked about it or let anyone else copy it. (This was always very important as a mitigating factor in such cases.) A search of the peasant's hut revealed 'herbs', a copy of *The Dream of the Virgin*, a *zagovor* for going before a judge or important person, another for sowing discord between man and wife, and a *mesechnik* (lit. 'month book' or possibly 'moon book') which gave predictions on good and bad days for travel.[142]

The eating of bewitched objects is common in this kind of magic. For example, if you speak a spell over a spice-cake and give it to a girl she will fall in love with you when she eats it. A more complicated version requires the young man to catch a dove, kill it, use its fat to make a dough, bake the dough and give it to the girl to eat, saying: 'As the doves live together in love, so may servant of God N. love me'.[143] Similarly, for women, a spell spoken over the food, drink, clothes or footprints of a man will make him love her.[144] The same effect may be achieved by breathing over things connected with the object of the spell. In a case in 1770 a peasant was accused of obtaining a charm to win the affection of a widow: he had to write certain words and breathe them into a bottle of wine which he would then get her to drink.[145] Perhaps because of the breathing element the winds are commonly involved in love spells: sometimes the aid is sought of three brother winds,[146] or seven winds,[147] or, in spells against love, whirlwinds (hostile demonic forces in Russian folk belief) may be invoked.[148]

Another theme in love spells is fire: 'In the stove the fire burns and flames, the logs blaze and glow, so may the heart glow and burn of the servant of God N'.[149] In one spell folkloric elements and parts of other spells (e.g. that mentioned above in connection with St Sisinnius), are invoked; the twelve *Triasavitsy* (fevers, snakes, daughters of Herod) are asked to take the fire out of the white stone Alatyr' so that the fiery serpent (sometimes associated with falling stars and a sign of impending death: snakes are a common feature of Slavonic folklore, in particular in marriage ceremonies and as phallic symbols)[150] may inflame her heart with love.[151]

A more elaborate, and passionately incoherent spell with many typical features reads, in approximate translation:

In the name of the Father, the Son and Holy Spirit. I, the servant of God (name), shall arise and bless myself, crossing myself I shall leave the hut by the doors, I shall leave the yard by the gates. I shall go out onto the wide road with my face to the east and my back to the west. I shall bow and pray. In the open country (*chistoe pole*) on the wide plain there are four brothers, the wild winds, east, west, south and north. As you [winds] served the true Christ, the king of heaven, so may you serve me, the good servant of God (name). Take from me, the servant of God, grief and dryness, and black misery, take them away and do not let them drop against the wind or with the wind, against the sun or with the sun, against the stream and with the stream, and through the flowing brooks and swift rivers, through high mountains and dark forests, through iron fences. Walking from the hall, or sitting on the stair or bed, or lying on the bed, or sitting at the table, with his father or mother or sister or brother, or friend or all his family, take him by the white hands and instil in his white body and ardent heart and black liver and seventy-seven veins (sinews) and seven joints[152] that he may not live without me, servant of God N, nor eat nor sleep, that he may agonize with a deadly anguish, an anguish he may not eat or drink away, or wash away in the bathhouse, but only run after me, take me by the neck, kiss me on the lips, and look no more on his father or mother, or sister or family or anyone at all; so may he think of me, servant of God N, during the day in sunlight and at night by moonlight, at dawn and sunset, at the new moon and the old moon and at the quarters of the moon and on the days in between. May my words be firm for ever and ever, Amen![153]

Min'ko describes a number of methods of securing someone's affections in Belorussia: you can wear two belts for three of the days of Easter, you can introduce some of your own sweat into the food or drink of the object of your affection;[154] you can wear a hawk's head next to your belly; you can fast for twelve Fridays (a practice condemned in Peter the Great's *Spiritual Regulation*); you can walk round the victim three times with three candles taken from a church; you can take a bat, put it into a new pot, cover it with a new cloth, put the pot into an anthill, go home without looking back and with your ears stopped so as not to hear the squeaks of the bat, and return after three weeks for the bones, with which you will be able to draw the object of your desire to you.[155] An identical procedure in Bohemia, but with a frog instead of a bat, is described in *The Golden Bough*,[156] and similar methods have been used in Great Russia to become invisible (see below). Min'ko further records a court case in Brest in 1950 when a *koldun* was accused of charlatanism by promising to get runaway husbands to return by boiling their underclothes in a pot and giving the water to the wives to sprinkle on their doorsteps.[157] Having caught their spouse the Belorussians guarded the subsequent marriage from the hostile magic of witches by wearing onions and garlic,[158] a well-known specific against witchcraft and the Devil in many parts of Europe.

Shirts, like the undergarments mentioned above, because of their intimate contact with the body, are often found in this kind of spell: one method of using them was to burn part of the shirt and sprinkle the ash on the food of the husband, saying: 'As this shirt was on the body, so may the husband be to the wife'.[159] This is even part of the wedding ritual in the Vologda region, where the bride wears in the steam bath clothes which she has prepared as a present for her husband.[160]

Associated with spells on clothes are spells involving perspiration and spittle. For example, a man must work up a sweat, wipe it off with a cloth, wipe the woman with the cloth and say: 'Just as my sweat boils and burns, so may the heart of N. boil and burn for me',[161] or he must spit on his hand, speak a spell over the spittle and then suddenly slap his victim over the heart.[162] Perspiration magic is recorded, and condemned by the Church with six weeks penance, as early as the twelfth century in a list of canonical questions and answers, which claims that women get men to drink the water in which they have washed in order to ensure their affection.[163]

Amatory curses for destroying love (*otsushka*) also exist. They are employed against rivals, often by wives with errant husbands. A spell of this kind was included in the evidence in the Krasnopol'skii case described above. One such spell, appropriately demonic, for sowing discord between a newly married couple, runs:

I, servant of the Devil N., will arise, not bless myself, go without crossing myself from door to door, from gate to gate, and go into the open field to the

Devil's bog.[164] In the open field stand fir trees and on them sit forty magpies, the forces of the Devil. And in the Devil's bog is the white stone Latyr, and on the white stone Latyr sits the Devil himself, and I shall go to the white stone Latyr and I shall bow to Satan and beg him: Oh you mighty Satan, just as you brought together this the bride and groom, so find a way to separate them so that they should not love each other but stab each other with knives. For I am your slave now and forever.[165]

5.4. *Spells for impotence.* This category is fairly consistent in its imagery.[166] One seventeenth-century spell against impotence 'that the member should not bend'. reads:

I, servant of God N., shall arise, blessing myself and I shall go crossing myself into the open field under the beautiful sun, under the bright new moon, under the crowding stars, past the grave of the bones of the giants,[167] and just as the bones of the giants do not bend or break so may my member (*firs*, from Greek for 'rod', a surprisingly learned source for a vulgar term) not bend or break against woman's flesh and parts and memorial bones (*pamiatnye kosti*). And I, servant of God N. shall take my red elm stick (*viaz*) and go into the open field and if the three-year old bull goes into the open field, tossing up its head and looking at the sky and moon and Great Bear, then I shall go with my red elm stick and strike the three-year-old bull on its horns with my red elm stick; and so with me, servant of God N., may my member not bend or break against woman's flesh or parts or memorial bones.[168]

Bones representing desired erections are even more prominent in another spell:

There is a bony mountain, on it a bony chair. On this bony chair sits a bony tsar leaning on his bony staff. His hat on his head is of bone, the gloves on his hands are of bone, the boots on his feet are of bone. The whole of this tsar is of bone, all his seventy-three members are of bone and his standing member is of bone. So may I, servant of God X, have all my seventy-three members of bone and my standing member of bone, and stand a hundred and a thousand times times at the little place of women and girls, black, brown, red and white and of every kind, at the new moon, at the old moon, and at the quarters of the moon.[169]

Other spells against impotence invoke the image of the stout oak and cockerel ('Just as the cock stands on the oak, rises early, raises its head and crows gaily, so may my seventy-seven and one sinews rise early ... ').[170]

Spells and other magical methods may also be used to cause impotence in a rival or as vengeance: for example, a thread from a shroud passed through the eye of a needle which is then stuck into the clothing of a woman would make her husband impotent. Alternatively one could cut off the end of a church bell-rope at sunrise, tie three knots in it, and recite the spell: 'Just as the bell hangs down so may the member of [name] hang down before [female name], now and for ever, Amen'.[171] A particular form of magical attack on the testicles which caused them to swell to a great size was called '*kila*'. Mark Ridley in the late sixteenth century described it as 'a swelling of the coddes by witchcraft',[172] and Richard James in 1618 records 'khila, the disease of the stones bewicht into an exceedinge swellinge bignesse'. Ivan the Terrible was reported by Sir Jerome Horsey to 'grievously swell in his cods' in his last illness. Horsey noted the magical circumstances of Ivan's death but also the sexual excesses of which Ivan had boasted.[173]

(On impotence and sterility caused by malefic magic see Ch. 3.4.)

5.5. *To guard against evil spirits, malefic spells and avert the Evil Eye.* Most of the spells and prayers in this chapter are, of course, designed to counteract demons, malefic magic and the Evil Eye in one way or another, since illnesses and misfortunes are usually personified as evil spirits or put down to hostile magic. *Porcha* ('harm; spoiling') was normally thought of as a sickness of man or livestock or crops brought on by magic and it usually required the efforts of a specialist to produce a successful counter-spell.

There are many spells for protecting flocks and cattle from *porcha*; a relatively short one collected by Rybnikov is:

Take from every beast some hair from between the horns and put it in wax; read this spell three times while walking round with an icon in a clockwise direction (lit. according to the sun)[174] dragging an axe behind you, then bury the wax where no one can see you or know about it. Read: 'If anyone should have evil designs on me or my dear beasts let his tongue be twisted, his hamstrings burst, his eyes pop out of his head, let him have no peace day or night till his dying hour, Lord, for ever and ever, Amen.[175]

Rybnikov also quotes protective *zagovory* for use at weddings; they end in spitting three times in the door lock and turning the key.[176]

One spell against the Devil takes the form of a prayer to one's guardian angel:

My guardian angel, preserve my soul, strengthen my heart every day, every hour every minute. I rise in the morning, I wash in dew, I wipe with a towel the icon of the Saviour. Enemy-Satan depart from me a hundred, a thousand versts – I am wearing the Cross of the Lord. On this Cross are written Luke and Mark and Nikita the martyr. They suffered for Christ – may they pray for us to God. The most pure locks are locked with keys, sealed with locks, now, always, and for ever, Amen.[177]

(For belief in the Evil Eye in general, and precautions against it, see Ch. 2.2. The very many herbal and talismanic alternatives to verbal spells are described in Chs 8 and 9.)

5.6. *Malefic spells*. Malefic spells are many and varied.[178] Spells may be short, as in the following specimen of seventeenth-century Russian necromancy: 'As X (if you do not know his name call him Ivan) died unshriven so may you die unshriven', but with elaborate accompanying rituals such as, in this case, going secretly at sunset to the grave of a person known to have died unshriven, carrying a hen's egg and an axe with a steel tied to it. Ask the corpse's permission to take earth from his head and offer him a gift of a white swan, symbolized by the egg, and ask for his help. Go home without looking back, stand on a stone near your home and draw a circle round the stone with the axe while reciting the protective spell: 'Save servant of God X from the enemy'. Then throw the axe to the north, and after a while fetch it and untie the steel. At a convenient opportunity throw the earth at the breast of the victim while reciting the spell.[179] Spells may also be elaborately long, as in some spells against rivals in love.

Malefic spells may include the almost universal practice of making dolls in the image of the person to be harmed and doing to the doll what you would like to be done to the victim. In a modern and no doubt facetious example of both this and the personification of disease, the wife of the Russian writer Mikhail Bulgakov recorded in her diary that on New Year's Eve of 1939–40 the family toasted the New Year, then made a doll to represent the writer's illness; the doll was thereupon shot.[180] Similar magic may be done with part of the victim's clothing or body (e.g. nail clippings) or even the earth on which he has walked: in 1689 one Ivan Bindakov admitted under torture that he had picked up the earth from the footprint of Prince V.V. Golitsyn for magical purposes.[181]

Hostile spells made by a *koldun* may in fact be simple poisoning (and indeed malefic magic and poisoning are so often linked both in Russia and elsewhere that it is clear that for many people they could hardly be distinguished as suspected causes of illness – see Ch. 9.2) usually include a spoken or whispered spell, and may also include magical ingredients such as herbs or roots, or, as in the case quoted above, graveyard earth,[182] or parts of human bodies,[183] or 'dead soap' which has been used to wash a corpse,[184] or water which has been used to wash a corpse (a specific employed by women for reducing breasts thought to be of excessive proportions),[185] or a 'dead candle' made from human fat from graves which will send to sleep or kill.[186] A similar belief would seem to lie behind an English newspaper report in 1889 of a trial in Kursk in which four peasants were convicted of chopping up a girl of eleven to make tallow candles which would enable them to carry out burglaries unseen; the court was told that this belief was very widespead in Russia.[187]

'Dead candles' were not the only ones with magical power; in fact any church candle, like other Christian ritual objects, could be used for magical purposes, as is evident elsewhere in this book. For malefic magic they could be placed upside down and a memorial prayer offered for the victim (a variety of cursing by inversion of a Christian practice).[188]

To return to the subject of corpses and malefic magic, Afanas'ev published a Russian folk tale which describes the use of a 'dead hand' by a witch.[189]

Kostomarov states that 'then as now [!]' thieves would use the hand of a corpse to ensure that the owners of a house slept soundly while the house was burgled.[190] A similar result was expected from communion bread over which a spell had been uttered.[191]

The first major travel writer on Muscovy, Herberstein, noted in 1557 that bishops had to deal with cases of witchcraft, poisoning and heresy (significantly grouped together as linked categories), and the spoliation of tombs or removal of portions of images or crucifixes for purposes of magic.[192] Graveyard dust could be administered in a potion; one recorded spell to go with it is: 'As the dead do not stand up, may Fedor not stand up; as the body of this dead man has disappeared so may Fedor disappear completely'.[193] In the Gomel' region of Belorussia even today the way to harm an enemy is to sprinkle graveyard dust under his house.[194] Coffin nails also had malefic power; if they were thrown into your victim's stable his horses would become lame.[195]

In the seventeenth century fear of spells directed against members of the court was constant and all members of the tsaritsa's household had to swear not to make spells or keep herbs or roots. These, it was feared, might be sprinkled, with an appropriate spell, in the path of, or in the entrance to the homes of the victim.[196] When in the early seventeenth century Tsar Mikhail Fedorovich's linen was taken to the river for laundering, it went under lock and key in a trunk covered by a red cloth (red is often found as a protective colour against witchcraft or the Evil Eye), accompanied by a lady of the court to supervise the washing as a precaution against witchcraft.[197]

A minor form of malefic magic was to inflict hiccups on your victim. One way of doing this was to remove your cross, put it under your heel, and say: 'I deny God and his life-giving cross. I give myself into the hands of the Devil'. Then whisper over some salt: 'Misery-hiccups, afflict this man [name], shake and torment him to the end of his life'. Then take the cross out of your boot and put it on back to front; this should cause devils to appear. A day later move the cross round to the front and sprinkle the salt where the intended victim will walk, saying: 'As this salt will dry up so may this man dry up'.[198] In 1815 a peasant, Mikhail Chukharev, was found guilty in court of inflicting on his cousin an evil spirit in the form of hiccups by using this spell. The guilty peasant was condemned to thirty-five blows of the knout and public penance. In this, as in the other court cases recorded, not all the circumstances are known. Local malice, hysteria, or unstated aggravating factors may have been responsible for this harsh sentence (scourging with the knout was often fatal) in a case which even in the eighteenth century might well have been dismissed. It was not only peasants who had recourse to malefic magic: at about the same time Martha Wilmot observed in her memoirs of life with the Russian aristocracy:

New storys too are coming to light about Mme S[hcherbenin] who has been plotting with sorcerers the Destruction of her Mother, Sister in Law, & me. A powerful Charm was to have bewitch'd us, alienated our reason or kill'd us'.[199]

Amulets are normally protective, but sometimes can be used malignantly. The knotted cord amulet, for example, which is discussed in Ch. 8.4, can be used with a spell against an enemy. For this purpose taken a length of woollen yarn, tie in it eight double knots, saying as you tie: '1. I go out onto the road, 2. I throw into the open field, 3. into the distance (?crossroads), 4. between the homesteads, 5. into the fields, 6. into the seas, 7. into the forest, 8. into the quaking bog'. The cord must then be left where the victim will step on it. More elaborate is a thirteen-knot thread for which the accompanying spell is:

> In the late evening I go out onto the road, and I renounce Jesus Christ, and the earthly Tsar, and Almighty God, and the Orthodox faith, and father and mother. I bind myself to the unclean spirit, to the accursed power, and I invoke his aid to help me against N. the thief and bandit, the daylight robber, the night robber. I want to pull him down, I want to harm him, be it in day time or at night, in the open country or in dark forests or in quaking bogs, be it sleeping or drowsing, in an upper room, or at oaken tables with honeyed viands, may he stumble and curse himself. Accursed spirits, help and aid me, so that N. has no peace by day, no sleep by night, not enough strength for an hour, nor endurance for a half-hour. May he be seized by hernias or internal pains,[200] may they grip him in a minute or two, and may he know every grief and woe.

The person making this curse does it at night, having removed his cross. It is recommended that a black cat be killed to strengthen the curse. As soon as the victim steps on the knotted thread he will stumble, and if he then swears the curse will begin to take effect.[201]

(For the Evil Eye, which may be the inadvertent influence of a person thought to have it, or the deliberate act of a *koldun*, especially at weddings, see Ch. 2.2.)

5.7. *To attract the benevolence of superiors, rulers, judges, etc.* Maikov lists several *zagovory* of this kind,[202] and a number of court cases mention them: in one a deacon is accused of giving a magic powder to a peasant by which he could gain the favour of his master.[203] Amulets such as the *Dream of the Virgin* (q.v.) could also be taken to court as magical protection.

One spell for this purpose reads:

> I shall arise and bless myself, I shall go crossing myself to the barn, into the open country, facing east. To the east stands a church with twelve cupolas. In this church sits the most holy Mother of God. Holy Mother of God, pray to your son Jesus Christ for your servant Ivan. Save him from tsars and kings, from unjust judges and evil men. For ever and ever, Amen.[204]

Another spell is to take a twig from a trembling birch and say: 'As this twig trembles so may my opponent and his tongue tremble in court'.[205]

A more elaborate method recommended by a *koldun* was to kill a black snake with a sabre or knife and take out its tongue; wrap this in green and black taffeta and put it into the left boot; then leave the spot without looking back and say nothing to anyone (a common requirement in spells); when required as protection in court or in battle the snake's tongue was to be put into the boot with three cloves of garlic and a towel tied over the right breast.[206] Another amulet for the same purpose was the herb called *khvalikha*, which had four flowers: red, black, green and blue, with ten leaves on each side.[207] Dal' quotes a saying that gentian and toads' bones soften the anger of the authorities, a belief going back at least to Pliny.[208]

If you were out of favour with the tsar or a prince magical help could be obtained by wearing under the left arm the right eye of an eagle caught at midnight on St John's Eve and stabbed to death with a sharp stick at a crossroads; the left eye of the same eagle, mixed with cow's blood and feathers, if dried and wrapped in a clean blue kerchief, was an excellent amulet for fishermen and hunters.[209]

Analogous spells can be found elsewhere.[210]

5.8. *To hide or find treasure*. Notions of spirit-guarded treasure are, of course, worldwide, and the search for treasure, usually by means of magic, is an ancient occupation and a staple theme of folktales.[211]

Traditional beliefs in northern Russia, and stories incorporating them, often attributed hoards of buried treasure to the activities of bandits or the *pany*, i.e. Polish adventurers in the so-called Time of Troubles at the beginning of the seventeenth century, or to the Chud' (variously a Finnic tribe with a magical reputation, or the legendary people who built the burial mounds of Siberia).[212] No-one seems to have doubted the existence of these hoards, and indeed the habit of burying valuables seems to have been strong in Russia – a Dutch diplomat in Russia wrote in 1610:

> I do not believe that there was a single piece of money or article of jewellery in the town, for everything was hidden in the ground. For in moments of danger it is the general custom in Muscovy to bury one's money and precious objects in the woods, cellars and other waste places.[213]

Popular belief about treasure includes the reification or personification of treasure (as, for example, a child, old man, dog, horse, cockerel, lamb, corpse, or wooden board, which will turn into money if struck, or, in the case of the corpse if you say 'Amen' over it).[214] The corpse and wooden boards variants are recorded in a North Russian legend, one of many concerning *pany*, the Polish soldiers in the early seventeenth century mentioned above, who were thought to have buried their booty when they left. In this story a corpse was found and when the finder said 'Amen' over it, it dissolved into a treasure hidden by a *pan*; the finder took some of the money but died three years later, according to local belief because he broke the taboo and told someone else about the incident.[215]

The other frequently occurring theme is that of the demonic guardian,[216] often manifested by mysterious lights, especially at Easter.[217] For the guardian spirit there is a special name, *kladovik* (or variant).[218] The ways of overcoming the magic protection of a treasure, be it in the form of the *kladovik* or a spell or curse, include magic books, formulas or herbs such as the *razriv-trava* (also known as *prygun, skakun, spryg-trava, gremuchaia trava, zhelezniak* and more). The *razryv-trava* flowers at midnight on the eve of the feast of St John (24 June), and only for as long as it takes to recite the Lord's Prayer, the prayer to the Virgin and the Creed; it opens locks and bolts, yields up treasures, and prevents blacksmiths from working. If a scythe breaks on the eve of the feast of St John the herb on which this happens will be *razryv-trava*.[219] The same magical plant, with the alternative name of *světi-tsvět*, will burst open in your hands when held over a treasure.[220] Most variants of this belief, throughout the Slavonic world, identify the plant which has these remarkable characteristics as the fern,[221] but in the trans-Baikal region it may also be hemp.[222]

A literary expansion of the theme of the fern which will discover treasures at midnight on St John's Eve occurs in Nikolai Gogol''s story *St John's Eve* with the further gory detail that a child must be sacrificed to obtain the treasure.[223]

The herb, or fern (its botanical identification varies), is clearly connected with beliefs about the magical properties of iron, and the stories about it are either cognate with or derived from the beliefs found with varying local coloration in England, France, France, Germany, Austria and Italy, where the gathering of fern seed on St John's Eve was forbidden by the Synod of Ferrara in 1612.[224]

Other plants are specified elsewhere: a professional treasure-hunter of the Simbirsk province, Andrei Mikhailov, a landowner who died in 1854, left a note about the treasure of Solomon and its demonic guards, and the means of overcoming them. This mentions *ogneia* (usually one of the names of the fever demons or *triasavitsy*, the daughters of Herod), *tsar'-trava, petrov krest* and *plakun* (see Ch. 9 for these). The *plakun* was to be gathered on St John's Eve, and its top twisted over; it was to be kept until Trinity Sunday when it was to be taken with its root to the church, where the priest's prayer over the herbs would make it good for discovering treasure.

After the priest's blessing the herb was ready for use with the following spell:

I, servant of God N., approach this treasure. I ring it with a circle in breadth and depth and affirm it by the word of God. Send me, Lord, the angel Uriel as a helper to drive off the power of the demon, the heretic and the sorcerer from this circle. Send, Lord, dread Elijah the Prophet with his fiery chariot, to destroy with thunderbolts the unclean spirit guarding this treasure. I affirm this treasure on the Alatyr stone, I open the lock in heaven, the key is in the sea. As the sea is not fiery, so may none except me take the key from the sea nor unlock the lock. Amen.[225]

One can only wonder how this 'professional' treasure-seeker made a living! The *plakun-trava* 'weeper-herb' employed in this procedure was a herb on which the Virgin's tears fell at the Crucifixion,[226] of which Dal' (s.v. *plakat'*) says that it makes devils and witches weep; its root is collected on St John's Eve and will protect you from temptation.

Another 'professional' treasure-seeker was a *koldun* in the Viatka region who was interrogated by the Synodal court in 1744. Most of his activities were related to healing and fortune-telling, but he also confessed to invoking the help of wood demons to find treasure. He brought three pea puddings and forty-five red eggs into the forest and called out a *prigovor*: 'Spirits of the woods, here are presents – show us the hidden money'. He asserted that the *leshie* had remained invisible but had given clearly audible instructions on the location of the treasure. These were followed, but alas, no treasure was found.[227]

Another method employed by treasure-seekers was to throw a fern flower into the air: the flower would float over it like a star and then fall to earth where the treasure was hidden.[228] In this it resembled the *perelet-trava* ('flying herb') which was sought on St John's Eve and guaranteed good luck.[229]

Treasure-seekers in Belorussia claimed that to find treasure you had to take with you a cockerel which had crowed on the third day of its life.[230]

It will be seen that the search for buried treasure, because it was usually protected by magic or a demon, was a dangerous business, and the magic employed to overcome this demonic protection was itself often of a demonic nature. For example, according to legends in the Volga region, the way to find one of the hoards hidden magically by the famous seventeenth-century rebel leader Stenka Razin, was to shoot an arrow into the heart of an icon of the Virgin.[231]

The discovery of treasures is closely allied with the making visible of other hidden things. One of the guardians of treasure was the White Serpent, the queen of serpents – in the Archangel region, it was thought that if you killed her you would gain the power of seeing hidden treasure.[232] The fern was reputed also to have this property when it flowered on Easter (or St John's) eve. For the latter purpose, in one account, you had to take a cloth on which an Easter cake has been blessed, go into the forest, trace a circle with a knife round the fern, spread the cloth within the circle, sit down on it and watch the plant. When 'Christ is risen' was sung in church the fern would bloom; you had then to seize it, cover yourself with the cloth, and rush home without looking back. Then you had to cut your hand with the knife and insert the blossom: thereupon hidden things would become visible.[233] Another version of this is quoted by De Gubernatis from a Russian correspondent: On St John's Eve take a cloth, cross, Gospel book, glass of water and a watch; draw a large circle, spread the cloth in it; place the Gospel book, glass of water and watch on it; look at the watch – at midnight it will flower and if you see it flower you will also see other marvellous things: three suns (for multiple suns in other contexts see Ch. 5.4) and a brilliant light which will reveal everything, even hidden things. You will also hear demonic laughter but on no account must you turn around; if you do the Devil will tear your head off and your soul will go to Hell.[234] If you do not panic you will learn everything that is happening or will happen in the world, have immense power, be able to become invisible and have the favours of any woman you wish.[235] In yet another description it was the Devil who tried to break off the flower as soon as it bloomed; you had therefore to draw a protective circle and wait for the Devil to call. He would be imitating the voice of someone close to you. You had not to listen or turn your head. If you were able to seize the flower yourself you would be able to find treasure, become invisible, be invincible on land or sea, and defy the Devil.[236]

Other methods for making secret things visible were to eat the remains of a serpent's meal,[237] or to light a candle made from human fat (see 5, Malefic spells, above). Stephen Graham, travelling in Russia just before the Revolution, was assured by a peasant worker in a Moscow tavern, that 'if you make a candle from human fat and light it, you will see all'.[238]

There are rituals and spells for burying a treasure, and curses placed on anyone stealing them.[239] These occur frequently in folktales about misers. They are often very brief, e.g. 'May only those hands which buried this dig it up again', and sometimes the finder avoided the curse by using the hands of the dead miser to dig up the treasure. The idea of hidden treasure protected by magic which could be circumvented by those with the proper knowledge is reflected in a folk saying: 'Those who know how can even dig up a spell-bound treasure'.[240] Frequently the *zagovor* includes the motif of having to place the same number of heads (e.g. a hundred sparrow heads, the heads of three brave lads) over the site of the treasure in order to obtain it as were put there at its burial.[241] A variant on this theme is the belief that if a treasure is buried 'with forty heads' the first forty treasure-hunters who try to dig it up will fall victim to the curse but the forty-first will be successful.[242] A more elaborate spell is the following:

> I, the servant of God (name), place [this treasure], with a stone barrier about it, closed with a stone door, locked with three times nine locks and three times nine keys, with one key and one lock let no one cross this barrier, no bird fly over it; As Jerusalem is fixed on the earth so may the earth here be fixed, let my curse be from east to west, from the seventh heaven to the third abyss; I shall give the key to the angel Michael, Michael will give it to the angel Gabriel, Gabriel will give it to our mother the Holy Mother of God and she will give it to the white fish in the River Jordan.[243]

Keys and locks have been noted elsewhere as having talismanic value (for protecting cattle, in the house of the deceased after a funeral, as a charm for a happy marriage, and as a contraceptive) and have indeed been found in the excavation of hoards.[244] The binding power of the key is no doubt the reason why in Siberia children were forbidden to play with keys, and especially to put them in their mouths, for fear of incurring a speech impediment.[245] The motif of stone walls or iron fences is a common one and has obvious application in any kind of protective spell, for persons, livestock, houses and treasures.

Klad, the word for treasure, may also be personified, as mentioned above, and the word was particularly used for will-o-the-wisps, who, as in other parts of Europe, were supposed to guard treasure.[246]

Dowsing for treasure seems not to have been a practice in Russia, but there is one (incomplete) text on the subject, evidently compiled or translated by a student sent to Germany in the time of Peter to study mining. The methods described are: choose forked hazel twigs to detect silver, cherry for copper, pine for tin and lead; cut the twigs at dawn, midday or sunset on the second, eighth, tenth, or twelfth day of the month; pronounce the prayer 'In the name of the Father, Son, and Holy Ghost, Jesus, Mary, Almighty ever-merciful God, to You, O Creator of the whole world, Amen'; the forked twig is to be held in both hands with the fingers pointing upwards and the twig slanting upwards; it will twitch when you are over a deposit. An alternative was to cut or break the twig at sunrise saying: 'I greet you, twig, and beg you to let me find gold, silver, copper, tin, lead and iron ores. In the name of the Father, etc.'.[247]

Another magical method for acquiring wealth was to secure a cock's egg (a malformed or immature chicken's egg), carry it for six weeks in one's left armpit, and when a serpent hatched, go to sleep for the night in a deserted hut or bathhouse; the Devil would appear in a dream and give the serpent powers to bring you gold in return for making a pact with him. This Russian-sounding belief has been examined in a short essay by Boris Uspenskii.[248] He relates it to a number of other Russian beliefs and mythological motifs; but it is worth noting that the whole procedure of the messy generation of a serpent which then brings you gold in exchange for a diabolical pact is very similar to one given in the *Grimorium verum vel probatissime Solomonis Claviculae*.[249]

5.9. *Protection from thieves*. The various gruesome magical practices employed by thieves to ensure success are described above in the section on malefic spells, and some methods of detecting thieves are described in Ch. 4.6.2. A Siberian spell for catching a thief is to take a thread from a shroud, the length of the corpse, walk three times round the house, barn etc. which are to be protected, then wind the thread round a stick and push this into the ground in the circled area, and say: 'As this corpse, servant of God N., will not get up and come out of the grave, so may this sinful person not be able to get out of the circle. For ever and ever, Amen'.[250]

5.10. *Protection in battle*. Up to the Revolution, and no doubt later, soldiers went off to battle with crosses, icons, and copies of the *Dream of the Virgin* (see Chs 8.6 and 10.5). There were also spells for this occasion:

> In the lofty chamber, at the river mouth, beyond the river Volga, a fair maiden stands, stands and decks herself, commends herself to valorous folk, glories in deeds of war. In her right hand she holds bullets of lead, in her left bullets of

copper, on her feet bullets of iron. Do thou, fair maiden, ward off the guns of the Turks, the Tatars, the Circassians, the Russians, the Mordvins, of all tribes and foes; smite with thy invisible might the hostile weapons. If they shall shoot from their guns, may their bullets not hit, but strike the moist earth, the open field. May I be whole and uninjured in this war, and my steed whole and uninjured, and my dress stouter than armour. I close my decree with a lock and I hurl the key into the Ocean-sea, on the burning stone Alatyr. And, as it is not to the sea to dry, as the stone may not be seen, the keys not be reached, so may I not be hit by bullets for all my life.[251]

For spells specifically designed to heal wounds see above under medical spells. Spells were also made for the protection of common soldiers from officers: a Belorussian spell reads:

The child came from the womb; it had no mind, no reason, no eyes, no words, no wicked heart. So my commander have no mind, no reason, no eyes, no words, no wicked heart against me, servant of God.[252]

5.11. *Spells on weapons.* Any weapon could have a *zagovor* placed on it, either by the owner to make him successful in hunting or invincible in battle, or by an enemy with the opposite intention. The idea of weapon spells is encountered all over Europe and beyond – Saxo Grammaticus for example mentions several occasions when swords were blunted by enemy spells.[253] In the case of firearms the consequences of a misfire could be unfortunate both medically and professionally and were serious enough to encourage the user to seek magical reassurance. One method of guarding against a dangerous misfire was to wipe the gun barrel with blood,[254] a Belorussian variant in Poles'e being that the blood had to come from the little finger of the right hand,[255] while a Karelian variant requires the warm blood of a magpie. In the Karelian case the hunter had also to buy from the *koldun* a magic hunting licence listing the animals which could be killed and in what numbers.[256] Another method was to speak a spell over the gun or even have the spell engraved on it. In Mogilev the hunter had to wash the gun in water from three wells, pour part of the water to the left and say: 'Thunder roars, lightning strikes, St Peter guides the lead [bullet]'. These spells were often performed by blacksmiths.[257] S.T. Aksakov in sketch 3 of his autobiographical *Semeinaia khronika* recounts how his grandfather in late eighteenth-century Russia dealt with a 'gun spell':

My grandfather in general was no believer in magic. A magician once tried to deceive him by telling him that he could bewitch guns so that no one could fire them. My grandfather handed over his own gun to be experimented with, and then calmly fired it, after the enchanter had secretly withdrawn the charge. The latter was very much upset, but recovered himself, and solemnly declared that my grandfather was also one of the 'Elect'.[258]

In western parts of Russia a gun which never missed was called a *iordanka* because it had a spell put on it at the Jordan (the hole in the ice made for blessing the water at the Epiphany).[259] On the other hand if a hunter was blasphemous enough to load a gun on a feast day, it would be 'spoiled'.[260] A spell for counteracting a spell put on a gun by an enemy reads as follows:

> In the name of the Father, Son and Holy Spirit. There is a holy ocean sea, in that holy ocean see there is the [A]Latyr' stone, and on that Latyr' stone there are three brothers, three bosom friends: one judges, the second acts, the third charms away spells from me and from my gun, my lead and powder, my firearm. The three brothers, the three bosom friends have made a circle round me, servant of God N, an iron wall from heaven to earth, from east to west and south to north. From the depths of the sea comes the tsar of the sea with three times nine locks and three times nine keys; he locks the locks and throws the keys into the sea. From the depths of the sea, from a cavern comes a pike fish; it swallows the keys and goes off into the sea. As fishermen may never catch it so, so may I, servant of God N, never be caught and my gun, lead and powder, my firearm, never be taken or bewitched by anyone, now and for ever, Amen.[261]

The last example was intended to counteract hostile spells on weapons such as:

> Five knots will I tie for every unfriendly [i.e. enemy] and unfaithful [i.e. pagan] shooter – on the guns, on the bows, on every weapon of war. O knots, shut against the shooter all highways and byways, close up the guns, put all the bows out of order, string together all the weapons of war; in my knots let there be almighty virtue.[262]

Another way of preventing a hostile spell from spoiling your hunting was to keep the shot in your mouth until you were ready to load.[263]

Eleonskaia quotes an example of a German prisoner teaching Russians gun-spells,[264] and Peter the Great lists gun-spells among the magic practices for which severe penalties were imposed in the code of military law, the *Voinskii artikul* of 1716 (see Ch. 16).

It was not only hunters and soldiers who used gun spells; criminals were notoriously superstitious (see 7.5.6 above), and one Cossack brigand in the middle of the nineteenth century believed that he could not be wounded or killed because he could put spells on guns.[265]

5.12. *For hunting and fishing.* Beside the gun-spells mentioned above, there were other magical procedures which could be followed by hunters and anglers. In Siberia the ritual to be observed for making hunting guns and fishing tackle successful was to place them under the table with 'Holy Thursday pitch', i.e. pitch which was put out on the eve of the feast in memory of the torches in the garden at Gethsemane. This pitch also had therapeutic properties.[266] A spell for a successful hunt (to be spoken over salt) is:

> Michael Archangel, just as the people of God gather at the church, so may there flock to me, servant of God N, white animals, bandy-legged black-eared hares, from all four quarters, east and west, south and north.[267]

An elaborate *zagovor* showing even more clearly the eclectic nature of the genre and the incantatory use of lists is:

> Lord bless me, I go to sleep and cross myself, I rise and wash in cold dew, dry myself with a blessed cloth. I shall pray to the Saviour, to Cosmas and Damian, to the Virgin, Gabriel and all the heavenly host. Bless me Lord and all the heavenly host to go out into the open country to the east to the ocean sea. In the ocean sea on the isle of Buian stands a temple of the Lord, all golden, holy, apostolic. In this church on a golden altar sit the Virgins of Tikhvin and Vladimir [two icon types of the Virgin]; pray to them to go out into the forest and field and set golden traps [there follows a list of types of trap and a list of animals] at all times, now and forever, Amen.[268]

There were also many superstitions and omens connected with hunting. For example, if when the hunter set out he met a woman, especially one with an empty bucket, this was a bad sign; if he met a man, it was a good sign.[269] When he reached the forest a placatory offering to the *leshii* or wood sprite, usually a piece of bread with a pinch of salt on top, the traditional gesture of hospitality, would ensure a good hunt.[270] Fishermen could ensure a good catch by having their nets woven at midnight by a pregnant woman,[271] and Belorussian fishermen evidently benefited from the Classical tradition in Polish education: one spell calls on Tsar Neptune as well as the Virgin Mary to bless the fishing.[272]

5.13. *For agriculture, including weather.* The greater part of agricultural magic involved either fertility rites, especially at sowing or harvesting times, or protective rituals and spells, especially at such times as the first pasturing of livestock after the winter. Typically these require a spoken spell or prayer (usually to one of the patron saints of flocks: St George, St Nicholas), some symbolic action (drawing a circle or walking around the thing to be protected), and a magical object (often symbolic of physical protection: a lock, knife, axehead, or of spiritual protection: candle, incense; but also many other objects), and an offering (e.g. bread, salt, a candle before an icon).[273]

One such practice required taking a handful of an unreaped cereal crop, with the hand protected by the sleeve, and either twisting it to the ground or twisting it into a wreath, saying: 'Here Elijah-beard, bring us corn, oats, barley and wheat'. Sometimes the heads of corn were tied with a red ribbon and buried with bread and salt and the words: 'God grant a good harvest next summer'.[274] (As we have seen elsewhere bread and salt are the traditional offerings of hospitality, and red ribbons, threads, etc. are a widely used protection against witchcraft.)

A ritual from the Olonets region in the north found in a seventeenth-century spell-book requires the owner of a herd to get up before dawn, take a bear-spear which has been in a bear, make a triple ring about the cattle which are to be sent out to pasture, go to the other side of the yard and recite: 'May an iron fence encircle my herd, as many as are sent out'; then put the spear on the other side of the gate and recite: 'My cattle, may you look like tree stumps, logs and stones to all black, grey and hunting wild beasts, from this day for the whole summer until the first snow'; then place a candle before the icon of St George. He was then to pray for the safety of the herd, place a candle stump, and arrange a dinner of fresh pike, and not clear away the bones of that day's meal. When dinner was over, he had to move the table back, touch nothing, put out the candle, pray to St George, go out into the yard with the whole family, and, with a blessing, let the cattle out of the yard. After that he was to place himself opposite the spear, take the spear and put it in a secret place so that no one could touch it while the cattle roamed the woods until the white snow came. Then going back into the house, he had to tidy the table, not giving the bones to the dogs nor anything to anyone else.[275] A similar set of rituals for the protection of livestock was performed in some regions on January 6: the owner was to bring home some water from the Blessing of the Water ceremony, put a sheaf of mixed cereal crops in the form of a cross in the farmyard, and then drive in the livestock. The owner's wife was to put on her sheepskin coat inside out, draw a circle with an axe three times round the sheaves and livestock while holding in the other hand an icon and a candle. The owner followed her sprinkling the blessed water over the sheaves and animals with a bunch of heads of rye. The wife then threw the axe over the animals.[276]

A St George's day ritual surviving into modern times was recorded in Nikol'sk in 1969. Here the last sheaf of corn from the previous year, which had been blessed in church and preserved in the corner where the icons were kept, was brought out to feed the cattle. The priest would carry the icon of St George round the herd three times, and the cowherd would cut a little hair from the hide of each, mix all the hair together, burn it and say the spell: 'May the cows stay together as this hair burns together'.[277]

There are also any number of weather and crop predictions based on the calendar, and forms of divination such as haruspicy which are described elsewhere, and magical practices such as burying a live cat in a field to keep down the weeds, a result which could also be obtained by pulling up a weed and replanting it upside down so that it grew away from the crops.[278]

A sub-category is spells or magical practices for bringing rain. The latter could involve throwing a priest on the ground and drenching him, dipping a figurine of St John into water on St John's Day, or throwing a passing stranger into the river;[279] in Belorussia all the widows of the village would strip naked and run around the village at night, steal a plough and hang it on a fence, or steal jugs and throw them in the well, or else gates would be taken down and thrown on the ground or into a marsh.[280] Other methods included ritual processions with prayers round the fields, weaving special cloths, rituals by wells or by the graves of 'unclean' corpses (i.e. those of magicians, suicides, and those who died violently or from alcohol), digging up roads or dried up river beds, destroying anthills, killing snakes and frogs.[281] As recently as 1965 it is recorded that the workers on a collective farm in Smolensk were ordered to bathe in the river in order to end a drought.[282]

Verbal charms, in particular for and against rain, are common.[283] One such is: 'As water puts out fire so may my words subdue the storm'.[284] One spell involves the belief described elsewhere that drought and crop failure are caused by burying the corpses of magicians, suicides, drunkards and victims of murder; it describes seeing the coffin of a magician on which the rain never falls, cutting an aspen stake and driving it into the belly of the corpse and then reburying it in a bog. The collector of this spell (in 1866) observed that in the provinces along the Volga peasants would often match their actions to their words.[285] Licit prayers for rain are known, e.g. the prayer of Patriarch Philotheos Kokkinos.[286] Rain could also be conjured by sprinkling the field with water from seven (in some places three) wells.[287]

The kind of weather for which magic might be invoked depends, of course, on locality. In northern Siberia clouds could be summoned after a long spell of clear frosty weather by a woman collecting pieces of wool or rags (as resembling clouds), throwing them into the fire and saying: 'Lord Tsar Fire, give clouds, give warmth to my child'. On the other hand a period of wet cloudy weather could be banished by throwing a piece of mammoth bone into the fire and saying: 'Be clear, be clear'. The same result could be obtained by persuading a man who had been born in calm clear weather to strip naked and run across the tundra crying: 'Be clear, be clear, be like the day I was born'.[288] In the same region extended windy periods could be brought to an end by the old folk reciting the *byliny* (folk epics) of Sadko, and shouting: 'Sadko, rich merchant, subdue the weather' (in the poem Sadko, merchant and minstrel, is able to calm the elements by playing music).[289]

Witches were frequently thought to be able to control rain,[290] and sorcerers to be able to blight crops and livestock (see Ch. 3). Min'ko lists a number of spells for protecting livestock from misfortune and witchcraft in Belorussia: these include placing a lock at the entrance to a field when cattle are driven there for the first time (this would protect them by locking up the jaws of wolves), pouring blessed mercury from a thermometer into a hole drilled into a cow's horn (to protect her from witches), hanging a dead magpie in a stall to protect the horse; using church candles when handling bees with smoke.[291] Cattle could be protected from plague by 'living fire' or 'wood fire' which was obtained by friction from wood, usually at the time of the midsummer festival of Ivan Kupala.[292] Various other practices for protecting domestic animals are described in Chs 8 and 9.

Lost livestock could perhaps be restored by a *zagovor* in the form of a letter to the *leshii* or wood-demon and the spirits of the earth and water. One such is:

> I write to the tsar of the forest, the tsaritsa of the forest and their little children; to the tsar of the earth . . ., to the tsar of the water . . . I inform you that servant of God X has lost a [black, brown, etc.] horse [or cow, etc.]. If it should be found in your realm send it back without delaying an hour, a minute, a second. And if you do not I shall appeal to the megolomartyr George and Tsaritsa Aleksandra.

This letter was to be written *right to left*, an magical inversion appropriate to dealings with a *leshii*, in triplicate, on birch bark. One copy was to be nailed to a tree, another buried, the third tied to a stone and thrown into water.[293]

A set of no fewer than six prayers and spells was required in one part of the Ukraine when setting up new beehives; for the last one it was necessary to go round the beehives three times with blessed olive oil, and say: 'Just as the Christian world cannot go without olive oil, so may the swarms of bees for ten miles around be unable to do without my beehives'.[294]

5.14. *Setting out on journey*. There are many popular superstitions about setting out on a journey: you must not begin your journey on a Monday, and if it rains after you have set out this means good luck;[295] you must sit silently for a moment before leaving, and once out of the door you must not cross back over the threshold (this is still widely practised in Russia). Other bad omens connected with travel, such as a hare or a monk crossing your path, are discussed in Ch. 5.2.

There are several specific magical ways of finding out if circumstances are propitious for a journey, and several kinds of more general methods of fortune-telling which may offer advice. An 'astrological' method involving the star 'Aravan' is described in Ch. 15.3. There are also ways of protecting oneself when setting out on, or during a journey: an icon was essential and a variety of amulets could also be employed. These are described elsewhere in this book. *Zagovory* may also be employed – an example is:

> [Saint] George the Brave is riding his white horse, he wears a gold crown, he is armed with a blade of finest steel; he meets a thief of the night and addresses him: Where are you going, thief of the night? [The thief replies:] I am going to kill people and rob passing merchants. But George would not yield the road to him, he protects the Orthodox and guards them on their journey.[296]

A *zagovor* to enable you to make a journey unseen, and thus safely, is given below (15), and one addressed to the 'Tsar of the forest Onoprii' to help you when you have lost your way is mentioned in n. 292 above.

5.15. *Trade.* Merchants would reward or punish icons to which they prayed for success in business (see Ch. 8.6). There were also spells. One brief example is: 'As the wild bees swarm and fly together so may the merchants flock to these traders' (this is said over honey with which you then smear yourself).[297] This is perhaps the most appropriate category in which to mention the *nerazmennyi rubl'*. This is a coin which the owner will always have no matter how often he spends it; it crops up from time to time in folk tales together with flying carpets and other magical aids. It can be obtained by tying up a black cat with tarry twine and selling it for a rouble (an improbable deal),[298] or by swaddling a black cat, taking it to the bathhouse at midnight, and speaking the words: 'Here is a child for you – give me an everlasting rouble'. Then throw the cat into the bathhouse, run out, make three circles around you with a cross, and say the magic protective word *chur*.[299] In one popular belief freemasons were thought to be a people living in a far land who possessed such coins.[300]

5.16. *To become invisible, fly, turn into an animal.* Invisibility was one of the characteristics of an evil spirit in Russia. *Nevidimka* 'an invisible being' and *nevidimaia sila* 'an invisible force' are two of the very many names for the sprites of the Russian popular imagination.[301] The *shapka nevidimka* 'cap of invisibility',[302] like the *kover-samolët* '= magic carpet' and *sapogi-samokhody* '= seven-league boots', the *skatert' (suma)-khlebosolka, kotoma dai pit' i est'*, or *skatert' samobranka* '= the ever-full tablecloth (bag)', *karty odnozolochnye* or gold cards which would always win,[303] and the *nerazmennyi rubl'* or 'everlasting rouble', is a common folk-tale motif in Russia as elsewhere. The idea that a person, witch or otherwise, can become invisible, is well known in Russian and Ukrainian folklore. Here is a specimen instruction and spell:

> If you find a large anthill with twelve paths leading from it, then light a fire and boil water in a pot; then soak the whole anthill, rake it level and soak it again; then you will find a hole in the ground, put a brass or pewter button into it as far as it will go;[304] then dig for two and a half to three sazhens (=fathoms) and you will see the king of the ants on a red or blue stone; pour boiling water on the king of the ants and he will fall from the stone; wrap the stone in a taffeta kerchief and start digging again; he will ask you 'have you found it?' but you must say nothing but keep the stone in your mouth and wipe yourself with the kerchief, and you will be invisible as you walk. Thou sky my father, thou earth my mother, thou sacred root, bless me to success(?)[305]

Another method quoted in the same source is to take the herb *erek* which grows by a middling river in a middling place and has blue and red flowers; leave it in church for three days, then take it and sew it into your hat, saying over it: 'As this herb has lain in church for three days and not been noticed so may the servant of God (name) be unseen and unheard whatever he does by day or night'. This must be said over the herb on three dawns. A similar popular superstition has it that the *kostochka-nevidimka* or 'bone of invisibility' can be obtained by boiling a black cat which has not a single white hair until the bones are clean, then you will find the special bone which will make you invisible and enable you to open locks.[306] The use of a 'dead candle' made from human fat to attain invisibility is described above under malefic spells.

A spell for becoming invisible while making a journey is quoted by Iatsimirskii: catch a bat and pick out its right eye with a brass pin while saying 'Just as you, accursed bat, cannot see with your right eye, so may I, servant of God Gregory, walk the earth unseen',[307] and magical procedures for making secrets visible are described above in the section on finding treasure.

The ability of a witch to fly or to turn into an animal or bird is discussed in Ch. 3, where a *zagovor* for becoming a werewolf is also given. A witch who has turned herself into a were-animal could be forced to change back by striking her with a rod of ash; and a person who has been changed by a spell could be restored by putting on him a girdle which has been knotted, and 'Lord have mercy' recited while each knot was being tied.[308]

5.17. *Moving into a new house.* There were various superstitions about where a new house could be built, and the advice of the *koldun* could well be sought. Moving into the new house was best done on one of the twelve major religious feasts, preferably the Presentation of the Virgin (21 November). Before entering the new house it was best to send in a cock or a cat – if anything untoward was going to happen it would happen to them. If all was well then you could enter the house yourself, carrying bread, salt, and an icon, if possible at night at the time of the new moon. You were to put a piece of bread under the stove for the house-sprite (*domovoi*). In some places the lady of the house would run barefoot round the house three times before dawn and pronounce the spell:

> I place an iron fence around about this home (*dvor*). Let no wild beast jump over the fence, nor serpent crawl over it, nor evil person set foot over it, and may the grandfather woodsprite not look over it.[309]

Some of these practices are reported more recently from Karelia, with the added details of burying a copper coin under the icon corner, putting a cross of pitch by the windows to keep out lightning, and starting the first fire with coals taken from the old house.[310] Another ritual is designed to persuade the house-sprite from the old house to move into the new house. The owner must go to the new house and leave a whole loaf with salt on it and a cup of milk, then go to the old house at night and, standing in nothing but his shirt, say: 'I bow to you, father-landlord (*batiushka-khoziain*), and ask you to come to stay with us in our new dwelling. We have a warm corner there for you and a meal'.[311] Curiously enough there are in Britain similar customs of putting salt in the hearth as the first act on moving into a new house, although any notion of it being a gift to a resident sprite seems to be absent.[312]

5.18. *Protection from fire.* The frequent occurrence of fire in the wooden towns and villages of Russia was always a matter of concern. Protection from fire seems to have been more a matter of ritual and the use of talismans than of verbal magic, although there is a record of Russians learning spells to put out fires from a German prisoner-of-war.[313] Good weather at the feast of the Annunciation (25 March),[314] a cuckoo flying though a village, or a hare running through a village, or a dog howling with its head lifted, or mice or cockroaches leaving a house, or a cricket entering a house, were all signs of an impending fire,[315] as was the omen of all the egg white sinking to the bottom when poured into a glass of water.[316] This misfortune could be prevented by leading a bear round the house three times,[317] or if a bear was not to hand, stripping naked and running three times round the burning house with a piece of communion bread in your mouth.[318] If that failed, an icon, especially of St Nicholas, would prevent the spread of the fire;[319] and in the last resort the SATOR magic square would put out the fire,[320] as would an egg used for the first Easter greeting if thrown over the fire.[321] In a Siberian variant of this a *znakharka* whispers a spell over an egg before throwing into the fire.[322] A fire started by lightning, 'by the grace of God', could be put out with eggs, beer, kvas, milk, or a white dove,[323] but some regarded lightning fires as acts of God, hence their name (*bozhii ogon'*) 'fire of God' and any attempt to extinguish them as blasphemous.[324] A Ukrainian method of putting out a fire involves waiting until a snake begins to swallow a toad, then forcing the toad out of the snake's jaws with a stick, then running round the fire three times with the stick.[325] The impossibility of being able to do this in an emergency suggests that this, like some other recorded spells and rituals, are a part of joke-lore; some recorders of folk wisdom no doubt believe you can catch birds by putting salt on their tails.

* * *

Most of the *zagovory* quoted above fall into the category of magical charms, and where a Christian element is involved it is often apocryphal, if not heretical. There are many charms and prayers, however, in which the addition or omission of a word or two makes all the difference between a licit prayer and a magic spell. And the fact that *zagovory* were condemned by the Church does not mean that the clergy did not resort to them: indeed, being more likely to be literate than their parishioners, and to be called to the bedside of the sick, priests were often specified as being necessary for the reading of a *zagovor* and, as we have seen elsewhere, were occasionally taken to court for possession of written copies. There can be little doubt that the clergy were often closely involved in magic of this kind, just as they were among the South Slavs, and in varying degrees in other parts of Europe. For most of the people who resorted to charms to cure themselves of illness or protect themselves from pestilence, violence, lawlessness, injustice or tyrannical masters, there was little else they could turn to.

Notes

1. Maikov, 'Velikorusskie zaklinaniia', p. 464.

2. On the early history of the combined use of amulet and incantation in the Greek world see Kotansky, 'Incantations', esp. pp. 108–10.

3. For a good discussion see Levin, 'Supplicatory Prayers'. For the West see Gifford, 'The Charm', p. 56. For a very pertinent discussion of the Greek situation see Stewart, *Demons*, ch. 9. Stewart remarks that on Naxos the same word is used for 'prayers' and 'spells', and that villagers, and perhaps even the priests, were unable to tell the difference between Orthodox and supposedly superstitious practices (p. 243).

4. See Speranskii, *Russkaia ustnaia slovesnost'*, p. 444. Pp. 436–53 on *zagovory* in general are still of value. See also Rozanov, 'Narodnye zagovory v tserkovnykh Trebnikakh', pp. 30–5.

5. For bibliography see de Santos Otero, *Die handschriftliche Überlieferung*, II, pp. 237–40.

6. For an analysis of actual recorded performances see Astakhova, '"Sound Shaping" of East Slavic Zagovory'.

7. Eleonskaia, *K izucheniiu zagovora i koldovstva v Rossii*, p. 18, mentions Tatars and Mordvinians. One seventeenth-century spell book described by Eleonskaia includes Vepsian (Finnic) spells.

8. Loc. cit. Eleonskaia mentions the case of a German prisoner teaching Russians spells for guns and for putting out fires. Prisoner-of-war contact is also witnessed by a manuscript fortune-telling book (involving 'fifty planets'!) translated from Swedish by Russian prisoners in the Great Northern War (1700–21): *Opisanie rukopisei sobraniia Chertkova*, p. 84. It is also interesting to note the beliefs and practices of the Volga Germans (settlers introduced into Russia by Catherine II in the later eighteenth century) which often parallel the beliefs of their Russian hosts: see Koch, *The Volga Germans*, pp. 163–70.

9. For a survey of Cosmas and Damian in Russian folklore see Makashina, 'Sviatye Kosma i Damian'.

10. This by no means exclusive list is given in Zabylin, *Russkii narod*, p. 273.

11. No doubt because of her narrow escape from rape by enchantment at the hands of St Cyprian before his conversion: see Ch. 1, p. 13.

12. Rovinskii, *Russkie narodnye kartinki*, 1881, III, p. 418 and Tarasov, *Ikona i blagochestie*, pp. 74–5.

13. As always Dal's dictionary has much to offer, but for recent work see, for example, Kondrat'eva, *Metamorfozy sobstvennogo imeni*, and for some discussion of such names in the north of Russia see Cherepanova, *Mifologicheskaia leksika*, pp. 39–40.

14. A *prigovor* is a short verbal formula or saying which accompanies some action, sometimes but not necessarily magical; *nashepti* are whispered spells (cf. Latin *murmur* and *susurrus*.).

15. Hastrup, 'Iceland', p. 387, remarks that words were the principal weapon of Icelandic magicians.

16. Krinichnaia, *Predaniia russkogo severa*, no. 248: 'Bogatyr' Pashko i razboiniki'.

17. Chikachev, *Russkie na Indigirke*, p. 146.

18. See Dal', *Tolkovyi slovar'*, s.v. *zaklinat'*.

19. See Vlasova, *Novaia abevega*, s.v. *urok*.

20. Dal', *Tolkovyi slovar'*, s.v. *chert*.

21. See Uspenskii, 'Religiozno-mifologicheskii aspekt', p. 207.

22. Maikov, 'Velikorusskie zaklinaniia'. Many are also quoted in Afanas'ev, *Poèticheskie vozzreniia*; Sakharov, *Skazaniia*, and Zabylin, *Russkii narod* (mostly compiled from Afanas'ev and Sakharov or

other published sources). For Belorussian *zagovory* see E.R. Romanov, *Belorusskii sbornik* (vol. V. *Zagovory, apokrify i dukhovnye stikhi*), and more recently Bartashevich, *Magichnae slova*. A collection of spells and magic prayers collected in the twentieth century is published in Adon'eva and Ovchinnikova, *Traditsionnaia russkaia magiia*.

23. Tikhonravov, *Pamiatniki*, pp. 351–60. Specimens from the sixteenth century onwards.

24. Pypin, *Lozhnye i otrechennye knigi*, pp. 167–8. Contemporary specimens from the Saratov region.

25. See Iatsimirskii, 'K istorii lozhnykh molitv' v iuzhno-slavianskoi pis'mennosti'. South Slav spells, but many of them are found also in Russia.

26. Quoted from Andreev, *Russkii fol'klor*, p. 32. This is repeated in later manuscripts: see Smirnov, *Materialy*, p. 49. This practice is much the same as the magical exorcism of fever spirits by writing the names of 'accursed Hellenic gods' on an apple which is then eaten by the sufferer: see Granstrem, 'Otgolosok visantiiskogo sueveriia'. Granstrem derives this practice from the tenth-century Byzantine *Geoponica*, which recommends that the injunction 'Taste and see that the Lord is good' (Psalm 34: 8) be written on an apple and put into wine to prevent it turning sour. The connection is a little tenuous and the *Geoponica* seems otherwise not to have been known in Russia. The Byzantine romance of *Kallimachos and Chrysorrhoe*, 1206–1412, contains an episode in which a charm written on an apple could kill or revivify.

27. See Zguta, 'Witchcraft and Medicine in Pre-Petrine Russia', p. 444, for some discussion of the views of Mansikka and his critics.

28. Eleonskaia, *K izucheniiu zagovora i koldovstva v Rossii*, p. 18; Gromyko, *Trudovye traditsii*, p. 148.

29. Kieckhefer, *Magic in the Middle Ages*, pp. 2–6.

30. The requirement that magical books featuring in court cases be burned is an old one – see Kieckhefer, *Forbidden Rites*, p. 2. Some of the works of the English magician of the first half of this century Aleister Crowley were seized and burned by the authorities, probably more for their indecency than their magical content. The continuing choice of this method of destruction for items thought to be socially abhorrent seems to meet a symbolic need beyond official disapproval – brassières and flags spring immediately to mind.

31. Vinogradov, *Zagovory, oberegi, spasitel'nye molitvy*, 2, pp. 28–9.

32. Smilianskaia, '"Suevernaia" knizhitsa'.

33. For a specific comparison with Assyrian see Miller, 'Assiriiskie zaklinaniia i russkie narodnye zagovory'.

34. Thomas, *Kentucky Superstitions*, no. 1112.

35. The structure and formulas of *zagovory* are discussed most recently in Iudin, *Onomastikon*, pp. 6–10. For an older non-Russian study see in Mansikka, *Russische Zauberformeln*. Iudin, op. cit., and Kliaus, *Ukazatel'* published their books in 1997 and both proposed a classification system. Iudin's is based on the subject of the invocation and the function of the spell; Kliaus's follows more the motif-index pattern. It is too soon to tell whether these taxonomies will be adopted by other scholars.

36. This quasi-legal tone is certainly not confined to Russian spells. It has been noted that the language of the many Latin curse tablets found in Britain is largely legal in tone: see Tomlin, *Tabellae Sulis*, pp. 70–71.

37. Chikachev, *Russkie na Indigirke*, p. 124, reports that Siberian shamans called to Russian patients also begin their rituals of healing magic by praying to the East. Storms, *Anglo-Saxon Magic*, gives examples of the same formula (which he relates to sun-worship) in Anglo-Saxon spells (pp. 6–7, 175). Several of the spells given in a fifteenth-century Latin magic manual also require the performer to be

clean and face east: see Kieckhefer, *Forbidden Rites*, pp. 59, 114, 117; in two experiments the demon to be conjured is actually called Oriens.

38. For discussion of this usage in Greek see Faraone, 'The "Performative Future"'.

39. One Belorussian incantatory list of such tsars even includes 'the English tsar': Romanov, *Belorusskii sbornik*, p. 51. For detailed analytical lists of names invoked in spells see Iudin, *Onomastikon* and Kliaus, *Ukazatel'*.

40. For recent study of medical magic involving narrative incantations in Europe as a whole see Bozóky, 'Mythic Mediation in Healing Incantations'.

41. Maikov, 'Velikorusskie zaklinaniia', p. 431. On the stone Alatyr' (and various other forms); see also Ch. 8.4.) Buian has been variously identified either as a derivative of the adjective *buinyi* 'wild, strong etc.' or the noun *buian* 'a high point in an open place', or as a corruption of the name of the island of Rügen, a holy place of the ancient Baltic Slavs. See Afanas'ev, 'Iazycheskie predaniia ob ostrove Buiane'; Vilinbakhov, 'Taina ostrova Buiana'; Kondrat'eva, *Metamorfozy sobstvennogo imeni*, s.v. For all names in spells see now Cherepanova, *Mifologicheskaia leksika russkogo severa*; Iudin, *Onomastikon*; Kliaus, *Ukazatel'*.

42. Rybnikov, *Pesni*, 1910, II, p. 631.

43. Adon'eva, Ovchinnikova, *Traditsionnaia russkaia magiia*, no. 296.

44. Ibid., no. 299.

45. For some etymological discussion of this see Iudin, 'Ob imenakh zvezd «pomoshchnits»'.

46. See Kieckhefer, *Magic in the Middle Age*s, p. 3, for two spells from the fifteenth-century Wolfsthurn handbook.

47. This form of dramatic presentation is commonly found in spells in many other culture areas. For Greek analogues of this element in Russian spells see Stewart, *Demons*, ch. 9, esp. pp. 238–9. See also Bozóky, 'Mythic Mediation in Healing Incantations' for some Latin specimens.

48. Pliny, *Naturalis historia*, XXVIII.iii.11.

49. Origen, *Contra Celsum*, I, 25.

50. Shein, *Materialy*, II, pp. 555–6.

51. Maikov, 'Velikorusskie zaklinaniia', p. 431.

52. This is common in magic in many parts of the world. For Greek amatory spells whispered over wine see *Papyri graecae magicae*, VII, pp. 285–9, 619–27, 643–51; for analogous Anglo-Saxon practices see Storms, *Anglo-Saxon Magic*, pp. 62–3.

53. Most scholars have more or less followed Maikov in grouping spells by their area of application. I have followed Maikov's principle, but not his order of groups (which anyway has never become a norm), mainly because in this chapter I have been deliberately discursive and have included some non-verbal magic when it seemed closely linked to the concerns of users of particular spells.

54. For a study of this category see Vetuchov, 'Zagovory'. See also Popov, *Russkaia narodnobytovaia meditsina*, pp. 224–49. The texts of many Russian *zagovory* of this kind are given in Iatsimirskii, although his main subject is South Slav texts. Belorussian medical spells are given in Romanov, *Belorusskii sbornik* (vol. V. *Zagovory, apokrify i dukhovnye stikhi*).

55. *Stoglav*, p. 46.

56. Strakhov, 'Na Sviatogo Nikolu . . .', p. 65.

57. Zhuravlev, *Domashnii skot*; pp. 111–13.

58. Dal', *Tolkovyi slovar'*, s.v. *opakhat'*; Popov, *Russkaia narodno-bytovaia meditsina*, pp. 190–1. Popov relates this practice in particular to cholera.

59. For a survey of the practice see Zhuravlev, *Domashnii skot*; pp. 101–13; Zelenin, *Russische (ostslavische) Volkskunde*, pp. 66–8.

60. Maksimov, *Nechistaia sila*, p. 261.

61. Eleonskaia, *Skazka, zagovor i koldovstvo*, pp. 219–20. Eleonskaia states that at the time of writing this custom was still widespread in Russia. For some analysis of the songs sung during *opakhivanie* see Zhuravlev, *Domashnii skot*; pp. 140–2.

62. Loginov, *Material'naia kul'tura i proizvodstvenno-bytovaia magiia russkikh Zaonezh'ia*, p. 34.

63. Blum and Blum, *The Dangerous Hour*, pp. 104–5.

64. Quoted from various sources by Strakhov, 'Vostochnoslavianskoe *chur*', pp. 72–3.

65. See Frazer, *Golden Bough*, abr. version, pp. 70–1; on encircling a house to exclude disease in ancient Egypt, with a modern Texan analogue, see Ritner, *Mechanics*, p. 60.

66. Iudin, *Onomastikon*, pp. 233–61 and *passim*.

67. Cherepanova, 'Tipologiia', p. 45; Dal', *Slovar'*, s.v. *ospa*. Note the female spirit of the measles in a Siberian (non-Russian) shamanistic ritual: Siikala, *The Rite Technique*, pp. 175–83.

68. Sveshnikova, 'O nekotorykh zagovornykh formul', comparing Rumanian and East Slavonic spells, notes in particular the banishing of illnesses to distant parts of the earth, into fish, into trees.

69. Iatsimirskii, 'K istorii lozhnykh molitv', pp. 46–52.

70. Maikov, 'Velikorusskie zaklinaniia', no. 72. Voronezh region.

71. Maikov, 'Velikorusskie zaklinaniia', no. 81. This is to be recited three times over an aspen branch.

72. Truvorov, 'Volkhvy i vorozhei', p. 709.

73. Iatsimirskii, 'K istorii lozhnykh molitv', pp. 42–3.

74. For variants see B.R. Townend, 'The Narrative Charm with Reference to Toothache', *British Dental Journal*, LXXXV, July, 1948.

75. Cockayne, *Leechdoms* I, p. 394, III, p. 64. For later English versions see also Opie and Tatem, *Dictionary*, s.v. *toothache*.

76. See Barb, 'The Survival of Magic Arts', *Paganism and Christianity in the Fourth Century*, Oxford, 1963, p. 123.

77. *Vita sancti Leogisili*, no. 6.

78. See Barb, 'Der Heilige und die Schlangen'. An Armenian prayer amulet is given in Feydit, *Amulettes*, pp. 295–301.

79. For a recent study and several texts of snake-bite prayers see Kagan-Tarkovskaia, 'Drevnerusskie vracheval'nye molitvy'.

80. Described in *Zapiski Otdela rukopisei*, vyp. 46, Moscow, 1987, p. 53, no. 9 (fond 735, no 33).

81. Romanov, *Belorusskii sbornik*, pp. 107–19, 176–87.

82. Shein, *Materialy*, II, p. 518. The actual spell he repeated was in verse and is quoted on pp. 548–9. On p. 548 another spell is quoted in which the serpent tsar is called Sukhodym (lit. Dry-Smoke). For some speculation on the origin of Ur (Ir) see Uspenskii, *Filologicheskie razyskaniia*, pp. 59–60.

83. Markevich, *Obychai* (reprint), p. 120.

84. Systerova and Liakhova, *Fol'klor Dal'nerech'ia*, p. 100.

85. Iatsimirskii, 'K istorii lozhnykh molitv', pp. 16–29; Bulgarian specimens are given in Kristanov and Duichev, *Estestvoznanieto*, pp. 550–2. Zabylin publishes ten Russian spells to staunch the flow of blood: Zabylin, *Russkii narod*, pp. 290–1.

86. The Jordan appears in many spells and other magical practices: see below and index, also Mansikka, *Über russische Zauberformeln*, ad indicem.

87. Iatsimirskii, 'K istorii lozhnykh molitv', pp. 30–9. For some discussion, with Greek and German analogues, see Rozanov, 'Narodnye zagovory v tserkovnykh Trebnikakh'. The use of Greek (and Hebrew) words as *voces magicae* is also found elsewhere – for example in English spells: see Gifford, 'The Charm', p. 49; Storms, *Anglo-Saxon Magic*, p. 269: 'Against every evil witch and against possession by elves write this in Greek letters'. On Hebrew in magical medicine in England see Zier, 'The Healing Power of the Hebrew Tongue'. As late as 1804 a Dorset vicar cured his bewitched child with a 'phylactery inscribed with sacred words in the original character': Thomas, *Religion and the Decline of Magic*, p. 276.

88. Rybnikov, *Pesni*, p. 209, see also p. 319, s.v. *les*, where Rybnikov notes that the name may be Musaila-les and that he has blue blood. Maksimov, *Nechistaia*, pp. 69–70. Afanas'ev, *Poèticheskie vozzreniia*, II, p. 235 mentions both Musail and Mafusail as the name of the chief *leshii*. Here the Russian may be following the Byzantine tradition of creating Hebrew-sounding names of angels and demons ending in -il or -el. For some examples of pseudo-angel names of this type see Iudin, *Onomastikon*, pp. 58–61.

89. Maikov, 'Velikorusskie zaklinaniia', no. 141. From an Old Believer manuscript. For other spells of this type see Zabylin, *Russkii narod*, pp. 290–1. For three Polessian spells and some discussion see Strakhov and Heretz, 'Disappearing Atlantis', pp. 166–70.

90. Eleonskaia, *Sel'sko-khoziaistvennaia magiia*, p. 169.

91. See Opie and Tatem, *Dictionary*, s.v. *Grave, earth/dew from: cures.*

92. See Listova, 'Nekotorye verovaniia russkikh krest'ian', pp. 26, 28). Amulet belts for pregnant women were a commonplace in Europe as a whole.

93. Zabylin, *Russkii narod*, p. 187.

94. Passing a baby under the father's legs was a way of breaking a spell on the child among the Volga Germans: see Koch, *The Volga Germans*, p. 166. In Anglo-Saxon England a pregnant woman would step over her husband to ensure the birth of a healthy child: see Cockayne, *Leechdoms*, III, 67.

95. *Na putiakh iz zemli permskoi v Sibir'*, p. 279.

96. For example, Semenova-Tian-Shanskaia, *Zhizn' Ivana*, p. 9, quotes several of them from the southern Black Earth region.

97. Maikov, 'Velikorusskie zaklinaniia', no. 49; Romanov, *Belorusskii sbornik*, p. 53–64.

98. Romanov, *Belorusskii sbornik*, pp. 53–64.

99. See Strakhov, '"Kuvada" po starobriadcheskoi rukopisi', pp. 104–5, quoting V.N. Dobrovol'skii, *Smolenskii ètnograficheskii sbornik*, pt. 2, St Petersburg, 1893, p. 369. It is, of course, possible that a quite different part of the body was being pulled.

100. Maikov, 'Velikorusskie zaklinaniia', nos. 51–54.

101. G. Popov, 1903, p. 260.

102. Dal', *Poslovitsy*, 1989, p. 363.

103. De Gubernatis, *La Mythologie des plantes*, I, p. 7, quoting Dragomanov and identifying the plant as *Enjugium campestre*. See also Zabylin, *Russkii narod*, p. 428.

104. For other examples of laughter as a sign of the demonic see Index.

105. Popov, *Russkaia narodno-bytovaia meditsina*, 1903, p. 25.

106. Together with a kopek piece, a tuft of flax, and a piece of pie, according to Lebedeva, 'Material'nye komponenty', p. 213. This is in the Tobol'sk region of Siberia.

107. For this belief in England see Hazlitt, *Dictionary*, s.v. *glass, looking.*

108. *Na putiakh iz zemli permskoi v Sibir'*, p. 285.

109. The 'Incredible Enchantress, Astounding Sibyl, the Magician, the Wise Woman of Murom' was one of the alleged sources of a fortune-telling compendium first published in Moscow in 1814: *Astrolog drevnii i novyi ili orakul gadatel'nyi polnyi Martyna Zadeka, Iosifa Muta, Tikhobraga, i Lafatera.*

110. Quoted from Aleksandr Blok, 'Poèziia zagovorov i zaklinanii', p. 101. Blok gives no source and says this is not the end of the spell. The last sentence of the spell is unusual in its patriotic and prematurely elegiac sentiment and one must hope that the eminent poet was not gilding the lily.

111. Maikov, 'Velikorusskie zaklinaniia', no. 58, Novgorod region, mid-nineteenth century.

112. Popov, *Russkaia narodno-bytovaia meditsina*, pp. 24, 232. See also Cherepanova, 'Tipologiia', p. 45, for another version of a 'dawn spell'. The names of 'dawns' and evening or morning stars found in women's spells are often rhyming, or reduplicating, and have an incantatory quality; cf. Maikov, no. 63, a spell against toothache which invokes the sisters 'Zakharii and Makarii [!], Dar'ia and Mar'ia'.

113. *Na putiakh iz zemli permskoi v Sibir'*, p. 284.

114. Kondrat'eva, *Metamorfozy sobstvennogo imeni*, s.v. *Solomonida*; Maikov, *Velikorusskie zaklinaniia*, no. 51; Adon'eva, Ovchinnikova, *Traditsionnaia russkaia magiia*, no. 330; Perunov, *Liubovnye, tselitel'nye i okhranitel'nye zagovory*, no. 144.

115. Dal', *Poslovitsy*, 1989, I, p.

116. The word also means simply a tearful baby, and in the plural is the popular word for the persistent crying of a sick child: see Dal', *Tolkovyi slovar'*, s.v. *krichat'*.

117. Romanov, *Belorusskii sbornik*, pp. 31–4.

118. See Toporkov, '«Perepekanie» detei'. The use of 'water from three wells' goes back at least to Pliny, *Naturalis historia*, XXXVIII.xi.46. On the notion of the special efficacy of water from several sources see Faraone, 'The Mystodokos and the Dark-Eyed Maidens', esp. pp. 316–17.

119. See, for example, the late seventh-century *Penitential of Theodore* and the early eighth-century penitential ascribed to Bede, and the twelfth-century penitential of Bartholomew Iscanus: McNeill and Gamer, *Medieval Handbooks of Penance* (reprint 1965), pp. 199, 229, 350. For the practice among the Volga Germans see Koch, *The Volga Germans*, p. 166.

120. Prokop'eva, 'Zhenskaia rubakha', p. 61.

121. Smirnov, *Materialy*, p. 47.

122. Popov, *Russkaia narodno-bytovaia meditsina*, p. 327; Listova, '«Nechistota» zhenshchiny', p. 162.

123. Listova, '«Nechistota» zhenshchiny', p. 165.

124. Semenova-Tian-Shanskaia, *Zhizn' Ivana*, p. 73. Another way of achieving this was to swear fidelity on 'Mother Moist Earth' and then eat earth. See also Agapkina, 'Slavianskie obriady', p. 138, and *passim* for a detailed study of other beliefs and rituals of the Slavs, some magical, relating to menstruation; also Listova, '«Nechistota» zhenshchiny', esp. pp. 168–9, for similar material in Russia only.

125. Weideger, *History's Mistress*, p. 129.

126. Levin, 'Childbirth', p. 53. Levin lists canon law prohibitions of this practice and French analogues.

127. Vinogradov, *Zagovory*, p. 33.

128. Makarenko, p. 91 n. 2. The question: 'where did you sleep?', and the answer given, are found in several spells and at the beginning of some versions of the *Dream of the Virgin.*

129. Cherepnin, 'Iz istorii drevnerusskogo koldovstva', p. 87.

130. De Gubernatis, *La Mythologie des plantes*, II, p. 181; quoting a Russian correspondent.

131. See von Boehr, *Dolls and Puppets*, p. 58.

132. In addition to other sources quoted here, a convenient collection of spells with sexual or childbirth content is published by Kliaus and Smilianskaia in *Russkii èroticheskii fol'klor*, pp. 344–70.

133. Almazov, *Tainaia ispoved'*, p. 408.

134. See for example *Russkii èroticheskii fol'klor*, pp. 348, 351–3, 358–60, 364–5.

135. Caesarius, *Dialogue on Miracles*, bk XII, ch. 27.

136. Artsikhovskii and Ianin, *Novgorodskie gramoty*, p. 120.

137. Zabelin, 'Sysknye dela', p. 477.

138. Kostomarov, *Ocherk*, p. 190.

139. Ibid., p. 481.

140. Min'ko, *Sueveriia*, p. 42, quoted from Novombergskii, *Koldovstvo*, p. ix.

141. 'Whispering over paper, herbs and drink' were among the magical practices listed as criminal offences under Catherine the Great in the later eighteenth century: see Popov, *Sud i nakazanie*, p. 381.

142. Popov, 'Rozysk o Moisee Churine'.

143. Maikov, 'Velikorusskie zaklinaniia', no. 22. Perm' region.

144. Maikov, 'Velikorusskie zaklinaniia', pp. 423, 425, 440.

145. *Opisanie dokumentov i del* (t. 1, 1770), Petrograd, 1914, no. 169.

146. Maikov, 'Velikorusskie zaklinaniia', no. 4.

147. Maikov, 'Velikorusskie zaklinaniia', no. 3.

148. Maikov, 'Velikorusskie zaklinaniia', no. 3. For whirlwinds see Vlasova, *Novaia abevega*, s.v. *vikhor*.

149. Maikov, 'Velikorusskie zaklinaniia', no. 5.

150. See Uspenskii, *Filologicheskie razyskaniia*, pp. 89, 103, 164 and 65; Ralston, pp. 370–1. Ralston also gives an English translation of a *prisushka* at p. 369. On the link between some star and serpent names in *zagovor* spells see Iudin, 'Ob imenakh zvezd- «pomoshchnits »'. On Russian serpent beliefs in general see also Vlasova, *Novaia abevega*, s.v. *zmei*.

151. Blok, 'Poèziia zagovorov i zaklinanii', p. 62.

152. Sevens and seventies are commonly the number of veins, sinews and joints referred to in medical spells. For a Greek example see Stewart, *Demons*, p. 289 n. 14. Numbering the parts of the body to be freed from an illness is common in other traditions: a number of Jewish fever amulets, for example, call on the sickness to depart from the 248 parts of the patient: see Naveh and Shaked, *Amulets and Magic Bowls*, amulet no. 9; Schiffmann and Swartz, *Hebrew and Aramaic Incantation Texts*, pp. 88, 163; and 365 limbs are often mentioned in Abraxas amulets: see *Abh. Rheinisch-Westphalischen Akademie der Wissenschaften*, Sonderreihe Papyrologia Coloniensia, XVI, 2, *Supplementum Magicum*, II, Cologne, 1991, p. 12. For the German tradition see *Handwörterbuch der deutschen Aberglauben*, III, s.v. *Glieder*, col. 866.

153. Rybnikov, *Pesni*, pp. 214–5. Another spell for a young man to bewitch a young woman is given on p. 216. For an analogous ancient Greco-Egyptian *defixio* see Faraone, 'The Agonistic Context of Early Greek Binding Spells', p. 14.

154. Cf. the addition of sweat from the bride's wedding bath to the bridegroom's food or drink with an appropriate *prisushka* in the wedding ritual in the Vologda region: *Russkaia svad'ba*, pp. 105–6.

155. Min'ko, *Sueveriia*, pp. 49–50. The use of bats in amatory magic goes back to the ancient magical papyri: see Luck, *Arcana mundi*, p. 101.

156. Frazer, *Golden Bough*, II, p. 345. Similar practices in Britain are given in Opie and Tatem, *Dictionary*, s.v. *toad's or frog's bone* and for Kentucky see Thomas, *Kentucky Superstitions*, no. 3507. Toads' bones are also a specific against the anger of rulers – see below p. 188.

157. Min'ko, *Sueveriia*, p. 54.

158. Min'ko, *Sueveriia*, p. 52.

159. Kostomarov, *Ocherk*, p. 189.

160. *Russkaia svad'ba*, pp. 105–6.

161. Maikov, 'Velikorusskie zaklinaniia', no. 23. Perm' region.

162. Maikov, 'Velikorusskie zaklinaniia', no. 25.

163. Beneshevich, *Pamiatniki*, col. 60. The text is called 'Questions of Kirik, Savva and Il'ia with the answers of Nifont, Bishop of Novgorod'.

164. In Russian and Belorussian magic spells devils and various kinds of folk demons often live in bogs.

165. Maikov, 'Velikorusskie zaklinaniia', no. 48, Novgorod region. Maikov quotes other love spells addressed to the Devil: e.g. nos. 16 and 24.

166. A dozen such spells are published in Kliaus, 'Zagovory', pp. 353–6.

167. According to Dal', *Tolkovyi slovar'*, s.v. *volot* 'giant', this was the popular interpretation of mammoth bones; a Siberian belief has it that a whole race of *voloty* had disappeared underground. This is perhaps an echo of the incarceration of Gog and Magog in the *Alexander Romance*, a Russian version of which provides the first instance of the use of the word: see *Slovar' XI–XVII*, s.v. See also Unbegaun, 'Les Contemporains de Avvakum en présence des fossiles'. The alternative belief recorded by Richard James (62.12) that they are the teeth, horns and bones of a giant sea elephant which lives underground, from which chessmen are made, is elaborated in the eighteenth century by Tu Li-Chen, the Chinese envoy to the Kalmuks in 1713, who says that near Eniseisk it is thought that they are the bones of a giant animal which burrows underground and dies if exposed to the air; its flesh, being cold, is a remedy for fever: see *Puteshestvie kitaiskogo poslannika*, p. 53. This legend may also lie behind the odd description of the 'Indra' or 'Indrik' (variously identified as Unicorn and Hydra, or both), 'the father (or in some versions mother) of all beasts', who looks after wells and streams and 'goes where he wishes underground' in the *Golubinaia kniga*, p. 41. Fossil bones were also known as 'Adam's bones': see Dal', *Tolkovyi slovar'*, s.v. *kost'*, although Ludolph, *Grammatica Russica*, p. 92, identified this as fossilized wood (he also identifies 'mamotovoi kost'' as elephant ivory). Trade in mammoth ivory via Khorezm and Khorasan is known at least from the twelfth century: see Dubler, *Abū Ḥāmid*, p. 54.

168. Maikov, 'Velikorusskie zaklinaniia', no. 130. From a court case of 1660.

169. Vinogradov, *Zagovory*, p. 34.

170. Zabylin, *Russkii narod*, p. 368.

171. Kliaus, 'Zagovory', pp. 356–7.

172. Ridley, *Dictionarie*, p. 174.

173. Berry and Crummey, *Rude and Barbarous Kingdom*, p. 304.

174. Turning three times clockwise is also a feature of an Anglo-Saxon agricultural spell: see Grendon, 'The Anglo-Saxon Charms', p. 173.

175. Rybnikov, *Pesni*, p. 231.

176. Rybnikov, *Pesni*, pp. 218, 233–5. For Belorussian spells against the Evil Eye, malefic magic witchcraft, etc., see Romanov, *Belorusskii sbornik*, pp. 3–31.

177. Maksimov, *Nechistaia*, p. 29.

178. For a specific study see Eleonskaia, *Sel'sko-khoziaistvennaia magiia*, pp. 162–71.

179. Eleonskaia, *Sel'sko-khoziaistvennaia magiia*, pp. 162–71. From a spell-book from the Olonets region which contains other complicated spells and rituals in which the dead are summoned, together with forest and water sprites, to attack the victim. Eleonskaia also notes that in another spell in the same spell-book a dead person may invoked to protect the supplicant from other dead persons who may have been magically sent against him (p. 170). For the magical power of corpses and earth from the churchyard (the latter often beneficial) in England see Thomas, *Religion and the Decline of Magic*, pp. 32, 230–1.

180. See review by Jane Grayson of J.A.E. Curtis, *Manuscripts Don't Burn*, in the *Slavonic and East European Review*, 70, 2, 1992, pp. 323–5.

181. Hughes, *Russia and the West*, p. 88. On footprint magic more generally see Frazer, *Golden Bough*, I, pp. 207–12.

182. Maikov, 'Velikorusskie zaklinaniia', p. 431.

183. Cherepnin, 'Iz istorii drevnerusskogo koldovstva', p. 98.

184. This would cure certain illnesses: see Prokop'eva, 'Zhenskaia rubakha', p. 63. It could be used by magicians to draw round a diseased place: see Maikov, *Velikorusskie zaklinaniia*, no. 210. In general soap in Russia was an amulet against malefic magic: Dal', *Tolkovyi slovar'*, s.v. *mylo*.

185. Nikiforovskii, *Prostonarodnye primety i poveriia*, p. 264, no. 2061. For a similar English superstition with regard to corpse's washing water see Opie and Tatem, *Dictionary*, s.v. *corpse's washing water*.

186. Markov, 'Derevenskii koldun', p. 18. This article is in general very contemptuous of peasants for mixing religion and magic. Nikiforovskii, *Prostonarodnye primety i pover'ia*, p. 262 no. 2052, states that the fat must be from the corpse of a man killed by the thief himself; he has then to shield the light from the candle and walk round the house in order to make the occupants unwakeable.

187. Quoted in Elworthy, *Horns of Honour*, p. 191, and Frazer, *Golden Bough*, I, p. 236. This would appear to be a belief in Britain also; see an account of burglars' superstitions quoted from the *Ashton-under-Lyne Reporter* for 22 April 1905 in the *FLS NEWS. The Newsletter of the Folklore Society*, 17, June 1993, p. 15. See also Hazlitt, *Dictionary*, s.v. *hand*, which quotes from, among others, *Les Secrets du Petit Albert*, 1751. See also n. 190 below. Baranov, *Moskovskie legendy*, p. 125, notes that in the 1920s it was still commonly believed that in the University of Moscow the corpses of orphans were used to make fat to be used in medical preparations. See Kieckhefer, 'Avenging the Blood of Children', for accusations of this kind in fifteenth-century French witchcraft trials.

188. See Listova, 'Nekotorye verovaniia', p. 27.

189. Afanas'ev, *Narodnye russkie skazki*, 1984–5 edn, no. 265.

190. Kostomarov, *Ocherk*, p. 191. For identical beliefs in Britain from 1440 onwards see Opie and Tatem, *Dictionary*, s.v. *corpse's hand holding candle*. For references to this belief in other European countries see Brand, *Observations on Popular Antiquities*, which quotes in particular *Les Secrets du Petit Albert* (in an edition of 1751, one of many after 1704; for the text and publishing history see *Le Grand et le Petit Albert*, ed. Husson); H.L. Strack, *Das Blut*, pp. 51–3; Frazer, *The Golden Bough*, I, p. 149; Elworthy, *Horns of Honour*, pp. 178–93; see also Hazlitt, *Dictionary of Faiths and Folklore*, s.v. *hand*, and Waite, *The Book of Ceremonial Magic*, ch. 8, §4, where the details of preparing the hand for use are given. An illustration of such a hand is given in one of the plates appended to *Superstitions anciennes et modernes, préjugés vulgaires*, I, Amsterdam, 1733 ('Main de gloire ou main de pendu dont les voleurs se servent pour voler la nuit'). For many English readers this practice will immediately bring to mind

'The Hand of Glory' in the *Ingoldsby Legends* ('The Nurse's Story') and Sir Walter Scott's *The Antiquary* (1816), which also contains the method of preparation. The Whitby Museum, Yorkshire, actually has a preserved 'hand of glory'. I am grateful to Roger Pickles, Hon. Curator of Whitby Museum for drawing my attention to this and for communicating information about North Yorkshire 'hand of glory' legends. A Cairo Genizah Jewish formula for finding treasure also requires the use of the hand of a corpse: Schäfer, 'Jewish Magic Literature', p. 89; this use is also recorded in Stith Thompson, *Motif-Index*, D 1314.5. The first reference in literature to the magic (here therapeutic) use of the hand of a corpse appears to be Pliny, *Naturalis historia*, XXVIII.vi.11. The practice of removing parts of bodies from graves for magical purposes was made a crime in England by James I: see Forbes, *The Midwife and the Witch*, p. 119.

191. Zabylin, *Russkii narod*, p. 410.

192. Herberstein, *Rerum Moscoviticarum commentarii* – see the English translation in *Description of Moscow and Muscovy 1557*, p. 52. Robbing graves was condemned as sinful from the early days of the Church and is mentioned in several Latin penitentials: see for example Schmitz, *Bussbücher*, I, p. 297.

193. Novombergskii, *Koldovstvo*, p. 67.

194. Min'ko, *Sueveriia*, p. 30.

195. Zabylin, *Russkii narod*, pp. 399–440.

196. For several cases see Cherepnin, 'Iz istorii drevnerusskogo koldovstva', pp. 96–7.

197. Zabelin, 'Sysknye dela o vorozheiakh', p. 475.

198. Maikov, 'Velikorusskie zaklinaniia', no. 244. Archangel region.

199. Wilmot, *Russian Journals*, p. 290.

200. In Russian *strely*, lit. 'arrows', for which Dal', *Tolkovyi slovar'*, s.v. *strela*, says that in the Archangel region it means inflammation of the lungs or sharp stabbing pains, usually brought on by a malign *koldun*.

201. Zabylin, *Russkii narod*, p. 396. Recorded in Mezen' near the White Sea. Eleonskaia, *Sel'sko-khoziaistvennaia magiia*, p. 173, mentions a curative nine-knotted thread amulet; nine-knot amulets are described by Frazer, *Golden Bough*, III, pp. 301, 303, 304, in places as disparate as Scotland, India, and Pliny's *Naturalis historia*.

202. Maikov, *Velikorusskie zaklinaniia*, nos. 562–571. See also Iatsimirskii, 'K istorii lozhnykh molitv', pp. 90–91.

203. *Opisanie dokumentov i del*, t. 1, (1770), no. 402.

204. Sokolovy, *Skazki i pesni Belozerskogo kraia*, p. 526.

205. Kostomarov, *Ocherk*, p. 190.

206. Kostomarov, *Ocherk*, p. 190.

207. Rybnikov, *Pesni*, p. 209. Rybnikov also gives two spells for use in court (p. 217).

208. Dal', *Tolkovyi slovar'*, s.v. *tirlich*. See Opie and Tatem, *Dictionary*, s.v. *toad's or frog's bone* for the Pliny and later English references. Pulverized toads were widely used in plague amulets in Western seventeenth-century medicine: Baldwin, 'Toads and Plague', pp. 227–47.

209. Kostomarov, *Ocherk*, p. 189.

210. For an Anglo-Saxon spell see Cockayne, *Leechdoms, Wortcunning, and Starcraft*, III, p. 291.

211. A motif index of treasure stories in Arizona, for example, contains analogues to most of the Russian beliefs and practices: see Granger, *A Motif Index for Lost Mines*. For English treasure-seeking see Thomas, *Religion and the Decline of Magic*, pp. 234–7. For a hilarious account of the lifelong search by magic means for hidden treasure by an English aristocratic politician of the late seventeenth

century who had a slight connection with the Russia Company, and possibly with Peter the Great, see Clark, *Goodwin Wharton*. For German beliefs and general remarks see *Handwörterbuch des deutschen Aberglaubens*, s.v. *Schatz*. For a Western Christian conjuration of a spirit guarding a treasure see Waite, *The Book of Ceremonial Magic*, ch. 9 (quoting the *Verus Jesuitarum libellus*).

212. Krinichnaia, *Predaniia russkogo severa*, pp. 83–90; see also motif index at end. See also Krinichnaia, *Russkaia narodnaia istoricheskaia proza*, pp. 97–109 (on the various and intermingled meanings of *pan*, including the meaning given here, and also the Chud', the mythical or real ancient inhabitants of a place); pp. 109–18 (on folk legends about buried treasure). For a survey in English of the legends of the Chuds and Pans, but with no discussion of the treasure motif, see Oinas, 'Legends of the Chuds and Pans'. For wider consideration of stories about buried treasure and their relation to real historical events see Sokolova, 'Predaniia o kladakh'. Sokolova also states that brigand treasures were normally supposed to be buried with a protective spell (p. 174). See also Bogdanov, *Den'gi v fol'klore*, esp. pp. 17–19, 63–5. In the older literature Maksimov, *Nechistaia sila*, has a short chapter on buried treasure, as does Dal', *O pover'iakh*. For Ukrainian stories about buried treasure see Dragomanov, *Malorusskie narodnie predaniia*, pp. 78–88.

213. Massa, *A Short History*, p. 103.

214. See Sokolova, 'Predaniia o kladakh', p. 170; Matveeva, *Mifologicheskie rasskazy*, pp 287–90; for the Ukraine see Markevich, *Obychai* (reprint), p. 61.

215. Krinichnaia, *Predaniia russkogo severa*, no. 153. The same account refers to the belief that the '*pany*' could place a curse on the treasure which would kill anyone violating its terms, in this case transmitted by a dream.

216. A widespread belief. See Stith Thompson, *Motif-Index*, N 571.

217. This theme is common to all the Slav peoples, according to Sokolova, 'Predaniia o kladakh', p. 170.

218. See Vlasova, *Novaia abevega*, s.v. *kladovoi*.

219. See Dal', *Tolkovyi slovar'*, s.vv. *razryvat'*, *trava*, *kupat'*.

220. Dal', *Tolkovyi slovar'*, s.v. *svět*.

221. Afanas'ev, *Poèticheskie vozzreniia*, II, pp. 375–89. Afanas'ev notes that the magical flower is called the flower of Perun (the Slav god of thunder) in Croatian, which is why it flowers with a blinding light.

222. Bolonev, *Narodnyi kalendar'*, p. 84.

223. First published in 1830 as part of a series of Ukrainian stories which eventually became the *Evenings on a Farm near Dikanka*. Gogol', *Sobranie khudozhestvennykh proiszvedenii*, pp. 66–70.

224. See Frazer, *Golden Bough*, XI, ch. VIII 'The Magic Flowers of Midsummer Eve', pp. 65–6. Frazer notes that the Russian *koldun* would dig up purple loosestrife on St John's day at dawn without using an iron tool, and that its root and blossom would subdue spirits and drive off witches and the spirits which guard treasures (features which normally identify the *plakun* plant – see Chap. 9). On the very many German beliefs about *Schlüsselblume*, *Wunderblume* and *Springwurzel* which will also open locks, reveal secrets and treasures, etc.: see *Handwörterbuch der deutschen Aberglaubens*, VII, pp. 1228–30, see also index, s.vv.; also *ERE*, VIII, col. 125a (*The key-flower*; also Brand, *Observations on Popular Antiquities*, p. 751 on moonwort; Hazlitt, *Dictionary*, s.v. *fernseed*.) From a terminological point of view the *razryv-trava* may be linked with another magical herb, *neodolim-trava* 'the unconquerable herb', which, when wound round a cross, will protect cattle from witches: Matveeva, *Mifologicheskie rasskazy*, p. 315.

225. Maikov, 'Velikorusskie zaklinaniia', no. 268.

226. See Malyshev, *Drevnerusskie rukopisi*, p. 180.

227. Golikova, 'Derevenskii koldun', p. 103.

228. Sakharov, *Skazaniia*, p. 90; De Gubernatis, *La Mythologie des plantes*, II, pp. 145–6. This belief is recorded for Lithuania in Stith Thompson, *Motif-Index*, D 1314.7.

229. Dal', *Tolkovyi slovar'*, s.v. *pereletyvat'*. Dal' puts a question mark after his identification of this herb with the fern.

230. Shein, *Materialy*, I, 1, p. 220.

231. Bogdanov, *Den'gi v fol'klore*, p. 65.

232. Vlasova, *Novaia abevega*, s.v. *belaia zmeia*.

233. Afanas'ev, *Narodnye russkie skazki*, II, p. 379, first edn. For other examples of ferns in Russian magic see Pomerantseva, *Mifologicheskie personazhi v russkom fol'klore*, p. 179. Fern-seed in England would keep away evil spirits (Thomas, *Religion and the Decline of Magic*, p. 624) and make persons invisible: Opie and Tatem, *Dictionary*, s.v. *fern*.

234. For other examples of laughter as a sign of the demonic see Index.

235. De Gubernatis, *La Mythologie des plantes*, II, pp. 145–61; Pokrovskii, *Istoricheskaia khrestomatiia*, p. 129.

236. Markevich, *Obychai*, p. 85.

237. This in a story about a soldier quoted in Pomerantseva, *Mifologicheskie personazhi v russkom fol'klore*, p. 179. Cf. the notion, recorded in Pliny, *Naturalis historia*, X 137, XXVI 4, XXIX 72n, and widely found thereafter, that eating serpent's flesh will enable you to understand the language of animals and birds. In Olaus Magnus, *Description of the Northern Peoples*, bk 3, ch. 29, a Norwegian called Erik acquired this power when the saliva of vipers dropped into his food. In the thirteenth-century Icelandic *Volsungs Saga*, ch. XIX, Sigurd inadvertently drank the blood of the monstrous serpent Fafnir and immediately understood the language of the birds. A similar story was told of the medieval bishop-magician Michael Scott: see Briggs, *Dictionary of Fairies*, s.v. *wizards*. See also Chs 9.4 and 11.2 on the herb *chernobyl*.

238. Graham, *The Way of Martha and the Way of Mary*, p. 69.

239. Some of these are examined in Makarov, 'Magicheskie obriady', pp. 261–4. See also the use of the word *slovo* on p. 166 above.

240. Dal', *Tolkovyi slovar'*, s.v. *zaklinat'*.

241. Dal', *Tolkovyi slovar'*, s.v. *klad* and *zaklinat'*; Makarov, 'Magicheskie obriady', p. 261.

242. Zabylin, *Russkii narod*, p. 439. Zabylin also gives a folktale in which the eighteenth-century rebel Stenka Razin, who was reputedly also a sorcerer, hid his great treasure away under a spell.

243. Makarov, 'Magicheskie obriady', p. 261.

244. Makarov, 'Magicheskie obriady', pp. 262–3.

245. Chikachev, *Russkie na Indigirke*, p. 135.

246. Dal', *Tolkovyi slovar'*, s.v.; see motif N 532 in Thompson, *Motif-Index*; for the German tradition see *Handbuch DA*, VII, p. 1007; for the Scandinavian belief see Olaus Magnus, *Description of the Northern Peoples*, bk 3, ch. 11, and bk 20, ch. 20, and more recently Johansen, '"Now We've Got It"', pp. 220–34.

247. *Letopis' zaniatii Arkheograficheskoi komissii, 1862–3*, 2, pp. 23–60.

248. Uspenskii, *Filologicheskie razyskaniia*, pp. 162–3.

249. Published 'Chez Alibeck l'Egyptien, Memphis, 1517', but in the opinion of Waite, who gave a

description in English in his *Book of Ceremonial Magic*, pp. 312–13, more probably published in Rome in the middle of the eighteenth century. The British Library catalogue gives 1817.

250. Maikov, 'Velikorusskie zaklinaniia', no. 352.

251. Quoted in *ERE*, VIII, cols 305b–306a.

252. Romanov, *Belorusskii sbornik*, p. 51.

253. For one example see Saxo Grammaticus, *History*, p. 111.

254. See Dal', *Poslovitsy*, p. 205.

255. Min'ko, *Sueveriia*, p. 148, also noted by Nikiforovskii, *Prostonarodnye primety i pover'ia*, no. 2047.

256. *Ètnokul'turnye protsessy v Karelii*, p. 45; Loginov, *Material'naia kul'tura i proizvodstvenno-bytovaia magiia russkikh Zaonezh'ia*, p. 49. The *koldun* in this area no doubt shares some of the reputed powers and responsibilities of the shaman, one of which was to assist hunters to find game.

257. Min'ko, *Sueveriia*, p. 148.

258. Quoted from the English version: Aksakov, *Chronicles of a Russian Family*, pp. 86–7, fn. 1.

259. Dal', *Tolkovyi slovar'*, s.v. *iordan'*.

260. Dal', *Tolkovyi slovar'*, s.v. *ruzh'e*.

261. Maikov, 'Velikorusskie zaklinaniia', no. 313.

262. Quoted from *ERE*, III, col. 466a. Another spell designed to spoil a hunter's gun is quoted by Maikov ('Velikorusskie zaklinaniia', no. 317); it is addressed to Moses and Elijah.

263. Shein, *Materialy*, p. 555.

264. See n. 8 above.

265. Shipov, 'Istoriia moei zhizni', pp. 138–9.

266. Makarenko, *Sibirskii narodnyi kalendar'*, pp. 154–5.

267. Maikov, 'Velikorusskie zaklinaniia', no. 295.

268. Vinogradov, *Zagovory, oberegi, spasitel'nye molitvy*, 2, pp. 5–6.

269. Min'ko, *Sueveriia*, p. 147. These omens had in fact more general significance – see Ch. 5.2.1.

270. Afanas'ev, *Poèticheskie vozzreniia*, II, p. 337. Afanas'ev also quotes a spell which calls on all 'Satanails, devils, and wood sprites' to drive game into the hunter's traps.

271. Min'ko, *Sueveriia*, p. 149.

272. Romanov, *Belorusskii sbornik*, V, p. 49.

273. The literature on magic of this kind is considerable: see, among many, Eleonskaia, *Sel'skokhoziastvennaia magiia*; Uspenskii, *Filologicheskie razyskaniia*; Propp, *Russkie agrarnye prazdniki*; Zhuravlev, *Domashnii skot*.

274. Propp, *Russkie agrarnye prazdniki*, pp. 65–6.

275. Eleonskaia, *Sel'sko-khoziaistevennaia magiia*, p. 146.

276. Gromyko, *Traditsionnye normy*, p. 120.

277. Mazo, '"We don't summon Spring in the Summer"', p. 79.

278. Belorussian practices described in Min'ko, *Sueveriia*, pp. 106–7.

279. Frazer, *Golden Bough*, I, p. 277 (these practices are evidently Ukrainian or Belorussian as well as Russian).

280. Min'ko, *Sueveriia*, p. 135.

281. Listed in Lysenko and Ostrovskii, 'Logicheskie skhemy okkazional'nykh obriadov', pp. 108–19. See also Tolstoi, 'Vyzyvanie dozhdia'.

282. Mazo, '"We don't summon Spring in the Summer"', pp. 78–9.

283. Kachanovskii, 'Molitva s apokrificheskimi chertami'.

284. Maikov, 'Velikorusskie zaklinaniia', no. 359. Maikov gives a good many agricultural charms; most are very short like this one, but one (no. 285), for protecting cattle, runs to eight pages.

285. Zelenin, *Izbrannye trudy*, p. 117, quoting a spell recorded by V. Iurlov in 1866 in the Simbirsk region.

286. See Prokhorov, 'K istorii liturgicheskoi poèzii', p. 147.

287. Min'ko, *Sueveriia*, pp. 134–5. Cf. the water from three wells mentioned in n. 118 above.

288. Chikachev, *Russkie na Indigirke*, p. 132.

289. Chikachev, *Russkie na Indigirke*, p. 133.

290. Ralston, *Songs of the Russian People*, pp. 382–3; Afanas'ev, *Poèticheskie vozzreniia slavian na prirodu*, III, p. 450.

291. Min'ko, *Sueveriia*, pp. 142–6. For quicksilver in amulets elsewhere, including the shores of the Caspian (in a nutshell or quill sealed with wax), see Seligmann, *Die magischen Heil- und Schutzmittel*, p. 175. Quicksilver in a quill sealed with wax is recorded as a talisman against impotence caused by maleficium in a Latin text ascribed to Constantine of Africa (eleventh century): see Hoffman, 'Beiträge', p. 7, 8. For the same use of dead magpies among the Volga Germans see Koch, *The Volga Germans*, p. 164.

292. For a wide-ranging survey of the use or invocation of 'Tsar' fire', 'living fire', 'wooden fire', 'new fire', etc., in particular with reference to the magical protection of livestock, see Zhuravlev, *Domashnii skot*, pp. 113–39.

293. Vinogradov, *Zagovory*, p. 75. A Belorussian spell for those lost in the forest also invoke the 'tsar of the forest', in this case called Onoprii: Romanov, *Belorusskii sbornik*, V, p. 3.

294. Miloradovich, 'Zhit'e-byt'e lubenskogo krestianina' (reprint, p. 238). This series of articles also contains a further eleven prayers and spells relating to bee-keeping (pp. 24–41) and many more on other aspects of agriculture and animal husbandry in the Ukraine.

295. Chulkov, *Abevega*, pp. 189, 191.

296. Maikov, 'Velikorusskie zaklinaniia', no. 258.

297. Maikov, 'Velikorusskie zaklinaniia', no. 326.

298. Dal', *Tolkovyi slovar'*, s.v. *nerazmĕnnyi*.

299. Maikov, 'Velikorusskie zaklinaniia', no. 269. Voronezh region.

300. Kondrat'eva, *Metamorfozy sobstvennogo imeni*, s.v. *armizon*.

301. See Cherepanova, *Mifologicheskaia leksika*, p. 70.

302. For a Western 'cap of invisibility', obtained from demons, see Kieckhefer, *Magic in the Middle Ages*, pp. 7–8.

303. Afanas'ev, *Narodnye russkie skazki*, no. 193.

304. The Devil was thought to fear brass and silver buttons: Pomerantseva, *Mifologicheski personazhi v russkom fol'klore*, p. 178.

305. See, for example, Rybnikov, *Pesni*, III, p. 209; the source quoted is 'an ancient manuscript'.

306. Bolonev, *Narodnyi kalendar'*, p. 60; Dal', *Tolkovyi slovar'*, s.v. *kost'*.

307. Iatsimirskii, 'K istorii lozhnykh molitv', p. 84. From a nineteenth-century prayerbook.

308. Zabylin, *Russkii narod*, p. 255.

309. Maksimov, *Nechistaia sila*, p. 31.

310. *Ètnokul'turnye protsessy v Karelii*, p. 46.

311. Maikov, 'Velikorusskie zaklinaniia', no. 363. Belozero region. For an alternative version see Dal', *Tolkovyi slovar'*, s.v. *milyi (milost')*.

312. See Opie and Tatem, *Dictionary*, s.v. *house*. The notion of domestic fairies who move house and even emigrate with the family of the house is, however, known in Britain and Ireland. see Briggs, *Dictionary*, s.v. *Tom Cockle*.

313. See Eleonskaia, n. 8 above.

314. Dal', *Tolkovyi slovar'*, s.v. *pozhar*.

315. See Ch. 5.2.2

316. See Ch. 4.5.1.

317. Nekrylova, *Russkie narodnye gorodskie prazdniki*, p. 37.

318. Nikiforovskii, *Prostonarodnye primety i pover'ia*, no. 1029

319. See Ch. 8.6.2.

320. See Ch. 10.8.

321. Dal', *Tolkovyi slovar'*, s.v. *iaitse*; similarly in Romanov, *Belorusskii sbornik*, p. 50.

322. Zinov'eva, *Ukazatel'*, motif GI 34.

323. Dal', *Tolkovyi slovar'*, s.v. *pozhar*.

324. Dal', *Tolkovyi slovar'*, s.v. *ogn'*.

325. Markevich, *Obychai* (reprint), p. 121.

8

TALISMANS AND AMULETS

1. *Introduction*

The nature and extent of the use of talismans and amulets among the Slavs are much as in other parts of Europe. Archaeological evidence from pre-Christian Russia up to more modern times, and recent or contemporary ethnographic evidence, shows an extensive range of objects which may be considered definitely or probably talismanic. Talismans in general can cross the boundaries between what have variously been called learned and popular, high and low, or great and little cultures, not to mention many of the religious and linguistic barriers which might have been expected to limit their semeiotic range. Most of the objects which will be discussed in this chapter are essentially part of the popular magic or popular religion discussed in Ch. 2, but since the subject is extensive, with historical, literary, iconographic, religious, and medical dimensions, it has been divided into three chapters, this on objects as talismans, and the following two on *materia magica* (Ch. 9) and texts as talismans (Ch. 10).

The amulets and talismans of antiquity, from engraved gems to spells written on papyrus, are fairly well documented and general discussion of the subject will be avoided except insofar as it helps to place a Russian object, practice, or belief, or where such objects are actually found in a Russian context. Precious stones with magic virtues are also omitted here since they are discussed in Ch. 13. Suffice it to say that almost all the popular medical books of the *Hortus sanitatis* tradition, which were popular in Muscovy from the sixteenth century onwards, gave details of the talismanic properties of stones. Other materials which have magical properties but are not necessarily in the form of specific objects, although they may well be used in amulets, are discussed separately in the next chapter.

It is, of course, usually impossible to tell how far an individual, or for that matter any segment of society at any particular time, actually believes in the magical properties of talismanic objects: levels of belief must vary from the total through various levels of lesser superstition, social convention and religious practice, to the purely decorative or iconographically persistent.

Frazer in his *Golden Bough* remarks: 'No doubt amulets often degenerate into ornament'[1] and the reverse is certainly true, as, for example, the presence of exotic coins on charm bracelets demonstrates. And on another level a pertinent observation is made by Keith Thomas, when discussing the apparent credulousness of well-educated Englishmen of the seventeenth century: 'many seventeenth-century prescriptions which seem magical to us were in fact based on obsolescent assumptions about the physical properties of natural substances'.[2]

For the purposes of this and the following two chapters we shall take as a working definition that a talisman is a natural object or purpose-made artefact credited with various magic properties, usually to avert evil influences or illness or to bring good luck, and an amulet is a talisman for wearing about one's person.

The most general term for both talismans and amulets in Russian is *obereg*. Dal' gives this word, which means literally 'protector', as being northern dialect for all kinds of spells, charms, talismans, etc. with *obereshchik* (fem. *obereshchitsa*) and *oberegatel'*, (fem. *oberegatel'nitsa*) as terms for those who make or use such things. The word is used in a general sense in modern Russian, and includes ritual gestures and utterances, whistling, etc., but the word seems not to be attested in Old Russian. The words *khranilishche*, *khranitva* (lit. a safe place or container), and *khranil'nik* (a maker of talismans) are listed in Sreznevskii, *Materialy*, which quotes several passages from Old Russian literature that give examples of texts being carried as amulets. Normally the word occurs as a translation of the Greek *phylaktērion* and is used to designate Hebrew phylacteries. In Russian scholarly work the terms *amulet* and *talisman* are also used; these are relatively modern learned words probably borrowed from Latin via French or German in the eighteenth century. Terms for special types of amulet such as the *zmeevik*, *nauz*, and *ladanka* are discussed separately below.

2. *Everyday Objects as Amulets*

This category includes archaeological and ethnographic material which may be considered as having its origin in the pagan beliefs of the Slavs or their neighbours.

In the 1950s B.A. Rybakov made an analysis of the small carved or cast material of this kind in archaeological collections and produced a classification scheme and an estimate of the place of production and extent of trade in amulets.[3] Later work has supplemented this and there is now a small but respectable literature of the subject.[4]

The largest category of such objects is that of pendants. They are found throughout East Slav territory: in eleventh or twelfth-century burial grounds in north-west Russia in the regions of Smolensk, Polotsk, Novgorod, Rostov-Suzdal'skii, and the eastern Baltic littoral (mainly in rural rather than urban areas). A few pendants of the same types as those found on Slav territory have been also been found in Scandinavia and in the Komi (Finnic) territory of Perm' in the west near the Urals. The centres of production seems to have been the Smolensk area and the lower reaches of the Western Dvina (Düna) near present-day Riga (i.e. a non-Slavonic area). The distribution of these amulets indicates an area of use, particularly in connection with women's dress, which encompasses East Slav, Baltic and Finno-Ugric communities, and indeed graves of the twelfth–thirteenth century have been excavated on the Kola peninsula which contain items typical of all these.[5] The amulets found here include a key and a horsehead comb. These pagan amulets are typical of the northern part of Russia. The south yields far more Christian remains crosses, metal miniature icons, etc.,[6] as well as axes and crescent moons.[7] In the case of axe amulets, these have been found in most East Slav areas, in particular in the eleventh and twelfth centuries, but almost exclusively among the grave goods of males.[8]

These amulets fall into several clearly defined categories: zoomorphic (usually horses, combs with horse-head ends primarily in the Smolensk region; also birds and fish); spoons and ladles (primarily in the Smolensk region); knives (primarily in the East Baltic region); keys (primarily in the Finno-Ugrian Ladoga region). They are usually cast in bronze or low-grade silver or sometimes made of bone, and may be found together as a collection of charms, together with little bells, teeth and possibly other items, even crosses, attached by links to a semicircular pendant-holder).[9]

The origin and application of these amulets is only partially clear. Russian research has, until very recently, tended to ignore the evidence of Western comparative scholarship and concentrated primarily on Byzantine and Finnic analogues. The search for local origins without reference to a possible common European tradition is unlikely to be fruitful. One study of burial practices and grave goods in Kiev Rus' in the tenth to thirteenth centuries demonstrates both the continuity of pre-Christian amulets (with specimens of most of the types mentioned above) in graves also containing amulets with Christian motifs, and also the fact that Christianity did bring with it new types of amulet.[10]

Analogues for most of the types of amulet found in Russian graves can be found over a wide area and in many historical periods. For example the horse's head design, which is regularly linked with a similar motif in Russian wooden architecture and folk art, is usually held by Russian scholars to be a survival of a solar cult and connected with Finnic motifs.[11] One should, however, also note the existence of comb and horse amulets in other parts of Europe such as South Germany and Austria, although admittedly of more recent date.[12]

In fact knife, spoon, key and comb, either singly or as composite amulets such as charm bracelets, are common from Northern Europe to North Africa, and may go back at least to Classical Antiquity.[13]

The knife amulet is ancient and widespread, one of its functions being to guard against witchcraft.[14] The spoon as an amulet is also well known in other parts of Europe, not least as a bringer of luck to new-born children[15] – hence the silver spoon as a christening present.

The keys are particularly difficult to interpret in a purely local context in Russia since they appear both in a Finnic locale at a time when mechanical locks of the Western type were probably unknown, except perhaps as exotic foreign items, and also in southern Russia (with locks). It seems far more likely that these key amulets are borrowings of foreign amulet motifs as such, regardless of the local existence of real keys: keys have been well known since antiquity in the Mediterranean, Western Europe, and North Africa, primarily as a love amulet, and also as a luck-bringer and guard against disease.[16] They are also associated with Hecate, in various manifestations, as the keys of the underworld.[17] As an attribute of St Peter (Matthew, 16, 19: 'I will give you the keys of the kingdom of heaven and whatever you bind on earth shall be bound in heaven, and whatever you loose on earth shall be loosed in heaven'), the key lends itself to a wide variety of magical interpretations in the Christian world. The concluding section of many spells in Russian include an 'affirmation' or binding formula involving locks and keys, and some 'magical prayers' have this as the main element: two Russians charms against witchcraft run: 'O Michael Archangel, protect me with an iron door and lock it with three times nine locks and keys' and:

> Michael Archangel, Gabriel Archangel, merciful Nicholas, come down from heaven and bring keys and lock up the wizard and witch, the warlock and hag. And Nicholas the Merciful will come down and bring iron and place it from earth to heaven and lock it with three golden keys and throw the keys into the ocean-sea.[18]

A similar spell for protecting a treasure is given below.

Locks and keys may also be used physically in a variety of folk cures in Russia – Ralston describes holding a key in each hand or allowing blood to drop through a locked padlock.[19] In England keys down the neck are still a cure for nosebleeding, the key of the church door was once an antidote to the bite of a mad dog,[20] and the use of keys in various divinatory practices, usually in combination with the Psalter or Bible, is well known in several parts of Europe, including both Russia and England.[21]

The symbolic use of locks in modern Russia can also be seen in the practice of placing an unlocked lock under the threshold of the house which is about to be entered by a newly married couple. The key is then thrown into a well in the belief that this will ensure a harmonious marriage.[22] In one area of Belorussia a lock would be thrown into a new grave with the corpse so that no more members of the family would die. Similarly the village midwife would place a lock beneath a dying child; the key would then be thrown into a well and thereafter children born to the family would not die.[23] In the Vologda region on St George's day (23 April) the owner of a herd would walk round his cattle three times carrying a lock and key; he would then turn the key in the lock and throw the key into the river. This would protect his herd from wild beasts and illnesses.[24]

A largely ornamental function of these amulets made of miniaturized everyday objects is suggested by the fact that they are found often as part of female dress. Indeed the identification of some types of Anglo-Saxon composite miniature objects, very similar to the Russian sets, as toilet sets and status symbols not always of demonstrable amuletic status, may be relevant to the Russian finds.[25] On the other hand a diffusionist view of the history of amulets is supported by the evidence of trade in amulets, often over considerable distances. Scarabs and other probably amuletic objects of the ancient world have been found, often in graves, in Scandinavia and in both the south and north of the territory now occupied by the Slavonic peoples.[26] If *zmeeviki* and scarabs were current in medieval Russia, in more modern times the collecting activities of scholars and princes, not to mention looting by soldiery, thieves and pirates, have also helped to disseminate magical objects, and sometimes even belief in them. Catherine the Great, for example, owned several of the Abraxas gems which were common in antiquity, and which she chose to regard as good luck charms.[27]

Perhaps related to amulets of this kind are the small engraved or repoussé *ex-voto* tablets of silver or tin which can be found placed on icons, or as pendant amulets, at least from the seventeenth century in Russia (Fig. 5). Tsar Aleksei Mikhailovich, for example, in 1646 took two silver *ex-voto* teeth to the church of St Antipii (see pp. 239–40 below). These seem not to have attracted serious study.[28] Stephen Graham, writing just before the First World War, described and photographed a number of these which he had found on Old Believer domestic icons. They represent cows, horses, human figures, hands, eyes, ears, etc. and were evidently intended either to prevent or to cure illnesses, or as a thank-offering for a cure. They were evidently produced in quantity and were sold by hawkers and sometimes by priests.[29] Exactly the same kind of object is found in the Balkans and Greece and it is entirely possible that the custom, perhaps even the *ex-voto* plates themselves, are of Greek origin.[30]

To catalogue exhaustively and describe in detail the enormous variety of popular practices and superstitions relating to talismanic objects in Russia of more recent date, as recorded by ethnographers and folklorists, is beyond the scope of this survey. Some of these have been mentioned above and a representative sample of particular categories is given below.

3. Other Domestic Talismans

In his study of the folklore of St Nicholas, Uspenskii mentions the *skotii bog* ('cattle god') and the *kurinyi bog* ('chicken god'). The first term may be applied to various items, including phallic symbols, which protect cattle: the second, often a stone or vessel with a hole in it, which has evident sexual symbolism, serves to protect chickens and is employed in the treatment of a variety of medical conditions.[31]

These are part of a whole range of objects which served, or serve, as talismans in Russian life, and in most respects they have Western analogues. It is lucky to have an adder, swallow (but see below under Birds), stork, or horseshoe in your house, or a candle from a church lit during a thunderstorm or fire. Soap worn at the breast is a countercharm to malefic magic.[32] And the Ukrainian *koldun* favours grass which has grown through the eyeholes of a horse's skull.[33]

4. Other non-Christian Amulets: Knots and Stones

4.1. *Knots, nets and threads*. Magic knots are universal, and are recorded from ancient Mesopotamia onwards.[34] One name for an amulet in Russian is *nauz* (*nauzd, nauza, nauzok*), an old term which is evidently connected etymologically with the notion of tying.[35] Dal's dictionary defines *nauzy* as a part of a horse harness, or horse brasses or other harness decoration such as a plume attached to the harness. (Harness talismans are a fairly common phenomenon, from English horse brasses to a variety of amulets from Egypt.)[36] Formerly these would have been magic roots or spells on pieces of paper, or other talismans against the Evil Eye or malefic magic. The current dictionary of Old Russian defines *nauz* as a knot or talisman worn round the neck or tied to the arm to ward off evil spirits, illness or misfortune.[37] It cites one of the sermons of the twelfth-century Bishop Cyril of Turov which lists the wearing of *nauzy* as a sin, together with witchcraft, lying, robbing and banditry, and a sixteenth-century polemic against paganism which says 'some believe in dreams or wear *nauzy* and tie them to their children'.

A *nauznik* (f. *nauznitsa*) Dal' defines as a synonym of *koldun, vorozheia, znakhar'*.[38] A *nauznik* is classified in another sixteenth-century text with wizards and *oblakoprogonniki* (cloud-dispersers). Sreznevskii gives a long list of condemnations of *nauzy* and *nauzniki* and notes Czech cognates.[39] Further examples are given under the heading of *uz"l* (knot), and *uz"l'nik* (a practitioner in magic knots) including one from the Novgorod *Kormchaia* (book of canon law) of 1280 which excommunicates anyone engaging in witchcraft, the conjuring of demons, casting horoscopes, or making knots round the neck or limbs. These prohibitions correspond with the banning of amulets called *ligatura* in Latin penitentials.[40]

In more modern times a *nauz* could be simply a knotted thread: red wool tied round the arms and legs averted fever and nine loops round a child's neck would keep off scarlatina.[41] Knot magic is common in many cultures, including that of the ancient Near East and classical antiquity. It was also popular in more modern times in Jewish communities, where, as with the Russians, crimson thread and foxtails were employed to avert the Evil Eye from horses.[42]

One common magical use of thread is to cure illnesses by transference: the thread is used to measure the sick person, or affected limb, then buried or thrown on the wind, with or without an accompanying spell.[43]

Closely allied to knotted threads are girdles and belts which were also widely employed as protection against malefic magic and illness.[44] Specific examples such as the use of a belt to induce prophetic dreams, the use of a priest's girdle as a pregnancy amulet, the removal of belts and girdles when performing magic and divination, are discussed elsewhere (see Index). The magical significance of belts and girdles is underlined by a number of popular religious practices and beliefs, in particular among the Old Believers, who invented the term *bespoiasniki* (lit. 'unbelted people') as a term of abuse for their modernizing antagonists. These beliefs are enshrined in the popular sayings: 'When praying you must lower your belt below the navel'; 'To make the sign of the cross across your belt is a sin'.[45] Negative figures in Russian folklore are often described as being 'without cross or belt'. Samuel Collins, the court physician of Tsar Aleksei Mikhailovich in the sevententh-century and a shrewd observer of Russian customs and beliefs, wrote that neither men and women leave off their belts for fear of divine punishment.[46] Both he and Herberstein particularly noticed that Russians wore their belts very low.[47]

There is often a clear sexual as well as magical significance in the removal of belts and girdles, as the examples given here and elsewhere demonstrate. In one Siberian *bylina* (folk epic fragment) two brothers at a court feast are chided by the prince for not engaging in the ceremonial boasting.[48] They thereupon boast about the beauty of their sister. The young lover of the sister rises and in his turn boasts drunkenly that he has seen her in her shift without her girdle. This shames the two brothers, who pursue and kill the young man. This story might seem to have nothing to do with the magic significance of belts and girdles, were it not for the fact that the young lady who removed her girdle was called Sofiia Volkhovnitsa, i.e. Sophia the Witch.

Another type of magic knot is used by the *koldun* in malefic magic: if he ties a knot (*zakrut*) in a tuft of grass or a growing plant this will blight the harvest (see Ch. 3.3).[49] Probably associated with knots is the use of nets (i.e. multiple knots) as amulets.[50] These would give protection against sorcerers, and Ralston mentions them as being a part of the marriage ceremony in some parts of Russia;[51] in the Vologda province they were obtainable from a monastery[52] (Fig. 6). Fishermen could ensure a good catch by having their nets woven at midnight by a pregnant woman.[53] The knotted cord used in protective magic may also be used with hostile intent; spells for this are given in Ch. 7.5.6.[54]

4.2. *Stones.* Yet another kind of amulet, which may also, confusingly, be called a *nauz* is the *gromovaia* (*gromnaia*) *strela*, literally 'thunder arrow' and *gromovoi toporok*, literally 'thunder axe'. These may be naturally occurring. Dal' (s.v. *strela*) remarks that they are also called 'Devil's fingers' and quotes a saying that 'For bellyache drink or wash from a *gromovaia strela*' (i.e. from water in which it has been placed), a common folk-medicine practice which may also employ crosses, objects of silver, icons, or stones from Athos or Jerusalem.[55] Amulets of the 'thunder arrow' kind are fairly widespread and ancient in Europe. They are described in Pliny's *Naturalis historia* (**XXXVIII.LI.LV**) as being sought by wizards for their practices (51) and for Moon divination (59) and this information is repeated in medieval lapidaries such as Marbod's.[56]

In view of their ubiquity the Russian use could well be native, and the use of the words *strela* and *toporok* as well as *grom* suggests that both aeroliths and prehistoric arrowheads are involved, but equally the notion of these stones as amulets could have come to Russia from Byzantium, perhaps via the Balkans;[57] certainly they were condemned in the fourth-century *Canons of Laodicea* (no. 36) and continue to be condemned in later florilegia in a tract attributed to Athanasius of Jerusalem or Athanasius of Alexandria, in which it is alleged that they are used against fevers and to exorcize demons.[58] Both thunder arrows and axeheads were condemned in the mid-sixteenth century in the *Domostroi* (see Ch. 1.6 above).

The *gromovaia strela* was evidently thought to be a powerful talisman: one specimen, a flint spearhead set in silver, was found in the excavation of a house in ancient Novgorod which was supposedly that of a *volkhv* or wizard,[59] and amulets of this type were often buried with the later type of wizard called *koldun*.[60]

In the Indigirka region of northern Siberia pieces of meteorite called *sata* are thought to have magical qualities.[61]

A quite different type of 'magic' stone is the *sledovik* cult stone found in many of the forest areas of northern and eastern Europe. This must certainly have been non-Christian in origin but often has acquired Christian associations, even to the extent of being built into churches.[62] Frequently, even in modern times, offerings are left beside them by sufferers seeking healing. Zabylin records that in the Odoevskii district of Tula province there was a local cult of two stones called Bash and Bashikha on which offerings were left, which would afterwards go to the local church. Earth from under these stones had magical curative properties, increased the fertility of cattle, and kept off the Evil Eye; fragments of the stone would cure toothache. (The association of stones with teeth is common in curative spells.) Sometimes cult stones have natural or man-made patterns in them; the alleged footprint of St Alexander of Osheven, for example, was an object of pilgrimage and would cure ailments of the feet.[63] In the Novgorod province there is a village in which there is a rock marked with the footprint of St Zosima of Solovki. Peasants would pray there and drink the water which collected in the 'footprint' as medicine.[64] Belorussia has a considerable number of cult stones of this kind.[65]

The 'Christian' stone cults described are probably a late phenomenon which developed in the fifteenth to seventeenth centuries, but the notion of magic stones in general is well attested in folklore.

The best known of these is the *Alatyr'* which often occurs in the formulaic introduction to stories, spells and magic prayers (see also Ch. 7.4).[66] In folklore this stone is the 'mother of stones', in the *Golubinnaia kniga* 'the stone of all stones' near which the text had fallen from heaven, and which was brought from Sinai (or Tabor) and placed by the Saviour in the foundation of the temple of Sion as an altar (in some versions it is the stone on which the skull of Adam reposes at the foot of the Cross).[67] In one copy of the *Beseda Ierusalimskaia* (a curious conversation of four 'tsars': Votolomon, Ioakim, Iezeki, and David, containing material similar to the *Golubinnaia kniga*) it is said to be found at the mouth of the Volga and all the fishes swim up to it on St Nicholas's Day.[68]

5. *Magic Rings, Wands, Mirrors, Books, Dolls*

5.1. *Magic Rings.* Magic rings are common enough in literature and folklore, often as part of the equipment of wizards. The tale of Solomon's magic ring with which he controlled demons, apparently first attested in Josephus's *Antiquities* (8.2.5), is known in Slavonic literature, in particular in the text known as *Solomon and Kitovras* (sc. the Centaur),[69] as is another story not apparently attested elsewhere in which Solomon inscribes all his wisdom on a ring (see Ch. 15.3). A magic ring bearing a talisman, and a variety of rings set with precious stones possessing magical properties, was part of the secret wisdom allegedly given by Aristotle to Alexander the Great in the *Secretum secretorum*, known in Russia certainly from the sixteenth century (see Chs 1 and 13). In the seventeenth-century tale of Ieruslan Lazarevich, which may be distantly related to Firdausi's *Shah-nameh*, the hero wins a magic ring by defeating a three-headed dragon. Although all these examples are from translated texts, it is clear that the concept of the magic ring is fully assimilated into Russian folklore. Sufficiently so in fact that the idea is mocked in two ribald stories recorded in Afanas'ev's nineteenth-century collection of 'indecent' folktales in which a 'magic' ring controls the length of a peasant's penis.[70]

A more modern, purely Russian, ring legend is that of Pushkin's ring which he believed contained his genius and which was supposedly destined to be passed on to whoever was the greatest writer in Russia.[71] In another popular anecdote the Tsar Nicholas II was supposed to have a ring containing a relic of the True Cross which was thought to preserve him from harm. It had been given to him by the Pope and he would go nowhere without it.[72]

As artefacts with magical properties rings are found in a variety of Russian popular beliefs; for example, water poured through a wedding ring was thought to have therapeutic properties, as had rainwater from a thunderstorm if caught in a bowl with rings placed in it. In the divinatory process of pouring wax, lead etc. into water to produce prophetically suggestive shapes (see Ch. 4.5.1), pouring through a ring is sometimes specified. Under certain circumstances a young girl looking through a ring will see her future husband.[73]

Rings may also be involved in selection procedures in bibliomancy (see the discussion of the *Divinatory Psalter* in Ch. 11.4), or in that form of ancient divination called dactylomancy in which a suspended ring will answer a question by turning towards a person or a letter in a circle.[74] In a particular version of this a bewitched Russian could turn to a wizard for help; the wizard would take a snake ring, suspend it by a woman's hair, and wait for it to start to swing. The direction of swing would indicate where the hostile wizard lived who had bewitched the client.[75]

Rings may also be used in the guessing games accompanying the *podbliudnye pesni* ('under-the-bowl songs') at the New Year and Epiphany. In these, rings or other small personal objects are dropped into a bowl which is then covered. After each song a ring is taken out at random and the owner interprets the words of the song just finished as an omen (see Ch. 4.4).

Magic rings in Russian folk tales have much the same characteristics as magic rings in the folk tales of other lands: they may be used to summon demonic servants, as in the translated Solomon story mentioned above;[76] they may show you the road when you are lost;[77] or enable you to turn into a horse.[78] Magic rings appear to have been condemned by Peter Mogila, metropolitan of Kiev in the seventeenth century, in his 'Rules for the confession of faith'.[79]

5.2. *Magic Wands.* Magic wands are very common in the fairy tales of Western Europe,[80] but although the Bible offered a striking model in the rod of Moses, they are not so commonly found in the literature or folklore of Russia. This is despite the fact that the most popular literary work in Old Russian was the Pseudo-Callisthenes Alexander book, which contains at the very beginning a passage in which Nectanebus, the wizard king of Egypt, dons magic robes, takes up his magic wand and summons gods, spirits of the air and demons. The sixteenth-century *Illuminated Chronicle* contains a version of the *Alexander Romance* with an illustration of Nectanebus holding a magic wand.[81] And one may, perhaps, mention in this context the staff of Ivan the Terrible which was set with magic stones, as described by Sir Jerome Horsey (see Ch. 13.4), and the magic rod inscribed with Russian characters mentioned by Olaus Magnus.[82] One has to conclude that the standard dictionary of literary Russian, in listing 'magic wand' and 'magic mirror' as the first two examples of the use of the word *volshebnyi* are reflecting a usage which has come into Russian literature from translated Western literature.[83]

5.3. *Magic Mirrors*. Magic mirrors do occur occasionally in Russian literature, folklore, and popular belief. In folk tales the magic mirror will tell you what is going on somewhere else, or tell you the truth about what is really happening, as in the Russian version of the Snow White story.[84] Mirrors and other reflective surfaces are also used in popular divination, mostly for displaying the features of a future husband or for predicting the size of one's family (see Ch. 4.3 – 5). The Old Believers regarded mirrors as the invention of the Devil, probably for a variety of reasons including disapproval of vanity, the reversing properties of mirrors, their common use in divination, and not least because glass mirrors were for the most part a luxury import from the West. And there are common superstitions in Russia, as elsewhere, that to smash a mirror is bad luck and that mirrors should be covered after the death of a member of the household in case the spirit of the dead person (which in Russian belief remains in the house until after the wake), not realizing that it is dead, should look in the mirror and be frightened when it does not see a reflection.[85]

5.4. *Magic Books*. One of the terms for magic in Russian is *chernoknizhie* (lit. 'black-bookery'). This looks like a calque, although no reliable etymology has been proposed, and the word is not given an early date in any dictionary.[86] D'iachenko's idiosyncratic dictionary notes that 'black book' (*chernaia kniga*) was a popular term for the printed books of arithmetic which appeared in the eighteenth century, and suggests that to simple people they would have seemed magical.[87] This typically amateur etymology collapses when confronted with the fact the adjective *chernoknizhnyi* was used in accusations of witchcraft against Maxim the Greek in the early sixteenth century (the date and circumstances suggest a Greek rather than Latin or Western vernacular source for the word),[88] the noun *chernoknizhnik* ('wizard') is found in the mid-sixteenth-century *Domostroi*, and the noun *chernoknizhstvo* was used in the 1660s by Grigorii Kotoshikhin in a serious description of the Russian legal system, and yet again in Peter the Great's military law of 1716 (see Ch. 16).[89]

Old Russian texts which refer to magic or magicians (by any of the possible terms) not infrequently mention 'magic books' (e.g. the *volkhv* in the seventeenth-century *Tale of Savva Grudtsyn*), and indeed magic is often regarded in early Christian and medieval Western literature also as a pursuit of men of learning. This notion, together with the magical notebooks (*tetradki*) which often feature as evidence in Russian witchcraft trials, and which indeed existed in the form of books of remedies (some of which were magical) or the divination books described in other chapters, were no doubt the source of the 'magic books' occasionally to be found in folk tales. These, depending on the story, would tell you the answer to anything you wanted to know, reveal what is hidden, and give the answer to riddles.[90]

5.5. *Magic dolls*. The role of the magic mirror and the magic book is to some extent shared in folk tales by the magic doll which will tell you the truth and give you true advice.[91] In real life dolls may figure in malefic and fertility magic (see also Ch. 2.3.5 and 2.5). Siberian stories recount how a doll may be used by a *koldun* to introduce into a house a *kikimora*, a kind of house-sprite which causes havoc at night by throwing utensils and items of furniture about the room.[92] This can only be got rid of by burning the doll.[93] The notion of dolls as the vehicles of evil spirits can also be seen in the practice of Kursk doll-makers who leave the faces of their dolls as a piece of plain linen, completely featureless, for fear that if given faces the dolls would become animated by demons and harm children playing with them.[94] A set of twelve dolls representing the fever spirits or *triasavitsy*, the evil daughters of Herod, is described below. Dolls were frequently part of seasonal festivities, and are usually described as survivals of fertility rites. Figures called *kukushka* (cuckoo), *kupalo*, *kostroma*, *semik*, *mara*[95] and *maslenitsa* (the names of seasonal festivals) were known in many parts of Russia, Belorussia and the Ukraine.[96] These were often personifications of seasons (or in one case SS. Cosmas and Damian),[97] and the festivities usually involved their destruction and often burial. An example is the burying of a straw doll personifying Maslenitsa, or Shrovetide, on the last day of that season. This was done by the women of the village, one of whom would dress as a priest and lead the women from one end of the village to the other, singing songs, shouting and generally making a noise. At the end of the procession the doll would be undressed, pulled to pieces and buried.[98] In several areas, usually around the feast of St Peter (29 June), straw effigies of women called 'Kostroma' were dressed in festive clothes and either carried to a field of rye in a mock funeral procession or thrown into the river. This marked the end of the summer festivals and the beginning of the harvest season and was probably connected with the ritual of getting rid of *rusalki* or water sprites in *rusal'skaia nedelia*, the seventh week after Easter, also called *zelenye sviatki*.[99]

The use of dolls representing babies to encourage conception is a more specific kind of fertility magic. In some areas a doll of this kind is placed in the bed of a couple on their wedding night.[100] A similar symbolism combined with the

magical use of icons can be seen in the pilgrimage which childless Russian
women would make to Smolensk in the hope of conceiving a child. Here there
was a wonder-working doll of the infant Jesus which they would rock in their
arms while a nun prayed for them.[101]

6. *Christian Objects as Talismans*

These are not always easy to assess as amulets for the reasons outlined at the
beginning of this chapter. The difficulty of distinguishing between magic and
religion in this matter is reflected in the apparently contradictory attitude of the
Christian churches, not to mention Judaism and Islam, in which magic is
frequently condemned, but just as frequently practices are condoned, or even
encouraged, which for many people are unquestionably magical. Thus Thomas
Aquinas, perhaps aware that he was trying to control the uncontrollable, declared
that the wearing of medals or scraps of paper bearing scriptural quotations was
not superstitious provided that it was not mixed with non-Christian symbols.[102]
On the magic which flourished alongside medieval Christianity a later Thomas
writes: 'Most of the magical claims made for religion were parasitic to its teaching
and were more or less vigorously refuted by ecclesiastical leaders'.[103]

In the Greek and Russian Orthodox Churches regular prohibitions were made
of both texts and practices which were regarded as being contrary to religion.
(These are discussed in more detail in Chs 1 and 16.) To judge from the extent to
which such artefacts survive, these had no more effect than the equivalent
condemnations in the West, and many cases display a syncretism which would
certainly not meet the criteria of Thomas Aquinas. Indeed many must have been
produced by institutions of the church: the Byzantine clay pilgrim tokens of St
Symeon Stylites the Younger, with an image of the saint on one side and a hand
on the other, were clearly an early manifestation of the pious souvenir trade
which has flourished ever since, and equally clearly were thought of as
prophylactic amulets.[104] Pilgrim tokens, however, seem not to have been a
popular amulet in Russia.[105]

On the other hand the wearing of amulets was certainly a matter of concern to
the Russian Church in the seventeenth century, the period in which magical
practices in Russia, both real and imagined, seem to have been at their most
widespread, a number of penitentials advise priests on the questions which
should be put to penitents during confession, and the wearing of amulets is one of
the striking list of pagan and diabolic practices mentioned (these include
worshipping idols, making offerings to the Devil, trampling on the cross,
indulging in Psalter divination, and shaving off the beard).[106] Minor objects
associated with religious practice which could be used for magico-medical
purposes are church candles, drops of wax from candles at each of twelve gospel
readings on Holy Thursday, icon oil (especially if gathered from nine different
lamps at the time of childbirth), communion bread.[107] Major categories are
discussed below.

6.1. *Crosses and Icons*. Whatever its origin and uses in other cultures, within Christian cultures from quite early in the Christian era the Cross has been the most important symbol. As has already been remarked, the dividing line between religion and magic with symbols of this kind is particularly difficult to draw. At one end of the scale crosses may be worn as an ornament, part of the insignia of an order or rank, as an official part of clerical vestments, or as a symbol of identity, in particular in a society where Christianity is only one of several religions.

In the last case the shape of the cross may be significant: in Russia from the mid seventeenth century onwards, for example, the iconography of the Cross, the making of the sign of the Cross, and the depiction of a hand raised in blessing, may depend on whether the artist, and consequently the user, was a member of the official Orthodox Church or of one of the schismatic sects known as the Old Believers which refused to accept textual and liturgical reforms and broke away from the official state Orthodox Church in the seventeenth century. Old Believers insisted on continuing to make the sign of the Cross with two fingers, the reformed official church used three. The official church often used the single-barred cross while the Old Believers recognized only the three-barred 'Russian' cross,[108] and considered the single-barred cross heretical, even demonic.

At the other end of the scale a cross may be carried for completely superstitious, prophylactic or apotropaeic reasons. And perhaps somewhere in between might come the cross or icon as heraldic device, vexillum or palladium. The Cross was thought to be an antidote to evil from the patristic age onwards.[109] Its employment in the liturgy must have had magical implications for many observers, and as a vexillum or palladium, beginning with the famous legend of Constantine and 'In hoc signo vincis', we have already moved into a system of pagan political rhetoric and close to the realms of magic – a banner with a strange device is both practical and magical in time of war.

Ecclesiastical support for the use of the cross as an amulet could even be deduced from a careless reading of a blameless patristic authority: St John Chrysostom in his eleventh baptismal instruction states: 'But the Cross has the strength of a wonderful amulet and a mighty incantation'. This, of course, occurs in the context of a denunciation of such practices but could easily be misinterpreted.[110]

The sign of the Cross is also used routinely as a blessing, and from that to the sign of the Cross as a magical operation is but a short step; a common Russian practice was to cross the mouth if one yawned to prevent the Devil from entering. As any devotee of horror films knows, the cross protects against demons and unwholesome creatures such as vampires, which is one reason why it is worn as an amulet and why it is often a component part of the design of Christian talismans.

Pectoral crosses, usually worn outside the clothing, appear in Russian as local versions of Byzantine *encolpia*. Early (eleventh–twelfth-century) enamelled crosses, evidently used as amulets (they are found in grave goods on suspension thongs with other amulets) and as part of female decoration, are known from archaeological research.[111] They were usually produced by casting, and later by pressing,[112] and the trade in mass-produced metal crosses, medallions, triptychs, etc., certainly continued until recent times, and will no doubt flourish again in the new climate of entrepreneurship and popular piety. (See Fig. 7 for nineteenth-century specimens.)

One particular type of thaumaturgic cross was the *Levanidov krest*, i.e. made of cedar of Lebanon.[113] Another distinctly magic cross was the *mertvyi krest* or 'dead cross', a pectoral cross which had to be taken from a corpse in a grave and would make you so thin that you could avoid conscription into the army.[114] At the same time it could also cure fever, fright, and nervous illness.[115] If this failed in its purpose, conscripts when setting out to join the army would take a St Nicholas icon with them as protection.[116]

Most Russians wore a pectoral cross, often the one given them at baptism, which they removed (according to many sources), either for practical or magical reasons, only during sexual intimacy,[117] or in the bathhouse, or when performing certain magical rites. As mentioned above, to trample on one's cross was a requirement of becoming a magician and a sign of demonic magic, against which confessors in seventeenth-century Russia were advised to be vigilant.

The belief in the power of the cross to disconcert demons goes back to the early centuries of Christianity and was widespread in Western Europe.[118] It is remarked very early in Russian literature: in the entry for 1068 in the *Russian Primary Chronicle* there is a digression on the power of the cross, its importance in the swearing of oaths, its value as a vexillum, and: 'if a man be importuned by devils, a sign of the Cross on the face drives them away'.[119] In 1071, in the same chronicle, a man of Novgorod visits a Chud' magician to have his fortune told, but the magician is unable to summon up his devils because the man is wearing a cross.[120] The sixteenth-century *Radziwiłł Chronicle* contains two miniatures which show the Devil being repulsed by a cross or Sign of the Cross. In Old Believer tracts the power of the cross to drive out demons is accorded only to the three-barred cross, the single-barred cross being seen as either Roman and heretical, or a sign of the Antichrist, or both. In more modern times a popular name for the cross is *chortogon* ('devil-chaser').

There are other talismanic uses of pectoral crosses in later popular belief. In Karelia a cross buried in a path will ensure the recovery of a stray cow (in case this method fails, one has to consult a *koldun* or a miller),[121] and in Siberia it is believed that a bullet made from a melted-down metal cross is the only means of killing a *koldun* (wizard),[122] a notion very similar to that of the silver bullet which will slay a vampire, or the silver or brass buttons which occasionally figure in Russian stories as bullets against supernatural targets such as a *leshii* or *rusalka* (wood and water sprites).[123]

Crosses may also be drawn: on the eve of the Epiphany a cross drawn on a door will keep witches at bay;[124] in the Volga region doors, windows and wells are marked with a chalk cross at the Epiphany;[125] in Siberia domestic animals used to be herded into pens and sheds on New Year's Eve and a cross would be painted in pitch on the door as a precaution against the witchcraft of 'heretics'; then, on the eve of the Epiphany, the same thing was done with chalk, or coal if the hut or barn was white.[126] An interesting variant of this is mentioned in Dal' *Tolkovyi slovar'*, s.v. *sviatoi*: *sviat-mel* is 'holy chalk' with which peasants in western regions would make crosses on their doors on the same night and which would thereafter serve as a medicament.

In medieval Russia, as in Byzantium and elsewhere, the Cross as a guarantee of good faith and witness to oaths was extremely important; to 'kiss (the cross)' is the normal term in Old Russian for swearing an oath or pledging loyalty and from the end of the fifteenth century the term *tseloval'nik* (lit. 'kisser') was used for many types of elected and sworn officials. Cross-kissing was one of the 'judgment of God' procedures which were part of the normal court practice in Muscovite Russia. The law code introduced by Tsar Aleksei Mikhailovich in 1649, the *Ulozhenie*, includes a whole chapter of ten articles on swearing by the cross, together with patristic justification for the practice and a list of penalties for swearing falsely. The first article of the first chapter of the same code condemns to death by burning anyone who profanes the cross.[127]

Large crosses are comparatively rare in magical practices, being normally high up on the top of a church, but an example of the magico-medical veneration of standing crosses may be seen in the practice associated with St Alexander of Osheven, whose 'magic footprint' in a stone was mentioned above. Here sufferers, employing a simple association of ideas, would tie headscarves to the top of one of the four crosses set up near the stone to be relieved of headache, and to the cross-piece for backache, or place shoes at the bottom to be cured of pain in the legs and feet.[128]

Metal pendants other than crosses include the Virgin and Child and the Dormition of the Virgin.[129] The medallions which have both Christian and pagan motifs are described below under *Zmeeviki*.

Crosses and icons were a normal part of the life of the peasantry as well as of the clergy and upper classes. An icon would be in every peasant hut in the right-hand corner facing the door, and in many of the rooms of the houses of merchants and nobles.[130] Peter Henry Bruce recounts in 1714:

> A Russian once coming to me with a message, looked about the room for an image, and seeing none, asked me, Where is thy God? I answered, In heaven: upon which he immediately went away without delivering his message. I told the general this circumstance, and he directly ordered a saint's picture to be hung up in my room, to prevent giving any farther offence of that kind.[131]

A pectoral icon would commonly be given to a young man being taken off to serve in the army, often the icon of St Nicholas mentioned above. Elizabeth Dimsdale notes in the journal of her trip to St Petersburg in 1781 that: 'A Russian Woman of the lower ranks would not go a Journey without her tutelar Saint and

in case she was to forget it, would expect some great Misfortune to befal her
before she returned home'.[132] A similar observation is made by the entertaining
Martha Wilmot, the Anglo-Irish friend of Princess Dashkova in the early years of
the nineteenth century. She further notes in her memoirs the use of an icon as an
oracle, not by a peasant but by Aleksandra Kochetova, neice of the princess and
a *demoiselle d'honneur* at the imperial court:

> Some days ago Alexandra Kotchetoff told me that when there was a question
> of her marrying M. de – a very excellent Match which her father wish'd her
> exceedingly to accept she wrote the word 'Yes' on one scrap of paper and 'No'
> on the other. Then she gave the two papers to someone to mingle & throw
> behind an Image of a Saint which her Mother had given her, resolv'd & even
> *bound by a promise* to adopt whatever advice the Saint should give. She then
> pray'd before it and at the end of some time shut her eyes, made the Sign of
> the Cross & drew out a paper. It was the answer to her question 'Shall I marry
> M. de –'. The Saint answer'd 'No', & from that time she say'd no power on
> earth could ever tempt her to become his Wife. The Princess Alexandra
> Gallitzen went a pilgrimage to know whether the Saints council'd her to marry
> General Loptoff! On this occasion they answer'd 'Yes', & she became his Wife.
> 'tis true the Lady's inclinations in both cases were the same as the tutelary
> Saints'; but there are many moments when the lot of life depends on accidents
> as trivial as the Caprice of a Saint, & I would have given half my fortune to
> have had one at my elbow last Winter when the Question 'Shall I go to Engd
> or remain in Russia' cost me so very near dear & was at last decided more by a
> terror panic than by anything which my reason can now justify.[133]

This type of icon oracle was apparently quite common, and at all social levels.[134]

The prayer before consulting the icon-oracle and the random selection
procedure are, of course, common to many types of divination and have been
mentioned elsewhere, but the latter is perhaps redundant in this case if the saint
is supposed to decide the matter! The choosing or foreseeing of a husband was
one of the commonest purposes of popular fortune-telling in Russia and is
discussed further in Ch. 4.5.

The use of icons as witnesses was one of the 'judgment of God' procedures in
Muscovite court actions. In one case of a land dispute in 1494 the boundaries
were marked by both parties carrying an icon,[135] the assumption being that the
fear of divine retribution would prevent a miscarriage of justice. What was
supposed to happen in the case of an honest mistake is not recorded.

6.2. *Wonder-Working Icons.* Many individual icons, or even local icon types, were,
often still are, regarded as having miraculous, usually healing, powers in both the
Eastern and Western churches,[136] but the number is too great to be discussed in
detail here – the number of wonder-working icons of the Virgin alone, which are
recognized by the Russian Orthodox Church, exceeds two hundred, and many of

these have given rise to legends in Old Russian literature.[137] Particular icon types of the Virgin had particular functions: the Virgin of the Unburning Bush would protect a home from fire; the Virgin of Kazan' would cure blindness; the Fedorov Virgin would help in a difficult childbirth; children would be protected by the Virgin of Tikhvin; the Hodigitria was prayed to before setting out on a long journey.[138] The belief in the power of the icon itself, or of a particular icon type, is quite evident in the various prayers, spells and magical practices in which, for example several separate versions of the image of the Virgin or St Nicholas may be invoked in succession.

The belief in the thaumaturgic powers of icons was well established in Byzantium and indeed was part of the argument in favour of images in the Iconoclast controversy. The ninth-century apocryphal *Letter of the Oriental Patriarchs to the Emperor Theophilus* includes a list of the twelve most potent miracle-working icons. They are: 1. The Mandylion of Edessa (King Abgar's image of Christ 'not made by human hands' – see below); 2. An image of the Virgin at Lydda, again 'not made by human hands'; 3. St Luke's portrait of the Virgin; 4. An image of the Virgin which appeared miraculously in Lydda in the time of Peter; 5. A mosaic on Cyprus which bled when shot in the knee by an Arab; 6. A mosaic on the façade of the church of the Nativity of Bethlehem which protected the church from Persian destruction; 7. An icon of the Virgin at Alexandria which could put to death those who insulted it; 8. An icon which blinded a man who threw a stone at it; 9. An icon of Christ at Berytus which bled when stabbed by a Jew; 10. An icon in St Sophia in Constantinople which bled when stabbed by a Jew and continued to bleed after it was thrown into a well; 11. An icon which saved itself during Iconoclasm by walking over the water to Rome; 12. An icon of St Andrew at Lemnos which, when mutilated by an iconoclast priest,[139] caused the eye of the priest to jump out and replace the mutilated eye in the icon.[140] Later Russian beliefs in the miraculous properties of icons will be seen to follow a similar pattern.

The people of Kiev Rus' were quickly introduced to Byzantine beliefs in the miraculous powers of icons: the *Russian Primary Chronicle* for the years 863–866 records how Patriarch Photius took the vestment of the Virgin from the church at Blachernae and dipped it in the sea, whereupon a great storm arose and scattered the invading fleet of the godless Rus'. Further manifestations of the offensive and defensive powers of icons in war are discussed below.

Icons in Russia may be involved in wide range of popular practices, including divination: for example, in a 'Christian' variation on the ancient and common practice of koskinomancy, or sieve divination, if you wanted to find a thief in Archangel province you had to place bread on a table, place an icon on the bread, place a sieve on scissors: it would tilt away if an innocent person approached but towards the guilty party;[141] the icon of St Nicholas is part of another kind of divination with rings; and icons may also perform as oracles, responding to written messages submitted to them.

The reputed power of icons to bless water in which they are placed is attested by several customs: icons may be dipped in water and placed in graves to help the dead; water drunk from an icon is widely thought to have healing properties.[142] The blessing of water by dipping icons or relics into it was condemned by the *Stoglav* Council of 1551 – triple immersion of a single cross was stipulated as the acceptable method of sanctifying water.[143] As usual, condemnation at one level did not prevent the practice from continuing at another. Russians in the Indigirka region of northern Siberia until fairly recently baptized their children without a priest by dipping a silver cross in water and then dipping the head and feet of the child in the water.[144] The icon of the Virgin of Akhtyrka, which 'manifested itself' in 1739 and was copied in popular prints in the eighteenth and nineteenth centuries (Fig. 8), was believed to turn water in which it was dipped into a cure for fever.[145]

Although all icons were popularly supposed to have thaumaturgic properties, some individual icons are particularly famous. One such is that of the Bogoliubskaia Virgin icon. A miraculous icon of this type was brought from the village church of Zimarovo in the Riazan' province to Moscow in 1771 to cure plague victims and was the catalyst to the plague riots of that year which resulted in, among other things, the murder of the patriarch; another was credited with saving several towns and villages from the plague in the mid-nineteenth century.[146]

Another popular thaumaturgic icon is that of St Nicholas at Zaraisk – indeed, as the many examples given elsewhere in this book demonstrate, St Nicholas is known in a host of manifestations in Russian popular belief. For example, his icon will protect flocks (a duty otherwise performed by bear's head or bear's paw amulets), in which he merges with pre-Christian deities.[147] Herberstein in his description of Muscovy (1557) mentions only St Nicholas under the heading of saints in his chapter on religion:

> Of Saints. They revere St Nicholas, who lies at Bari in the kingdom of Naples, above all others and tell of his many wondrous deeds, one of which is said to have taken place but a few years ago. An illustrious Muscovite soldier called Michael Kisaletski had routed a notable Tatar, and Michael could not catch the Tatar up. He cried aloud to St Nicholas: 'Help me to catch the Tatar!' The Tatar heard this and spoke: 'Nicholas, if he catches me with your help it will be no miracle. But if you save me, who do not know you, then great will be your fame'. They tell how Michael's horse stood still and the Tatar escaped him. From then on this same Tatar sent Michael each year a quantity of honey to be given to the poor in honour of St Nicholas, with a portion for himself and a splendid marten coat.[148]

Samuel Collins, in his *The Present State of Russia* (1671) recounts:

> They will hold their Gods[149] to the fire, trusting they can help them, if they will. A fellow, thinking to have staid the fire by that means, held his Mikola [i.e. icon of St Nicholas] so long, that he had like to have been burnt himself,

and seeing he did him no good, he threw him into the midst of the fire, with this curse: 'noo chert, i. e. The Devil take thee'.[150]

This story, true or not, must join the list of travellers' *loci communes*. Peter Henry Bruce, in a passage describing a great fire in Moscow in 1713, tells it as follows:

> On this occasion a poor superstitious man, seeing the fire advancing to consume his all, took a picture of St Nicholas and holding it between him and the fire, prayed fervently for that saint's protection, but in vain for the flames soon seized his house, for which he became so enraged at the saint, that he threw him into the fire, saying, since he would not save him, he might now save himself: this coming to the ears of the clergy, the poor man was sentenced to be burnt alive.[151]

The notion that St Nicholas could intervene in fires is perhaps related to the belief that he was the protector of carpenters, although one might have thought that fires were in fact good for that trade in the predominantly wooden towns of Russia. In fact icons of any kind were thought to be fire-resistant: Prince Kurbskii in the sixteenth century recounted two incidents in his history of Ivan IV in which icons of the Virgin remained unscathed in fires.[152] A painting by N.S. Matveev called 'The Fire' (1891) shows a peasant woman in front of her wooden hut holding an icon of the Unburning Bush as a protection against fire. The association of ideas is obvious.[153]

The punishment of non-performing icons described above is also known from other sources, and together with the blinding of an 'heretical' icon also mentioned above, does indeed suggest that for many the icon possessed a kind of magic life which could be affected in the same way that the witch-dolls in the likeness of an enemy could be pierced or placed under a spell which would harm the person represented.[154] A seventeenth-century incident involved punishing icons in a manner which has distinctly magical associations: during the Polish intervention the inhabitants of Smolensk fled into the forest to escape the invading troops of Poland-Lithaunia; they hung their icons on the trees upside down and shouted at them 'We pray to you but you do not protect us from the Lithuanians'.[155] An icon which failed could be punished in another way: it was customary for merchants to reinforce their prayers for commercial success by embellishing the appropriate icons with silver and jewelled covers; if they failed in their enterprise the disappointed donor would often repossess the gift.[156]

Icons, because of their holy nature, could not be bought. Simony was avoided by icon-sellers silently ignoring inadequate 'offerings' from would-be purchasers and handing over the icon only when a suitable 'offering' was made. This casuistry was noted by a number of foreign visitors to Russia, from Samuel Collins in the seventeenth century right up to the nineteenth century, and Kostomarov indicates that it was already the custom in the sixteenth century.[157] In fact this method of hallowing trade in sacred objects was certainly known to the Russians much earlier, and was not invented by them: the Russian Abbot Daniel in the early twelfth century described in his account of a pilgrimage to the Holy Land how he gave a small present to the guardian of the Holy Sepulchre, who, 'seeing his love for the Lord's Tomb', broke off a piece of the rock and gave it to him as a relic, after swearing him to silence.[158] Daniel had clearly been forewarned of local conventions. Icons which were beyond repair were burned at the crossroads to the accompaniment of prayers in several parts of Russia, although this was more generally thought to be sacrilegious.[159] Soloukhin says he found this custom in three places and adds that the commoner method of disposal was 'by water', i.e. by being floated face upwards down the river. Kostomarov also describes these practices, adding that one must never actually refer to an icon or church burning but use a euphemism. Moreover, one had to beg the icon's forgiveness by saying 'prosti!' before consigning it to the river; it was thought to be a sign of grace to find a floating icon.[160] Samuel Collins, the English personal physician of Tsar Aleksei Mikhailovich, who has already been quoted on the subject of icons, has a different interpretation of *prosti* but otherwise tells the same story. He states:

> An obliterate image they put into the river, and crossing themselves, bid it *prosti*, i.e. Farewell Brother. And if any of their brethren meets with Jove, he turns into Neptune, and they, crossing themselves, cry, *prosti, brat*, God be with you Brother. In time of fire they arrive above all things to save their images: but if they escape not the conflagration they must not be said to be burnt, but gone up. If a church be bur'nd, they say it is ascended, they must not say burn'd.[161]

Cast metal icons which became so worn that the features of the saints were not discernible were thought to be no longer able to see and would be discarded either by burying or in water.[162] This notion that icons could see has already been encountered in the 'blinding' of an 'heretical' icon mentioned above. Covering or turning icons to face the wall during sexual activity similarly suggests that the icons were thought to be able to see: Jodocus Crull recorded in the seventeenth century that:

> The *Muscovites* exercise the Veneral Act with a great deal of Gravity and Circumspection; for they will never have to do with a Woman, unless they first take off the little Cross which is hang'd about her Neck when she is Christned; and they are so Considerate in their Love-Passion, as first to cover the Images of their Saints, if there be any in the Room.[163]

6.3. *Palladia and Vexilla.* These may be considered a sub-division of the previous category. The prime model for the use of a Christian symbol as a vexillum is, of course, the Emperor Constantine's use of the cross, and the type of Byzantine icon known as the Nikitirion, the conquering cross, continues a theme which was also known in Western iconography. In Russia the best known examples are to be found in the use of icons as offensive or defensive weapons (sometimes both), and in this they are also following Byzantine precedents.[164]

In the battle between the men of Novgorod and Suzdal' in 1169, itself the subject of an icon,[165] the icon of the Virgin of the Sign was brought out onto the ramparts by the besieged Novgorodians and was pierced by the arrows of the attacking Suzdalians. As a result the icon wept and the Virgin sent help to Novgorod in the form of Saints Boris and Gleb, George, and Demetrius of Salonika (the personal appearance of warrior saints leading an army on to victory is common in Byzantine and Slavonic legends and chronicle-writing).[166]

The icon of the Virgin of Vladimir, painted, according to legend, by St Luke, was thought to have banished Tamerlane from Russia in 1395 and to have saved Moscow from the army of Makhmet-Girey in 1521. In 1613, when the monastery of Tikhvin was besieged by the Swedes, another icon of the Virgin was put to a similar use, and in 1619 Richard James, chaplain at the English factory in the White Sea, wrote '. . . when the Emperor goes into the field the *Spasova obraz* [i.e. icon of the Saviour] is carried before him'.[167] This custom, according to Bogoslovskii, was probably last observed by Peter the Great in the Azov campaign against the Turks in 1696.[168] The icon itself is now in the Kremlin Armoury museum in Moscow.

In fact the custom may well have continued into more recent times. If one is to believe Solzhenitsyn, the icon of 'The Virgin Appearing in a Vision to St Sergius', painted on a piece of wood taken from the coffin of the blessed saint himself, was taken into battle by Russian armies over three centuries; it was with Tsar Aleksei Mikhailovich in his Lithuanian campaign in the seventeenth century, with Peter the Great at Poltava, with Alexander I in the Napoleonic wars, and was sent by the Tsar to the General Headquarters of the Russian Army in the Russo-Japanese War. Notwithstanding the spectacular failure of the icon in that conflict Nicholas II sent it to help the army again in 1914.[169]

Even if Solzhenitsyn's story is told largely for satirical effect, it is nevertheless worth observing that Peter the Great's transformation of Russia into a secular state certainly did not end the use of religious emblems as military standards. Most of the new regiments he founded were given standards bearing the picture of the crucified St Andrew, the emblem of the Order of St Andrew created by Peter.[170] In the case of the dragoons this was supplemented by the motto 'In this sign *I* shall conquer', a version of the Roman Emperor Constantine's vision which the more educated of the Old Believers might well have seen as yet another example of Peter's blasphemous hubris.

In less exalted military contexts icons played the same role. An illuminated manuscript of about 1700, the *Remezov Chronicle*, recounts the history of the Russian conquest of Siberia, in particular the exploits of the sixteenth-century adventurer Ermak and his Cossack band. This leans heavily on the hagiographic tradition, even to the extent of recording miracles performed by Ermak's armour after his death. It also shows many battle scenes, in almost all of which the Cossacks are shown with banners bearing an image of Christ or St Nicholas or the Cross, which on several occasions did miraculous deeds. One picture shows the icon of Christ moving by itself in front of the Cossack boats and protecting them from the arrows of the pagans; another shows a miraculous apparition of Christ which paralysed the arms of the enemy archers when they shot at it. The chronicle ends with pictures and stories of the twelfth-century Prince Andrei Bogoliubskii going into battle with an icon of the Virgin and Child, 'arming the troops with unconquerable weapons better than sword or spear', and the intervention of SS. Boris and Gleb, with halo and sword, who personally slew the soldiers of the Tatar Mamai on behalf of Prince Dmitrii Donskoi in 1380.[171]

As the example of St Nicholas just mentioned will show, it was not only icons of Christ or the Virgin which could be used as palladia and vexilla: the personal intervention of warrior saints in battles mentioned above could extend to other areas and could include their icons. A further example of the power of the warrior saint Demetrius is the account in the tale of the siege of Pskov by the Polish King Stephen Batory in 1580–82 of how the icon of Demetrius won the day.[172] Another Russian story tells of a pagan chieftan who captured two maidens during an unsuccessful siege of Thessalonica and carried them off to his own country. He tells them:

> I hear that you have a great God called Demetrius, who works many miracles. Embroider me his likeness on an image, so that I might venerate him and defeat my enemies, while I carry his image in front of my armies.

In one version of the story the embroidered image becomes a magic carpet which rescues the two maidens and flies them home.[173]

Most of the examples quoted have been of icons in their offensive role as vexilla, but there are more passive types in which they serve as palladia. The icon theme of St Nicholas of Mozhaisk holding in one hand a sword and in the other a model of a town or monastery is clear enough in its symbolism, and is analogous with West European paintings showing patron saints holding a model of the town they were supposed to protect. A comparatively recent example of military protection afforded by an icon occurred during the bombardment by the gunboats HMS *Brisk* and *Miranda* of the Solovetskii monastery on the White Sea during the Crimean War. The icon of the Virgin over the cathedral door thereafter bore the legend:

> Call upon me in the day of trouble. The Heavenly Mother defended the Solovetsk Obitel during a nine hours' bombardment by the English, and was pleased to receive in the icon a blow from a 96 pound ball; this last shot was fired while ringing for Vespers, July 7, 1854. Mother of God, vouchsafe victory over his enemies to our Tsar, that we may in his peace live in all piety and purity.[174]

This episode survives in the folk memory of the north, which ascribes the failure of the British to hit the monastery, except with the one shot mentioned, to a procession with a cross on the ramparts of the monastery, and to a miraculous downpour of seagull droppings following prayers to SS. Zosima and Savatii.[175]

6.4. *Relics.* The miraculous power of relics was, and in many places still is, widely believed in by both Eastern and Western Christianity (with some diminution after the Reformation). Indeed, the 'odour of sanctity', non-putrefaction of the body, and miracles performed at the grave of, or by relics of putative saints are commonplaces of hagiography and canonization processes. If Dostoevskii is to be believed, provincial Russians in the nineteenth century could still be shocked when a reputed holy man (Father Zosima in *The Brothers Karamazov*) did not remain uncorrupted after his death.

By the twelfth century the practice of making a pilgrimage to the Holy Land was well established in Russia. The visiting of religious sites and the viewing, and if possible the acquisition of relics was a large part of the purpose of the pilgrimage.

The Abbot Daniel, who visited Jerusalem in 1106–8, notes that pilgrims, presumably including Russians, take home the holy dust from the tomb of St John at Ephesus to cure every kind of ailment;[176] he also describes a cross of cypress containing a nail from the cross of Christ erected by St Helena on Cyprus which performed miracles and cured all manner of sicknesses,[177] and a holy oil which exudes from the wall of the tomb of St Joseph at Nazareth and is collected for curing the sick.[178] Similar to the last example is the *miron* which was supposed to flow from the relics of the warrior saint Demetrius in Thessalonica.[179] This had therapeutic and apotropaic powers, in particular if applied as an unction before a battle,[180] and was taken home by pilgrims as many take home Lourdes water in the West today. Jordan water, earth from Golgotha, stones from Christ's tomb, oil from the relics at Kiev, or indeed any icon oil, were also prized for their therapeutic properties.[181] A more sinister pilgrim 'relic' was water from the Dead Sea. Stephen Graham, who went on a Russian pilgrim ship to the Holy Land just before the First World War, recalled a conversation with a Russian peasant pilgrim who told him that some less than God-fearing pilgrims took home with them water from the Dead Sea for sale to witches. Graham also described other practices, some more magical than religious, which were maintained up to 1917 by the enormous numbers of Russian peasant pilgrims to the Holy Land: the Russians would bathe in the Jordan in shrouds and caps which they would then take home and keep for their own funerals; they would also light lanterns from the Holy Fire (i.e. candles thought to have ignited miraculously on Holy Saturday in the Holy Sepulchre)[182] and attempt to keep the flame alight throughout the journey home, and some would bathe in the Dead Sea as a remedy for rheumatism, the king's evil, and the influence of the Evil Eye.[183]

One particularly noteworthy therapeutic relic was a tooth of St Antipii Velikii (an early Christian martyr Antipas, Bishop of Pergamon), a saint who was reputed to have healing powers and to whom sufferers from toothache would pray.[184] One of the saint's teeth was a prized possession of Tsar Ivan the Terrible, who had it mounted in silver and wore it with a variety of crosses, all containing precious stones of therapeutic virtue. A later tsar, Aleksei Mikhailovich, also employed this relic. In 1646 he went to the church of St Antipii to pray and bought two silver *ex-voto* teeth on the way at the silver market to present to the church, presumably for placing on the icon of the saint.[185]

6.5. *Bells.* Bells were used for magical purposes in Byzantium,[186] ancient Egypt and modern Europe.[187] They were also used in Russia, where small round bells can be found as amulets (*bubentsy, bubenchiki*),[188] in particular, like English horse brasses, to protect horses from the Evil Eye.[189] These small bells were usually found in odd numbers (most commonly seven, nine, or eleven) attached to horse harness and in particular to horse collars.[190] In Karelia it was considered to be a sign of misfortune if the head of a herd lost its bell, a belief which is perhaps fairly practical in origin.[191]

The casting of large bells, magical artefacts in several cultures, was invariably accompanied in Russia, as elsewhere,[192] by religious ceremonies.[193] A detailed account of a bell-founding and blessing in a Russian village in the Tambov province at the end of the nineteenth century can be found in a travel book by Maurice Baring.[194]

An instance of the power which can be attributed to a bell is the incident in which the bell of Uglich was held to be responsible for the riots which followed the death of Dmitrii, Ivan the Terrible's infant heir, in 1591. As a punishment for raising the alarm which triggered the riots the bell had its clapper and 'ears' cut off and was exiled to Siberia.[195] It was pardoned and returned to Uglich only in the late nineteenth century. Another bell was punished for a similar offence by Catherine the Great after the Plague Riot in 1771.[196] The punishment of these bells may be compared with the punishment of non-performing thaumaturgic icons.[197] One might add that the fall of the clapper of the great Moscow bell during the 'Time of Troubles' in the early seventeenth century was regarded at the time as a bad omen.[198]

Although Russian bells may be treated as live creatures with names (as in England),[199] and indeed contain sometimes fantastic beasts from folk art in their decoration, they do not appear to carry the kind of apotropaeic inscriptions against war, pestilence, lightning, and the Devil to be found widely in German *Wetterglocken* or in analogous English beliefs.[200] Dal' does, however, record a saying from the Viatka guberniia, that the Spasskii bell foretells rain, adding the rational explanation that it could only be heard in a certain region when the wind was in the south.[201]

Bells are also in some areas thought to drive away the Devil by their sound and *klikushi*, hysterical 'possessed' women, were sometimes placed under bells to exorcise the evil spirit which was possessing them.[202] Bell-towers were thought to be the haunt of demons which had inhabited the bodies of dead magicians but they were obliged to flee each time the bells rang.[203] Bells are involved in certain types of divination when listened for at a crossroads (see Ch. 4.5.5). Water in which the clapper of a bell has been dipped acquires healing properties.[204]

6.6. *Zmeeviki*. *Zmeevik* is the modern Russian name for medallion and pendant amulets with a Christian motif one side and an ancient pagan motif involving serpents on the other. (This is usually a Gorgon-like head with radiating snakes, or an anguipedal human figure or half-figure with serpents issuing from the waist or legs.) The word itself is not attested in Old Russian texts or in Dal' but is found in the 1816 French-Russian Lexicon of Tatishchev in technical senses as a calque of French *serpentin, serpentine*.[205] The term was taken up in the nineteenth century by Russian scholars, presumably because of the snake motif (*zmei* 'snake' in Russian) and associations which can be claimed with serpent themes in literature and folklore and a supposed ancient cosmic serpent cult among the Slavs (a popular theme with some scholars),[206] but the folksy appearance of the term is misleading; for all its syncretistic iconography and antique pagan and Judaeo-Christian or Gnostic origins the *zmeevik* is in Russia, and among the Balkan Slavs, a primarily Christian amulet which in Old Russian texts has a Christian, albeit uncanonical, interpretation.

Russian knowledge or use of Hellenistic, Byzantine, and Near Eastern talismans in general seems to have been relatively limited, if the literary evidence is a guide: a description, taken from the Byzantine chronicle of George Hamartolos, of the methods used by Apollonius of Tyana to protect cities from scorpions and earthquakes, appears in the twelfth-century *Russian Primary Chronicle* under the year 6420 (912);[207] the *Explanatory Palaia* of 1477, describing the planets and their spheres, remarks that the Hellenes call the moon Hecate and depict her in a chariot with a twining serpent.[208]

The one type of ancient amulet to survive and develop in Russia to any significant extent was the *zmeevik* pendant (Fig. 9). Specimens datable to the eleventh century have been found and they have been in more or less continuous production ever since, with new local Russian types appearing from the fifteenth century. Indeed, it has recently been claimed (presumably on the dubious basis of the number of extant specimens) that they were more popular in Russia than in Byzantium, and that in the nineteenth century it was common in the northern provinces of Russia for a peasant to wear a *zmeevik* together with his pectoral cross.[209] *Zmeeviki*, especially copper specimens, were apparently popular among the traditionalist Old Believers, who reinterpreted them in the sense of Moses's bronze replica of a snake mentioned in Numbers 21: 8, 9 as a protection against snakebite.[210]

The models for the Russian *zmeevik* are Byzantine and Near Eastern. They are found in bronze, copper, lead, silver, gold, terracotta or stone.[211] They may be cast, struck, or engraved, and their workmanship varies from the most skilled to uncomprehending crude copying. Typically they have a Christian or Judaeo-Christian motif on one side and a pagan motif on the other; the armbands and rings with similar motifs did not become popular in Russia.[212]

The 'Christian' motif in amulets of this type is often a figure with a nimbus, on horseback, piercing with a lance a female figure, demon, serpent, lion, mermaid or some kind of monster. This mounted figure has been identified with the so-called 'Thracian rider' motif,[213] and is similar to the conventional icon representation of St George. Campbell Bonner, in a study of an amulet of this type,[214] declares that they are never labelled as St George, and Christopher Walter has questioned the assumptions made by scholars in assimilating the Thracian rider and St George motifs.[215] One can, however, assert quite properly that in late antiquity amulets existed which carried the representation of a mounted man spearing a recumbent figure and that the same figure appears on later amulets with an inscription identifying the rider as Solomon, St Sisinnius, or a warrior saint. Christopher Walter has recently proposed a rough chronology for the iconographic development of the rider motif on amulets, beginning perhaps in the third century with representations of Solomon, and assuming the character of warrior saint by the sixth century.[216]

An alternative treatment by Jeffrey Spier of the later Byzantine amulets of this type concentrates on the other side of the amulet (which Spier regards as the obverse), and sees the significance of the amulets primarily in the 'hystera' formula.[217] A comparatively recent catalogue of icon and reliquary amulets from the territory of the former Yugoslavia shows that at least in later Balkan examples of this motif the identification with St George is normal.[218] The assertion by Nikolaeva and Chernetsov[219] that amulets of this kind are practically unknown among the South Slavs needs modification; it is not impossible that, as with certain other magical objects and texts, later South Slav examples are in fact not directly Byzantine in origin but are mediated through Russia and the Ukraine.

The rider figure may also be identified with St Demetrios,[220] or Solomon,[221] or his Byzantine replacement St Sisinnius. The figure of the horseman's victim has been seen as representing the illness to be guarded against, or as a variety of manifestations of she-demons such as Gillo, Alabasdria, Antaura or Lilith, the foetus-destroying and child-stealing first wife of Adam in Jewish myth.[222]

More common Christian motifs in Russian amulets may be the Cross, plain or with the figure of the crucified Christ, IHS (i.e. one of the monograms for Jesus), the Virgin and Child (mostly the icon types of the Virgin of Tenderness and the Hodigitria), St John the Baptist, the Baptism of Christ, SS. Cosmas and Damian,[223] Mina, Constantine and Helena and the Cross, St Theodore Stratilates,[224] St Charlampios, the Seven Sleepers of Ephesus,[225] St Achileos, St Nicholas killing the Devil, SS. Boris and Gleb (the only exclusively Russian saints so employed), the Archangel Michael.

In 1925 the Russian scholar Orlov devised a classification of the *zmeeviki* in the important collection of some 160 specimens in the State Historical Museum in Moscow.[226] This has been the basis of many other articles but is now superseded by the monograph of Nikolaeva and Chernetsov, the most authoritative work on the subject to date,[227] which proposes an iconographic classification based on the obverse images which may be summarized as follows:

1. Archangel Michael. Five types, 11–15th century. Two with the inscription EFROSIN are associated with Novgorod, the others are Kievan or southern.
2. Icon type of the Virgin of Tenderness (Virgin of Vladimir). 12–15th century. This is the commonest category. There are several types, both round and arch-topped, the latter appearing from the 13th century onwards.
3. Icon type of the Fedorov Virgin. End of the 13th century to the 17th century. Often in triptych form.
4. Icon type of the Virgin of Tikhvin. 14–18th century. Several types both round and arch-topped.
5. Icon type of the Virgin of the Sign. Two types: one with triangular ornament, 13th century; the other with a circular inscription, 12th century. Very common but found only in the Novgorod area.
6. The Baptism of Christ. 13–15th century.
7. Two saints on horseback (Theodore Stratilates and George). From 13th but more commonly 14th century.
8. St George on horseback. 14th century. Two types, one Novgorodian.
9. St Theodore Stratilates, standing. Not very common. From end of 12th century.
10. St Nikita flogging the Devil.[228] Two types: one small octagonal, 13th century onwards; the other arch-topped with a reverse showing the 'gorgon' motif and St Theodore Tiro, another warrior-saint, thrusting a spear into the mouth of a serpent, 14th–17th century.[229] In one case Theodore is replaced by 'Zesinii', i.e. Sisinnius. The arch-topped type is unusual in showing both the Christian and the pagan motifs on the same side.
11. SS. Cosmas and Damian. From 13th century. Mostly Ukrainian. Serpent-killing motif.
12. SS. Boris and Gleb. From 13th century. Serpent-killing motif.
13. Crucifixion. Two types.

In shape these *zmeeviki* are most commonly circular with a suspension ring at the top. A less common form is octagonal, or square with an arched top and a suspension ring, in some cases with hinged sides forming a triptych (similar to the small cast icons called *skladen'*). Some cases of engraved gemstone *zmeeviki* are also known: for example, a twelfth–thirteenth-century gem from Suzdal' depicting the Seven Sleepers of Ephesus[230] and a Gorgon head with six snakes, and a fourteenth-century gem with Christ Enthroned on one side and a Gorgon head pattern on the other.[231]

The last two gemstone *zmeeviki* mentioned are particularly interesting in one respect – the first carries an inscription containing the names of the local princely family and the second was part of a benefaction by Tsar Ivan the Terrible to one of the principal monasteries of Russia, the Laura of the Trinity and St Sergius. The same monastery had a seventeenth-century icon in the iconostasis of its Trinity Cathedral in which the centre-piece was an inset gilt brass *zmeevik* of the Virgin of Tenderness, with a Gorgon head on the reverse.[232] These examples, added to the fact that some *zmeeviki* were made of gold and carried the name of the person who had ordered it, show fairly clearly that even at the highest levels of church and society the mixture of pagan and Christian in these amulets was not thought incongruous or reprehensible. Indeed, one *zmeevik* is known to have been used as *panagia* for liturgical purposes.[233] In the case of the benefaction of Ivan the Terrible it is hard to draw any conclusion – as will be clear from other episodes connected with this tsar described elsewhere in the book Ivan was both a practitioner and a persecutor of magical practices. One has to assume that for some the pagan magic design had still sufficient significance to invite censorship; one *zmeevik* is known which has had its pagan side ground off and a cross engraved in its place.[234] For others it must have become simply a meaningless decorative feature, with the protective power of the amulet residing in its Christian image.

As already mentioned, medallion amulets also frequently carry magical or prayer inscriptions, either in Greek or in Church Slavonic, such as 'One God, vanquisher of evil',[235] the Trisagion, 'Mother of God protect', 'Seal of God', 'Seal of Solomon', or parts of Psalm 90(91). This psalm promises comprehensive insurance, not least from the midday demon who is often found in Slavonic and Greek belief: 'For he will deliver you from the snare of the fowler and from the deadly pestilence; . . . You will not fear the terror of the night nor the arrow that flies by day, nor the pestilence that stalks in darkness nor the destruction that wastes at noonday. A thousand may fall at your side, ten thousand at your right hand; but it will not come near you.'[236]

The reverse side of the amulet in its non-Russian forms carries a magic motif; this is most commonly the Evil Eye, usually with knives and animals attacking it,[237] or a 'Gorgon's head' – a head with from five to twelve snake-heads radiating from it. The notion of Solomon vanquishing the Gorgon (or sometimes the womb or black demon of internal sickness called the Hystera) may, it has been suggested, be connected with the late antique *Testamentum Salomonis*.[238]

In Russia *zmeeviki* may have Greek inscriptions, and thus perhaps be imports from Byzantium or copies of Byzantine models, or Slavonic inscriptions, indicating more probably Balkan or Russian workmanship. Some may have both Greek and Slavonic inscriptions. One gold *zmeevik* with St Michael (?) and the Trisagion inscription on one side and a 'Gorgon head' on the other is supposed to have belonged to Vladimir Monomakh, Grand Prince of Kiev in the early twelfth century.[239]

6.6.1. *Sisinnius and the Daughters of Herod.* The figure of St Sisinnius and references to him in some of the amulet inscriptions suggest at least one of the purposes of *zmeeviki*. Sisinnius is associated in several legends which contain pagan, Christian, and Bogomil elements.[240] In Russian texts and folklore he appears as Sisinii, or corruptions of the name such as Sozont, Saksenii, Sinei, or Zesinii; he cures 'shaking fevers' (*triasavitsy*) personified as twelve (usually, but also seven, forty, seventy-seven) evil women, who are often further identified as Herod's (rarely

Cain's) daughters,[241] and may also be identified as *rusalki*, usually a type of water-sprite.[242]

A curious variant of this theme is the belief in the Orel province that a fever (*vorogushka*, a diminutive of *vrag* 'enemy; demon') is one of the forty sisters of Herod, who inflict illness on people by visiting them at night in the form of white moths and biting their lips while they sleep.[243] Dal', *Tolkovyi slovar'*, s.v. *marii-zazhgi-snega* (lit. 'Mary set fire to the snow', the folk name of 1 April), mentions Mar'ia Irodovna, i.e. Mary, Herod's daughter, as the name of a fever, against which the possibly jocular spell was 'Mar'ia Irodovna, come to me yesterday'.[244] This kind of spell formula intended to misdirect a demon is not uncommon – for example if you think you hear someone calling your name, this is probably the *domovoi* or house goblin preparing to trick you in some way; a way of dealing with him is to repeat to yourself silently the same spell: 'Mary, daughter of Herod, come yesterday'. Under *likhoradka* Dal' also lists the popular names of the twelve fever daughters of Herod as *likhoradka, likhomanka, triasukha (triasuchka), gnetukha (gnetushka), kumokha, kitiukha, zheltukha, blednukha, lomovaia, maial'nitsa, znobukha, trepukha*, all of which names suggest some illness or symptom of illness.[245] A further tradition identifies seventy-seven fevers as daughters of Herod turned into seventy-seven evil winds,[246] or seventy-seven flies. A separate cure for each was required; alternatively, in a procedure which is almost an anthology of popular magical beliefs, you could boil an egg from a black hen before sunset in water from three places, cut it into seventy-seven pieces, tie them in a rag, go at sunset to a lake or river and throw it into the water with the left hand while muttering a spell, then run home without looking back. As soon as the rag hits the water the fever sisters rush to get their bit of egg and in the confusion the patient is freed from his fever.[247] A prayer to St Makarii, which was used as an amulet, mentions seventy-seven evil sisters with loose hair and would appear to be part of the same tradition.[248] And two wedding spells recorded in the 1880s and 1906 seek protection for the bride from, among several things, witches and wizards, ravens and magpies, and maidens with unbound hair.[249] A rather more distant variant on the Herod and female relative theme is a diminishing spell in which Herod has nine wives who disappear one by one until the pain disappears.[250] Yet another manifestation of the 'daughters of Herod' theme is in a spell from the Baikal region of eastern Siberia to inflict a *khomut(ets)* (the worst kind of *porcha* or malefic magic, usually fatal) which would seal up the penis of the victim. In this spell: '. . . on the accursed sea there is a golden bathhouse; in this bathhouse there are the twenty-four daughters of Herod, and the twenty-fifth who cut off the head of John the Baptist . . .'; the names of the twenty-four are mostly similar to the fever names found in the fever spells.

In the Greek Sisinnius legend the saint and his brother Sisinorus defend the children of their sister Miletina from the evil child-killing demon Gillo (also Gello and various other spellings), mentioned above in connection with Solomon/Sisinnius as the mounted lancer. The method of dealing with this demon consists in reciting all its twelve and a half names (twelve and twenty are the commonest alternatives).[251] Veselovskii notes the tradition of the twelve names as the twelve daughters of Herod, and quotes a Greek version in which the twelve and a half names are: Gylou, Mōrra, Byzou, Marmarou, Petasia, Pelagia, Bordona, Apletou, Chamodrakaina, Anabardalaia, Psychanospastria, Paidopniktria, and Strigla.[252] The extra half name has been interpreted, at a time when solar myths could explain everything, as the difference between the solar and lunar years.[253] Some versions of the *zagovor* employ garbled Greek names,[254] which certainly underlines the Greek origin of the story, and the elaborate repetition of the names of the *Triasavitsy* does recall the point made by Barb in his discussion of Gillo/Lilith, that on no account must one leave the demon a loophole by omitting one of the names. The apparently Greek character of these names in *-eia*, and *-iia* may, however, be misleading. Iudin has drawn attention to the frequency of this type of name formation in the names of serpents invoked in Russian *zagovor* spells; in one case a 'serpent' name (Neveia) coincides with the name of a *Triasavitsa*.[255]

A Slavonic version of the story of Sisinnius appears in an eleventh-century Glagolitic Euchologion,[256] but was soon classified as apocryphal and is condemned in the earliest (fourteenth-century) Russian index of banned books as being the invention of the Bulgarian Bogomil priest Jeremy.[257] This mentions St Sisinnius on Mount Sinai, the angel Sikhail, seven fevers, the daughters of Herod, and objects to the text on the biblically correct grounds that only one person asked for the head of John the Baptist, and she was the daughter not of Herod but of his brother Philip! It further quotes Patriarch Sisinios (evidently Sisinios II, patriarch of Constantinople between April 996 and August 998) to the effect that he was 'not the false Sisinios of whom the priest Jeremy had written to deceive the simple'.[258]

I have been able to find only a few representations of Sisinnius in Russian art, though it seems likely that the subject was well known. One is a silver triptych with some gilding and niello dated 1412 and signed by the maker Lukian. The signature, date, and quality of workmanship are all most unusual for this period. The triptych was made to private order in the Suzdal area of central Russia and may be seen as a composite amulet: its central panel shows Christ enthroned, with the Archangel Michael above St John the Baptist and the Virgin on one side and the Crucifixion above St Peter and the women bearing myrrh on the other, but the panels on the back show St Sisinnius and the angel Sikhail, a guardian angel, the Seven Sleepers of Ephesus, St John the Baptist, St Nicholas, St Demetrius of Salonika, St Cosmas, the prophet Elijah, and the Virgin Mary, all of whom are commonly invoked for medical problems. The triptych also includes a highly unusual inscription: the words 'life' and 'death' over a male and female face. The specifically pagan elements of a *zmeevik* are omitted, but there can be no doubt that this is in fact a *zmeevik* sanitized to a sufficient degree that it was able to repose in the treasury of the Annunciation Cathedral in the Moscow Kremlin for centuries.[259]

The second representation is a nineteenth-century popular print which shows a rock rising from the sea, and twelve scantily dressed women of different colours with loosened hair;[260] on one side stands St Sisinnius with outstretched right hand; above are the four Evangelists holding rods, and below them an angel is diving down with rods in hand to beat the women [Fig. 11].[261]

The third representation is another nineteenth-century icon, tentatively ascribed to Mstera, a major icon-painting centre. This shows the Archangel Michael holding a triple-barred Russian cross extended to form a spear with which he appears to have driven the twelve *triasavitsy* into a cave. They are all naked, in several different colours, and with long hair.[262] Above the cave stand St Sisinnii 'the Wonderworker' dressed as a bishop and holding a book, and the 'Holy Martyr Fotinia' (probably Photina, the Samaritan woman with whom Jesus talked at the well of Jacob, and who by tradition was martyred under Nero).[263]

A fourth representation is in the form of a set of twelve small dolls in brightly coloured clothes, probably of the nineteenth century, which used to hang on the side of a stove in a Russian house (Fig. 12), and are described as the twelve daughters of Herod turned into demons by the curse of God because of the death of John the Baptist.[264]

One eighteenth-century Russian prayer lists the twelve women by name (all recognizable as words for fever) as the daughters of Herod and states that the prayer must be accompanied by the common magical practice of drinking water in which a cross has been immersed.[265]

A very similar version of the story exists in the form of a *zagovor* or spell against fever, apparently with the benefit of clergy. The *zagovor* is worth quoting in full since it is a good example of a fusion of antique, dubiously Christian, and folktale elements. Particularly noteworthy is the way in which each of the fever demons in turn names and describes herself: this is the formula found in the *Testament of Solomon*.[266] The *zagovor* reads:

By the Black Sea stands a stone column; on the column sits the holy and great apostle Sisinnius and he sees how the sea rises up in a storm to the clouds and out of it come twelve women with unbound hair – a cursed devilish vision. And these women say: We are the Triasovitsy, the daughters of Tsar Herod. And St Sisinnius asks them: Accursed devils, why have you come here? They reply: We have come to torment the human race. If anyone crosses our path we shall set on him and torment him, anyone who oversleeps morning service or does not pray to God or does not observe the fast days but eats and drinks early after rising. And St Sisinnius prayed to God: Lord, Lord, save the human race from these accursed devils. And God sent to him two angels, Sikhail and Anos, and the four evangelists. And they started to beat the Triasovitsy with four iron clubs and gave them three thousand wounds each every day. And the Triasovitsy begged them: Holy great apostle Sisinnius and Sikhail and Enos and you four evangelists, Luke, Mark, Matthew, John, do not torture us! Wherever we hear your holy names and in whatever family your names are revered we shall shall avoid that place by three days and three leagues! And the holy apostle Sisinnius asked them: What are your devilish names? The first said: My name is Triaseia (*triasti* = to shake. *Triasuchka* and variants are dialect and Old Russian for fever).[267] The second said: My name is Ogneia (*ogon'* = fire. *Ognevaia* is Old Russian for fever). Just as the stove is heated by pitchy logs, so Ogneia burns the bodies of men. The third said: My name is Ledeia (*led* = ice). Just as ice Ledeia makes men shiver so that they cannot warm themselves even by the stove. The fourth said: My name is Gneteia (*gnesti* = to press, oppress; *gnetukha* is dialect for fever). Gneteia lies on a man's ribs and churns up his insides, and if he wants to eat, let him, but his soul will depart. And the fifth said: My name is Grynusha (*gryzt'* = to gnaw. *Gryzuchka* is dialect for a kind of fever). Grynusha lies in a man's breast and his lungs rot and he coughs. The sixth said: My name is Glukheia (*glukhoi* – deaf). Glukheia settles in the head, blocks the ears and hurts the head, and the man becomes deaf. The seventh said: My name is Lomeia (*lomat'* = to break). Lomeia breaks a man's bones and back, as a strong storm breaks a dry tree. The eighth said: My name is Pukhneia (*pukhnut'* = to swell). Pukhneia brings dropsy to the human race. The ninth said: My name is Zhelteia (*zheltet'* = to yellow). Zhelteia is like the yellowing of a field. The tenth said: My name is Korkusha (*korchi, korkota* = convulsions).[268] This one is the most accursed of all; it cramps the sinews of the arms and legs. The eleventh said: My name is Gladeia (*gliadet'* = to look; perhaps with the connotation of being unable to shut one's eyes, or possibly connected with *glazit'* 'to put the Evil Eye on'). And this is the most accursed of all and does not let a man sleep at night, and devils come to him and he goes out of his mind. The twelfth said: My name is Neveia.[269] Neveia is their eldest sister, the dancer who cut off the head of John the Baptist. She is the most accursed of all and if she catches a man he will not survive. If a priest is about he should say this prayer over a man sick with a Triasovitsa: In the name of the Father, Son, and Holy Spirit! Accursed Triasovitsy, I exorcize you by the holy great apostle Sisinnius and the holy evangelists Luke, Mark, Matthew and John. Then he says: You, accursed Triaseia, and you (etc. for each name). I exorcize you by the holy great apostle Sisinnius, SS. Sikhail and Anos, and the four evangelists Luke, Mark, Matthew and John. Flee from the servant of God [name] for three days and three leagues and if you do not leave this servant of God [name] I shall call down on you the great apostle Sisinnius and SS. Sikhail and Enos and the four evangelists Luke, Mark, Matthew and John and they will torment you and every day they will give you four thousand wounds each. Saying this over the man ill with a Triasovitsa, the priest gives him to drink water in which a cross has been dipped and then says: The Cross the guardian of the universe, the Cross the ornament of churches, the Cross the glory of the apostles, the Cross the symbol of power of tsars, the Cross the affirmation of Christians and cure of ills, the Cross the illumination and decoration of the fathers, the Cross the expeller of demons, the Cross the expeller of Triasovitsy and idols, the Cross is the protection of the servant of God [name].

There exist other spells in which either Sisinnius or the daughters of Herod, or both, are absent, but appear to be nevertheless in the same tradition. For example:

> On the Mountain of Athos there is an oak, and under the oak thirteen sages with the Sage Pafnuti. To them there go twelve maidens, fair, with simple [i.e. unbound] tresses, and simple girdles. And the Sage Pafnuti with the twelve sages says: Who are these who have come to us? And the twelve maidens say: We are the daughters of King Herod, we journey across the earth to freeze up bones and torture the body. And the Sage Pafnuti spake to his sages: Break off three rods and we will beat them for three dawns and three gloamings. The twelve maidens besought the thirteen sages but in vain. And the sages began beating them saying: Hail, ye twelve maidens! Be ye turned into water-sprites, and weakened, and live in the chilled water; nor enter the world, nor afflict bones, nor torture bodies.[270]

A simpler Ukrainian version of this spell involves St Pafnutii and seventy-seven fair maidens rising from the sea; they confess to inflicting fevers on men and are beaten by the saint who inflicts seventy-seven wounds. The maidens beg for mercy and say they will not attack anyone wearing his name (this spell was to be worn round the neck as an amulet).[271] A similar Belorussian spell against fever, also beginning with an oak, invokes three saints Michael the Archangel, Cosmas-Damian, St Moses. St Moses meets twelve maidens who are naked, barefoot, with wild loose hair, who are travelling the world spreading misery. They beg St Moses not to beat them and promise not to afflict those who repeat the prayer.[272] A (?Siberian) spell invokes St Simon who meets twelve misshapen women who say they are going to Holy Russia to drink the blood of the people. Another has St Nicholas meeting Herod's three sisters who are going into the world to break bones and suck out the marrow.[273] The idea of the meeting of the deity/ angel/saint with the evil force causing illness or unhappiness and vanquishing or banishing it is a commonplace of spells and amulet inscriptions both Christian and pagan.[274]

A less elaborate appeal to St Sisinnius is to be seen in a fourteenth-century Rumanian lead amulet with a Slavonic inscription containing a prayer to Christ and St Sisinnius to exorcize the Devil and drive away fevers.[275] A Serbian prayer to 'St Sison' is similar to the prayers quoted above invoking Michael and the evangelists and ending in the invocations to the Cross, but is closer to the original story in that there is only one demon-witch, who has twenty-one horrible names and who can be restrained by writing them all down. The prayer is accompanied in the manuscript by a picture of the witch: she has long hair down to the ground, fiery eyes, and blood-stained arms.[276]

It can be seen that the Russian tradition of Sisinnius has developed in a distinctive direction; the motif of Miletina and her children and the demon Gillo have gone, Sisinnius himself makes only a short appearance, and the feverish daughters of Herod have taken over the story. One must assume that the twelve (usually) snakes of the Gorgon's head on the *zmeeviki* are associated with the twelve (usually) daughters of Herod, the *Triasavitsy* (lit. 'shakers' = fevers), personifications of fevers, for which there are analogues in other literatures.[277]

The demonization of Herod in popular culture is, of course not hard to account for. Indeed in the eighteenth century under Peter the Great, a bogus 'holy fool' was accused of murder, rape, making the sign of the cross with only two fingers (i.e. the Old Believer practice), doing evil magic (*eretichestvo*), having devils at his command, of whom the chief was called Herod, and whom he used to jam watermills (such malfunctions were commonly ascribed to witchcraft) and to bring treasure from Greece, Turkey and Sweden. I cannot, however, pin down a source for the extension of this demonic reputation to Herod's mythical daughters. But whatever its origin the idea caught the Russian popular imagination, as the variety of examples I have quoted shows. I will give one more example: the so-called Old Believers, those Russians who in the seventeenth century refused to accept church reforms, conducted a pamphlet war against all diabolical Western innovations such as coffee, tea, potatoes and tobacco. The potato, for example, was described as the 'Devil's apple' or the 'apple of Sodom', and in the rich religious polemic style of the time was portrayed as growing out of the anus and genitals of a either a dead oriental magician, or alternatively a daughter of Herod who had had carnal relations with a dog. In the latter case, when the two were discovered together they were both killed, and after burial from the grave of the dog there grew potatoes, and from that of the girl, tobacco.[278]

As mentioned above, the Gorgon head is not the only pagan magical motif to be found on the reverse of Russian *zmeeviki*. A few are found with serpent-footed figures which are clearly derived from another ancient magical talisman, the anguipedal motif of talismans of the Abraxas type, which has been linked by some scholars with Gnostic beliefs. There are, however, no inscriptions or other details on Russian *zmeeviki* which might lead one to suspect that there is a serious tradition of this type of amulet. On the other hand some *zmeeviki* carry an inscription on the obverse which is a spell not against Gillo or fevers or their personifications but against the *dna*. This rather rare word of obscure etymology seems to mean, depending on context, 'the womb; internal organs; internal disorders; internal disorders personified as a demon; death; gout; aching bones;[279] it is also one of the Old Russian or Church Slavonic words used to translate Greek *hystera*, which is found on some Byzantine amulets of the *zmeevik* type. This is another common type of ancient talisman, and as with the Sisinnius amulets the literary evidence for the prayer or spell against the demon of sickness is stronger than the relatively few extant amulets of this type might suggest. Prayers against the *dna* can be found in Balkan Slav and Russian Euchologia (*trebniki*) and in childbirth spells; they contain details which clearly indicate that, as in Greek and some Western traditions, the Hystera was a mobile sickness demon (in both Greek and Russian prayers it roars like a lion, bellows like a bull and leaps like a goat) which could affect either sex and had to be induced to go back quietly and curl up in its proper place.[280] An interesting late Latin analogy calling upon the womb to return to its proper place can be found in a ninth-century St Gall manuscript medical recipe which includes the words 'conjuro te matrix . . . revertaris in locum suum'.[281] The earliest Slavonic prayer against the *dna* is found in a late tenth-century Glagolitic Euchologium. This is evidently translated from Greek and appears to be designed to help a *male* sufferer afflicted by the *dna*, a creature which has one hundred and thirty claws and afflicts the arms and legs and whole body.[282] Later Russian prayers from a *trebnik* of the fifteenth or sixteenth century mention blackness and redness, roaring like a lion, bellowing like a bull, being bound by three archangels, and being told to sleep like a lamb.[283]

When discussing whether the *zmeevik* is a charm *for* the womb, *against* a sickness of the womb, or *against* any internal sickness, or *against* any sickness classified popularly as a fever, we have also to consider linguistic evidence which suggests a confusion or conflation of ideas which could well mean that any or all of these interpretations are possible. The semantic chain connecting the womb with fevers and other illnesses is based on the word for gold (*zoloto* in Russian, *zlato* in Church Slavonic and sometimes in older Russian), and symbolism motivated by popular etymology. The word *zlatenitsa*, first attested in the 1499 Gennadii Bible (Leviticus 26, 16), probably in the sense of scrofula, was occasionally used in popular speech to mean the Herod's daughter fevers.[284] This word, which one might translate as 'the golden one', is possibly is a euphemism, possibly simply a generalization of a name for an illness, but the word is also clearly linked with a word of the same origin *zolotnik*, or *zolotnik-donnitsa* 'womb', which in Russian and Belorussian childbirth spells may also be told, as was the *dna*/Hystera, to go back to its proper place and be quiet. This 'proper place' is often a golden armchair (*kreslo*), and the association of ideas also requires the Blessed Virgin to employ her golden keys to unlock the gates of the womb, or to lock them until the proper time in the case of a feared miscarriage.[285] Further associations of 'gold' words with the women's reproductive organs are *zolotaia dyra* 'golden hole' and *pozolochennoe kol'tso* 'gilded ring' for the vulva,[286] and *zolotukha*, usually scrofula but in one seventeeth-century text an internal sickness of women.[287] A spell against erysipelas (*rozha*, a word probably, and perhaps significantly, connected with the verb *rodit'* 'to give birth') recorded in the Russian Far East in this century calls on the *zolotnik* to go back to its place in its golden armchair.[288]

A Polessian spell reads:

I pray to the Lord God, I beseech the Lord God. The sunrise [var.: sunset] is a good time The Mother of God walked in Heaven, carrying keys. The keys fell and [they] picked up the *zalat'nik* [=womb]. Oh *zalat'nik*, little *zalat'nik*, take your seat at your place, on your golden chair. The father created you, God made you, your mother gave birth to you, and put you into your place. The midwife cut the navel-string, and charmed against witchcraft and the Evil Eye. (Take some water in a jug, read this spell three times, and give it to the sick person to drink. Read over the water and blow on it.)[289]

Strakhov, who published this spell, was apparently unaware of the tradition of the 'wandering womb', and explains the 'putting in place' as massage by 'wise men'; he also doubts the translation of *kreslo* as chair and prefers a derivation from Church Slavonic *kresla* (pl. tant.) 'underbelly'. Whatever the etymology, it is clear from the usage in spells that 'chair' is indeed the understood meaning. One spell for newborn children, evidently to protect them from sickness and harm, uses several typical spell motifs, and mentions a golden throne (*prestol*):

> On the Latyr' stone there is a cathedral, and in the cathedral there is a golden throne, and on the golden throne sits Solomonida. She swaddled Christ and took away his gripes and pains . . .[290]

A further spell in which the holy woman Solomonida sits in a golden chair also mentions a golden bed into which the Solomonida puts illnesses and covers them with a blanket for ever.[291] Clearly the golden throne of Solomonida, the apocryphal midwife who delivered Jesus, is a part of the same complex of ideas as the golden chair of childbirth spells.

The association of ideas based on the various meanings of a word and its derivatives, or on popular etymology of the word, in this case gold, is a common enough phenomenon in spells, as we have seen elsewhere. This particular association of ideas and words connected with gold would appear to be exclusively Russian. There are, however, some very similar Latvian spells which are addressed to 'the mother' and also call upon her to be quiet, sit down in a golden chair and rest in a golden bed.[292] In the absence of any argument to the contrary, one has to suspect that these are spells derived from Russian models but with the etymological links lost in the process of translation – the 'mother' of the spell comes no doubt from the Russian word *matka*, a diminutive of *mat'* 'mother' and a commoner Russian word for womb than *zolotnik*.

The further magical association of Solomon with the sickness demons, the womb, and the stealing or deforming of unborn children appears to be very old, as may be seen in a late antique Jewish spell from the Cairo Genizah. This includes a list of demons to be invoked and the phrase '. . . you seven spirits about which Ashmedai, king of the demons, taught King Solomon, who enter the wombs of women and deform their offspring . . .'.[293] Even in Russia the magic used to expel a *triasavitsa* or fever demon could still be associated with Jews. A condemnation of such magic is found in a Russian canon law text of Byzantine origin which was to be employed when baptizing a Jew. It lists the various accursed Jewish practices which the candidate for baptism was supposed to abjure, some of which are clearly popular magic; the text associates spells against *triasavitsy* with the beginning of the indiction and the Feast of Trumpets and the use of red dye.[294]

6.6.2. *Zmeeviki and seals.* We may also note in connection with Russian and Byzantine amulets the figure of a rider with a spear killing a serpent who appears on the first seal of Muscovy in the fifteenth century. In general it is hard not to see some connection between certain types of seal and amulets. The earliest (tenth- to twelfth-century) Kievan Russian seals are usually of a Greek type with a saint and the inscription 'Lord help your servant X' at first in Greek, later in Russian.[295] This type continues to be found in princely and ecclesiastical seals up to the fifteenth century. Also in use were antique gems with a variety of designs, including one of a lion devouring a serpent,[296] and, in the fourteenth century, Mongol seals with six-pointed stars and designs of the 'Knot of Solomon' type.[297]

The mounted man with spear is found as a Muscovite seal from the 1390s. The rider has no nimbus but is often wearing a crown or antique helmet. He is interpreted as St George only from the seventeenth century, and then only in foreign accounts.[298] He is quickly incorporated as a central medallion into the double-headed eagle which the Muscovite Grand Princes began to use as their emblem as part of their claim to be the rulers of the Third Rome.[299] The Russian interpretation of this seal until recently was that the rider represents the prince, or Russia, defeating national enemies; this interpretation is not supported by the iconography of any other artefact nor by any very clear textual evidence[300] – indeed, the notion of a relatively complex emblem suddenly appearing without any signs of earlier development, without analogues, and without explanation, is unconvincing. In fact the iconography, shape, size, method of production, and symbolic nature of both seals and amulets, the known use of antique pagan gems as seals by Russian princes, not to mention the fact that the Byzantine amulets often bear the inscription 'Seal of Solomon' or 'Seal of God', seems very suggestive, to put it no higher. Interestingly enough the State Coat of Arms of the Russian Federation, established by decree of Boris Yeltsin in 1993, revives the old pre-Revolutionary emblem – it is a double-headed eagle with three crowns, holding a sceptre and orb, and on its breast a shield bearing the mounted man with a spear killing a dragon. The official book outlining the history of the Russian coat of arms which was published to commemorate the five hundred years of its existence does not identify the mounted figure with a saint, or offer any explanation of its significance.

To end this section on pendant amulets, there should be some mention of other types of pendant which may have magical uses. There is, for example, a group of decorative pendants of Byzantine origin, but without any Christian associations, which are probably amulets. These are the enamelled *kolty* from Kiev which have themes such as the aerial journey of Alexander, Sirens or other fantastic birds.[301] And in more modern times the possible use of *dukachi* (imitation gold coins used primarily for dress decoration) as amulets, perhaps because of confusion with *zmeeviki*, has been observed in the Ukraine.[302]

7. *Ladanki*

Dal' explains a *ladanka* as a little bag of incense (*ladan*) or some other holy object worn round the neck with a cross, a talisman or amulet or other pendant often of a superstitious nature. In fact, as Ralston notes, they could contain a variety of things: herbs, roots, embers, bats' wings, snakes' heads, etc.[303] None of the dictionaries of Old Russian record this meaning, from which we may perhaps deduce that it is a comparatively recent usage. An older term for a small amulet bag of this kind is *otnos*.[304]

Some specific examples recorded in 1831 are: an amulet against growing old containing a piece of snakeskin, a dried bat's wing, and a piece of incense; an amulet against death containing pieces of coal, sulphur, and salt; an amulet against theft consisting of a cord with forty knots.[305]

These amulets may contain written spells – one is recorded which contains the diminishing spell AVRAAM, AVRAA, AVRA, AVR, AV, A.[306] This appears to be a variant of the commoner ABRACADABRA spell which could be worn as a triangular inscription attached to a cross, or written on paper and given to a sick person – one letter was to be cut off each day until only A was left and the patient cured.[307] The first reference to ABRACADABRA appears to be in the work of the late Roman physician Quintus Serenus Sammonicus.[308] It was an amulet against ague which was to be worn around the neck, and its use over the centuries has been remarkably consistent. Daniel Defoe in his *Journal of the Plague Year*, first published in 1722 but relating to the Great Plague in London in 1664–5, gives a long description of the magical remedies and prophylactics used by the panic-stricken Londoners; it includes the Jesus symbol IHS (to be written by a Jesuit!) and the diminishing ABRACADABRA spell for wearing about the body as a protection from the plague.[309]

The SATOR magic square, discussed in more detail in Ch. 10.8, could also be sewn into a *ladanka* as a precaution against fever. Non-verbal magic characters, so common in Byzantine, Hebrew, and Arabic spells and amulets, and in their West European derivatives, are not common in Russia, or at least are not much recorded. Exceptions may be some of the graffiti found in the cathedrals of St Sophia in Kiev and Novgorod, although their status is not firmly established,[310] and their origin in any case is not necessarily Slavonic.

Notes

1. Frazer, *Golden Bough*, XI, p. 156 n. 2.

2. Thomas, *Religion and the Decline of Magic*, p. 189.

3. Rybakov, 'Prikladnoe iskusstvo i skul'ptura' and 'Iskusstvo drevnikh slavian', pp. 39, 68–9. Rybakov's classification is based on his own symbolic interpretation of these objects which he does not relate to any objects or research outside the former Soviet Union.

4. See in particular Zhurzhalina, 'Datirovka drevnerusskikh privesok-amuletov'; Uspenskaia 'Nagrudnye i poiasnye priveski'; Sedov, 'Amulety kon'ki iz drevnerusskikh kurganov'; Riabinin, 'Zoomorfnye ukrasheniia drevnei Rusi X–XIV vv.'; Riabinin, 'Iazicheskie priveski-amulety drevnei Rusi'; Motsia, 'Nekotorye svedeniia'.

5. See Ovsiannikov and Riabinin, 'Srednevekovye gruntovye mogil'niki Terskogo berega'.

6. See Rybakov, 'Sbyt produktsii gorodskikh remeslennikov v X–XIII vv.', pp. 94–5.

7. See Bobrovskii, *Mifologicheskii mir drevnikh kievlian*, pp. 82–8.

8. Makarov, 'Drevnerusskie amulety-toporiki', 1988, p. 31, and *idem*, 'Drevnerusskie amulety toporiki', 1992, pp. 41–56.

9. On all these points see Riabinin, 'Iazicheskie priveski-amulety'.

10. Motsia, 'Nekotorye svedeniia', esp. pp. 124–9.

11. On horse-head decoration see Kondrat'eva, 'Krest'ianskie zoomorfnye metallicheskie grebni'. This deals with combs with horse-heads at either end from northern Russia. The Finnic element is noted. See also her 'Greben' v pogrebal'nom obriade'.

12. Hansmann and Kriss-Rettenbeck, *Amulett und Talisman*, pp. 165–6.

13. For a fairly modern general study with copious illustrations and bibliography of more specialized studies see Hansmann and Kriss-Rettenbeck, *Amulett und Talisman*, esp. pp. 162–7. At p. 163 they show a 'St George' amulet from Macedonia or European Anatolia with a whole range of charms attached to the rim, including a key, spoon and knife. Another 'holy rider' amulet with a key on its reverse side is published in Maguire and Duncan-Flowers, *Art and Holy Powers in the Early Christian House*, pp. 8–9.

14 Hansmann and Kriss-Rettenbeck, *Amulett und Talisman*, pp. 166, 167.

15. Hansmann and Kriss-Rettenbeck, *Amulett und Talisman*, pp. 162–7.

16. Hansmann and Kriss-Rettenbeck, *Amulett und Talisman*, pp. 164, 167. See also *ERE*, VIII, cols 123b–125a (*Locks and keys in magic*).

17. See Aune, 'The Apocalypse of John and Graeco-Roman Revelatory Magic', pp. 486–8 and n. 43.

18. Uspenskii, *Filologicheskie razyskaniia*, pp. 27–8.

19. Ralston, *Songs of the Russian People*, p. 96.

20. See Thomas, *Religion and the Decline of Magic*, p. 32.

21. See *ERE*, VIII, col. 124b. The practices include the detection of witches and thieves, removing spells and curing bleeding from the nose.

22. Zabylin, *Russkii narod*, p. 242.

23. Bulgakovskii, 'Pinchuki', pp. 186, 188.

24. *Narodnyi prazdnik*, p. 11.

25. Meaney, *Anglo-Saxon Amulets and Curing Stones*, ch. 5 'Manufactured amulets' and pp. 245–62 on women's amulets.

26. See most recently Davidan, 'Skarabei iz Staroi Ladogi' and Kargapol'tsev and Bazhan, 'O odnoi kategorii ukrashenii-amuletov'.

27. Pyliaev, *Dragotsennye kamni*, pp. 201–2.

28. A recent Russian article dealing with some aspects notes the lack of literature or even informed opinion on the subject: see Ostrovskii, 'Lechebno-magicheskii kompleks'. Ostrovskii says that the tablets are found in Russia, the Ukraine, and Bulgaria, and are sometimes ascribed to Catholic influence. The Ethnographic Museum in St Petersburg has a small collection of these *ex-votos* and there are a few in the Elworthy Collection in the Pitt-Rivers Museum in Oxford.

29. Stephen Graham, *Undiscovered Russia*, London, 1914, pp. 50–51 and plate facing p. 46.

30. For Greek items (*tamata*) of this kind see Kriss and Kriss-Heinrich, *Peregrinatio neohellenika*, esp. pp. 2–13. A very well-produced plate displaying such *ex-votos* is published in *Ikonen und ostkirchliches Kultgerät*, p. 195.

31. For a survey of this large subject see Uspenskii, *Filologicheskie razyskaniia*, pp. 150–56, 'Self-bored stones' have magical properties in England also (they are often called 'witch stones'), in particular for protecting horses from fairies: see Briggs, *A Dictionary of Fairies*, s.v., and Opie and Tatem, *Dictionary*, s.v. *stone with hole*. Stones with holes, or necks of bottles, are used as talismans among the Russians of Karelia: see *Ètnokul'turnye protsessy v Karelii*, p. 43.

32. Dal', *Tolkovyi slovar'*, s.v. *mylo*. See also Ch. 7.5.2, spells for childbirth.

33. Sumtsov, 'Kul'turnye perezhivaniia', p. 449. This is a variant of a belief recorded in Pliny, *Naturalis historia*, XXVIII.xi.46. For English and Irish beliefs about the curative properties of moss growing on a skull see Opie and Tatem, *Dictionary of Superstition*, s.v. *skull*.

34. See examples in *ERE*, VII, cols 747a–751b; Frazer, *Golden Bough*, III, pp. 293–317, and a useful discussion in Cockayne, *Leechdoms*, pp. xli–xliv. For some Mesopotamian examples see Scurlock, 'Baby-snatching Demons', pp. 135–83, esp. 136–7. For comparable English beliefs and practices see Opie and Tatem, *Dictionary of Superstitions*, s.v. *knot*. For some discussion of knots and threads in Russian magic, viewed comparatively, see Eleonskaia, *Sel'sko-khoziaistvennaia magiia*, pp. 171–8.

35. For further discussion of knots and threads in Russian witchcraft see Eleonskaia, *Skazka, zagovor i koldovstvo v Rossii*, pp. 171–8: 'Uzly i niti v russkoi narodnoi koldovskoi praktike'.

36. See, for example, Hildburgh, 'Some Cairene Amulets'.

37. *Slovar' russkogo iazyka XI–XVII vv.*, s.v.

38. Dal', *Tolkovyi slovar'*, s.vv.

39. Sreznevskii, *Materialy*, s.v.

40. See, for example, Schmitz, *Bussbücher*, I, p. 312. Like *nauz* the Latin *ligatura* means primarily a knot but could be used more generally to mean an amulet.

41. Ralston, *Songs of the Russian People*, p. 388. Red thread (wool is often specified) was use in magic from ancient times: in Theocritus, *Idylls*, 2, a thread of purple wool is referred to as part of an amatory binding spell. W. B. Yeats, himself a magician, wrote in his *Fairy and Folk Tales of the Irish Peasantry*, p. 61: 'Red is the colour of magic in every country and has been so from the very earliest times'. In Macedonia red and white thread tied round the wrist was a charm against sunburn: see Abbott, *Macedonian Folklore*, p. 23. Red thread in Herzegovina protected against witches: see Vukanović, 'Witchcraft in the Central Balkans. II', p. 221. Similar precautions were taken in Rumania (as in Bulgaria) against the Evil Eye: see A. Murgoci, 'The Evil Eye in Rumania', p. 126. For British beliefs in the curative and prophylactic power of red thread and ribbon see Opie and Tatem, *Dictionary*, s.v. *red thread*. The dictator of Panana, General Noriega, was alleged in the American media in 1989 to wear red underpants as a protection against magic – but they did not protect him from the US army or the barrage of extremely noisy pop music with which it drove him from his refuge.

42. Trachtenberg, *Jewish Magic and Superstition*, pp. 127, 133. For the alleged Jewish use of red dye in spells see p. 252 below.

43. See Eleonskaia, *Sel'sko-khoziaistvennaia magiia*, p. 172, for several examples.

44. Zabylin, *Russkii narod*, pp. 420–1; Lebedeva, 'Znachenie poiasa', p. 232.

45. Dal', *Poslovitsy russkogo naroda*, 1989, p. 34. Cf. the Muslim belief that the Koran must not be held below the girdle: Hughes, *Dictionary of Islam*, p. 521. On belts in Russian, Ukrainian and Belorussian magic and folk customs in general see Lebedeva, 'Znachenie poiasa'.

46. Lebedeva, 'Znachenie poiasa', p. 231.

47. Herberstein, in the Hakluyt Society English version, *Notes upon Russia*, I, p. 100.

48. *Russkaia epicheskaia poèziia Sibiri i Dal'nego Vostoka'*, nos 108–111.

49. For this practice elsewhere see Frazer, *Golden Bough*, III, pp. 305–6.

50. For references to the magic of knots and nets in early Russian texts see Tolstoi, '*Set' (mrezha)*'.

51. Ralston, *Songs of the Russian People*, p. 390. Frazer, *Golden Bough*, III, p. 300, mentions a net as a wedding amulet on Lesbos.

52. Fig 6 is a specimen from this region: Ethnographic Museum, St Petersburg, coll. 4005, no. 5 'merezhka, setochka'.

53. Min'ko, *Sueveriia*, p. 149.

54. See also Eleonskaia, *Sel'sko-khoziaistvennaia magiia*, p. 173.

55. For water made magical by a 'thunder arrow' or other object see below, *passim*, and Popov, *Russkaia narodno-bytovaia meditsina*, p. 35; Cherepnin, 'Iz istorii drevnerusskogo koldovstva', p. 93; Seligmann, *Schutzmittel*, p. 197; for washing in water in which silver has been placed (to bring prosperity) in Subcarpathian Ruthenia see Bogatyrev, *Actes magiques*, p. 42.

56. See Saintyves, *Pierres magiques*. Saintyves notes that amulets of this kind in fact include aeroliths, stone implements, and stones resembling animals.

57. Vukanović, 'Witchcraft in the Central Balkans II', p. 221; here they are a protection against witches and the Evil Eye.

58. Arkhangelskii, 'K izucheniiu drevne-russkoi literatury', pp. 15–16.

59. Sedova, 'Amulet iz drevnego Novgoroda', pp. 166–7 and fig. 1.

60. Rybakov, *Iazychestvo*, p. 299.

61. Chikachev, *Russkie na Indigirke*, p. 160.

62. See Lotman and Uspenskii, 'The Role of Dual Models', p. 29.

63. For a survey and bibliography of this subject see Makarov and Chernetsov, 'K izuchenii kul'tovykh kamnei', pp. 79–90; see also Dubov, *I poklaniashesia idolu kamenu*, ch. 5. More specifically for the Archangel region see Shevelov, 'Kul'tovye kamni v Kargopol'e'.

64. Popov, *Russkaia narodno-bytovaia meditsina*, p. 259.

65. See Shein, *Materialy*, pp. 437–45.

66. See Veselovskii, 'Razyskaniia v oblasti russkogo dukhovnogo stikha. III'; Mansikka, *Über russische Zauberformeln*, *passim*; Ralston, *Songs of the Russian People*, pp. 368, 370, 376–77; Korobka, 'Kamen' na more i kamen' alatar'', p. 422.

67. For a summary of theories about the name of this stone see Vasmer, *Ètimologicheskii slovar'*, s.v. *alatyr'*. *Altar* and *elektron* are the most commonly cited source-words.

68. MS St Petersburg, Pushkinskii dom, IMLI 7, ff. 31–43v published in Malyshev, *Drevnerusskie rukopisi Pushkinskogo Doma*, p. 180.

69. For text see *Izbornik*, pp. 370–4 (74). *The Testament of Solomon* (?third century, probably written in Greek by either a Jew or a Christian), the source of much of the later Solomonic literature, was not known in Russia. See Duling, 'The Testament of Solomon'.

70. Afanas'ev, *Russkie zavetnye skazki*, pp. 45–51.

71. Pyliaev, *Dragotsennye kamni*, pp. 370–71.

72. Bratley, *The Power of Gems and Charms*, p. 11.

73. Matveeva, *Mifologicheskie rasskazy*, p. 320.

74. On the practice in antiquity see Jones, *Finger-Ring Lore*, pp. 111–12.

75. Sakharov, *Skazaniia*, p. 39.

76. See also Afanas'ev, *Narodnye russkie skazki*, 1984–5 edn, nos 159, 190, 191; Zelenin, *Velikorusskie skazki Permskoi gubernii*, nos 21(55), 22(12), 40(87), 41(46).

77. Afanas'ev, *Narodnye russkie skazki*, 1984–5 edn, no. 214.

78. Afanas'ev, *Narodnye russkie skazki*, 1984–5 edn, no. 209.

79. D'iachenko, *Polnyi tserkovno-slavianskii slovar'*, s.v. *perstni*.

80. For a convenient survey see Philippe Ménard, 'La Baguette magique au moyen âge'.

81. Chernetsov, 'Medieval Russian Pictorial Materials on Paganism and Superstitions', pp. 101–2.

82. Olaus Magnus, *Description of the Northern Peoples*, bk 3, ch. 37.

83. *Slovar' sovremennogo russkogo iazyka*, 2nd edn, Moscow, 1991, s.v.

84. See Afanas'ev, *Narodnye russkie skazki*, nos 123, 210, 211, 236; Zelenin, *Velikorusskie skazki Permskoi gubernii*, 52(44).

85. Dal', *Tolkovyi slovar'*, s.v. *zerkalo*. Turning the mirror to the wall or covering it after death is a common European custom: Opie and Tatem, *Dictionary of Superstitions*, s.v. *mirrors turned to wall*; *ERE*, VIII, col. 696b; Frazer, *Golden Bough*, III, pp. 94-6. See also Barber, *Vampires*, 33, 180.

86. The *OED* gives 'black book' as a book of necromancy, but the 1842 example quoted, the Rev. Barham's *Ingoldsby Legends*, cannot add to the argument.

87. D'iachenko, *Polnyi tserkovno-slavianskii slovar'*, s.v. *chernaia kniga*.

88. Pokrovskii, *Sudnye spiski*, p. 149.

89. The contention that a *chernoknizhnik* is 'a person who plies his trade with the aid of a black book' (Worobec, 'Witchcraft Beliefs and Practices' , p. 169), is an over-literal guess.

90. See Afanas'ev, *Narodnye russkie skazki*, nos 134, 198, 212, 236, 239, 240, 273, 275. Rybnikov, *Pesni*, II (repr. 1990), pp. 105–7 records the *bylina* of *Van'ka Udovkin syn and Tsar Volshan Volshankii*, in which Tsar Volshan, whose name suggests an oriental wizard, consults a magic book which speaks and gives him advice.

91. See Afanas'ev, *Narodnye russkie skazki*, nos 104, 114, 225, 291, 294.

92. See Vlasova, *Novaia abevega*, s.v. *kikimora*.

93. Zinov'eva, 'Ukazatel' siuzhetov', motifs BIV 7a and GII 13a.

94. Perevezentseva, *Russkaia narodnaia igrushka*, n.p., n.d. (1990s), unpaginated.

95. *Mara* is also a dream, illusion, ghost or a kind of house sprite: Dal', *Tolkovyi slovar'*, s.v.

96. Kondrat'eva, *Metamorfozy*, s.v.; Warner, *Russian Folk Theatre*, pp. 18–35, gives a good survey of these ritual carnival figures.

97. *Narodnyi prazdnik*, p. 17.

98. Shein, *Velikoruss v svoikh pesniakh*, 1, p. 333.

99. See *Poèziia krest'ianskikh prazdnikov*, pp. 598–600.

100. Warner, *The Russian Folk Theatre*, 1977, p. 51.

101. See Boehr, *Dolls and Puppets*, p. 58. The author gives no source for this information. Normally three-dimensional images were forbidden by the Orthodox Church but they could nevertheless be found; moreover Smolensk before the treaty of Andrusovo in 1667 was for much of its history governed by Catholic Poland, which had a different attitude to images. The first reference to puppets in Russia is in 1636 (by Olearius): Peretts, *Kukol'nyi teatr*, p. 12.

102. *Summa theologica*, II, 2, 96, 4.

103. Thomas, *Religion and the Decline of Magic*, p. 46. This does seem to be a more judicious interpretation of the general situation in the Middle Ages than the quite opposite view of Valerie Flint in her *The Rise of Magic* that the Church had in fact deliberately adopted magic for its own purposes.

104. Vikan, 'How St Symeon made House Calls', p. 22.

105. But see Graham, *With the Russian Pilgrims*, p. 239 below, on the preservation of candles lit in Jerusalem and shrouds in which the owner had bathed in the Jordan.

106. Almazov, 'Tainaia ispoved' v pravoslavnoi vostochnoi tserkvi', pp. 405, 408; see also Smirnov, *Materialy*.

107. Popov, *Russkaia narodno-bytovaia meditsina*, p. 260.

108. For the significance of this in the overall context of the cultural clash of the schism see Uspensky, 'Schism and Cultural Conflict', esp. pp. 106–7.

109. See, for example, the introduction to St Athanasius, *Contra gentes*.

110. I quote the English version: Harkins, *St John Chrysostom: Baptismal Instructions*, p. 168.

111. Mal'm, 'Krestiki s emal'iu', p. 116.

112. For a wide-ranging analysis of types and functions of Russian pectoral crosses, in particular silver crosses of the seventeenth and eighteenth centuries, see Ostrovskii's articles, 'Pravoslavnye nagrudnye kresty'. For earlier particular groups see Darkevich and Putsko, 'Proizvedeniia srednevekovoi metalloplastiki'; also Sedov, 'Ob odnoi gruppe drevnerusskikh krestov'.

113. Vasmer, *Ètimologicheskii slovar'*, s.v. *Levanidov*. 'Chuden krest Levanidovskoi' occurs in a song in Kirsha Danilov's collection: *Drevnie rossiiskie stikhotvoreniia*, p. 259.

114. Dal', *Tolkovyi slovar'*, s.v. *meret'*.

115. Nikiforovskii, *Prostonarodnye primety i pover'ia*, p. 275.

116. Bolonev, *Narodnyi kalendar' semeiskikh Zabaikal'ia*, p. 79.

117. See n. 153 below.

118. See Flint, *The Rise of Magic*, ch. 7.

119. *Russian Primary Chronicle*, p. 149.

120. *Russian Primary Chronicle*, pp. 153. This incident is illustrated in the late fifteenth-century *Radziwiłł Chronicle*: see Chernetsov, 'Medieval Russian Pictorial Materials on Paganism and Superstitions', p. 102.

121. *Ètnokul'turnye protsessy v Karelii*, p. 40.

122. Matveeva, *Mifologicheskie rasskazy*, p. 316; Zinov'eva, *Ukazatel' siuzhetov*, motif GII 19.

123. Several instances are listed by Ivanits, *Russian Folk Belief*, pp. 67, 73.

124. Ralston, *Songs of the Russian People*, p. 386, quoting Afanas'ev. This is a Walpurgis Night practice in Silesia and Central Germany according to Frazer, *Golden Bough*, IX, 160, 162.

125. Shapovalova and Lavrent'eva, *Traditsionnye obriady*, p. 18, no. 49.

126. Makarenko, *Sibirskii narodnyi kalendar'*, pp. 46, 50.

127. See *Ulozhenie*, I, 1.

128. See Makarov and Chernetsov, 'K izucheniiu kul'tovykh kamnei', p. 86.

129. See Sedova, 'O dvukh tipakh privesok ikonok'.

130. Crull, *The Antient and Present State of Russia*, I, p. 150. He probably obtained this information from Olearius.

131. Bruce, *Memoirs*, p. 121.

132. Cross, *A Lady at the Court of Catherine the Great*, p. 47.

133. *The Russian Journals of Martha and Catherine Wilmot*, pp. 373–4.

134. For example, it is recorded as a practice in the Volga region: Shapovalova and Lavrent'eva, *Traditsionnye obriady*, p. 25, no. 149, and in the Kostroma region: Smirnov, 'Narodnye gadaniia v Kostromskom krae', p. 46.

135. See Kleimola, *Justice in Medieval Russia*, p. 67.

136. A valuable collection of papers on wonder-working icons mostly in Byzantium and medieval Russia is *Chudotvornaia ikona v Vizantii i Drevnei Rusi* (1996); unfortunately it does not address topics discussed here. A good essay on the popular veneration of wonder-working icons in Russia appears in Tarasov, *Ikona i blagochestie*, pp. 53–80.

137. For an example of how complicated the history of such legends can be see Kulakovskii, 'Sostav Skazaniia o chudesakh ikony bogomateri Rymlianini'.

138. Tarasov, *Ikona i blagochestie*, p. 72.

139. The mutilation of images by putting out their eyes is frequent enough in Eastern and Western Europe (e.g. in English churches after the Reformation) to suggest a common impulse in the psychology of iconoclasm. In Russia a well-known instance is the putting out of the eyes of icons by the Patriarch Nikon on the grounds that they were painted in a Western heretical style – see Uspenskii, *Semiotics*, p. 22 n. 18, commenting on the contemporary account of Archdeacon Paul of Aleppo.

140. See Cormack, 'Miraculous Icons in Byzantium and their Powers'.

141. Efimenko, *Materialy po ètnografii*, p. 167.

142. For details and bibliography see Uspenskii, *Filologicheskie razyskaniia*, pp. 63, 184–5, 110. See also Frazer, *Golden Bough*, I, pp. 277, 307–8, on the use of images dipped in water to produce rain.

143. *Stoglav*, ch. 41, p. 128.

144. Chikachev, *Russkie na Indigirke*, p. 117.

145. Sytova, *The Lubok*, no. 94.

146. See *Polnyi pravoslavnyi bogoslovskii entsiklopedicheskii slovar'*, St Petersburg, 1913, s.v *Bogoliubskaia ikona*; on the icon and the Plague Riots see Alexander, *Bubonic Plague in Early Modern Russia*, pp. 187–90.

147. For an immensely erudite discussion of St Nicholas in Russian history, literature and folklore see Uspenskii, *Filologicheskie razyskaniia*. Uspenskii is primarily concerned to show the persistence of the cult of the ancient Slav god Volos (Veles), in particular with respect to his identification with St Nicholas (and to a lesser extent SS. Florus and Laurus, Peter, George, Basil and Blaise!). Problems arise at some points in this interpretation where there are analogues of Russian beliefs and practices in cultures ignorant of both Volos and the Russian tradition of St Nicholas. On the subject of bear amulets and St Nicholas see ibid. p. 100.

148. Herberstein, *Rerum Moscoviticarum comentarii* – see the English translation, p. 94.

149. Russian icons were often referred to as 'gods' in Russian, indeed this meaning of *bogi* is recorded by Dal'; this apparently idolatrous usage regularly provoked comment in foreign travel accounts of Russia: see Uspenskii, *Filologicheskie razyskaniia*, pp. 118–22. As late as 1876 an English traveller could refer to icons as 'Russian idols': see Burnaby, *A Ride to Khiva*, ch. VI.

150. Collins, *The Present State of Russia*, p. 25.

151. *Memoirs of Peter Henry Bruce*, London, 1782, reprinted London, 1970, p. 97.

152. Fennell, *Kurbsky's History of Ivan IV*, pp. 110–11, 114–15.

153. See Tarasov, *Ikona i blagochestie*, p. 71 for a reproduction. The painting was in the Museum of the History of Religion in St Petersburg.

154. For the punishment of non-performing thaumaturgic icons see Uspenskii, *Filogicheskie razyskaniia*, pp. 114–6, 182–186. For beliefs about the evil influence of 'incorrect' icons see Uspenskii, *Semiotics*, p. 22 n. 18.

155. Tarasov, *Ikona i blagochestie*, p. 76.

156. Kostomarov, *Ocherk*, p. 204.

157. Kostomarov, *Ocherk*, p. 205.

158. *Jerusalem Pilgrimage*, pp. 170–1.

159. Soloukhin, *Searching for Icons in Russia*, p. 87.

160. Kostomarov, *Ocherk*, p. 205. For some discussion of the methods of disposing of old icons and books see Uspenskii, *Semiotics*, p. 29 n. 54, and *idem, Razyskaniia*, p. 185.

161. Collins, *The Present State of Russia*, quoted from Cross, *Russia under Western Eyes*, p 116.

162. Vera Beaver-Bricken Espinola, 'Copper Icons in Daily Use in Old Russia', *Russian Copper Icons and Crosses from the Kunz Collection: Castings of Faith*, ed. R.E. Ahlborn and V. Beaver-Bricken Espinola, Washington, 1990, pp. 8–10 (9).

163. Crull, *The Antient and Present State of Russia*, I, p. 150. Crull had not visited Russia and probably gained his information from Olearius.

164. For a brief account see Herrin, *The Formation of Christendom*, pp. 314–5: 'The Eighth Century Cult of Icons'; also Cormack, 'Miraculous Icons in Byzantium and their Powers'.

165. On this icon see Antonova and Mneva, *Katalog drevnei russkoi zhivopisi*, I, pp. 152–3; for the legend of this event see *Pamiatniki starinnoi russkoi literatury*, I, pp. 241–2; for a study of both the iconography and the literary history of the legend see Dmitriev, *Zhitiinye povesti russkogo severa*, pp. 95–148.

166. See Walter, 'The Thracian Horseman', p. 660, for an interesting account of warrior saints who intervene in battles and the possible derivation of this notion from pagan myths such as that of the Dioscuri who fought alongside the Romans at the battle of Lake Regillus, and who are also often described as being mounted on white horses.

167. Larin, *Russko-angliiskii slovar'-dnevnik Richarda Dzhemsa*, p. 189.

168. Bogoslovskii, *Petr I*, I, pp. 283, 347.

169. Solzhenitsyn, *August 1914*, p. 621.

170. See *Pamiatniki russkoi kul'tury pervoi chetverti XVIII veka*, pp. 230–2, and on the emblem of the order in general Vilinbakhov, 'K istorii uchrezhdeniia ordena Andreia Pervozvannogo'.

171. For a facsimile see Armstrong, *Yermak's Campaign in Siberia*, esp. pp. 129, 131, 137, 139–40, 220, 250, 254, 256.

172. *Povest' o prikhozhenii Stefana Batoriia na grad Pskov*, pp. 85–6.

173. See Obolensky, 'The Cult of St. Demetrius'.

174. Quoted in Trevor-Battye, *A Northern Highway of the Tsar*, pp. 99–101.

175. Krinichnaia, *Predaniia russkogo severa*, nos 295, 298.

176. *Jerusalem Pilgrimage 1099–1185*, p. 124.

177. Ibid., p. 125–6.

178. Ibid., p. 163.

179. See Obolenskii, 'The Cult', p. 13. St Demetrius was held in such regard that even reputed pieces of his horse were regarded as relics with apotropaic virtue: see Paul of Aleppo, *Travels of Macarius*, p. 8.

180. See Walter, 'The Thracian Horseman', p. 664.

181. Popov, *Russkaia narodno-bytovaia meditsina*, pp. 259, 265.

182. This is first recorded as a Russian practice by Daniel the Abbot in the twelfth century (see *Jerusalem Pilgrimage*, pp. 166–70). Quantities of such candles were preserved as treasures by the tsars, together with other items from the Holy Land such as incense. An old palace inventory notes that they were mainly of new wax, green in colour and wrapped in gold foil: see Zabelin, *Domashnii byt russkikh tsarei*, p. 294

183. Stephen Graham, *With the Russian Pilgrims*, pp. 198, 290. The Russian Palestine Society used to provide subsidized transport and accommodation for pilgrims. By 1913 around 20,000 per annum were making the trip.

184. Tikhonravov, *Pamiatniki*, II, p. 356 gives the text of a prayer from 1476 which requires the sufferer to bow twelve times, say the *Kyrie* forty times and, significantly, place his jaw on a rock, then have a mass said in honour of St Antipii and give an offering according to his means.

185. Zabelin, *Domashnii byt russkikh tsarei*, pp. 293, 297. On the popular print of the saint see Rovinskii, *Russkie narodnye kartinki*, II, p. 293.

186. See Russell, 'The Evil Eye in Early Byzantine Society', p. 543.

187. See Hansmann and Kriss-Rettenbeck, *Amulett und Talisman*, pp. 182–3 for illustrations.

188. Riabinin, 'Iazicheskie priveski-amulety drevnei Rusi', p. 58.

189. *ERE*, V, col. 614a.

190. The only article on this subject known to me is Ganulich, 'Kollektsiia russkikh upriazhnykh bubentsov A.K. Ganulicha'. It does not discuss the bells as amulets.

191. *Ètnokul'turnye protsessy v Karelii*, p. 38.

192. *ERE*, VI, col. 315a notes that in Western Europe bells are often elaborately christened.

193. See Williams, *The Bells of Russia*, pp. 117–21, 124–5.

194. Baring, *What I saw in Russia*, pp. 358–64. For the baptism of bells in the West see Hazlitt, *Dictionary*, s.v. *Bells, Baptism of.*

195. Williams, *The Bells of Russia*, pp. 47–50.

196. Ibid., pp. 58, 60.

197. See Uspenskii, *Filologicheskie razyskaniia*, pp. 114–16.

198. Massa, *A Short History*, p. 169.

199. Dal', *Tolkovyi slovar'*, s.v. *kolokol.*

200. See for examples Schulze, 'Wetterglocken und Dreikönigsglocken' and idem, 'Wetterglocken im Rheinland'. For England see Opie and Tatem, *Dictionary*, s.v. *church bell*; Thomas, *Religion and the Decline of Magic*, p. 31.

201. Dal', *Tolkovyi slovar'*, s.v. *kolokol.*

202. Novichkova, *Russkii demonologicheskii slovar'*, s.v. *kolokol'nyi mertvets*, p. 271.

203. Loc. cit.

204. Dal', *Poslovitsy*, 1989, I, p. 352.

205. See Shanskii, *Ètimologicheskii slovar' russkogo iazyka*, II, 6, Moscow, 1975, s.v.

206. Most recently Veletskaia, 'O genezise drevnerusskikh «zmeevikov»'. On serpents in Russian folktales in the general context of serpent myths see also Propp, *Istoricheskie korni volshebnoi skazki*, esp. pp. 216–22. Comets and meteors are called 'Fiery serpents' in several areas and occasionally in the chronicles – see Afanas'ev, *Poèticheskie vozzreniia slavian na prirodu*, II, p. 150; Vysotskii, *Narodnaia meditsina*, p. 68. For some remarks on the interaction of star and serpent mythonyms see Iudin, 'Ob imenakh zvezd-«pomoshchnits»'.

207. See *Pamiatniki literatury drevnei Rusi. Nachalo russkoi literatury. XI–nachalo XII veka*, p. 54.

208. *Tolkovaia paleia 1477 goda*, f. 15v. This text in its earliest Russian form probably dates from the thirteenth century.

209. Nikolaeva and Chernetsov, *Drevnerusskie amulety-zmeeviki*, p. 5. A.B. Ostrovskii of the Ethnographic Museum in St Petersburg stated in an interview on the subject of *oberegi* in Smena (18 May 1995, p. 4) that he had seen contemporary Russian villagers wearing amber bead and bear's claw amulets on the same neck cord as their crosses (see Fig. 11 for an example). See also his 'Pravoslavnye nagrudnye kresty'.

210. L.V. Dal', 'Zametki o mednykh grivnakh XII veka', p. 76.

211. On Byzantine terracotta amulets as distinct from pilgrim tokens see Russell, 'The Evil Eye in Early Byzantine Society', p. 542.

212. On the latter see Vikan, 'Art, Medicine and Magic in Early Byzantium', pp. 77–80.

213. See Kazarow in Pauly-Wissowa, *Realencyclopädie*, Suppl. III, 1132–48.

214. Bonner, 'Two Studies in Syncretistic Amulets'. See also his *Studies in Magical Amulets*, Ann Arbor, 1950.

215. Walter, 'The Thracian Horseman: Ancestor of Warrior Saints'.

216. Walter, 'The Intaglio of Solomon', pp. 33–42.

217. Spier, 'Medieval Byzantine Magical Amulets'. Spier traces the *hystera* formula from its ancient origins to its use in medieval western and Slavic Europe and in Jewish magic. Its use on amulets he dates to a tenth-century revival of interest in amulets in Constantinople.

218. Radojković, *Filakteriji, enamluci, pripojasnice*, pl. XI, XXVI, XXVII.

219. *Drevnerusskie amulety-zmeeviki*, p. 5.

220. Radojković, *Filakteriji, enamluci, pripojasnice*, pl. XXXV.

221. Schlumberger, 'Amulettes byzantins', has a rider saint and the inscription 'Flee vile creature, Solomon is pursuing you. Sisinnarios.' and on the other the Evil Eye with three daggers and attacking animals, and an inscription which reads 'Seal of Solomon'. On Solomon as a horseman see Bonner, *Studies*, pp. 210 ff.; Goodenough, *Jewish Symbols in the Greco-Roman Period*, II, pp. 227–35 (notes the occasional adaptation to SS. Sisinnius or George in Christian iconography); Delatte and Derchain, *Les Intailles magiques gréco-égyptiennes* (notes that the inscription on the back is usually 'Seal of God'); Schwartz and Schwartz, 'Engraved Gems' (pp. 184–7: 'Solomon the Cavalier'). See also Bagatti, 'I Giudeo-cristiani e l'anello di Salamone'. Variants of this type are common in Palestine and Syria – see Mouterde, 'Objets magiques'.

222. See Gaster, 'Two Thousand Years of a Charm against the Child-Stealing Witch'; Barb, 'Antaura. The Mermaid and the Devil's Grandmother'. Bonner, *Studies*, p. 210, suggested that the Lilith figure may indicate that these amulets were designed for children. Gaster had already pointed out that the prayer to St Sisoe was an amulet placed by a cradle to protect the child (p. 139). A recent catalogue of amulets by L.A. Wolfe states the female figure to be Lilith without further discussion, although the figure is never identified by an inscription: *Objects with Semitic Inscriptions*, p. 59.

223. Spasskii, 'Tri zmeevika s Ukrainy'.

224. For an illustration see Popov and Ryndina, *Zhivopis' i prikladnoe iskusstvo Tveri*, p. 574.

225. Quoted by Uspenskii, *Filologicheskie razyskaniia*, p. 27, as a charm against lethargic sleep.

226. Orlov, 'Amulety – «zmeeviki» Istoricheskogo muzeia'.

227. Nikolaeva and Chernetsov, *Drevnerusskie amulety-zmeeviki*; see also for a brief account Blankoff, 'A propos du «dvoeverie»'.

228. For the history of this motif see Teteriatnikov, 'Representations of St Nikita flogging the Devil'.

229. The third–fourth-century soldier-martyr Theodore of Amasea, but often partially confused with Theodore Stratilates. The apocryphal *vita*, originally Greek, of Theodore was known in Russia, both as a *vita* and in the form of the popular religious songs known as *dukhovnye stikhi*, where it appears to have assimilated aspects of the story of Theodore Stratilates; the text itself had magical properties as an amulet. It is a fantastic story of fighting giant serpents, crossing the sea on the back of a whale (an echo of the *vita* of St Brendan?) and it promises to expel demons, cure the blind and deaf, provide abundant wheat, wine and oil and all good things to those who keep his memory holy. The serpent-

killing and demonifuge elements are clearly appropriate here. The saint is also invoked to find runaway serfs, and appears in a dice divination text: see p. 524. It is noteworthy, in the context of *zmeeviki*, that in one *dukhovnye stikhi* version the twelve-year-old Theodore is credited not only with slaughtering a whole Jewish army but also with killing a serpent with *twelve heads* in order to free his mother, and twelve young serpents who are sucking his mother's breasts. Text consulted: *Golubinaia kniga*, pp. 85–91. On the text see Veselovskii, *Razyskaniia v oblasti russkikh dukhovnykh stikhov. I. Grecheskii apokrif o sv. Feodore; Slovar' knizhnikov*, I, s.v. *Muchenie Feodora Tirona*.

230. The Seven Sleepers are also invoked in Western fever amulets: see Flint, *The Rise of Magic*, pp. 315–16.

231. There is also a Greek engraved heliotrope gem amulet with the Virgin on one side and Gorgon head on the other. Illustrated in Nikolaeva and Chernetsov, *Drevnerusskie amulety-zmeeviki*, p. 112; see also Laurent, 'Amulettes byzantines et formulaires magiques', pl. 5.

232. Nikolaeva and Chernetsov, *Drevnerusskie amulety-zmeeviki*, pp. 99–100.

233. Nikolaeva and Chernetsov, *Drevnerusskie amulety-zmeeviki*, p. 6.

234. Nikolaeva and Chernetsov, *Drevnerusskie amulety-zmeeviki*, p. 6.

235. On the 'One God' inscription see Erik Peterson, ΕΙΣ ΘΕΟΣ; 'Unus Deus' inscriptions can also be found on Western amulets: Hansmann and Kriss-Rettenbeck, *Amulett und Talisman*, p. 152, show two seventeenth-century German Tau Cross Trinity amulets including these words.

236. The midday demon is often thought of as the demon who steals babies. According to Dal', *Tolkovyi slovar'*, s.v. *pola*, in Siberia a sprite in the form of a ragged old woman called *poludnitsa* (derived from the word for midday) is used to frighten children from playing in the vegetable patch while the adults are having a midday rest. E. Zamiatin in his *A Provincial Tale* (1913) mentions a popular belief that sleeping or swimming at midday were dangerous because of the midday demon. For similar Greek beliefs see Stewart, *Demons*, p. 172; for a Greek exorcism of the midday demon from Mt Athos see L. Delatte, 'Un Office byzantin d'exorcisme byzantin', pp. 80–84, 109–110.

237. See for example Russell, 'The Evil Eye in Early Byzantine Society', pp. 240–41.

238. The associations of mermaids, Gorgons, Gyllou, Hystera, Lilith, Solomon and Sisinnius were imaginatively examined by Barb in 'Antaura. The Mermaid and the Devil's Grandmother'. See also Gaster, 'Two Thousand Years', pp. 158–9, who points to the story of Solomon and the evil spirit Obizuth, who is frustrated by the angel Raphael, and has wild hair like a dragon and an invisible body, i.e. something like the Gorgon head. See also Winkler, *Salomo und die Karina* and more recently Vikan, 'Art, Medicine, and Magic in Early Byzantium', pp. 77–80. In Greek popular tradition *gorgōnes* are demonic mermaids, the sisters of Alexander the Great: see Stewart, *Demons*, p. 252.

239. Rybakov, *Iazychestvo*, p. 654.

240. There are four saints called Sisinnius commemorated in the Russian Orthodox Church. Alfons Barb sees the name as a Christian adaptation of a probably Hebrew *vox magica* of uncertain meaning found in Hebrew magic inscriptions: see Barb, 'Three Elusive Amulets', pp. 13–15. One source of the Russian apocryphal story appears to be the Greek text, or texts, listed by Halkin, *Bibliotheca hagiographica graeca*, III, pp. 69–79 (Nos 2401–4: 'Sisinnius et Sisinnodorus fratres, cum Meletina sorore)' and *idem, Novum auctarium*, p. 259; see also Greenfield, 'St Sisinnios'.

241. See Mansvetov, *Vizantiiskii material dlia skazaniia o 12 triasavits*; Veselovskii, 'Molitva sv. Sisinniia i Verzilovo kolo'; Mansikka, *Über russische Zauberformeln*, ad indicem; Popov, *Russkaia narodno-bytovaia meditsina*, pp. 236–9; Vinogradov, *Zagovory, oberegi, spasitel'nye molitvy*, 2, p. 5–6; Romanov, *Belorusskii sbornik*, p. 101 (the saints involved here are called Susoi and Saksenii); Poznanskii, 'Sisinieva legenda-

obereg'. Recent important studies are Cherepanova, 'Tipologiia i genezis nazvanii likhoradok-triasavits', pp. 54–57, and *idem*, *Mifologicheskaia leksika russkogo severa*, pp. 92–4: 'Devy-triasavitsy' (this discusses the personification of fevers in general (usually 7, 10, 19, 40 or 77 in number), gives a selection of the names used, notes the widespread, but not obligatory, association with the daughters of Herod, and the frequency of the *zagovor* from the eighteenth century onwards) and Iudin, *Onomastikon*, pp. 233–61 and *passim*, which analyses the sources and frequency of the names in detail. See also Vlasova, *Novaia abevega*, s.v. *likhoradka*. A Belorussian spell against angina also gives a list of twelve names of sister diseases: see Romanov, *Belorusskii sbornik*, p. 89; and a rhymed spell against the Evil Eye from the Smolensk region asks for protection from twelve tsars, twelve kings and twelve maladies: Shein, *Materialy*, p. 531. Cf. a Dalmatian legend: 'When the child was seven, one night there came twelve witches and a wizard in a yellow cart and they stole this feverish child' — Pócs, *Fairies and Witches*, p. 48. A Western spell to exorcize 'Heradiana, deaf-mute mother of malignant elves [i.e. personified illnesses]' is quoted in Kieckhefer, *Magic in the Middle Ages*, p. 73.

242. Zelenin, *Izbrannye trudy*, ch. 5, §51, notes the identification of the 'daughters of Herod' with *rusalki* (water sprites) in some places, and also observes that *rusalki* in some cases seem to have the characteristics of the *poludnitsa*, the midday witch/demon who shares some features with the Gylou. Zelenin also notes (pp. 302–3) thirty fever-sisters called *viriavy* among the Mordvinians (i.e. not Slavs).

243. See Dal', *Tolkovyi slovar'*, s.v. *vorog* (*vrag* 'enemy') variously 'enemy; woodsprite; devil; magician'. See also Vlasova, *Novaia abevega*, s.v. *vorogusha*. On Slavonic beliefs (predominantly South Slav) about butterflies and moths as blood-sucking transformations of witches, or as the spirits of ancestors, see Ternovskaia, 'Babochka v narodnoi demonologii slavian'. Note that the Russian for butterfly (and often moth) is *babochka*, a diminutive of *baba*, which may mean 'witch'.

244. Kondrat'eva, *Metamorfozy sobstvennogo imeni*, s.v. *Irod*. The meanings of 'unclean spirit' and 'woman of easy virtue' are also listed here under *Irodia, Irodiada*. For some discussion of this formula for tricking demons of disease see Strakhov, 'Na sviatogo Nikolu . . .', pp. 65–6. He notes that in cases of fever 'come yesterday' used to be written in chalk under windows doors and gates in the Saratov province, and the same formula was chanted by the women performing the ritual of *opakhivanie* (see pp. 171–2).

245. But see now Cherepanova, *Mifologicheskaia leksika russkogo severa* and Iudin, *Onomastikon*, for much longer lists of possible names.

246. For the earlier association of 'evil wind' with this complex of spell traditions see Barb 'Antaura'.

247. Nikiforovskii, *Prostonarodnye primety i pover'ia*, pp. 274 nos. 2135–6; 266 no. 2154.

248. Sokolov 'Novyi material dlia ob''iasneniia amuletov', p. 168.

249. *Oberegi i zaklinaniia*, pp. 48, 52.

250. Adon'eva, Ovchinnikova, *Traditsionnaia russkaia magiia*, no. 457.

251. The two main variants of the Greek story of Gylou, one involving Sisinnios, the other St Michael, have been analysed most recently and in greatest depth in Greenfield, 'St Sisinnios'. Greenfield gives extensive bibliographical coverage and the text of a fifteenth-century version of the 'Life of Sisinnios'. For a comparatively modern Greek prayer against the *yalou* (*Gello*) resembling the Russian spell against the *Triasavitsy* see Stewart, *Demons*, pp. 100–1. An Armenian prayer to St Sisinnius used as an amuletic demonifuge is quoted in Feydit, *Amulettes de l'Arménie chrétienne*, p. 313. For a twelfth-century Latin spell involving three angels walking on Mt Sinai meeting seven demons of rheumatism who confess they are going to torment a victim and are banned from so doing, see

Bozóky, 'Mythic Mediation in Healing Incantations', pp. 85–6. The St Sisinnius legend appears also in Ethiopic magic scrolls (as Susenyos), interestingly enough in its probable original role as a protection for babies: three nineteenth–early twentieth-century specimens were sold at Christies's in London, 22 June 1983, cat. nos. 157, 160, 161.

252. Veselovskii, 'Razyskaniia v oblasti russkogo dukhovnogo stikha', SORIaS, XXXII, 4, pp. 47, 94. See also the note by Vasilievskii on Gillo at the end of Sokolov, 'Apokrificheskii material dlia ob''iasneniia amuletov'.

253. See Mansvetov, *Vizantiiskii material dlia skazaniia o 12 triasavits*, p. 13. It is worth noting however, that the 'and a half' element also occurs in the Greek, Serbian and Russian versions of the spell against snake-bite attributed to St Paul (see chap. 7), in which the saint curses the 'sixty and a half tribes of creature that crawl on the earth': Kagan-Tarkovskaia, 'Drevnerusskie vracheval'nye molitvy', p. 289.

254. E.g. the ninth fever may be *khampoia, khampeia, khameia* which corresponds to the ninth Greek name *kamodrakaina*.

255. Iudin, 'Ob imenakh zvezd-«pomoshchnits»', p. 70.

256. Cherepanova, *Mifologicheskaia leksika russkogo severa*, p. 93.

257. See Pypin, 'Issledovaniia dlia ob''iasneniia o lozhnykh knigakh', pp. 26–7.

258. See Émile Turdeanu, *Apocryphes slaves et roumains*, pp. 4–7.

259. Nikolaeva, *Drevnerusskaia melkaia plastika*, pp. 25–6, plates 39–41.

260. The motif of twelve maidens rising from the sea is also found in a song which is part of the ritual of *opakhivanie*, or ploughing a protective circle round a farm or village (see pp. 171–2): see Poznanskii, *Zagovory* (reprint), p. 315.

261. This has been quoted by Barb, 'Antaura. The Mermaid and the Devil's Grandmother', pp. 3–4, but he had not seen the print, and was apparently unaware of the *vita* of St Sisinnius. Barb notes that St Sisinnius is the most frequently invoked exorcizer of demons in Byzantine magic. See also Rovinskii, *Russkie narodnye kartinki*, 1881, IV, p. 658. The association of unbound and uncombed hair with witches and demons in Russian folktales and dialectisms is demonstrated by Cherepanova, *Mifologicheskaia leksika*, pp. 123–4. Wild hair as a demonic attribute has been mentioned elsewhere, and it has been noted in Byzantine iconography: see Greenfield, 'Fallen into Outer Darkness', pp. 66, 74. The magical connotations of nakedness are more or less universal.

262. Ethnographic Museum, St Petersburg.

263. See Tarasov, *Ikona i blagochestie*, plates 38–9. The icon is in the Museum of the History of Religion in St Petersburg.

264. These are preserved in the Ethnographic Museum in St Petersburg, coll. 5866, no. 144, purchased in Voronezh in 1936.

265. See Tikhonravov, *Pamiatniki*, II, pp. 351–3 for two versions; the prayer is no. 73 in Tikhonravov's list of banned texts (p. vii). also Vinogradov, 'Zagovory'. For folklore references to the daughters of Herod motif see also Efimenko, *Materialy po ètnografii*, p. 192; Minkh, 'Narodnye obychai', p. 51.

266. See Duling, 'The Testament of Solomon'.

267. These and similar names for fevers are also found unpersonified: see Cherepanova, pp. 63, 93–4. In Belorussia Traska-Chukhna was the name of fever but was also a taboo-word never to be spoken aloud: see Horoško, 'A Guide to Belorussian Mythology', p. 69.

268. Korkusha is the name of one of the women in the popular print shown in Fig. 11.

269. In the popular print shown in Fig. 11 the scantily clad woman in the lower left corner is called Nevra.

270. Quoted from *ERE*, VIII, col. 306a.

271. Dragomanov, *Malorusskie narodnie predaniia*, p. 26.

272. Shein, *Materialy*, p. 544.

273. Perunov, *Liubovnye, tselitel'nye i okhranitel'nye zagovory*, nos 69, 70.

274. In the Byzantine demonological texts, and in the *Testament of Solomon*, specific angels are usually invoked to deal with specific demons: see Greenfield, *Traditions of Belief*, pp. 222–5, 271–7.

275. See Năsturel, 'Autour du phylactère slavo-roumain de Budăneşti'. A Serbian prayer to St Sisinnius, together with a *Koliadnik*, a *Gromnik* and the *Twelve Fridays* is to be found in the thirteenth-century Serbian manuscript 'Sbornık popa Dragol'a'. see Stojanović, *Katalog*, IV, p. 361 (MS Belgrade, National Library 499 (555). For Bulgarian versions see *Stara bŭlgarska literatura*, pp. 313–14, 405–6.

276. Dujčev, 'Apocrypha byzantino-slavica'.

277. For some discussion see Mansikka, *Über russische Zauberformeln*, pp. 48–9, 57–60, 83–5, 102.

278. For a detailed study of potato legends see Nikiforov, 'Russkie povesti o kartofele'. The details mentioned are at pp. 24, 82. This is described as a Ukrainian belief in Blok, 'Poèziia zagovorov', p. 104. The motif of plants growing out of buried corpses is fairly common – see the description of *arkhangel*, *gorokh* and *simtarina* below.

279. The last two meanings are given in D'iachenko, *Polnyi tserkovno-slavianskii slovar'*, s.v. *dna*.

280. The most learned, but rather chaotic, discussion of this subject is Sokolov, 'Apokrificheskii material dlia ob"iasneniia amuletov', and *idem*, 'Novyi material dlia ob"iasneniia amuletov'; for further discussion in the context of later work see Nikolaeva and Chernetsov, *Drevnerusskie amulety-zmeeviki*, pp. 17, 38. For an exhaustive examination of the Hystera and its connection with amulets see Spier, 'Medieval Byzantine Magical Amulets'. For some discussion of Jewish 'exorcisms' of the womb and the Greek spells against Antaura (migraine) which have similar elements see Kotansky, *Greek Magical Amulets*, nos 13 and 51.

281. Addabbo, 'Le formule magico-mediche', p. 150, quoting MS Sangallensis 752.

282. Geitler, *Euchologium*, p. 67.

283. Porfiriev, 'Apokrificheskie molitvy', p. 10.

284. Dal', *Tolkovyi slovar'*, s.v. *zoloto*. Dal' mentions forty daughters in this case.

285. For texts see Romanov, *Belorusskii sbornik*, p. 51; Perunov, *Liubovnye, tselitel'nye i okhranitel'nye zagovory*, nos 107–9 (this is a popular booklet published in Novosibirsk – no sources are given).

286. As stated in Uspenskii, *Filologicheskie razyskaniia*, p. 150. Uspenskii speculates on an association of gold with prosperity, and thus fertility.

287 *Slovar' XI–XVII*, s.v.

288. Systerova and Liakhova, *Fol'klor Dal'nerech'ia*, p. 101.

289. Strakhov and Heretz, 'Disappearing Atlantis', pp. 169–70.

290. See Maikov, *Velikorusskie zaklinaniia*, nos 31, 67, 68.

291. Quoted in A. V. Pigin, *Iz istorii russkoi demonologii*, pp. 88–9.

292. Drexler, 'Alter Beschworungsformeln', pp. 603–5.

293. Schiffmann and Swartz, *Hebrew and Aramaic Incantation Texts*, p. 74.

294. Beneshevich, *Drevneslavianskaia kormchaia*, pp. 159–61.

295. See Kamentseva and Ustiugov, *Russkaia sfragistika i geral'dika*, pp. 62, 72–9.

296. Ibid., pp. 81–2.

297. Ibid., p. 78.

298. Richard Chancellor, in 1589, describes the seal as having on one side 'the image of a man on horseback in complete harnesse fighting with a dragon' which he does not identify as being St George: Hakluyt, *Principal Navigations*, p. 293.

299. Kamentseva and Ustiugov, *Russkaia sfragistika i geral'dika*, pp. 108 ff.

300. In the *Povest' o zhenit'be Ivana Groznogo na Marii Temriukovne* there is a statement that Ivan the Terrible sealed a document with his favorite ring on which he himself was depicted. See *Pamiatniki literatury Drevnei Rusi. XVII vek*, 2, p. 7. The annotation to this text (p. 586) states that in the sixteenth and seventeenth centuries the mounted figure on the tsar's seal was generally regarded as being a representation of the tsar. This is supported by the statement of Grigorii Kotoshikhin, a senior official under Aleksei Mikhailovich, who says that the personal seal of the tsar was a 'tsar on a horse conquering a serpent', and the state seal was the same in the centre of a double-headed eagle: Kotoshikhin, *O Rossii*, fols 55, 168. A recent study of St George in Russian culture also suggests that the Muscovite princes of the fifteenth to seventeenth centuries saw themselves as the mounted figure: see Senderovich, *Georgii Pobedonosets*, p. 81.

301. Bocharov, 'Russkie siuzhetno-ornamental'nye izdeliia'. Bocharov is primarily concerned with technique and style and only once mentions the possibility of these objects as love amulets (p. 244).

302. Spasskii, 'Tri zmeevika', p. 361.

303. Ralston, *Songs of the Russian People*, p. 387.

304. Fennell, *Kurbsky's History of Ivan IV*, pp. 204–5; Dal', s.v. *otnosit'*.

305. Malov, *Pis'ma k voinam*, p. 107.

306. Abramov, 'Chernigovskie malorossi', p. 548.

307. See Vysotskii, *Narodnaia meditsina*, p. 96. Vysotskii records a number of other inscriptions on *ladanki* at pp. 94–5. Russian diminishing spells are also described in Poznanskii, *Zagovory*, p. 95.

308. Quintus Serenus, *Liber medicinalis*, Leipzig, 1917, cap. 52. Third century AD.

309. Daniel Defoe, *A Journal of the Plague Year*, ed. L. Landa, London, 1969, p. 33. For the diminishing ABRACADABRA see Marquès-Rivière, *Amulettes, talismans et pantacles*, p. 48 for its Hebrew origin and pp. 115–6 for its alleged Gnostic use; for a Hebrew example see also Schire, *Hebrew Amulets*, p. 59, and Trachtenberg, *Jewish Magic and Superstition*, pp. 116–7, who mentions a Talmudic diminishing spell against the demon Shabriri and others such as TON . . . TETRAGRAMMATON in the *Clavicula Salomonis*; for European examples see Hansmann and Kriss-Rettenbeck, *Amulett und Talisman*, p. 138; for similar Anglo-Saxon counting-out spells and diminishing word amulets see Cockayne, *Leechdoms, Wortcunning, and Starcraft*, III, p. 63 and Storms, *Anglo-Saxon Magic*, pp. 151–5. Scandinavian diminishing spells beginning KULUMARIS (and variants) were published in B. av Klintberg, *Svenska trollformler*, p. 114. A twentieth-century specimen for the protection of cattle has been recorded in Wales: see Merrifield, *The Archaeology of Ritual and Magic*, p. 152. For the similar Greek diminishing 'wing' formula see A. Delatte, 'Études sur la magie grecque', p. 57 and Marquès-Rivière, *Amulettes, talismans et pantacles*, p. 116.

310. See most recently Nikitina, 'Risunki-graffiti iz Sofii novgorodskoi'.

MATERIA MAGICA

1. *Introduction*

This chapter will survey briefly the magical and medico-magical properties thought to be inherent in animal or vegetable or mineral matter as distinct from the specific objects which were discussed in the previous chapter. Since magical substances are mentioned in many places in this book, cross-references are given here only sparingly and the reader should go to the index for more information. The subject of the properties of precious stones is not discussed here but appears together with alchemy in Ch. 13.

2. *Herbs, magic, and poison*

The close relationship, both terminological and conceptual, between magic, herbs, and poison, is mentioned at several points in this book (for legal aspects see also Chapter 16), and is worth summarizing here. The word *zel'e* in Old Russian may mean 'herb; medicine; magic potion; poison'; the word *potvor* may mean 'magic and witchcraft, poisoning, poison, potion, herb'. It is found as a translation of Greek *mageia*, *goēteia*, *pharmakeia* and *pharmakon*). In this semantic grouping the Greek *pharmakon* is perhaps the most significant, since the Greek word is used regularly to mean 'poison', 'medicine' or 'magic' and is probably the source of the association of ideas in the Roman and the various Christian traditions.

In the Russian context the *Izbornik Sviatoslava* of 1076 contains condemnations of divination, witchcraft and poisoning from the *Constitutiones Apostolorum*; the Permian wizard Pam in the fourteenth–fifteenth-century *vita* of St Stefan of Perm' is also described as a poisoner,[1] and the sixteenth-century *Domostroi* or 'Book of Ruling the Household' condemns in one breath practising witchcraft and poisoning'.[2]

As the example of Greek *pharmakon* shows, the association of ideas is ancient, and its survival was certainly not confined to Russia: the *Lex Cornelia de sicoriis* mentions 'artibus odiosis tam venenis vel susurris magices homines occiderunt'.[3] Apuleius in the second century links 'carmina' and 'venena'.[4] Indeed, it has been suggested that there is a linguistic link – if *venenum* is cognate with Venus, its first meaning may have been that of 'love potion'.[5] The second-century *Epistle of Barnabas* links magic and poison (ch. 20); St Augustine describes the two magicians of the Pharoah who were bested by Moses as operating with 'veneficia' and magical incantations with the aid of evil angels (*De civitate Dei*, lib. 10, cap. 8); Isidore of Seville and the Venerable Bede make the same connection and one

Latin penitential has a gloss which reads 'Veneficio, id est maleficio quisque aut venenum aut herbas tribuit'.[6]

The probability that the association of poison with magic in Russia goes back to the ancient Mediterranean world is strengthened by the fact that it occurs almost exclusively in Russian canon law texts, or texts produced in an ecclesiastical milieu,[7] and not in the state law codes of the fifteenth to eighteenth centuries. The exception to this is Peter the Great's code of naval law, the *Morskoi ustav* of 1720 which also links black magicians and poisoners, together with blasphemers, as criminals liable to the death penalty by burning; this law was based on West European models (see Ch. 16).

3. *Herbs and Roots*

Specific uses of particular herbs are discussed in detail in other chapters at the appropriate places: see in particular Ch. 2.6 for the significance of the feast of St John for the gathering of magic herbs (often specified as twelve – seven and nine are more common in Western Europe), and Ch. 7.5.8 for the plants involved in discovering treasure. For plants used in divination see also Chs 4 and 5.2.3. The legal aspect of 'possession of roots' is discussed in Ch. 16.

Many plants in Russia, as elsewhere, have symbolic, religious or magical significance. The various apocryphal legends of the Tree of the Cross usually identify the cedar, cypress and olive.[8] The Old Believers typically regarded imported plants as diabolical: the potato, for example, was described as the 'Devil's apple' or the 'apple of Sodom', and, as mentioned in Ch. 8, was described as growing out of the anus and genitals of a dead oriental magician, or a daughter of Herod who had had intercourse with a dog; in the latter case they were both killed, and from the body of the dog grew potatoes and from the girl tobacco.[9] No less diabolical were the twice-accursed tea, and the thrice-accursed coffee. These, according to a chronologically preposterous Old Believer saying, were condemned at seven ecumenical councils.[10]

Magical herbs and roots (often worn in the collar or tied to a pectoral cross) are, of course, the stock in trade of the *koldun* and *znakhar'*, and their possession was frequently used as evidence against those accused of witchcraft in the seventeenth and eighteenth centuries. They are usually called *koren'* 'root' or *trava* 'herb, grass' in the texts, but these are in fact imprecise terms which could mean any kind of plant.[11] Indeed *koren'*, like *zelie* ('herb, grass; medicinal or magic potion; poison; gunpowder') could simply mean 'magic or medicinal remedy': Dal' lists *privorotnye koreshki, privorotnoe zelie* ('love-attracting herbs') and *otvorotnye koreshki* ('love-repelling herbs') as magical simples offered by village healers to attract or destroy love respectively, and records sayings such as 'ot starosti zelie mogila' (= the grave is the remedy for old age).[12]

The names of magic or magico-medical plants in popular belief and folk tales are often difficult to identify with actual plants, Dal' and Afanas'ev notwithstanding. The names of the plants and their properties are frequently confused and interchanged and subject to regional variation. Sometimes, as in classical antiquity and in other parts of Europe, plants have to be gathered at a special time, typically at dawn on St John's Day, or in a special manner, usually without the use of iron, or with gold or silver implements.[13] Sometimes a prayer or spell is specified in herbals; one such is: 'Lord bless me. And you Mother Fresh Earth bless me to cull this plant. You have brought it forth for man's use and thus I take you. From the earth a plant, from God a medicine. Amen'.[14] This is to be said three times. Another, described by Pypin in 1862 as being in current use, runs: 'Holy Adam ploughed, Jesus Christ gave the seed, the Lord sowed it, the Mother of God watered it, and gave it to all the Orthodox people as an aid'. This was to be said standing with one's back to the plant and after crossing oneself and spitting three times on the ground, otherwise the plant would have no therapeutic value.[15]

* * *

What follows is a selection of plant names and the magical properties attributed to them, culled from a variety of sources. Russian folk medicine was predominantly herbal and, as elsewhere, both the practitioner and the user probably made no distinction between what would now be considered genuine therapeutic and supposed magical properties. The village *znakar'* in the nineteenth century prided himself on a stock in trade of ninety-nine or seventy-seven herbs or roots, of which he would always keep twelve at home. The numbers themselves suggest magical significance.[16] The list could be considerably extended from the many extant herbal remedy books *(travniki)*, some of which are published, but much of the material would not qualify as unambiguously magical. Plants to which purely medical properties are attached, i.e. specifics for particular physical ailments, are therefore omitted here.

Adamova golova, 'Adam's Head'. This is variously identified by Dal' (who notes no magical qualities) as *mandragora* and *Centaurea scabiosa*.[17] Magicians were supposed to gather it on St John's Day and keep it hidden until Holy Thursday. It was used for the magical fumigation of the equipment used in duck-shooting on that day.[18] This 'tsar of herbs' was to be culled using a cross and a prayer; if brought into the house of anyone blighted by an evil spell or of a woman unable to conceive, they would be relieved if given the plant in a drink. If blessed with holy water and placed on the altar for forty days it would enable the wearer to detect demons and magicians. It could heal wounds in three days.[19] In the Ukraine its property was to attract gifts and ease childbirth.[20]

Adrian i Mar'ia, also called *Ivan da Mar'ia, Iokim i Mar'ia, trava Ivan*. Koren identifies *Ivan-da Mar'ia* as *Melampyrum nemorosum*.[21] It was used by *znakhari* to restore marital harmony as well as curing several illnesses.[22] It could also be gathered on St John's Day before sunrise, and placed at the four corners of a house as a protection from burglars.[23] Dal' lists only *Ivan-trava*, with several possible identifications, and no magical attributes.

Arkhangel, Arkharik, Arkhalim, (Tsar'-)Arkhilin, Arkhiton, Akhtonom, Tsar'-sil, Tsar'-simtarim (local variants and equivalents). Dal' lists *Arkhilin* as a fabulous plant. Seventeenth–eighteenth-century herbals say it grows from the ribs of a corpse and is culled with a gold or silver coin on St John's Day. Whoever wore it need fear no devil or sorcerer or evil man, would win cases in court, and all would love him. Prepared with milk it would remedy childlessness and ward off *porcha*.[24] See also *simtarina* below.

Artamon. St Artamon's day, 12 September, was the 'snakes' holiday'. A plant named after the saint was a specific against evil spirits.[25]

Atsarosha golova. This had to be gathered with a cross and three hundred repetions of the prayer 'Lord Jesus Christ, Son of God, have mercy on me, a sinner'. If taken as an infusion it would counter malefic magic (*porcha*) and help women in labour. Anyone wishing to detect the Devil or a 'heretic' (i.e. wizard) could soak the root in water and place it on the altar for forty days, after which he would be able to see the demons of air and water.[26]

Buzina, elder. Sticks of elder were thought protect a traveller from wild animals and evil men. The following extravagant procedure was recommended: on the eve of All Saints' Day cut a suitably sized elder stick, hollow out the soft centre of the bottom end, insert wolf's eyes, the tongues of three green lizards, the hearts of a dog and three swallows, all of which have been pulverized and mixed with powdered ironstone. The stick was then to be furnished with an iron ferrule, and could be used as a magic walking stick.[27]

Chernobyl and *polyn'* (wormwood, *Artemisia vulgaris*). A specific against witches and water-sprites (*rusalki*) and fevers.[28] This plant was gathered on St John's Eve and woven into a wreath (a practice also in medieval Western Europe) – if you looked through this at the Kupala bonfire you would be preserved from headache and sore eyes for the whole year.[29] Cows washed with an infusion of this herb would give more milk. The herb itself had apotropaeic powers against the Devil and lightning in Belorussia.[30] Its most magical quality (recorded in Russia, the Ukraine and Belorussia) was that, if you had acquired the gift of understanding what animals and plants are saying by eating serpents' flesh (an apparently ubiquitous belief at least as old as Pliny)[31] you would immediately lose this gift when you ate the herb or drank an infusion of it.[32] So powerful was this effect that even the name of the herb would nullify spells cast with the help of the Queen of Serpents. Rogovich quotes a story from the Starodub region in which a girl gathering mushrooms found herself in a cavern of serpents; the Queen of Serpents gave her the power of knowing the language and properties of plants on condition that she never used the word *chernobyl*. She later used the word inadvertently and immediately lost her powers.[33] A variant form of the name, *Chernobyl'nik* is given by Zabylin as a herb which, if gathered at the end of August or in the first days of September, sewn in the skin of a young hare and worn as an amulet, would enable a man to outrun the swiftest horse.[34] Beneath the plant would be found a piece of charcoal – this could be worn as an amulet to bring happiness and success.[35] Belief in the power of *Artemisia* to ward off witchcraft is also known in the West: it is mentioned for example in the fifteenth-century Wolfsthurn handbook.[36] (See also Chs 7.5.8 and 11.2.)

Chertopolokh ('devil alarmer'). Burdock or thistle. Afanas'ev and Dal' say this is the name of varieties of *Carduus* and *Cirsium*. Merkulova adds *Arctium*,[37] and gives *shishobar* (? 'devil-conqueror') as an alternative name in parts of northern Russia and Siberia. Toren adds that it is the same as *Tsar'-trava*.[38] It could drive off devils and witches, protect cattle, cure illnesses.[39] To drive the Devil out of an epileptic, one could draw a circle round him and then beat him mercilessly with this plant.[40] For the Amur region it is listed as *Bidens tripartita* (Water Agrimony), a remedy for scrofula and wakeful children.[41] Maikov published a spell to cure worms in livestock: 'Mordvin, Mordvin, you are the Tsar' herb *chertopolokh*. Take away the worms. If you don't take them away I shall take away your root'. This was to be said at three dawns and three sunsets facing east.[42]

Chesnok (garlic). As in other parts of Europe, this was thought to ward off evil spirits and hostile witches. In Belorussia it was worn by wives to protect their marriages from spells.[43] The tongue of a black snake with three cloves of garlic tied in a towel over your right breast was protection in battle or in court.[44] Richard James, in Russia in 1618–19, records in his glossary: '*odnazubka*, garlike without cloves of one round stringe which they use to some speciall inchantement'.[45]

Deviasil, for which the obvious etymology is *deviat'* 'nine' and *sila* 'power, strength' (cf. the German *Neunkraft*). Given thus in Zabylin. Dal' lists *devesil*, identified as *Inula Helenium* (*Elecampane*), a medicinal plant known from antiquity, with a number of other possible uses; he suggests it is a corruption of *divosil*, the etymology of which would appear to be *divo* 'marvel' and *sila* 'power, strength'; the local variants and cognates in other Slavonic languages, however, make this unlikely and point to a Common Slavonic origin based on the number nine, a common magic number.[46] In the sixteenth century Ridley listed it as a medicinal plant and identified it by its pre-Linnean name *Enula campana*.[47] The plant was to be picked on St John's Eve, dried, pulverized with rosin and made into an amulet. This was worn next to the body for nine days, then sewn secretly into the clothes of the object of one's desire as a love-spell. It is supposed to have nine different virtues.[48] The *Slovar' Priamur'ia* lists *deviatil'nik* as *Tanacetum boreale*, a remedy for nine illnesses. Whether the name suggested the belief or *vice versa* must remain an open question.[49]

Diagel', Diagil' (angelica).[50] A widely and long known medicinal plant in northern Europe. This plant was supposed to be of great utility in moments of danger by, for example, giving your horse an extra turn of speed.[51] This property it shared with *Ivan-da-Mar'ia*,[52] and *Iatryshnik* or *Kukushkiny slezy* (Cuckoo Tears – and *Orchis*, according to Dal', who adds that it is used by girls anxious to strike up an acquaintance), which had to be chopped up finely and added to the horse's oats. After this the legs and belly of the horse had to be rubbed with deer fat, and two wolf's teeth.[53]

Erek. This was supposed to grow near middling rivers in middling places; its flowers were blue and red. It was to be placed under the church for three days, then sewn into a hat and while reciting the spell: 'As no-one saw this plant under the church for three days, so may I, servant of God X not be seen or heard in any thing I do day or night, Amen'. This was to be done on three days at dawn.[54]

Galgan (galanga). An infusion of this in wine was reputed to give protection against *porcha* or Evil Eye.[55] Possibly this is the same as *galbel*, of which an eighteenth-century herbal says that if you hold it or a nettle in your hand you will be safe from the attacks of your enemies and from all witchcraft.[56] Also a contraceptive if held under the tongue by a woman.[57]

Golubets ('blue flower'). If you drank an infusion of this bears would not attack you.[58] It is not identifiable, since many blue flowers, and at least one variety of mushroom, may have this name in different localities.

Gorokh (peas). It was thought that if you killed a snake in spring, opened its belly and placed in it three peas, then buried the snake, and when the peas flowered picked the flowers at midday or midnight, then rolled the flowers in wax and placed the pills in your mouth, you would be able to know what anyone is thinking.[59]

Ibragim. A root which was used to attract a lover. It was placed behind a mirror; the woman employing it would gaze into the mirror and say: 'As I gaze into this mirror may he gaze upon me'.[60] Probably a corruption of the *obratim* described below.

Iova-druzhba. A marvellous plant which, like the *razryv-trava*, would open locks and bolts. Also thieves' jargon for a skeleton key.[61]

Khvalika. This had four flowers: red, black, green and blue, with ten leaves on each side and was a protection in court.[62]

Kochedyzhnik (fern). Originally the name of the fern (usually *paporotnik*) in the Tver' region.[63] This was protected by, or alternatively protected from, evil spirits. Although a non-flowering plant, it was alleged to flower with a great burst of light, but only for a moment at midnight before St John's Day.[64] For a more detailed description of the magical fern see Ch. 7.5.8 on spells for finding treasure. Many of the magical properties of the fern may be attributed to other magic plants such as the *plakun-trava*, *razryv-trava*, *perelet-trava*. The fern would also protect you from the evil designs of your enemy.[65]

Krapiva (stinging nettle). This was a protection against witches and demons.[66]

Koliuka. A name widely used for several prickly plants.[67] This was gathered by magicians on St Peter and Paul's day (29 June), the last day of the cuckoo and one much quoted in agricultural predictions. It was collected with the evening dew on it, dried, and preserved in cows' bladders. Its virtue was that if a gun was smoked with it it would never miss, and would also be proof against hostile gun spells.[68] Dal' (s.v. *kolot'*) lists it simply as a thorny plant, which its name implies, and does not attempt to identify it; but he does also add the information about fumigating guns with its magic smoke. De Gubernatis offers a variant in which an arrow if dipped in an infusion of the plant would never miss its target.[69] According to Afanas'ev the *koliuka* is the same as *prostrel-trava*, *odolen'-trava*, *chertopolokh*.[70] Koren gives *Koliuchnik* as *Carlina Biebersteinii* and another name for *chertopolokh*. This is apparently the same plant as the *chertagon* or *ispolokh*, described by De Gubernatis, which grew in or near a wood and was prickly with a blue flower; it cured childish fears and banished the Devil if placed under the pillow or used in an infusion for bathing children.[71]

Kupal'nitsa, kupava. Botanically the name of several plants which grow in or near water,[72] with magic properties derived from association with Ivan Kupala (the Midsummer festival) and *kupat'sia* 'to bathe'. It was one of the St John's Eve herbs and was scattered on the floor of the bathhouse.[73] It was straight like an arrow and had nine leaves on each side in four colours: black, green, red, and blue. Its power was that if you plucked it on St John's Eve and carried it with you, bound to a gold or silver coin, you need fear neither the Devil nor enemies, you would win any case in court and you would be in favour with the Tsar and princes. The root if ground and taken in water would enable childless women to conceive and would also drive away evil spirits.[74] A variant is *Agrafena-kupal'nitsa*, from the feast day of St Agrippina (Agrafena) on 23 June, and a festive bathhouse day.[75]

Kupena (*Polygonatum multiflorum*, Solomon's Seal). Used by girls as a counting-out oracle, and, when added to washing water, as a means of acquiring a white skin.[76] The latter use is also known in Italy.[77]

Liubistok see *zoria*.

Molodilo[78] A magic contraceptive root mentioned in a court case in the seventeenth century.[79] The form of the word suggests a meaning of 'something which makes one younger'. Dal' gives *molodilo*, *Sedum acre*, as a synonym of *utrobyshen'* without further comment. Since *utroba* means womb, this may well have been popularly thought to be an abortifacient. Dal', s.v. *mladoi* also gives *molodika* with a possible synonym *adalen'* (i.e. *odolen'* below).

Nechui-veter (lit. 'Not feel the wind', *Hieracium pilosella* [Hawkweed], according to Dal'). This grows by riverbanks and lakes. It was thought to subdue storms, save boats from sinking and catch fish without nets. It was gathered at midnight on New Year's Eve when the Devil, wandering about the waters, would throw it down to calm the waves. Only those blind from birth could detect it – they would feel a pricking in the eyes when they stepped on it. If they could pick it up in their mouths they would absorb all its powers.[80]

Neodolim-trava (lit. 'the unconquerable herb'). This protected cattle from witches.[81] Cf. the *odolen'-trava* mentioned by Afanas'ev as being a variety of *prostrel-trava*, *koliuchka* and *chertopolokh* which are demonifuges.[82]

Obratim (lit. 'the herb which turns'). This herb when placed on a mirror would make your husband love you.[83] Probably the same as *Ibragim* above, which seems to have been orientalized by popular etymology. This name, and the method of application, is recorded in a pitiful court case of 1635 when a woman in the entourage of the tsaritsa confessed under torture that she had acquired the root from a *vorozheia* in order to regain her husband's affection.[84]

Odan. A herb to attract a lover.[85] Probably the same as that listed by Dal' as *odalen'*, which may be the same as *Odolei, Euphorbium*.

Odolen', adalen' (from *odolet'* 'to overcome'). Usually *Nymphea*, although the name in other Slavonic languages is attached to *Valeriana*.[86] Mentioned by Afanas'ev as being a variety of *prostrel-trava*, *koliuchka* and *chertopolokh* which are demonifuges.[87] Vinogradov records it as a cure for poisons, for preventing flocks from scattering, for killing wild beasts and turning enemies into friends.[88] Herbals record two plants with this name. The first could be employed by placing its root in vinegar and drinking the infusion as a cure for a malefic spell; the flower could be rolled in wax and worn as an amulet to obtain respect, power, and dominance over enemies. The plant was to be plucked with a spell 'through wax or gold'. The other plant with this name will drive out poison 'above and below', cure toothache, and win the affection of those who do not like you.[89] It was also supposed to be a protection for travellers in foreign lands.[90]

Osina (the aspen tree). This was held to be accursed because it was the tree on which Judas Iscariot hanged himself, hence its other name *iudino derevo*, 'Judas tree'.[91] It had reputed power against wizards and was specified for making the stake with which the corpse of a *koldun* should be pierced to prevent him from rising from the grave.[92]

Paporotnik (fern) see *kochedyzhnik*.

Paramon. This plant has black hairs and a yellow cap and grows near bogs. Given in milk it would protect you from evil spirits and illness.[93]

Perelet-trava ('flying herb'). This was sought on St John's Eve and guaranteed good luck.[94] Dal' puts a question mark after his identification of this herb with the fern.

Perenos (*Eryngium*). This was a specific for snakebite and a demonifuge, the latter property being shared by *prostrěl* (probably *Pulsatilla*).[95] The plant *perekos* recorded by Vinogradov as being like a man and sending reptiles and men to sleep,[96] is probably a variant, perhaps even a copyist's misreading (*n* and *k* in some hands are very similar).

Petrov krest (lit. 'Peter's cross' – *Lathraea squammaria* according to Dal'). This protected from all harm, and if you were going to a feast would guard you from 'heretics' and sudden death. It was recommended in pulverized form, rolled in wax from candles which had burned before icons of the Saviour or the Virgin; it was to be worn on the pectoral cross of those who had an unhappy home life.[97] Fishermen tied it to their pectoral cross as an amulet against the Evil Eye.[98]

Plakun-trava (lit. 'weeper-grass'). Dal' identifies it with four different plants; Koren gives only *Lythrum salicaria*.[99] The *plakun-trava* 'weeper-grass' was, according to the *Golubinnaia kniga*, the 'religious song' which is a kind of anthology of folk cosmology, a herb on which the Virgin's tears fell at the Crucifixion, and this is why it is the 'mother of all plants'.[100] One version of the song states that the root is fashioned into crosses in Russia for the salvation of monks, old men and youths.[101] According to Sakharov magicians gathered it at dawn on St John's Day using a non-ferrous implement.[102] Its flower and root had the property of subduing demons, and driving them out of possessed persons, and magicians and treasure-hunters used it to frighten off the demons who guard treasure (see Ch. 7.4.6). When the plant had been dug up the magician would take it to church, stand at the altar holding the root and facing east, and recite a spell inviting the plant to 'drown in tears all devils and ancient Kievan witches'.[103] Sakharov declares tantalizingly that he cannot bring himself to describe what is done next, but claims that magic herb books have been imported from Poland and Belorussia which contain ceremonies associated with this plant which are contrary to religion.[104] Markevich notes that it is potent against the Evil Eye, sorcerers, demons, and house sprites (*domovoi*).[105] The *plakun* is one of the first magic plants to be recorded: in 1488 bishop Gennadii of Novgorod writes to bishop Nifont that among the religious abuses of the Novgorodians a priest had given a peasant a pectoral cross made of *plakun* with an 'indecent' depiction on it, and that a clerk had turned all the icons upside down.[106] This chance reference demonstrates that many examples of magical folk belief may well be much older than the obvious written sources reveal.

Poputnik (Plantago). This drove away snakes, was an antidote to poisons, and if boiled with honey and gunpowder would cure internal disorders.[107]

Posolnechnik (Sunflower). If gathered in August, bound up with a wolf's tooth, and worn on the belt, this would give you an ingratiating power over all you meet and drive away thieves.[108]

Prikrysh. Dal' (s.v. *prikryvat'*, 'cover, hide') mentions only *prikryt* for varieties of aconite. Possibly the name is cognate with *prikryi* 'bitter', but has become associated with *prikryt'* 'to hide' by popular etymology. This would explain the quality attributed to the plant in the Ukraine where the *prikryt* was thought to prevent spells or libellous calumnies against the bride at weddings.[109] In Russia the plant is gathered during the period 15 August to 1 October. It is used to counteract hostile spells at weddings: when the bride is being led to the marital home the *znakhar'* runs ahead and places some of this plant under the threshold. When the bride arrives she must jump over the threshold – if she steps on the plant any hostile spells will affect her, if not they will rebound on those who wished the couple ill.[110]

Razryv-trava, lit. 'split-open herb', the German *Springwurzel*, hence probably the alternative names of *Prygun, Skakun, Spryg-trava* 'Jumper'. Its name is explained both by the supposed manner of its flowering and by its reputed powers, the latter being no doubt the sympathetic extension of the former. This was allegedly a very rare herb known only to magicians. It could shatter metals (it was also known as *gremuchaia trava* ('exploding herb') and *zhelezniak* ('iron [herb]'),[111] break bonds, open locks, and prevent a smith from working if thrown into his smithy. Its main use was in hunting for buried treasure;[112] for detail see Ch. 7.5.8. It is perhaps saxifrage or *Impatiens* or *Noli tangere* according to Dal'.[113] Obviously associated with the *razryv-trava* are the *kliuch-trava* (lit. 'key-herb'), probably a variant in popular belief of the preceding but identified by Dal' (s.v. *kliuch*) as *Botrychium lunaria*, and the *zhivaia trava* (lit. 'live herb'), which may be confused with the preceding two, is known in folk tales and could be sought out with the aid of a snake, hedgehog, black woodpecker (*zhelna*) or *remez* (a kind of tomtit) – all these herbs were, of course, prized by thieves.[114] Dal', *Tolkovyi slovar'*, s.v. *spryg-trava*, mentions that there had recently (in 1882) been a court case in which a soldier confidence-trickster had raised money for a treasure hunt by showing people some seventeenth-century thalers which he said he had found with the help of this magic herb. One modern popular book on Russian nature beliefs states that, according to tradition, the *razryv trava* is revealed only to those who already have the fern flower and the *plakun*.[115]

Reven', rhubarb. This plant is reputed to roar and groan at sunset. This is more probably a popular etymology from the verb *revet'* 'to roar' than a quality shared with the mandrake. It could self-ignite and float against the current. If you took some in your mouth you too would easily be able to swim against the current. If you gave it to someone blighted by the Evil Eye he would reveal who blighted him; under its influence unfaithful wives would reveal the name of their lovers.[116] This last quality is perhaps linked with the fact that rhubarb was the most powerful laxative available in the seventeenth and eighteenth centuries. It was brought from Siberia under a Russian state monopoly and sold at high prices all over Europe.[117]

Riaska, raska, raiskaia, rokiia, etc. If administered to a wife on the 19th, 20th or 25th day of the month she would reveal with whom she has been, what she has talked about, against whom she has plotted mischief.[118]

Simtarina. Zabylin says that this is the same as *Tsar'-trava*, has six leaves of different colours, is gathered on St John's Eve, using a gold or silver coin or medallion. Beneath it lies a man and the herb grows from his rib (this suggests the mandrake tradition); take this man, cut open his breast and remove his heart. This is an infallible means of attracting love. Similarly the head of the man, if placed before an uncaring husband will immediately reinflame his love. The right hand of this underground man is also useful; the little finger ground up and administered as an infusion is a cure for infidelity.[119] See also *Arkhangel*.

Solomonidina ruchka ('Hand of Solomonida'), *Orepis latifolia*. By apocryphal tradition it was Solomonida (Solomoniia, Solomiia) who swaddled the new-born Jesus.[120] The plant named after her was used by *znakhari* in cases of impotence, feminine disorders, pains in the chest, and infant hernia.[121]

Son-trava (lit. 'sleep-herb'). Usually belladonna, but also other herbs.[122] Semenov-Tian-Shanskii identified it as *Pulsatilla albana*.[123] This was gathered in May to the accompaniment of spells and rituals (unspecified by Sakharov).[124] It was gathered with the morning dew and placed in cold water. At midnight it would begin to move. It was then placed under the pillow to induce prophetic dreams – a young man or woman meant good fortune; death, naturally enough, meant misfortune.[125]

Sova (lit. 'owl'). A fearsome plant which sent men mad if they came upon it, and made them lose their way. Its virtue was that if it were placed on the track of a thief he would be obliged to return.[126]

Strekil'. Mentioned as a 'magic herb' in a witchcraft case in Velikie Luki in 1628 in which a peasant woman, Katerinka, was accused of causing her mistress, the pregnant wife of Prince Fedor Eletskoi, to miscarry. The plant was one of several suspicious substances found in her house.[127] Dal' gives it as a Pskov' dialect word for *badiaga*, which he identifies as *Spongia* or *Bodiga fluviatilis*.[128] It was used as a remedy for jaundice (but according to Dal' was harmful), and by women and girls to rub on their faces to produce an inflammation – pink cheeks were much admired in Russian women, whose use of face-painting was much disparaged by foreign traveller writers. This was precisely what Katerinka claimed she was using it for but was not believed.

Tirlich or *tyrlych*. This was gathered on St John's Eve on Bald Mountain near Kiev, where the witches gathered for their Sabbath. For this reason, anyone wishing to gather some had to protect himself with some *plakun*, q.v.[129] The juice of this plant was squeezed out and rubbed under the armpits by were-animals when performing magic. Dal' identifies the plant as *Gentiana amarella* and adds the detail that *tirlich* and toads' bones calm the anger of those in power. He also gives *tirlich* as a synonym of *bad'ia*, identified as Typha.[130] Afanas'ev quotes the belief that this root can turn a man into a were-animal and enable him to fly. For this reason witches rubbed it into their armpits and the backs of their knees to give them the power to fly up chimneys.[131] The etymology of the word *tirlich* is given as 'unclear' in Vasmer, but the association with witches' sabbaths and flying ointment suggests a West European origin, and the association with were-animals further suggests a connection with German *Tier*.

Tsar'-trava see *Arkhangel, Chertopolokh, Simtarina*, also Ch. 7.4.6.

Vish'. Mentioned a witchcraft case in 1628 as a synonym of *strekil'*, q.v.

Zoria, also called *liubistok*. According to Dal' s.v. this is usually *Ligusticum levisticum* or *Levisticum officinalis*, lovage. It gave protection from fevers and *rusalki*, water-sprites who might tickle you to death.[132]

Many other plants may be associated with magical practices. For example heather and thistles gathered on Holy Thursday would protect a house from a hostile *koldun* if placed under the house or burned in the stove.[133] Birch twig wreaths were used in Trinity day marital divination, and *dukhovaia trava*, herbs that have been left in church during Trinity day, were a specific for cattle plague.[134] Any grass or cereal could be tied in a knot by a *koldun* in one variety of malefic magic (see pp. 75–6) and corn could be used in another kind of plant magic in which you had to hunt for a stalk of corn with twelve ears; when found this was kept until the next sowing when the grains were sown first, before the other seed corn, to ensure a good harvest.[135] One method of healing used by *znakhari*, or folk healers, was to take nine twigs from a tree struck by lightning, set them alight, then put them out by spraying a mouthful of water through them on to the patient.[136] In one seventeenth-century copy of the herbal called *Prokhladnyi vertograd* a method of determining virginity is described: leaves of horse sorrel were to be burned near the girl – if she turned pale she was not a virgin.[137] One can only wonder how many virgins could survive this ordeal with reputation intact.

4. *Food*

Apart from the specific magical use of herbs and roots, there are several varieties of food which may be used in magic or divination.

Pastry ladders, with seven rungs for the seven heavens, were baked as part of the funeral ritual, to enable the dead to climb to heaven.[138] Similar bread ladders were also baked in several regions of Russia for feast days which had obvious upwards connotations, such as the Ascension, Raising of Lazarus, St John Climacus.[139] Dal' records that in the Riazan' region these bread ladders were taken out into fields on Ascension day, and after prayers to the four corners of the earth were thrown into the air with the cry: 'May the rye grow that high!'. The bread was then eaten.[140] Communion bread could also be used in the same way by eating it during the first sowing or burying it in the cornfield.[141]

Pancakes, especially the first pancake of a batch, may be involved in a number of divinatory processes. Several of these are described in Ch. 4.[142]

5. *Human materia magica*

Several parts of the body or body fluids could be used for magical purposes in Russia. Urine features in several practices; perspiration and breast milk could be used in love magic; the apotropaic use of spittle is described in several other parts of this book, as is the use of blood, including menstrual blood, in a number of magical procedures. The use of parts of the body, and of corpses, in malefic magic is also described elsewhere.

Hair and fingernails are connected with particular beliefs. For example, human fingernails were used as amulets among the Old Believers as being useful for clambering out of the grave and up to heaven (sometimes thought of as being on top of a glass mountain).[143] There was also a popular belief that nail-parings and hair-clippings should be kept because at the Last Judgment one would have to account for every part of one's body.[144] It was for this reason that Peter the Great's edict forcing Russian men to shave their beards caused such dismay; Captain John Perry, writing in 1716, described a carpenter who had cut off his beard in conformity with the law, but kept the hair hidden inside his shirt so that he could eventually be buried with and thus be able to account for it to St Nicholas.[145]

Cauls of newborn infants (which they had to keep as an amulet for the rest of their lives), were and still are considered lucky.[146] To be born 'in a shirt' (*v sorochke* or *v rubashke*) is an expression still used of a fortunate person.[147] Beliefs about the caul are very ancient and can be found in most parts of Europe. In the case of Russia, as mentioned in Ch. 1, the recorded connection with magic goes back at least to 1044 when the Chronicle entry states that Prince Vseslav of Polotsk was conceived by enchantment and born with a caul which he wore as an amulet all his life. At the 1551 *Stoglav* Council in Moscow parish clergy were specifically forbidden to allow cauls to be placed on the altar during the liturgy to enhance their magic power.[148] It is a matter of some interest that the *benandanti*, the 'anti-witches' of Friuli, according to the Inquisition records so ably utilized by Carlo Ginzburg, followed the same practice. In 1580 Battista Moduco testified that he was a *benandante* because he had been born in a caul, that it had been preserved by his mother, baptized with him, and placed under the altarcloth at mass on many occasions both by his mother and by himself. He alleged that a priest had agreed to do this and had accepted an offering after so doing.[149] The parallel is striking, but although there is a Slavonic background to Friuli it is hard to imagine what the common source might be for what are essentially popular practices without there being any obvious social or textual link.[150] And in fact the practice of 'baptizing' cauls, often surreptitiously for magical purposes, was fairly widespread in Europe,[151] and is of considerable antiquity.[152] Other Slavonic beliefs about the caul are that its loss means trouble for the child and, in Belorussia, that it may be used as an amulet to ensure healthy cattle and a good harvest.[153]

In the Indigirka region of northern Siberia mothers used to save the remainder of the umbilical cord after it was detached from the child's navel and wrap it in a cloth in the belief that this would ensure that the child would have a good memory.[154] For the placenta as aid to conception or contraceptive specific see Ch. 7.

6. *Animals and parts of animals*

Certain animals could bring luck or be good or bad omens, as described in Ch. 5. Parts of animals and human beings, too, could have magical value, especially in magic medicine, in which their occasionally demonstrable genuine pharmaceutical properties in no way diminished the magical purpose of their user. They could also serve as talismans – horses' heads, bears' heads, paws and claws, bats' wings (a dried bat worn at the breast was a good-luck charm; water in which it has been boiled was a remedy for fever),[155] snakeskin, dried heads of snakes or frogs (against fever),[156] teeth, bones (especially mammoth bones), all had their uses, and hard-boiled eggs worn at the breast for forty days would prevent a miscarriage.[157]

A bear's head buried in the ground would increase the size of a flock, according to some herbals; bear's fat would prevent unfaithfulness in marriage; pork fat placed between the fingers of a sick man would predict the outcome of his illness (presumably by the degree to which it melted); the bones of whatever animal had been consumed at dinner on Easter Sunday were buried in cornfields as a precaution against hail.[158] Dried frogs and water in which a snake had been placed were specifics against marital disharmony,[159] and in the *bylina* of *Potuk Mikhaila Ivanovich*, in the version given in the Kirsha Danilov collection, the hero brings his wife back to life by rubbing her with the head of the serpent which he had killed in her grave.[160] I offer this as a gift to Freudians. A snake killed and hung on a birch tree would bring rain.[161]

The exact nature of the 'unicorn horn' set with precious stones and used by Ivan the Terrible as his royal staff (see p. 363) or that bought for ten thousand roubles by Tsar Aleksei Mikhailovich in 1655, and which was 'six spans in length and shining bright', is open to question, but most 'unicorn horns' elsewhere were narwhal. The French soldier of fortune Jacques Margeret, in Russia from 1590 to 1606, described being taken into the tsar's treasury by the pretender Dmitrii and seeing there:

> two intact unicorn horns and a crosier which the emperors carry [i.e. Ivan the Terrible's staff], the entire length of which is made of one piece of unicorn [horn]. The transverse part of the crosier, on which one leans, is made of another piece of unicorn[horn]. There is also another half unicorn [horn] which is for everyday use in medicines.[162]

'Unicorn' horn was a widely known and prized magico-pharmaceutical item, with a reputation as an antidote to poison.[163] For example, an alleged 'unicorn horn', identified as in fact from a narwhal, is listed in the posthumous inventory of valuables of the fifteenth-century Cardinal Francesco Gonzaga.[164] In English the term 'unicorn horn' was regularly used in the seventeenth and eighteenth centuries to denote narwhal ('sea-unicorn') horn as a trade commodity. In the Russian context, however, the 'unicorn horn' may well come from the remains of mammoths in Siberia, on which see Ch. 7.4.4.(n.).[165] The image of the unicorn as a horse-like creature with a long single horn was perfectly well known to the Russians and appears on royal seals in the sixteenth and seventeenth centuries from Ivan IV to Aleksei Mikhailovich,[166] perhaps significantly in view of his 'unicorn' staff described above. The association of Russia with 'unicorn horn' seems to be established at the more esoteric fringe of alternative medicine: a few years ago the author lectured to the Folklore Society and was asked by a member of the audience to recommend a source of supply of Russian unicorn horn, since contact had been lost with the Soviet supplier and stock was running low. Possibly the enquirer had in mind the various deer horn remedies derived from Chinese medicine which were much promoted at one time in the Soviet Union.[167] The identity of 'snake's horns', a cheaper magical remedy, is not clear.[168]

The Muscovite tsars, like the rich and powerful in Western Europe, are also known to have possessed bezoars (*bezui, bezoar, bezar, bezur, zabezat*), hard secretions found in certain animals which were well known in the lists of *materia medica* from Classical antiquity onwards (for Russian textual references see also Ch. 13) and which they employed both as talismans and as an ingredient in medicines against malefic magic.[169] In 1587 Maximilian of Austria sent to Tsar Fedor Ivanovich a bezoar taken from his father's treasury and 'it had great power to heal *porcha'*.[170] This suggests that the reputation of the stone may have come from the West.

7. *Fish*

The magical use of fish is not much recorded in Russia, notwithstanding the appearance of magic fish in Russian folktales, and the symbolism, often sexual, of fish in many cultures. There are, however, a few examples. The English clergyman Richard James, writing in 1619 in the Archangel region, includes in his annotated glossary of local Russian an inelegantly named fish used as an amulet:

> *Zaixa* aliter pisda [i.e. a Russian word, now only vulgar, for the female pudenda, presumably from some fancied similarity in appearance], a fish with a head which they drie and sell in the market to hange on their neckes whoe have agues with opinion that it will so be driven away.[171]

Possibly this is related to the *piskun*, noted by Zabylin as having an indecent name in the Vetluga region.[172] The naming of fish after the male and female genitalia, and their use in magic, was described in some detail in the second century by Apuleius.[173] The example here would appear to be a Russian manifestation of the widespead practice of displaying grotesquely exaggerated representations of the female pudenda to avert the Evil Eye and frighten off witches.[174] The display of actual genitalia by women to avert an enemy attack or thunder and hail storms is also known in Russia and among the South Slavs.[175] And no doubt there is sexual significance in the rubbing down of brides with a whole raw fish, later to be eaten by the bridegroom, a ritual still performed by magicians in the pre-nuptial bath ceremony in at least one northern area of Russia in the last twenty years (see p. 75), which one may perhaps compare with the more overtly sexual magic practice of stifling a fish in the vulva and then giving it to a man as aphrodisiac food to secure his affection, a practice condemned in a Latin penitential of the tenth or eleventh century.[176]

   Other aquatic creatures may also appear in magical medicine. A cure for fever is to drink water in which a crayfish has lain for twelve days, or a glass of vodka in which twelve crayfish have been dunked.[177] The reason for the number twelve, which adds a magical flavour to what otherwise might be simple folk pharmacy, is no doubt to be found in the Russian tradition of the fevers as the twelve daughters of Herod (see Ch. 8.6.6.1).

8. *Birds*

Birds are more commonly recorded than fish. The eyes, feathers and feet of eagles were used as both a medicine and an amulet: one seventeenth-century herbal recommends the right eye of an eagle placed on one's left breast to assuage the anger of tsars and princes (see also Ch. 7.5.7); eagles' feet guaranteed quick success in trade; the last feather in an eagle's wing would remedy childlessness; and the stones allegedly to be found in an eagle's stomach or nest would bring riches.[178] Eagle-stones, or aetites (a stone with another loose stone within it), have been reputed to have magical properties since the Assyrians.[179] Parings of eagles' claws could be used in place of finger nails for clambering out of the grave on the Day of Judgement (see above, p. 281)

Other birds of magical application were swallows, which were birds protected by God (see Ch. 5.2.2) and were reputed to secrete a stone with curative powers (they could to be worn under one's coat as an amulet);[180] magpies, which when hung in a barn would protect it from the *domovoi* or house sprite; and chickens The latter are often found in the New Year divinations, usually to discover a husband (see Ch. 4.5.11.1), but had a further amatory use in that their eyes could be ground up and made into a love potion.[181] The bones of an owl would protect a house from the Devil,[182] and owls' hearts when placed on a cloth at the left side of a sleeping woman would make her reveal in her sleep any infidelities she was guilty of in the absence of her husband,[183] while larks' hearts were given to wives in the habit of running away.[184] Sparrow fat or blood when rubbed on the limbs was supposed to protect the user from frost.[185]

9. *Minerals and Metals*

Various types of stone have been discussed in the previous section and in Ch. 13. Other substances used in medical talismans were coal, charcoal, verdigris and cinnabar. These could be used with incense or rosin and tied in a bag to the sufferer's pectoral cross.[186] The ashes of incense (called *kheruvimskii ladan* or *kherumvimskaia zola*) from a church thurible were also thought to have magical therapeutic qualities.[187] Earth from graves could be used in necromancy, and examples of this are given elsewhere; but it could also be used for curative purposes. The use of other substances may be mentioned incidentally in other chapters.

Of the metals, mercury was occasionally used in protection against *maleficium* but the most commonly found are silver and gold and iron. The first two are often mentioned in spells and records of magical practices elsewhere in this book, but a little more must be said about iron.

The curative and apotropaeic power of iron has been believed in from ancient times and is recorded by Pliny.[188] The curative value of iron is demonstrated by a Belorussian spell against syphilis which requires sores to be circled with iron.[189] The frequent use of iron (e.g. horseshoe talismans), iron fences, and locks and keys in the magical protection of livestock has been discussed elsewhere,[190] and references to iron in *zagovory* are quite common and can be found in Ch. 7 and 9.5. It is believed in some parts that the magic circles with which those attempting divination protect themselves from demonic forces should be inscribed with an iron implement.[191]

The avoidance of iron, presumably because it is inimical to sorcery, is also a feature of certain magical practices in Russia; in particular it is often specified that iron implements must not be used to dig up certain magical plants, such as those used in finding treasure (see Ch. 7.5.8) and those gathered on St John's Day. This too is a common belief outside Russia.

In the text of the widely known Old Russian apocryphal tale *Solomon and Kitovras* (the Slavonic version of *Solomon and Marculphus*), Kitovras (sc. the Centaur) is credited with the knowledge of how to hew stone without the use of iron, a skill which he used in helping Solomon build the Temple. This is evidently a magical interpretation of a passage in the biblical description of the building of the Temple (I Kings 6, 7), which is elaborated in the *Testament of Solomon* (2, 6–7), where it is stated that demons are terrified of iron.

The magic power of iron is inevitably linked with the magic power of blacksmiths, who are often reputed to be magicians, and who, in the Christmas divination songs (*podbliudnye pesni*) for example, can 'forge happiness'.[192]

10. *Water*

Water appears in a very large number of magical and divinatory practices. It can be symbolic, by association with washing and purity, or in rain-making ceremonies, or it can be used as a medium in which things can be floated or poured in several forms of divination, or as a reflective medium in catoptromancy. It can be given to the sick, or to intended victims, after it has been endowed with magical, usually curative properties by having immersed in it icons, crosses, rings, silver objects, bell clappers, roots, frogs, snakes, or aeroliths. Water from the river Jordan, water from any 'Jordan' (i.e. the place, or hole in the ice, where the Epiphany Blessing of the Water ceremony takes place), any blessed water, or water drawn from three (or seven) wells, rainwater, dew, or water from melting snow may all be used in magic, usually as a cure for some condition, while water (or soap) with which a corpse was washed,[193] or in which the clothes of the person towards whom a spell is directed was washed, or water from the Dead Sea can be used for more sinister ends.[194] Examples can be found throughout this book, and most of them have analogues in other cultures. Particular varieties of specifically magic water, *zhivaia voda* 'water of life' and *mertvaia voda* 'water of death' may be found in folktales, where they are the names of magical waters used for killing victims or reviving corpses, or restoring severed limbs.[195] There is also a superstition that water must not be drawn after dark because it is then 'sleeping'.[196] The tradition is live: Reuters (quoting TASS) reported on May 15, 1996, that a magic well had been discovered in a village in the Vologda region. Its water is claimed to have anti-alcoholic properties which cure hangovers and even turn alcoholics into teetotallers. (See also Ch. 2.7 on magic springs and wells.)

Notes

1. See Ch. 3.

2. *Domostroi*, p. 80.

3. See *Apulei Apologia*, commentary, p. 3, n. 15.

4. Apuleius, *Apologia*, 69, 17.

5. Ibid., commentary, p. 175, n. 17.

6. See Schmitz, *Bussbücher*, I, p. 307; see also Thomas of Chobham, *Summa de arte praedicandi*, cap. 6, l. 756: 'sortilegiorum vel veneficiorum'. For a survey of early Christian and Byzantine links see Troianos, 'Zauberei und Giftmischerei'.

7. The compilation called the *Izbornik Sviatoslava* of 1076 includes a passage from the fourth-century *Constitutiones Apostolorum*: 'You shall not divine, you shall not bewitch, you shall not poison, for "a sorcerer shall not live" [see Exodus 22,18 and Deuteronomy 18, 10] You shall not slay infants in the womb . . .'. See *The Edificatory Prose of Kievan Rus'*, p. 32.

8. For some discussion of Russian tales of the Tree of the Cross see Veselovskii, *Razyskaniia v oblasti russkikh dukhovnykh stikhakh. IV. Son o dereve v povesti grada Ierusalima i stikhe o golubinoi knige* and *X. Zapadnye legendy o dreve kresta i Slovo Grigoriiia o trekh krestnykh drevakh*.

9. For a detailed study of potato legends see Nikiforov, 'Russkie povesti o kartofele'. The details mentioned are at pp. 24, 82. The motif of plants growing out of buried corpses is fairly common – see the description of *arkhangel*, *gorokh* and *simtarina* below.

10. Dal', *Tolkovyi slovar'*, s.v. *kartofel'*; Kondrat'eva, *Metamorfozy sobstvennogo imeni*, s.v *sodomskie iabloki*; Dal', *Poslovitsy*, 1989 edn, I, p. 35. (A variant makes tea slightly less sinful in that it was condemned at only three councils.) In Old Believer tracts seven Ecumenical Councils were recognized (i.e. the councils generally accepted by both the Eastern and Western Churches, up to Nicaea II in 787) – the eighth was that of Patriarch Nikon, or the Antichrist.

11. See Dal', *Tolkovyi slovar'*, s.v. *koren'*, for a list of plants normally referred to as 'roots'.

12. Dal', *Tolkovyi slovar'*, s.vv. *zelie, koren'*.

13. The St John's day, avoidance of iron, digging at dawn, and placing under a church altar, are all found, for example, in Anglo-Saxon England: see Storms, *Anglo-Saxon Magic*, pp. 9, 10. For Germany and general remarks see *Handwörterbuch des deutschen Aberglaubens*, s.vv. *Johannes der Täufer; Neunerlei Kräuter*. For the ancient world see Delatte, *Herbarius*, ch. 1, Temps propice à la récolte'.

14. *Domostroi*, 1990, p. 239.

15. Pypin, *Lozhnye i otrechennye knigi*, p. 167. A similar spell is published in Maikov, *Velikorusskie zaklinaniia*, no. 253. No. 254 of the same collection, quoted from 'a wise woman', specifies complete nakedness as a condition for gathering the herbs.

16. Maksimov, *Nechistaia sila* (1993), I, p. 181.

17. See also Kondrat'eva, *Metamorfozy sobstvennogo imeni*, s.v. *Adam* for other identifications. Also Zabylin, *Russkii narod*, pp. 394–5.

18. Sakharov, *Skazaniia*, pp. 88–92.

19. *Domostroi*, 1990, p. 226. This gives the most likely identification as *Cypripedium calcedus*. For the magical power imparted by leaving on an altar see the discussion of cauls below.

20. De Gubernatis, *La Mythologie des plantes*, I, p. 7, quoting Dragomanov and identifying the plant as *Enjugium campestre*. See also Zabylin, *Russkii narod*, p. 428.

21. Toren, *Russkaia narodnaia meditsina*, p. 68. See also under *Ivan-chai* in Merkulova, *Ocherki*, p. 130 for botanical and etymological details.

22. Kondrat'eva, *Metamorfozy sobstvennogo imeni*, s.vv.; notes that the adjective *adamov* 'Adam's' can be attached to a wide range of plant names.

23. Makarenko, *Sibirskii narodnyi kalendar'*, p. 86.

24. *Domostroi*, 1990, pp. 226–7; Kondrat'eva, *Metamorfozy sobstvennogo imeni*, s.v.

25. Kondrat'eva, *Metamorfozy sobstvennogo imeni*, s.v.

26. Vinogradov, 'Zagovory', p. 31.

27. Zabylin, *Russkii narod*, p. 435.

28. See examples in Zelenin, *Izbrannye trudy: Ocherki russkoi mifilogii, ad indicem*.

29. Grieve, *Modern Herbal*, s.v. *mugwort*.

30. Min'ko, *Sueveriia*, p. 131.

31. See Frazer, *Garnered Sheaves*, ch. 4, 'The Language of Animals'.

32. Afanas'ev, *Poèticheskie vozzreniia*, pp. 574–5.

33. Rogovich quoted in De Gubernatis, *La Mythologie des plantes*, II, p. 17.

34. Zabylin, *Russkii narod*, pp. 434–5

35. *Domostroi*, 1990, p. 232.

36. Kieckhefer, *Magic in the Middle Ages*, p. 5.

37. Merkulova, *Ocherki*, pp. 93, 96.

38. Toren, *Russkaia narodnaia meditsina*, p. 82.

39. Afanas'ev, *Poèticheskie vozzreniia*, II, p. 415.

40. Merkulova, *Ocherki*, p. 96.

41. *Slovar' Priamur'ia*, s.v.

42. Maikov, *Velikorusskie zaklinaniia*, no. 201.

43. Min'ko, *Sueveriia*, p. 52.

44. Kostomarov, *Ocherk*, p. 190.

45. Larin, *Russko-angliiskii slovar'-dnevnik Richarda Dzhemsa*, 62.13.

46. See Merkulova, *Ocherki*, pp. 104–5.

47. Stone, *Dictionarie*, pp. 121, 474.

48. Zabylin, *Russkii narod*, p. 433.

49. See Merkulova, *Ocherki*, pp. 104–5 for botanical and etymological details.

50. See Merkulova, *Ocherki*, pp. 59–60 for botanical and etymological details.

51. These last two are mentioned in Cherepnin, 'Iz istorii drevnerusskogo koldovstva', p. 80. The property of giving speed to horses is attributed elsewhere in Europe to garlic: Grieve, *Modern Herbal*, s.v.

52. De Gubernatis, *La Mythologie des plantes*, II, p. 175.

53. Zabylin, *Russkii narod*, p. 435.

54. Rybnikov, *Pesni*, 1991 edn, p. 208. Not in Dal'.

55. Cherepnin, 'Iz istorii drevnerusskogo koldovstva', p. 189.

56. *Slovar' XI–XVII v.*, s.v. *opasnyi*.

57. Vinogradov, *Zagovory*, p. 33.

58. De Gubernatis, *La Mythologie des plantes*, II, p. 156.

59. Zabylin, *Russkii narod*, p. 426. A parallel Oriental practice for the same purpose employs five coriander seeds which are to be buried in the scooped-out head of a black raven, the resulting sprouts then to be eaten: Budge, *Syrian Anatomy*, II, p. 700.

60. Zabylin, *Russkii narod*, p. 409. Not listed in Dal'.

61. Kondrat'eva, *Metamorfozy sobstvennogo imeni*, s.v.

62. Rybnikov, *Pesni*, p. 209.

63. Merkulova, *Ocherki*, p. 119 for botanical and etymological details.

64. Sakharov, *Skazaniia*, pp. 88–92.

65. Cherepnin, 'Iz istorii drevnerusskogo koldovstva', p. 80. For other references to ferns in magic see Pomerantseva, *Mifologicheskie personazhi*, p. 179; Afanas'ev, *ad indicem*, Zabylin, *Russkii narod*, p. 78; Pokrovskii, *Istoricheskaia khrestomatiia*, p. 129.

66. Zelenin, *Izbrannye trudy: Ocherki russkoi mifilogii*, pp. 188, 245, 312.

67. Merkulova, *Ocherki*, p. 95 for botanical and etymological details.

68. Sakharov, *Skazaniia*, pp. 88–92.

69. De Gubernatis, *La Mythologie des plantes*, I, p. 127.

70. Afanas'ev, *Poèticheskie vozzreniia*, II, p. 415.

71. De Gubernatis, *La Mythologie des plantes*, I, p. 110.

72. Merkulova, *Ocherki*, pp. 34–5, for botanical and etymological details.

73. Perhaps one of the practices which provoked the ecclesiastical prohibition of 'bathing with herbs' mentioned on p. 32.

74. De Gubernatis, *La Mythologie des plantes*, II, p. 181; quoting a Russian correspondent.

75. Kondrat'eva, *Metamorfozy sobstvennogo imeni*, s.v. *Agrafena-kupal'nitsa*; Dal', *Tolkovy slovar'*, s.v. *kupat'*.

76. Merkulova, *Ocherki*, p. 35.

77. Grieve, *A Modern Herbal*, pp. 749–50.

78. Merkulova, *Ocherki*, p. 110 for botanical and etymological details.

79. Dubasov, 'Ocherki Tambovskogo byta', p. 663 mentioned, but no source or further detail given.

80. Sakharov, *Skazaniia*, pp. 88–92.

81. Kostomarov, *Ocherk*, p. 197.

82. Afanas'ev, *Poèticheskie vozzreniia*, II, pp. 415–17.

83. Kostomarov, *Ocherk*, p. 197; Zabylin, *Russkii narod*, pp. 409–10.

84. Zabelin, *Domashnii byt russkikh tsarits*, p. 538.

85. Zabylin, *Russkii narod*, p. 409.

86. See Merkulova, *Ocherki*, p. 34, for the botanical and etymological aspects.

87. Afanas'ev, *Poèticheskie vozzreniia*, II, pp. 415–17.

88. Vinogradov, *Zagovory*, p. 31.

89. *Domostroi*, 1990, p. 236.

90. Strizhev, *Kalendar'*, p. 271.

91. Kondrat'eva, *Metamorfozy sobstvennogo imeni*, s.v. *Iuda*.

92. Zabylin, *Russkii narod*, p. 275; Markevich, *Obychai* (reprint, p. 118).

93. Kondrat'eva, *Metamorfozy sobstvennogo imeni*, s.v.; *Domostroi*, 1990, p. 239.

94. Dal', *Tolkovyi slovar'*, s.v. *pereletyvat'*.

95. Kostomarov, *Ocherk*, p. 197.

96. Vinogradov, 'Zagovory', p. 31.

97. Zabylin, *Russkii narod*, pp. 431–2.

98. Kondrat'eva, *Metamorfozy sobstvennogo imeni*, s.v.

99. Toren, *Russkaia narodnaia meditsina*, p. 75; also listed with this meaning under *plakun* and *alyi plakun* in *Slovar' Priamur'ia* as a medicinal plant for heart complaints and fright.

100. *Golubinnaia kniga*, p. 39.

101. D'iachenko, *Polnyi tserkovno-slavianskii slovar'*, s.v. *plakun-trava*.

102. *Domostroi*, 1990, p. 237, gives the time of gathering as sunset on 1 August.

103. Dal', *Slovar'*, s.v. *plakat'*, also states that the plant is supposed to make demons and witches weep.

104. Sakharov, *Skazaniia*, pp. 88–92.

105. Markevich, *Obychai* (reprint, p. 117). A cross made of the plant will make the whole world fear you.

106. Skrynnikov, *Gosudarstvo i tserkov'*, p. 139.

107. Kostomarov, *Ocherk*, p. 197; *Domostroi*, 1990, p. 237.

108. Zabylin, *Russkii narod*, p. 433.

109. Markevich, *Obychai* (reprint, p. 117).

110. Sakharov, *Skazaniia*, pp. 88–92.

111. Dal', *Tolkovyi slovar'*, s.v. *gremet'*.

112. Sakharov, *Skazaniia*, pp. 88–92.

113. Dal', *Tolkovyi slovar'*, s.vv. *netron'*, *razryv*.

114. See Smirnov, 'Èpika Poles'ia', nos. 66, 67. Recorded in the Poles'e region of the Ukraine.

115. Strizhev, *Kalendar'*, p. 271.

116. *Domostroi*, 1990, p. 238.

117. Foust, *Rhubarb*.

118. *Domostroi*, 1990, p. 238. Note on p. 296 identifies this as *Glechoma hederacea*.

119. Zabylin, *Russkii narod*, p. 409.

120. Originally in the *Protoevangelium of James*: see Index for other occurrences.

121. Kondrat'eva, *Metamorfozy sobstvennogo imeni*, s.v.

122. See Afanas'ev, *Poèticheskie vozzreniia*, II, pp. 421–2.

123. Semenov, *Travels in the Tian'-Shan'*, p. 13.

124. According to De Gubernatis, *La Mythologie des plantes*, I, p. 291, quoting Rogovich, this plant is *Pulsatilla patiens* and has blue flowers which come out in April. Toren, *Russkaia narodnaia meditsina*, p. 79 gives *Pulsatilla pratensis*.

125. Sakharov, *Skazaniia*, pp. 88–92.

126. *Domostroi*, 1990, p. 238.

127. See Kivelson, 'Patrolling the Boundaries', p. 309.

128. Dal', *Tolkovyi slovar'*, s.vv. *strekat'*; *badiaga*.

129. Markevich, *Obychai* (reprint, p. 117).

130. Dal', *Tolkovyi slovar'*, s.v. *bad'ia*.

131. Sakharov, *Skazaniia*, pp. 88–92; Afanas'ev, *Poèticheskie vozzreniia*, III, pp. 458, 461.

132. See Zelenin, *Izbrannye trudy: Ocherki russkoi mifilogii, ad indicem*.

133. Zabylin, *Russkii narod*, p. 51.

134. Dal', *Tolkovyi slovar'*, s.v. *dukh*.

135. Andreev, *Russkii fol'klor*, p. 51.

136. Popov, *Russkaia narodno-bytovaia meditsina*, p. 54. Nine twigs are mentioned in the Anglo-Saxon 'Nine Herbs Spell': see Storms, *Anglo-Saxon Magic*, pp. 188–9.

137. Zmeev, *Russkie vrachebniki*, p. 72.

138. For a detailed survey of bread in Russian and East Slavonic beliefs see Strakhov, *Kul't khleba*, esp. ch. 2, section 4,1 on bread ladders.

139. Kititsina, 'Khleb', pp. 98–9; Strakhov, *Kul't khleba*.

140. Dal', *Tolkovyi slovar'*, s.v. *lestvitsa*.

141. See Vlasova, *Novaia abevega*, p. 27.

142. See also Strakhov, *Kul't khleba*, esp. ch. 1, section 5,1.

143. Afanas'ev, *Poèticheskie vozzreniia*, I, p. 120; Dal', *Tolkovyi slovar'*, s.v. *nogot'* (the nail clippings had to be saved and kept about one's person); Ralston, *Songs of the Russian People*, pp. 110–11; Frazer, *Folklore in the Old Testament*, II, p. 57. Beliefs in soul ladders are found in many parts of the world: ibid., pp. 52–8.

144. Zabylin, *Russkii narod*, p. 262; for similar Islamic beliefs in Iran see Donaldson, *Wild Rue*, pp. 185–6.

145. Perry, *The State of Russia*, pp. 196–7.

146. Zabylin, *Russkii narod*, p. 268.

147. Dal', *Tolkovyi slovar'*, s.v. *sorochka*. For widespread British beliefs in the caul as a luck amulet see Opie and Tatem, *Dictionary of Superstitions*, s.v. *caul*; Hazlitt, *Dictionary*, s.v. *caul*. According to a Kentucky belief infants born with a caul will have second sight: Thomas and Thomas, *Kentucky Superstitions*, no. 12.

148. Levin, 'Childbirth', p. 53, states that this practice could also apply to the placenta.

149. Ginzburg, *The Night Battles*, p. 163.

150. But against this see Klaniczay, 'Shamanistic Elements in Central European Witchcraft', where related beliefs in Central Europe and the Balkans and their possible common origin are described in detail.

151. See Forbes, *The Midwife and the Witch*, p. 102.

152. Duchesne in his edition of the *Stoglav*, p. 108, quotes the commentary of Balsamon on Rule 61 of the Trullan Synod (692), which tells of an abbot who wore a caul as an amulet against malicious gossip.

153. Ibid., pp. 101, 103.

154. Chikachev, *Russkie na Indigirke*, p. 116.

155. Zabylin, *Russkii narod*, p. 271.

156. Popov, *Russkaia narodno-bytovaia meditsina*, p. 189.

157. Popov, *Russkaia narodno-bytovaia meditsina*, p. 190.

158. Dal', *Tolkovyi slovar'*, s.v. *paskha*. Zabylin, *Russkii narod*, p. 53, mentions this as involving calf bones in Belorussia and Bulgaria.

159. Cherepnin, 'Iz istorii drevnerusskogo koldovstva', p. 88.

160. Danilov, *Drevnie rossiiskie stikhotvoreniia*, p. 154.

161. Dal', *Tolkovyi slovar'*, s.v. *zmii*.

162. Margeret, *The Russian Empire* (1607), p. 37, and n. 115. I quote from the modern English edition. The staff was apparently stolen by the Poles in 1611, cut up and distributed to mercenary soldiers.

163. For a photograph of a mounted narwhal horn from a German treasury see Lansmann and Kriss-Rettenbeck, *Amulett und Talisman*, p. 79. See also Massing, 'Ceremonial Staff' in *Circa 1492: Art in the Age of Exploration*, p. 126.

164. See Chambers, *A Renaissance Cardinal*, p. 164 and *passim*.

165. For some discussion of the unicorn in Slavonic literature and legend see Belova, 'Edinorog'.

166. See Vilinbakhov, *Gosudarstvennyi gerb Rossii*, pp. 28–32.

167. See Appleby, *A Selective Index*, pp. 28–33. In one recorded popular belief Rasputin cured the tsar's son with 'horn drops': Baranov: *Moskovskie legendy*, pp. 207–9.

168. Zabylin, *Russkii narod*, pp. 185–6.

169. Some are listed in the official inventories: see Zabelin, *Domashnii byt russkikh tsarits*, pp. 48 (in a

box, presumably therefore as a talisman); 54–5 (three valued at 215 roubles); 136 (white, with unicorn horn).

170. D'iachenko, *Polnyi tserkovno-slavianskii slovar'*, s.v. *bezar*.

171. Larin, *Russko-angliiskii slovar'-dnevnik*, p. 185. Larin gives no translation but presumably this is the *saika*, listed by Vasmer as a small fish in the Archangel region which is not eaten.

172. Zabylin, *Russkii narod*, p. 279. Vasmer, s.v. *pesok*, regards the word as a corruption of *peskar'*.

173. See Apuleius, *Apulei Apologia*, commentary, p. 84, n. 12; *Works of Apuleius*, p. 281.

174. For an interesting *tour d'horizon* of the subject, with particular reference to cowrie shells see Gobert, 'Le Pudendum magique'; also Andersen, *The Witch on the Wall*. D. Fraser, 'The Heraldic Woman', p. 81, discusses the notion that displayed female genitalia attracts good and repels evil. On the fish as a sexual symbol see Eisler, 'Der Fisch' (the Freudian interpretation) and the article by H. Bauman in the *Encyclopedia of World Art*, 12, NY and London, 1966, col. 895. For fish amulets and their sexual connotations see also Lansmann and Kriss-Rettenbeck, *Amulett und Talisman*, pp. 217–18.

175. See N.I. Tolstoi, 'vykhodila potaskukha v chem mat' rodila', *Zhivaia starina*, 1994, 4, pp. 6–7.

176. British Library MS Arundel 201, published in Schmitz, *Bussbücher*, I, p. 459.

177. Nikiforovskii, *Prostonarodnye primety i pover'ia*, p. 275.

178. Cherepnin, 'Iz istorii drevnerusskogo koldovstva XVII v.', p. 87.

179. See Barb, 'Birds and Medical Magic', pp. 316–22. For a note on its use as an amulet in England see *Proceedings of the Society of Antiquaries*, second ser., XXII, 1909, pp. 516–17 and Hazlitt, *Dictionary*, s.v. *aetites*.

180. *Lastochkin kamen', lastovik, lastochnik*: see Dal', *Tolkovyi slovar'*, s.v. *lastitsa*.

181. Cherepnin, 'Iz istorii drevnerusskogo koldovstva', p. 88.

182. Ibid., p. 88.

183. Zabylin, *Russkii narod*, p. 407.

184. Vinogradov, *Zagovory*, p. 33. For an essay on bird's hearts and the sexual organs of animals as an ingredient in Russian love potions see Kliaus, 'Serdtsa ptits i polovye organy zhivotnykh'.

185. Zabylin, *Russkii narod*, p. 262. Afanas'ev, *Narodnye russkie legendy*, Moscow, 1859, p 13.

186. Popov, *Russkaia narodno-bytovaia meditsina*, p. 189.

187. Dal', *Slovar'*, s.v. *kheruvim*.

188. Pliny, *Naturalis historia*, XXIV.14–15. The belief seems to be almost universal; for British beliefs, for example, see Opie and Tatem, *Dictionary*, s.v. *horseshoe, iron*.

189. Romanov, *Belorusskii sbornik*, p. 65.

190. For detailed discussion of Belorussian usage see Min'ko, *Sueveriia*, pp. 137–52.

191. Bolonev, 'O nekotorykh arkhaicheskikh elementakh', p. 70.

192. Bolonev, 'O nekotorykh arkhaicheskikh elementakh', p. 71.

193. For a Scottish example of this see Opie and Tatem, *Dictionary of Superstitions*, s.v. *corpse's washing water cures*.

194. Dead Sea water was apparently used by witches, probably as a 'water of death': see Graham, *With the Russian Pilgrims*, p. 198.

195. See Afanas'ev, *Poèticheskie vozzreniia slavian na prirodu*, esp. chapters 7, 16, and *passim*; Eleonskaia, 'Otgoloski drevnikh verovanii' on the literary and folklore ramifications of this idea, not least the phrase in the Acathistus to the Virgin: 'Rejoice, O most clear spring of life-giving water'. See also Ch. 15, p. 402 and n. 60 on James Bruce.

196. Vlasova, *Novaia abevega*, pp. 9–10.

TEXTS AS AMULETS

1. *Introduction*

T
he amuletic use of books or texts is widespread in many cultures.[1] In
Russia there is no lack of examples of written spells which have to be
worn about the body, or in some cases eaten, to be efficacious.
Commonly these amulets were worn round the neck or attached to the pectoral
cross, itself an amulet to most people, but textual amulets could also be carried in
other ways. The English doctor and observer of the Russian scene in the late
eighteenth century Matthew Guthrie describes 'bands or frontlets of parchment'
containing some sentence as an antidote or charm and worn on the forehead. He
also considers the names of the Slav letters as a 'didactic phylactery' – this
presumably is a reference to the Slavonic didactic 'Alphabet Prayer' in which the
first words of successive lines begin with the successive letters of the alphabet and
have as a result become the 'names' of the letters (*az, buki, vedi*, etc.),[2] or possibly
to the didactic versions of the SATOR square (see below, section 8).[3] These and
other uses of the written word for magical purposes are discussed in other parts
of this book; in this chapter we shall for the most part be considering only texts
which were originally written as religious literature, mostly apocryphal, and were
later employed as amulets.

The number of apocryphal texts used as amulets is considerable: *The Tale of
Adam and Eve, About the Tree of the Cross, About Heaven, The Lament of Adam, Adam's
Letter, About the Head of Adam, The Dream of the Virgin, The Jerusalem Scroll (The Letter
of Jesus about Sunday), The Journey of the Virgin through Hell, The Twelve Fridays*.[4]
Minkh remarks that the practice comes from Byzantium and that the *Dream of the
Virgin* is the commonest. In fact it is clear from catalogues of Russian manuscript
collections that the very many copies of the *Dream of the Virgin* from the eighteenth
century to the present day more often than not also contain the *Jerusalem Scroll*
and the *Twelve Fridays*.[5]

2. *The Letters of Christ and Abgar*

Perhaps the oldest text used as an amulet in Russian is the apocryphal exchange of
letters between Christ and King Abgar of Edessa.[6] This was certainly known in late
Antiquity. Eusebius in his *Ecclesiastical History*[7] gives one version of it, and another
fourth-century account is in the Syriac *Didascalia Addai* where the final promise is
given that Edessa should never fall to an enemy: the fourth-century lady pilgrim
Egeria, in the account of her journey to Jerusalem, remarks that the letter is still
preserved at Edessa and that Abgar did indeed save his city from attack by the

Persians by holding up the letter at the city gates.[8] The additional element of the picture of Christ is found from the sixth century onwards in the Syriac version and Byzantine writers such as John Damascene (675–749), Theodore the Studite (759–826), and the thirteenth-century Byzantine ecclesiastical historian Nicephorus Callistus.[9] This story is the source of the well-known icon-type 'The Saviour not made by human hands' (*nerukotvornyi*).[10] A sixteenth-century Russian version of the Abgar story was published by Tikhonravov in 1863;[11] in a footnote he says that this is a canonical work (as indeed it was often thought to be in some parts of the Christian world, in particular in the Orthodox churches),[12] which is included in indexes of prohibited books because of apocryphal accretions and because it was worn round the neck by superstitious people.[13]

To summarize the story: Abgar, king of Edessa sends to Luke the scribe and icon-painter and orders him to go to Jerusalem to paint an image of Christ. He meets Jesus who takes Luke's towel and impresses it with his face. He gives the towel to Thaddeus and sends him to Edessa with this image. A fiery column marks the place where Thaddeus rests and leaves an impression of Christ's face on a stone. The townspeople take this stone to the town and the blind, lame and lepers were healed by touching it. Eventually they come to Abgar who is healed of his gout. He sends a letter to Christ saying: we have heard how you cure without magic or herbs (potions); by your voice alone the lame walk and the deaf hear, lepers are cleansed, evil spirits are driven out by a word, and long-standing illnesses; the woman with an issue of blood was cured by touching the hem of your robe, and you have raised the dead. Either you are God come down from Heaven or you are the son of God. Come to me to heal here for I have heard that the Jews are murmuring against you and wish to kill you. Jesus sends a reply by Ananias the scribe blessing Abgar and promising health but saying he cannot come because of his imminent death and ascension.

Then follows a passage promising that anyone who wears this letter will be protected from all evil and illness, for it was written by the hand of the Saviour. The letter must be read three times with great reverence over a sick person with a prayer. The letter is sealed with seven seals (F T Kh E U R D : each of these letters is then given an interpretation). Then further instructions are given for an amulet made up of the various names for Christ very similar to another apocryphon, the *Seventy Names of God* (see below).

The nature of the Abgar story itself presumably prompted its use as a primarily medical amulet and magic prayer. The use of the letter of Christ to Abgar as an amulet in Bulgaria and Serbia is also well attested,[14] and a Bulgarian book actually called *The Abagar of Philip Stanislavov* was printed in Rome in 1651 and was used as an amulet.[15]

3. *The Seventy(-Two) Names of God*

As its name would suggest, this is a kind of litany of seventy (or seventy-two) names of God, usually followed by the same number for the Virgin.[16] Preceding the main text is a passage: 'If you read these you will be unconquered in battle and safe from all foes and sudden death and terror of the night and the deeds of Satan.' The theme of this amulet is fairly common: Jewish spells from the Cairo Genizah invoke the seventy names of God,[17] a Latin spell against fevers in Anglo-Saxon England conjures the fevers 'per septuaginta nomina dei sancta et immaculata'.[18] A French Cathar specialist, René Nelli, described a very similar prayer current in Languedoc from the twelfth to the twentieth century. It includes Greek and Hebrew words, and Nelli notes that it occurs in the so-called *Grimoire of Pope Honorius* and relates it, rather vaguely, to Cabalistic tradition.[19] An Armenian amulet also lists the seventy-two magical names of God.[20] In view of its date (it is not known before the sixteenth century) the Russian text is most probably of either West European or Byzantine origin, although the ultimate source is claimed by Gaster to be Hebrew.[21] The seventy(-two) names of God are certainly linked with other uses of seventy and seventy-two in magico-medical contexts such as the seventy-two veins, joints, or sinews, and the seventy-two illnesses, which occur in Greek and Slavonic spells and false prayers.

4. *The Letter to St Nicholas / St Peter*

This is the famous *Letter to St Nicholas* (in some versions to St Peter) which was placed in the right hand of Russian corpses about to be buried and which so intrigued foreign visitors to Russia. Travel accounts in several languages mention this letter: Richard Chancellor, who wrote an account of his voyage to Muscovy in 1553 (first published in Richard Hakluyt's *Principal Navigations* in 1589), notes that:

> . . . when any man dieth amongst them, they take the dead body and put it in a coffin or chest, and in the hand of the corpse they put a little scroll, and in the same there are these words written, that the man died a Russe of Russes, having received the faith and died in the same. The writing or letter they say they send to St Peter, who, receiving it as they affirm, reads it and by and by admits him into heaven . . .[22]

Giles Fletcher, writing a little later, in his *Of the Russe Common Wealth* (1591), asserts:

> About their burials also they have many superstitious and profane ceremonies: as putting within the finger of the corpse a letter to Saint Nicholas, whom they make their chief mediator, and as it were, the porter of heaven gates, as the papists do their Peter.[23]

It was no doubt on these sources that the poet John Milton relied when he included the same story in his *Brief History of Muscovia* (London, 1682).

In 1618–19 the chaplain of the Muscovy Company, Richard James, wrote a dictionary and phrasebook of the Russian language which he heard in Archangel;

it too records this story with the variant details that it is a favour granted only to the clergy, except in Lithuania where it is also given to the magnates and distinguished soldiers, and that the letter is addressed to SS. Peter and Paul.[24]

Adam Olearius, the diplomat from Holstein in the 1630s and '40s quotes the text of the letter as:

> We whose names are hereunto subscribed, the Patriarch or Metropolitan, and Priest of the city of . . . do make known and certify, by these presents, that the bearer of these our letters has always lived among us like a good Christian, professing our Greek religion; and though he has committed some sins, yet that he has confessed the same, and that thereupon he has received absolution for the remission of his sins: That he has honoured God and his saints; that he has said his prayers, and that he has fasted on the hours and days appointed by the church, and that he has carried himself so well toward me, who am his confessor, that I have no reason to complain of him, nor to deny him the absolution of his sins. In witness whereof, we have given him the present testimonial to the end that upon sight thereof, St Peter may open unto him the gate of eternal bliss.[25]

Samuel Collins, the tsar's English physician, in his version of the story (1671) says that this a letter from the local bishop to St Nicholas describing the life and behaviour of the dead man,[26] Jean Struys, in 1681, describes the letter as being signed and also sealed,[27] and both Peter Henry Bruce and John Perry, writing in the early eighteenth century, add that this is a certificate that the man is a Christian and should be admitted to heaven.[28] This view is also maintained by a French visitor to Russia in the same period, Jacques Jubé, who properly objects that 'passport' is a misnomer and it should rather be called a 'certificate of Christianity'. He adds the interesting detail that, according to Baronius, it was Vladimir I of Kiev (c. 956–1015), canonized by the Russian Church for making Christianity the state religion of Kiev Rus', who introduced this custom of the 'passport' as a way of preventing his subjects from relapsing into paganism.[29] By 1733 the practice was recorded pictorially in an engraving by Bernard Picart in the *Cérémonies et coutumes religieuses de tous les peuples du monde* (Amsterdam, 1733) (Fig. 13).

By the late eighteenth century these letters were being printed, with a blank space left for the name of the deceased; one such was obtained in 1781 as a curio by Thomas Dimsdale, the Quaker doctor who became physician to Catherine the Great, and survives in the Dimsdale family collection (Fig. 14).[30] Its text is much the same as that reported by Olearius.[31]

The custom was followed at all levels of society including the nobility and the tsar himself. In 1674 after the death of Tsar Aleksei Mikhailovich there was a dispute between the Patriarch and the tsar's chaplain as to which of them had the right to place the letter in the corpse's hand,[32] a matter of protocol which seems to have been dealt with in the eighteenth century by a division of labour:

Richardson describes how, at the funeral of Princess Kurakin, the princess's confessor handed the scroll to the bishop, who read it aloud, and then returned it to the confessor who placed it solemnly in the right hand of the dead princess. In an appendix Richardson gives a translation of the scroll: it is an unexceptionable prayer which, he says, has been 'ludicrously represented as a passport to be delivered to St Peter'.[33] Lady Rondeau, writing of the 1730s, describes the funeral of the youngest daughter of Prince Menshikov, Peter the Great's favourite, at which the same custom was observed.[34]

In fact the custom of placing a penitential prayer in the right hand of a corpse was, and is, part of the Russian Orthodox burial ceremony. But the notion that it was a 'passport' is too regularly noted by foreigners to be just a traveller's tale, and in any case the terms *propusk* (a pass) and *podorozhnaia* (an official order for post-horses – see Dal', *Tolkovyi slovar'*, s.v.) popularly applied to it in Russian shows that it certainly acquired an uncanonical colouring. An anonymous Protestant pamphlet of 1725, *Curieuse Nachricht . . .* , claims that Peter I had abolished the custom of the passport to St Nicholas.[35] If this is so, then clearly it was only the addressee and the more superstitious elements of the letter which were removed. The most recent notable example of the custom seems to have been at the funeral of Alexander III in 1894 (i.e. the last proper funeral of a tsar – the next and last tsar, Nicholas II, was disposed of uncanonically by the Bolsheviks), according to the reports in the English press at the time.[36]

The custom no doubt seemed to the English and other foreign writers a quaint practice typical of a barbarous land. In fact, by the time it had made its way into *The Turkish Spy*[37] it had become one of the standard humorous stories about Russia which tended to crop up particularly in the pseudo-oriental epistolary romances of the seventeenth and eighteenth centuries. This was not entirely unreasonable of foreigners since even a distinguished modern Russian scholar of popular religion regards the custom as one exclusive to Russia. Uspenskii in his account of the 'passport' traces its origin to the beginnings of Russian monastic life in the Kiev Monastery of the Caves, and states that the letter was probably originally a prayer by St Feodosii, founder of the monastery in the eleventh century. He adds that the prayer in current use for this purpose is taken from the liturgy of St James, and was probably introduced in the seventeenth-century reforms of the Patriarch Nikon.[38] But few customs are unique and in fact similar pious fictions have existed, perhaps still exist, in parts of the Western Church in the form of *Breve* or *Schutzbriefen*.[39] And we may also cite by way of analogy the story of St Vincent Ferrer, who wrote such a letter for a dying sinner and had the satisfaction of a letter in reply, signed by the Holy Trinity and delivered by air.[40] An analogous Islamic custom is also recorded, in which verses from the Koran are written on the winding sheet of a corpse as proof that the man was a true believer.[41] Since both Christians and Muslims regard God as omniscient, these written *aide-memoires* to a busy deity can have at best only the status of pious practice, and would certainly have been thought of as amulets by many.

5. *The* Dream of the Virgin

This is the most commonly found text amulet in Russia, but perhaps also one of the most recent. It is probably of medieval Latin origin;[42] it is known in several languages and may well have come to Russia from Poland,[43] perhaps via Belorussia where it was known from the sixteenth century,[44] and it was also well known in the Balkans and in Rumania.[45]

Not surprisingly, there are very many recorded examples, of which the latest I have seen is dated 1972.[46] Versions have been published or described by Veselovskii, Pypin, Karskii, Franko, and Minkh.[47]

The *Dream of the Virgin*, although deriving from a literary source, is not in fact a single text but essentially a story expressed in a variety of styles, and with varying local features. It may take the form of a dialogue of Jesus and Mary in which the latter confides that she had slept in Bethlehem (or Jerusalem) in a cave, or on an altar (sometimes even the day of the month is mentioned), and there she had a dream in which she foresees the passion and death of her son, a dream which Jesus explains to her. Alternatively the story may launch straight into the telling of the dream. Frequently the *Dream* contains other Biblical, apocryphal or folklore motifs (the Tree of the Cross, the river Jordan, the Isle of Buian). Normally the *Dream* ends with a list of promised benefits to those who keep, or read, or wear a copy of the text.

The version published by Pypin is fairly modern (no source is given) with Russian localisms and includes apocryphal elements such as the three trees which made up the wood of the Cross.[48] It promises that:

1. Anyone who writes down the dream and keeps it reverently at home will keep his home safe;
2. Anyone who wears it on a journey will be safe from thunder, war, storms and the devil;
3. Anyone who wears it in the forest will be safe from the woodsprite (*leshii*), snakes and unclean spirits;
4. Anyone who wears it at sea will be safe from drowning and the Devil;
5. Anyone who wears it before the tsar or important person will be safe from death and unjust judges and will always be the winner in court;
6. Anyone who goes to be married and wears it will be safe from evil men and spirits;
7. If a pregnant woman has difficulties in childbirth read it over her three times and place it over her head and she will have a painless delivery;
8. If anyone is ill or cannot sleep read it over him three times and place it over his head and he will be safe from illness and insomnia and will have a long life;
9. If anyone is dying without a priest, read it over him three times and place it over his head and then put it into the grave with him and he will go to heaven;

10. If anyone marries and wears it he will be safe from all evil men and
    enemies and no iron will wound him, nor will he be killed in battle;

11. This prayer, the Dream of the Virgin, was placed in the Holy of Holies in
    the holy apostolic church in Jerusalem and sealed by the fourth Patriarch
    of Jerusalem. And it was read by Peter and Paul and Cosmas and Damian
    and sealed with the cross of heavenly height, the cross of earthly breadth,
    the cross of the beauty of the church, the cross of the depth of the sea, the
    cross of praise of angels and archangels, the cross of the tsar's power,
    the cross of the confirmation of the faithful, the cross of the community of
    the Orthodox, the cross of help to me, servant of God, the cross of the
    curse on demons, the cross of victory over enemies, the cross of the
    expulsion of devils.

The Russian bibliophile Buslaev observed that the *Dream* was in every Russian
peasant home: it was carried everywhere as an amulet, especially when going to
court, or to comfort the dying; it was placed under the pillow of sick persons, and
it would bring a blessing to anyone who copied it nine times and gave it to nine
people (in other words an early version of the chain letter).[49] In the home it was
normally kept behind the icon case,[50] and, in Siberia, it would be taken out to
the fields and read out at the time of sowing the crops.[51] This fertility function
perhaps derives obscurely from the fact that the *Dream* promises benefits to those
about to marry, and to pregnant women, and was often placed beside women in
childbirth.[52]

Despite the innocuous nature of most versions of the *Dream of the Virgin*, it was
nevertheless an amulet and its possession could lead to trouble in court. In a *slovo
i delo* (treason) case in 1724 a certain Roman Krasnopol'skii was accused of
having a 'magic letter' for seducing women. He said that he had it from a
peasant, Moisei Churin. The letter was to be read over salt, which was then to be
put into kvas or food and given to the person desired. The peasant's hut was
searched and spells to be used when going before a judge, a paper listing which
days were lucky for travel, and a *Dream of the Virgin*, were found. In another case
before the Synodal court in 1770, part of the incriminating evidence found in
possession of a priest involved in an accusation of witchcraft was a magical
herbal, divinatory texts including the Tsar David text (see Ch. 10.10), illicit
prayers, and apocryphal texts including the *Dream of the Virgin*, one written by the
priest himself.[53]

Legal disapproval continued into the nineteenth century, and although there
seems to have been no difference between members of the official Orthodox
Church and the Old Believers in the use of this text, punishment for its
possession could be used as part of the periodic campaigns of harassment of
religious dissidents. The archive of the Tiumen' oblast' in Tobol'sk (Siberia)
contains a nineteenth-century copy of the *Dream of the Virgin* which has a note on
the cover stating that it was confiscated during an official search of the house of a
schismatic.[54]

The promise in one of the versions quoted above that the amulet would protect the wearer in battle is no doubt the reason why this text was popular with soldiers in both Russia and the Balkans. A curious work with the title *Letters to the Troops* appeared in St Petersburg in 1831. It was an attempt to persuade soldiers that their superstitious belief in visions, dreams, miracles and magic were against reason and good religion. Fortunately for the historian it describes, in what might have been thought to be unwisely specific detail, many of the practices it condemned. It gives a text of the *Dream of the Virgin* and instructions which read:

> If anyone keeps the Dream on his person he will go to heaven. If you keep it under your pillow or at your breast you will be safe from thieves and brigands and evil men and demons. If anyone does not believe in the Dream he will be anathema and prey to fevers of every kind and plague and blindness and deafness and eternal darkness.[55]

It also describes a case of a soldier who extracted large sums of money from some villagers by persuading them that he had had a vision of the Virgin Mary, and that she had given him the *Dream*.[56] The *Dream of the Virgin* in written form is often found in manuscripts which also contain one or more of the other texts mentioned here: the *Sunday Letter*, the *Twelve Fridays* and the *Golubinnaia kniga*; occasionally it is even conflated with elements of these texts and becomes itself a 'letter from heaven'.[57]

6. *The Letter of Jesus about Sunday (The Sunday Letter, Jerusalem Scroll, Letter from Heaven)*

This text, perhaps of Latin origin in the fourth or fifth century, is found in many versions in many languages both eastern and western, often together with the *Dream of the Virgin*, and sometimes with elements of the *Twelve Fridays* text.[58] In Anglo-Saxon England too this letter was used as an amulet and the method of its application was similar to that employed with many Russian talismans: 'if the evil is internal sing it over water, give him to drink . . . If it is external sing it on fresh butter and anoint the body with it'.[59]

Russian versions exist of both the first and second Greek recensions.[60] A Russian version published Pypin,[61] tells how a stone fell in Jerusalem and the Patriarch and congregation prayed over it for three days and nights. Then the stone opened to reveal a letter which rehearsed some Bible history, called for repentance for sins (which included speaking Hebrew!) and keeping Sunday holy as a fast day, and prescribed reading the letter on Sundays and feastdays. The cult of days of the week, sometimes disguised as saints (in particular St Paraskeva), is probably behind the popularity of this kind of amuletic text. It was sufficiently known among the Slavs to warrant tracts against it.

Malov's *Letter to the Troops* quoted in the previous section notes that there is a curse on anyone not paying for his copy of the *Sunday Letter*, a sure sign that the text was being used by confidence tricksters.[62]

One version has the note:

This holy letter, written by Our Lord in Hebrew in golden letters was found near Jerusalem and was interpreted by a seven-year-old orphan boy who up to that time had never spoken. It must be given to anyone who wants to copy it and a curse will be on anyone who hides it away for himself.[63]

Another version adds that the letter was in the tomb of Jesus in Jerusalem and the Pope of Rome sent it to his brother the king to help him against his enemy. It offers a forty-day indulgence and easy childbirth, day and night protection from serpents and from the Devil Iscariot.[64] This appears to be a conflation with the Charlemagne letter known in the West.[65] A Ukrainian version of this, designed to be worn as an amulet, states that it was found 'in the British land on the Mount of Olives'![66]

7. *The Twelve Fridays*

The text known as the *Twelve Fridays* has been mentioned several times above. It is both a set of instructions for serial devotions with their rewards and in itself an amulet. It exists in many forms including that of the 'religious song' and the various versions of it usually claim the authorship of Eleutherius or Clement of Rome.[67] It has a longer history in Russian than the *Dream of the Virgin* and its dubious status as a religious text is perhaps demonstrated by the fact that the monk-encyclopedist Efrosin in the early fifteenth century copied it with the advice that it should not be shown to everyone (something of a *topos* in 'secret' literature).[68] Afanas'ev states that in some Old Believer communities a tale about the Twelve Fridays acquired the status of Scripture.[69] It has a well-known analogue in the popular Catholic practice in the West, the nine First Fridays (associated with St Margaret Mary Alacoque and the devotion to the Sacred Heart of Jesus, which began in the seventeenth century).

In Russia in 1831 the *Letters to the Troops* tells us that it promises that if you fast:

on the first Friday you will be safe from sudden death, fire and water; on the second Friday you will be safe from murder and have all your sins forgiven; on the third Friday you will be safe from every enemy, will overcome any wizard, and will not be bitten by mad dogs; on the fourth Friday you will have a hundred-fold harvest and be safe from drowning; on the fifth Friday you will have a son if so far you have achieved only a daughter; on the sixth Friday you will be safe from headache, toothache and stroke; on the seventh Friday you will be saved from hell, have good horses and easy childbirth; on the eighth Friday you will have an obedient wife, beautiful children, and no *iazva* [this word may mean an ulcer, plague or the Evil Eye]; on the ninth Friday you will win in court cases, overcome the rich, remain unwounded in battle; on the tenth Friday your name will be inscribed on the throne of the Blessed Virgin, and angels will take your soul to heaven; on the eleventh Friday you will die without pain; on the twelfth Friday you will know all secrets and be inscribed on the staff of Moses.[70]

It will be noted that this comprehensive list of benefits suits both sexes and covers most preoccupations of village folk of a religious disposition. It is perhaps odd that the list should itself should have acquired amuletic status, almost as if the instructions on the label of the medicine bottle were thought to possess the same properties as the medicine. The actual practice of fasting for twelve Fridays in order to gain the listed advantages was condemned in Peter the Great's *Spiritual Regulation* in 1721, together with other beliefs relating to Friday.

The exact Fridays to be observed in this practice are not usually specified, but they are supposed to be consecutive. Afanas'ev in his study of Russian legends, however, gives a list: the Fridays are the one before the Annunciation, the first and tenth after the Ascension, the Fridays before Trinity, the Dormition, Elijah's day, the Decollation of St John, the Exaltation of the Cross, the Pokrov, the Presentation of the Virgin in the Temple, Christmas, and the Baptism of Christ (Epiphany).[71] Almost all the respondents in the Tenishev survey of folk customs and beliefs at the end of the nineteenth century mentioned this text as being common in Russian households.[72]

The use of the Twelve Fridays text as an amulet may be associated with the use of a prayer to 'St Friday' as an amulet against illness – for this and other beliefs relating to Friday as a saint see Ch. 14.8.

8. *The SATOR Square*

The words SATOR AREPO TENET OPERA ROTAS if written in a column form a palindromic magic square'.[73] They are sometimes found in reverse order, and since this is the form found at Dura Europos, this may be the older form. The square is also found in many garbled forms and in several scripts (Latin, Greek, Hebrew, Coptic, Cyrillic).

There is a very large literature on the subject, the greater part of it devoted to finding an origin and meaning for the words, and the sum of the evidence to date puts its date at some time before Christ, if one leans towards the Mithraic, Jewish, or Egyptian interpretations, or in the Christian era if one accepts the once widely held explanation that it is an early Christian anagram of 'Pater noster' with the addition of alpha and omega.

In magical and popular religious literature and practice there has been a colorful profusion of imaginative uses of the letters in the square as a talisman:[74] in Anglo-Saxon England it was a charm for pregnant women;[75] in Serbia an antidote to the bite of a mad dog; on Ethiopic crosses the five wounds of Christ;[76]

in Coptic a febrifuge amulet associated with the nails on the Cross;[77] in Cappadocia the names of the shepherds who worshipped the infant Jesus;[78] in Jewish magical texts the pentacle of Saturn and a love charm;[79] in Byzantine and early modern Greek it may occur in magical texts[80] or as the names of five of the forty martyrs of Sebaste;[81] in Germany it exists in many guises including that of a talisman to put out fires (see below n. 97); in Brazil it was employed against snakebite, ghosts, witches, and many ailments and misfortunes;[82] in the United States of America in the last century (and quite possibly still) one chapbook recommended it as a fire precaution, detector of witches, a specific against sorcery, pestilence and foul air, and good for cows.[83]

In Russian and South Slavonic manuscripts the SATOR square is common. It has been discussed briefly by Sobolevskii,[84] and, in its late printed form, by Rovinskii.[85] More recently individual specimens have been examined by Pennington[86] and Van den Baar.[87] The Russian versions, which date from the sixteenth century onwards, are often called 'The Seal of Solomon the Most Wise'. Some add an acrostic interpretation – a sentence for each letter containing a Biblical sentiment beginning with that letter and an attribution, either 'The Interpretation of the Most Wise Leo the Greek Tsar' or 'The Interpretation of the Holy Fathers'.

Very commonly these squares are found in manuscript miscellanies containing calendars, or divinatory texts, some with Jewish associations. One clearly links the five words with the legend of the tree of the Cross (in which Solomon figures) and the nails with which Christ was nailed to the Cross (left and right hands and feet).[88] One sixteenth-century specimen notes that it is copied from a translation of Gennadii, Archbishop of Novgorod at the end of the fifteenth century, i.e. the churchman involved in computing new paschal tables at the end of the 'seventh millennium', who was interested in acrostics, had links with men such as Dmitrii Gerasimov and Nicolaus of Lübeck who were interested in astrology, and was involved in combatting the Judaizer heresy.[89]

It is not clear from most of these texts whether the square was thought to have magical properties, but other evidence shows that it certainly was used as an amulet. One Serbian version adds the note: these words are [a cure] for a mad dog [bite]';[90] another nineteenth-century Serbian version, written by a priest, says that it is to be written on dough, cooked and eaten as a remedy for various medical conditions including the bite of a mad dog;[91] the same procedure is recommended in a nineteenth-century Belorussian spell.[92] Yet another Serbian version says that SATOR, etc. is a cure for toothache if you say ABRACADABRA three times first;[93] one study of nineteenth-century Russian folk medicine notes a charm very similar to an English one,[94] which involves writing the SATOR square three times on paper while saying the Jesus prayer – the paper is then to be eaten or sewn into a *ladanka* amulet for wearing.[95] Speranskii in his study of Russian folk literature notes that the square called 'Seal of Solomon' is used as an amulet against fevers.[96] Rovinskii says that in Russian belief the SATOR spell is so strong that if you write it on a plate and throw it into a fire, the flames will immediately be extinguished (this is possibly a practice imported from Germany where SATOR talismans, *Feuerteller*, were used for the same purpose);[97] this was probably as effective as the fire-extinguishing icon of St Nicholas described elsewhere, or the practice of stripping naked and running three times round the fire with a piece of communion bread in your mouth.[98] In a seventeenth-century Russian miscellany, after a set of Paschal tables, there is a SATOR inscription followed by the statement 'This seal, I, Feofan, archimandrite of the holy mountain of Athos, wrote while in prison' (presumably he thought of it as a charm for achieving freedom);[99] the early nineteenth-century Russian *Letter to the Troops*, which was intended as an antidote to superstition in the army, says 'Many sew the seal of Solomon on their pillows or tie it to their crosses, and one miser made it in steel and sealed all his trunks with it in the belief that neither thieves nor the evil spirit would touch it'.[100] The square may also have been used for a different kind of magic if we are to believe Sakharov's dismissive statement, perhaps based on no more than ignorance, that SATOR was used by witches in the villages to conjure up spirits and only they know what the words mean.[101]

Notes

1. On books as magical objects see most recently the papers of a Wolfenbüttl symposium largely devoted to the subject: *Das Buch als magisches und als Repräsentationsobjekt*, 1992. Individual papers in this volume are cited elsewhere.

2. For texts and history, with German summary, see Kuev, *Azbuchnita molitva*.

3. Guthrie, *Noctes Rossicae*, f. 39.

4. This list is given in Minkh, 'Narodnye obychai', p. 51; I have not found recorded cases of the use of all these texts as amulets.

5. See Deletant, 'Sunday Legend' for the same practice elsewhere. For details of texts and bibliography see de Santos Otero, *Die handschriftliche Überlieferung*, s.vv.

6. For texts and bibliography see de Santos Otero, *Die handschriftliche Überlieferung*, pp. 149–57.

7. *PG*, 20, 121–4.

8. See Wilkinson, *Egeria's Travels*, pp. 116–17, and an English text of the letters in the Eusebian version, with comment, at pp. 151–2.

9. See Dobschütz, *Christusbilder*, pp. 102–96. The most recent account of the history of the image is Cameron, 'The History of the Image of Edessa'. Professor Cameron argues that the icon story must be post-544 since it is not mentioned by Procopius.

10. In fact it has several variants of which the commonest are: 'wet-beard' (a Russian type with a pointed beard) and 'on a towel'. For the legends concerning this icon see Pokrovskii, *Siiskii ikonopisnyi podlinninik*, I, pp. 49–52.

11. Tikhonravov, *Pamiatniki*, II, pp. 11–17: text of MS Moscow, Russian State Library, Sin. 558, f. 7v, 16th c.

12. See Cabrol, *Dictionnaire*, II, cols 1807–10. This article notes that the Abgar letter was often found in conjunction with the SATOR square and was used as late as the eighteenth century in England as an amulet to protect houses.

13. This practice was indeed specifically condemned in the indexes of false books: see Kobiak, 'Indeks lozhnykh knig', p. 63.

14. Der Nersessian, 'La Légende d'Abgar'; Radojčić, 'Srpski Abagar'.

15. *Abagar na Filip Stanislavov*, Rim, 1651. A version of this edition, without the commentary, is printed as a roll and placed in a round leather case, presumably to emphasize its former amuletic function. For an Armenian version see Feydit, *Amulettes de l'Arménie chrétienne*, pp. 281–4.

16. Tikhonravov, *Pamiatniki*, II, pp. 339–44. Text of MS Moscow, Russian State Library, Mosk. Dukh. Akad. 181/554, ff. 292–7, 16–17th c.

17. Schiffmann and Swartz, *Hebrew and Aramaic Incantation Texts*, pp. 115, 151.

18. Storms, *Anglo-Saxon Magic*, p. 295.

19. Nelli, 'La Prière aux soixante-douze noms de Dieu'.

20. Feydit, *Amulettes de l'Arménie chrétienne*, pp. 99–104.

21. Gaster, 'Zur Quellenkunde deutschen Sagen und Märchen', pp. 203–4. Gaster quotes the *Sefer Raziel*. More recently on the ramifications of this subject see Dan, 'The Seventy Names of Metatron'. See also Gaster, 'The Sword of Moses', p. 8, on the seventy-two words or letters in the ineffable name of God. See also Izmirlieva, 'The Aetiology of the Seventy-Two Diseases' which appeared as this book was going to press, and A. Schimmel, *The Mystery of Numbers*, New York, 1993, pp. 263–8.

22. Quoted in the edition of Berry and Crummey, *Rude and Barbarous Kingdom*, p. 38.

23. Ibid., p. 235.

24. Larin, *Russko-angliiskii slovar'-dnevnik Richarda Dzhemsa*, p. 113.

25. Olearius, *Voyages and Travells*, pp. 290–1.

26. Collins, *The Present State of Russia*, p. 21.

27. Struys, *Les Voyages de Jean Struys en Muscovie . . .*, p. 138.

28. Bruce, *Memoirs*, p. 120; Perry, *The State of Russia*, p. 231.

29. Jubé, *La Religion des Moscovites*, pp. 84, 161. I have been unable to locate any such assertion by Baronius.

30. Dimsdale Collection, no. 90. Made available by the courtesy of Mr Robert Dimsdale.

31. Baroness Dimsdale gives a translation of it in the journal of her visit to St Petersburg in 1781: see Cross, *A Lady at the Court of Catherine the Great*, pp. 60–1.

32. Uspenskii, *Filologicheskie razyskaniia*, pp. 124–5.

33. Richardson, *Anecdotes of the Russian Empire*, pp. 115, 128.

34. Lady Jane Rondeau, *Letters from a Lady who Resided some Years in Russia*, London, 1775, quoted from Cross, *Russia under Western Eyes*, p. 178.

35. For this and other details of the subject see Uspenskii, *Filologicheskie razyskaniia*, pp. 122–5. Uspenskii also draws attention to a frequent confusion of the functions of St Peter and St Nicholas in Russian popular religion (pp. 125–7).

36. *Daily Telegraph*, Nov. 20, 1894 and *The Spectator*, Nov. 24, 1894, p. 733.

37. Giovanni Paolo Marana, *L'Esploratore Turco*. In the third volume of the English version it is stated that the spy knew, among other languages, Sclavonian: *The Third Volume of Letters written by a Turkish Spy*, London, 1691, preface.

38. Uspenskii, *Filologicheskie razyskaniia*, pp. 124–5.

39. See *Handwörterbuch des deutschen Aberglaubens*, s.v. *Schutzbriefen*. A fine eighteenth-century German example is published in Hansmann and Kriss-Rettenbeck, *Amulett und Talisman*, p. 127.

40. Brewer, *A Dictionary of Miracles*, pp. 436–7.

41. Donaldson, *Wild Rue*, p. 72.

42. de Santos Otero, *Die handschriftliche Überlieferung*, I, p. 196. For the most detailed study see Veselovskii, 'Opyty po istorii razvitiia khristiánskoi legendy, II'.

43. Pypin, *Lozhnye i otrechennye knigi*, III, p. 128, publishes a Polish version.

44. Lastoŭski, *Hystoriia belaruskaĭ (kryŭskaĭ) knig*, p. 636. For several versions, in prose and verse, see Romanov, *Belorusskii sbornik*, pp. 235–55. For five *dukhovnye stikhi* versions see Shein, *Materialy dlia izucheniia byta*, II, pp. 612–27, and for one short version serving as a spell against the Evil Eye see Shein, *Materialy*, pp. 532–3.

45. Gaster, 'Rumanian Popular Legends of the Lady Mary', and Tailliez, 'La Vierge dans la littérature populaire roumaine', pp. 286–8 ('La lettre et la songe de la Vierge'). The *Dream* was very popular in the Balkans where it is still current; see Kretzenbacher, 'Südost-Überlieferung zum Apokryphen "Traum Mariens"'.

46. See *Oberegi i zaklinaniia russkogo naroda*, pp. 40–2. This is from the Pinega region near the White Sea. The same anthology contains two other versions.

47. Veselovskii, 'Opyty po istorii razvitiia khristiánskoi legendy. II'; Pypin, *Lozhnye i otrechennye knigi*, pp. 126–8; Karskii, *Belorusi*, pp. 48–9; Franko, *Apokrifi i legendy*, IV, pp. 79–80; Minkh, 'Narodnye obychai', pp. 61–7. Minkh gives several variants of the *Dream of the Virgin* including one in verse (pp. 61–7). The variants in verse are *dukhovnye stikhi*, the 'spiritual verses' which used to be sung in Russia by itinerant groups of usually blind beggars.

48. Pypin, *Lozhnye i otrechennye knigi*, pp. 125–8. On the three trees which make up the wood of the Cross, an element of several apocryphal texts and often associated with Solomon, Seth and the oil of life, etc, see de Santos Otero, *Die handschriftliche Überlieferung*, II, pp. 129–47 for bibliography, and for magical connotations Mansikka, *Über russische Zauberformeln*, passim.

49. Buslaev, *Moi dosugi*, 46, 1911, pp. 112–13.

50. Sumtsov, 'Kul'turnye perezhivaniia', 5–6, p. 449.

51. Gromyko, *Trudovye traditsii*.

52. Veselovskii, 'Opyty', II, p. 345.

53. *Opisanie dokumentov i del*, L (1770), 1914, no. 322.

54. Dergacheva-Skop and Romodanovskaia, 'Sobranie rukopisnykh knig Gosudarstvennogo arkhiva Tiumenskoi oblasti v Tobol'ske', p. 119, no. 62.

55. Malov, *Pis'ma k voinam*, ch. 1, pp. 74–9.

56. Ibid., p. 41.

57. Veselovskii, 'Opyty po istorii razvitiia khristiánskoi legendy, II', pp. 350–1.

58. See *Slovar' knizhnikov*, I, s.v. *Epistoliia Iisusa Khrista o nedele*. This notes the wide variety of types of this text and its popularity in the Ukraine and Belorussia. See also Romanov, *Belorusskii sbornik*, pp. 255–61. For an exhaustive survey of the *Sunday Letter* text in Europe see Deletant, 'The Sunday Legend'. For an Armenian version see Feydit, *Amulettes de l'Arménie chrétienne*, p. 341. For contemporary use in Greece, apparently in printed brochure form, see Hart, *Time, Religion*, p. 155. For Germany and general comments see *Handwörterbuch des deutschen Aberglaubens*, s.v. *Himmelsbrief*.

59. Storms, *Anglo-Saxon Magic*, p. 273.

60. For texts and bibliography see de Santos Otero, *Die handschriftliche Überlieferung*, I, pp. 158–69.

61. Pypin, *Lozhnye i otrechennye knigi*, pp. 150–3, and Tikhonravov, *Pamiatniki*, II, pp. 314–22.

62. Malov, *Pis'ma k voinam*, ch. 1, p. 85. For variants see Dal', *Poslovitsy*, 1989, I, p. 36.

63. Minkh, 'Narodnye obychai', p. 67.

64. Loc. cit.

65. On this see Gougaud, 'La Prière dite de Charlemagne'.

66. Dragomanov, *Malorusskie narodnie predaniia*, p. 168.

67. Tikhonravov, *Pamiatniki*, publishes four versions, including two from the fifteenth century, of which one is Serbian, and one nineteenth-century Old Believer version. For a *dukhovnyi stikh* version, not before the seventeenth century, see *Golubinnaia kniga*, pp. 189–93.

68. See Lur'e, *Russkie sovremenniki Vozrozhdeniia*, p. 69.

69. Afanas'ev, *Russkie narodnye legendy*, p. 85.

70. Malov, *Pis'ma k voinam*, ch. 1, pp. 82–5. For several Belorussian versions see Romanov, *Belorusskii sbornik*, pp. 264–71.

71. Afanas'ev, *Russkie narodnye legendy*, p. 85. Much the same list is given for the Ukraine: Markevich, *Obychai* (reprint, p. 64.)

72. Gromyko, *Traditsionnye normy*, p. 128.

73. The only book-length study is Moeller, *The Mithraic Origin and Meanings of the ROTAS-SATOR Square*. Its title makes its position clear and it suffers from excessive numerological enthusiasm. The most extensive analytical survey is Heinz Hoffmann, 'Satorquadrat'. Much of what is said in this section is examined in greater detail in Ryan, 'Solomon, SATOR, Acrostics, and Leo the Wise'. This discusses the Russian context and twenty-nine examples of the square. A further two mid-nineteenth-century examples of the explanatory version with Biblical texts have been published in *Russkii risovannyi lubok*, nos 46 and 79, the latter ascribed to Leo the Wise.

74. The earliest medallion amulet bearing SATOR is of the fourth or fifth century from Asia Minor. For illustrations of SATOR medallions see S. Seligman, 'Die Satorformel', and Hansmann and Kriss-Rettenbeck, *Amulett und Talisman*.

75. Storms, *Anglo-Saxon Magic*, p. 281. A late nineteenth-century English SATOR charm (from Somerset; its owner died in 1924) is recorded in Merrifield, *The Archaeology of Ritual and Magic*, pp. 142–5.

76. Hoffmann, 'Satorquadrat'.

77. Alcock, 'A Coptic Magical Text'.

78. Marquès-Rivière, *Amulettes, talismans et pantacles*, pp. 167–70.

79. Macgregor Mathers, *The Key of Solomon the King*, p. 67, and idem, *The Book of Sacred Magic of Abra-Melin*, pp. xxix, xxx, 216, 219.

80. Delatte, *Anecdota atheniensia*, I, pp. 141, 457, 585.

81. *DACL*, s.v.

82. See the chapter 'Word Charms and the SATOR Mystery' in Forbes, *The Midwife and the Witch*, pp. 80–93.

83. *Albertus Magnus, being the approved, Verified, Sympathetic and Natural Egyptian Secrets; or White and Black Art for Man and Beast Translated from the German*, ?New York, c. 1880.

84. Sobolevskii, *Perevodnaia literatura*, p. 226.

85. Rovinskii, *Russkie narodnye kartinki*, 1881, III, p. 187; IV, pp. 581 ff. and atlas volume, no. 798; also in Rovinskii, *Russkie narodnye kartinki*, 1900.

86. Pennington, 'South Slavs in Malta'.

87. Van den Baar, 'On the SATOR Formula'.

88. MS St Petersburg, Pushkinskii dom, Pinezhskoe sobr. 40 (325), miscellany, nineteenth century. This is paralleled by German amulets of the seventeenth and eighteenth centuries and one quoted in a nineteenth-century American Pseudo-Albertus translated from German: see Seligman, 'Die

Satorformel', pp. 157–8 and *Albertus Magnus*. These contain references to the Cross and some garbled Greek.

89. The SATOR square is not normally found in cosmological contexts in the West, but see a Latin cosmological diagram including SATOR in a mid-fifteenth-century manuscript in Kremsmüster: *Die Kunstdenkmäler des Benediktinerstiftes Kremsmünster*, 2, 1977, 2. Teil: *Die stiftlichen Sammlungen und die Bibliothek*, pl. 502.

90. Pennington, 'South Slavs in Malta'.

91. Novaković, 'Apokrifski zbornik nasego vijeka', p. 81.

92. Shein, *Materialy*, p. 551.

93. *Kievskaia starina*, 1906, LV, 1–2, 248.

94. Forbes, 'Verbal Charms', p. 298: SATOR is written on paper and hung round the neck against ague and other diseases. Other formulas are written on bread and eaten.

95. See Vysotskii, *Narodnaia meditsina*, p. 97.

96. Speranskii, *Russkaia ustnaia slovesnost'*, p. 443.

97. See Rovinskii, *Russkie narodnye kartinki*, 1881, IV, p. 585; Hansmann and Kriss-Rettenbeck, *Amulett und Talisman*, p. 136.

98. Nikiforovskii, *Prostonarodnye primety i pover'ia*, p. 120, no. 1029.

99. See 'Opisanie rukopisei Solovetskogo monastyria', *Pravoslavnyi sobesednik*, 1892, June–July, no. 854(769).

100. Malov, *Pis'ma k voinam*, ch. 1, pp. 89–92.

101. Sakharov, *Skazaniia russkogo naroda*.

MAGIC OF LETTER AND NUMBER

1. *Introduction*

This chapter will somewhat arbitrarily deal with a variety of texts and practices which involve numbers, letters, calculations, tables, wheels of fortune, dice, cards and sundry other systematic fortune-telling devices. Inevitably the practices and methods described overlap with aspects of magic and divination described in other chapters. Geomancy, in particular, should properly be included here but is so large a subject that it has been dealt with separately in Ch. 12; the SATOR magic square and diminishing 'wing' spells of the ABRACADABRA type are discussed as text amulets in Ch. 10; lucky and unlucky days, and other types of calendar-based prediction, are treated under astrology in Chs 14 and 15. Magic spells may include *voces magicae* but the subject as a whole is dealt with in Ch. 7.

2. *Magic Words and Names in General*

Leaving aside purely stylistic phenomena such as the intricate ornate style called 'word-weaving' (*pletenie sloves*) of the fourteenth-fifteenth century, and letter-substitution cryptography, the more elaborate kinds of word play are not common in Old Russian literature before the seventeenth century, when the Baroque fashion for *carmina curiosa* reached Russia.[1] On the other hand puns on the names of saints are common in popular prognostications of the weather based on what the weather is like on a particular saint's day, and sometimes in spells and invocations – on these points see Chs 5.3 and 7.

If we exclude the names of saints, etc., and the names of various demonic creatures invoked in spells (for which see in particular Ch. 7), Russian spells and texts in general contain fewer specifically magic words or names than their equivalents in some other languages. Where *voces magicae* do occur they are as often as not, as in some Anglo-Saxon texts, transliterated and garbled Greek, or, in a few cases, the Finno-Ugric or other languages spoken in areas where Slavs lived in close contact with speakers of those languages.[2] The SATOR square and ABRACADABRA, almost certainly imports from Western Europe, are discussed in Chs 8.7 and 10.8. From the Christian liturgy the word 'Amen' was certainly thought to be a demonifuge – 'the verb *zaaminit*' means 'to render a demon harmless by repeating Amen three times'.[3]

Although most of the words for 'spell' are related to words meaning 'word, speaking, whispering', native Slavonic magic words are comparatively few; the commonest in Russian is *chur*, once thought to be the name of a Slavonic deity, but etymologically more probably a line or boundary, or in the opinion of one scholar 'penis'.[4] The word is used in a variety of childrens games and magical rituals either to establish a claim (cf. English 'Bags I') or in a protective sense to mean 'Keep away!'. This is used to keep sprites and the Devil at a distance during divinations, and its etymology may well be linked with the notion of the magic circle. It may be expanded to 'Chur, nashe mesto sviato' ('Keep away, our place is sacred').[5] A method which village women healers had to drive out magically induced illnesses was to cry 'gam, gam, gam' followed by prayers to saints to drive out the sickness demon.[6]

Taboo words are commoner:[7] among fishermen the words bear, hare, priest and fox must not be pronounced,[8] probably because they are usually considered to bring bad luck if met by chance (see Ch. 5.2.1);[9] and Antichrist is a word avoided by Old Believers (see 11.9 below). A curious taboo word of specialized application is the word *chernobyl* (*Artemisia vulgaris*, a variety of the herb wormwood), which has acquired a terrible modern significance from the catastrophe at the nuclear power-station in the town of that name. This word must on no account be used when conjuring with the aid of the Queen of Serpents or else the spell will be broken.[10] This would appear to be linked with the effect of the herb itself in cancelling the magical powers acquired by eating serpents' flesh (see Ch. 9.4). The more common word for wormwood, *polyn'*, has also a magical use: in the Ukraine *rusalki* (a kind of malignant mermaid, the soul of an unbaptized child) would accost young ladies on their way to draw water at the river and cry 'Wormwood or parsley!'. If she could answer 'wormwood', and had by chance or prudence some of that herb about her, she would be allowed to pass. If she was foolish enough to answer 'parsley', she would be seized and tickled to death.[11]

Associated with taboo words is the whole area of the use of foul language, especially that involving use of the word 'mother', for magical purposes. This area has been extensively surveyed by Uspenskii, who traces it, with compelling ingenuity, to the ancient Earth cult still very evident in the expression 'mat' syraia zemlia' ('mother-raw [or moist]-earth') found in folklore, and gives many examples of its use as magical inversion or anti-behaviour.[12] Uspenskii has also drawn attention to the magical and demonic significance popularly imputed to orthographic variants of words, especially *nomina sacra*, which occurred in revisions of texts in the seventeenth century, the role which was played in this by the coexistence of Russian and Church Slavonic in the written language of the Russians, and the consequent possibility of assigning negative connotations to one or other linguistic form. Indeed, the mere use of Church Slavonic, the language of Scripture, was itself a form of demonifuge, while Latin was the language of the Devil[13] who was also popularly supposed to dress in Western clothes.[14] This may be compared with the West where, for different cultural reasons, both demons and God responded most readily to Latin.[15]

But if specifically magic words are few, folk etymologies and word associations or punning with magical elements are fairly common. Thus rhubarb (*reven'*) is supposed to roar (*revet'*), a stove (*pech'*) seen in wax-pouring divination means grief (*pechal'*), on the feast of the Virgin of the Veil (*Pokrov*, a word derived from the verb to 'cover') girls might try a spell to catch a young man, and so on.

One may perhaps also mention here some miscellaneous specimens of name magic such as the practice of giving a false name (often taken from the first person met in the street) at the baptism of infants in order to mislead death, or demons, or the wizards who might turn it into a were-animal.[16] Elaborations of the same idea can be seen in the practice, in particular in families with a history of high infant mortality or in cases where a new born child was obviously weak, of calling a list of names up the chimney of the stove and noting at which name the child stopped crying (this name would be used for the child thereafter instead of its baptismal name); arranging a mock funeral or sale of the child to a passer-by and then taking the child back into the house under another name; sweeping the child out of the house with the rubbish and arranging for the godparents to bring it back into the house with a new name; or baptizing the child with an unpleasant name to make it unattractive to evil spirits.[17] In the Indigirka region of northern Siberia, a child might even be given as a second name the name of an animal in order that a disease or magic spell should not be able to find it.[18] For the same reason the naming of a bride on her wedding day was avoided.[19] Unbaptized and illegitimate children were often given the euphemistic protective name of Bogdan, i.e. 'God-given';[20] a Russian saying has it that 'a child without a name is a little devil'.[21]

3. *Bibliomancy*

The practice of using randomly selected passages in books to predict the future was well known in antiquity, in Byzantium, in the Muslim world, and in medieval and even modern Europe.[22] In the Western world the commonest works to be used for this purpose were the works of Vergil (the famous *Sortes Vergilianae*), the Psalter, and the Bible (from the time of St Augustine at least). Sacred books such as the Bible, Psalter, Koran, could also figure in the preparation to a divination as part of the ritual purification protecting the diviner from evil spirits, and, no doubt, as an attempt to give the appearance of legitimacy to practices frowned on in Christianity, Islam and Judaism.

In some cases the selection process could be quite complicated and compounded with other magical or divinatory procedures, in others the use of the book was itself a selection device in some other kind of divination, e.g. for selecting an answer from an 'oracle' or pre-existing list of predictions.

4. *The Divinatory Psalter*

Divination by the book, bibliomancy, was inherited from Byzantium.[23] The commonest book used for this purpose among the East and South Slavs was the Psalter, although the various types of Gospel books are known to have been used also. In Russia the Bible as a coherent canon in a single text was less common than in the West, and in any case not was not translated in full until the end of the fifteenth century. The single-volume Bibles often used in western Europe for divination are essentially the product of the introduction of printing, which came later in Russia and never achieved there the domestic status it acquired in the West, especially in Protestant countries. The practice of psalmomancy may have had its popularity in Muscovy reinforced by the fact that the Psalter was the sacred text most likely to be found in an ordinary household; it is often found with a calendar at the end, and was the book from which many learned to read.[24] The practice of psalmomancy was condemned by the Church: some Russian penitentials list it among the sins about which penitents should be questioned.[25] This did not, however, prevent the Orthodox and even their clergy from using it: Pakhomii, a Rumanian priest, consulted the Psalter in 1706 to discover if he would ever be promoted to bishop and whether he would die at home or abroad.[26]

There are several ways in which a Psalter can be used for divination:

1. It may be simply part of a hallowing process otherwise incidental to the divination. For example in the sixteenth-century geomantic text by Rykov summarized in Ch. 12, the diviner or appellant is advised before proceeding to the geomancy to 'fast, bathe, then with a pure and humble heart take the Gospels or Psalter, sing the *trisagion* three times, pray to God and cross yourself with the Gospels or Psalter'.

2. The Psalter may be used as a divinatory device but without reference to its text (onomancy presupposes literacy). One such practice involves: saying a prayer, taking a key and tying the ring end to the Psalter, then asking a passer-by to suspend the Psalter by lifting it with the index finger under the ward of the key. If the Psalter turns this is a good omen, if not, a bad one.[27] The key could also be placed at the beginning of the Gospel of St John in a gospel book.[28]

Similar practices, usually involving the Bible and a key, can be found in England and Germany.[29]

Perhaps the oddest example of the magical use of a Slavonic Psalter, in which the text can hardly be of relevance, is a copy of a 1596 printed (?Vilna) Psalter in the Herzog August library, Wolfenbüttel.[30] On the outer cover of this is pasted a portrait of Dr Faustus, apparently from a book printed in London (perhaps Christopher Marlowe, *The Tragical History of Doctor Faustus*, probably produced in 1588, or *The History of the Damnable Life and Death of Dr John Faustus* on which it was partly based and which in turn was a translation of a German *Volksbuch* published in Frankfurt in 1587), and the inscription 'D. Johann Fausts Nigromantia . . .' and a sketch of a black raven. On the reverse is the word 'kabala'. Between folios 111 and 112 there is a pasted-in engraving of Faust in his study with the Devil on a chain, and on the verso of f. 116 a different engraving of Faust with a raven flying away. It is hard to imagine exactly how this modified Psalter was used, but a magical context is clearly indicated, and one must assume that the mysterious Cyrillic characters must have suggested magic to a German, just as fertile minds since the Renaissance have found magical significance in runic inscriptions and the hieroglyphs of ancient Egypt.[31]

3. The Psalter may be opened at random either by the diviner or by a random passer-by.[32] The text may then be read from the top, or a passage or line or letter chosen by a previous random selection,[33] by either a passer-by or one of the many other methods of selection described in this chapter, and interpreted as desired. A variant of this method, in which a 'wise woman' opens the Psalter with a knife, is also used to discover thieves.[34] Often the procedure involves rotating the book three times above the head before commencing the divination,[35] a practice also known in Western Europe and Islam.[36]

4. Extracts (first lines) of the psalms could be copied into *tetradki* (notebooks, the usual term employed in court cases and denunciations for books of spells and recipes) and used for fortune telling; in 1647 a cathedral clerk admitted having such a booklet, and of telling fortunes from it by throwing a piece of wax.[37]

5. The Psalter may be used in conjunction with a set of oracular statements. This is the *Gadatel'nyi psaltyr'* or Divinatory Psalter.[38] In its simplest form it has one oracular statement attached to each Psalm: e.g. for Psalm 1 'From grief to joy'; for Psalm 53 'It shall be as you wish'. These are not always found in the same order and have no obvious connection with the text of the Psalm to which they are attached. Later versions have many 'fortunes' almost identical with those in the King David dice divination text discussed below (section 10.2) and some textual similarity, and similarity of method, with the *Circle of Solomon* (section 11 below), but the extremely fluid nature of texts of this kind does not permit a clear textual history to be discerned.[39] Ecclesiastical displeasure at the use of textually amended Psalters of this kind may be deduced from the fact that copies of the Psalter with the divinatory text rubbed out are common.[40] The earliest reference to psalmomancy in Russia is in a passage in the *Pouchenie* (Testament) of Vladimir Monomakh, Grand Prince of Kiev (?1117) where the prince opens the Psalter at random and finds the phrase 'Why art thou cast down, O my soul?' (Psalms 42:5 or 43:5).[41] A slightly later example in the *Novgorod Chronicle*, s.a. 1193, suggests that the divination could use three dice as the selection mechanism.[42] This was probably not the only method of number selection: a thirteenth-century Serbian divinatory psalter has a diagram of a divided circle and a divided spiral onto which a grain had to be thrown to select a number, just as in the later *Circle of Solomon* books.[43]

5. *The Passion of Christ*

This text, based primarily on the apocryphal *Gospel of Nicodemus*, was one of the most popular apocryphal works in the seventeenth century, in particular among the Old Believers. One version, evidently translated from Polish, found in a sixteenth–seventeenth-century miscellany from Sub-Carpathian Ruthenia was clearly used as a divinatory text like the Psalter and has forty-one predictions appended to it, one per page.[44] The Muscovite versions are relatively unresearched and no divinatory use of these versions has been recorded.

6. *Number Magic in General*

It might be expected that the system of alphabetical numerals used by the South and East Slavs, which was a variant of the Greek system, would lend itself very easily to number magic. In fact, although there are some examples of onomancy, described below in the sections on Onomancy and the Number of the Beast, and numerological aspects of astrology and geomancy which are discussed in their appropriate chapters, number symbolism and number magic were not much developed in Russia, partly perhaps because knowledge of mathematics itself was very limited. A recent study has shown that the names of various Russian systems of cryptography (*tainopis'*) could well be derived from Jewish Cabala,[45] but for any Russian interest in Cabalistic gematria we have to wait until the Rosicrucians of the eighteenth and nineteenth centuries.[46] Some fairly elaborate numerical riddles are known from the sixteenth century onwards (e g the 'Fable of the year' in Ch. 12.4.1.5, and the *pritcha* 'On the name of Christopher')[47] and from 1633 numerical ciphers were used for Russian diplomatic correspondence, but this does not seem to have fostered any interest in onomancy.

7. *Significant Numbers*

The significance of particular numbers in particular circumstances is discussed elsewhere as appropriate – see the Index. The significance of odds and evens, days of the week, month, etc. is discussed elsewhere, and in particular in Chs 4.5.6–8 and 14.8).

Three and threefold repetition are universal in folklore and are very common in Russian divination and magic spells or *zagovory* (see Ch. 7). *Trideviat'*, 'three nines', possibly a relic of an old counting system, is also found as a formulaic number both in folk tales and in spells. A relic of Pythagorean thought is mentioned in the Russian version of the *Secretum secretorum* (fifteenth–sixteenth century) where four and ten are described as perfect numbers because one plus two plus three plus four equal ten. Seven, and seventy-seven, in particular with reference to veins and sinews, are also common in spells (see Ch. 7). It is considered unlucky in Russia, as elsewhere, to sit thirteen at a table, a superstition no doubt deriving from the account of the Last Supper in the Gospel of St John, 6, 70–1.[48]

8. *Onomancy*

The earliest example of systematic onomancy in Old Russian literature is to be found in the pseudo-Aristotelian *Secretum secretorum* (for details of which see Ch. 1). This was translated in the late fifteenth or early sixteenth century from Hebrew, probably in the Grand Duchy of Lithuania, and is extant in some twenty complete or partial copies. This system of divination involves adding up the numerical values of the letters in the names of two antagonists, dividing the totals by nine and comparing the results in a table which will predict the winner (Fig. 16). According to the *Secretum* the table was used by Aristotle when giving advice to Alexander the Great, but despite the latter's pleas the secret was not revealed to him until Aristotle decided to write down all his secret wisdom for Alexander's benefit.[49]

Some copies of the Russian text include two pairs of names, Alexander and Porus, and Nestor and Lyaeus, as examples of the efficacy of the system. The first pair has an obvious enough source. The story of the single combat of Alexander of Macedon and the Indian king Porus resulting in the latter's death occurs in Pseudo-Callisthenes but in no other antique historical source. It was well known to Russians: the several Russian versions of the Alexander story of pseudo-Callisthenes were the most popular secular works in Kievan and Muscovite Russia with several hundred extant copies or fragments;[50] a further reference to this duel appears in the *Tale of the Battle of Kulikovo*,[51] and the subject appears in pictorial form in the sixteenth-century *Illuminated Chronicle*, in a form apparently derived from the late antique picture cycle,[52] and in a late popular woodcut (*lubok*).[53]

The second pair given as examples of the system, Nestor and Lyaeus, is rather more obscure, but lifts the text into the Christian tradition.[54] According to the legend in the *Passio* of Demetrius of Salonika, Nestor was a young disciple of St Demetrius in the time of Galerius. With the help of the saint's prayers he was able to defeat a giant Vandal gladiator called Lyaeus.[55] The story regularly appears in hagiographic icons of St Demetrius and in Russian popular prints.[56]

Since the *Secretum* was translated from Hebrew, we have to assume that the translator was a Jew. This part of the Russian text of the *Secretum*, therefore, must definitely have been added by a Christian copyist. The fact that the copyist, unlike most of his Western counterparts, added to his text only at this point seems to indicate that his interest, perhaps even his primary interest, lay in the occult aspect of the work, although in other respects the the Russian version of the *Secretum* differs from the various West European versions in its emphasis on the medical and political parts of the work. It is also noteworthy that the *Secretum* frequently appears in manuscripts containing other divinatory works.

Perhaps significantly, the *Secretum* is not the only divinatory text in which Nestor and Lyaeus appear. A seventeenth-century Belorussian version of the *Zagadki Tsaria Davida*, the dice divination text described below, includes the passage:

39. St Nestor by the prayers of St Demetrius defeated the great warrior Lyaeus, felling and crushing him with a great swing, and shaming the king so that he and all his nobles fled the scene in shame. So, O man, your enemies will scatter and the Lord God will be with you. This is good [i.e. a good throw].

This method of divination is in fact found in many places in various guises. A table identical to that found in the *Secretum* is given by Tannery to illustrate a

Greek text in which Pythagoras is credited with inventing the method and, instead of the two pairs of antagonists given in the Russian text, Hector and Patroclus are quoted.[57] Festugière has suggested that this system of divination originated in a neo-Pythagorean sect,[58] an opinion supported in late antiquity by Terentianus Maurus in his *De litteris*, which also mentions Hector and Patroclus.[59]

These ascriptions to Pythagoras and Aristotle are described by the historian of Arabic divination, Toufic Fahd, as characteristic of Greek and Islamic divination respectively.[60] Ibn Khaldūn, in his description of the many kinds of divination, also describes the system and gives as its source Aristotle's *Politics* (i.e. the *Secretum*).[61] In fact the tradition ascribing the system to Aristotle also belongs to the Christian East: the twelfth-century (?) text called by its publisher and translator *The Book of Medicines* contains this onomantic system (as well as several others), stating that it 'was made by Aristotle for King Alexander, his royal disciple, when he was waging war against Darius the Mede, and Aristotle conquered Darius'.[62] This gives us two more antagonists to demonstrate the efficacy of the system.

Most of the European versions of the *Secretum* are derived from the Arabic Long Form of the text and omit the onomancy. Only the Castilian short form of the text[63] and one English version retain the onomantic passage.[64] This method of prediction does, however, exist in a number of Latin and vernacular contexts apart from the *Secretum*, with a whole series of other pairs of antagonists.[65] Similar systems exist outside this tradition: one fourteenth-century German text (which includes some Greek words and is preceded by a short medical onomancy) is ascribed to the philosopher Phisitor,[66] and Trachtenberg in his study of Jewish magic describes a system which is similar but has no names attached to it. In this system the remainder after the division by nine predicts the winner of a dispute. If the antagonists are similar in type, both Jews, of the same trade and degree of learning then the larger number would prevail, if they were dissimilar the smaller number would win.[67]

9. *The Number of the Beast*

The South and East Slavs with their Greek-based alphabetical system of numeration might have been expected to have indulged in onomancy rather more than seems to have been the case. They certainly used the numerical values of letters in their cryptographic systems, in which the names and techniques of Jewish Cabalistic influence has been seen,[68] and indulged in speculation on 666, the 'Number of the Beast' in the Apocalypse. In the more lurid kind of eschatological writing, which still flourishes,[69] this is usually held to be a cryptogram of the name of the Antichrist, a being who, textually speaking, is quite distinct from the Beast. The early identification of the Antichrist with Simon Magus and the belief of St Cyril of Jerusalem that the Antichrist would be a magician show that the later association of 666 and the Antichrist with demonic magic has deep roots.

The first rulers to be identified as the Antichrist were Nero and Caligula, but they had many successors, especially at the time of the Reformation when both Luther and Pope Leo X, and many lesser figures, were by various arithmetical manipulations discovered to be the Antichrist.[70] The papacy has continued to be officially labelled as the Antichrist in many of the more exclusive Protestant sects,[71] and most major figures in world history have at one time or another been identified in this way: Mahomet, the Sultan, Napoleon I, Napoleon III,[72] Roosevelt, Lenin and Stalin, and most major figures in Soviet history, including Khrushchev; more recently Bible-belt Americans have discovered him in the firm of Proctor and Gamble (their trademark of the Man in the Moon allegedly has 666 in the curls of his beard),[73] a Washington taxi-driver pin pointed the President of the European Assembly,[74] and a Rumanian interviewed on BBC television at the end of 1989 during the revolution in Bucharest was in no doubt that the Antichrist was President Ceauşescu. Indeed, such is the continuing power of superstition, aided no doubt by the spate of occult horror films, that in 1989 in Britain the Driver and Vehicle Licensing Centre was obliged to cease issuing vehicle licensing plates bearing the number 666.[75] Perhaps the most improbable Antichrist accusation was that made by Gennadii Ziuganov, leader of the Russian Communist Party, against his rivals in the presidential elections in 1996: 'Let's remember what is in the Apocalypse. The Devil has sent two beasts from hell. The first has a mark on his head [i.e. Mikhail Gorbachov, who has a prominent birthmark on his head], and the second has a mark on his hand [i.e. Boris Yeltsin, who has two fingers missing]'.[76] An article in *Komsomolskaia Pravda* at the end of 1997 states that 1998 would be the year of the Antichrist and would be marked by an upsurge of satanic rituals.[77]

The Russians were familiar with the notion of the Antichrist quite early. It came to them through a variety of mostly supposititious texts: the *Seven Words on the Second Coming of Christ* ascribed to St Ephraem the Syrian (known in Church Slavonic translation from the eleventh century), tracts attributed to Hippolytus of Rome on the Antichrist and the end of the world (known in Church Slavonic from the end of the twelfth century),[78] the *Revelations* of pseudo-Methodius of Patara,[79] who also told them about Gog and Magog (very quickly recognized in the Tatars),[80] and the *Questions of St John the Divine to the Lord on Mount Tabor*. The Antichrist could be associated with Jews and judaizing Christians,[81] and was easily associated in the fifteenth and sixteenth centuries with the part-eschatological, part-political notion of 'Moscow the Third Rome' and the 'New Jerusalem' and, as with the Protestants from whom the notion was probably borrowed, the Pope was often seen as the Antichrist. There were plenty of, for example, English and Dutch merchants in Muscovy who were quite happy to promote this idea, and the tsars, though usually suspicious of Protestantism, had little love for Rome.[82] The notion of the Antichrist in Russia received a new impetus from the seventeenth century onwards in the controversy between the official Orthodox Church and the schismatic Old Believers, who identified first Patriarch Nikon, then Tsar Aleksei Mikhailovich, Peter the Great (the title of *imperator*, new to Russia and bestowed on Peter by his grateful Senate, added up to 666 in Russian letter numerals if you used the single-stroke letter I and left out the letter M),[83] and subsequent rulers of Russia, as the Beast of the Apocalypse.[84] The precise nature of the Antichrist, and whether he was to be understood literally or symbolically, was a matter of dispute between the various sub-sects of Old Believers.[85] By the late nineteenth century the Antichrist was expected to come not from Palestine or Western Europe but from China.[86]

Boris Uspenskii has pointed out that Peter the Great was brought up in this tradition and actually encouraged his own cult, either as God or as Antichrist, both by the titles he took and by continuing in his 'All-Jesting Synod' the 'anti-behaviour' of blasphemous parodies of religion which had begun with Ivan the Terrible in the sixteenth century.[87] Uspenskii asserts that the drunken debauch of the mock-marriage of Peter's old tutor Zotov, appointed 'Patriarch of Mirth', was performed by a real priest in a kind of 'black mass', and that one of Peter's followers kept the Tsar's portrait in the icon corner among his sacred images. In fact this seems to be more a continuation of the medieval tradition of the 'abbots (or lords) of misrule' known in many parts of Europe, and thought by some to derive from the Roman *Saturnalia*. Against Uspenskii's interpretation can perhaps be counted the fact that many Orthodox were persecuted, even executed, for publicly denouncing Peter as the Antichrist.[88] Moreover, although the example of Peter is the most obvious, he is not unique in this respect, for the implied divinity of the monarch can be found in icons and texts reflecting the rhetoric of official ideology both from before the time of Peter (e.g. in particular Tsar Aleksei Mikhailovich), and after him (e.g. Catherine the Great and Alexander 1).[89]

Successive Russian governments in the eighteenth century were worried by the political implications of the various eschatological 'letters' and 'gazettes' about the Antichrist and the end of the world which were circulating, in particular in the army, and several investigations at the highest level were carried out.[90] The Old Believers, among whom the *Revelations* of pseudo-Methodius was a very popular text, and mindful of the text of Revelations 13.16 ('and he causeth all . . . to receive a mark in the right hand'), saw the Seal of the Antichrist in the mark placed on the hands of recruits to Peter the Great's army, or alternatively in the tokens issued as evidence of payment of the beard tax which they were obliged to pay for refusing to obey Peter's 'blasphemous' law against beards,[91] and even in the official stamp on scales and weights.[92]

Later, in the reign of Catherine the Great, it was the smallpox vaccination scar which became the Seal of the Antichrist.[93] Vaccination was one of a list of things held in abomination by the Old Believers; others were potatoes ('Devil's apples' or 'apples of Sodom' or the 'bread of Antichrist' (*antiev khleb*)), tobacco, and marriage. In the eighteenth century vaccination was an important issue in Russia since Catherine II had submitted to it at the hands of Dr Thomas Dimsdale. This was an inexpensive, if fairly courageous, way of promoting her image as an enlightened monarch. It was even the subject of a court spectacle in 1768, an allegorical ballet entitled 'Prejudice Overcome' in which Minerva (goddess of wisdom, the arts, etc., and a regular iconographic representation of the Empresses Elizabeth and Catherine II), seated in the Temple of Aesculapius (medicine), consents to inoculation and then persuades Ruthenia (Russia), seated in the Temple of Ignorance, to follow her example; they break into a 'grand dance' of hope to celebrate the expulsion of Ignorance and Superstition.[94]

According to one nineteenth-century source the various sub-sects of the Old Believers had specific beliefs about the Antichrist: the Chernobol'tsy believed that the state identity document was the Seal of Antichrist; the Pastukhovshchina, who refused to walk on paved roads, would not touch coins or passports because they were the Seal of Antichrist (they bore the head of the tsar);[95] and the Samokreshchentsy would wash only in rainwater because any other kind was used by the Antichrist.[96] Some Old Believers believed that the chariot of Antichrist had a single shaft to which the horses were attached (a non-Russian method) and that it was therefore a sin to travel in any conveyance so drawn,[97] and that the population census was a device of the Antichrist for collecting tribute from the living and the dead (this was the primary element of the plot of Gogol's famous novel *Dead Souls*).[98]

Various groups of Old Believers were sufficiently convinced that they were living in the reign of the Antichrist, and thus in the last days of the world, that they were given to mass suicide by burning. The last case of this was in the late nineteenth century.[99] 'Antichrist' even became a taboo word and was replaced by 'Antii' or 'Anchutka', which by a popular association of ideas also came to mean the Devil or a *leshii* (wood demon),[100] or other demons of folk belief, in particular the bathhouse demon.[101] In a final semantic twist the word acquired the meaning of 'police informer' in pre-Revolutionary criminal argot.[102]

In 1812, during the French invasion of Russia, the Russian authorities used the popular belief in the Antichrist to good effect by trying to convince the populace that Napoleon was the Antichrist.[103] This must have presented a problem for the Old Believers, who believed at that particular time that Tsar Alexander I was the Antichrist – indeed a police search of the Preobrazhensk merchant community in Moscow discovered a portrait of the tsar with horns and tail.[104] Nevertheless, for the rest of the population the promotion of the image of Napoleon as Antichrist was simply adopting a common theme in Europe in the Napoleonic period. It is still memorable in Russia because of its satirical treatment in Tolstoi's *War and Peace*. In that novel one of Pierre's masonic acquaintances revealed to him that by treating the letters of the roman alphabet in the same way as Hebrew letter-numerals the words 'L'Empereur Napoléon' add up to 666, and that Napoleon was forty-two years in age, which was the number of years of the rule of the Beast foretold in the Book of Revelation. Pierre is much impressed and after several absurd manipulations of his own name he discovers that if he describes himself in elided French as 'L'russe Besuhof', he too adds up to 666, and his fate is therefore bound up with that of Napoleon, whose assassination he then contemplates.

Tolstoi is here not only mocking the Old Believer interpretation of 'Imperator' but also invoking an alternative newer tradition of belief in the Antichrist and the

Number of the Beast, one which prevailed not at the simple level of the conservative Old Believers but rather in aristocratic Westernized society where Freemasonry of several varieties, and Rosicrucianism, flourished in the eighteenth and early nineteenth centuries. The poet G.R. Derzhavin, for a while the secretary of Catherine the Great, was prevented by his aunt from having anything to do with Count I.I. Shuvalov, Curator of Moscow University, because the count was one of the masons, who were 'apostates, heretics, blasphemers, and given over to the Antichrist', and were able to kill their enemies a thousand miles away.[105] (This last attribute gives the accusation a more popular Russian flavour since it was a power thought to be possessed by the Russian *koldun* or village wizard.) And an eighteenth-century polemic verse against Freemasonry declares: 'Freemasons, your laws are full of lies and your mystery consists in counting up to 666!'[106] In popular language freemasons, *frankmasony*, became *farmazony*, and then *armizony*, a fabulous people in a far land who, in the popular imagination, possessed magic money which still remained however much you spent (cf. the *nerazmennyi rubl'* on p. 199).[107]

The curious but typically inconsistent attempt to destroy the Antichrist, who is by definition both inevitable and indestructible by human agency, can be seen again in Russia a little later in the attempt of a Russian peasant woman to assassinate Rasputin; when questioned she would only reply: 'He is the Antichrist.'[108] The rather eccentric English wandering writer and enthusiast for 'Holy Russia' Stephen Graham, writing in 1914, describes the murder of a woman by peasants in Russia after she had confessed to being the Antichrist (a point of interest for feminist theologians), and notes that this name was also given to unusual-looking babies.[109,110] The most unusual recent Russian manifestation of 666 of which I am aware, is its use in a prison-camp tattoo where it appears under a horrific fanged skull in a horned helmet in a rogues' gallery of underworld tattoos which includes Marx, Lenin, Stalin, Hitler, Mussolini, and Margaret Thatcher.[111] The multiplicity of Antichrists so far discovered, like the various dates of the end of the world which have passed without incident, seems not to have embarrassed those of an apocalyptic disposition and, as some of the above examples testify, the seductive numerological method of detecting demons is even now being employed to find new Antichrists – it appeals to too many instincts ever to disappear.

10. *Dice and Cleromancy*

10.1. *Dice in Russia: Divination, Lots and Gambling.* Dice are known as far back as the civilization of Sumer and the Indus valley, and can be found in one form or another in most subsequent cultures, including that of the Slavs.[112] In fact, in one of the few accounts we have of pre-Christian divination among the Slavs, a passage in the *Gesta Danorum* of Saxo Grammaticus which mentions the magical practices of the Baltic Slavs, we find a reference to the casting by the pagan priests of three pieces of wood of which one side was white and the other black: the white side signified good fortune, the black ill fortune.[113]

This would appear to be the first description we have of anything among the Slavs resembling the Russian *zern'*. These are small bone pieces with black and white sides which can be tossed like a coin and were used for betting at odds-and-evens.[114] Guthrie in his *Noctes Rossicae* describes small stones coloured in this fashion, which he says were called *kruchki* (*?kruzhki*)and used for divination: a preponderence of white meant good, black meant bad.[115]

Binary selection mechanisms of this kind are very commonly found in magic and divination, and Russia has the same customs as most other parts of Europe: the 'good and bad days' inherited from antiquity; the notion of the Devil not liking odd numbers (because they were favoured by God: 'Numero Deus impare gaudet', Vergil, *Eclogues*, viii, 75); tossing a coin; counting-out rhymes of the 'she loves me, she loves me not' type, and so on. In the Pinsk region of Belorussia if a corpse was washed by an odd number of helpers this meant that it would become a *rusalka*, a vexatious water-sprite.[116]

The practice described by Saxo Grammaticus survives in several kinds of folk divination. For example, the casting of three loaves to see in what proportion they fall crust-side uppermost (This was part of a house-building divination: three crusts up was a good omen, two – fair, one or none – bad),[117] or the simple Russian peasant method of determining the success of a mushroom expedition by singing a special song and throwing the basket ahead to see which way up it will land (bottom down means a full basket, bottom up, none, sideways, half a basket).[118] It would appear that some such practice is the source of the Jewish popular fortune-telling device, allegedly from 'Esclavonia', in which a piece of wood from which the bark had been peeled on one side was utilized. The smooth side was called the 'woman' and the rough side the 'man'. It was tossed in the air twice – if the 'man' fell uppermost the first time, followed by the 'woman' this was a good omen; the reverse was a bad omen and two of a kind was taken to be neutral.[119]

The use of dice had been condemned as an occasion of sin in the early Church by Clement of Alexandria (c. 150–c. 215) in his *Paedagogus* (III, 11) and two centuries later by John Chrysostom in his *Ad populum Antiochenum homilia* (XV, 4). It is further condemned in the seventh century at the Sixth Ecumenical Council (Third Council of Constantinople)[120] and in the ninth century in the *Nomokanon* of Photius, where it is linked with chess. Dice appear to have been used as part of bibliomantic divination in twelfth-century Novgorod – see section 4 above. Chess and dice (*leki* or *zern'*) continue to be condemned in later Russian versions of the *Nomokanon* known as the *Kormchaia*,[121] and the *Stoglav* council of 1551 condemns in its chapter 42 the servitors of the tsar (*deti boiarskie*) and boyars (*liudi boiarskie*) for gambling at *zern'*, drunkenness, riotous behaviour and neglect of their duties.[122] This seems to have been a continuing concern at the Muscovite court, for Tsar Mikhail Fedorovich felt obliged, about 1630, to forbid Russians to sell their land to foreigners on the grounds that they were in the habit of spending the money on drink or losing it at *zern'*.[123]

Although the *zern'*, whatever it is made of, appears to be a cube used for random binary selection, and *leki* were more probably numbered dice; both terms are found from the Kievan period onwards, and it is not always clear that the words have distinct referents. Mark Ridley, in his late sixteenth-century dictionary of Russian, gives the plural *zerni* for 'dice' without further comment and presumably therefore recognized the Russian dice as being much the same as English,[124] a probability strengthened by Turberville's verse description quoted below. Either *zern'* or *leki* could could have been the 'magic bones' condemned in the sixteenth-century manual of proper behaviour and good husbandry, the *Domostroi*,[125] although in another place that text condemns *zern'* by name, together with chess and draughts (*tavleia*).[126] The practice of *metanie* ('casting'), which probably means throwing dice, and is referred to in literature from the early fifteenth century and in indexes of banned books from the sixteenth century onwards, is nowhere actually described.[127]

Another term, *boby* (lit. 'beans') is also found in descriptions of casting lots in the seventeenth century;[128] although this may also be a variety of geomancy which was certainly known in the nineteenth century (see Ch. 13, p.), it has been suggested that this does not mean that beans were used but refers to the spots on the dice.[129]

The Church ban was not simply a mechanical copy of earlier Byzantine canon law without reference to Russia, as can sometimes happen: in 1647 a peasant was condemned to exile for 'sorcery, casting bones (*kosnoi razvod*, i.e. dice), and making spells (*nagovory*)';[130] after him there is a whole series of cases in which fortune-telling by both men and women with 'bones', or the possession of such 'bones' or sometimes 'magic' or 'divinatory bones' (*volshebnye* or *gadal'nye kosti*) is part of the evidence.[131] Neither this, nor his father's *ukaz* mentioned above, prevented Tsar Aleksei Mikhailovich in 1667 from selling licences to trade in *zern'* (but see below under 'Playing Cards'). The normal modern Russian for dice is *igral'nye kosti* 'gaming bones'.

It is significant that an alternative word, *zhrebii*, *zherebii* and variants, means a die, lot, and fate. Random selection by dice or a variety of other methods could be considered as the expression of fate, or the judgment of God. The judgment of God (*sud bozhii*) was a normal judicial procedure in Muscovite Russia. It included cross-kissing, using an icon as witness, judicial duel, and drawing lots.[132] Examples of decisions being taken by the drawing of lots are found from at least the early fifteenth century.[133] In the sixteenth century in Muscovy the casting of lots could be used in place of trial by combat to settle legal disputes. The method was to roll up the names of the litigants into two equal wax balls, place these in a hat, and invite a bystander to draw out one at random.[134] *Zherebei* and its diminutive *zherebeika* are regularly used from the seventeenth century onwards of any kind of cube or block, or of a coin used for casting lots, or for making a decision (as nowadays at the beginning of a sports contest), or random selections in land allocation or recruiting into the army.[135] *Zhereb'evka* meant drawing lots or recruiting by lot.

There is also fairly early evidence for the existence in Russia of numbered dice (probably the *leki* mentioned in early Russian canon law) of the Roman and modern type, with one opposite six: one illustration in the fourteenth-century *Radziwiłł Chronicle* shows three spotted dice, showing the numbers 6, 5, and 4, being used to draw lots to choose a sacrificial victim.[136] Gambling with *zern'* has already been mentioned as a serious worry to Tsar Mikhail Fedorovich in the earlier part of the seventeenth century, and wild gambling with numbered dice seems to have been no less common. It certainly excited comment from foreign visitors: the English writer and scholar George Turberville, the secretary to Sir Thomas Randolph on his mission to Russia in 1568–9, wrote three letters in verse to friends in England, which describe Muscovy, its inhabitants, and their customs, including gambling, chess and dice, in unflattering terms:

> Again they dice as fast: the poorest rogues of all
> Will sit them down in open field and there to gaming fall.
> Their dice are very small (in fashion like to those
> Which we do use); he takes them up and over thumb he throws, . . .[137]

A similar comment comes from Richard James in 1618: '*Sem-odenatset* [i.e. seven-eleven],[138] a plaie at dice with which the Russes playe even their wives and children, and themselves into their naked creation, shirt and all.'[139]

10.2. *Dice Divination Texts*. Most writers commenting on the *Rafli* which figures in later lists of banned books had assumed that this was a book of dice divination, partly because of the entry for the word *raffla* (cf. English 'raffle' and cognates in other European languages from the fifteenth century onwards) in Du Cange, which identifies it fairly securely as dice divination.[140] Pypin was the first to publish the text of dice divination ascribed to King David, in the belief that it was the *Rafli*.[141]

In fact it is now established that the *Rafli* was a geomancy (see Ch. 12) and the term should not be applied to the *Gadaniia Tsaria Davida* or 'Oracle of King David', several versions of which exist. Rybnikov published a popular version,[142] another version was published in 1905,[143] and a Rumanian version also exists.[144] A very similar seventeenth-century Belorussian version of the King David text has also been published.[145] For those unable or too lazy to interpret the dice, the text itself could be used as a *zagovor* or spell,[146] and possession of amulets and divinatory texts including the King David text was part of the incriminating evidence against a priest at a Synodal court in 1770.[147]

The text could well be of Western origin. All attested copies of it are late, as are references in the literature, and the only Byzantine dice text of which I am aware is an astrological work with no similarity to the Russian text.[148] Texts of this kind are common in Western Europe,[149] many of them stemming from Lorenzo Spirito's *Libro della ventura ouer libro della sorte*.[150] This Italian fortune-telling book contains series of twelve 'oracles' of twelve prophets (which includes

Balaam and David), selected by throwing three dice. One German version (P. Pambst, *Loosbuch*, 1546) has a King David and dice divination on the same page. Spirito's book itself seems to be derived from the *Sortes XII Patriarchum*, the earliest extant version of which is declared by Skeat to be of the eleventh century.[151] Skeat considers an Arabic source for this text to be improbable, but it would be better to keep an open mind: the illustrations of Alfonso the Wise's book of games,[152] very many of which include three dice, and other kinds of oriental divination using dot-numbered dice, in for example Persia and Tibet, demonstrate the ubiquity of the practice.[153]

The predictions in the Russian 'Oracle of King David' are arranged in descending numerical order: 666, 665, 664 . . . 111. Individual predictions are about fifty words long; typically they consist of a quotation from a Psalm or description of an incident in the Bible or religious, sometimes apocryphal, literature or folktales, then an interpretation, sometimes with a proverb, and sometimes with a final statement as to whether the cast indicated good fortune or not. The predictions offer advice on a limited number of subjects: almost all advise on the outcome of an illness, most also advise on journeys, and may also have predictions for domestic life, a move to a new home, loss, enemies, general well-being. In structure these predictions with their *historiola* are very similar to *zagovor* spells, as the following examples from the version published by Pypin will demonstrate:

3.3.2. When Moses led the Israelites out of Egypt he parted the Red Sea with his staff. The Israelites crossed the sea, the Egyptians drowned in the sea and the waters covered them. From this comes the saying: the hare flees and the hunter drowns. O man, what you have in mind is your enemy, and you should beware of this enemy; if you ask about a journey or moving to a new house, do not do this. This cast is not in your favour.

5.5.5. Tsar Abgar in his palsy lay down on his bed to sleep, and the Lord sent his angel to him and Abgar rejoiced at the teaching of the Lord. So you O man rejoice at your lot: if you ask about illness it will pass; if about domestic life all will be well in your house; if about something lost it will be found; if about a journey it will be a good one.

6.1.1. St Theodore Tiro took his falcon,[154] mounted on his horse, and went out into the open country, and his falcon caught a falcon and Theodore rejoiced at his catch. So you, O man, rejoice at your lot, God comes to your aid. If you ask about an illness or journey your journey will be happy; if you wish to take a loan take it, but with care; you will overcome your enemies.

The incomplete version published by Kuznetsov-Krasnoiarskii is essentially in the same tradition and shares some of the same material but it includes some predictions which have no religious content:

5.5.2. Do not mix lead with silver nor good thoughts with bad. If crystal falls on the floor it will smash. So you O man, do not do whatever you intended or were divining about; if you wish to go on a journey do not; wait for a good time. Protect yourself from your enemy on all sides; throw again for this throw is not good.

An alternative tradition of dice numbered one to four may also have existed in Russia.[155] At all events there exists a seventeenth-century text (c. 1632–3) giving predictions based on throws of three such dice.[156] This is quite different in tone and has no religious or folktale element, the predictions are brief, followed by a letter T (for *tolkovanie* 'interpretation') which gives more detail. The type of circumstance for which predictions are offered, however, is the same. The prediction for 2.1.2. reads:

2.1.2. This indicates that everything you are thinking of will be terrible and there will be illness and great grief to your body, and loss. T. If you seek for profit you will not find it, and if you go to war this means death, and if you move to a new place you will lose your old profit and there will be loss and death to livestock.

The manuscript is incomplete but contains a separate section at the end giving predictions 'for the heart' which contain instructions for an alternative interpretation of the dice when they are turned over. (The King David text occasionally invites you to throw again when there is a particularly bad prediction.)

The various popular fortune-telling books of the eighteenth century, usually of foreign origin, may contain dice or cleromantic sections. The only one devoted exclusively to this appears to be the *Popytka ne shutka*, which claims to be translated from German, published in St Petersburg in 1785.[157] This allows members of either sex to discover the answer to questions by the simple casting of two dice.[158] And a last use of dice for use as a random selection device was a curious musical game with dice, for the composition of music, which was published in 1795 in St Petersburg in a musical 'Pocket-Book'.[159]

11. *Wheels of Fortune and the Circle of Solomon*

The 'Wheel of Fortune' is frequently referred to in Russian literature of the sixteenth and seventeenth centuries, in particular in the many abecediaries which appeared in this period. The references appear to derive from the polemic articles of Maxim the Greek (Michael Trivolis),[160] the former humanist who had worked in Italy as a translator of the Greek classics and then, having become a monk on Mt Athos, was sent to Russia to help with the correction of the scriptures in Church Slavonic. Maxim's descriptions of these wheels are clearly based on the various representations in Western art of this theme, but he is quite definite that the notion of the 'Wheel of Fortune' is part of pagan belief in astrology going back to Zoroaster which had dominated the classical world and was now corrupting the Western church. He accuses Nicholas Bülow, the tsar's physician, of bringing it into Russia. In the Russian abecediaries these 'Wheels of Fortune' are understood as being condemned books of astrology.[161] These references to a 'Wheel of Fortune', however, are to a large extent part of the *topos* of Latin and Hellene aberrancy and do not, as far as I can discover, relate to anything actually existing in Muscovite Russian literature or art.

Pictures of 'Wheels of Fortune', either as symbolic representations of the fickleness of fate, or as fortune-telling devices, are probably imported into Russia and the Balkans as popular prints and chapbooks not before the eighteenth century.[162] The earliest representation I have seen is, improbably, near the end of the *Remezov Chronicle* (c. 1700), an illuminated chronicle of the conquering of Siberia in the sixteenth century by the Cossack Ermak.[162] The figures on the wheel are in Russian dress and the text begins with the text from Ecclesiastes: 'Vanity of vanities'.[163] It was evidently not intended for fortune-telling.

Circles with radial or spiral divisions each bearing a number, letter or text, from which a random selection can be made by dropping on to it a grain, bean or pebble, have been known from antiquity.[164] They may contain predictions within themselves or be selection mechanisms for an 'oracle'. Popular prints containing divination systems of this kind have been common all over Europe, and are still published. As has been said, in Russia and the Balkans these prints and booklets appear relatively late and show every sign of importation from Western Europe.

Best known of these was the *Circle of Solomon* (Fig. 15), a booklet which appeared in many versions but usually with a front page showing an engraving of a bearded man supporting on his shoulders a circle with the face of the sun at the centre and the numbers 1 to 100 (or 150) in a clockwise spiral from the centre outwards. The instructions below tell the user to drop a grain of wheat on the centre and see which number it falls on, for which reason it is sometimes called *Zernometka* (lit. 'grain-throwing').[165] This is the key to a list of predictions which follow; as with several other kinds of divination the predictions are in fact quotations from the Bible or apocryphal works. It is not clear why this particular type of fortune-telling, with its echo of the iconography of Atlas, should have been ascribed to Solomon in Russia but nowhere else – Solomon's reputation as a magician was as widespread in the Western Europe as it was in Orthodox Europe and among the Jews (see SATOR in Ch. 10.8). The historian of Russian popular prints, Rovinskii, tells us that this, together with dream books, formed one of the favourite evening diversions in Russian peasant, merchant and *petit bourgeois* households in the nineteenth century;[166] he considered the text to be probably of French origin, but offers no identification. A well-known picture, 'The Book-stall' ('Knizhnaia lavochka'), painted in 1876 by V.M. Vasnetsov and now in the Tret'iakov Gallery in Moscow, shows the *Circle of Solomon* in a prominent position among other popular prints (the other recognizable items are all religious: icons and a 'Last Judgement' with apocalyptic horrors). The *Circle of Solomon* continued to be sold in the twentieth century; an article in the main Russian ethnographical journal in 1907 stated that Solomon books were on sale in Moscow at the time of writing, and that the sun picture containing the numbers was used as the design for the wrappers of sweets.[167] The *Gromnik* thunder divination text had already, in 1899, come to the same sticky end (see p. 379)

There appears to have been some conflation of the *Circle of Solomon* text with the older indigenous *zagovor* tradition among the Old Believers of the trans-Baikal region who use the invocation 'Tsar Solomon, tell me the real truth' before making a throw.[168] A version of the *Circle of Solomon* entitled *The Latest Card Oracle* (*Noveishii kartochnyi orakul*) also exists. It has pairs of playing cards instead of numbers, a grain as the selection mechanism, and predictions in rhyming couplets.[169]

Rovinskii claims that 'Wheel of Fortune' prints, ostensibly of an exclusively moralizing character, and based on the West European tradition, were also used for divination. He offers no proof of this but he did know his subject well.[170] The topic is complicated by the fact that at least one edition (a lithograph dated 1883) of what is normally labelled *Circle of Solomon* appeared with the title *Krug schastiia* ('Circle of Fortune') with the word *charodei* ('wizard') beneath the bearded figure. Another early eighteenth-century popular print of a similar kind, probably from a French original, includes a love oracle of twelve pictures and a circle with thirty divisions as a selection device.[171]

Fortune-telling books of this type are usually anonymous or fathered preposterously on some sage of classical or biblical antiquity, but one improbable love oracle of the eighteenth century, the *Liubovnaia gadatel'naia knizhka* ('An Amorous Fortune-Telling Book'), was written by the poet Aleksander Sumarokov, known principally for his classical dramas and triumphal odes. Sumarokov selected sixty-six verse couplets from his own tragedies, arranged them in six chapters and invited his gentle readers to indulge in the pleasant pastime of selecting a fortune in love by casting dice, first to find the chapter, then to select the verse.[172] The intended user of this very literary oracle was not, one may assume, the peasant or minor merchant.

With the exception of Sumarokov's little book, all these booklets and prints are very similar to the kind of popular fortune-telling publications sold in west European countries. One difference, however, is that almanacs, part calendar and part prognostication, which formed the bulk of Western publications of this sort and are still published in astonishing numbers in England,[173] were a far smaller part of the Russian output, perhaps because in 1739 and 1780 ukazes were issued restricting purchases of almanacs to those published by the Academy of Sciences, and in 1800 and 1830 further ukazes gave the Academy exclusive rights of publication which were rescinded only in 1865. The profitability of almanacs was potentially vast and the right to publish them had been a matter of bitter legal dispute in England also in the seventeenth century, with the Stationers' Company desperately defending its royal monopoly against the universities of Oxford and Cambridge, almost the reverse of the later Russian situation.[174] In fact the divinatory element in the Russian almanacs of the later eighteenth century is relatively small compared with that in English almanacs, perhaps because of the Academy connection. On the other hand fortune-telling books of the kind described above, as well as dream books (see Ch. 6.1), were frequently produced, despite the fact that their use was in theory proscribed by law, by the printing houses of government-controlled bodies such as Moscow University and the various cadet and military colleges.

12. *Playing Cards*

Playing cards were certainly known in Muscovy by the end of the sixteenth century: the word *karty* is first registered in 1599 in the manuscript dictionary of the English doctor Mark Ridley,[175] written while he was court physician in Moscow, and the earliest record of card-playing terminology (mostly from German, through Czech to Polish, thence to the Ukraine and on to Russia) is to be found in the Russian-English glossary of Richard James, chaplain to the embassy of Sir Dudley Digges in 1618.[176] These sources are not mentioned in the current dictionary of Old Russian,[177] which does, however, quote the sixteenth-century Prince Andrei Kurbskii on the subject of Western monarchs who 'stay up all night amusing themselves at cards and other devilish lunacies'.

Despite this hostile opinion and the fact that cards were very quickly associated with a dissolute way of life, the import of playing cards through the northern ports (i.e. in all probability mostly from England) reached considerable proportions in the seventeenth century.[178] Russian monarchs tended to vacillate between God and Mammon in their attitudes to popular vices: liquor was a profitable crown monopoly from the sixteenth century and the use of tobacco was at different times a capital crime or a lucrative source of licence revenue; chess and draughts, though often condemned, were certainly to be found in the seventeenth century even in the tsaritsa's quarters.[179] In 1667 Tsar Aleksei Mikhailovich, having been tempted into selling licences to trade in playing cards and *zern'*, felt obliged to cancel the licences in the following year, perhaps because there was no way of distinguishing the gaming uses of dice and cards from the divinatory (if indeed cards were so used at this period) but also because games even as games were regularly condemned by the church as pagan, 'Hellenic', and occasions of sin.

By the eighteenth century the moral objections to cards, though not to gambling,[180] had diminished (indeed the clergy became the most notorious devotees of card-playing), and the Moscow Foundling Home, one of Catherine II's enlightened projects, was partly funded by a tax on cards, including the fortune-telling cards produced by the Ivanov factory.[181] Interestingly enough, the first recorded occasion of fortune-telling from a spread of cards seems to have been in Russia in 1765, and the fortune-teller was a young Russian serf girl who had been bought by the celebrated adventurer Giacomo Casanova and became his mistress. The authors of the generally authoritative history of the occult Tarot, *A Wicked Pack of Cards*, express surprise that an uneducated Russian peasant girl should have practised cartomancy of this kind while the worldly Casanova, who recorded the incident in his memoirs, appeared to have been unfamilar with it.[182] And indeed the incident is puzzling, especially if the girl really was Russian (Casanova called her Zaire) and really was a peasant.

At least nine books on card games were published in Russia in the course of the century,[183] including two versions of Hoyle on whist,[184] and two manuals of cartomancy: *A True and very Simple Method of Fortune-Telling with Cards* (St Petersburg, 1782) and *The Open Secret of Fortune Telling by Cards* (Moscow, 1795).[185] The more general books of pastimes and fortune-telling also contained sections devoted to cards.

To judge from published titles, the popularity of games and books about them, conjuring or scientific tricks, and fortune-telling by cards or other means as semi-serious social pastimes at most levels of society, was really established in Russia from the 1760s onwards and, taken together with the kind of entertaining literature, especially fiction, which was being translated at the same time, it marks a new phase in Russian social manners in which the notions of leisure and pastime (*vremiaprovozhdenie*) became important and the middling urban population and the gentry on their estates began to amuse themselves in much the same way as their counterparts in other parts of Europe. The seriousness with which such social fortune-telling was taken clearly varied from person to person, but we may note that at the beginning of the nineteenth century Alexander I's Greek (but Italian-educated) Foreign Minister Capodistria consulted a ninety-five-year-old Finnish fortune-teller to have his fate told from cards and coffee-cups.[186] Cartomancy was evidently taken seriously also by the Freemasons of Russia, for whom it was one of the secrets of the craft.[187] Indeed, a good case has been made for a masonic numerological and cartomantic interpretation of Pushkin's story *The Queen of Spades* (1834),[188] and as we have seen in Ch. 4.3, Pushkin was no stranger to divination.

The Tarot, though known in Russia from at least one publication, seems not to have had any impact in Russia,[189] though Papus (Gérard d'Encausse), occultist, head of the revived Martinist Order at the end of the nineteenth century and one of the main propagators of the Tarot and the myth of its ancient origin, visited Russia and had a following there.[190] The major dictionaries, including that of Dal', do not record the Tarot.

Notes

1. On this subject see Drage, *Russian Word-Play Poetry*. The *carmina cabalistica* described there are disappointingly just verses with a particular alphanumerical method of encoding a date. The *carmina arithmetica* come closer to divination: the aim was to compose verses which, by another alphanumerical process, would select fifteen out of thirty names of passengers to be thrown overboard to lighten a sinking ship, in such a way that Jews would be sacrificed and Catholics saved (p. 85).

2. Karelian and Vepsian *zagovory* in Cyrillic are mentioned in Turilov and Chernetsov, 'O perspektivakh'.

3. Vlasova, *Novaia abevega*, p. 373.

4. Tolstoi, 'Russk. *chur* i chush''.

5. Kondrat'eva, *Metamorfozy sobstvennogo imeni*, s.v. For a long discussion of this word in both its ludic and its magic senses see Strakhov, 'Vostochnoslavianskoe *chur*'; see also Tolstoi, 'Russk. *chur i chush*'.

6. Vlasova, *Novaia abevega*, s.v. *urok*.

7. In general for Russian taboo words see Zelenin, 'Tabu slov'.

8. Zelenin, *Russische Volkskunde*, p. 78.

9. In the case of the bear the taboo is also related to bear cults, common among the non-Russian peoples of northern Russia and Siberia, and probably to some extent also among the Slavs. The Russian word for bear, *medved'*, itself a euphemism, is replaced in Siberia by the word *dedushka*, 'grandfather', and the bear is thought to be the brother of 'Tsar Fire' with water as its sister: Chikachev, *Russkie na Indigirke*, p. 133.

10. Demich in *Zhivaia starina*, 1912, p. 49.

11. Markevich, *Obychai* (reprint), p. 114. The association of parsley with the Devil, bad luck and death is also made in England: See Opie and Tatem, *Dictionary of Superstitions*, s.v.

12. Uspenskii, 'Religiozno-mifologicheskii aspekt', pp. 197–302. This has a very extensive bibliography.

13. Uspenskii, 'Language Situation', pp. 365–85. See also his 'Dualisticheskii kharakter' and 'Schism and Cultural Conflict', esp. 113–19.

14. Zelenin, *Izbrannye trudy*, p. 331, in the commentary by E.E. Levkievskaia.

15. See Kieckhefer, *Forbidden Rites*, pp. 16–17.

16. Chulkov, *Abevega*, p. 206; Eremina, 'Zagovornye kolybel'nye pesni', p. 30. On varieties of this practice elsewhere see Frazer, *Golden Bough*, III, p. 319f. A brief but informative overview of the ritual deception of diseases among the Slavs is given in Usacheva, 'Ritual'nyi obman'.

17. Eremina, 'Zagovornye kolybel'nye pesni', p. 30. This idea of deceiving Death can also be seen in the practice of ripping the shirt off a sick man, tearing it to pieces, burning it and then burying it: see Prokop'eva, 'Zhenskaia rubakha', pp. 60–1.

18. Chikachev, *Russkie na Indigirke*, p. 117.

19. Tudorovskaia, 'O vnepesennykh sviaziakh narodnoi obriadovoi pesni', p. 84.

20. Kondrat'eva, *Metamorfozy sobstvennogo imeni*, s.v.

21. Dal', *Tolkovyi slovar'*, s.v. *chert*.

22. See for Britain in particular Opie and Tatem, *Dictionary*, s.v. *Book*.

23. It is also found among the Copts: see Henein and Bianquis, *La Magie par les Psaumes*.

24. There were no fewer than forty-four printed editions of the Psalter in seventeenth-century Russia, out of a total for all books of 483, and print-runs could be well over a thousand: Luppov, *Kniga v Rossii v XVII veke*, pp. 28–30. To put these figures in perspective it should be noted that for most of the time there was effectively only one printing house in Muscovite Russia.

25. Almazov, 'Tainaia ispoved' v pravoslavnoi vostochnoi tserkvi', p. 409.

26. Iatsimirskii, *Slavianskie i russkie rukopisi rumynskikh bibliotek*, pp. 86–7.

27. Sakharov, *Skazaniia russkogo naroda*, p. 127.

28. D'iachenko, *Polnyi tserkovno slavianskii slovar'*, s.v. *kliuchevolkhvovanie*.

29. See *ERE*, VIII, col. 124b. Used for the detection of witches and thieves, removing spells and

curing bleeding from the nose. As late as 1870 in a court case at Southampton the bible and key oracle was the only evidence brought against a thief: Lea, *Superstition and Force*, p. 277. See also Opie and Tatem, *Dictionary*, s.v. *Bible and key*, which notes, among other things, the popularity of this method among fourteen-year-old girls in Ayr (Scotland) in the 1960s as an oracle to discover the names of future boy-friends.

30. Bibel, S.588a.

31. Reported in Demkova, 'Drevnerusskie rukopisi', p. 380.

32. Sakharov, *Skazaniia russkogo naroda*, p. 127.

33. Burtsev, *Obzor russkogo narodnogo byta severnogo kraia*, p. 10: here two numbers are chosen, one for page and one for line, and the passage thus selected is read out and interpreted.

34. Levenstim, 'Sueverie v ego otnoshenie k ugolovnomu pravu', p. 208.

35. For an example in the Arkhangel region see P. Efimenko, *Materialy*, p. 192; for a Podolian example see Simashkevich, 'Ob obychae gadat' na knigakh', pp. 457–65: this involves placing a knife, scissors or key on the Bible or Psalter, making a sign of the Cross with them, then opening the book with the implement.

36. For Islam see Fahd, *La Divination arabe*; in the West one may also cite the practice of holding the Gospel over the head of a bishop during his consecration, and the subsequent bibliomantic consultation: see Elukin, 'The Ordeal of Scripture', who dates the practice to post-1000 (p. 138).

37. Cherepnin, 'Iz istorii drevnerusskogo koldovstva', p. 103.

38. For studies of this text see Speranskii, *Iz istorii otrechennykh knig. I. Gadaniia po psaltiri*, p. 21, and V. M. Istrin's review of Speranskii in *Letopisi Istoriko-philologicheskogo obshchestva Novorossiskogo universiteta*, Odessa, 1901, 9, pp. 153–202. Speranskii's introduction to the text is long, detailed and still very informative on divinatory books in general, their origins and the history of their reception – it is also rambling and disorganized.

39. See Speranskii, *Iz istorii otrechennykh knig. I. Gadaniia po psaltiri*, sections VIII and IX.

40. See Meshcherskii, *Istochniki*, p. 46.

41. For text see *Izbornik*, pp. 146–7.

42. See Speranskii, *Iz istorii otrechennykh knig. I. Gadaniia po psaltiri*, p. 6, n. 1.

43. Ibid., p. 53.

44. Iavorskii, 'Novye rukopisnye nakhodki', p. 62 (text at pp. 110–11). This manuscript also contains a *zagovor* against the Devil in the name of the Cross and the archangels (p. 112) and a *Koliadnik* ascribed to the prophet 'Esdrom' (i.e. Esdras) (p. 113). A text was published by N. Tupikov in *Pamiatniki drevnei pis'mennosti i isskustva*, 140. On the text see Karskii in *Izvestiia Otdeleniia russkogo iazyka i slovesnosti*, 65, 8, pp. 9–12, 18–28. On the Muscovite versions of the text (without recorded divinatory additions) see Voznesenskii, *Staroobriadcheskie izdaniia*, pp. 125–30.

45. Arkhipov, 'O proiskhozhdenii drevneslavianskoi tainopisi', pp. 79–81 and *idem, Iz istori gebraizmov*, pp. 13–15 (summarizing the author's *kandidat* dissertation).

46. For some discussion see Leighton, 'Gematria in "The Queen of Spades"' and *idem*, 'Puskin and Freemasonry'; Baehr, *The Paradise Myth*, pp. 96, 102, 108, 243 n. 87.

47. For texts with some notes see *Drevnerusskaia pritcha*, pp. 381–93, 490–2.

48. For the English superstition see Opie and Tatem, *Dictionary of Superstition*, s.v. *Thirteen in company or at table*.

49. On the onomantic table in the Russian version see Ryan, 'The Onomantic Table' and *idem*, 'The *Passion of St Demetrius* and the *Secret of Secrets*'.

50. The so-called 'Chronograph Alexander' of the eleventh or twelfth century is derived from the β version of Pseudo-Callisthenes. It was published in Istrin, *Aleksandriia russkikh khronografov*. The fifteenth-century 'Serbian Alexander', not in fact in Serbian but so called because the earliest Slavonic MSS were found in Serbia, derives from the ε version of pseudo-Callisthenes via the *Middle Greek Alexander Book*. It was published in *Aleksandriia. Roman ob Aleksandre Makedonskom po russkoi rukopisi XV veka*, Moscow–Leningrad, 1963. A conflation of the two versions with other works appeared in the *Chronograph* of Pakhomii Logofet in 1442 and in subsequent reworkings. A Belorussian version of the *Historia de preliis* also exists: see *Aleksandryia*, Minsk, 1962.

51. See *Povest' o Kulikovskoi bitve*, p. 30.

52. See Ross, *Alexander Historiatus*, p. 42.

53. See Rovinskii, *Russkie gravery*, p. 139.

54. For a more detailed discussion see Ryan, 'The *Passion of St Demetrius* and the *Secret of Secrets*'.

55. See Migne, *Patrologia Graeca*, 116, cols 1171, 1179, 1191. Lemerle, *Les Plus Anciens Récits*, pp. 198–200, notes that the connection of the Nestor episode with Demetrius is very tenuous.

56. See Ryan, 'The *Passion of St Demetrius* and the *Secret of Secrets*', pp. 61–2.

57. Tannery, 'Notice sur des fragments d'onomatomancie arithmétique', p. 248.

58. Festugière, *La Révélation*, pp. 336–9. The system is also described in Bouché-Leclerq, *Histoire de la divination dans l'antiquité*, pp. 261–3.

59. ed. Santen, II. 250, 272, 273.

60. Fahd, *La Divination arabe*, p. 217.

61. For this and letter magic in the Islamic world in general see Ibn Khaldūn, *The Muqaddimah*, I, pp. 234–45; III, pp. 171–227.

62. Budge, *Syrian Anatomy*, II, pp. 540–1.

63. Kasten, *Seudo Aristóteles Poridat de las Poridades*, pp. 92–3.

64. Manzalaoui, *Secretum secretorum. Nine English Versions*, pp. xviii, 15–16.

65. See Burnett, 'The Eadwine Psalter', for a detailed study.

66. Eis, *Wahrsage texte des Spätmittelalters*, pp. 13–16, text at pp. 49–52.

67. Trachtenberg, *Jewish Magic and Superstition*, p. 217.

68. See Archipov, 'O proiskhozhedenii drevneslavianskoi tainopisi'.

69. In 1991 in Moscow there appeared a reprint of the 1912 fifth edition of *Znameniia prishestviia Antikhrista* ('Signs of the coming of the Antichrist'), a booklet published with the imprimatur of the Moscow religious censorship committee.

70. The literature of the subject is extensive: for a good general survey of the medieval tradition but one which ignores Russia, see Emmerson, *Antichrist in the Middle Ages*. McGinn's *Antichrist* devotes six pages (263–9) to Antichrist in Russia but only in the literature of the late nineteenth and twentieth centuries.

71. One seventeenth-century German (Swedish Hanoverian) publication manages to find that both Pope Alexander VII and Sultan Mehmed IV were the Antichrist and gives a family tree showing that they were in fact blood relations: Wallich, *Religio Turcica*, 1659.

72. A book by an English clergyman, Revd M. Baxter, *Louis Napoleon, The Destined Monarch of the World*, London, 1861, demonstrated at length, and with enormous Biblical and numerological ingenuity, that Louis Napoleon was the Antichrist.

73. In fact this particular representation of the moon is quite common: it can be found for example on one buttock of the *Papstesel* in Reformation anti-papal prints (which to some would support the

Antichrist theme), but, on the side of the angels, it is also shown on the shield of St Demetrius in the Stroganov icon-painters handbook.

74. 'Up and Down the City Road', *The Independent*, 20 May 1989.

75. Ian MacKinnon, 'Drivers register 666 reasons for new numbers', *The Independent*, February 1990, p. 1.

76. Reported by Phil Reeves in *The Independent*, 12 June 1996, p. 9. Mikhail Gorbachov, the last head of the Soviet state, had long been known as 'Mikhail mechennyi' (Michael the Marked), a not always jocular reference both to the Apocalypse and to the popular appellations of medieval monarchs.

77. Reported by Alan Philps in *The Daily Telegraph*, January 1, 1998, p. 11.

78. See *Slovar' knizhnikov*, vyp. 1, s.v. *Slova i Skazanie sviatogo Ippolita ob antikhriste*.

79. For Russian bibliography see *Slovar' knizhnikov*, vyp. 1, s.v. *Otkrovenie Mefodiia Patarskogo*.

80. See in general Alexander, 'The Diffusion of Byzantine Apocalypses' and *idem*, *The Byzantine Apocalyptic Tradition*, esp. pp. 193–225 'The Legend of the Antichrist'.

81. See a series of anti-Jewish and anti-Judaizing anathemas in MS Moscow State Historical Museum, Barsov 1395, ff. 61–61v: 'I curse all who await the coming of the Antichrist and who expect to prepare a feast for him'.

82. See most recently De Michelis, *I nomi dell'avversario*.

83. See Gur'ianova, 'Staroobriadcheskie sochinenia', pp. 140–1; also, with more general reference to Old Believer piety, Tarasov, *Ikona i blagochestie*, pp. 107–27. The fashion for discovering the name of the Antichrist was not confined to Old Believers; indeed Stephan Iavorskii, bishop of Riazan and Murom, one of Peter the Great's supporters and a signatory to his *Spiritual Regulation* of 1720, wrote on the subject and has left a number of numerological interpretations, e.g. *Alithis vlaveros* (Greek, 'truly harmful'), *Kakosodikos* (Greek, 'evil leader'), *Lateinos*, a Latin, or Westerner. Quoted from D'iachenko, *Polnyi tserkovno-slavianskii slovar'*, s.vv.

84. For a convenient English survey and some bibliography see Billington, *The Icon and the Axe*, esp. pp. 141–4, 682–3.

85. Discussed most recently in Pokrovskii, 'Staroobriadchestvo', pp. 183–5.

86. Novichkova, *Russkii demonologicheskii slovar'*, s.v. *antikhrist*.

87. Uspenskii, 'Historia sub specie semioticae'. Both here and in other works Uspenskii has drawn attention to the magical significance of both Ivan the Terrible and Peter the Great.

88. See Cracraft, *Church Reform*, p. 241, for some discussion of the executions of Grishka Talitskii and Varlaam Levin.

89. For detailed discussion and examples of the rhetorical deification of Russian monarchs see Baehr, *The Paradise Myth*, esp. pp. 22–33.

90. For a valuable case study see Pokrovskii, 'Narodnaia èskhatologicheskaia «gazeta» 1731 g.'

91. Kondrat'eva, *Metamorfozy sobstvennogo imeni*, s.v. *antikhrist*.

92. Dal', *Poslovitsy*, 1989, I, p. 35.

93. Ralston, *Songs of the Russian People*, pp. 402–3.

94. See Baehr, '"Fortuna Redux": The Iconography of Happiness', p. 116.

95. Some even issued their own 'passports' identifying themselves as 'citizens of the Heavenly Jerusalem': see Chistov, *Russkie narodnye sotial'no-utopicheskie legendy*, pp. 244–5.

96. Malov, *Pis'ma k voinam*, pp. 150–3.

97. A popular print of the late eighteenth century depicts the scene: see Pera, *I Vecchi Credenti*, facing p. 131.

98. Dal', s.v. *antikhrist*.

99. For recent studies and bibliography of Old Believer beliefs and texts about the Antichrist see Gur'ianova, *Krest'ianskii antimonarkhicheskii protest*, esp. ch. 2 'Staroobriadcheskoe uchenie o Petre I–antikhriste'; Eleonskaia, 'Gumanisticheskie motivy v «Otrazitel'nom pisanii» Efrosina'; Pera, *I Vecchi Credenti e l'Anticristo*.

100. Kondrat'eva, *Metamorfozy sobstvennogo imeni*, s.vv. *antikhrist, anchutka*. Dal' lists *anchutka* only in the plural in the sense of satanic imps; he adds the expression 'dopit'sia do anchutkov', 'to drink to the point of seeing little demons'.

101. See Novichkova, *Russkii demonologicheskii slovar'*, s.v. *anchutka*.

102. V.F. Trakhtenberg, *Blatnaia muzyka*, St Petersburg, 1908, s.v. Also recorded for the Soviet period as slang for the Devil or an unreliable person: Baldaev *et al.*, *Slovar'*.

103. See Hartley, 'Russia in 1812', p. 186.

104. Kelsiev, *Sbornik pravitel'stvennykh svedenii o rasskolnikakh*, I, p. 43.

105. Derzhavin, *Sochineniia Derzhavina*, VI, pp. 427–8. I am obliged to Professor Isabel de Madariaga for this and the following reference.

106. Vernadskii, *Russkoe masonstvo*, p. 7.

107. Kondrat'eva, *Metamorfozy sobstvennogo imeni*, s.v. *armizon*.

108. A newspaper item quoted in Solzhenitsyn, *August 1914*, p. 60.

109. Graham, *Undiscovered Russia*, pp. 46–7.

110. It would be a pity to ignore one or two further Russian literary associations. The writer P. Boborykhin, writing in the journal *Golos* in the 1860s used the *nom-de-plume* of 666, and the notorious English 'black magician' and confidence-trickster Aleister Crowley, who called himself 'The Beast 666', spent some time in Moscow in 1913 as promoter of a *risqué* dance troupe called 'The Ragged Ragtime Girls' (they played violins while dancing seductively in scanty clothing). See Ryan, 'The Great Beast in Russia'.

111. *Slovar' tiuremno-lagerno-blatnogo zhargona. Rechevoi i graficheskii portret sovetskoi tiur'my*, Moscow, 1992, pp. 451, 484–6.

112. For a useful general history of dice see Grandjouan, *L'Astragale et le pari*.

113. Saxo Grammaticus, *Gesta Danorum*, XIV, p. 567.

114. See Dal', *Tolkovyi slovar'*, s.v. *zerno*; Kostomarov, 'Ocherk domashnei zhizni', p. 92.

115. Guthrie, *Noctes Rossicae*, f. 83v.

116. Bulgakovskii, 'Pinchuki', p. 185.

117. Sumtsov, *Khleb v obriadakh i pesniakh*, p. 187. Cf. the English superstition that a loaf upside down means bad luck: see Opie and Tatem, *Dictionary*, s.v. *Loaf*.

118. Shein, *Velikoruss v svoikh pesniakh*, vyp. 1, p. 37.

119. Trachtenberg, *Jewish Magic*, p. 217. Trachtenberg does not elaborate, but the form 'Esclavonia' suggests that it was Spanish Jews who ascribed this practice to the Slavs, and Moorish Spain had many Balkan Slav and Russian slaves.

120. Trullan canons, L: Mansi, *Collection conciliorum*, XI, col. 967.

121. See *SRIa, s.v. lek, zern'*. See also Linder, *Shakhmaty na Rusi*, pp. 98–102.

122. *Stoglav*, pp. 137–8. In ch. 92 of this work 'On the Playthings of Hellenic Devilry' the Sixth Ecumenical Council is invoked against *zern'*, chess and draughts.

123. *Zakonodatel'nye akty*, p. 156, no. 198.

124. See Stone, *A Dictionarie*, p. 157.

125. *Domostroi*, p. 22.

126. *Domostroi*, p. 80.

127. Speranskii, *Iz istorii otrechennykh knig. I. Gadaniia po psaltiri*, p. 107.

128. See *Slovar' XVIII v., s.v. bob: vorozhit', razvodit' bobami*.

129. Mordovina and Stanislavskii, 'Gadatel'naia kniga', pp. 324–5.

130. Zabelin, *Domashnii byt russkikh tsarits*, p. 248.

131. See Ch. 16.

132. For an overview see Kleimola, *Justice in Medieval Russia*, pp. 58–68.

133. *Slovar' XI–XVII*, s.v. *zherebei*. See also Kleimola, *Justice in Medieval Russia*, pp. 66–7.

134. See Butler, 'Foreign Impressions of Russian Law', pp. 78–9.

135. See Dal', *Tolkovyi slovar'*, s.v. *zherebei*.

136. See *Radzivillovskaia letopis'*, f. 46v. See Chernetsov, 'K izucheniiu Radzivilovskoi letopisi', p. 284.

137. Quoted in the version published in *Rude and Barbarous Kingdom*, p. 82, letter to Parker.

138. As in English, the various number combinations have been given slang names by Russian gamblers: by the nineteenth century for seven and eleven these would be *komitetskaia* and *s pudom* – see Dal', *Tolkovyi slovar'*, s.v. *kost'*.

139. Larin, *Russko-angliiskii slovar'-dnevnik Richarda Dzhemsa*, p. 127.

140. Du Cange, *Glossarium*, s.v. *raffla*. For some discussion of this see Veselovskii, 'Zametki k istorii apokrifov'.

141. Pypin, *Lozhnye i otrechennye knigi*, pp. 161–6. On this see also a detailed but confused discussion in Speranskii, *Gadatel'nyi psaltyr'*.

142. Rybnikov, *Pesni*, IV, pp. 248–50. He also publishes at pp. 211–13 another set of eighteen predictions from the manuscript of a *znakhar'* which are very similar but have no indication of how they are selected.

143. Kuznetsov-Krasnoiarskii, *Rafli*. Review by S.K. K-v in *Etnograficheskoe obozrenie*, 1905, 4, pp. 129–32. Incomplete, 17–18th c.; a further copy dating from the 1780s is in the Russian Academy of Sciences Library, MS 45.1.198.

144. Gaster, *Literatura populară romănă*, pp. 502–3.

145. Romanov, *Belorusskii sbornik*, 4, pp. 213–33. See also Karskii, *Belorusi*, 1920, pp. 51–2.

146. E. Eleonskaia, *K izucheniia zagovora*, p. 18.

147. *Opisanie dokumentov i del*, L (1770), no. 322.

148. Delatte, *Anecdota*, pp. 392–6.

149. A still useful survey of 'Books of Fate' is the appendix to Bolte, *Georg Wickrams Werke*, p. 276–348.

150. Vicenza, c. 1185 (first edn 1483).

151. Skeat, 'An Early Medieval "Book of Fate"', p. 50.

152. See *Libro de ajedrez, dados y tablas de Alfonso X el Sabio*.

153. Arabic and Persian geomancy may use four dice, arranged on a spindle so that there are only four numbered faces, as an alternative to random marking in sand, etc.: see Skinner, *Terrestrial Astrology*, pp. 31–2; Savage-Smith and Smith, *Islamic Geomancy*, p. 9, and Massé in *Encyclopedia of Islam*, II, p. 761. A Tibetan three-dice oracle is described in *Divination and Oracles*, p. 17.

154. In the Kuznetsov-Krasnoiarskii version this prediction is for 6.3.1. and Theodore is replaced by St Agapius. The apocryphal *vita* of Theodore is a fantastic story of fighting giant serpents (on the

text see Ch. 8.6.6, n. n). It promises to expel demons, cure the blind and deaf, provide abundant wheat, wine and oil (an indication of Greek origins) and all good things to those who keep his memory holy.

155. On the history of dice numbered one to four see Grandjouan, *L'Astragale*, pp. 86–95.

156. Moscow, MS RGADA, Prikaznye dela starykh let, fond 141, no. 71, ch. 1, ff. 126–33 published in Mordovina and Stanislavskii, 'Gadatel'naia kniga XVII v. kholopa Pimena Kalinina'.

157. Described in *SK dop.*, no. 163 (not seen. WFR).

158. The word used is *kostochki*, lit. 'little bones'. Normally dice are *kosti* and *kostochki* are fruit stones, which were used as counters in games, some kinds of divination, and in the sixteenth century for calculation on the counting board, whence their use in the sense of bead on a Russian abacus.

159. See Seaman, 'An Eighteenth-Century Russian Pocket-Book', pp. 270–1. This was apparently borrowed from England. Musical dice composition has been variously attributed to C.P.E. Bach, Haydn and Mozart.

160. For the text of the 'Epistle of the monk Maksim the Greek to a certain monk of the rank of abbot concerning the German (i.e. West European) falsehood called Fortune and about her wheel' see *Pamiatniki literatury Drevnei Rusi. Konets XV–pervaia polovina XVI veka*, pp. 456–65.

161. See Kovtun, 'Planida – furtuna – schastnoe koleso'. Kovtun suggests that the references to 'fatum and fortuna' in fact reflect Maxim's familiarity with Coluccio Salutati's *De Fato et Fortuna*.

162. Published in Armstrong, *Yermak's Campaign in Siberia*, p. 274.

163. One nineteenth-century popular print of the wheel of fortune ('Fartuna'), also with the 'Vanity of vanities' inscription, is published in Ivanov, *Russkii narodnyi lubok*, p. 132, no. 86.

164. Delatte, *Anecdota*, pp. 388, 392, notes two such circles in Byzantine texts, the first as part of a geomancy, the second astrological.

165. See Kirilov, 'Interes izucheniia narodnoi i tibetskoi meditsiny', p. 108. Kirilov is describing Old Believer practices in Russian Asia beyond Lake Baikal.

166. Rovinskii, *Russkie narodnye kartinki*, 1881–4, V, pp. 94–5. An illustration of the text is published in Rovinskii, *Russkie narodnye kartinki*, 1900, col. 176, and a Bulgarian version, evidently of Russian origin is published in Tomov, *Bulgarische Ikonen*, no. 104. The earliest dated version I have found recorded was printed in Moscow in 1829 by T. Selivanovskii.

167. Kharuzina, 'Po povodu zametki P. Andre', p. 102.

168. Bolonev, *Narodnyi kalendar' semeiskikh Zabaikal'ia*, p. 60.

169. Reproduced in Ivanov, *Russkii narodnyi lubok*, p. 104, no. 47. An Old Believer print also showing a man with the globe on his shoulders and very similar to the Solomon print is given at no. 77.

170. Rovinskii, *Russkie narodnye kartinki*, 1900, cols 171, 174.

171. Rovinskii, *Russkie narodnye kartinki*, 1881–4, I, p. 358, no. 136.

172. Sumarokov, *Polnoe sobranie vsekh sochiinenii*, IV, Moscow, 1781. I am grateful to Professor Charles Drage for drawing my attention to this text.

173. See Capp, *Astrology and the Popular Press*, pp. 268–9, on the ubiquity and influence of almanacs in late Victorian England.

174. See Capp, *Astrology and the Popular Press*, pp. 37ff.

175. See Stone, *A Dictionarie*, p. 172.

176. See Unbegaun, 'Cards and Card-Playing in Muscovite Russia'. A brief but thorough recent survey of the history of playing cards in Russia is to be found in Burnett, 'Russian Playing Card History'.

177. *Slovar' XI–XVII vv.*, s.v. *karta*.

178. Unbegaun, 'Cards and Card Playing in Muscovite Russia', pp. 256–7.

179. Several sets, including one 'crystal' chess set, are listed in the official inventories: see Zabelin, *Domashnii byt russkikh tsarits*, p. 47.

180. A Moscow popular print of 1853 entitled 'The Demon of Gambling' shows a dragon whose body is decorated with playing cards and dice guarding a treasure of gambled-away property, breathing fire over a city which it holds in its hand: published in Sakovich, 'Moskovskaia narodnaia graviura', p. 146.

181. *Materialy dlia istorii Moskovskogo vospitatel'nogo doma*, p. 22.

182. Decker, Depaulis, and Dummett, *A Wicked Pack of Cards*, p. 74.

183. On the subject of cartomancy and popular fortune-telling in the eighteenth and nineteenth century in Russia, see now the detailed study by Faith Wigzell, *Reading Russian Fortunes*.

184. In 1769 and 1791: *SK*, nos 1461–2.

185. *SK*, no. 5075 and *SK dop.*, no. 24.

186. Woodhouse, *Capodistria*, p. 71. Sakharov, *Skazaniia russkogo naroda*, p. 116–17, notes that telling fortunes by coffee grounds was an urban not rural practice. It was also evidently a practice confined to women: Dal', *Tolkovyi slovar'*, s.v. *kofe* mentions only the feminine form *kofeinitsa*.

187. Leighton, 'Russian Freemasons'.

188. Leighton, 'Gematria'.

189. Wigzell, *Reading Russian Fortunes*, pp. 33–4.

190. Decker, Depaulis, and Dummett, *A Wicked Pack of Cards*, pp. 253–4.

12

GEOMANCY

1. *Introduction*

Geomancy as a term has a number of possible meanings. Two of them apply to divinatory systems known in Russia. The first of these is earthquake divination, known from the fourteenth century onwards in a Balkan Slav translation of the Greek *Seismologion* which is found as part of the thunder divination text *Gromnik* or *Gromovnik* (in Greek *Brontologion*), and is discussed together with that text in Ch. 14. The second, a more widely known divinatory system which will be discussed here, is based on the interpretation of arbitrarily drawn series of dots, originally in sand but later on other media. It is possible that some such divination was practised by the pre-literate Slavs – the tenth-century Bulgarian monk Khrabr, in a treatise defending the use of a Slavonic alphabet, wrote: 'Formerly the Slavs had no writing but, being pagans, counted and performed divinations with lines and cuts'. Saxo Grammaticus, two centuries later, records a similar practice among the Baltic Slavs.[1]

In general, however, the practice of geomancy appears to be Arabic in origin. It was known in North Africa at least from the ninth century and the earliest extant manual dates probably from the twelfth century. Thence it passed into Jewish literature and practice,[2] and Greek and Latin translations and reworkings followed from the twelfth century and in their turn gave rise a number of vernacular texts.[3]

The Arabic term for this system of divination is *raml* 'sand', and from this word the Byzantine terms for geomancy *raboulion*, *ramblion* and variants are supposedly derived, as is the system itself. The most recent works mentioning the subject in Russian consider these Greek words to be the source of the Russian term *rafli*, and abandon the easier, and perhaps still the better, etymology of medieval Latin *raffla*, 'game or divination by dice'[4] (cf. English 'raffle') proposed in the earliest Russian studies by Pypin and Veselovskii.[5] What is now undisputed is that there were geomantic texts in Russia and that they were called *Rafli*.

The word *Rafli* is not found in the earlier lists of banned books[6] but appears first in lists of forbidden books and practices in two sixteenth-century texts: the *Domostroi* (a manual of domestic behaviour), which condemns 'spell-casting and wizardry and amulets, stargazing, *Rafli*, almanacs, black-bookery, crow-cawing, Six Wings, axe amulets, medical amulets, magic bones . . .' etc.,[7] and the *Stoglav* or record of the Council of One Hundred Chapters convened by Ivan IV in Moscow in 1551, which condemns the following 'evil heresies' (as in most lists of this kind it is not always clear whether books or practices are being referred to): '*rafli*, Six Wings, crow cawing, astronomy, zodiac signs, almanac, stargazing,

Aristotle, the Gates of Aristotle'.[8] (For the *Stoglav* and *Domostroi* in more detail see Ch. 1.6.)

Only recently, however, has it become possible to say definitely what the Old Russian *Rafli* was. Indeed, the first Russian text to be published which purported to be the *Rafli* (despite the absence of the word from the text)[9] was in fact not a geomancy but a quite different form of divination involving three dice, and is described in Ch. 11.10.

2. *The Geomancy Ascribed to the Prophet Samuel/Khail*

A semi geomantic Serbian Church Slavonic text was published by Speranskii in 1899.[10] Speranskii had started out in the wrong direction and introduced a great deal of confusion into his learned but rambling discussion of the *Rafli* (at pp. 59–75 and 159–65) so that although he recognized this text as having similarity with Western geomantic texts he was not prepared to recognize it as being the same as the *Rafli*.

The text, taken from two seventeenth-century Serbian manuscripts,[11] has a defective heading 'The benificent, ancient and truthful [?prophecy] . . . this wisdom was revealed to the prophet Samuel by the angel of the Lord in sixteen figures and he prophesied to the people about future things'. It begins with instructions on how to make a divination: you must fast, then with a pure and humble heart take the Gospels or Psalter, sing the Trisagion three times, pray to God and cross yourself with the Gospels or Psalter.[12] Then, keeping your question in your heart,[13] you open the book and choose the first word of the first line on the left-hand page; if the letter is Greek *a, g, e, z, i, l, n, r, t, f, ps* [i.e. the odd numbers in Greek and Slavonic alphabetic numeration] then you must write down a line; but if the letter is Greek *v, d, ĭ, m, ks, y, p, s, u, ch, ō* [i.e. the even numbers] then write two lines; do this for four lines and then compare with the sixteen figures (*obrazy*). These figures have the following names [the usual Latin names of the geomantic figures are given in square brackets for comparison]:

  1 .... Way [*Via*]
  2 :::: People and gathering [*Populus*]
  3 ::.. The Great Fortune of Christ [*Fortuna Major*]
  4 ..:: The Minor Fortune [*Fortuna Minor*]
  5 :::. Misfortune and grief [*Tristitia*]
  6 .::: Good fortune and happiness [*Laetitia*]
  7 .::. Misfortune [*Carcer*]
  8 :..: Riches [*Acquisitio*]
  9 ..:. Good War [*Puella*]
  10 :.:: Physical labour and bloodshed [*Rubeus*]
  11 ::.: White silver [*Albus*]
  12 .:.. Lesser War [*Puer*]
  13 .:.: Perdition [*Amissio*]

14 :..: Union [*Conjunctio*]
15 :... Head [*Caput*]
16 ...: Tail [*Cauda*]

Each of these categories is followed by a short prediction. It is clear that although there are some variations – there are no 'standard' divination texts – these are essentially the sixteen figures and predictions of geomancy, shorn of all further derived figures and associations, and with a selection procedure drawn from bibliomancy (i.e. by random reference to a book), as in lot-books.[14] A Byzantine text is known which is almost identical, even to the Prophet Khail, the detail of the Gospels and Psalter and the unusual ninth, eleventh and twelfth houses: 'Good War',[15] White Silver' and 'Little War'. Delatte, who published this text from a fifteenth-century Greek manuscript containing three versions of the text, recorded six copies in Paris alone, two of which have alternative names for the prophet (Chaleth and Charouth).[16] This type of divination, whether or not it derives ultimately from an Arabic source, seems to have been common, at least in late Byzantium, and its transmission to the Orthodox Slavs is unproblematic. Similar semi-geomantic texts exist in the West. A fifteenth-century German 'Geomancy of the Sixteen Judges' offers a set of sixteen answers (one for each figure) from each of sixteen 'Judges' (all of whom have Hebrew names, often garbled).[17] A Latin text using the geomantic figures as the key to an 'oracle' (an answer to each of twenty-five questions is given for every figure) was published in Frankfurt am Main in 1693 with the title *Tabulae geomanticae seu liber singularis de tribus ultimis ex antiquo manuscripto de anno MDXXXV jam primo luci datus annexis duabus tabellis huic studio mire inservientibus caeteroquin utilibus & jucundis.*[18]

3. *The Geomantic Figures in the* Radziwiłł Chronicle

Evidence of a geomantic consultation in Russia is to be seen in an illustration in the late fifteenth-century Russian illuminated chronicle known as the *Radziwiłł* or *Königsberg Chronicle.* Here, below a battle scene, is an almost complete geomantic consultation in its characteristic triangular shape of eight *matres* and *filiae* in the top line, four *nepotes* below, and below them the two *testes* (one erased) and the *iudex.* This was previously thought to be an abacus calculation but was correctly identified in 1977 by Chernetsov.[19] The compiler of this prediction, which appears to be of approximately the same date as the main text of the manuscript, must have been familiar with a full geomantic text, such as the *Rafli* described below (or possibly a West European manual, in view of other Western influences in the manuscript), and not simply a basic text of the Prophet Samuel/Khail type. Who might have made this so far unique geomantic consultation, and why, and where, remains a mystery.

4. *The* Rafli *and the* Gates of Aristotle

In 1985 an important and hitherto unknown text was published by Chernetsov and Turilov which not only calls itself *Rafli* but is in fact a geomancy.[21] It is unusual in many respects – it is long, it has a named and identifiable Russian author (probably a cleric), it appears to be partly of apparently oriental origin[22] but obviously reworked extensively for a Russian, Christian, readership, and it forms part of a compendium of minor astrological texts.

Chernetsov and Turilov note in their edition that the date of composition is probably 1579; the manuscript is much later (seventeenth–eighteenth century), in three parts in different hands (the first two Great Russian, one of them being possibly Pomorian Old Believer, and the third being Ukrainian cursive); the author, Ivan Rykov, was probably a Pskovian in the entourage of Ivan IV; the introduction resembles that of the calendrical texts *Mirotvornyi krug* and *Sviattsy*; the language of the text is Great Russian with some Belorussian and Polish influence and evidence of oriental origin (e.g. the use of *vrata* 'gates' for 'chapters', probably ultimately from Arabic *bāb*), perhaps indicating that the underlying text of the *Rafli*, before its reworking by Rykov, had some connection with works such as the *Logika* (the description in both of Aristotle as 'the head of all philosophers') and *Secretum secretorum* (all three texts are divided into *vrata*), translated from Hebrew in the late fifteenth or early sixteenth centuries, probably in the Grand Duchy of Lithuania, and possibly connected with the Judaizers (see Ch. 1.5).

The work quotes from the Old and New Testaments and the late fourteenth-century *vita* of Stefan of Perm' by Epifanii Premudryi, as well as employing apocryphal motifs like Seth's columns of stone and clay; the manuscript containing the *Rafli* also contains a number of minor calendrical and astrological texts known independently, including part of a curious astrological Solomon text,[23] and 'The Divination of Tsar David', a dice prediction text similar to that incorrectly identified as the *Rafli* by Pypin.[24] These are discussed in more detail in Ch. 11.10.

In view of the interest of this text and the entirely new light it sheds on the possible extent of interest in divination and the esoteric in sixteenth-century Muscovy, I give a summary of it below (my numeration). It should be noted that the text is at some points physically defective and at others has suffered from scribal errors such as omission and repetition. Its sense is therefore occasionally unclear or ambiguous:

I.1 [f. 1] 'Preface to the calendar [*sviattsy*, church calendar of saints' days], the work of the sinful servant Ioann Rykov'.[25] The author's preface which follows indicates that the work was compiled for 'brother Kir Ioann' in Pskov (which suggests that both men were clerics – the title Kir normally indicates a member of the higher clergy). Ioann is addressed regularly throughout Book 1.[26]

I.2. Rykov states his intention of explaining the *Sviattsy* (church calendar of saints) and the *Mirotvornyi krug* (calendar cycles from the date of the Creation) and the great and lesser indictions. [f. 2] The use of the 'scroll given by God to 'Seth the son of Adam' and the *Ruchnaia paskhaliia* (mnemonic hand calendar) to find the Jewish Passover.

I.3. The seven great luminaries; quotes 'Athanasius and other fathers' on the origin of the Zodiac. Recommends John Damascene's *De fide orthodoxa*.

I.4. [f. 3] 'A brief account of the year, and matters relating to it'. The allegory of the year: the Tsar is the solar year; [f. 4] four tsars who serve are the seasons, which are equivalent of the four elements, air, fire, water, earth; the twelve animals (*sic*) of the Zodiac are the months; the fifty-two passers-by (*prekhoditeli* – evidently the weeks); 365 members of the household are the days; the twelve gold coins are the hours of daylight, the twelve copper coins are the night hours; one lesser slave is the bissextile day; the two gold-measurers are the two equinoxes, the two gold-collectors are the two solstices; the thirty-six noble youths are the thirty-six days of the kalends. The Tsaritsa is the lunar year; the twelve princes are the months; the 354 slaves are the days of the lunar year. The four seasons are the four ages of man: youth, maturity, old age; sickness and death.[27] The number of days in each month. The reason for, and constitution of, twelve months instead of the ten instituted by Romulus [f.5].

I.5. 'On the solar year'. Brief discussion of why the year should begin in March (see below, para. 8). The world was created on March 25, [f. 6] the calendars of the Arabs, Persians, Romans, Egyptians, and the Roman Christians [ff. 6–7].[28]

I.6. Finding the number of the solar cycle in the *Ruchnaia paskhaliia*.

I.7. Finding the number of the lunar cycle [f.8].

I.8. 'Preface concerning March'. God made the seven planets and the Zodiac and gave Seth and Japhet, the first scribes (*d'iaki*),[29] a scroll [f. 9] containing everything in the zones of the firmament. For this scroll they made two pillars, one of stone, the other of clay, so that if God should punish mankind for its sins by fire or water one or other of the pillars would survive. After the Flood the scroll was rescued from the stone pillar. The importance of the month of March: Moses, the month of the Creation, Exodus, conception of Christ, Romulus and the building of Rome [f. 10],[30] St Stefan of Perm' fixes the 25 March, the Annunciation, as the first day of the year for his newly converted flock of Permians and Zyrians.[31]

II. 1. [f. 11] Address to his brothers 'kir Ioann and Zakharii' and the brotherhood of Pskov to study how to use the calendrical cycles without suspicion of heresy or schism. First reference to *rafli*. Repetition of the story of the scroll of wisdom: this time it is brought by Gabriel to Seth and contains knowledge of the sun and moon and the other five planets and the Zodiac.[32] [f. 12] And the descendants of Seth guarded this knowledge for two thousand years; they built two columns in Assyria, one of stone, the other of clay. The stone column was found by the sons of Noah after the Flood and they took the scroll and read it, and built the Tower of Babel in Babylon in case of another flood. The Assyrians used the tower for astronomical observations, and from them the Hellenic kings, and Aristotle and the wizard Nectanebus[33] and Ptolemy in Egypt, and the wise men of Persia derived their wisdom, which comes from the stars and this book *Rafli*, or in Slavonic *sviattsy*.[34]

In Persia there were four wise men: Iuda, Khariz, Shmoil and Avengasan. [f. 13] They fell out over the wife of Khariz, Amorra, who after their various violent deaths married Eptai and gave him the book called *Rafli*. Eptai has a young and handsome disciple called Ivash. Amorra tries to persuade Ivash to kill Eptai and take her away. She drags him into her bed; Eptai returns and finds them; Amorra stabs him to death. [f. 14] The two then take Eptai's gold and the *Rafli* and flee to the Arabs and settle by the Ethiopian river. Ivash is punished by God by being struck dead by lightning. Amorra is left alone and hands over the *Rafli* to the Arabs, after which she too is destroyed by fire. Rykov adds that the *Rafli* was translated into Slavonic without adding anything and without any heretical or schismatic intent.

III. 1. Instructions on how to use the *Rafli*. The four elements called tsars; these are East, West, North, and South and are the first four houses of the Rafli;[35] add to these the elements of fire, air, water and earth, and you will have eight houses. [f. 15] The first house is summer, the second spring, the third winter, the fourth autumn. The last four are the shining column of night, the shining column of day, the winter solstice, the summer solstice.

III.2. Of the twelve signs of the Zodiac and their houses and influence. [ff. 16–17] Table of Zodiac signs with their associated planets, months, temperaments, etc. From the letters calculate the value of the appellants name and that of his mother. Divide the first by seven and the second by nine: the remainder will indicate the planet. In the third series of numbers up to 25 the remainder will indicate your Zodiac sign [for comparable onomantic operations in the Old Russian *Secretum secretorum* see Ch. 11.8].

III.3. Reveal your desire to God and pray from the Psalm 'O Lord how wonderful is your name over all the earth' [i.e. Psalm 8, 1]. Write down your star, of that day and hour and do your divination. The sky should be clear and quiet, after the third hour of the day or night and three hours before evening or morning.

III.4. [f. 18] 'The first planet is the sun, its day is Sunday, its sign is Leo; | | . | , .. | | . 'Concerns the ruler and his children, state affairs and all humanity and children'. Similarly for the other planets: Venus . | | ., . | . | , Mercury | .. | , | | | | , Moon .... , | | .. , Mars ... | , | | | ., . | | ., Jupiter | . | ., . | | | , | ... , Saturn .. | ., | . | | [36] Planetary and zodiacal symbols are given; the terminology is Greek-based, as is normal in Russian before the seventeenth century.

Say the Jesus prayer, the Trisagion, and the Paternoster, then make your divination.

III.5. [f. 19] How to make a judgement (*sud* – geomantic literature usually has 'judge' for this) from the eleven houses of this book. Take a pen and think of the matters which concern you one after another. Then make lines of dots like the four fingers of your hand, one longer than the next,[37] but without counting; then mark them off in twos. These are the first four houses of the *Rafli* or, in Slavonic, the seasons of the year. Then count off these lines in twos and where one is left write a dot, where two a stroke. From this you generate the first house. This house is called Aries or March, the first of the months and the renewal of everything living and of the annual cycle. In the *Rafli* the sixteenth house is called the mentor (or shepherd – Russ. *pastyr'*) of all the houses. How to generate the *filiae* (no special term in the Russian text).

[f. 20] How to generate the *nepotes* (no special term in the Russian text).

[f. 21] Make four hands of dots, like the fingers of a hand, with one longer and another shorter, and do this without thinking about the number, but it should be not less than twelve and not more than sixteen. Erase them from the back end in twos; if one is left write a dot, if two a stroke. If the fifteenth house has a favourable figure but the upper ones have unfavourable figures then generate a second four figures and from them the ninth, tenth, eleventh and twelfth figures. From these figures will be generated two columns. If the fifteenth house is favourable then your case is unfortunate but good will come later. Other interpretations follow.

III.6. About the houses; these are favourable 1, 4, 5, 7, 10, 11, 13, 14; these days are favourable 1, 2, 4, 6, 7, 8, 9, 11, 12, 13, 14, 15, 17, 18, 24.

Ist house: life, soul, body, nature, health, etc. This house tells all about [the appellant's] life.

2nd house: possessions, profit, good fortune in trade, cattle, gifts, marriage, etc.

3rd house: brothers, friendship, science, engaging in war, litigation, travel, etc.

4th house: parents, inheritance, parent's grave, land, home, farms, old age, sleep, etc. [f. 23]

5th house: sons and fathers, envoys, pregnant women, sowing of wheat. This house is called the house of the son.

6th house: illness, servants, cattle, etc.

7th house: taking of wives, contract with a partner, litigation(?) over fields and vineyards, discovery of hidden foes.

8th house: death, fear, mourning, wretchedness, heartbreak, guilt, grave, shame, harm.

9th house: long journeys, guests, external wisdom, happiness of people, fear God, news.

10th house: royal fortune, rank, honour, etc.

11th house: hope, mercy, love, wealth, love, peace, outcome of waiting.

12th house: enemies, evil-doing, labour, grief, shame, mockery, dishonour.

13th house: good and evil.

14th house: past and future and the end of things.

15th house: true judgement and mentor (*pastyr'*) of all the houses.[38]

16th house: same as fifteenth. If both are good then your situation is good. If one is good and the other bad, then so is your situation.

[f. 24] Good houses are 1, 5, 10, 11; average are 2, 3, 7, 9; bad are 4, 6, 8, 12.

Interpretation of figures and houses ('If there are good figures in a good house, all will be good.', etc.) [f. 25]

The thirteenth house is the mentor of houses one to four, the fourteenth house is the mentor of houses 5, 6, 8, 12, 15, and the fifteenth house is the mentor of all the houses and 13 and 14 are his witnesses.

III.7. From summer to winter solstice belongs to Venus, from winter to summer, Mercury.

The strong signs are Taurus, Leo, Scorpio, Aquarius. Interpretation of combination with strong houses.

[f. 26–27] Evidence of the witnesses, one each for the eastern and western houses, and its interpretation.

III.8. Do not consult the *Rafli* at the time of the new moon or two days either side of it, nor at the full moon or in stormy weather or strong frost, nor on Saturday or Monday. And be sober and clean and in the right spiritual frame of mind, and consult it three hours before sunrise or sunset. Do not consult it twice in one hour, and only at a favourable time and sign. The day should be clear, without wind or rain or any other aerial disturbance.[39] [f. 28] And this Aristotle, the chief and first of philosophers, did. And the Troparion, tone 4, and the Kondakion, tone 3, show how the stars foretold the birth of Christ.[40] [f. 29]

III.9. When you consult say this prayer: 'O God who created heaven and earth and all that moves in the heavens and on earth. Lord Jesus Christ, son of the living God, you have created man in your own image and likeness and with your hand you have placed him over all things. I, your sinful servant X have come to you, your sinful servant having no one else to turn to, but with fear and trembling I cry out to you. Show, O Lord, of your mercy, all my intentions clearly. For now there is no prophet and we your sinful servants are saved from all evil that may befall by your holy deeds, now and for ever, Amen.'[41]

III.10. The names and indications of the sixteen houses:

1st house: soul, life, the path to salvation. .|||

2nd house: goods, money, people, servants, treasure. |.||

3rd house: brother, sister, brother-in-law, short journey.|.|.

4th house: father, household, village. |||| [f. 30]

5th house: son, daughter, envoy, news, treasure, village. ..|.

6th house: illness, misfortune, loss. .||.

7th house: comrade, lover, woman. |||.

8th house: death. |.||

9th house: journey, crowd. ||.|

10th house: great prince, happiness, mother. ..||

11th house: friend, guest. ||..

12th house: enemy, prison, jealosy, captivity. .||.

13th house: rules houses 3, 4, 9, 10; likes to be in figures |.|., ||||, ||.|, ..||

14th house: likes midday; mentor of houses 7, 8, 11, 12, 14. |.|.

15th house: judges true, son of all the houses. |..|

16th house: shows what will be, good or ill; mentor of all the houses and the house of the sons of Israel. ||||

These are the deeds of the triune God, Father, Son, and Holy Spirit, Amen.

III.11. Repetition of the story of Iuda, Khariz, Shmoil, and Avengasan, who are men, not idols or Mohammedan heresiarchs. [f. 31] Added references to Balaam, the first to prophesy the coming of Christ, and to the Three Wise Men who brought gifts.

III.12. The stars which rule good and evil:

1st house: journey from home. Moon. [predictions] ....

2nd house: change of fortune, journey, meeting. Mercury. [predictions] ||||

3rd house: coming together (conjunctio). Mercury. [predictions] |.|. [f. 37]

4th house: captivity. Saturn. [prediction] .||.

5th house: lowering the head (= *tristitia*). Mercury. [predictions] |||.

6th house: raising the head (= *laetitia*). Jupiter. [predictions] .||.

7th house: property entering. Jupiter. [predictions] |.|.

8th house: property leaving. Venus. [predictions] .|.|

9th house: young man. Venus. [predictions] .|..

10th house: warrior. Mars. [prediction] ..|.

11th house: red. Mars. [prediction] |.||

12th house: white. Moon. [predictions] ||.|

13th house: exiting part. Sun. [predictions] ..||

14th house: honour (part) will enter. Sun. [predictions] ||..

15th house: *Caput Draconis*. [predictions] |...

16th house: *Cauda Draconis*. [predictions] ...|

Further predictions follow. A heading in f. 39 reads 'The first Arabic houses and figures of Eptai and Ivash, that is the calendar'; in f. 40 'The second Arabic houses and figures of Ektai and Ivash, from Mercury'; in f. 42 'Third Arabic calendar,[42] the houses and figures of Ektai and Ivash'; in f. 43v 'Fourth calendar, houses and figures, that is the four seasons and twelve months. These are the houses and figures of Ektai and Ivash'; in f. 45 'Fifth Arabic calendar the young man of Ektai and Ivash'; in f. 46 'Sixth Arabic calendar – property leaving and the figures of Ektai and Ivash'; in f. 47v 'Seventh Arabic calendar – prison of Ektai and Ivash'; in f. 48v 'Eighth Arabic calendar – the Star. Figures of Ektai and Ivash'; in f. 49v 'Ninth Arabic calendar of Ektai and Ivash'; in f. 51 'Tenth Arabic calendar of Ektai and Ivash – exiting part'; in f. 52 'Eleventh Arabic calendar of Ektai and Ivash. Figure white, that is, the star'; in f. 53 'Twelfth calendar of Ektai and Ivash and its figure is the star Prikol which in the evening precedes all the other stars';[43] in f. 54 'Thirteenth Arabic calendar of Ektai and Ivash. Red'; in f. 55v 'Fourteenth Arabic calendar of Ektai and Ivash'; in f. 56v 'Fifteenth Arabic calendar of Ektai and Ivash. Dragon'; in f. 58 'Sixteenth Arabic calendar of Ektai and Ivash. Figures of the Dragon'. [f. 59]

III.13. 'Account of the twelve stars which serve the seven planets' (the sun serves Leo, etc.; 'Account of sidereal love, which star loves which, and the strength and weakness they give on earth' (Aries with Gemini, etc.); 'Second account of sidereal love . . .' (Aries with Sagittarius and Cancer, etc.)[44]

III.14. [f. 60v] 'To know the houses and figures of terms' – how to calculate the time of a prediction: the figures for distant years are .||., .|.|, ||.., |. . ., |.|. means you will live for 31 years, |... means you will live for seven years. And so on for months, weeks, [f. 61] days, hours.

III.13. Affinities: air with fire, water with earth.

III.14. Predictions, each preceded by a prayer, short religious statements, or biblical quotation. Then follows the influence of the planets (e.g. the sun rules the 'Roman land in the west', Mars rules Hungary and the Czech land, Saturn rules Russia, Lithuania, Novgorod and Moscow). [f. 63v]; then predictions (mostly agricultural and meteorological) based on the day of the week on which Christmas falls (i.e. the text which exists independently as the *Koliadnik* – see Ch. 14) and the day of the new moon (i.e. one of several texts known as the *Lunnik* – see Ch. 14).

III.15. Final address to 'beloved brother Kir Ioann' emphasizing that all this is the wisdom and mercy of God.

III.16. [f. 70] Book 2. (In the text of MS Moscow, GIM, Muz. sobr. 1226, ff. 292–307, a very similar text is preceded by a preface 'This book is called the Gates of Aristotle the Wise [and belonged to] Alexander the Tsar of Macedon'. It says that the diviner must be clean and fasting and think only of the matter in hand. It offers two methods of selection: dice or dots with pen and ink. Cf. bean divination in Chs 4.6.4 and 11.10.) There follow agricultural predictions based on the time of the appearance of the new moon.

III.17. [f. 71–113v] List of seventy-one chapters of predictions from 'serdobol' na chuzhoi strane' (lit. 'heart pain in a foreign land', or 'heart pain on the other side'); then series of predictions under each heading (called *vrata* 'gates') accompanied by geomantic figures, e.g. 'Third gate. Concerning journeys, whether to travel or not. |.|., ||.., |..., ..|| – he will go and return but there will be loss on the way. ...|, |||., .|||, |.||, .||., .|.|, ||.| – he will go soon and his journey will be with great benefit. ..|., .|.. – he will not go soon and there will be evil on his way'.

III.18. [f. 118–123] Book 3 (end missing). Further interpretations of geomantic predictions arranged by house.

* * *

It has not been possible to trace all the elements in this text to their source but some points can be illuminated a little.

First the story of Seth and the divine origin of geomancy: this contains elements of great antiquity.[45] It is most probably a Hellenistic conflation of several legends, possibly with later Byzantine and Arabic additions. Some elements occur in first-century AD Jewish literature (*Book of Jubilees*, *Vita Adae et Evae* and the much later *Zohar*). It seems to have been a popular theme in Gnostic literature. Ch. 2 of Flavius Josephus's *Antiquities of the Jews*, quoted here in Whiston's translation, says:

> They [the children of Seth] were also the inventors of that peculiar sort of wisdom which is concerned with the heavenly bodies and their order. And that their inventions might not be lost before they were sufficiently known, upon Adam's prediction that the world was to be destroyed at one time by the force of fire, and at another time by the violence and quantity of water, they made two pillars; the one of brick, the other of stone: they inscribed their discoveries on them both, that in case the pillar of brick should be destroyed by the flood, the pillar of stone might remain and exhibit those discoveries to mankind; and also inform them that there was another pillar of brick erected by them. Now this remains in the land of Siriad to this day.[46]

An analogous story involving God, an angel, astronomical wisdom given to Seth and inscribed by him on stone tablets, and the rediscovery of the tablets after the Flood is to be found in Greek.[47]

The outline of the story of the transmission of the wisdom of Seth would not have been new to Russians. Although there was no Slavonic version of the *Antiquitates*, the essentials of the Josephus account are to be found in the Byzantine chronicles of John Malalas and George the Monk (Hamartolos), the main sources of world history in Russia. George the Monk adds a detail or two – Seth was the first to know the Hebrew letters, and it was Arphaxad who rescued the wisdom after the Flood and wrote books of geometry and astronomy.[48] Apocryphal stories from the *Palaea historica*, a Greek compendium of elaborations on Bible stories translated at an early date into Slavonic,[49] contain several other elements of the Seth story, e.g. Seth as the second seed of Adam, the searcher for the oil of life, the inventor of (Hebrew) writing, and he 'named the four seasons of the year and the years and the months and the stars, but the Lord named the sun and moon'.[50] The idea of Enoch as the man to whom divine secrets were entrusted for preserving in writing was also familiar to the Orthodox Slavs from the *Book of Enoch*.[51] The remaining elements of the story, however, are new in Russian, although they crop up in other literatures. The ninth-century Arabic astrologer Abū Maʿshar, in a discussion of the Hermetic tradition, says of Hermes that he is Enoch in Hebrew and Idris in Arabic and that:

> he was the first to speak of upper things, such as the motion of the stars, and his grandfather, Adam, taught him the hours of night and day. He was the first to build sanctuaries and praise God therein, the first to think and speak of medicine. He wrote for his contemporaries many books of rhythmic poems, with rhymes known in the language of his contemporaries, about the knowledge of terrestrial and celestial subjects. He was the first to prophesy the coming of the Flood and saw that heavenly plague by water and fire threatened the Earth. His domicile was the Saʿid of Egypt, which he selected for himself, and he built there the sanctuaries of the pyramids and the temple towns. It was because of his fear that wisdom might be lost that he built the temples, namely the mountain known as al-Barbā, the temple of Akhmʾimm (Panopolis), engraved on their walls drawings of all techniques and their technicians, made pictures of all the working tools of craftsmen, and by inscriptions indicated the essence of the sciences for those who were to come after him. In doing so he was guided by the desire of preserving science for later generations and by fear that its trace might disappear from the world. In the tradition handed down from the ancestors it is stated that Idrīs was the first to study books and to think about sciences and that Allah revealed to him thirty pages (of the Heavenly Book).[52]

The motif of the pillars on which the divine wisdom was preserved is probably linked to another Hermetic story, ascribed to the Egyptian priest Manetho, in which Hermes engraved his wisdom on *stelae* from which it was recovered after the Flood.[53] An Armenian version of the story has Enos (Enoch) writing on two pillars the names given to things by Adam. In this case the pillars are of bronze and clay; bronze in case of flood and clay in case of fire.[54]

The identification of the divine wisdom with geomancy is not explicit in these sources; the tradition is rather one of astrology, particularly among the Byzantine chronographers,[55] and the account given in Josephus was used in the Middle Ages, and as late as Annius of Viterbo in the sixteenth century, to legitimize astrology.[56] An alternative hostile interpretation of the two columns occurs in a seventeenth-century Russian treatise by the schismatic archpriest Avvakum (on whom see Ch. 15 for more detail). He states that Nimrod practised divination using the antediluvian wisdom found on the two columns and as a result ordered the building of the Tower of Babel as a challenge to God. This he sees as the origin of the 'devilish almanac-mongers' (*almanashniki* – a term he invented) of his own time.[57]

The notion that Seth's wisdom was communicated to the Magi was a Gnostic and Syriac Christian tradition.[58] In Samaritan literature, however, this wisdom is described as being contained in books possessed by Adam called 'The Book of Wars', 'The Book of Astrology', and 'The Book of Signs' and the last was the book which was given to Arphaxad.[59] In some Islamic traditions Gabriel brought geomancy either to Idris or to the prophet Daniel,[60] and Seth either had fifty scrolls of knowledge revealed to him by God or inherited them from Adam, or both, and also built the Ka'ba of stone and clay (cf. the two pillars of stone and clay);[61] other stories make the Ka'ba the navel of the earth and a temple of the planets.[62]

One element of the story occurs in Latin in the prologue to the thirteenth-century geomancy of Bartholomew of Parma, where Shem rather than Seth is given as the transmitter of geomancy, and also in the anonymous *Estimaverunt Indi*.[63] The story of the columns of stone and clay in the Latin West becomes involved with the stories of Jubal and Tubalcain and the origins of music, and is regularly linked with the iconographic representation of music.[64] The story of Seth and the columns is referred to in Peter Comestor and Rabanus Maurus and was apparently believed by the English chemist Robert Boyle.[65] It was used as the basis for an elaborate poetical conceit (the fourth part of the second day of the second week, entitled 'The Columns') by the sixteenth-century French Protestant poet Guillaume du Bartas in *La Seconde Semaine* (1584), the second part of his long poem on the creation. Du Bartas, presumably taking his theme from Josephus, surveys at some length the mathematical sciences which were revealed by the columns in an imaginary conversation between Heber, son of Shem and ancestor of the Hebrews, and his son Phalec (Genesis, 11:16).

The novelistic continuation of the Seth story involving the four Persian magi appears to be of multiple origin; their names sound like a mixture of Arabic and Hebrew; the reference to Aristotle, Nectanebus and Alexander almost certainly comes from Pseudo-Callisthenes; the transmission to the Arabs was presumably added by an Arabic writer. The claim by the Russian compiler, Rykov, that this text was translated into Slavonic from Arabic is a *topos* of pedigree and cannot be taken at face value – there are no authenticated translations of any literary text from Arabic into Old Russian. The improbability of the claim does not, of course, entirely exclude its possibility.

Two remaining points: the Samuel/Khail text is too close to the Byzantine text to be anything but a translation from Greek; the address and frequent exhortations to 'brothers', and in one case 'spiritual children', is surprisingly consonant with a *topos* of Hermetic literature.[66] Indeed, this text must be regarded as being in the Hermetic tradition, even if Hermes is not mentioned.[67]

The Rykov geomantic manuscript, which is quite remarkable in a Russian context, is known only in this one late copy. Clearly it is a conflation of several texts: a major manual of geomancy, possibly with some Jewish influence ('Shmoil' for 'Samuel' and 'gates' for 'chapters', as in several other Russian texts translated from Hebrew), considerably reworked for a Russian milieu; a minor arithmomancy of Byzantine origin; a collection of basic astrological texts of late Byzantine provenance, most of which probably appeared in Russia in the late fifteenth century. Most of the minor texts in this compilation exist independently in several copies, scattered through the very many *florilegia* of Muscovite Russia. Possibly the size and patently occult nature of the main geomantic text made it vulnerable to suppression, notwithstanding the frequent pious interjections and explanations of the divine origin of the text (which are *loci communes* for the genre), while the small texts passed unnoticed in the large miscellanies. Certainly possession of texts such as the *Gates of Aristotle* was enough to merit severe punishment in the seventeenth and even eighteenth centuries. An interesting example is Simon, abbot of the Pishchegovskaia Pustyn' monastery, who in 1721 was arraigned before the Synodal Court for the political indiscretion of paying respect to the nun Elena (i.e. ex-tsaritsa Eudoxia, the first wife of Peter the Great, who had been banished to a nunnery), and also for telling fortunes by casting dice and cubes of bread and possessing magic books. These allegedly included a prayer to the Devil, the 'Gates of Aristotle of Alexander of Macedon' (the further description mentions 'signs in dots' and 'casting bones' and is clearly the geomancy described by Speranskii), a Divinatory Psalter, and the 'Voice of the Prophet Balaam the Wizard'. As punishment Simon was forbidden to say mass and was exiled for life to the Solovetskii monastery in the far north.[68]

It is very possible that it is this method of divination which is mentioned by Richard James in his manuscript phrasebook of 1619 under the name of *Vorota* ('Gates'), with the observation that it is practised on Christmas Eve, an indication that it had been assimilated to folk divination, which is very frequently practised only at certain 'magic' times, usually the eve of a major feast such as Christmas or the feast of St John (these approximate roughly to midwinter and midsummer), or New Year's Eve.[69]

This is the sum of the evidence for the existence of geomancy in Russia and one might therefore conclude that it was not widespread. It is, however, possible that the practice was more popular than the extant written evidence indicates – in the eighteenth century Tatishchev talks of the fortune-telling charlatans who practise casting dice or beans, drawing dots on paper, and pouring wax or tin.[70] 'Drawing dots on paper' is certainly a description of the method of geomancy given in Rykov's manuscript and does not suggest any other practice which might have incurred censure. In the reign of the enlightened Catherine the Great 'drawing on the ground' was included in a list of magical practices which were made criminal offences.[71] This too could be geomancy, but possibly also the inscribing of the magic circles required in some forms of divination (see Chs 2.5 and 4.2).

Notes

1. Vaillant, *Textes vieux-slaves*, p. 57 (French translation, II, p. 47). See also Saxo Grammaticus, *Gesta Danorum*, XIV, p. 567.

2. See *Jewish Encyclopedia*, 5, 1903, s.v. *geomancy*.

3. The main studies are Tannery, 'Le Rabolion' (this includes a note by Carra de Vaux on Arab geomancy, on which see also Fahd, *La Divination arabe*, pp. 195–204, and Savage-Smith and Smith, *Islamic Geomancy*; Charmasson, *Recherches* (chapters one and two are on Arabic and Byzantine geomancy respectively); Skinner, *Terrestrial Astrology*, esp. ch. 2 '*Raml* and Islamic Origins'.

4. Du Cange, *Glossarium*, s.v.

5. Pypin, 'Dlia istorii lozhnykh knig', pp. 15–27; Veselovskii, 'Zametki k istorii apokrifov' – Veselovskii was also the first to propose the Arabic derivation in his 'Gadatel'nye knigi na Zapade i u nas', p. 896.

6. See Iatsimirskii, *Bibliograficheskii obzor*, pp. 72–3.

7. *Domostroi*, p. 22.

8. *Stoglav*, p. 139.

9. See Pypin, *Lozhnye i otrechennnye knigi*, pp. 161–6; Kuznetsov-Krasnoiarskii, *Rafli* (and review by S. K. K-v in *Etnograficheskoe obozrenie*, 1905, 4, pp. 129–32).

10. Speranskii, *Iz istorii otrechennykh knig. 1. Gadaniia po Psaltiri*, Prilozhenie, pp. 15–20.

11. Sobr. P.I. Šafarik, 5, ff. 397r–397v and Vienna, Staatsbibliothek, 108, f. 81 et seq. Two other manuscripts are quoted by Turilov and Chernetsov: a fifteenth-century Serbian (Bosnian) Psalter, MS Sofia, National Library, 771 (381), ff. 200v–204v (this also includes a passage of planetary medicine and a version of the spell involving three angels on the Jordan which in this case will cure constipation in horses: see Tsonev, *Opis*, II, p. 443.) and MS Vienna, Staatsbibliothek 143, ff. 2v–4. The first of these is published in Turilov and Chernetsov, 'Otrechennaia knig Rafli', pp. 342–4, where the text is attributed not to Samuel but the prophet 'Khail'.

12. Similar requirements of purity, cleanliness, fasting and prayer are commonplaces in Hermetic literature (see Festugière, *La Révélation*, p. 361.) and medieval divination (see Skeat, 'An Early Medieval "Book of Fate"', pp. 42–4). Prayer and fasting are also required for catoptromancy: see Delatte, *La Catoptromancie*, p. 58. In Islamic divination the Koran replaces the Christian books but the requirement of purity and prayer before divination remains the same: see Hughes, *Dictionary of Islam*, p. 73. For an elaborate example in Jewish magic see Gaster, 'The Sword of Moses', p. 8.

13. The importance of keeping your desire firmly in mind is emphasized elsewhere; for the Iranian geomantic belief see Donaldson, *The Wild Rue*, p. 195.

14. A very similar procedure is still being published in English in popular fortune-telling books under the title of 'The Oracle of Napoleon'. In this the geomantic method of making dots at random is followed but each figure comprises five rows instead of four. The figures are then interpreted by reference to an 'oracle' list of answers, rather as in the *Divinatory Psalter*. In this case, as with the major Arabic and Latin texts and the Russian text by Rykov discussed below, a mysterious and seemingly authoritative provenance is given. This varies from book to book: in the case of my copy, which is in *Everybody's Book of Fate and Fortune*, pp. 295–363, the author assures us that he had it from an old French professor whom he met on a train, who in turn had it from his grandfather, whose father worked in the Imperial court! The earliest version of the Napoleon story seems to be that of Kirchenhoffer, *The Book of Fate* (London, 1822): the text was supposed to have been found on the breast of a mummy by one of the scholars on Napoleon's Egyptian expedition. The preposterous

story is told with relish by Alphons Barb in 'Mystery, Myth, and Magic'. He would no doubt have been amused to know that at the date of writing this book, in Dillon's University Bookshop in London, not a hundred yards from the Warburg Institute where Barb wrote his piece, no fewer than three competing versions of this *Oracle*, with totally different accounts of its origin, are on sale today.

15. The standard form of the Greek geomantic houses is given in Charmasson, *Recherches*, p. 88.

16. Delatte, *Anecdota*, I, pp. 557–61. One of the selection devices described uses dots, single or double, corresponding to odd or even values of letters chosen at random from a book.

17. Eis, *Wahrsage texte des Spätmittelalters*, pp. 7–13, text at pp. 29–48.

18. The copy consulted was bound with *Fasciculus geomanticus*, Verona, 1687, and geomantic texts ascribed to Fludd, and 'Alfakini'.

19. See Chernetsov, 'Ob odnom risunke Radzivillovskoi letopisi'.

20. See Chernetsov, 'K izucheniiu Radzivillovskoi letopisi', p. 284. Chernetsov notes that another illustration in the manuscript shows divination by three dice.

21. MS Moscow, GBL, fond 439, karton 21, ed. khr. 3, *sbornik*, seventeenth to eighteenth century, from the collection of V.A. Desnitskii. The contemporary binding has an embossed emblem of the Moscow Printing House (*Pechatnyi dvor*). For the complete text and detailed introduction see Turilov and Chernetsov, 'Otrechennaia kniga Rafli'. For further discussion see Simonov, Turilov, Chernetsov, *Drevnerusskaia knizhnost'*.

22. A short article by Khodzhiev, 'K voprosu o vostochnykh predshestvennikakh pskovskoi gadatel'noi knigi', puts forward the claim that this a direct translation from Arabic, made in the 'Arabo-Tadzhik-Persian cultural milieu', mainly on the basis of the quantity of geomantic texts found in Arabic, but is unable to point to an immediate source, nor does it address the obvious problems of both syncretism and conflation of textual traditions.

23. Published in part by Sobolevskii, *Perevodnaia literatura*, pp. 428–33. For some discussion see Ryan, 'Solomon, SATOR, Acrostics and Leo the Wise', pp. 56–7 and *idem*, 'Curious Star Names', pp. 144–6.

24. See Pypin, *Lozhnye i otrechennye knigi*, pp. 161–6. A very similar seventeenth-century Belorussian version is published in Romanov, *Belorusskii sbornik*, 4, pp. 213–33. See also Karskii, *Belorusi*, 1920, pp. 51–2.

25. Another moon divination text by Rykov is known – MS Moscow, GBL, Barsov (fond 17, No. 518). It is dated 1579. See Turilov and Chernetsov, 'Otrechennaia kniga Rafli', p. 274, 276. A further text of astrological medicine perhaps ascribable to Rykov ('sinful Ioann') is published in Sobolevskii, *Perevodnaia literatura*, p. 132.

26. In the many manuscripts containing the very similar introduction to the *Mirotvornyi krug* but without the geomantic sections, the addressee is Sofronii, the Tsar's *knigchii* (scribe – exactly what rank or duty this implies is not clear).

27. For analogous texts of the 'Fable of the year' see Sobolevskii, *Perevodnaia literatura*, pp. 128–9. This text appears in various forms sometimes with, sometimes without an explanation, in calendrical texts and florilegia. Sobolevskii notes its frequent occurrence, often with illustrations, in seventeenth and eighteenth-century miscellanies. Rykov's use of the text points to an earlier origin than previously thought. For a recent edition with some notes see *Drevnerusskaia pritcha*, pp. 381–91, 490–1.

28. It is not clear why the Jewish and Orthodox calendars are omitted here.

29. This I assume to be Rykov's meaning – in Muscovite Russia a *d'iak* could be various kinds of secretary or official. The word comes from Greek *diakonos*, a servant.

30. With the exception of the passage on Seth, astronomy and the pillars, this is essentially the same text as that which appears in MS Leningrad, GPB, Kir. Bel. sobr. XII, ff. 311–312v, one of the encyclopedic florilegia of Kiril Belozerskii, founder of the monastery at Belozero at the end of the fourteenth century, which was to be the home of the later encyclopedist Efrosin (see Ch. 1). This manuscript also contains calendrical and eschatological information about the end of the millennium and the coming of the Antichrist, and also the first medical texts of any substance to appear in Russia 'Galen on Hippocrates' and 'Alexander on conception'. The argument about March is an ancient *topos* – Brock, 'A Dispute of the Months and Some Related Syriac Texts', p. 186, notes that *Nisan* appears to win the dispute, a matter of some importance in the Semitic world with its conflicting calendars, and that the Greek and Roman literatures lack this motif. The Bible (Exodus 12:2) required the Jews to begin their year with March. We may note, however, in view of the reference to Romulus, that the Byzantine chronographer George the Monk in his chronicle (I.xiv) states that Romulus built the temple of Mars and called the month March instead of its earlier name, Primus. In Kievan Russia there was in fact a problem – the Byzantine year began in September but the Russian year began in March. This is called the 'March' or 'ultra-March' year depending on whether the March following or preceeding a given Byzantine year is taken to be start of that year in Kiev-Rus'. The September year began to be used in Russia in the new Paschal tables of 1492, possibly as part of the putative *translatio imperii* following the fall of Byzantium. This makes Rykov's inclusion of this text on the priority of March something of a curiosity.

31. This includes a short quotation from the *vita* of St Stefan by Epifanii the Wise (fourteenth–fifteenth centuries), which has a lengthy historical justification, beginning with Moses, for beginning the year with March: for the text of the *vita* see *Pamiatniki starinnoi russkoi literatury*, IV, pp. 130–1. Epifanii's defence of March is very similar to that of Kiril Belozerskii mentioned above.

32. The connection of Seth with astronomy also finds pictorial expression; in the Church of the Assumption at Volotovo Pole (destroyed during the Second World War) there was a fresco, painted *c.* 1380, depicting Seth holding a large disc with what appear to be stars around the outer edge: Alpatov, *Freski tserkvi Uspeniia*, fig. 35.

33. Nectanebus was well known to Russians as a magician from the very popular *Aleksandriia*, the South and East Slavonic versions of Pseudo-Callisthenes.

34. A puzzling statement: *Sviattsy*, lit. 'saints', is in fact the name of the Orthodox calendar of saints. Later in the text the seasons are described as '*rafli*'.

35. Evidently the geomantic *matres* – some confusion arises from the use of *dom* to mean both house and figure, although *izraz* is also used for the latter. These groups of four, which have already been prominent in the astronomical articles at the beginning of the manuscript, are very characteristic of geomantic texts, probably because the sixteen figures encourage such associations.

36. These are only occasionally the same as the correspondences given in Charmasson, *Recherches*, for Arabic, Greek or Latin.

37. For a similar passage in a thirteenth-century Latin geomancy translated from Arabic which is ascribed to Hugo Sanctallensis see Tannery, 'Le Rambolion', p. 374: MS Paris, BN, latin 7354, f. 2v.

38. This was previously stated to be the sixteenth house. The houses, strictly speaking, are twelve in number – once again there is some confusion of the concepts of 'house' and 'figure'. The meanings of the houses correspond fairly well with the list given in Charmasson, *Recherches*, p. 49.

39. The same requirement is given in the Latin version of an Arabic text ascribed to Hugo

Sanctallensis – see Tannery, 'Le Rambolion', p. 374: 'nec sub inbrium decursu aut uentorum rabie'. This passage is also noted by Charmasson, *Recherches*, p. 102.

40. Orthodox liturgical hymns.

41. This prayer seems to be a mixture of biblical quotations. A version of it is found as preface to the Divinatory Psalter: see Speranskii, *Iz istorii otrechennykh knig. I. Gadaniia po psaltiri*, prilozhenie, p. 21.

42. 'Calendar' is my *ad hoc* translation of *sviattsy* in the Russian text, where it is stated to be the Slavonic for *Rafli*.

43. Apart from *dennitsa* 'Morning Star' the Russian folk names for stars are rarely found in written documents. *Prikol* (or *Kol*) normally means the Pole Star or Ursa Major (see Dal', s.v. *kol*) but here apparently means the Evening Star.

44. This section is notable for considerable variation in the form of the names of the signs of the Zodiac. Gemini is found in the form *bliznetsy, bliznets, blizniata* of which the last two are less common. *Tur* (i.e. aurochs) for Taurus I have only found in two other manuscripts (Leningrad, BAN 11.8.9, Belorussian *sbornik*, 16th c. and Moscow, GBL 921, a 16th-c. copy of the Slavonic version of the *Hexaemeron* of Severianus of Gabala) and *inorog* ('unicorn') for Capricorn appears to be unique.

45. For the most detailed discussion see Klijn, *Seth in Jewish, Christian and Gnostic Literature*, esp. pp. 24–5; also von Erffa, *Ikonologie der Genesis*, pp. 400–4.

46. Whiston, *The Genuine Works of Flavius Josephus*, p. 27.

47. *CCAG*, VII, p. 87. On this and other fragments of the story see Festugière, *La Révélation*, pp. 334–5.

48. Istrin, *Khronika Georga Amartola*, I, p. 53; *idem*, 'Khronika Ioanna Malaly', p. 6. This is presumably the source for the Seth story in the 1512 Russian *Khronograf*. Maxim the Greek alludes several times to the Seth story, using both the Suda lexicon and George the Monk as his sources: see Bulanin, *Perevody i poslaniia Maksima Greka*, p. 72. For the Greek texts see Migne, *PG*, 97, col. 69 ('Anonymi chronologica') for Malalas, and 110, bk I, 1, for George the Monk. For comment on these see Klijn, *Seth in Jewish, Christian and Gnostic Literature*, pp. 61–7.

49. See Vassiliev, *Anecdota graeco-byzantina*. Flusser, 'Palaea historica', pp. 50–2, draws attention to the Seth story as told in this text.

50. *Palaia* of 1494, MS Moscow, Lenin Library, no. 453, ff. 40–2, quoted in Pypin, *Lozhnye i otrechennye knigi*, pp. 9–10. This conflicts with a commonly found apocryphal fragment in which the name of Adam is derived from the first letters of the Greek names of the four corners of the earth, *arktos, dusis, anatolē, mesembria* (these often appear in garbled form), which four archangels were sent to gather and which are interpreted as being the names of stars; this cosmological notion seems to have entered Russia in the Slavonic *Book of Enoch*. It can also be found, usually without the detail of the archangels, embedded in a number of early Christian and medieval West European texts. See Ryan, 'Curious Star Names', and Turdeanu, *Apocryphes slaves*, pp. 380, 405, 425–30. The detail of the archangels is also found in an Old Irish text and in the Old English *Life of Adam and Eve*: see *Lebor Gabála Érena*, ed., transl. R.A.S. Macalister (Irish Texts Society, vol. 34), Dublin, 1938, pp. 55–7, 226–7. I am obliged to John Carey for this reference.

51. Vaillant, *Le Livre des secrets d'Hénoch*, p. 27. On the links between the stories of Seth and Enoch, and Seth and Hermes Trismegistus, see Adler, *Time Immemorial*, pp. 59, 105.

52. See Plessner, 'Hermes Trismegistus and Arab Science', pp. 51–2, and *idem*, 'Irmis' in *Encyclopedia of Islam*. Plessner notes that this is the earliest such story in Arabic but that the later *Treasure of Alexander* has a passage with some similarities. He also notes parallels with the *Book of*

Jubilees and Berossus, where, as in several traditions, the record of ancient wisdom is buried rather than placed on pillars. Plessner regards the underlying story as Babylonian, transmitted to Greece and thence to the Arabs and medieval Jewish and Latin writers. See also Pingree, *The Thousands of Abū Maʿshar*, pp. 14–16.

53. See Festugière, *La Révélation*, I, pp. 74–5. Festugière remarks (p. 319) on the popularity in literatures of all countries of the theme of the discovery of secret books and engraved columns. Klijn regards the story of the punishment by fire and water and the two pillars as evidence of Egyptian influence: Klijn, *Seth in Jewish, Christian and Gnostic Literature*, pp. 121–4.

54. Stone, 'The History of the Forefathers', pp. 81–2.

55. See Klijn, *Seth in Jewish, Christian and Gnostic Literature*, pp. 48–53.

56. See Bokdam, 'Les Mythes de l'origine de l'astrologie', pp. 57–61.

57. *Pamiatniki literatury Drevnei Rusi. XVII vek*, pp. 446–7.

58. Klijn, *Seth in Jewish, Christian and Gnostic Literature*, pp. 53–60.

59. Klijn, *Seth in Jewish, Christian and Gnostic Literature*, p. 30 (cf. the report of George the Monk mentioned above).

60. See Savage-Smith, *Islamic Geomancy*, pp. 1–2; Donaldson, *The Wild Rue*, p. 194.

61. *The History of al-Ṭabarī*, pp. 325, 335.

62. *Shorter Encyclopedia of Islam*, s.v. *Kāba* and *Shīth*.

63. Charmasson, *Recherches*, p. 152.

64. See Beichner, *The Medieval Representation of Music, Jubal or Tubalcain*.

65. Thorndike, *History of Magic and Experimental Science*, VIII, p. 188.

66. See Festugière, *La Révélation*, pp. 347–54: 'L'influence du motif de la *traditio* sur le *logos* hermétique'.

67. Hermes is rarely mentioned in Russian literature (he appears in the Malalas Chronicle as 'Ermin tr'velikii, a wise man'). When he is referred to in the Russian *Secretum secretorum* it is in the form 'Romas' – the translator was unable to reconstruct the name correctly from his Hebrew original and obviously mistook the first syllable for the article; the inserted vowels were evidently inspired by Rome.

68. *Opisanie dokumentov . . . Sinoda*, 1, cols 272–6.

69. For text see Larin, *Russko-angliiskii slovar'-dnevnik Richarda Dzhemsa*, p. 153.

70. *Slovar' XVIII v.*, s.v. *vorozhba*.

71. *PSZ*, XX, no. 14392; XXI, no. 1539: see Popov, *Sud i nakazaniia*, p. 381.

ALCHEMY AND
THE VIRTUES OF STONES[1]

1. *Introduction*

There are only two modern book-length studies of alchemy in Russian[2] and they are concerned with alchemy as a cultural phenomenon in general without reference to alchemy in Russia. Modern general histories of Russian science which deal with the history of chemistry for the most part have, until recently, avoided alchemy as a 'pseudo-science', more to be condemned as an intellectual aberration than examined historically. Rainov's standard *Nauka v Rossii XI–XVII vekov* (1940) has no entry in the index for the subject, the Academy of Sciences *Istoriia estestvoznaniia v Rossii*[3] denied, probably correctly, that Russian craftsmen ever engaged in alchemy or that there is any evidence for the existence of alchemy in Russia before the fifteenth century, and Kuzakov[4] correctly notes that some non-alchemical works of Albertus Magnus, Ramon Lull, and Michael Scott, whom he describes as 'West European alchemists'[5] were known in seventeenth-century Russia but incorrectly states, as will be shown below, that not a single alchemical treatise in Russian is known.

2. *Byzantine Sources*

We have no knowledge of any indigenous Slavonic beliefs or practices from the pre-Christian and pre-literary period which might be described as alchemical. Certainly the Slavs employed fire to work materials and used a variety of substances for culinary, medicinal, and decorative purposes, but in the absence of textual evidence we have no means of knowing how far such use might have been given a magical significance.

For the period of Kiev Rus' the situation is much the same. There is archaeological evidence of artefacts manufactured in iron, copper, bronze and precious metals, and in glass, including enamel and mosaic.[6] There is literary evidence for the existence of monastic hospitals but it is not extensive or detailed and the nature of the medicinal preparations used is not known, although the use of the word *zel'e* to mean both 'herb' and 'potion' (as well as 'gunpowder', a calque of the German soldiers' slang *Kraut*[7]) suggests that treatment was primarily herbal.[8] And there is the evidence of icons, wallpaintings, and manuscripts which indicates knowledge of the methods of preparation of pigments, glues and inks. There is, however, no evidence of anything resembling alchemy, unless one accepts Granstrem's suggestion that the earliest Slavonic alphabet, the Glagolitic, is based on Greek alchemical symbols. This theory has not found favour with philologists despite one-to-one correspondences and the fact that some Greek manuscripts use these signs to mark glosses (i.e. they are not found in alchemical texts alone), and notwithstanding the perhaps indicative error of no less a scholar than M.P. Alekseev, who mistook for Glagolitic letters a series of planet and zodiac signs used in a manuscript as a cryptographic system.[9]

At the same time those who could read would have become acquainted at least with the notions of the four elements, the humours, and the microcosm-macrocosm from references in literature, usually *florilegia*, translated from Greek into Church Slavonic and arriving for the most part by way of Bulgaria.[10] The main sources are two works by John the Exarch of Bulgaria (tenth century): the *Hexaemeron*, a miscellany based mainly on Basil the Great and a partial translation of John Damascene, *De fide orthodoxa*.[11]

The Orthodox Slavs also had access to at least part of the same lapidary lore as had medieval Western Europe. The stones listed in the Bible (the twelve stones in the breastplate of the High Priest in Exodus 28, 17–20; the covering of the King of Tyre in Ezekiel 28, 13 and the stones in the foundations of the Heavenly City in Revelations 21, 19–20) naturally gave rise to exegetical speculation and symbolic or magical interpretation. The discussion by the fourth-century bishop Epiphanius of Salamis[12] of the origin and virtues of the stones in the breastplate of the High Priest, together with the reference to them in the *De bello judaico* of Josephus (which was translated into Church Slavonic in the twelfth century) and the *Physiologus*, a moralized natural history probably translated from Greek in the eleventh century, would appear to be the source for their further appearance in the twelfth- or thirteenth-century Slavonic version of the *Christian Topography* of Cosmas Indicopleustes (an almost canonical work in Muscovy), the Chronicle of George Hamartolos, the *Hexaemeron* of John the Exarch of Bulgaria (tenth century), the *florilegium* called the *Izbornik Sviatoslava* of 1073, the *Aleksandriia* (the Slavonic version of Pseudo-Callisthenes, translated in one version in the twelfth–thirteenth century), as well as the later *Tale of the Indian Kingdom* (the Prester John legend appearing in Russian versions in the thirteenth–fourteenth century)[13] and the *Life of Stefan of Perm'* by Epifanii Premudryi.[14] The Orthodox Slavs, then, were not unfamiliar with the notion of sacred or symbolic importance being attached to precious stones. The contention of Simonov, that the Russians were not interested in mystical lapidary lore but only in the decorative use of precious stones,[15] is not entirely supported by the evidence, as this chapter demonstrates. Alchemy, however, in any of its manifestations whether concerned with mystical and cabalistic concepts, or with the philosopher's stone or transmutation or universal solvents and panacaeas, seems not to have been available to them, if the surviving literature is a fair guide, before the translation from Hebrew of the pseudo-Aristotelian *Secretum secretorum*.[16]

3. *Muscovy – the* Secretum secretorum

In Muscovy, however, in particular in the late fifteenth and sixteenth centuries, the picture with regard to both science and magic begins to change. For alchemy the crucial text is the *Secretum secretorum* (in Russian *Tainaia tainykh*), which is discussed in detail in Ch. 1. It was translated from Hebrew Short Form of the text,[17] possibly in the late fifteenth century, probably in the Grand Duchy of Lithuania. The Short Form of the *Secretum secretorum* differs from the Long Form Arabic versions and their European derivatives in many respects and not least in the sections on alchemy, the greatest poison, the magic ring, and the magical and medical properties of precious stones (both with and without talismanic engravings), for which the other versions have alternative texts.[18] The Old Russian version inherits this information, together with instruction in the divinatory practices of physiognomy (see Ch. 6.2) and onomancy (see Ch. 11.8), and medical interpolations from works by Maimonides,[19] and in fact is the first Old Russian or Church Slavonic text to offer its readers these benefits of classical and oriental erudition.

It is tempting to conclude that increased awareness in the sixteenth and seventeenth centuries of the chemical and pharmaceutical properties of substances was in some way linked to the translation of the *Secretum secretorum*. A closer look at the text, however, tends to dispel this thought, at least with regard to the alchemical section. In fact the Old Russian text is corrupt and barely comprehensible at some points, and a serious impediment to understanding is the insertion of two sections of the text (as defined by Gaster in his edition of the Hebrew version) into the section preceding them – this was not noticed by Speranskii, the editor of the first published version of the work[20] (the second published version is only partial and does not include this part of the text[21]). Since all the manuscripts have this transposition, one can only assume that the Jewish translator was working with a Slav assistant (there is other evidence of this) and that between them they made an error of direction.

Notwithstanding these difficulties, the Old Russian *Secretum* is historically interesting in many ways. Not only does it contain the first and probably the only alchemical text in Old Russian, and certainly the first to give instruction in the making of talismans,[22] it is also one of the first to use several philosophical, medical and pharmacological terms derived either by direct loan or by calque from Hebrew and Arabic. In view of its significance the entire text is given below in translation:[23]

> TEXT: *(Gaster 124)* [Chapter 10. Of special wisdoms and hidden secrets[24] and of precious stones Saturday][25] Alexander, I have many times written to you that the essence[26] of the whole world is one and that there is no variety in its substance[27] but only in its accidents[28] and that it is in its forms[29] and elements[30] that it varies. It does not vary of its own accord but only on account of something else and there is no change except in material[31] nature.[32] But

I shall not enlarge on this but only mention this great secret; therefore read this book from end to end and you shall know the truth of it. Next I shall write to you about stones for it is necessary that you should know of their great virtue.[33]

(Gaster 125) [A necessary wisdom] To know [how to make] silver and gold. To know [how to make] them in truth is impossible, however, because it is not possible to equal God in his actions, but these *pripravy*[34] when you make them as is fitting then they will be very good. Take a *zolotnik*[35] of arsenic[36] and put it in vinegar[37] until it turns white, then take some quicksilver and silver in the same way and mix them all together and heat them in a fire until white [*Here sections Gaster 126 and 127 on the ring and poison are interpolated in the Russian manuscripts*] and mix with oil of egg[38] and vinegar as I have told you. If it comes out white and pure then it is good. If not put it in again until it is good. And mix in one part to seven of Mars[39] (i.e. iron) and a half measure of Moon[40] then take it quickly[41] and mix it and feed the Falcon[42] until it is green and add galena[43] or verdigris or wax with oil of egg and mix one part to two of the Moon equal to them and it will be good.

(*Gaster 126*) [About the Ring]. Make a ring out of silver and gold and red jacinth[44] and carve on it the image[45] of a girl[46] swaggering and riding on a lion[47] and six [men] bowing down. And do this on Sunday early, at the hour of the sun and in the planet (sic) Leo and the Moon should be in the ascendant[48] and malevolent ones [i.e. planetary influences] far away[49] from her. And whoever wears this ring on his hand shall be honoured and obeyed and his enemy shall not prevail against him.

(*Gaster 127*) [1. Bashman[50] this is] one of the greatest poisons[51] but only some [can] taste it for it is not more bitter than the *mara efieva i namelova*[52] and the orpiment[53] one should not be without these because they are of great virtue and increase the realm as I have told you before. But take strength from that good planet under which you were born, and it is fitting that you make a special seal of every land.[54] Ponder this as is befitting for it is very wonderful.

(*Gaster 128*) Alchemy[55] is in truth ploughing and ploughing[56] and sowing[57] and for this reason should be favoured in your eyes and by them, God willing, you shall extend your realm.

(*Gaster 129 – no heading in Sp. or O.*) And concerning this there is in stones a great virtue as I have myself tested and I shall write to you about this in brief.

(*Gaster 130*) [The stone Bezoar][58] It is of two kinds, one yellow like wax, the other streaked like a snake,[59] and the yellow is best and it comes from the lower land[60] and it is said that it is found in the gall[61] of great serpents and it is hung on a silk thread and is white and soft. Thus it is an antidote to animal, mineral, and vegetable poison and if it is powdered and two grains[62] of it are drunk it will save from death. And if anyone wears it in a ring he shall be honoured by all who look upon him and if it be ground up and spread on a snake bite it will draw out the poison and even if that place should begin to putrefy it will heal it. And if two barleycorns weight be ground up and dissolved in water and poured into the mouths of poisonous [animals][63] then they will die.[64] And if it be hung above a child so that no evil accident befall him then nothing bad will happen.[65]

(*Gaster 131*) [The stone Jacinth]. These are red and yellow and black[66] and if anyone wear it on himself and and should happen to be in a town where there is *ulochi*[67] there will be no sore on him and nothing will happen to him. And if anyone should wear a red jacinth it will strengthen his heart and men will honour him. And if anyone should engrave on it the figure of a lion and the planet (*sic*)[68] Leo and do this in the middle of the day of the Sun and *zavady* far from it,[69] will be much honoured and shall attain what he desires in abundance and shall see no bad dreams in his bed.

(*Gaster 132*) [The stone Emerald].[70] It is good for the liver and it is good for the stomach of anyone who wears it, and if he drinks it this is a remedy for snake poison and if he wears it in his ring it takes away the disease of palsy when it is put on before the onset of the illness.

(*Gaster 134*) The stone Albogat.[71] It is soft and red[72] and bright and cold. Fire has no power over it nor can it burn it. It is a remedy for all hot illnesses, for a great cold will seize the man who holds it and whoever looks too long at it will become dazed and its owner will be honoured. Whoever wears it in war will be withstood by none, therefore lay in a great store of it in your court and use them as I have taught you.

(*Gaster 133*) The stone Feroza.[73] It is collected in treasure-houses by great emperors and they prize it and its virtue is that no one who wears it can be killed. It has never been seen on a murdered man and if it is ground up and drunk it is a remedy against snake poisons and many ills.

4. *After the* Secretum secretorum

At the end of the fifteenth century, when the first foreign doctors were arriving in Muscovy, and at about the same time as the translation of the *Secretum*, a German medical text seems to have made its appearance in Muscovy. There is some confusion over the identity of this text but it is usually held to be the *Gart der Gesundheit*, compiled by Iohann Wonnecke von Cube, town physician of Frankfurt-am-Main, probably in the expanded Low German version printed by

Steffan Arndes in Lübeck in 1492 and 1520, and translated into Russian in 1534, probably by Nicolaus Bülow from Lübeck (and/or possibly Gottlieb Lansmann, also from Lübeck, if we accept the suggestion of I.L. Anikin).[74] It was an important and influential work in its time, and was widely copied and adapted. It produced in Muscovy a whole genre of manuscript *hortus* literature (*vertogrady*) of inconsistent content but very often containing a section entitled 'The Instruction (*nauka*) of Moses the Egyptian to Alexander of Macedon', i.e. the medical sections of the Old Russian *Secretum secretorum* proper (*not* the Maimonidean interpolations).[75]

The commonest early texts of this kind are the *Blagoprokhladnyi vertograd*, the translation ascribed to Nicolaus Bülow mentioned above, and typically they include not only the basic herbal, lapidary and urinoscopy, but also sections on bloodletting, childbirth, medical astrology and a passage ascribed to a certain 'Filon' (possibly Philo Judaeus, less probably Philo of Tarsus)[76] which, depending on the manuscript, may be concerned with the ages of man, seasonal medicine, or *Lunaria* predictions according to the days of the lunar month (see Ch. 14.5.2).

The various magico-medical properties of stones given in many of the *lechebniki* or medical manuals of the sixteenth and seventeenth century are derived either from the *Secretum* or from the *Blagoprokhladnyi vertograd*.[77] As an example of the genre here are descriptions of the properties of the diamond and the lodestone:

> Of the Diamond. The diamond stone is like sal ammoniac in colour but darker than crystal inside, and it sparkles; it is hard and strong so that it neither burns in fire nor can be harmed by any other substance. But it can be softened in the following manner: place it in goat's meat with blood, the goat having been previously fed on wine and parsley. The size of the stone is no greater than a hazelnut, and it is found in Arab lands and on Cyprus. If a soldier wears a diamond on his head or on his left side when armed, it will guard and protect him from the enemy and in frays and from the attacks of evil spirits. And this diamond, if anyone should wear it on his person, will drive away sins and dreams at night. This stone reveals deadly poison; if a poisoner approaches it the stone will sweat [cf. Ivan IV's belief as recorded by Horsey below]. The diamond should be worn by all who sleepwalk or are visited by ghosts at night. If a madman is touched by a diamond he will be cured of his malady.

> Of the Magnet. The magnet stone is obtained from India, from mountains near the sea, like iron . . . And if anyone should pulverize it and take it in French wine with sugar it will expel thick blood and moisture; anyone who wears it will have a strong voice and happiness. If a man wears it he will be kind to his wife and if his wife wears it she will be the same to him. When the stone is placed at his wife's bedhead, if she is faithful to him then she will immediately embrace him in her sleep, but if she is cuckolding her husband she will immediately be thrown from the bed as if someone had kicked her.

And this stone brings terrible and frightening nightmares. If the stone is ground up finely and sprinkled on hot coals such wonderful and fearful things will appear that it will be impossible not to flee.[78]

Most of the details here are of ancient provenance. They occur, for example, in the eleventh-century *Lapidarium* of Marbod,[79] and in the antique and late antique *Orphei Lithica*, *Orphei Lithica kerygmata* and Damigeron-Evax (apparently Marbod's main source).[80] The curious notion of goat's blood softening diamonds also occurs in Pliny.[81] These details also recur in many late derivative works, for example in Albertus Magnus, and in the many vernacular versions, still published in recent times, of pseudo-Albertus's *Book of Secrets*, and *Le Grand Albert*.[82]

Folktales may also contain references to 'magic stones', such as the *alatyr'* and variants (see Ch. 8.3 4) or the *antavent*.[83]

In the sixteenth century the subject of alchemy and the magical properties of stones acquired great interest. Ivan IV, who, like his grandfather Vassilii III, consulted Finnish magicians (see Ch. 2.4 above) had a knowledge of the virtues of precious stones, as he related to Sir Jerome Horsey, the English merchant and diplomat:

'The loadstone you all know hath great and hidden virtue, without which the seas that compass the world are not navigable nor the bounds nor circle of the earth cannot be known. Muhammed, the Persians' prophet, his tomb hangs in their Ropata [temple] at Derbent most miraculously'. Caused the waiters to bring a chain of needles touched by this loadstone, hanged all one by the other. 'This fair coral and this fair turquoise you see; take it in your hand; of his nature are orient colours; put them on my hand and arm. I am poisoned with disease; you see they show their virtue by the change of their pure colour into pall; declares my death. Reach out my staff royal, an unicorn's horn garnished with very fair diamonds, rubies, sapphires, emeralds, and other precious stones that are rich in value, cost seventy thousand marks sterling of David Gower from the folkers of Augsburg. Seek out for some spiders.' Caused his physician, Johan Eilof, to scrape a circle thereof upon the table; put within it one spider and so one another and died, and some other without that ran alive apace from it. 'It is too late, it will not preserve me. Behold these precious stones. This diamond is the orient's richest and most precious of all other. I have never affected it; it restrains fury and luxury and abstinacy and chastity; the least parcel of it in powder will poison a horse given to drink, much more a man.' Points at the ruby. 'O! this most comfortable to the heart brain, vigour and memory of man, clarifies congealed and corrupt blood.' Then at the emerald. 'The nature of the rainbow, this precious stone is an enemy to uncleanness. Try it, though man and wife cohabit in lust together, having this stone about them, it will burst at the spending of nature. The sapphire I greatly delight in; it preserves and increaseth courage, joys the heart,

pleasing to all the vital senses, precious and very sovereign for the eyes, clears
the sight, takes away bloodshot, and strengthens the muscles and strings
thereof.' Then takes the onyx in hand. 'These are God's wonderful gifts,
secrets in nature, and yet reveals them to man's use and contemplation, as
friends to grace and virtue and enemies to vice.'[84]

Not long afterwards, in 1586, Tsar Boris Godunov offered the fabulous salary of
£2000 p.a., and all provisions free, to the English magus and mathematical
advisor to the Muscovy Company John Dee to enter his service;[85] his son Arthur
Dee, who was also an alchemist, actually went to Moscow and had a successful
career there as a royal physician and subsequently in England. He actually wrote
his *Arcana arcanorum* in Moscow.[86]

The Muscovite tsars, like most European rulers and magnates, were quite
happy to pay enormous sums for curative stones. Tsar Aleksei Mikhailovich
possessed, beside the narwhal horn mentioned in Ch. 9, which he bought for
10,000 roubles, a nephrite drinking vessel set in silver which cost 6000 roubles
and had curative powers when drunk from or worn.[87]

Interest in alchemy was common throughout Europe in the sixteenth and
seventeenth centuries, and after Paracelsus the growth of iatrochemistry would
have made it inevitable that a good proportion of the physicians seeking their
fortune in Muscovy (and many were little more than adventurers) could have
pretended to at least some alchemical doctrine, not to mention astrology and
other arcane skills – indeed it seems to have been a required part of their
qualifications: Dr Timothy Willis, who was sent on a diplomatic mission to
Moscow in 1599, reported on his return:

> . . . before my coming thether the great duke had procured 3 or 4 physitiones
> to be provided him in germanie: which wear not come when I departed from
> Moskovie, bycause they demannded great soms of prest monie and a greater
> yearlie pensione then he useth to give to his physitions. It is thowght that the
> duke will satisfie them in all, the rather bycause some of them profes great
> power in nigromancie and conjuring.[88]

The habit of calling in both foreign doctors and Lappish witches was in fact very
suspect to the Orthodox who, in one Russian interpretation of the canons of the
Trullan Synod in 692, had been declared anathema if they consulted Jewish or
German doctors, or those of other heretical faiths, or a Russian wizard or Lapps
or Samoyeds, or to bathe with Jews.[89] But the Russian situation is far from
unique; the exotic appeal which a foreign healer or magician can exert has an
ancient history – the Bible has condemnations of those who follow strange gods,
and almost any oriental cult or medical fad has been able to find enthusiasts from
ancient Rome to modern Europe and America. The Spanish rulers of the
sixteenth century certainly employed Jewish and Morisco physicians and
magicians, and the contemporary of Ivan IV, that most orthodox of Catholic

monarchs Philip II of Spain, employed Morisco diviners to find new springs for his palaces, used Morisco prophecies to undermine the Morisco rebellion, and even called in Morisco healers to treat his children when his Christian court physicians had failed.[90]

As we have seen above in the case of Dee, these physicians with occult leanings were not only Germans, and Willis himself was later to write two alchemical books. Indeed, English doctors who served in Russia often had some occult or disreputable connections;[91] Eliseus Bomel, a Cambridge-educated Westphalian doctor, who had been imprisoned in England for astrology, became, on Queen Elizabeth's recommendation, court physician and astrologer to Ivan IV; he was reputed to have been the official poisoner of those who fell under Ivan's disfavour and his fate, like that of several earlier court physicians,[92] was unpleasant – when he tried to flee the country he was caught, accused of treason, tortured with the strappado and rack and roasted on a spit, and died shortly after (?1574).[93] The writer of the *Pskov Chronicle* described him as a *koldun* and a *liutyi volkhv* (ferocious wizard) and one modern historian has suggested that Bomel introduced Ivan to magic.[94] A later English doctor-alchemist, Francis Anthony (1550–1623), presented his 'aurum potabile', a preparation which had made him rich in England,[95] to Tsar Mikhail Fedorovich.[96]

The medical and alchemical adventurers were not necessarily all foreigners, and what could just possibly be a purely Russian attempt at transmutational alchemy appears to be described in the *Piskarev Chronicle* under the year 1596 when two men appeared in Tver' claiming to 'distill' (*propuskat'*) silver and gold. They were summoned to Moscow by Tsar Fedor Ivanovich to demonstrate their skill. When they failed they were punished by being tortured and forced to drink their own mercury, from which they died painfully.[97] This punishment was analogous to that meted out to counterfeiters of coin, who had their molten base metal poured down their throats.[98] The chronicle text does not state that the two 'alchemists' were foreign, as it probably would if this were the case, but it is difficult to account for Muscovites, who were rarely allowed outside their own country, acquiring the expertise to practice alchemy even at this apparently crude level; and they could hardly have been using the *Secretum* as their guide! The likeliest explanation is that they came from the Grand Duchy of Lithuania, which was much more open to Western influences, but whose Ukrainian and Belorussian citizens were not entirely foreign in language and religion.

The existence of official 'alkimisty' (most, apparently, foreign[99]) in the Tsar's Apothecary Department (*Aptekarskii prikaz*) in the seventeenth century, perhaps dating back to the time of Ivan the Terrible in the sixteenth century, suggests at first sight that Ivan, like his contemporary Rudolph II, had begun the official promotion of alchemy, but in fact the duties of these 'alchemists' seem to have extended no further than the preparation of medicines and the enormous quantities of distilled cordials consumed by the tsar's household.[100]

Other aspects of West European Hermeticism were not entirely unknown in seventeenth-century Muscovy – the Western-educated court poet and cleric

Simeon Polotskii owned John Dee's *Monas Hieroglyphica* and Caussin's *Symbolica Aegiptiana Sapientia*, and the Greek clerical adventurer and writer of 'oracles' Paisios Ligarides refers in a letter to 'the prophetic sphinx' and 'Trismegistus Mercurius'.[101] Tsar Aleksei himself had a picture of an obelisk with hieroglyphs.[102]

Despite this evidence of occasional interest in alchemy, in particular at the level of the court,[103] there are no further alchemical manuscripts in Russia, as far as I can tell, until the freemasons, Rosicrucians and Martinists of the eighteenth century, some of whom made translations of Basil Valentine, Roger Bacon, John Fludd, Paracelsus, etc.,[104] as well as being, one imagines, the main consumers of the extraordinary stock of West European alchemical and occult literature which was kept by the Rosicrucian Nikolai Novikov, the publisher, printer, bookseller and leading figure of the Enlightenment in Catherine II's reign (1762 96), and confiscated by order of the Moscow censor.[105] Only a handful of alchemical works was published in Russian in the eighteenth century, three of them by the Moscow Rosicrucian I.V. Lopukhin.[106]

In the nineteenth and twentieth centuries alchemy became, as in most Western countries, simply the eccentricity of some freemasons and occultists. One of the less desirable results of the relaxation of censorship and Party control of literature following the Gorbachev reforms in the late 1980s, and the subsequent collapse of the Soviet Union, has been the reappearance of the kind of catchpenny popular fortune-telling literature which flourishes in the non-communist world and is encouraged there by the tabloid press. So far this has taken the form of reprints of pre-Revolutionary popular books and pamphlets, and cheaply duplicated typescript *samizdat* broadsheet fortune-telling books, and, most pertinent to this chapter, a pamphlet called 'A Talisman for You: Secrets of Precious Stones'. This describes the birth stones appropriate to each of the signs of the zodiac and lists their magical and medical properties with historical examples. It appears to be derived entirely from popular Western sources.[107]

Notes

1. Much of the material published in this chapter has appeared previously in Ryan, 'Alchemy and the Virtues of Stones in Muscovy', and Ryan, 'Alchemy, Magic, Poisons and the Virtues of Stones in the Old Russian Secretum Secretorum'.

2. See Rabinovich, *Alkhimiia kak fenomen srednevekovoi kul'tury*, and *idem*, *Obraz mira v zerkale alkhimii*.

3. *Istoriia estestvoznaniia v Rossii*, ch. 4 'Khimiia', p. 90.

4. Kuzakov, *Ocherki*, pp. 213–14.

5. All three appear to have had some knowledge of alchemy but the many works ascribed to them are supposititious. The works known in Russian translation are pseudo-Albertus, *De secretis mulierum, item de virtutibus herbarum, lapidum et animalium* (Amsterdam, 1648, translation 1670) – this was published together with pseudo-Michael Scott, *De secretis naturae*, which was also translated into Russian, presumably as part of the same exercise (see Sobolevskii, *Perevodnaia literatura*, p. 157, who characterizes the language as 'bad Church Slavonic with Polonisms'), on Lullian literature in late seventeenth-century Russian (a translation of the *Ars brevis* and compilations based on the *Ars magna*

and later Lullian commentators such as Agrippa, all by the poet and diplomatic interpreter Andrei Belobotskii, with an abbreviated version of Belobotskii's *Ars magna* by the Old Believer leader Andrei Denisov), see Gorfunkel', 'Andrei Belobotskii', and *idem*, '«Velikaia nauka Raimunda Liulliia» i ee chitateli', also Zubov, 'Quelques notices'.

6. For a general survey of chemistry in Kiev Rus' see *Istoriia estestvoznaniia v Rossii*, ch. 4 'Khimiia'. On the making of glass in Kiev Rus' see Shchapova, *Steklo Kievskoi Rusi*; *idem*, 'O khimii i tekhnologii stekla', and *idem*, 'Elementy znanii po khimii neorganicheskikh soedinenii v Drevnei Rusi'.

7. See Unbegaun, 'Les Slaves et la poudre à canon'.

8. See Russell Zguta, 'Monastic Medicine in Kievan Rus' and Early Muscovy'.

9. See Granstrem, 'O proiskhozhdenii glagolicheskoi azbuki'; Alekseev, *Slovari inostrannykh iazykov*, pp. 66–7.

10. For a good survey of this literature see Rainov, *Nauka*; Grmek, *Les Sciences*; Ihor Ševčenko, 'Remarks'; Ryan, 'Science in Medieval Russia', and more recently, on the Bulgarian dimension, Georgiev, 'Osnovni cherti' and Cholova, 'La Cosmologie'. For texts see Kristanov and Duichev, *Estestvoznanieto*.

11. The best discussion of the theory of the elements, humours, etc. in these works is in Sokolov, *Ocherki*.

12. *De duodecim gemmis quae erant in veste aaronis liber* in Migne, *Patrologia graeca*, 43, col. 293–371.

13. For a survey of this material see Aksenton, 'Svedeniia o dragotsennykh kamniakh'.

14. On the symbolic interpretation of the stones in this work see Konovalova, 'Sravnenie kak literaturnyi priem v *Zhitii Stefana Permskogo*', p. 131.

15. Simonov, 'O metodologii', p. 8.

16. Shchapova notes two pieces of 'alchemical laboratory glassware' of the twelfth century found on Russian territory but concludes from their location that they were not used for alchemical purposes: Shchapova, 'Elementy', p. 22.

17. I use Manzalaoui's terminology: see Manzalaoui, 'The Pseudo-Aristotelian *Kitāb Sirr al Asrār*: Facts and Problems', pp. 147–257.

18. Spitzer, 'Hebrew Translation', pp. 45–9, suggests a close link between the Eighth Discourse of the Short Form and the Tenth Discourse of the Long Form.

19. Ryan, 'Maimonides'. Maimonides's medicine is for the most part distinctly practical and non-magical; even his love potions are essentially pharmacological.

20. Speranskii, *Iz istorii otrechennykh knig. IV. Aristotelevy vrata ili Tainaia tainykh*, Pamiatniki drevnei pis'mennosti i iskusstva CLXXI, St Petersburg, 1908.

21. Bulanin in *Pamiatniki literatury Drevnei Rusi. Konets XV – pervaia polovina XV veka*, pp. 534–91, 750–4.

22. The concept, however, was not new to the East Slavs: a description, taken from the Byzantine chronicle of George Hamartolos, of the methods used by Apollonius of Tyana to protect cities from scorpions and earthquakes appears in the twelfth-century *Russian Primary Chronicle* under the year 6420 (912) – see *Pamiatniki literatury drevnei Rusi. Nachalo russkoi literatury. XI – nachalo XII veka*, p. 54.

23. A more detailed edition of this text is given in Ryan, 'Alchemy, Magic, Poisons'. The translation is from the Russian text of MS Bodley Laud Misc. 45, pp. 124–7 (O. in the notes) unless otherwise indicated (Sp. = the Speranskii edition). For convenience the text is divided up according to the numbered sections of Gaster's translation of the Hebrew text. The square brackets enclosing headings are in the original manuscript (an unusual feature). Some comparison is made with the

Latin translation from Hebrew published by Achillini. Note that the Old Russian text not only interpolates Gaster 126 and 127 into 125 but also reverses Gaster 133 and 134.

TEXT REFERENCES (all page numbers refer to Speranskii's edition of the Old Russian *Tainaia tainykh* except where otherwise indicated):

Speranskii = M.N. Speranskii, *Iz istorii otrechennykh knig. IV.*

Gaster = M. Gaster, 'The Hebrew Version of the *Secretum Secretorum*'.

Achillini = the Latin text published in R. Steele, *Secretum secretorum … Fratris Rogeri*, Opera hactenus inedita Rogeri Baconi, fasc.5, Oxford, 1920, pp. 173–5.

A = Maimonides, *Treatise on Asthma* (interpolated in the Old Russian *Secretum*).

G = *Galinovo na Ipokrata*, in Tikhonravov, *Pamiatniki otrechennoi russkoi literatury*, II, pp. 405–10.

O = Oxford, Bodleian Library, MS Laud Misc. 45, *Secretum secretorum*, Russian, late 16th c.

P – Maimonides, *Treatise on Poisons* (interpolated in the Old Russian *Secretum*).

R = Rhazes' physiognomy (interpolated in the Old Russian Secretum).

S = Maimonides, *Treatise on Sexual Intercourse* (interpolated in the Old Russian *Secretum*).

SS = *Secretum secretorum.*

24. In text *tainitsa*, possibly meaning 'treasurehouse'. I have read it as *taina* 'secret', as in Gaster. The Arabic is *nāmūs* 'confidential' from Greek *gnōma* for 'hidden'.

25. The continuous system of text division by the names of the days of the week runs through all the texts in the manuscripts of the Russian *Secretum*, beginning with Sunday. This is considered by Speranskii to be the Jewish system of daily readings but see Arkhipov, *Drevnerusskaia Kniga Proroka Daniila*, p. 13, n. 26, who disputes this and leaves open the question of the purpose of the day-name divisions. Usually the day name occurs in the margin but here it has been absorbed into the main text.

26. *estvo.* Cf. *estestvo* in G 405.19. Modern Russian *estestvo* 'nature, essence; Nature'.

27. *samost'*, also in line P 204.9. Substance. One manuscript of a logical text also translated from Hebrew (St Petersburg, Academy of Sciences Library, Arkh. sobr. 210, f. 112) has the marginal gloss *sushchestvo* 'essence; creature' for this word.

28. *prikliuchenie (prikluchenie, priluchenie)*, also found in P 204.9 and S 210.5. Accident (as a philosophical term).

29. *obraz* could mean 'form, shape, image, icon, map'.

30. *veshch'*, also in G 405.7. Cf. *osnovanie* in line P 204.8, also in the Church Slavonic translation by John the Exarch of John Damascene, *De fide vera* (see Tikhomirov, *Russkaia kul'tura X–XVIII vekov*, p. 108) and John the Exarch's *Shestodnev*. John the Exarch also uses the not uncommon *stukhii/stikhiia* Greek *stoicheion* 'element' (as does G. but in the sense of 'humours').

31. *giiul'nyi*: material. <Hebrew *hiyuli* <Greek *hulē*, with Russian adjectival suffix.

32. *prirozhenie* also in line A 218.19. Nature. Polish *przyrodzenie.*

33. Lit. 'help' but the verb *pomogat'* here often means, as it can in modern Russian, 'to be a remedy for'.

34. Not clear, perhaps for *prikliuchenie.*

35. Drachm. 4.2 g, 1/72 or 1/96 of a *funt*. Originally the weight of a coin.

36. *zarnikh* Arsenic. <Arabic *zarnīkh.*

37. *vinnik*, also in line P 207.20. Vinegar.

38. Extracted from baked egg yolks.

39. In Sp. *arr'ris*, in O. *urris*. Mars (here as the alchemical name of the metal iron). A transliteration from Greek *arēs*, commonly found in Russian as *arei, aris, arris, areris.*

40. The alchemical name of silver.

41. 'A large amount'?

42. *krechet* in O., *krechat* in Sp. Probably *krechet* 'falcon'. Gaster has 'the bird Paras, in Arabic *akab*': this is probably Arabic *'uqāb* 'eagle', one of the symbols of Sophic Mercury and one of the several bird names used as alchemical terms.

43. *galina*. The compound antidote galena (from Greek *galēnē*). The phrase 'galesnu ili iari ili vosku' corresponds to Gaster '*shsbuzag* and wax'.

44. One manuscript of the Latin version of the medieval Arabic compendium of magic called *Picatrix* describes a 'ring of Venus' in which 'sculpatur in lapide acuty [i.e. jacinth] mulier'. The rest of our talisman, however, is much closer to the talisman of Virgo, quoted from the *Liber imaginum* of Hermes Trismegistus in the same work: 'Virgo. Forma eius est muliebris involute et equitantes super leonem . . . et fiat ex argento vel auro in die et hora Solis . . .'. See Pingree, ed., *Picatrix*, pp. 240 and 84 respectively.

45. *obraz* here = talisman.

46. In Russian *btulin*, i.e. a Russian adjective formed from the Hebrew *betula* 'young girl; Virgo' – it is not clear why the translator could not translate this word.

47. The text has the Hebrew *kfir* here for some unclear reason. See previous note.

48. In the text *saraf* from Arabic *sharaf* 'exaltation'. The word seems to have puzzled all the translators; Gaster has 'Shrf in Arabic', Achillini has 'in gradu decimo celi, quod vocatur Seraph in Arabico'.

49. *zly dalekii* in Sp., *zlyi paleki* in O. Achillini has 'et erit rethe a remotioribus ex eo', which Gaster, following the Latin as he often does when puzzled, renders 'and the net(?) far away from it'. Possibly there is a confusion with the other talisman below, which has *zavady*, possibly meaning nets (Dal', s.v. *zavodit*') but more likely is an error of translation from Arabic *rudī*.

50. The poison *Bish*, aconite. On this see Ruska, *Tabula Smaragdina*, pp. 96–7, where *bish* is part of the 'Treasure of Alexander the Great'; Yule, *Hobson-Jobson*, s.v. *bish*; *Oxford English Dictionary*, s.v. *bikh*.

51. The text has *arasim*, i.e. Hebrew *eresin* 'drops (of poison)' <Latin *virus*.

52. Not clear in Sp. or O. Gaster has 'asp or leopard'; Achillini has: 'sicut in basilisco aut felle'. The Arabic text seems to give the sensible advice not to use the poison because its presence is betrayed by its bitter taste.

53. *Ruda zolotaia* 'gold ore'.

54. Not in other versions. The reference may be to talismans or a universal talisman or, more prosaically, a map if that is the correct interpretation of an earlier passage in the Russian version of the *Secretum* which recommends Alexander to have an image (map?) of all his lands (Sp., p. 149). This too is not in other versions and could also mean a talisman.

55. *kimiia*, misread in Sp. as *kimi*. Alchemy. Arabic *kīmīyā'* <Greek *chēmeia*.

56. Hebrew reduplication indicating intensification.

57. The other versions appear to say that alchemy is *not* a true science, unlike ploughing and sowing. See Spitzer, 'Hebrew Translation', pp. 47–8.

58. *Badzagir*, bezoar. From Arabic *bāzahr* <Persian *padzahr*. see Yule, *Hobson-Jobson*, s.v. *bezoar*.

59. Gaster has: 'like a sallow piece of leather' and this was repeated by Steele, p. 253. Achillini has 'viridis sicut oliva'. M. Manzalaoui has kindly informed me that the Short Form Arabic reads: 'like the skin of a yellow snake' – evidently Gaster's manuscripts and the Hebrew manuscript from which the Old Russian version derives simplified the text in different directions.

60. Gaster: 'land of Tsin' (i.e. China, in Arabic ṣīn). The Russian *nizkii* is possible by metathesis.

61. Gaster: 'poison'; *rosh* in Hebrew is both gall and poison.

62. Lit. *chachki* but probably the same as *zr"něs dvěiachnykh* below.

63. Gaster: 'vipers and reptiles'.

64. This is the virtue of the stone *achates* in Epiphanius.

65. The tsars are known to have possessed bezoars which they employed both as talismans and as an ingredient in medicines against malefic magic. Some are listed in the official inventories: see Zabelin, *Domashnii byt russkikh tsarits*, pp. 48 (in a box, presumably therefore as a talisman); 54–5 (three valued at 215 roubles); 136 (white, with unicorn horn, a medicine against *porcha*, malefic magic). See also Pyliaev, *Dragotsennye kamni*, pp. 201–2.

66. In text *surmit* which should probably be *surmist* 'of antimony, kohl'.

67. = swelling? Not clear. Gaster has 'a town where the illness called *tamun* is raging'. *Suhāj* has Al-tāʿūn. '(bubonic) plague'.

68. Astronomical texts in Old Russian or Church Slavonic were not very common and there is frequently a confusion of terms. Even the learned Pamva Berynda in his *Leksikon slavenorosskii* (Kiev, 1627) uses the Latin-derived *planeta* in the sense of 'sign of the Zodiac' while also using the Greek-derived alternative form *planita* to mean 'planet'.

69. Not clear. The Latin has 'scientias (i.e. radiis) elongaverit ab eo'. Quite possibly there is a confusion of Arabic *radī'* and Latin *radii* and *rethe* and a confusion with the ring talisman above, q.v., which mentions nets in Gaster and Steele. None of these versions has an obvious reading of either of these two talismans.

70. *izmaragd*, also in P 207.4. Emerald. From Greek *smaragdos*, one of the stones mentioned in the Bible and therefore well known in Church Slavonic; the doublet *izumrud*, derived from Arabic *al-zumurrud* (which gives the *zamrad* of the Latin text) is not found in these texts. The title is missing in Laud Misc. 45 which runs on from the preceding section without break.

71. A possible but unattested Arabic derivation might be *al-baht*. In Gaster: *Alkahat*. Steel gives Latin 'Alchahat' with the marginal note 'agate?'.

72. In Gaster: black. Red, *cherlennyi, chervlennyi* and black, *chernyi* are similar in spelling and often confused in Old Russian texts.

73. *feroza* : Turquoise. Cf. at line 176.1 *zerkost' ferzina* 'turquoise blue'. Modern Russian *biriuza*. Arabic *fārūz* 'turquoise'. Gaster: '*ahlamah, Firzag* in Arabic'. The medical miscellany *Prokhladnyi vertograd* of 1672, copies of which often contain the 'Instruction of Moses the Egyptian to Alexander the Great' (See Ryan, 'Maimonides') includes in its section on precious stones : 'Beriuza ili theriuza … Aristotel' premudryi pishet pro nego chto umnozhivaet ego tsari v sokrovnitsakh svoikh i chestvuiutsia ikh' (Florinskii, *Russkie prostonarodnye travniki*, p. 154), i.e. a reference to this section of the *Secretum*.

74. Research on this in Russian has been inadequate but see most recently Anikin, 'K proiskhozhdeniiu pamiatnikov vrachebnoi pis'mennosti'. In Western bibliography and library catalogues also there has been great confusion over the names and identities of incunable herbals, e.g. the *Gart der Gesundheit, or Ortus sanitatis*, first printed in Mainz by Peter Schoefer in 1485, and the *Herbarius latinus*, also printed in Mainz by the same printer but in the previous year, and the Latin *Hortus sanitatis* (Mainz, 1491). For a recent summary of the extensive literature on the subject see Keil in *Die deutsche Literatur des Mittelalters. Verfasserlexikon*, IV, 1, 1983, s.v. *Hortus sanitatis* and longer articles by the same author (see bibliography). Three Lübeck editions (1492, 1510, 1520) are identified by

Schreiber, *Die Kräuterbücher*, pp. XXV–XXVII; of these the 1510 edition is a ghost – see Borchling and Claussen, *Niederdeutsche Bibliographie*, I, no. 475. The Lübeck editions appear to be derived from the 1485 *Gart* with elements of the later Latin *Hortus sanitatis* of 1491. This book is described as 'a remarkable work' by W.T. Stearns in his annotations to the third edition of Arber, *Herbals*, p. 309. On Ghotan and Bülow see also Miller, 'The Lübeckers Bartholomäus Ghotan and Nicolaus Bülow'. It is noteworthy that 1534 is also the date of the first Polish printed herbal: it was written by Stefan Falimirz, based on the Latin *Herbarius* and *Ortus sanitatis*, and printed in Cracow by Florian Ungler – see Kuźnicka, 'The Earliest Printed Herbals', p. 260).

75. See Speranskii, *Iz istorii otrechennykh knig. IV. Aristotelevy vrata ili Tainaia tainykh*, pp. 126–7 and Zmeev, *Russkie vrachebniki*, pp. 76, 77, 79, 83, 91, 108, 188. Zmeev, while noting the frequency of occurrence of this text, fails to identify the Old Russian *Secretum* as the immediate source of the text and does not recognize 'Moses the Egyptian' as Maimonides. The text of the *Instruction of Moses the Egyptian to Alexander of Macedon* is published in Florinskii, *Russkie prostonarodnye travniki*, pp. 184–7; it has recently been republished in *Pamiatniki literatury Drevnei Rusi. Konets XVI–nachalo XVII vekov*, pp. 524–7, 607–13, with a commentary but still no identification. It appears after ch. 340 of the *Prokhladnyi vertograd* in Florinskii's version (in the manuscripts it appears variously as ch. 341, 342, sometimes ch. 343), differs slightly from the usual *Secretum* text and has an extra section on the Dog Days 'un amon, ezhe est' pesii mesiats'.

76. In chs 35–6 of the *De opificio mundi* Philo Judaeus quotes Solon and Hippocrates on the seven ages of man, which he discusses as part of his general essay on the cosmic significance of the number seven. None of the several known medical doctors called Philo seems to fit this text.

77. Many of the texts were first published in Florinskii, *Russkie prostonarodnye travniki* and still the best survey of the contents of this type of literature is Zmeev, *Russkie vrachebniki*. For the most recent discussion of the genre (some 400 manuscrits are now known) and publication of the main text on the virtues of precious stones see *Pamiatniki literatury Drevnei Rusi. Konets XVI–nachalo XVII vekov*, pp. 516–23 (text), 607–13 (commentary by V.V. Kolesova).

78. *Pamiatniki literatury drevnei Rusi. Konets XVI–nachalo XVII vekov*, pp. 516, 522.

79. See Riddle, *Marbode of Rennes' (1035–1123) De Lapidibus*, pp. 57–8.

80. See *Les Lapidaires grecs*, s.v.

81. *Naturalis historia*, 37. 15. 59.

82. See the entries for magnet and diamond in *The Book of Secrets of Albertus Magnus*, pp. 26, 93, and *Le Grand et le Petit Albert*, p. 106.

83. Rybnikov, *Pesni*, 1991 edn., III, p. 314 s.v.

84. As published in Berry and Crummey, *Rude and Barbarous Kingdom*, pp. 304–6.

85. See Hakluyt, *Principal Navigations*, I, p. 573, also State Papers Foreign Addenda XXIX, p. 1414.

86. British Library, Sloane MS 1876. For further detail and bibliography see Figurovskii, 'The Alchemist and Physician Arthur Dee'; Appleby, 'Arthur Dee and Johannes Bánfi Hunyades'; *idem*, 'Some of Arthur Dee's Associations'; Abraham, 'Arthur Dee'.

87. Zabelin, *Domashnii byt russkikh tsarei*, p. 279.

88. Evans, 'Doctor Timothy Willis', p. 61.

89. Mansikka, *Der Religion der Ostslaven*, p. 269.

90. See Goodman, *Power and Penury*, pp. 17–19, 38–9, 221.

91. See Appleby, 'Arthur Dee', p. 99. Appleby notes that 'It is a curious fact that several British doctors, besides Arthur Dee, were connected both with Russia and alchemy'.

92. A Jewish doctor from Italy, Leon, was court physician to Grand Prince Ivan III and was executed for failing to effect a cure; in this he followed a German doctor put to death in 1485 for the same reason: see Florinskii, *Russkie prostonarodnye travniki*, p. v. They were followed in 1687 by the German physician Daniel von Haden, who was hacked to death for practising witchcraft and possessing a snakeskin (a not uncommon ingredient in amulets and magical potions). The possible connection between poison, magic, and foreign doctors clearly evoked potent fears.

93. See Hamel, *England and Russia*, pp. 201–6, and *Dictionary of National Biography*, s.v. *Bomelius*.

94. Skrynnikov, *Gosudarstvo i tserkov'*, p. 343.

95. Simonov, 'Russkie pridvornye matematiki', p. 79.

96. Appleby, 'Arthur Dee', p. 100. See also *DNB*, s.v.

97. Kuzakov, *Ocherki*, pp. 214–15.

98. According to Struys, *The Voiages and travels of John Struys*, p. 140; Kotoshikhin, *O Rossii*, fol. 171, who mentions also adulterers of gold and silver and specifies molten tin and lead.

99. A known exception is Tikhon Anan'in, one of the lower grade of Russian *khimiki*, who studied under an *alkimist* and eventually reached that grade himself: see Rainov, *Nauka*, pp. 327–8.

100. See *Istoriia estestvoznaniia v Rossii*, pp. 101–3, and more recently Lokhteva, 'Materialy Aptekarskogo prikaza'.

101. See Longworth, *Alexis*, pp. 205–6. On Ligarides see V. Grumel's article in the *Dictionnaire théologique catholique*, pp. 749–57.

102. See Waugh, 'Azbuka znameni lits'.

103. Iakov Villimovich Brius (James Bruce), Peter the Great's scientific adviser, was popularly reputed to be a wizard (see ch. 15.5), and certainly possessed a number of alchemical works in his considerable scientific library: see *Biblioteka Ia. V. Briusa*.

104. See Vernadskii, *Russkoe masonstvo*, pp. 126–7, 150–3; more generally see Ryu, 'Moscow Freemasons and the Rosicrucian Order'; de Madariaga, *Russia in the Age of Catherine the Great*, ch. 33 'The Role of Freemasonry'; *idem*, 'Freemasonry in Eighteenth-Century Russian Society'; the discussion and notes in ch. 8 of Jones, *Nikolay Novikov, Enlightener of Russia*; also, on literary aspects, Baehr, 'The Masonic Component in Eighteenth-Century Russian Literature'; *idem*, *The Paradise Myth in Eighteenth-Century Russia*; Leighton, 'Puškin and Freemasonry'.

105. For a list of these works see 'Podlinnye reestry knigam vzyatym, po vysochaishem poveleniiu, iz palat N.I. Novikova v Moskovskuiu dukhovnuiu i svetskuiu tsenzuru', *ChOIDR*, 1871, 3, pp. 17–46.

106. See *Svodnyi katalog*, nos 3042, 5150, 6456.

107. I am obliged to Dr Faith Wigzell for supplying me with copies of some of these curiosities.

ASTROLOGY –
THE BYZANTINE TRADITION

1. *Greek Learning and the Slavs*

The elaborate system of astrology as it was in the Greco-Roman world in the age of Ptolemy, and as it was further refined by the Arabs, required a knowledge of mathematics and observational astronomy, the compilation of tables, and the development of instruments. In Western Europe some aspects of astronomy and astrology survived in Latin from antiquity, but for the most part they were reconstructed by means of texts and instruments imported from the non-Christian Mediterranean world with the help of Muslim and Jewish scholars in Spain, Provence and Italy in the Middle Ages, and later, in the Renaissance, directly from Greek texts. In Byzantium, on the other hand, in the thousand years of its history astrology knew periods of both enthusiastic application and decline, but the textual basis remained more or less intact.

This knowledge was not transmitted to the Slavs, even though the 'apostles of the Slavs', Cyril and Methodius, were learned men of their time who had received a good education. The *Vita Constantini* lists geometry and astronomy among the sciences which Cyril had studied, and he taught philosophy in succession to his teacher, the famous Patriarch Photius.[1] These lists of disciplines known, or frequently boasted about as *not* being known, by saintly members of the clergy are a biographical *topos* in Old Russian as in other medieval literatures but in this case the claim would appear to be accurate.

In the general historical context this non-transmission of science was not entirely surprising, for reasons outlined in Ch. 1. To this should be added, in the case of astronomy and astrology, a lack of of all but the most basic mathematics and the absence even of the concept of angular measurement, which made the development of mathematical astrology an impossibility.

This does not mean, of course, that there was no knowledge of mathematics at all in Kiev Rus'. The mathematical text of Kirik of Novgorod (1136), even if it is based on a Greek *computus* (as seems probable – creative original writing in such subject areas, especially at this time and place, is not to be expected), was clearly compiled for a Russian milieu,[2] and part of one manuscript of the first Russian law code, the *Russkaia pravda*, show that in matters of calculation for trade and taxation the people of Kiev Rus' knew what they were doing and may have been acquainted with the abacus of classical antiquity.[3] No doubt the Tatar invasion, that general scapegoat, hindered progress thereafter; at any event no further development in mathematics or astronomy is observable until the late fifteenth century when Jewish and West European influences began to alter Muscovite perceptions. This will be discussed in the next chapter.

The practice of astrology, or the consultation of astrologers, is referred to in every index of banned books.[4] The Novgorod canon law code called *Kormchaia* of 1280, for example, condemns 'astrological nativities',[5] and several versions in both Greek and Church Slavonic of the *Kormchaia* require those who convert from Islam to forswear the worship of 'Aphrodite, the Morning Star called in Arabic Khovar, or great'.[6] Further condemnations could be found in the works of theologians, such as John Damascene, translated from Greek,[7] and in Russian penitentials. As in many other matters (and especially with regard to the clergy), such as mixed bathing, cross-dressing, marriage, sexual impropriety, abortion, or playing dice, the Russian Church's attitude to astrology was no doubt determined by the oft-quoted canon 61 of the Trullan Synod (692).[8] This authority is specifically quoted in the acts of the *Stoglav* Council of 1551, and the condemnation carries over into the *Domostroi*, which contains a very similar list of proscribed texts and practices: almanacs, horoscopes, signs of the zodiac, astrology, etc.[9]

In any case the Bible, bible commentaries, and a number of apocryphal and historical texts known to the Orthodox Slavs contain references to astrology and magic which cannot have been lost on their readers. In particular we may note the legends which tell of Seth or Enoch being given the secrets of the heavens (see the discussion of Rykov's geomancy in Ch. 12) and the conversion of the wizard Balaam into a Persian magus who bequeathed his books of astrology to the Three Magi, thus enabling them to identify the star of Bethlehem.[10] The patristic view of this was that astrology ceased to be licit with the birth of Christ and that the Magi were the last to practice astrology licitly,[11] thus distinguishing the old dispensation from the new in this respect. No Slavonic text appears to make this clear distinction.

The early Slavs would have been unusual if they had not attributed some meaning to events in the heavens, and what little we know from non-Slav sources, and what has been conjectured from apparent survivals from pagan times, suggests a celestial element in early Slav religious beliefs. However, since there is no literature in a Slavonic language from before the conversion of the various Slavonic peoples to Christianity we can really only talk about the belief in celestial portents in the Christian period. Here the notion of celestial phenomena as portents was familiar not only from the Bible but also from the *De bello judaico* of Flavius Josephus, and the chronicle of George Hamartolos which copies the episode from Josephus, in which the fall of Jerusalem is preceded by the appearance of a comet. The Slavonic version, which dates from the eleventh century (manuscripts extant in Russia from the fifteenth), describes the portent as: '. . . a star above the city, like a spear, which remained all summer, and its name was Komitis, which means all hairy'.[12]

Thereafter comets are regularly noted in the Russian chronicles, usually as portents of disaster, and are usually described as being 'like a spear', 'bearded' or 'hairy', although this is probably often a convention rather than a description of their actual appearance. This is roughly in line with Seneca's remark about the three types of comet distinguished by the Greeks.[13] The Greek text of Josephus has *hromfaias*, 'sword' at this point, and another Greek word for sword or dagger, *xifias*, is also found in the sense of 'comet', for example in Johannes Lydus. The reason for a change to the spear image is not clear, unless it had already become a fixed term. We may note also that the *Novgorod Fourth Chronicle*, s.a. 6732, states: 'there appeared a star Dokit, which is to say like a spear' which presumably derives from Greek *dokos*, 'a rod, shaft', and Pliny (*Naturalis historia*, II.22.89) lists both *acontia* and *hasta* as a type of comet in Latin.[14] Whatever the reason for this translation, it is clear that the notion of the comet as a weapon in the sky foretelling bloodshed became firmly fixed in Old Russian literature. The notion of comets as signs accompanying disasters, and the specific disaster of the death of princes, dates from antiquity,[15] and was certainly known in Russia. As particularly apt evidence that Russian and Western beliefs in this matter were not far apart, we may note the account of Sir Jerome Horsey, which describes the blazing star and other prodigies seen in the sky over Moscow at the time of the death of Ivan the Terrible. Horsey observes that this is liable to happen on such occasions.[16]

Although literary evidence for that other universal celestial portent of disaster, the eclipse, occurs quite early in Russian literature, in the *Tale of the Campaign of Prince Igor* (at the earliest late twelfth century, if indeed it is genuine),[17] I know of no divinatory text in Russian relating to eclipses, although there is a short Bulgarian text.[18] Eclipses continued to be interpreted as portents of disaster, or, with a slight shift of emphasis, as signs of divine wrath, in the various Russian chronicles. In the seventeenth century the archpriest Avvakum, leader of the Old Believer resistance to the reforms of Patriarch Nikon, interpreted an eclipse as a divine comment on Nikon's 'innovations' (see Ch. 15.2 and 15.5).

The Slavonic *Alexander Romance* (not later than the mid-thirteenth century in the version in which it appears in the Chronographs, fifteenth century in the version known as the 'Serbian Alexander') was another source of information about magic and astrology – the 'Chronograph' version tells how Nectanebus lost his royal dignity by indulging in witchcraft; he dispensed with weapons and armies and conquered all his enemies by making spells over a copper bowl. He would put on the dress of a priest and take an ebony wand and summon up his gods and infernal demons. He would make wax effigies of his enemies and their ships which he would sink in the water in the bowl so that the real ships would sink at sea. (It was, no doubt, this kind of perception of the power of magic which made heads of state from the Roman emperors to European, and Russian, monarchs of the seventeenth century, regard its practice as seditious.) The story recounts how eventually Nectanebus looked into the bowl and his gods told him that the Egyptian kingdom was finished. He shaved his beard and head and, promising to return again as a young man (i.e. as Alexander), fled to Pella in Macedonia where he set up as a magician, claiming skill in astrology, horoscopes, interpretation of dreams and signs and lambs (?haruspicy or scapulimancy). He had a wonderful gold and ivory tablet with the images of the seven planets and the horoscope; and the sun was of crystal, the moon of diamond, Saturn of serpentine, Venus of sapphire, Mercury of emerald, and the horoscope of marble. He was consulted by Olympias, wife of King Philip, and seduced her in a complicated fashion by making spells over a wax image of her, burning magic herbs and giving her a false astrological reading which told her she must sleep with the god Amon and bear his child, then visiting her disguised as Amon, wearing a gilded ram's head and carrying his ebony wand. From what followed Alexander was born and as he grew up he excelled in everything, including astrology.[19]

This piece of Egyptian wishful thinking is in no way censored or subject to hostile comment in the Slavonic text in either version; indeed part of this story recurs in the sixteenth-century *Tale of the Princes of Vladimir*, a political work intended to provide the Grand Princes of Moscow with an ancient imperial pedigree to match those claimed by royal and aristocratic families of the Renaissance West. Here, a few generations after Shem, whose great-grandson is alleged to have invented astronomy, we find the wizard-pharaoh Nectanebus listed as the father of Alexander and a precursor of Augustus Caesar, whose brother Prus was supposed to have been the ancestor of Rurik, the Varangian first Prince of Kiev, from whom the Muscovite tsars claimed descent.[20]

2. *Astronomical Knowledge in Kïev Rus'*

The extent of astronomical knowledge available to Kiev Rus', as distinct from the references to astrology listed above, can only be judged from the surviving texts, all of which are translated from Greek into Church Slavonic and some of which are no longer than an article in a *florilegium*. In some cases Russian redactions are known only from the fifteenth century and we cannot always be sure that texts known in Bulgaria or Serbia were also known in Kiev Rus'.

These texts represent not the highest levels of Byzantine achievement in the subject, but rather the popular cosmology of late antiquity and patristic Bible exegesis. They provide the world view of the Orthodox East Slavs up to the seventeenth century, when excerpts are particularly common in *florilegia* and abecediaries, and have a continuing existence in manuscripts, particularly of the Old Believers, into the present century. These texts are: the *Izbornik* of 1073 (the first miscellany written for Prince Sviatoslav, which was taken from an early tenth-century Bulgarian miscellany of Greek patristic texts, mostly Anastasius Sinaiticus, Basil the Great and Gregory of Nyssa) – this, incidentally contains the first, and for a long time the only pictorial representations of the signs of the zodiac;[21] the *Tolkovaia paleia* (*Explanatory palaia* or commentary on bible history), dating probably from the twelfth or thirteenth century;[22] the Slavonic *Book of Enoch* (Greek original lost, but evidently different from the Coptic and Hebrew Enoch books), first translated in the tenth or eleventh century and amplified in

Russian versions of the fifteenth century onwards;[23] the *Hexaemeron* (commentary on the six days of creation) of John the Exarch of Bulgaria, written *circa* 915, taken largely from the fourth-century work of the same name by St Basil (manuscripts of a Russian redaction extant only from the fifteenth century); parts of the eighth-century *De fide orthodoxa* of St John Damascene, translated by the same John the Exarch; the *Hexaemera* of Severianus of Gabala and George of Pisidia;[24] the *Christian Topography* of Cosmas Indicopleustes;[25] various simple encyclopedic works in dialogue form such as the *Dialogues* of Pseudo-Caesarius or the *Lucidarius* (of Latin origin).

3. *Astrological Texts*

Although it is usually pointless to try to separate the concepts of astronomy and astrology before modern times, it must be said that these basic astronomical or cosmological texts have little about them which is astrological. For the magical and divinatory aspects of the subject we have to turn to a different category of text, small works of prognostication involving a degree of astronomical and calendrical information. These are the *Brontologion* (or *Gromnik*, *Gromovnik* in Slavonic), the *Seismologion*, which in Slavonic texts is integral with the *Gromnik* and has no separate title, the *Selenodromion* (in Slavonic *Lunnik*), and the *Kalandologion* (*Koliadnik* in Slavonic), and a variety of smaller texts.[26] These all take their origin in the ancient world,[27] and very similar texts can be found in the *Liber de ostentis*, the Byzantine anthology of such material which was compiled by Johannes Lydus in the sixth century.[28]

Some of these are known in South Slavonic manuscripts from at least the thirteenth century.[29] In Russia they appear to have gained currency from the later fifteenth century onwards, together with other non-astrological divinatory texts of Byzantine or presumed Byzantine origin such as the *Trepetnik* (divination from involuntary movements), *Lopatochnik* (scapulimancy), the *Divinatory Psalter*, the geomancy ascribed to Samuel, and the dice divination ascribed to King David which are discussed elsewhere. Delatte mentions the prevalence of texts of this kind in the monastic libraries of Mt Athos,[30] and it seems fairly clear that literature of this nature was the province of the lesser clergy in later Byzantium and among the Orthodox of the Balkans and Mediterranean area, and began to spread in Russia after the fall of Constantinople through the medium of clerical refugees. It is obvious from the catalogues of manuscripts in Russian, Bulgarian, Serbian, and Rumanian collections that the Byzantine influence in the matter of astrology continued into the post-Byzantine and modern period.

Texts of this kind, though quite clearly primitive by comparison with the elaborate horoscopes described by Neugebauer,[31] are nevertheless not easy to place in binary cultural models of 'high' and 'low' culture. An emperor as sophisticated as Constantine Porphyrogenitus in the tenth century recommends in his *De ceremoniis aulae Byzantinae* that emperors should always take with them on their campaigns a *Biblion sunantematikon*,[32] a Dream Book (*Oneirocriticon*), a

Thunder Book (*Brontologion*) and an Earthquake Book (*Seismologion*). This can hardly be considered a 'low' cultural context.[33]

Five centuries later the Greek theologian, philosopher and astrologer Demetrius Chrysoloras, who was one of the agents of the Byzantine Emperor who helped set up the Council of Florence, interpreted as an evil omen an earthquake in 1437, which supposedly occurred at the exact moment when the papal galleys touched Byzantine soil[34] – a primitive prediction from one of the more sophisticated men of his time.

In fact, the existence of Byzantium more or less continuously for a thousand years does not mean that there was a steady cultural development over that period, or even that there was a real cultural continuum at all. The science and learning of the Hellenistic world faded and was rediscovered more than once, and surviving texts are the only guide to the level at which they were pursued: if St Cyril really was learned in mathematics and astronomy, how far did his learning extend? The available evidence suggests that mathematical astronomy and astrology were more or less dormant for long periods in Byzantium, and when there was a serious interest in astronomy, this was not transmitted to the Slavs. In some cases where textual evidence points to some interest among the South Slavs, this does not extend to the East Slavs; a case in point is the work of the eleventh-century neo-Platonist Michael Psellus.[35]

The simple astrological and divinatory texts such as the *Brontologion* have a continuous existence from late antiquity to the present day; they do not in themselves have a 'cultural level', they simply circulate in different kinds of society at different times. In Russia they flourish mainly in monastic *florilegia* and only in the seventeenth century begin to be restricted to the level of popular culture as a distinct 'educated' culture starts to emerge. Even then Tsar Aleksei Mikhailovich (d. 1676), who ordered the translation of relatively learned Western almanachs and scientific works, was as terrified of popular malefic magic as any of his peasants.

4. *The* Gromnik *and the* Molniak: *Predictions by Thunder, Lightning and Earthquake*

As has already been indicated, divination by thunder is of great antiquity, and texts of systematic thunder divination have a long tradition. The Slavonic text of the *Gromnik* (or *Gromovnik*) is derived from a Byzantine source, as apparently are the Georgian and Hebrew versions.[36] The Slavonic versions are usually ascribed to the seventh-century Byzantine emperor Heraclius, as are many of the Greek versions found in the *Corpus codicum astrologorum graecorum*, although one manuscript ascribes it to 'Moses the Thunder Witness',[37] and another ascribes it to King David.[38] As with the other small 'astrological' texts there is little uniformity of text, details being altered to suit localities, but all are clearly in the Byzantine tradition until the eighteenth century when texts are often markedly different from the earlier versions and may be a newer importation from the

West.[39] The last appearance of the *Gromnik*, Peretts declared optimistically in 1899, was on the toffee papers of the Zhurkin factory![40]

It is not known when the first translation was made but the survival of several comparatively early manuscripts of the text suggests that it was common at an early date among the Orthodox Slavs. A Bulgarian version is referred to in the thirteenth century.[41] Later versions from the fourteenth and fifteenth centuries are known in Serbian and Russian Church Slavonic,[42] and from the Slavonic world pass to Rumania, presumably by way of the Orthodox clergy.[43] Books of thunder divination are regularly condemned in the Russian indexes of banned books from the fourteenth to the eighteenth century.[44] Thunder and lightning are also found in popular divination and as omens – see Index.

5. *The Lunnik: Lunar Predictions*

5.1. *General.* The word *lunnik* ('moon-book') is used as the title of a number of quite separate texts, both in the original manuscripts and by later scholars. It may even be applied to the innocuous lunar tables used in the calculation of the Church calendar.

5.2. *Lunaria with Prophets.* In many of the medical compendia derived from the *Hortus sanitatis* and circulating in Russia from the sixteenth century onwards there are articles ascribed to a certain Filon (Philo?). Sometimes these are an account of the seven ages of man,[45] but sometimes they are *lunaria*, a set of predictions for days of the lunar month, with an Old Testament event attached to each. The biblical events are: Day 1. Adam was created by God; 2. Eve was created; 3. Cain was born; 4. Abel was born; 5. Cain brought an unworthy sacrifice to God; 6. Seth was born; 7. Cain killed his brother Abel; . . . 29. The Jews came to the promised land; 30. Samuel was born. The predictions for the seventh day, on which Cain killed Abel, are:

> This day is bad. Beware it. Do not set out on a journey, buy or sell. The sick will die; the fugitive will not be found. Do not cut your hair. If a child is born it will not be healthy. Do not plant the vegetable garden. If you have a dream it will come true on the second day. Clean lambs and sheep. It is good to let blood at any time of day.[46]

Another version of the text, possibly a quite independent translation, with considerable difference in detail and without the attribution to Philo, was published from a sixteenth-century manuscript by Tikhonravov.[47] The two Russian texts, though differing in much detail, both belong to group two of Weisser's classification of German and Latin texts in that they combine the predictions for fugitives and lost objects, and do not differentiate male and female in the birth prognostications.[48] They have, however, a distinctive feature in that they add an indication of the 'bad hour' at the end of the prognostication for most days. (This is not found in the Latin and German versions.) They also omit the quotation from the Psalms found in many Latin and German manuscripts of this group.

This tradition of Old Testament *lunaria* was shown by Cumont to be an adaptation, probably by a Jew, of a more ancient system of divination involving classical mythology.[49] There are many copies of these *lunaria*. They may vary in detail and in some cases even very late specimens of Greek versions may retain traces of their pagan origin – one thirteenth-century manuscript contains a version headed *Selenodromion etoi profetologion to selenaion* in which most of the days are given as the day of birth both of a pagan god and of an Old Testament figure.[50] A nineteenth-century manuscript, in which the text is ascribed to David and Solomon, still gives day 7 as the day of Apollo's birth.[51] The textual tradition is extremely loose; the Latin versions, of which the earliest extant manuscripts date from the ninth century, do not correspond very closely to the Greek, but are nevertheless presumed to be derived from a Greek text (or texts),[52] and in their turn give rise to the vernacular texts.[53] There is also an oriental tradition recorded in the Syriac *Book of Medicines* in which neither the classical Gods nor the prophets nor the psalms are involved and in which the 'fugitives' are unambiguously identified as fugitive slaves.[54]

6. *The* Koliadnik: *Calendar Predictions*

This takes a variety of forms but essentially is a set of predictions arranged for the days of the week on which Christmas, the New Year, etc. occur. The earliest extant versions are Latin, not later than the ninth century, although the text has similarities with the 'Treatise of Shem' (?first century BC) in which the predictions are based on the sign of the zodiac in which the year begins.[55] St John Chrysostom in the fourth century seems to have been the first to condemn this belief as superstitious.[56]

There are many subsequent Latin and vernacular versions, including the German *Bauern-Praktik* and the versions of *Erra Pater*, mocked in Butler's *Hudibras*, published at least a dozen times in English between 1536 and 1640, and re-issued in the eighteenth century as the work of the astrologer William Lilly.[57]

In the South and East Slavonic versions (usually in fact Church Slavonic), usually known as *koliadniki* (*koliada* <Latin *calendae* and cognates in other Slavonic languages means the Christmas period and/or festivities), this text is usually ascribed to the prophet Esdras (Ezra), as it is in many of the Greek *kalandologia*, West European ('Signum quod estendit Dominus Esdrae prophetae') and Hebrew versions.[58] (Esdras vies with Solomon in popularity as the putative author of astrological and divinatory texts.)

Copies are known from the thirteenth century in Bulgarian,[59] the fourteenth century in Serbian,[60] and fifteenth century onwards in Russian.[61] As with most texts of this type there is considerable fluctuation in content and wording; there is, however, sufficient consistency to suggest that all the East and South Slavonic versions are in the same tradition and derive from Byzantine Greek versions.

7. Lucky and Unlucky Days

There are several traditions of calendrical superstition in Byzantium, the simplest of which is the ascription of good or bad luck to odd and even dates, a process which may be elaborated by any number of onomantic systems (for which see Ch. 11.8).[62] Egyptian days, the unlucky *dies aegyptici*, originally two in each month, go back to before the third century AD.[63] One suggestion is that they were originally the days following senatorial meetings. The Roman calendar marked days as F (for *fasti*) or N (for *nefasti*), days on which business could or could not be done. The 'Egyptian Days' were well known throughout Europe in the Middle Ages, although belief in them was regularly condemned by the Church. In Anglo-Saxon calendars they were marked as days on which blood-letting was dangerous and one should not begin any enterprise or journey.

Among the Slavs this belief found literary expression from the very beginning of their Christian history.[64] The earliest calendrical advice given in an East Slav manuscript is in the *Izbornik Sviatoslava* of 1073, which gives prohibitions of food, drink, or ablutions for each month in the article on the Roman months.[65] The more specific 'good and bad days' texts take a variety of forms, almost always short articles in miscellanies or at the end of psalters. They cannot easily be dated. There are, for example: a short list of good and bad parts of the days in the lunar month (e.g. 'Day 1, morning: bad');[66] these are a list of two days in each month (beginning with September 3 and 24) on which you should not do anything such as planting or pruning vines or olives or fruit trees, or trading or travelling, or healing or cupping or getting married or receiving guests;[67] advice on behaviour when the moon is in each sign of the zodiac – if it is in a favourable sign (Aries, Gemini, Virgo, Pisces) then do whatever you wish, if in a bad sign (Cancer, Leo, Capricorn) do nothing, if in a neutral sign (Taurus, Libra, Sagittarius, Aquarius) then act but do not cup or take medicine;[68] good and bad hours for each day of the week (e.g. Sunday: hour 1 is good, hour 2 is good, hour 3 is bad, hour 4 is neutral).[69]

A psalter of about 1500 gives a list of good and bad days, days on which to sow, let blood, etc.;[70] another sixteenth-century psalter is followed by astrological articles (predictions from the star Chigir, lunar tables, medical zodiac) and a list of unlucky days ascribed in this case to Moses.[71] A psalter of the seventeenth century gives a list of good and bad days for planting, etc. with paschal tables.[72]

One of the encyclopaedic florilegia of Kiril Belozerskii, founder of the monastery at Belozero at the end of the fourteenth century, contains calendrical and eschatological information about the end of the millennium and the coming of the Antichrist, medical and dietary advice for the four seasons; a lunar almanac giving the times of waxing and waning of the moon, and eclipses, followed by a list of the hours in each day on which planting and sowing, pruning, tree-felling, slaughtering of cattle, blood-letting, haircutting, etc. may be done with advantage, and a list of days on which this should not be attempted.[73]

The originally Byzantine tradition is reinforced in Russia by Western influences such as the *Hortus sanitatis* literature,[74] almanacs, which normally listed good and bad days, and calendars, which marked days which were favourable for cupping. It is perhaps worth noting that Western almanacs of the fifteenth,[75] sixteenth and seventeenth centuries (and to a lesser degree ever since) included precisely the same kinds of divination as the Russian manuscripts: *Erra Pater*, for example, contains lucky and unlucky days, thunder divination, lunar divination, and calendrical divination, etc.[76] One nineteenth-century Russian manuscript miscellany of prayers includes a 'Table left by the Great Albert of the whole year in which there are thirty-two days on which nothing should be started and nothing important done'.[77] This presumably comes from the same source as the chapbooks common in England and France which appeared under the name of Albertus Magnus.

In 1831 Malov's *Pis'ma k voinam* (Letters to the Troops), a book written to dissuade Russian soldiers from superstition but which in fact describes these superstitions in curious detail (see Ch. 10.5–8), published a 'Spisanie o chernodnevie' (List of black days). This gives two days in each month, beginning with September 2 and 21, which are bad and on which one should not let blood, pull teeth, go hunting, or sew a new kaftan. On those days too the *spryg-trava* will not do its customary magic duty of opening locks and finding treasure (see Ch. 9.4, s.v. *razryv-trava*).

Apart from unlucky dates, the Russians also had pagan cults of the days of the week. These were reinforced by the Byzantine sacralization of days, especially Friday, which, from being Holy Friday, the day of Christ's Crucifixion, became Saint Friday (Paraskeva-Piatnitsa). St Paraskeva, or Piatnitsa, was the patron saint of women, with her own icon representation, shrines at crossroads and folklore attributes. These included wandering the land punishing women who ignored proper observation of the day, which meant refraining from many kinds of work.[78] Thomas Consett, chaplain to the English merchants in Moscow in the time of Peter I, remarked that 'St Friday seems to be the same with Venus of the Heathen, and antiently worship'd by the Russians'.[79] This remark is a footnote to a description of the banning of several Friday superstitions in Peter the Great's *Ecclesiastical Regulation*. These would have included women refusing on that day to spin, wash clothes, or clear ashes from the stove, and men refusing to plough, superstitions which had already been condemned at the *Stoglav* Council in Moscow in 1551. St Friday was thought to influence health, cereal crops and the fertility of livestock, and to punish those who offended by afflicting them with whitlows and eye infections. A prayer to her could be used as an amulet against various sicknesses when worn round the neck, or for headache if bound round the head.[80]

Popular beliefs about Friday are not peculiar to Russia. Byzantine beliefs have been mentioned; British beliefs about Friday as an unlucky day, the unwisdom of beginning anything on a Friday, or setting out on a journey on that day are well documented.[81]

Sunday, sometimes personified as St Anastasia,[82] was also an object of worship. A sermon against this practice, evidently from the early days of Christianity in Russia, is extant in copies from the fourteenth century onwards.[83]

The days of the week are often classified as 'clean' or 'unclean' – the latter were usually Monday, Wednesday and Friday, but sometimes the other way round. Dal', s.v. *ponedel'nyi*, quotes sayings that on these days nothing should be undertaken; that Monday and Friday are 'heavy' days but Tuesday and Saturday are 'light'; popular belief has it that if you give someone money on a Monday you will be obliged to spend all week. Friday's 'unclean' status may perhaps be linked with the fact that it is the day of the Crucifixion and the favoured day for divination (see Ch. 2.5). On the significance of sneezing on the various days see Ch. 6.5.[84] This confusion may due to the conflict of the Christian week, which began on a Sunday, and the traditional week which, as the Russian day names for Tuesday, Thursday and Friday (i.e. *vtornik, chetverg, piatnitsa* 'second day, fourth day, fifth day') indicate, began on a Monday. Peter the Great's edict bringing the Russian *anno mundi* calendar into line with the Julian calendar in 1700 also had the effect of making Sunday ('clean') fall on what was previously a Wednesday ('unclean'). As can be imagined, this was seen by the Old Believers as yet one more proof that Peter was the Antichrist, and led to one group (known as *sredniki*, i.e. 'Wednesdayers') even celebrating the new Wednesday as Sunday.[85] Despite the published disapproval of the State and the Official Church of many of the popularly observed bans on working on certain days, the local peasant communes (*obshchina*), which functioned as the lowest level of court in Russia in the nineteenth century, are known to have upheld popular custom by imposing fines on those who defied the local rules.[86]

8. *Astrological Terminology*

We know relatively little about early Slavonic star lore and the paucity of all but borrowed astronomical terms in the early East and South Slavonic translations from Greek suggests that there was not a developed terminology. Moreover, the fact that close analogies for almost all Slavonic star names can be found in Finnic, Germanic or other languages, suggests that most of them are borrowed. What there is, however, suggests that the Slavs, like the Greeks, Arabs, and most other cultures, were inclined to mythologize the heavens, and in particular to see animals in them.

For example, the world was supposed to stand on (usually) three whales in the *Golubinnaia kniga*[87] and a number of texts recorded by folklorists, and *los'*, reindeer, for Ursa major, obviously a northern term, was first recorded in Afanasii Nikitin's account of his voyage to India (*Khozhenie za tri moria*) in the late fifteenth century. It also occurs in a seventeeth-century Archangel sailors' text which contains a 'Regiment of the Pole Star' (diagram for finding the pole star from Ursa Major): 'Los' po nemetski telega' ('the reindeer, in German waggon'). *Los'* is not found in other Slav languages although Hungarian and some Finnic languages have words for elk or reindeer in this sense, which suggests a Russian borrowing. *Los'*, together with *Kolo* ('ring') for Orion, and *Volosiny* (etymology unclear) for the Pleiades are the only popular names of constellations attested in Russian before the seventeenth century.

Learned texts before the fifteenth century which touch on astronomy and astrology are, as we have described above, translated from Greek into Church Slavonic, often via a Bulgarian or, later, a Serbian Church Slavonic version. The translators were obliged, of course, to find some way of translating the Greek astronomical terminology, and in particular the names of the planets and signs of the zodiac. The names of the planets in Church Slavonic and Old Russian are all transliterated from Greek, sometimes with minor modifications to suit Slavonic morphology. The commonest forms are *kron, zeves, aris, afrodit, ermis*. An occasional exception is Venus, the only astral body apart from the sun and moon which regularly has a Slavonic name, even in rare cases in learned texts. This is usually *dennitsa* ('day-star'), *utrenitsa* ('morning star') or *zoryanka* ('dawn-star') or cognate forms. These terms survive in folk usage, occasionally in the sense of 'shooting star'. In the latter sense a *dennitsa* may be a fallen angel or the soul of a child, and may be captured by a witch and kept in a jar. Venus may also be called *Volch'ia zvezda* ('wolf star') in Great Russian folk terminology. In the case of the zodiac, however, the names of the constellations, many of them animal names, are translatable and are in fact almost invariably calqued.

The zodiac itself, i.e. the band on either side of the ecliptic which is divided into the twelve signs, is rarely referred to. The earliest term is *krug zhivotnyi* ('animal circle') in the *Shestodnev* of 1263. This is a calque of the Greek *zodiakos kuklos*. This is alternatively calqued as *zhivoe nebo* 'living heaven' in a seventeenth-century manuscript; in an eighteenth-century source it is *zhivotnyi*: 'Zodiak sirech' zhivotnyi ili znamenosets' (this usually means a sign of the zodiac or the adjective 'zodiacal'). Simeon Polotskii in 1667 in his *Orel rossiiskii* uses *zverinets*, more commonly a zoo! This is followed in 1719 by *zverilnyi krug* and *zverilnitsa* in a more academic work, the *Zemnevodnogo kruga kratkoe opisanie*, a translation of Johann Hübner, *Kurtze Fragen aus der neuen und alten Geographie* (1722).

In fact the zodiac is most commonly referred to periphrastically as 'the twelve signs' or 'the twelve zodii' or 'the twelve animals'. The words for 'sign' are many. *Znamia, znamenie* as calques of Greek *semeion* are common at all periods, with *znak* coming in in the seventeenth century. But equally common are *zhivot* 'animal' from the *Izbornik Sviatoslava* of 1073 up to the seventeenth century; *zhivotina* in a fourteenth-century Serbian Church Slavonic *Gromnik*; *zhivotna* in the *Shestodnev* of 1263; and *zhivotno, zhivotnyi* in many sources from the fifteenth to the seventeenth century. Signs can also be known, mostly in the sixteenth and seventeenth centuries, simply as *zvezda* 'a star'. *Zverie*, apparently a plural, is used by Simeon Polotskii in his *Orel rossiiskii* in 1667. From earliest times the modified transliterated loan *zodii* or *zodio, zodie, zodiia, zadei*, even *zodiak* are found, but are commonest from the seventeenth century onwards, together with adjectival forms *zodiachnyi, zodiatskii, zodiinyi, zodiiskii, zodeichnyi* and a derivative noun, apparently coined in the seventeenth century as a term of abuse by the schismatic leader archpriest Avvakum, *zodeishchik* for astrologer.

The term used for a planetary sphere was usually *poias*, a semantic calque from Greek *zōnē* 'belt'. Occasionally it is given as *krug* 'circle', a word which in Old Russian could mean a circle, disc, cylinder, sphere, orbit or cycle.

In fact a little thought will show that the signs of the zodiac are not all animals and the animal association is based on a defective calque, as is the German *Tierkreis*. The Greek *zōon* means animal or painted figure; its diminutive *zōdion* normally means only a figure.

Astrology and astronomy are not terminologically distinguished in a consistent way in Church Slavonic or Old Russian until the eighteenth century, a little later than in the rest of Europe.[88]

The Greek *astrologia* is found transliterated as *astrologiia* in the *Izbornik Svatoslava* of 1073 but is normally calqued as *zvezdoslovie* ('star-words'). Similarly Greek *astronomia*, though found transliterated in the *Vita Constantini* (and whenever the Quadrivium is in question), and in an eleventh-century translation of Gregory of Nazianzum, it is more commonly calqued as *zvezdozakonie* ('star-law'). *Astronomiia* is also found in indexes of banned books as the name of an unidentified text (or possibly simply as the name of a banned practice). Examples of *astronomiia* and *astrologiia* from the fifteenth century onwards are most probably direct loans from Latin. Variant calques, or calque-type words are *zvezdochetie* ('star-counting, star-reading') which is is quite common, and less commonly *zvezdōchitanie*, *zvezdoskazanie*, *zvezdozakonnitsa*, *zvezdozrenie*, *zvezdochislenie*, *zvezdobliudenie*. Only rarely is it possible to say that any of these words refers specifically to what would now be called astrology. The same is true of the names of the practitioners of astronomy and astrology, which are formed in the same way (e.g. *zvezdoslov*, *zvezdoslovets*, *zvezdoblaznitel'*, *zvezdozakonnik*, *zvezdogadatel'*, *zvezdobliustel'*, *zvezdnik*, *zvezdober'ts*, *zvezdozorets*, *zvezdar'*, *zvezdozritel'*).[89] Other specifically astrological terminology is rare before the fifteenth century. One may quote the single eleventh-century specimen of *godinozrenie* 'hour observing', a loan translation of Greek *hōroskopos*, the ascending sign at birth, which can have done little to clarify the text for the reader. In another text, the *Hexaemeron* of John the Exarch in a version of 1263, this is rendered no less confusingly as *zvezda chasobliudivaia* 'the time-observing star'. Most confusing of all perhaps is the *strazh chastnyi* 'guardian of fate (time?)' for 'horoscope' in one of the versions of the Slavonic *Alexander Romance*. More generally genethliacal prediction is referred to in passing in several works by the term *rozhestvoslovie*, a calque of the Greek *genethlialogia*, and a curious association of ancient Slav fertility gods with stars can be seen in the thirteenth-century story of the Magi, the *Skazanie Afroditiana*: 'We have seen the *rozhshaia* and *rozhennyi*, stars which show a royal child'.[90]

Notes

1. In this text see *Slovar' knizhnikov*, I, s.v. *Zhitie Konstantina*. On the academic and ecclesiastical career of Constantine (Cyril) 'the Philosopher' see Dvornik, *Byzantine Missions among the Slavs*, ch. 2.

2. See *Slovar' knizhnikov*, I, s.v. *Kirik Novgorodets*, and Simonov, *Matematicheskaia mysl' Drevnei Rusi*. For text see Zubov, 'Primechanie'.

3. Simonov, *Matematicheskaia mysl'*, pp. 44–62.

4. Iatsimirskii, *Bibliograficheskii obzor*, pp. 64–5.

5. See Sreznevskii *Materialy*, s.v. *uz'l*.

6. Beneshevich, *Drevneslavianskaia Kormchaia*, p. 143.

7. For some discussion see Sokolov, *Ocherki*, pp. 41–2.

8. See Mansi, *Collectio conciliorum*, vol. 11, *passim*, and col. 974 on astrology, quoting 2 Kings 21 on the reign of Manasseh, a devotee of magic and astrology. The other chapters dealing with these pagan practices are 62, 65, 77.

9. See Ch. 1.6 for these two texts.

10. This is found in some versions of the apocryphal *Tale of Afroditian*, known in Russia from the thirteenth century and included in lectionaries under 25 December: Franko, *Apokrifi*, II, pp. 2–18; on this text see *Slovar' knizhnikov*, I, s.v. *Skazanie Afroditiana*.

11. See, for example,Tertullian, *De idololatria*, IX; the argument is repeated in Isidore, *Etymologiae*, VIII, IX, 25–6.

12. Meshcherskii, *Istoriia iudeiskoi voiny*, p. 420, ll. 6–7. See also *Slovar' knizhnikov*, I, s.v. *Istoriia iudeiskoi voiny*.

13. Seneca, *Naturales quaestiones*, vii, 11, 2. It is interesting that it is precisely these three categories which are given in the Syriac *Book of Medicines*: Budge, *Syrian Anatomy*, II, pp. 652–3.

14. For some of these terms for comets in classical and medieval literature see dall'Olmo, 'Latin Terminology', pp. 10–27.

15. E.g. Tacitus, *Annals*, XIV, 22.

16. Berry and Crummey, *Rude and Barbarous Kingdom*, pp. 305–6. For the same beliefs in England from Bede to 1910 see Opie and Tatem, *Dictionary of Superstitions*, s.v. *comet*.

17. For a survey of the interpretations of this passage see *Entsiklopediia «Slova o Polku Igoreve»*, I, pp. 73–6.

18. Kristanov and Duichev, *Estestvoznanieto*, pp. 435–6. This gives short predictions for each month; since these include a bad harvest in Armenia for December and the Greek emperor making war on Egypt for September, the text was unlikely to excite much interest in Russia.

19. For the 'Chronograph Alexander', edited and translated into modern Russian by O.V. Tvorogov, see *Izbornik*, pp. 236–79 (the Nectanebus story is at pp. 236–48) See also *Slovar' knizhnikov*, I, s.v. *Aleksandriia khronograficheskaia*. The 'Serbian Alexander' is published in *Aleksandriia. Roman ob Aleksandre Makedonskom*. The Nectanebus story at pp. 8–10 is less detailed. For bibliography see *Slovar' knizhnikov*, II, 1, s.v. *Aleksandriia serbskaia*.

20. See Dmitrieva, *Skazanie o kniaziak vladimirskikh*, pp. 172–3.

21. *Slovar' knizhnikov*, I, s.v. *Izbornik 1073*. On the zodiac illustrations and in particular Capricorn, which is shown as a unicorn, see Girshberg, '«Koz'l'rog» v Izbornike Sviatoslava'.

22. *Slovar' knizhnikov*, I, s.v. *Paleia tolkovaia*.

23. *Slovar' knizhnikov*, I, s.v. *Apokrif ob Enokhe*.

24. *Slovar' knizhnikov*, I, s.v. *Shestodnev*.

25. *Slovar' knizhnikov*, I, s.v. *Khristianskaia topografiia*. Cosmas is described in the ninth century by the Greek Patriarch Photius as 'more a teller of fables than a recounter of the truth': see Migne, *PG*, 88, cols 17–20. He acquires almost canonical status in the Russian Church and is included in the *Chetii*

minet (Reading Menaion) for August 23–31. One of the objections brought by the Church to a star map published in the reign of Peter the Great was that it was not in conformity with the Holy Father Cosmas.

26. These texts were examined in detail in the 1930s in a series of now rather outdated and slightly tendentious articles by Andreeva, 'Politicheskii i obshchestvennyi èlement'. Andreeva gives a good deal of useful textual material but her emphasis was on demonstrating a connection with Johannes Lydus, and with South Slav manuscripts.

27. E.g. for omens of the moon on the first day of the month, haloes round the sun and moon, position of the moon's cusps, thunder, earthquakes, etc. in ancient Mesopotamia, see Thomson, *The Reports of the Magicians*, pp. xxxiii–lxv.

28. ed. C. Wachsmuth, Leipzig, 1887.

29. For a good survey and bibliography of the origins of this literature, although with particular reference to its Bulgarian manifestations, see Kristanov and Duichev, *Estestvoznanieto*, pp. 390–400 on divinatory texts (texts at pp. 400–36); pp. 496–8 on good and bad days and hours, etc. (texts at pp. 498–514); pp. 536–44 on spells and magic prayers (texts at pp. 544–57). For a more recent analysis of Old Bulgarian texts of this kind see Angusheva-Tikhanova, *Gadatelnite knigi v starobalgarskata literatura*, Sofia, 1996. For a seventeenth-century Serbian Church Slavonic compendium of remedies, spells, and divinatory texts of this kind see Jagić, 'Opisi i izvodi'.

30. Delatte, 'Note sur les manuscrits astrologiques', p. 110. Capane, 'La magia a Bisanzio', p. 239, confirms the impression that Byzantine magic in the fourteenth century was essentially lower-class suburban, and typically the province of the clergy.

31. Neugebauer, *Greek Horoscopes*.

32. This may be the *Putnik* of Russian indexes of banned books: see Granstrem, 'Grecheskii original', pp. 72–4.

33. For some useful thoughts on the interpretation of references to magic in Byzantine sources see Greenfield, 'Sorcery and Politics'.

34. Laurent, *Les 'Mémoires' du Grand Ecclésiarque*, p. 172–5.

35. For a summary see Grmek, *Les Sciences*, pp. 14–16.

36. See Peretts, 'Gromnik', pp. 30–1. This is the only work of monograph length devoted to the subject, but it is very concerned to show Jewish parallels and discusses this at length, although it is probably of little relevance.

37. Peretts, 'Gromnik', p. 38.

38. *CCAG*, VIII/3, p. 168.

39. Peretts, 'Gromnik', pp. 41–3.

40. Ibid, p. 44.

41. Begunov, *Kozma Prezviter*, p. 134: a thirteenth-century anti-Bogomil *sbornik* including astrological articles, the *Gromnik*, *Koliadnik*, and a prayer of St Sisinnius against the Devil. On Bulgarian texts and the *Gromnik* in general see Kristanov and Duichev, *Estestvoznanieto*, pp. 390–400, texts at pp. 400–32.

42. Texts are published in Pypin, *Lozhnye i otrechennnye knigi*, II, pp. 361–76; Rybnikov, *Pesni*, p. 207. Iatsimirskii, 'Melkie teksty', p. 429, notes a composite text of *Gromnik*, *Molniak*, *Seismologion*, written by the monk Pakhomii in Serbia in the late fourteenth century. A later Serbian version is given in Jagić, 'Opisi', pp. 121–4.

43. See Gaster, *Literatura populară română*, pp. 506–9.

44. See Iatsimirskii, *Apokrifi*, pp. 64–5.

45. One version of this short article, ascribed to both Philo and Hippocrates, is published in Lakhtin, 'Starinnye pamiatniki meditsinskoi pis'mennosti', pp. 1, 109. Philo Judaeus wrote on the mystical significance of the number seven and there are several Philos known from medical texts, of whom the best known was Philo of Tarsus, inventor of a famous medicine. None seems to fit this text. See Pauly-Wissowa, *Realencyclopädie*, s.v. *Philo*.

46. Florinskii, *Russkie prostonarodnye travniki*, pp 187–91.

47. Tikhonravov, *Pamiatniki*, II, pp. 388–95.

48. Weisser, *Studien zu mittelalterlichen Krankheitslunar*, pp. 18, 67–8.

49. Cumont, 'Les Présages lunaires', pp. 259–70.

50. *CCAG*, III (Codices mediolanenses), pp. 12, 32–9.

51. *CCAG*, X (Codices athenienses), pp. 122–6.

52. See Svenberg, *Lunaria et zodiologia latina*, p. 6.

53. For an older but useful discussion and bibliography of lunation texts in general, and English in particular, see Metham, *Works*, pp. xxxviii–xlii, text at pp. 148–56. Greek versions of the lunar day prognostication texts, mostly late, occur fairly frequently in the *Corpus codicum astrologorum graecorum*; some are mentioned above. The most recent study of the Latin and German versions of the text is by Weisser (see n. 48 above).

54. Budge, *Syrian Anatomy*, pp. 560–5.

55. See Fiensy, 'Revelation of Ezra', pp. 601–4.

56. Chrysostom, *In kalendas*, in Migne, *Patrologia graeca*, 48.

57. Thomas, *Religion and the Decline of Magic*, p. 295. For discussion and fifteenth-century English texts see Metham, *Works*, pp. xxxii–xxxvii; Cockayne, *Leechdoms*, pp. 195ff (1120). German versions are known from the fourteenth century and the text is referred to by Bede: see Eis, *Wahrsage texte*, pp. 24–6, text at pp. 66–8.

58. A Hebrew version ascribed to Esdras is mentioned in Peretts, 'Gromnik', p. 82.

59. Begunov, *Kozma Prezviter*, p. 134: a thirteenth-century anti-Bogomil *sbornik* including the *Gromnik*, *Koliadnik*, and a prayer of Sisinnius against the Devil.

60. Iatsimirskii, 'Melkie teksty', pp. 423–75 (p. 429 notes a composite text of *Gromnik*, *Molniak*, *Seismologion* written by the monk Pakhomii in Serbia in the late fourteenth century.; pp. 436–8 a *Koliadnik* about 1345 copied for Tsar Aleksandr Asen). Jagić, 'Opisi', pp. 115–19, gives a number of Serbian versions.

61. For texts see Tikhonravov, *Pamiatniki*, II, pp. 377–81 (Russian and Serbian, fifteenth century); Pypin, *Lozhnye i otrechennye knigi*, III, pp. 155–8; Rybnikov, *Pesni* (pp. 207–8 good and bad days; p. 207 *Koliadnik*, *Gromnik*, nineteenth century, Olonets region.). Other copies are mentioned in Iavorskii, *Novye rukopisnye nakhodki* (seventeenth-century manuscript containing a dream book, a *zagovor* against the Devil in the name of the Cross and the archangels, and a *Koliadnik* ascribed to the prophet 'Esdrom' (i.e. Esdras) (p. 113); Viktorov, *Opisi rukopisnykh sobranii*: p. 99, 185 (1823) (a late seventeenth-century *sbornik* of the Antoniev-Siiskii Monastery including a *Koliadnik* and horoscopes at the end); Arsenii, *Opisanie slavianskikh rukopisei* (no. 762 (1881), a fifteenth-century *sbornik* including *Paskhalia*, *Gromnik*, *Koliadnik*, *Galen*. A late (nineteenth century?) Rumanian version is published in Gaster, *Literatura populară romāna*, pp. 514–16.

62. For a brief survey see *Cambridge Medieval History. VI. Byzantine Empire*, pt 2, pp. 298–9, marred by the evident distaste of the author for the 'pseudo-sciences'.

63. The subject of tabooed days in general was surveyed extensively in Hutton Webster, *Rest Days*.

64. Late ninth century in Bulgaria: see Kristanov and Duichev, *Estestvoznanieto*, p. 496. In general see Pypin, 'Dlia istorii lozhnykh knig', pp. 15–27.

65. Pypin, *Lozhnye i otrechennye knigi*, III, p. 159. Monthly regimes of this kind are a commonplace in both the Eastern and Western medical traditions.

66. Tikhonravov, *Pamiatniki*, II, pp. 382–4, fifteenth-century Russian manuscript.

67. Tikhonravov, *Pamiatniki*, II, p. 386, fifteenth-century Serbian manuscript, includes the heading: 'The Days which God revealed to his Priest Sikhar'. A different list is given in Pypin, II, p. 159.

68. Tikhonravov, *Pamiatniki*, pp. 386–7.

69. Tikhonravov, *Pamiatniki*, II, p. 385.

70. See Arsenii, *Opisanie slavianskikh rukopisei*, no. 46 (833), ff. 91v–97.

71. Iatsimirskii, *Slavianskie i russkie rukopisi rumynskikh bibliotek*, p. 359, no. 58(1198), f. 226v.

72. Viktorov, *Opisi rukopisnykh sobranii*, p. 174: *Psaltyr' sledovannaia*, MS Aleksandro-Svirskii Mon. 7 (11).

73. See Prokhorov, 'Knigi Kirill Belozerskogo', pp. 50–68: MS Leningrad, GPB, Kir. Bel. sobr. XII, ff. 311–312v. For more examples see Rybnikov, *Pesni*, pp. 207–8; Franko, IV, p. 102; Kerenskii, 'Drevnerusskie otrechennye verovaniia', pp. 70–1 (on Kirik of Novgorod and good and bad days).

74. E.g. MSS Leningrad PD, Peretts 327, *Prokhladny vertograd*, 18th c.; op. 23, no. 157, *Travnik*, 18th c. See Gruzdev, 'Rukopisnye lechebniki', pp. 345, 347. In some manuscripts of this type the text may be ascribed to Philo: see Florinskii, *Russkie prostonarodnye travniki*, p. 187.

75. See for example Brevant, 'The German *Volkskalender*'.

76. On *Erra Pater* and similar popular works see Capp, *Astrology and the Popular Press*, p. 31.

77. *Zapiski otdela rukopisei*, 45, 1986, p. 102, no. 283, mid-nineteenth-century miscellany at ff. 172–5v.

78. See Uspenskii, *Filologicheskie razyskaniia*, index, s.v. *dni nedeli*; Gromyko, *Traditsionnye normy*, pp. 125–9 on 'banned' days in general, esp. p. 127 on the ban on women's work on Fridays. For some discussion in English, including translations of tales in which days are personified, see Ralston, *Russian Folk-tales*, pp. 198–204. For Ukrainian beliefs see V.P. Miloradovich, 'Malorusskie narodnye pover'ia i rasskazy o piatnitse', *Kievskaia starina*, 1905, no. 5. On the various saints called Paraskeva see Walter, 'The Portrait of Saint Parasceve'. For icons of 'St Sunday' and 'St Friday' see Scheffer, 'Days of the Week in Russian Religious Art'.

79. Consett, *The Present State and Regulations of the Church of Russia*, II, p. 26.

80. See Afanas'ev, *Russkie narodnye legendy*, pp. 85–8.

81. Opie and Tatem, *Dictionary of Superstitions*, s.v. *Friday*.

82. Sunday in Modern Russian and in later Old Russian texts is *voskresenie*, i.e. resurrection, because Easter Sunday was the day of the Resurrection of Christ. The Greek for resurrection is *anastasis*, hence Anastasia.

83. See Likhacheva, 'K izucheniiu «Slova o tvari i o dni, rekomem nedelia»', pp. 68–71.

84. Cf. Serbian belief that anyone born on a 'masculine' day (by gender of the day-name) is safe from witches: Vukanović, 'Witchcraft in the Central Balkans. II: Protection against Witches', p. 221.

85. See Uspenskii, 'K simvolike vremeni u slavian: "chistie" i "nechistie" dni nedeli', pp. 70–5. See also Tolstaia, 'K sootnosheniia khristianskogo i narodnogo kalendaria', pp. 154–68 (examples are mostly from Poles'e). For a comparison see the Macedonian 'unlucky days' in which every day except Sunday was unlucky depending on the activity undertaken: Abbott, *Macedonian Folklore*, pp. 189–91.

86. Gromyko, *Traditsionnye normy*, p. 125.

87. A slightly mysterious text of popular cosmology and eschatology variously translated as the 'Book of the Dove' or 'Book of the Depths': see Index for other references to this work.

88. For some discussion of terminological and conceptual distinction in the ancient world see Hübner, *Die Begriffe 'Astrologie' und 'Astronomie'*.

89. For further discussion of the topic of astronomical terminology see Ryan, *Astronomical and Astrological Terminology*; *idem*, 'Astronomy in Church Slavonic', and *idem*, 'Curious Star Names in Slavonic Literature', pp. 144–6.

90. Tikhonravov, *Pamiatniki*, II, p. 4. In *CCAG*, II (Codices mediolanenses), a 'Sichar' is mentioned in the *Oraculorum decades CIII* of Astrampsychus (MS A45 Sup.). Perhaps this is the Biblical Sirach: a sixteenth-century Greek geomancy ascribed to the Prophet Sirach is mentioned in *CCAG*, IX, 2, p. 89: Leiden Bibl. Publ. Gr. 74J, f. 52v.

Astrology –
Post-Byzantine Influences

1. *Mathematics and Astronomy*

The lack of mathematical skills in the period of Kiev Rus' was only partially remedied in Muscovite Russia. In the sixteenth century the *schety* or bead calculator was probably first used in Muscovy.[1] This instrument, the origin of which remains mysterious, was in fact a powerful tool for fast arithmetical calculation, and one which existed nowhere else in Europe at that time; but once again its use, as far as can be ascertained, did not extend beyond trade and tax calculation.

As late as the eighteenth century the common foreign view of Russian mathematical ability was that it did not exist. Captain John Perry, who served Peter the Great as shipbuilder and hydraulic engineer in the first decade of that century, blinded to the potential of the *schety* by the habitual contempt of westerners for Russian backwardness and perhaps jaundiced by Peter's repeated failure to pay him his agreed salary, remarked:

> They did not know the use of figures (I believe not twenty men in the whole country) but they made use of a kind of beads which they set upon wires in a frame like that which our women in England use to set their smoothing irons on, which they placed units, tens, hundreds, thousands and tens of thousands . . .[2]

Certainly in the matter of calendar computation the Muscovites of the late fifteenth century had not advanced much beyond what Kirik of Novgorod had written in the twelfth.[3] When the 'seventh millennium' and its calendar came to an end, and the world did not, despite an ominous total eclipse of the sun in 1491, and faced with a dissident judaizing group which had at its disposal the astronomically superior *Six Wings* of Emmanuel Bonfils, they had to resort to Western Catholic clergy (since Byzantium was no more) for assistance in computing a new calendar.[4]

But if the instrumental possibilities for arithmetical calculation were considerable, and backwardness in the knowledge of calendar computation was overcome in the sixteenth century, the lack of geometry and understanding of angular measurement was still a factor limiting the understanding of astronomy and preventing the application of astrology. The first Russian geometry text, indeed the only one before the end of the seventeenth century, was a translation made in 1625 of part of Aaron Rathborne's *The Surveyor* (London, 1616); it was so literal and so bad as to be unusable.[5]

When geometry in any real sense arrived in Russia, it was through the medium of a good up-to-date textbook on Western lines, Leontii Magnitskii's *Arifmetika* (1703), and courses in navigation at a modern secular school, the Moscow Mathematics and Navigation School.[6] This was the age of Peter the Great (reigned 1682–1725), who was interested in many things but did not, it seems, share the belief of his father, Tsar Aleksei, or his sister, the Regent Sofiia, in magic and divination. As far as the Tsar, court, military and departments of state were concerned, Russia had joined Europe, where for most educated people the time for astrology as a serious preoccupation was over.

2. *Attitudes to Astrology*

For the most part the attitude of the Orthodox Church in Muscovite Russia, and to a large extent in the Ukrainian and Belorussian parts of the Grand Duchy of Lithuania, continued to be that of its Byzantine past, as described in the last chapter. Astrology continues to appear in the indexes of banned books, and its condemnation is reinforced from a rather unexpected quarter. Michael Trivolis (later known in Russia as Maxim the Greek), a well-connected aristocrat who had studied in Corfu with John Moscos, went to Florence with John Lascaris, was well acquainted with the humanists of the time, and worked on the Aldine edition of Aristotle, had a spiritual conversion under the influence of Savonarola and eventually, in 1505 or 1506, joined the Vatopedi monastery on Mt Athos. In 1518 he was sent to Moscow at the request of Grand Prince Vasilii III, who needed a learned translator. Here he was much involved in ecclesiastical polemics, was accused of heresy in his translations, of sorcery, and of spying for the Turks; he was never allowed to return home. Much of his extensive writing is directed against the corrosive influence of the West, and in particular its liking for the ancient pagan philosophers and the consequent corruption of Western theology. He was, nevertheless, quite happy to quote Socrates, Plato, and Aristotle, as well as the first-century poet Leonidas of Alexandria and St Augustine,[7] in support of his polemic against astrology. In particular he was hostile to the court physician and astrologer Nicolaus Bülow of Lübeck, a Catholic who was further suspect in that he advocated a reunion of the Orthodox and Catholic Churches.[8] Maxim's attack on astrology was primarily based on the fairly standard Christian view of the irreconcilability of astrology with belief in God's omnipotence and man's free will; he also attacked Johannes Stöffler's almanac, which had been translated into Russian by the above-mentioned Nicolaus Bülow, for predicting a second world-wide flood in 1524. In an epigram Maxim repeats a well-worn *topos* by mocking Bülow for foretelling the end of the world while being unable to foresee critical moments in his own life.[9]

Some of Maxim's epistles attacking Catholicism and astrology were written to the aristocrat and senior Muscovite diplomat Fedor Karpov. From Maxim's words it would appear that Karpov believed that astrology was a science necessary to a ruler (this is the view expressed in the *Secretum secretorum*), and that ignorance of it in Muscovy was a matter of shame. Maxim denied that he was against true learning and distinguished the 'astronomy' of the Quadrivium (which he accepted as necessary for the calculation of time) from 'mathematikia', and the 'devilish astrological art' which falsely claimed to foretell the future, and which even the foremost pagan philosopher, Plato, excluded from the realm of true philosophy.

Since only Maxim's side of the polemic survives, in epistles to Karpov, Bülow, and 'a certain abbot' (to whom a letter about the 'wheel of fortune' was addressed), we cannot know exactly what views were held by the recipients of the letters. In the case of Bülow it is not hard to establish his position, but for the two Russians the situation is not clear. Certainly it is not possible to proceed, as some writers have done, from Maxim's epistles to Karpov to the assumption that Karpov, or any other Russian in the sixteenth century, actually practised astrology. To accept such a view would mean that, since Maxim's writings were widely copied and continued to be influential long after his death, especially in Old Believer circles, their popularity reflected a genuine concern about the practice of astrology in that fundamentalist milieu.

Maxim's attack on the almanacs is no doubt the reason why the word 'almanak' appears in the list of banned texts and practices of the *Stoglav* Council convened in 1551 by Ivan the Terrible. This list includes: '*rafli*, Six Wings, crow-cawing, astronomy, zodiac, almanac, stargazing, Aristotle, the Gates of Aristotle'.[10] Of these condemned texts and practices (many of apparently Western origin, for the first time in Russian lists of 'evil books'), five are evidently aspects of astrology, and most of them appear in another text of the period, the *Domostroi*.[11]

Although Maxim's epistle's on astrology continued to be copied after the sixteenth century there was little new added to the literature of the subject until the later part of the seventeenth century.

In 1671 Nikolai Spafarii, as he was known in Russia, a Moldavian educated in Greece and Italy who had translated the Bible into Rumanian and had served several masters in various diplomatic capacities, entered Muscovite service as a diplomatic translator and wrote several treatises in Russian full of humanist erudition. In one of these, a treatise on the liberal arts, he drew a clear distinction between astronomy and astrology, although he did not condemn the latter as unscientific.[12]

Perhaps more typical of older 'low-brow' attitudes was that of Avvakum, one of the leaders of the schismatic Old Believers, who in about 1673 wrote his famous autobiography (called *Zhitie*), in the preface to which he condemned astrology, on the authority of Pseudo-Dionysius. With typical inconsistency he went on to declare, on the same authority, that the solar eclipse of 1654, and the outbreak of plague at about the same time, was a sign of the wrath of God against the apostasy, as he saw it, of the then patriarch, Nikon, and his reform of the Russian Church. Avvakum, like Maxim the Greek before him, also condemned almanacs (see below).

All the evidence about attitudes to astrology in Russia quoted above is literary or documentary. As with other matters discussed in this book, we can sometimes find revealing statements of popular attitudes in the accounts of foreign visitors. Richard James in 1619 recorded that when he asked Russians about the parhelia seen on January 13 at Kholmogory near Archangel, one said 'God is judging us'. This kind of opinion of unusual celestial phenomena could, of course, have been expressed anywhere (John of Salisbury in the twelfth century said that a parhelion was supposed to foretell floods),[13] and one should add that two more Russians when asked the same question by James said that it meant a severe frost, which could indeed be true.[14]

The inconsistency of the Russian Church (as of the Western Church) in the matter of astrology was never really resolved: astrological texts and astronomical texts of ambivalent status could evidently be copied, even commissioned, in Russian monastic scriptoria up to the end of the seventeenth century without difficulty. For example, the Antoniev-Siiskii Monastery records show that in 1695 an illuminated sheet showing the planets and zodiac was copied for the monastery at a cost of ten altyns by the scribe Trofim Kuznetsov and icon-painter Ivan Mefodiev.[15]

3. Jewish Influences

In 1899 in his important study of the *Brontologion* V.N. Peretts called for more study of possible Jewish origins of divinatory literature in Russia.[16] This has not yet happened and what follows is a non-Hebraist's inevitably partial account of the subject.

The first Jewish sources to leave their mark on the Slavonic understanding of the universe were, of course, Biblical, and their influence was indirect, by way of Greek. The same can be said for the texts which followed, the Slavonic *Book of Enoch*, the *De bello judaico* of Josephus, and some of the sources of the *Palaia*.

A more direct Jewish influence can be seen in later expanded versions of the Slavonic *Enoch* in which the Hebrew names of the heavens are given.[17] This gave rise to a curious divinatory text, extant in seventeenth- and eighteenth-century manuscript miscellanies, about a star called Aravan (a corruption of Aravoth, the empty heaven).[18] This is confused with another star called Chigir which is discussed below.

At the end of the fifteenth century, however, a number of texts were translated directly from Hebrew, which have a bearing on astronomy and astrology in Russia.[19] The first of these was the *Shestokryl* or *Six Wings* of Emmanuel Bonfils of Tarascon, a set of lunar tables allegedly used by the Judaizers in Novgorod. This alarmed Gennadii, the Archbishop of Novgorod, because the Russian church was suffering a calendrical crisis and could not match this Jewish expertise in an area which it considered essential to its identity vis-à-vis both Jews and Catholics.

The second 'Judaizer' text was the *De sphera* of Sacrobosco, an early thirteenth-century Latin work of astronomy which became a standard university textbook over the following three centuries and was still in serious use in Western Europe in the seventeenth century.[20] Neither of these two texts was in itself astrological, although the instructions for predicting eclipses and the references to the *caput* and *cauda draconis* and the zodiac in the *Six Wings* may have looked like magic to Russian readers, and it is listed with magic and astrology as an abomination before the Lord in at least one seventeenth-century abecediary.[21]

Another work, however, the *Secretum secretorum* (see Ch. 1), that compendium of magical, political and medical advice which purports to have been written for Alexander the Great by Aristotle and deposited in the Temple of the Sun, and which was probably translated from Hebrew in the same Judaizing milieu, does present, as part of the esoteric knowledge needed by a ruler, a defence of astrology. It speaks of Alexander's lucky star, advises that nothing should be undertaken without first consulting the stars, and describes the astrologically proper time for making certain talismans. It tells the story of the astrologers who cast the horoscope of a weaver's son who, it appeared, was destined to become a counsellor of the king, and the King of India's son for whom the stars predicted only the skill of a blacksmith. Although the astrologers kept these predictions hidden they nevertheless came true, which proved, claims the *Secretum*, the immutability of fate as seen in the stars.

A further text with clear signs of Jewish influence is a relatively unresearched miscellany of mainly Solomonic texts of very eclectic content. It appears with alternative titles: *Begi nebesnye* ('The Heavenly Courses') and *The Tale of Tsar Solomon, his great seal, how and when it came to him*, and is divided internally into sections called 'The First (Second, etc.) Wisdom of Solomon'. Sobolevskii dated the text as not later than mid-sixteenth-century and described it as Muscovite Russian based on Greek and Judaizer sources.[22]

In summary, the text tells of how Solomon became king at the age of twenty-five and how all the other kings rose up against him. He asked God for wisdom not a kingdom (cf. Wisdom of Solomon 7:7–8: 'I called upon God and the spirit of wisdom came to me. I preferred her to sceptres and thrones . . .'.); God gave him wisdom and the knowledge of astronomy, astrology, the calendrical cycles, leap years, the number of hours, minutes and seconds in a day, year, etc. (an amplification of Wisdom of Solomon 7:19) and at what hour to travel or do battle. Then follows a lurid and garbled version of the classical myth of Chronos and the birth of Jupiter. After this comes the story of how Solomon ordered an emerald to be brought from Ethiopia, and had it set in a ring of pure gold and had an inscription engraved on it which encapsulated all his wisdom (the actual letters of the inscription vary slightly in the manuscripts but they appear to be a clerical joke – they read 'Wisdom of Solomon' in one of the systems of Russian cipher!). Next comes an episode about Solomon, the Sibyl, and the Tree of the Cross taken from the apocryphal text *The Tree of the Cross*. Solomon's ring, by which he was able to make demons work for him (this is from another well-known Solomonic story), also contained geometry and philosophy in the Chaldean, Persian, Athenian, Hellene, Latin, Roman, Scythian and Slavonic(!)

tongues. There then follows a cosmology: there are seven heavens with different ranks of spirits, a description of the planet in each heaven (these are strange names and include Kolo and Chigir, of which more below). The text may end with a passage about Solomon's magic mirror which darkens the reflection of anyone who thinks evil,[23] and a moon-halo divination table (which also exists as a separate text). This extraordinary mixture also includes references to Juvenal and St Paul, and to the 'gates of the sun' (probably from the Slavonic *Book of Enoch*) and may be accompanied by the SATOR square (see Ch. 10.8). Both the probable date of the text and the mixture of Jewish and Christian esoteric and apocryphal material prompt comparison with the miscellany of geomantic and other divinatory texts by Ivan Rykov described in Ch. 12.4.

Probably extracted from the Solomonic miscellany is a divinatory text about the star Chigir, which is one of the planets in Solomon's cosmology.[24] In one manuscript it is called 'Solomon's star' and 'the Syrian star' and also Aravan, a pseudo-star name which arises from a misunderstanding of a passage in a late interpolation in the Slavonic *Book of Enoch* where *Aravoth* is the name of the eighth or tenth heaven.[25]

The references to Aravan are usually in the form: 'In the eighth heaven is the star Aravan which gives strength to all other stars', but one (MS St Petersburg GPB Q.XVII.117, 'Ostrologiia', 17th–18th c., f. 3) gives a geocentric diagram (Fig. 17a) showing eight heavens with the zodiac and month names outside the eighth sphere and at the top the inscription 'The star Aravan called Chigir by some'. Another manuscript says 'This star Chigir before the fall [of the angels] was the right hand of angelic pride', which seems to indicate that Chigir is Lucifer or Venus, which is confirmed in the Solomon text by the statement that it precedes the sun, and gives substance to the suggestion that the name could be derived ultimately from Hebrew *zohar*.[26] The Chigir divination seems to have had wider circulation than might have been expected; from a presumably exotic setting in a translated text to a general purpose magical recipe book from around 1730, where it occurs as 'Skazanie of zvezde Tsygiretskoi' in company with other ancient divination texts such as the *Brontologion* and two physiognomies.[27]

The divination text involving the star Chigir runs as follows:

An account of the star Chigir' [in one manuscript *Kolo* 'circle; wheel; waggon']/[28] and where it stands. If anyone wishes to travel and Chigir' is in front of him on that day, then he should not travel. But if Chigir' is behind him or to the side then he can go and will be safe and gain much good. But if Chigir' is beneath the earth or stands in the middle of the sky then he should go nowhere, and if he does go he will not be safe and harm will come to him and his property. On days 1, 11, 21 of the moon it stands in the east;

On days 2, 12, 22, it stands between the east and the south . . . , etc. On days 10, 20, 30 it stands in the middle of the sky.

This corresponds very closely with a curious late Greek text *Hermeneia peri tou ofiomimetou asteros* except that in the Greek the directions are given as the names of the winds.[29] Essentially the same text is found in a Rumanian manuscript of 1750 in which the star name is *Ţigâra* (and variants).[30]

Even closer to the Russian text, however, with the same identification of the days on which one should not travel and an identical diagrammatic presentation (see Fig. 17b), are the Turkish and Arabic texts published by Geoffrey Lewis in 1988, and about which there has also been considerable scholarly confusion. Lewis concluded convincingly that the star was originally called *Şigir Yılduz* and that it could have been influenced by the Sanskrit for Venus, *Sukra*, mediated by Uighur *Şükür*, and that the association with the number eight (there are eight stars in some texts) is a graphic or folk etymological confusion. He also notes that the belief in the star is attributed in one Arabic and two Persian texts to the Turks, and in a Turkish text to 'the sages of India, Cathay and Khotan', and suggests that the origin is India.[31]

It is not clear at present what the relationship is between the Slavonic, Rumanian, Greek, Arabic and Turkish texts. It seems most likely that the malevolent star and the text describing its influence are indeed of Turkic origin: transmission to the Slavs, Rumanians and Greeks in the post-Byzantine world is unproblematic, although in the case of the fairly modern Rumanian text there is also the possibility of translation from a Russian (or Ukrainian) source. The 'serpent-imitating star' of the Greek text sounds like a mistranslation: Lewis quotes one Arabic manuscript which states that the star is 'in the shape of an excited Bactrian camel, opening its mouth and swallowing any who confront it', which suggests that identification of the star as a zoomorphic demon is part of the tradition. The route by which this piece of popular oriental astrology entered the extraordinary Russian Solomonic text remains mysterious.

4. *Oriental Influences*

Although there are many close parallels between Oriental and Western magic, either deriving from antiquity or the result of the cultural eclecticism found at popular level in the Byzantine Empire, there are few unmediated and specifically oriental influences in Russian magic and divination. Exceptions are the Chigir text described in the preceding section and a curious astrological text occasionally associated with it.[32] This is a short piece, usually in diagrammatic form, entitled 'The Uighur cycle of twelve years containing the Polovtsian years'. I have found it in five manuscripts of the seventeenth and eighteenth centuries.[33] The texts of these manuscripts are not identical but clearly they have a common origin. Text 1 is a series of concentric circles divided into twelve. The first circle contains the adjectival form of the names of the twelve animals of the oriental duodenary cycle: Mouse, Ox, . . . , Pig. The next circle contains the Russian names of the signs of the zodiac, the next shows the favourability of the sign: good, medium, bad. The last carries the first letter of the month name:

Mouse	Aries	Good	March
Ox	Taurus	Medium	April
Panther	Gemini	Good	May
Hare	Cancer	Bad	June
Serpent	Leo	Bad	July
Snake	Virgo	Good	August
Horse	Libra	Medium	September
Sheep	Scorpio	Bad	October
Monkey	Sagittarius	Medium	November
Chicken	Capricorn	Bad	December
Dog	Aquarius	Medium	January
Pig	Pisces	Good	February

Text 4 contains, beside the circular diagram, a mnemonic hand diagram of the kind used in the 'Hand Paschal Tables' in which the joints and sections of the fingers are used to memorize numbers (see Fig. 18). It is captioned 'Polovtsian hand for twelve years'. Text 5 differs in that it gives the parts of the body, etc. governed by each sign and offers predictions (remarkably limited in scope) instead of indications of favourability:

Libra	There will be wars	Waist	Monkey's
Scorpio	There will be hail	Thoughts(?)	Chicken's
Sagittarius	There will be rain	Shins	Dog's
Capricorn	Many waters	Secret parts	Pig's
Aquarius	Strong prince will destroy	Feet	Serpent's
Pisces	Many dense waters	Head	Sheep's
Aries	Great hail will fall	Man	Mouse's
Taurus	There will be war	Eyes	Ox's
Gemini	Death to animals	(?krani)	Monkey's
Cancer	Many fish	Shoulders	Hare's
Leo	Great rains	Soul	Horse's
Virgo	It will be dry	Breast	Snake's

The animal cycle is out of correct order here and the parts of the body are not in their normal relationship.

The origin of the oriental animal cycle is still a matter of some debate. In combination with a cycle of five it produced a cycle of sixty which was used by the Mongols and Chinese for calendrical purposes. It has been known in the West at least since Marco Polo, and in Russia was known from the dates of Tatar official documents written in Russian (*iarliki*). It is to be noted, however, that Tatar *iarliki* use the words only for the years, and, although these texts claim to indicate the years, in fact the names are attached to the months and signs of the zodiac. One other Russian text gives an account of the Mongol calendar and the religious and agricultural customs associated with it. This is an article in a late seventeenth-century *Chronograph* and it includes some of the names from the animal cycle as being the names of the months: March – panther, July – lion, December – pig, January – mouse, February – bull.[34] This cycle is not known in the context of astrology in Europe, although in one Byzantine astrological text the mouse appears as the regent of the year in a prognostication for 1336.[35] A Byzantine source for this text is not excluded – a description of the Uighur calendar appears in at least one Byzantine manuscript[36] but in general the source of the text, which could well be a good deal older than the extant manuscripts, and the reason for its propagation, remain mysterious. The fact that several copies are found in manuscripts of very eclectic content, including Jewish, tells us only that the small world of those with esoteric tastes in seventeenth-century Russia would take up anything exotic indiscriminately so that it is unlikely that a satisfactory textual history will be possible.

5. *West European Influences: Almanacs, Horoscopes, Popular Astrology*

Perhaps the first serious East Slavonic astrological writer, certainly the first to publish, was a Ukrainian from the Carpathians, Iurii Kotermak of Drohobych, sometime rector of the University of Bologna and author of the *Judicium prognosticon anni 1483 currentis Magistri Georgii Drohobicz de Russia almi studii bononiensis artium et medicinae doctoris* (Rome, 1483) as well as several other small works surviving in manuscript. His activity was confined to Italy and Poland and although he could conceivably have taught both Copernicus and the humanist Conrad Celtis when he was a university professor in Cracow, he probably had no contact with, or influence on, the Orthodox Ukrainians and Muscovites of his time.[37]

The first astrological almanac appeared in Muscovy in the fifteenth century. This was a translation probably by Nicolaus Bülow of Lübeck, court physician of Ivan III, of the *Almanach nova* of Johannes Stöffler (Venice, 1518). It was the occasion of the attack on astrology by Maxim the Greek described earlier, on the familiar gound that it derogated from God's omniscience, and for another reason quite novel in Russia, that it had been condemned by Aristotle.

Calendars and almanacs with some astronomical and astrological content (e.g. the signs of the zodiac, the dates of eclipses and propitious times for blood-letting) were published in the Grand Duchy of Lithuania: for example the *Malaia podorozhnaia knizhitsa*, published in Vilna in 1522 by the Italian-educated Belorussian scholar Francis Skarina, included the zodiac and dates of eclipses, taken from Johannes Stöffler's calculations, which probably prompted the remark in the 1598 Ostrog Psalter that 'calendars should not be used for astrological magic'.[38] Calendars of saints' days (*sviattsy*), also carrying such information, were printed in Vilna in 1601 and Kiev in 1628.[39]

In Muscovy there was a story that a merchant brought almanacs to sell in Moscow in the reign of Ivan IV (the Terrible, 1530–84) but the Tsar bought them all up for fear that the people would learn too much.[40] Ivan certainly seems to have been interested in magical astrology – contemporary accounts describe the summoning in 1584 of sixty 'wizards and witches' (*kudesniki i koldunii*, i.e. male and female) to foretell the time of his death. This duly happened at the appointed time, although poison has also been suggested.[41]

No further almanacs seem to have appeared until the reign of Aleksei Mikhailovich (1645–76). This tsar was fascinated by astrology and astronomy. He had an armillary sphere placed over his foreign ministry building, a zodiac room in the Kremlin and an astronomical ceiling including the zodiac painted in his new palace at Kolomenskoe.[42] The latter was described by the court poet Simeon Polotskii, in a poem welcoming the the tsar to the palace, as the eighth wonder of the world. One of the leading boiars of the time, Prince V.V. Golitsyn, a statesman with Western tastes, is also supposed to have had the ceiling of the dining room in his Moscow house painted with the sun, stars, and zodiac, with the planets in his bedroom.[43] In this, of course, the Russian tsar and his boiar could be thought of simply as late-comers to a fashion beginning perhaps with the reputed magus Leo the Wise, Emperor of Byzantium,[44] but more probably in the palaces and villas of the Italian Renaissance.

Tsar Aleksei had translations made of a variety of foreign almanacs, presumably for use by himself and his advisers, and the practice continued into the early eighteenth century. Most of these almanacs were not known to the populace in general, to judge from the very small number of extant copies. Among the translated almanacs (often entitled *Kalendar'* or *Mesiatseslov*) of the seventeenth and early eighteenth century were: a translation by Semion Lavretskii of the *Nowy i stary kalendarz* of Stanisław Słowakowicz;[45] the *Kalendar' Korvina Kvasovskogo*;[46] and a late seventeenth-century 'Almanak' translated by Ivan Tiashkogorskii from a Swedish almanac by the Swedish royal mathematician Johann Heinrich Focht.[47] Sobolevskii, in his *Perevodnaia literatura*, lists translations of Focht almanacs for 1684, 1685, 1690, 1691, 1695, 1696, almanacs by W.H. Adelung and J.H. Focht for 1706, 1707, 1708,[48] and an almanac ('A Calendar of Cunning Mathematical Subtleties') translated in 1697 by Petr Shafirov of the Posolskii prikaz (Foreign Ministry) from an original by Paul Galken of Buxtehude.[49] The first native Russian almanac was that of Brius (see below).

Short articles of medical astrology also continued to appear in medical compendia (*lechebniki*), certainly from the middle of the seventeenth century. These *lechebniki* varied considerably in content and often contained small articles of a magical nature. One small translated text of astrological medicine «*Nauka midicheskaia ot matematiki*» is found in some seventeen manuscripts of the seventeenth and eighteenth centuries.[50]

Other seventeenth-century works with astrological content are translations of a Polish work *Klucz prognostykarsky*, giving the arms of the monarchs and states of Europe with appropriate astrological predictions,[51] Conrad Lycosthenes, *Prodigiorum ac ostentorum chronicon* (Basle, 1557), and Stanisław Niewieski, *Komety roku 1680 widziane, o ktòrych jest tu relacyaz prognostikiem do roku 1686 służącym* (Zamość, 1681).[52]

It was, no doubt, Tsar Aleksei's interest in almanacs which prompted another clerical denunciation, this time from the redoubtable archpriest Avvakum (1621–82), one of the leaders of what was to become the sect of Old Believers, a man who was burned at the stake for his opposition to innovations. In a series of attacks on the Nikonian reforms Avvakum made it clear that he considered the apostasy of the official church to be in part the result of foreign influences, in which he included astrology. In his fourth *Beseda* he lamented that Russia had adopted foreign ways: one of these was the change of the name of St Nikola to Nikolai, a German name, he alleged, and the name of a heresiarch in the Acts of the Apostles, and of the notorious German physician and astrologer of Ivan III (1440–1505) Nicolaus Bülow (who appears in several other places in this book). In his fifth *Beseda* Avvakum railed against 'Almanac-mongers, star-gazers, and zodiac-peddlers' ('almanashniki, i zvezdochettsy, i vsi zodiishiki'),[53] and all the clever pagans, Plato and Pythagoras, Aristotle and Diogenes, Hippocrates and Galen, who had all gone to hell, before going on to berate the 'learned swine' who had become 'Russian Germans' and changed the style of icon-painting and the liturgy, so that on Sundays when hard-working Russians went to church to pray, all they could hear was women street entertainers singing in Latin' ('po-latyne poiut pliasavitsy skomorosh'i')![54]

But Avvakum's splendid and splenetic invective was in vain. The influence of the West was becoming stronger. The court poet, the cleric Simeon Polotskii (d. 1680), mentioned above as author of a poem describing an astronomical ceiling, began a new fashion for elaborate baroque poetry on the Western model, complete with Classical allusions and symbolism. His *Orel rossiiskii* ('The Russian Eagle'),[55] a glorification of the Russian ruler, used extended astrological imagery and cannot be understood without some knowledge of astrology and classical mythology. Polotskii was for a long time considered to be the author of a not entirely positive horoscope of the future Peter the Great, but doubt has now been cast on this.[56] The knowledge required for casting horoscopes was certainly possessed by a few individuals in Muscovy at this time, but the written examples are few and it is not possible to establish how widely known the practice was, and whether it was Russians or non-Russians who were involved (Polotskii was a Belorussian).[57]

By this time astrology was not only a fad for the court. The colloquial language had begun to use the word *planita* (*planida*) to mean fate or luck,[58] and eventually even the popular epics called *byliny* (of some antiquity but regularly updated and adapted and not collected before the eighteenth and nineteenth centuries) could include astrological notions as well as their older magic. One *bylina* in the Dobrynia Nikitich cycle has the passage:

Vidno ty, chado moe miloe
zarodilsia ty v tu zvezdu
v tu minutu bezschastnuiu, ne v talannuiu
(Evidently, my dear child, you were born under an unfortunate star at an unfortunate and inauspicious moment).[59]

The reign of Peter the Great (1682–1725) was marked by an even greater increase in Western influence in Russian culture. For the most part this took a very practical direction in favour of the applied sciences and reorganization of the institutions of the state, but we may note that while new Western-style legislation against magic was introduced, and indeed invoked in the courts (see Ch. 16), Peter's own scientific advisor, and Russia's first astronomer and constructor of its first observatory, James Bruce (Iakov Villimovich Brius), was popularly regarded as a wizard who possessed the 'water of life' and a 'black book' which would cause the appearance of demons in search of work if anyone should chance to open and read it.[60] He also published Russia's first printed almanac, which, together with astronomical information, also contained astrological predictions of the kind commonly found in western almanacs.[61] Indeed, Bruce has the dubious distinction of joining Aristotle, Albertus Magnus, Erra Pater, and Old Moore, as the eponym for a whole sub-genre of popular pseudo-scientific literature – the calendar carrying his name continued to be published in various forms until 1917.[62] His memory as a magus has been preserved in popular legend into the twentieth century: in Moscow urban legends recorded in the 1920s in cheap teashops and taverns, Bruce was supposed to have hidden in Moscow a library of magic books, and was credited with the invention of a perpetual clock, and an automaton-girl made out of flowers, and with designing and piloting a flying-machine; his plans for aeroplanes, telephones and telegraph were alleged to have been smuggled out to Germany.[63]

These almanacs were by no means the preserve of the simple or semi-educated. As with their western counterparts they could be found at all levels of society – a sketch by Viktor Vasnetsov dated 1871 in the Tret'iakov Gallery in Moscow is entitled 'Bruce's Calendar'; it shows a well-dressed elderly gentleman in apparently affluent surroundings engrossed in his 'Bruce'.

While Avvakum's attacks on astrology in the seventeenth century failed to halt the spread of this pernicious Western import, the same West also offered antidotes in the form of rationalistic Enlightenment attitudes which found their way into print in the translated works of men such as Fontenelle, Voltaire, Diderot, and the original works of Russian writers. At a relatively simple level we find an anti-astrological piece in the *intermedia*, the short comic interludes which were performed between the acts of the school dramas on the Jesuit model. This was called *Astrolog* and consists in the monologue of an astrologer who repeatedly looks into his telescope and makes grandiose predictions but is surprised when he is soaked by a shower of rain, and then, in an ancient *topos*, falls into a pit.[64] The obvious moral is delivered at the end by a passing peasant.

Intermedii, however, were probably not known outside the world of the seminary, and the works of writers of the Enlightenment must also have had a very limited circulation by comparison with the almanacs and fortune books'.[65] Since this was also the case, more or less, in England and Western Europe, one can see that Russia, in astrology as in other matters, was beginning to conform to a general European model of cultural development, with astrology surviving for the most part in primitive form in almanacs[66] and fortune-telling chapbooks or as a private interest of a few eccentrics. The occult revival of the late nineteenth century affected Russia and led a renewed public interest until it was more or less extinguished by the Revolution of 1917. Since the collapse of the Soviet regime there has been an enormous outpouring of cheap fortune-telling books (often reprints), frequently with a crude astrological content of the kind found in West European newspapers, and one or two more elaborate publications. The restoration of free-market capitalism has provided a benign environment for facile syncretism of the New Age kind, together with cynical entrepreneurship. One may expect popular astrology to continue to flourish.

6. *Astrological Terminology*

In the previous chapter an outline was given of the origins of astronomical and astrological terminology in Church Slavonic and Old Russian. The terminology of the period of Byzantine influence to some extent survived the Westernization of Russia, but inevitably a newer terminology based on Latin and Western vernaculars came into use when translation from those languages began. The most obvious and common sign of Western influence is the use of the Latin planet names, usually denuded of their case endings, occasionally disguised by arriving via Polish (e.g. the occasional *Iovish*, from the Latin genitive *Jovis*) and in the case of *Venera*, Venus, with her sex restored, to a Slavonic eye, by adding an -a to the Latin oblique case stem. The word for planet in general is now more commonly *planeta*, from the Latin, but the Greek-based form *planita* (sometimes *planida*, this often having the sense of 'fate' see above, n. 58) is still found.[67] In one seventeenth-century Ukrainian dictionary of the contemporary learned language, predominantly Church Slavonic, both forms are given: *planita* for planet and *planeta* for sign of the zodiac![68]

The names of the signs of the zodiac remain the same as they were in earlier texts of Greek origin because translation from the Latin terms of course gives the same result as translation from the Greek. In addition, however, to the various words beginning *zhivo-* which continue in use for 'sign of the zodiac' we now find very commonly *znamia, znamenie, znak*, all semantic calques from Latin *signum*, in some cases by way of German or Polish.

The other main difference is that terms for horoscopic calculation begin to be required as more sophisticated texts are translated. The concept of aspect from the seventeenth century onwards may be rendered as *aspekt*, the modern term and a modified transliteration loan from Latin *aspectus*, or a straight loan from Polish or German; or by *vzgliad, vozgliad* (nowadays 'gaze, glance'), a loan translation of Latin *aspectus*, in some cases via the occasional German *Anschauung*, and/or Polish *wzgliąd*; or by synonyms such as *vzor* 'gaze'.

The names for the aspects themselves vary from translation to translation: the subject was presumably too arcane for any standard terminology to emerge.

'Conjunction' is usually *sovokuplenie*, which more commonly means coitus. One or two other words may occasionally be found: e.g. *stechenie* 'confluence', and in the eighteenth century one may also often find *soedinenie* 'union'.

'Opposition' is rendered in one fifteenth-century manuscript as *dvomerno* 'in two measures', as *protivlenie* in the *Shestokryl* (a fifteenth-century translation of the Hebrew *Six Wings*), thereafter with a variety of words including the element *protiv-* 'against' (*protivno, protivny, protivnyi, protivnik, protivopolozhnost', protivopolozhenie, proitvostoianie, soprotivlenie, protivnyi vozgliad, protivnyi vzor*). The cases of *protivosiianie* and *protivnoe siianie* 'contrary shining' are evidently translations of the German *Gegenschein*.

A similar calque from German is found for 'Trine' in the form of *treugolnoe siianie*, lit. 'triangular shining' together with a whole variety of terms including the various forms of the word for three or third or triangle: *tretii, tret'iak, treugolnik, triugolnik, troeugolnik, troinik*.

'Quartile, quadrature' is found as *chvartak, chvarty, chetvertak* in several texts of Polish provenance, and as *chetverik, chetvernik, chetvertyi, chetverugolnik*, all terms based on the word for 'four', and in two late manuscripts as *kvadrat* 'square'.

'Sextile' is found in a number of terms based on the word for 'six': *shestnyi, shesterik, shesterichnyi aspekt, shestiugolnik, shesterougolnik, shestak, shostak* (these last two from Polish), *shesterougolnoe siianie* (from German *Gesechtsschein*).

The notion of ruling is regularly calqued as *gospodstvovat'* or *vladet'* 'to rule', or *derzhat'* 'to hold' (probably ultimately from Latin *tenere* which could be used in this sense).

House is regularly translated by the word *dom*, and in one case *obitel'* 'dwelling', but the Russian texts not infrequently fail to distinguish 'house' and 'sign'.

The strength of a planet is usually given as *sila*, occasionally as *potuga* (from Polish). Degrees of favorability are usually *fortuna*.[69]

Current popular astrological publications are not consistent in their terminology; indeed translated texts often show a complete misunderstanding of more complicated concepts such as aspects.

Notes

1. See Spasskii, 'Proiskhozhdenie i istoriya russkikh schetov'; Ryan, 'John Tradescant's Russian Abacus'.

2. Perry, *The State of Russia*, p. 211.

3. See Ch. 14.1.

4. For a convenient study in English see Huttenbach, 'Muscovy's Calendar Controversy'.

5. See Ryan, 'Rathborne's *Surveyor*' with additional information in Kosheleva and Simonov, 'Novoe o pervoi russkoi knige po teoreticheskoi geometrii'.

6. For the most recent study see Ryan, 'Navigation and the Modernization of Petrine Russia'.

7. St Augustine of Hippo was known only by repute in medieval Russia; a Latin *vita* was translated in the sixteenth century, but none of Augustine's works was translated into Russian (or Church Slavonic) until comparatively modern times. Maxim was clearly familiar with Augustine's theology, which he had presumably read in Latin in his Italian period.

8. In general on Maxim see Haney, *From Italy to Muscovy*; for Maxim's attacks on astrology see pp. 154–60, also Ivanov, *Literaturnoe nasledie Maksima Greka*, pp. 119–27, and Sinitsyna, *Maksim Grek v Rossii*, esp. pp. 75–103.

9. Sinitsyna, *Maksim Grek v Rossii*, p. 90.

10. See *Stoglav* (1863 edn), p. 139.

11. For these two texts see also Ch. 1.6.

12. See Belobrova, *Nikolai Spafarii*, p. 45.

13. John of Salisbury, *Policraticus* (in partial English text by Pike, p. 60). John also offered a scientific explanation.

14. Larin, *Russko-angliiskii slovar'-dnevnik*, pp. 156–7.

15. Kukushkina, *Monastyrskie biblioteki*, p. 54.

16. Peretts, 'Gromnik', p. 81.

17. Vaillant, *Le Livre des secrets d'Hénoch*, p. 95.

18. For more detailed discussion see Ryan, 'Curious Star Names', pp. 138–9.

19. First described in Sobolevskii, *Perevodnaia literatura*, pp. 413–19 (text but no tables). The most detailed current research on the 'Judaizer' astronomical texts and their provenance, with English translations, is Taube, 'The Kievan Jew Zacharia and the Astronomical Works of the Judaizers'. This lists and supersedes most of the earlier work.

20. See Thorndike, *The Sphere of Sacrobosco*. For the Russian text, translated from the Hebrew version, see Zubov, 'Neizvestnyi russkii perevod', and now Taube, 'The Kievan Jew Zacharia and the Astronomical Works of the Judaizers', with English translation.

21. Karpov, *Azbukovniki*, p. 197.

22. Sobolevskii, *Perevodnaia literatura*, pp. 428–33. No evidence is offered for the 'Judaizer' assertion. For more discussion of the text see Ryan, 'Curious Star Names', pp. 142–6 and *idem*, 'The *Passion of St Demetrius* and the *Secret of Secrets*', pp. 56–7.

23. Solomon's mirror also appears in the *Key of Solomon*, and magic mirrors were supposedly possessed by Leo the Wise and Alexander the Great as well as a variety of oriental princes: see Delatte, *La Catoptromancie grecque*, pp. 100, 115, 123, 139, 199.

24. The only Russian article on the subject of the star Chigir is Sviatskii, 'Skazanie o Chigire zvezde'. It does not discuss the divination text but is concerned to show that sixteenth-century Russians were aware of the observations of Galileo of the rings of Saturn and the satellites of Jupiter! The star is also mentioned in Kerenskii, 'Drevnerusskie otrechennye verovaniia', p. 73.

25. Probably originally the seventh heaven: see H. Odeberg, *3 Enoch or the Hebrew Book of Enoch*, Cambridge, 1928, p. 62.

26. See Sobolevskii, *Perevodnaia literatura*, p. 428 and Ryan, 'Curious Star Names', p. 145.

27. Described in Smilianskaia, '"Suevernaia" knizhitsa'.

28. MS St Petersburg, GPB Q.XVII.176, miscellany, 17–18th c., f. 83. Kolo as a star name is also found in Afanasii Nikitin's fifteenth-century account of his journey to India – it has been interpreted as Orion but could be a calque of Greek *hamaxa*, i.e. one of many words in the Slavonic languages meaning 'waggon' and used as the name of Ursa Major; see Gibbon, *Popular Star Names*, pp. 145–59.

29. Athens, Bibl. Publ. 1275: see *CCAG*, X (Codices athenienses), pp. 126–8, and Erlangen University MS 93: ibid., VII, 1908, pp. 75–6.

30. See Gaster, *Literatura populară romănă*, pp. 502–3. A sixteenth-century psalter with lunar tables

and the Chigir divination (f. 226), a medical zodiac, and the 'Good and bad days of Moses' is quoted in Iatsimirskii, *Slavianskie i russkie rukopisi*, p. 359.

31. See Lewis, 'The Eight Stars that Never Were'. The list of days is quoted by Lewis from Princeton MS Yahuda 933, a seventeenth-century Arabic manuscript. This also contains a diagram of essentially the same construction as the Russian one, and containing the same information.

32. For more discussion, in particular of background and terminology see Ryan, 'The Oriental Duodenary Animal Cycle'.

33. 1. MSS Moscow, Russian State Library, Undol'skoe sobr. 440, Paschal tables, 17th century f. 2v; 2. Undol'skoe 447, 17th–18th century, miscellany with Paschal tables; 3. Muzeinoe sobr. 1372, miscellany, 18th century, f. 59, containing also a *Mirotvornyi krug* (Paschal table), an astrological text called *Planetnik*, a description of the star *Aravan* (for which see previous section) and a calendrical article apparently of Jewish origin; 4. MSS St Petersburg, Academy of Sciences Library, Arkh. sobr. C. 204, miscellany, 17th century, f. 170v, also containing a *Mirotvornyi krug* and a SATOR square; 5. St Petersburg, GPB Q.XVII.176, miscellany, 17th or early 18th century, also contains a *Planetnik*, a garbled SATOR square, Paschal tables and the article about the star *Aravan*. MS Und. 447 was published in 1996 in Belobrova, 'K istorii knizhnoi miniatiury', p. 80, as an example of continuing Byzantine tradition but with no mention of the animal cycle.

34. See Tikhomirov, 'O dvenadtsati mongol'skikh mesiatsakh v starinnoi russkoi pis'mennosti', *Sovetskaia etnografiia*, 1958, 3, pp. 21–7.

35. *CCAG*, VIII, 1908, p. 157, l. 6.

36. See Neugebauer, 'Studies in Byzantine Astronomical Terminology', describing MS Vat. Gr. 1058, f. 331v.

37. See Isaevich, 'Redkaia inkunabula'; *Iurii Drohobych: bibliohrafychnyi pokazchyk*, Lvov, 1983; and Longo, *Iurii Drogobich* (this contains a facsimile of the *Iudicium prognosticon*).

38. See Golenchenko, '"Kalendar'" Frantsiska Skoriny', p. 39.

39. Oxford, Bodleian Library, A.22.th.B.S. and Arch.A.v.103.

40. Peretts, 'Lunnik', pp. 22–3.

41. For some discussion see Simonov, 'Russkie pridvornye «matematiki»', pp. 79–80.

42. See Zabelin, *Domashnii byt russkikh tsarei*, pp. 223–5. A plate allegedly depicting this is given in Rovinskii, *Russkie narodnye kartinki*, 1900, plate V. The history of this image and some comments on Rovinskii's attribution is given in Belobrova, 'K istorii knizhnoi miniatiury', pp. 71–81. The architect and artist were 'engineer and colonel Gustav Dekepnin'. Zabelin also notes (p. 270) a large Venetian clock 'with planets' in an inventory of the tsar's belongings of 1634.

43. See Ainalov, 'Ocherki'.

44. He was supposed to have had a palace in which the sun, moon, and stars revolved: Mango, 'The Legend of Leo the Wise', p. 74.

45. MS St Petersburg, BAN, Arkh. 860, ff. 1–14. 1689. The Polish version appeared in several editions from 1666 onwards: see Górska, *Katalog kalendarzy*, nos. 299–301.

46. Rovinskii, *Russkie narodnye kartinki*, II, p. 434, no. 666.

47. MS St Petersburg, BAN, 16.17.15, ff.1–15v.

48. MS St Petersburg, GPB, Pog. 1760.

49. Pekarskii, *Nauka*, I, pp. 287–8.

50. For text see Simonov, '«Nauka midicheskaia ot matematiki»'.

51. See Belobrova, 'K istorii knizhnoi miniatiury', p. 77.

52. Sobolevskii, *Perevodnaia literatura*, p. 146.

53. My translation: *almanashniki* and *zodiishyki* are Avvakum's own coinings and are clearly intended in a pejorative sense.

54. *Pamiatniki literatury Drevnei Rusi*, XVII, 2, pp. 418, 420–1.

55. Published in the OLDP series as no. 133 in 1915.

56. See Pluzhnikov and Simonov, 'Goroskop Petra I'.

57. Some recorded examples are Viktorov, *Opisi rukopisnykh sobranii*: pp. 99, 185 (1823) (a late seventeenth-century *sbornik* of the Antoniev-Siiskii Monastery including a *Koliadnik* and horoscopes at the end); Waugh, *The Great Turkes Defiance*, p. 273: a Posolskii prikaz copy of Pseudo-Aristotle, *Problemata* with a horoscope, in a manuscript copied for the Swedish diplomat J.G. Sparwenfeld in 1684–7.

58. See Kovtun, 'Planida – furtuna – schastnoe koleso'.

59. Rybnikov, *Pesni*, II, p. 376.

60. See Chistiakov, 'Narodnoe predanie o Briuse'; also Chulkov, *Abevega*, p. 73. 'Water of life' and 'water of death' are common ideas in folklore – see Ch. 9.

61. See Chenakal, 'Iakov Vilimovich Brius', p. 8. For a full account of Bruce in English see Boss, *Newton and Russia*. On the almanacs see Kerenskii, 'Drevnerusskie otrechennye verovaniia'; Rovinskii, *Russkie narodnye kartinki*, II, p. 360, no. 658.

62. See Wigzell, *Reading Russian Fortunes*, p. 40. One version appeared in a composite work including household remedies and magic spells – it reached its fifth edition in 1917 (ibid., p. 55).

63. For texts of legends about Bruce recorded in the 1920s see Baranov, *Moskovskie legendy*, pp. 20–66.

64. See *Russkaia dramaturgiia poslednei chetverti XVII i nachala XVIII v.*, pp. 287–9.

65. For this whole genre see the very detailed account in Wigzell, *Reading Russian Fortunes*.

66. A regrettably brief summary of a conference paper by Simonov and Khromov, 'Astrologicheskie pripiski v gravirovannykh (lubochnykh) kalendariakh kak otrazhenie otnosheniia obshchestva k sokrovennym znaniiam i knige', in *Kniga v prostranstve kul'tury*, Moscow, 1995, pp. 53–5, draws attention to the value of annotations on calendars and almanacs as evidence of popular belief in astrology.

67. See Lepskaia, 'K istorii slova *planeta*'. Although full of useful information, this article makes the almost certainly erroneous assumption that the distinction between the two forms is dialectal.

68. Berynda, *Leksikon slavenorosskii*, s.v.

69. These terms are documented and discussed in more detail in Ryan, *Astronomical and Astrological Terminology*.

MAGIC, THE CHURCH, THE LAW AND THE STATE

T he attitudes of the Eastern and Western Churches towards magic and divination have generally been condemnatory, both on theological grounds and because of biblical or patristic precept. It takes a shrewd theologian, however, to distinguish miracles from magic, and most ordinary people of any period would have seen no difference. In practice the Christian Churches have found difficulty in ensuring that their official view of the matter prevailed, not least because some of those who practised magic and divination, from the earliest times up to the present, were themselves members of the clergy, and because at least some forms of divination (e.g. the interpretation of dreams) are reported in Scripture, hagiographic and patristic writing, not to mention medieval and post-medieval works, by otherwise fairly orthodox Christian writers, as normal and legitimate activities.[1] The fourth-century Council of Laodicea found it necessary to forbid the clergy to practise magic and divination, and many local councils and synods over the centuries have condemned magic and divination in general or in particular aspects. [2]

Russian penitentials, expositions of canon law, episcopal denunciations, and lists of banned books are as varied as their Western counterparts, but most catalogues of sins, again like their Western counterparts, display a concern with sexual behaviour and magic. (Since the concentration on sexual behaviour in many of the penitentials and moral treatises in the Western Church has often been blamed on the influence of St Augustine, as has the pre-Reformation theology of witchcraft, it is worth noting that Augustine was hardly known in Russia, and certainly not before the sixteenth century.) This association is not fortuitous; as Kieckhefer has reminded us 'The glorification of the transgressive and the vilification of persecutors has perhaps too often blinded us to the recognition that much magic was intended for sexual coercion and exploitation'.[3] As in Western medieval penitentials and other texts cataloguing sins, many of the items listed in Orthodox texts are simply survivals from, or even specific references to, more ancient councils and synods. The commonest source in Russia appears to have been the acts of the Sixth Ecumenical Council (III Constantinople, 680–81) and its successor the Trullan Synod of 692. Among other things these acts lay down rules for marriage and sexual behaviour; forbid association with Jews; forbid mixed bathing, going to horse-races, mimes, animal shows, theatrical dancing, consulting diviners, sorcerers, cloud-chasers, purveyors of amulets; forbid celebrating the Calends, Vota and Brumalia, wearing comic, satyric or tragic masks, and jumping over fires at the beginning of the month (see Ch. 1.6 for detail). It is impossible to establish now how many people in any given community actually confessed voluntarily to some of the sins listed in penitentials, or how far the parish clergy went in seeking out such sins, or indeed, how far the recitation of such lists actually encouraged beliefs and practices which had not hitherto existed, just as the preconceptions of inquisitors and judges appear to have prompted the evidential detail in many witchcraft trial confessions in Western Europe. The occasional contemporary or local colouring of these lists, however, can be taken as an indication at least of some new ecclesiastical concern.

The florilegium called *Izbornik Sviatoslava*, compiled in 1076 for Sviatoslav, the Grand Prince of Kiev, contains condemnations of divination, witchcraft and poisoning abstracted from the fourth-century *Constitutiones Apostolorum*, and quotes Athanasius of Alexandria on magic and demons.[4] A list of canonical answers by the Metropolitan of Kiev, Ioann II, written in the 1080s condemns in strong terms those men and women who practise witchcraft and enchantments ('volkhovanie i charodeianiia'), but adds that they should not be killed.[5] A twelfth-century list of canonical questions and answers (the *Voproshanie Kirika*) which continued to circulate, more or less modified, as a kind of penitential at least until the seventeenth century, stipulates six weeks penance for taking a child to a wizard ('volkhv') – and the same for taking him to a 'Frankish' priest. (These two sins are discussed in the same breath as Lesbian love-making.)[6] This list is apparently aimed more specifically at women than are other documents of this kind. Other penitentials do not mention the Western clergy, but do seem to link magic, devil-worship, and deviant sex: a penitential of the fourteenth–fifteenth century condemns the consultation of wizards and prescribes four years' penance, but makes no reference to Catholic priests;[7] a mid-fifteenth-century penitential, *The Rules of the Holy Apostles* (evidently based on the *Constitutiones Apostolorum* mentioned above), condemns bestiality, unapproved positions in coitus, seeking the help of devils, going to wizards for fortune-telling or amulets.[8] It adds that anyone believing in charms is serving the Devil. Another sixteenth-century list of sins condemns the use of herbs or potions (*zelie*) for murder, procuring abortions, or conceiving a child, also believing in dreams, fortune-telling, or praying to Satan.[9] The linking of magic with family law and sexual misbehaviour as areas falling under ecclesiastical jurisdiction seems to have arisen in Russia in the twelfth century. It has been suggested that this was part of a reform designed to secure the funding of the episcopate by extending its area of competence,[10] but the association of these subjects is generally much older and would certainly have been known to the Russians from the acts of the Sixth Ecumenical Council and the Trullan synod mentioned above.

More than a millennium after the Council of Laodicea had condemned the practice of magic by clergy, it was still found necessary, in the acts of the *Stoglav* Council convened in Moscow by Ivan the Terrible in 1551, to forbid the parish clergy specifically, under pain of ecclesiastical ban, to accept salt, soap, or the cauls of newborn infants for placing on or under the altar in order to give them magical properties (see Ch. 1.6 for detail).[11]

The *Stoglav* quite specifically classifies magical practices and texts as heresy, and in this follows an association of ideas going back to early Christianity. Until quite recently a widely accepted view among historians writing in English was that this association, like 'demonic magic' and the 'demonic pact' and flying witches, were the invention of 'the Inquisition'. A closer study of the Russian, Byzantine, and late antique evidence, which is rarely quoted in the debate, tends to dispel this simplistic idea (which probably owes something to the Black Legend) and supports the subtler analysis of contemporary scholarship.[12]

The opposition of the early Church to magic had not only sound theological, pastoral, and polemic reasons, but also, once Christianity became respectable in the Roman Empire, this opposition had solid support in the pre-existing hostility and suspicion of the State towards magic and divination as potentially seditious or even actually treasonous.[13] The fear that diviners might discover the name of the next emperor was real, and the possible political or dynastic damage which might result from such presumed knowledge was considerable and continued to worry rulers of later periods;[14] indeed, in the 1580s in Russia the wizard Andriusha Mochalov was arrested and brought to Moscow following allegations that he had been asked by Michael Nagoi (from a family with some dynastic claims to the throne) to predict how long Tsar Fedor would reign.[15]

The image of Nectanebus, in the various versions of Pseudo-Callisthenes' Alexander story, destroying an enemy fleet by doing nothing more expensive than bewitching model boats floating in a bowl, must have been terrifying to a credulous ruler as nullifying at no cost the economic and military basis of his power.

Once Christianity was officially accepted in the Roman Empire, it became very easy to blur the distinctions between paganism, (malefic) magic, false prophecy, heresy and treason, and indeed to redefine them.[16] The gods of the old order, though they might sometimes be popularly reinterpreted as saints or angels in the new, more often were cast in the role of the demons who could be summoned to perform magic. And the fear of magic, often linked with poisoning,[17] as a weapon of sedition resurfaces again and again in later European history,[18] not least, as we shall see, in Russia.

In countries officially professing Christianity the civil law has normally either deferred to canon law in the matter of magic or itself made the practice of magic or divination a punishable offence. In earlier times among the Orthodox Slavs the punishment specified by the Church for such practices was often relatively mild. For example, a tenth-century Glagolitic Euchologion specifies four years on bread and water for 'praying to devils'.[19] Early princely law in Kiev Rus' tended to treat magic and divination as a naughty domestic practice of women which was best left to husbands to deal with. This view was still prevalent in sixteenth-century Russia, if the *Domostroi* is a fair guide (see Ch. 1 above). On the other hand a twelfth-century traveller from Moorish Spain found the treatment of suspected witches in Kiev Rus' worth including in his short account of the country. Suspects were, he says, tied up and thrown into the river: if they floated they were witches and were taken out and burned.[20] This example of 'swimming' witches serves to place Russia in an ancient and widespread tradition.[21]

Even in the acts of the 1551 *Stoglav* Council mentioned above (and in more detail in Ch. 1.6), a council in fact summoned by Ivan the Terrible to deal with specific abuses in the Church and in the popular religious practices of Russians (apparently listed by the Tsar himself), and one of the few Russian documents to list current popular vices, superstitions, and abuses of religion, the specified punishments for practising magic or owning magic books were purely ecclesiastical (excommunication or, revealingly, suspension from clerical duties). Comparison with law other than canon law at this point is also illuminating. Ivan the Terrible's attempt to codify and regulate the administration of justice, the *Sudebnik*, drawn up in the previous year and submitted to the *Stoglav* Council for approval, has no mention of witches, magic or superstitious practices. A later semi-official version of 1589, probably adapted for the free peasant (*chernososhnye*) communities of northern Russia,[22] mentions witches (*vedun'ia*; in one copy *ved'ma*) but only in the context of specifying levels of compensation for offences against the honour (*beschestie*) of the various categories of citizen, for which purpose they came at the bottom of the list with harlots![23] Male magicians are not mentioned, nor is there any trace of any other concern with magic, superstition or poisoning. We have to conclude from this that female witches were at this time a distinct category in village communities, at least in northern Russia, and that although canon law and occasional ukazes from the tsar in particular circumstances might condemn magic and witchcraft and their practitioners, codified Muscovite law in the form of the *Sudebniki* of 1497, 1550, and 1589 mentions only female witches, and only in the context of their legal *rights*! The situation, as far as codified non-canon law is concerned, was to change with the *Ulozhenie* of 1649, i.e. the law code introduced by Tsar Aleksei Mikhailovich (which incorporated many provisions for canon-law offences), and the military code (*Voinskii artikul*) of Peter the Great of 26 April 1715, of which more will be said below. In these codes witchcraft was a crime against the sovereign or state and punishable by death.

These punishments, however, appear to be directed primarily at the clergy, who were not subject to civil law. By the late fifteenth century, when members of the laity were accused of witchcraft or practising magic, as often as not this was an accusation of a particular form of treason, i.e. the magic was malefic magic directed against the ruler or a person of high rank.

This political dimension goes back a long way. In Kiev Rus' the chronicles record a number of cases in which pagan *volkhvy* were put to death or driven out; there were executions in Suzdal' in 1024, in Novgorod in 1071 and 1227.[24] In the last of these cases it is recorded in the *Novgorod Chronicle* that magicians of various kinds, male and female (*volkhvy*, *veduny*, *potvornitsy*) were seized by the people of Novgorod and thrown into a fire.[25]

In the early Muscovite period under Ivan III (1462–1505) three 'evil women' were arrested for the possession of herbs while visiting the Tsar's wife. They were punished by being pushed through holes in the ice in the Moskva river. This was a not unusual punishment for common criminals in Muscovy.[26] The close association of witchcraft, heresy and treason may be seen in the accusations brought against Maxim the Greek (the ex-humanist Michael Trivolis – see Ch. 15.2) in his trials in 1525 and 1531. These included charges of having 'evil intentions' towards the grand prince, communicating with the Turks in order to help them wage war with Russia, practising sorcery against the grand prince, heresy, judaizing.[27] The most precise accusation was that 'by magical Hellenic tricks he had written on his palms in vodka and then held out his hands against the Grand Prince and others, making magic' and later that he indulged in Hellenic and Jewish black magic and witchcraft.[28] These accusations bear all the marks of political witch-hunting rather than of genuine theological concern.

Later in the sixteenth century Prince Andrei Kurbskii, who had fled from Muscovy and conducted an acrimonious correspondence with Ivan IV, protested in his first epistle to Ivan that he, Ivan, had 'falsely accused the Orthodox of treason and magic and other abuses'. In his typically trenchant and syntactically insecure reply Ivan declared: 'As for your mentioning "treachery and magic" – well, such dogs are executed in all countries'.[29] Magic was indeed known and feared in Ivan's Russia, both at court and among the people. In 1547, after a great fire in Moscow and a subsequent uprising, Princess Anna Glinskaia, Ivan's grandmother, was accused by the people of Moscow of being a witch; Ivan's court physician, poisoner and astrologer Bomel (see Ch. 13.4) was tortured to death for treason, and under interrogation implicated a number of highly placed persons, including Leonid, Archbishop of Novgorod. Leonid was accused of running a coven of fifteen witches; he was found guilty and disgraced and the witches were burned.[30]

From the time of Ivan IV onwards the central administration of the Muscovite state was increasingly concerned with 'political crimes' and courts began to look for evidence by means of search as well as interrogation.[31] Frequently this involved both an accusation of treasonable words and actions and the discovery of possession of herbs and roots or other suspicious substances, or documents (including spells and heterodox texts). The process of denunciation and investigation became known as 'slovo i delo gosudarevo'. This phrase, literally 'word and deed of the sovereign' describes a procedure which anyone could invoke if he or she wished to make an accusation of behaviour or speech inimical to the tsar's health or honour, or relating to uprising or other treasonable activities (known in the sixteenth century as *kramola*). It was an offence not to denounce anyone suspected of such activities. Both the accuser and accused were immediately arrested and interrogated under torture. The affair had to be referred to one of the *prikazy* (departments of state) and the results would be passed a single department (from 1650 to 1676 this was the Tainyi prikaz) or to the tsar himself. In the eighteenth century denunciations were normally dealt with locally and only the more serious passed on to the state departments which at various times dealt with state security (under Peter this was for a short time the Preobrazhenskii prikaz, then from 1718 the Tainaia kantseliaria). The history of the procedure is obscure; it probably began in the reign of Tsar Mikhail Fedorovich (1613–45),[32] but there seems to be no documentary evidence of its establishment or of rules for its conduct apart from the second chapter of the *Ulozhenie* law code of 1649. It was most widely invoked in the reign of Peter the Great (sometimes renamed as *gosudartsvennye prestupleniia*, 'state crimes'), when even a critical remark could be regarded as treason. It was eventually abolished by Catherine the Great in 1762.

The fear of the tsar and his officials of hostile magic directed against the ruler and his officials is very evident. In 1598 Boris Godunov, on becoming tsar after fourteen years as regent, exacted an oath from those in his service which required that neither in eating nor in drinking, neither in their clothing nor in anything else would they attempt to devise evil; that they would not send to him any of their people bearing sorcery or noisome roots; that they would not hire wizards or witches, that they would not efface his footprints with any magical design, that they would not by means of magic send any evil upon him by the wind. (The last two were types of malefic magic well known in Russia.)[33] In particular, access to the stables was forbidden 'so that no evil-disposed person should place noxious herbs or roots in the Tsar's saddle, bridle, belt or gloves'.[34] Several people were in fact accused of using magic against the tsar, either because Boris really believed this to be true or because it was a convenient method of disposing of political and dynastic opponents (e.g. the Romanov family).[35] A similar oath was demanded from the people of Moscow later in the seventeenth century by Tsar Vasilii Shuiskii.[36] According to one historian, foreign doctors, who were regularly employed as court physicians from the fifteenth to the eighteenth century, were expected to give a written oath not to practise magic against the Tsar's household.[37] In fact members of the tsars' household were themselves not infrequently accused of magical offences, as will be seen below. Outside Muscovy the other two Orthodox East Slav territories, the Ukraine and Belorussia, were for the most part in this period under Polish rule, and the treatment of witches was largely dependent on Polish practices and the prevailing local law (mostly the Lithuanian Statute and Magdeburg Law). There are plenty of cases documented of burning at the stake for witchcraft. One case in 1615 involved the burning of two women and the son of one of them.[38]

The assumption made in some modern popular writing on witchcraft, especially feminist writing of the more extravagant kind, is that an accusation of witchcraft is in fact a cover for something else (anything from class warfare to the global male conspiracy against women). While it is certainly true that the politically and spiritually heterodox, as well as foreigners and the socially obnoxious or mentally disturbed, have always been particularly susceptible to charges of witchcraft, lycanthropy, possessing the Evil Eye, and other kinds of 'demonic' or 'magical' behaviour, this must not obscure the fact that people did, and do still, indulge in practices which they and their neighbours considered magical, and did, and do still, claim to be witches. These practices and claims may be felt in many communities to be both real and threatening, particularly at times of panic due to some crisis or natural disaster, such as drought, plague, or cholera epidemics. The use of petty magical practices and folk remedies was also so widespread that a malicious accusation of witchcraft could easily be given some colour – the number of cases in which the accuser and accused were members of the same household is significant.[39]

In the Russian context Boris Uspenskii has suggested, with a wealth of examples, that sorcery, royal imposture, parody of religion, and the promotion of things foreign, are all examples of 'antibehaviour' in a binary model of culture, and indeed that they may be equivalent.[40] (It is worth noting that although writers in the Moscow-Tartu school derive their semeiotic method from certain traditions in linguistics, mere deviance, which might satisfy a linguistic model, is not usually enough to create a cultural opposition; for this a full symbolic inversion is invoked, with varying degrees of plausibility.) The most telling example is the case of the False Dmitrii, the early seventeenth-century pretender to the Russian throne, who married a Polish noblewoman, adopted Polish manners, and briefly seized power with Polish help. It is possible that both he and Tsar Boris Godunov, like Ivan IV before them, really did have an interest in sorcery. Certainly in contemporary accounts and accusations and in folklore Dmitrii was regarded as a sorcerer who practised 'gypsy sorcery and every kind of devilish magic . . . like Julian the Apostate who did sorcery with devils'[41] and 'cast spells with devils', and indeed, after his death his body was adorned with the mask and pipe of the *skomorokhi*, the wandering minstrels often accused of witchcraft and pagan practices, and he was buried as a *koldun*. Dmitrii's un-Orthodox conduct included, allegedly, getting married on the feast of St Nicholas and despoiling young nuns and boys.[42] In one historical song he is described as going to the bathhouse with his wife while the princes and boiars went to church – behaviour popularly imputed to the sorcerer – and his Polish wife Marina, described as an 'evil heretic atheist', escaped the bloody end suffered by her husband by turning herself into a magpie and flying away[43] – in other words she was a witch.[44]

These examples of fear of witches in the sixteenth and early seventeenth century do not add up to anything on the scale of the witch craze of parts of Western Europe. Certainly there were not arrests, denunciations, trials and executions on the scale that occurred in some areas of Europe. And insofar as there was a witch-hunt in Russia at all, it must be said to have taken place mainly in the seventeenth century,[45] and to have been fostered by Aleksei Mikhailovich (1629–76), tsar from 1645, who, rather like his near contemporary James I of England (d. 1625), was both interested in the occult and fearful of malefic magic directed against his household. Perhaps the nearest that Muscovy came to a witch panic was the case of Lukh, a small town to the north-east of Moscow in 1656–60 (i.e. after the publication of the *Ulozhenie* law code). The Lukh episode involved a considerable number of people of both sexes, mainly as a result of denunciations by accused persons under interrogation. In this case there was no obvious political context. Many of the details of the accusations were typical of

Russian popular magic and beliefs about witchcraft: the alleged witches were accused of crying out like wild animals, possessing herbs and roots, placing a cross under the heel (the usual Russian method of performing demonic magic, according to later accounts), performing magic at weddings (one of the main roles of the Russian *koldun* or magician), sending spells 'on the wind' (a particular type of exclusively malefic magic well known in Russia), scattering salt. Five men were eventually executed (the method is not stated in the documents).[46]

The Lukh case notwithstanding, the association of witchcraft with conspiracy against Church or State has always been widespread, and the Russian experience goes some way to supporting the sweeping claim of Muchembled that 'witch-hunting is fundamentally not a religious but a political phenomenon'.[47] In 1638, in the reign of Mikhail Romanov, a serving woman, D. Lamanova, was accused of burning a smock and sprinkling the ash in the path of the tsaritsa as part of a magical attempt to win her favour.[48] In 1647, in the reign of Aleksei, Mikhailovich, a peasant, with the complicity of the boiars Semen and Ivan Danilov, was accused of using magical love spells on Prince Waldemar of Denmark and Princess Irina Mikhailovicha.[49] On 22 April 1670 Artamon Matveev, a senior army commander, was accused of attempting to influence the Tsar's choice of bride by sorcery.[50] In 1671 one of the Tsaritsa's serving women, Marfa Timofeevna, was accused of stealing some salt and a mushroom which had been prepared for her mistress. When observed, she had spilled the salt. Although she confessed to stealing the salt and mushroom, which she said she wanted to eat herself, she was tortured 'na dybakh' (i.e. the Russian version of the strappado: her wrists were tied behind her back and she was then lifted into the air by them so that her shoulder joints were wrenched out of place), and then by fire, but confessed to nothing else. It is clear that this was not so much a punishment as an attempt to discover whether malefic magic or poisoning were intended.[51] In 1675 Prince F.F. Kurakin was accused of harbouring a witch, an old blind woman called Fen'ka. She confessed under torture and died; the case had wide ramifications.[52]

Grigorii Kotoshikhin, a senior official of the Russian diplomatic service in the reign of Aleksei Mikhailovich, fled to Sweden and wrote (at some time in the 1660s) an account of the internal politics and manners of the Russian court and state at the beginning of the second half of the seventeenth century. It included the information that it was the Razboinyi prikaz (the highest authority dealing with criminal cases at that time) which dealt with *koldovstvo* and *chernoknizhstvo* (sorcery and black magic – it is not clear what distinction was intended, if any), which were listed together with blasphemy, theft of church property, sodomy and false interpretation of Scripture. The penalty for all these was, according to Kotoshikhin, to be burned alive if the condemned person was a man, or beheaded in the case of a woman.[53]

The death of Aleksei in 1676 did not bring changes in this matter; the Regent Sofiia and her entourage seem to have had occult interests, and in the enquiry of 1689–90 into an alleged plot on the life of the young Tsar Peter, Prince V.V.

Golitsyn and Silvester Medvedev were accused of employing astrology and magic to achieve their ends. Golitsyn was accused of asking a Polish wizard to prophesy whether or not he would marry Sofiia, and of keeping a peasant sorcerer in his bathhouse to prepare love potions which would ensure Sofiia's love;[54] and Iuda Boltin, an associate of the leader of the alleged conspiracy, the state secretary (*dumnyi d'iak*) Fedor Shaklovitii, was accused of sprinkling herbs and roots where the tsar would walk.[55]

These accusations were certainly politically motivated, but the young Peter, for all his modern technical interests, had been brought up in an atmosphere where such things mattered a great deal, and whether he believed in them or not he certainly introduced very severe punishments for magic and witchcraft in his code of military law (the *Voinskii artikul* of 1715). In article 1 of its first chapter, 'On the fear of God', this states:

> If any soldier is found to be an idol-worshipper, black magician (*chernoknizhets*), gun-charmer, or superstitious and blasphemous enchanter (*charodei*), depending on the nature of the offence he shall be placed under close arrest, put in irons, made to run the gauntlet, or be burned to death. Interpretation: Death by burning is to be the normal punishment for black magicians if they have harmed anyone by magic, or had dealings with the Devil. If he has not harmed anyone or had dealings with the Devil then he should be punished by one of the other punishments listed above, and made to do public church penance.

Article 2 of the same law states that anyone who hires a magician or encourages anyone else to do this so that he harms someone shall be punished in the same way as the magician. Article 3 lays down that any soldier guilty of blasphemy shall have his tongue burned through with a hot iron and then be beheaded.[56] Most cases were in fact punished with lesser penalties and public penance.[57]

In fact Peter's military code was based largely on the 1683 edition of the Swedish military code introduced by Gustavus Adolphus in 1621–2, which was itself derived from earlier models. The Swedish law also devotes its first article to 'the fear of God' and forbids magic and gun-spells with similar severe penalties.[58] The Swedish code, written at a time when fear of witchcraft in Sweden was very strong, though not yet at its peak, is based in part on the *Constitutio criminalis Carolina*, the law code drawn up at the order of Emperor Charles V in 1532, which had the intention of providing a common legal structure for the whole of the Holy Roman Empire,[59] and various Danish and French ordinances. In fact the Roman law distinction between magic which harms and magic which does not, and the punishment of the former by burning to death, is taken by the *Voinskii artikul* directly or indirectly from article 109 of the *Carolina* (although that article does not contain the demonic/non-demonic distinction).[60] The requirement in the *Carolina* that confessions should be extracted by torture was already normal practice in Russia. The derivative nature of Peter's code was rarely even mentioned in Soviet commentaries on Russian law.

Similar legal provisions can be found in the seventeenth and eighteenth centuries in many parts of Germany, and it must remain a matter of debate to what extent Peter was simply following an established North European model in punishing the practice of magic and witchcraft in his *Voinskii artikul* and to what extent it was a matter of genuine concern to him. Certainly it would appear that Peter was concerned that his military law should be 'European'; on 3 July 1699 his aide General-Major Adam Weide reported to him that all the articles for the new military code were ready, and that he had borne in mind 'what is the custom of other great monarchs'.[61] It may be the case, however, that Peter, or his administrators, had second thoughts about the witchcraft provisions of the military code: in the code of naval law, the *Morskoi ustav* of 1720 (which was compiled from contemporary French, English, Swedish and Dutch naval regulations),[62] the legislation against magic has slipped from first place to chapter 4; it omits the references to gun-spells, satanism, and employing magicians, and associates magic with idolatry, superstition, and blasphemy. The 'interpretation' of this law (each article is followed by an interpretive gloss on how it should be administered) nevertheless still states that that burning is to be the normal punishment of black magicians, poisoners, and blasphemers.[63] This law, however, seems not to have been invoked in recorded witchcraft trials.

The introduction in Russia of a military law condemning witchcraft, outside any supporting framework of Russian legal precedent, is an oddity. And the fact that the two codes of military law contained the first non-ecclesiastical laws in Russia in which magical practices were specifically made a crime with a stipulated punishment, is one reason why soldiers appear fairly often in witchcraft cases in the eighteenth century. Another is that the life of the soldier in Russia was wretched and precarious. In the eighteenth and nineteenth centuries he was taken from his family as a young man and spent all or most of the rest of his life in military service.[64] In this relatively closed society superstitious gossip and alarmist stories flourished and often posed problems for the authorities. The wandering mode of life of the soldier (often deliberately posted to regions far from his home), and perhaps also of the pilgrim, was probably one of the reasons for the relative consistency of superstitious and magical beliefs over the vast distances of Russia and Siberia. In 1721 the first priest of the navy, Markel Radyshevskii, noted in a report that there were large numbers of magical booklets (i.e. spell books) circulating among the officers and men of the army.[65]

The other prominent category of accused persons was the clergy, and for a similar administrative reason, although it must also be admitted that, as discussed earlier, the lower clergy does seem to have been very interested in popular magic[66] – a survey by M.N. Speranskii of privately-owned *florilegia* in the eighteenth century showed that of the four categories of owner, peasants, clergy, merchants, the minor service class, and the military, only the clergy possessed 'magical' texts.[67] The clergy appear not only among the accused but also among the plaintiffs – one priest petitioned the tsar, alleging that a couple had put an evil spell on his daughters.[68]

The effective bureaucratization of the Church under Peter enabled him to introduce measures abolishing the secrecy of confession, on the specific grounds that duty to the state in matters deemed to be of state interest represented the higher good.[69] This and similar requirements more or less turned priests into state informers and, together with the Westernized education of the clergy in the seminaries established in the eighteenth century, went a long way to changing the status of the parish (white) clergy from an uneducated and largely unconsidered element of the Church differing very little in culture from their parishioners, to a half-educated closed caste of badly paid minor functionaries in the employ of the state and largely alienated from their parishioners. (Most priests were sons of priests; the brighter seminarians were often moved into other areas of state service.)

The confusion of civil and ecclesiastical law was made worse by Peter the Great's church reforms. Peter abolished the patriarchate of the Russian Orthodox Church and established, in his *Ecclesiastical Regulation* in 1721, a Synod to govern it instead. This was essentially a branch of the apparatus of the state, and insofar as it served as a court, the distinction between civil and ecclesiastical authority became very blurred, and the Church was deprived of jurisdiction in many areas of law.[70] In particular, the only specific laws against witchcraft in this period are found in the codes of military and naval law mentioned above, although in 1722 the Synod did obtain Peter's confirmation that it had jurisdiction in cases relating to marriage, blasphemy, heresy and *volshebnye dela* (magical matters).[71]

The severe treatment prescribed for those suspected of practising magic continued after Peter; *ukazy* of 20 March 1731 and 25 May 1731, in the reign of the Empress Anna, prescribe death by burning for 'deceivers' who practise magic and the knout or in extreme cases death as the punishment for consulting magicians (the words used indicate that male magicians were envisaged).[72] The use of the word 'deceivers' (*obmanshchiki*) suggests that the law now regarded witchcraft as a species of fraud, even if the punishment was that associated with older views of magic and heresy.

In the eighteenth century the Synodal court dealt with some sixty cases of witchcraft and superstition, and the number of cases dealt with in lower ecclesiastical and criminal courts runs into hundreds.[73] Indeed, in the episcopal oath of 1716 all bishops had to ensure that superstition was not practised in their dioceses, and in Peter's *Ecclesiastical Regulation* (1721), reinforced later by an *ukaz* of Empress Anna in 1737, all bishops and abbots were obliged, under threat of trial for negligence, to send biannual reports to the Synod of any occurrences of witchcraft or superstition which became known to them.[74]

In one such report the Bishop of Suzdal' stated despairingly that he was unable to stem the rising tide of black magic, in particular the cursing of births and weddings, even in his own household. Most bishops were more politic, and evidently deciding to let ubiquitous customs well alone, sent in bland reports that all was well in their dioceses.[75]

It is noteworthy that in the eighteenth century even non-magical religious activity thought to be deviant, such as seeing signs and wonders or prophesying, was liable to be treated as a political issue. This was not without reason since such activities often heralded movements of popular discontent. In 1720 a priest in a Novgorod monastery reported seeing a comet and strange signs in the sky (i.e. signs popularly thought to be portents of the death of the monarch, or of some national disaster). He was sent to the Tainaia kantsellariia, tortured and eventually exiled to the Solovetskii Monastery in the far north (a great fortified monastery on the White Sea which was often used as a place of exile, especially for dissident nobles and clergy).[76] In another even more remote monastery, the Yakut Spasskii Monastery in Iakutia (eastern Siberia) a certain Maksim Malygin was kept in solitary confinement as a punishment for 'secret and blasphemous communing with the Unclean Force'. This was in the early eighteenth century, and his jailers reportedly prevented him from having water, on the ground that the Devil would help him escape into the water, despite his chains and guards.[77] At the end of the reign of Catherine the Great a monk foretold the date and time of the empress's imminent death and was promptly incarcerated in the Schlusselburg fortress; he was released by the perhaps grateful son of Catherine, Paul I, who had little love for his mother, and sent to an 'appropriate' monastery.[78]

* * *

The records of the Synodal court contain a number of interesting examples of cases of alleged witchcraft and the practice of magic, and sometimes give details of how they were were dealt with:

1. Case no. 266(271), 11 May–18 October, 1722. This was sent to the Synod by the Tainaia kantseliariia (in effect the secret police) and concerned Simon, at one time a married deacon, who, after the death of his wife became a monk and for twenty years served as *riznichii* (sacristan, steward) of the bishop's house. He was then sent as abbot to the Kuz'ma Monastery in the Vladimir region. This he left voluntarily and went as an ordinary monk to several other monasteries before returning to become abbot of the Nikolaevo-Pishchegovskaia Pustyn' (monastery). In 1721 he was arraigned for the political indiscretion of paying respect to the nun Elena, the ex-tsaritsa Eudoxia, first wife of Peter the Great, and also for possessing magic *tetradki* (sheets of paper made up as a pamphlet – this the common description of magical texts in these cases) and 'strange letters'. These included the 'Gates of Aristotle of Aristotle of Alexander of Macedon', with instructions on how to tell fortunes by throwing dice, a Divinatory Psalter, a 'Voice of the Prophet Balaam the Wizard', a 'Predictions of the prophet Balaam the wise', a prayer of St Cyprian for driving out evil spirits,[79] a prayer against the Devil, and a letter about the appearance of St Cosmas the Wonder-worker, to whom Simon had made a complaint. The record notes a fact that was evidently thought significant, that some of these documents were in cursive but some were in semi-uncial with rubrication (i.e. had an ecclesiastical appearance). Simon was

also accused of fortune-telling by throwing dice and *zherebeiki* (in this case squares of bread), and other things unbecoming in a monk. Evidently the political crime was on this occasion considered not very important, which is why the case was transferred to the Synod. Simon was forbidden to say mass and exiled for life to the Solovetskii Monastery 'which is on the ocean sea'.[80]

2. Case no. 306(270), 2 June–14 May 1722. Vasilii Efrimov, sexton (*d'iachok*) of the Trinity church in Novgorod, was accused of inventing and publicizing a 'false miracle' (pretending that the icons had sprinkled holy water and burned incense).[81] The Synod referred the case to the Iustits-kollegiia for civil punishment, recommending execution. The Iustits-kollegiia decided on death by fire.[82]

3. Case no. 18(602), 5 January–4 April 1723. Ivan Kraskov, a retired soldier of the Vyborg Regiment, was found to possess suspicious booklets (*tetradi*) and letters, wooden *zherebeiki* (a kind of dice), herbs and roots. He claimed under interrogation that he had found the documents on Vasiliev Island and inherited the *zherebeiki* from his nephew, also a soldier. He had used the *zherebeiki* for two years to foretell his own domestic needs, health, and time of death. He had learned the art from from his cousin, a horse-doctor, and had never told fortunes for anyone else. The herbs too were for his own exclusive use. He denied charges of idol-worship, blasphemy, black magic, putting spells on guns, and communing with the Devil. The regimental doctor gave evidence that the herbs and roots were of genuine medical value and nothing to do with malefic magic. Ivan was sentenced to run the gauntlet six times (which he can hardly have survived) and then do elaborate public penance. The *zherebeiki* were to be burned.[83]

4. Case no. 149(382). A 'false holy fool' called Vassilii, aged twenty, was accused of murder, rape, making the sign of the cross with only two fingers (i.e. the Old Believer practice), doing evil magic (*eretichestvo* – lit. heresy), having devils at his command, of whom the chief was called Herod, and whom he used to jam watermills (such malfunctions were commonly ascribed to witchcraft) and to bring treasure from Greece, Turkey and Sweden. Instead of throwing out this extraordinary farrago the court referred the case to the Iustits-kollegiia (Ministry of Justice) because of the accused's 'wizardry and having devils'.[84]

5. Case no 211(269), 1731. Captain Alexander Bredikhin of the Preobrazhenskii Guards accused Ivan Miakinin, former chief administrator (*landrat*) of Novgorod, of practising magic. The accused was found to possess a variety of spells and prayers for childbirth, bewitching guns and so on, also for having the *Dream of the Virgin*, the *Predictions of Tsar David*, a medical book (*lechebnik*) and a variety of herbs, roots and coloured stones in bags. Miakinin claimed he inherited all these and knew nothing about magic. He was sentenced to do public penance.[85]

6. Case No. 644(741), 1729. A priest was accused of performing marriages within the prohibited degrees of consanguinity and of having 'heretical' letters, including a prayer to Baba Iaga (the evil old witch of Slavonic folklore), and an enticement spell.[86]

7. Case no. 453(452). A priest, Ivan Ivanov, was accused by his bishop of having roots sewn into his collar and hat, and in wax. The bishop was told not to present cases without due form and evidence.[87]

8. Case no. 115(450). A clerk (*pod'iachii*), Fedor Sokolov, was accused of practising magic and was found to possess five love spells.[88]

9. Case no. 229(187). Parodies of the Lord's Prayer were found on a monk.[89]

10. Case no. 501(434). A deacon, Vasilii Ivanov, was found to possess spells for weapons, and against 'heretics' (wizards), bandits, and the Evil Eye. He also owned an apocryphal text (the *Khozhdenie Bogoroditsy po mukam*). Although it was agreed by all that these had simply been left to him in his grandfather's chest, he was found guilty under article 149 of the Army Code.[90]

11. Case no. 434(206), 1731. The deacon Stefan Koz'min of Chernigov Cathedral had been found in possession of magic books (*tetradki*) which included instructions for calling up devils: these specified removing your cross and crushing it under your right heel, removing your belt, denying Christ, the Virgin, the Apostolic Church, the apostles, the twelve great feasts of the Church and your own parents. The devils summoned included Cheremis, Crimean, Saxon and other devils from overseas, with names such as Veliger, Has, Herod, Aspid, Basilisk, Enarei, Semyon, Indik and Khalei. One of the spells ran 'Balaam, Valgel and Galilei (!), cure the servant of God N of this illness, Amen, Amen, Amen'.[91]

12. Case no. 163(361), 1731. Brigadir Dmitrii Poretskii was accused by his wife under the *slovo i delo* procedure for treason. In the evidence it appeared that he beat her and did not live with her. She had placed a spell on his pillow to make him treat her better.[92]

13. Case no. 74(225), 1732. Petr Osipov, an unfrocked priest, was accused of celebrating religious rites illicitly, of living in sin and of possessing magic books.[93]

14. Case no. 17(107), 1734–40. Archimandrite Mitrofan of the Kursk Znamenskii Bogoroditskii Monastery was accused of eighty-nine offences, taking up 486 sheets of evidence, including immorality, luxurious living, sale of church goods, extortion and witchcraft.[94]

15. Case no. 428(286), 1740. Il'ia Chovpilo, the servant of a colonel, was accused of writing, in blood, a pact with the 'prince of devils' for thirty years.[95]

16. Case no. 328(431), 1740. Iakov Iarov was accused of witchcraft. In his possession were found roots, herbs, bones, spells, books of divination, and a dictionary. He was alleged to have told fortunes using dice and the Psalter. Under torture he admitted denying Christ and calling on Satan. He admitted knowing another wizard in Simbirsk. His wife said that he used to turn the icons to face the wall, wore no cross or icon, refused to wash, and when she was pregnant said: 'If it is a boy, give it to the Devil'. Iarov's clients said in his defence that he only healed by using herbs. The case was heard in 1740 but the wizard had already been put to death by burning in 1736.[96]

17. Case no. 294(292), 1746. A peasant was arrested by the St Petersburg police for possessing a copy of the *Dream of the Virgin*. He was sentenced to be whipped 'mercilessly' and sent for hard labour to the Ipatievskii Monastery.[97]

18. Case no. 17(429), 1754. In 1761 a priest and his wife were accused of going to a witch for a spell to enable them to have children.[98]

19. Case no. 528(349), 1754. Porfirii, Bishop of Suzdal', reported that magic and witchcraft were rife and could be found in practically every home, and especially at the time of weddings and childbirth. He wished to be relieved of his duties.[99]

20. Case no. 114(214), 1759. Nikolai Serebriakov, a corporal in the Ingermanland Dragoon Regiment, was found to have a letter to Satanail. He was sentenced by a military court to have his tongue burned through with a hot iron, and then to be burned alive.[100]

21. Case no. 169(61), 1759. A peasant trying to secure the affections of a widow had whispered over a bottle, blown into it, and then given the widow a drink from it. He claimed he did not know that this was magic. He was sentenced to be whipped.[101]

22. Case no. 322(382), 1771. An accusation brought against a boy in Kolomna for using animal cries in magic,[102] – in fact this turned out to be a false accusation designed by a priest to implicate a *d'iachok* who allegedly had put a spell on the priest's wife. A search of the priest's house revealed a quantity of 'magical' texts, including the *Dream of the Virgin*, the *Jerusalem Letter*, various other apocryphal and eschatological texts, a Tsar David text and a herbal.[103]

23. In 1770 a certain state peasant, Artemii Sakalov, in the remote Altai region of Central Asia was arrested on suspicion of being a schismatic and was further

accused under the *slovo i delo* procedure. After interrogation by a church court he was sent on to the provincial chancery of Siberia for investigation of the political charges. These were found to be baseless, but he was sent back to the church court because the interrogation had brought to light a series of religious misdemeanours which the accused himself had written down, before his arrest, in a private list of sins. These included details of banditry, murder, arson, robbing churches and pagan graves, dealing with the Devil, making magic spells by invoking the Devil (whom he called father), Christ, and three of the ancient gods of the Slavs: Perun (whom the court notes identify as a Jewish heretic!), Vikhor' and Koliada! He also interpreted dreams and used beans and the Psalter for divination.[104]

Other cases described in the literature include a soldier, Petr Shestakov, sentenced in 1740 to run the gauntlet for possessing a spell;[105] another soldier, Petr Krylov, accused in 1751 of writing four blasphemous letters in his own blood with the intention of becoming rich and important, claimed he had been taught by a peasant, who in turn said he had obtained an enticement spell addressed to Satan, from a monk.[106] In 1756 priests Makarii Ivanov and Ivan Osipov were expelled from the priesthood and together with Ivanov's brother Stakhei and sexton Ivan Kuz'min were sent to a civil court for punishment after investigation revealed their possession of satanic spells.[107]

It is very noticeable that many of the accused, and accusers, in these cases are persons, sometimes of quite senior rank, in the employ of the State or the Church, and that the accusations were as likely as not to be brought under military law or the older *slovo i delo* provision of denunciation for treason. The accused were usually men; the accusations, however bizarre, were usually supported by evidence (most commonly the possession of herbs and roots, apocryphal texts such as the *Dream of the Virgin*, popular *zagovor* spells); diabolism was occasionally involved. In the case of the Synodal court it is not surprising that many of the cases involved the clergy; the clergy was the one area where the Synod could still claim some jurisdiction and it was a relatively small and tightly organized section of society. Some parallel could perhaps be drawn with the significant proportion of ecclesiastics among those accused of witchcraft in heresy trials in Italy by the Roman Inquisition,[108] although, unlike the Inquisition, which did not allow the evidence of a person accused of witchcraft to be used against others, the Russian practice both before and after Peter's military law seems to have been always to suspect plots and to try to extract from the accused the names of others indulging in the same practices. The situation changed to some extent when counter-accusations by persons condemned to death were disallowed in an *ukaz* of 10 April 1730, which was designed to protect the innocent from malicious accusations.

It should also be borne in mind that before the late eighteenth century there was no academic law or legal profession in Russia; essentially law was the administration of the country by edict of the tsar (*ukaz*) as interpreted by the tsar's officials.[109] Indeed, the attempts at a codification of national law in Muscovy, the *Sudebniki* of 1497 and 1550 and the *Ulozhenie* of 1649, were a mixture of canon law of Byzantine origin, rules for administrative procedure, and political statements about the relationship of the Tsar, the nobility, and the rest of the people. In the *Ulozhenie* the areas of jurisdiction of Church and civil courts are to some extent codified; there is nothing explicit in it concerning witchcraft and magic, although it does introduce measures in chapter 1 against *bogokhul'stvo* (blasphemy and sacrilege). On the other hand the Russian legal historian Tel'berg has argued that the very first words of the first article of chapter 2 of the *Ulozhenie* (i.e. the first chapter to deal with secular law, and specifically with crimes against the majesty, authority, and well-being of the Tsar) 'if anyone should have evil designs against the health of the Tsar' in fact has witchcraft in mind, and specifies death as the penalty. This does seem very probable; it was under this article of the *Ulozhenie* that four men accused in 1689, in the so-called Shaklovityi case, of plotting with magic and 'sending spells on the wind' against the young Peter I and his family were found guilty and executed, by burning at the stake in the case of the two magicians, and by beheading in the case of those who hired them.[110] Tel'berg cites several other cases where it is clear that the 'evil designs' were indeed magical;[111] it would be extraordinary if the new code of law were to contain nothing on the subject, given the fear of witchcraft at the Russian court in the seventeenth century, the nature of the oaths which the servants of the Tsars had to swear, and the fact that accusations in cases of witchcraft had so often a political colouring.

In fact the treatment of those convicted of 'magical' crimes in the eighteenth century was extraordinarily inconsistent; although a convicted person could indeed be whipped, knouted, branded, mutilated, exiled or executed, he could also be let off with a penance or a caution. This could often happen when the case was transferred from a civil to an ecclesiastical court. For example, in a *slovo i delo* (state security) case sent on to an ecclesiastical court in 1727 a certain Roman Krasnolpolskii gave evidence that, wishing to possess women other than his wife, he had copied down a spell from the words of the peasant Moisei Churin. He was to read this letter over salt, put the salt in kvas or food, and give it to girls and women.[112] He swore he had never used it, talked about it or let anyone else copy it (this was always very important as a mitigating factor in such cases). A search of the peasant's hut revealed 'herbs', a copy of *The Dream of the Virgin*, a *zagovor* for going before a judge or important person, another for sowing discord between man and wife, and a *mesechnik* (lit. 'moon book' or possibly 'month book') which gave predictions on good and bad days for travel.[113] In this case the judge, Archbishop Varnava, decided that the accused had caused no harm, there was no petition against him, he was of good repute, and his parish priest reported that he had never confessed to using magic books (an example of how Peter the Great's abolition of the secrecy of the confessional worked in practice). He was sent home on probation (*na poruki*) and told to behave himself in future. He was lucky – one eighteenth-century list of penances specifies 105 prostrations and 230 prayers per day over six years for 'wizardry' which involved no more than casting three bread squares (a kind of dice) and divining with a key and the Psalter.[114]

The Synod was in fact aware of its own inconsistency and in April 1722 requested guidance from the tsar as to how disseminators of superstition should be punished. Peter, ever practical, decided that the appropriate punishment was to slit the nostrils of the guilty person and send him to hard labour in the galley fleet.[115]

Not all cases of magic and witchcraft, however, were referred to the Synodal court. For example, in 1753 a group of peasants on an estate near Suzdal' was arrested for trying to kill the landowner by magic and poison. They had gone to the *vorozheia* Maksim Markov, a former village scribe, to offer him one rouble for a fatal spell. Markov's method was to bewitch a piece of wax by reading a spell-book in front of an icon, doing a somersault over a knife stuck in the floor, and then directing that the wax should be rubbed on the victim's bed, shoes and door threshold. The magician and the plotters, who had also tried arsenic, were arrested and sent to Moscow to the Sysknyi prikaz (criminal investigation office) where they were tried under Empress Anna's *ukaz* of 8 January 1733 forbidding the sale of poisons, and under Peter's military code. After the obligatory torture they confessed. They were condemned to death by burning under Peter's military law and under Anna's *ukaz* of 20 March 1731. This was commuted to seventy blows with the knout, slitting the nostrils and hard labour in the dockyards for life, i.e. Peter's prescription mentioned above.[116]

In Catherine the Great's reign (1762–96) a number of attempts were made to modernize and regularize the law in Russia. An *ukaz* of Empress Elizabeth of 17 May 1744, had established that all convicts condemned to death had to have their sentences suspended and details of the case were to be sent the Senate. In consequence, at the very beginning of Catherine's reign the Ruling Senate received via the Archangel province chancellery a report of a case tried in a local court in which a peasant, Andrei Kozypin, admitted after interrogation and torture that he had learned 'charodeistvo' (enchantment) and 'volshebstvo' (magic in general) in Siberia from a certain Ivan Poskotin. Kozypin stated that Poskotin used to summon devils to perform his magic, and that he, Kozypin, had seen them and had himself used magic to harm ('isportil') some ten persons, men and women. The local court, apparently still following the Petrine instruction, had condemned the man to be knouted, to have his nostrils slit and his forehead and cheeks branded, and to be sent to the galleys. The Ruling Senate was clearly unhappy with this and ordered that Kozypin should be kept under guard until it had received a proper detailed account of the case, including the name of the person who had brought the charge, what measures had then been taken, and whether or not any of the alleged victims of witchcraft had died. It further added that torture was to be used only with the greatest circumspection. (Catherine later abolished it.)

In 1775 the Statute on Provincial Administration (*Uchrezhdenie dlia upravleniia gubernii*) was issued. It included a chapter (26) on the setting up of a 'Conscience

Court', an idea very typical of the Enlightenment, which some have seen as the work of S.E. Desnitskii, pupil of Adam Smith and Russia's first professor of jurisprudence. Among the social ills which the Conscience Court would deal with, and in one sense decriminalize, was the practice of *koldovstvo* (which could embrace the whole area of magic, witchcraft and divination), which it saw as the consequence of ignorance, stupidity and fraud.[117] Catherine's 'Police Statute' (*Ustav blagochiniia ili politseiskii*) of 1782 returns to this subject in article 224, in which it is confirmed that *koldovstvo* and suchlike deceptions arising from ignorance, superstition or fraud are forbidden by law. These include *koldovstvo*, *charodeistvo*, *kurenie* (the second probably means 'casting spells', the third 'enchanting by smoke'),[118] frightening with monstrosities, fortune-telling by air or water, dream interpretation, treasure-hunting by magic, ghost-hunting, whispering over paper, herbs or drink.[119]

Catherine, however, despite her stated intentions, did not overhaul the whole legal system. The first codification of national law since the *Ulozhenie* of 1649 was not made until 1833 when Emperor Nicholas I promulgated the *Svod zakonov Rossiiskoi imperii* based on the work of his chief minister M.M. Speranskii.[120]

Nevertheless, one important new element entered official and legal thinking about witchcraft in eighteenth-century Russia. The condemnation of magical practices, as well as religious fakery within the official church, because of their effect on the simple and gullible, was a prominent feature in Peter the Great's reform of the Russian Orthodox Church. In Peter's case contact with Western, including English, divines and natural philosophers no doubt played a part; in the case of Catherine the influence of Enlightenment writers ensured a similar attitude, although the punishments imposed for superstitious practices throughout the eighteenth century were often anything but enlightened. The concern of legislators with magic and witchcraft as fraud continued in Russia in the nineteenth century: in 1890 a law was introduced which again mentions superstition, ignorance and fraud, and which forbade anyone to claim to be a *koldun*, to tell fortunes or sell magic potions.[121]

I have mentioned above that servants at court, and state officials in the seventeenth century, and soldiers, clerics and officials in the eighteenth, are prominent categories of person accused of witchcraft for whom records survive. Given the social circumstances and legal system under which accusations of witchcraft were made in Russia, the differences between the Russian experience and that of most of the rest of Europe can be seen to be more apparent than real. In fact the vast territory of Imperial Russia was in many respects very under-administered, and offences by serfs were normally dealt with outside the formal structure of the courts.[122] The majority of persons suspected of witchcraft would have been serf villagers who were not necessarily taken to a court in which the written laws of the land were administered. They could have been dealt with summarily by their owners or neighbours, or taken to the local assemblies (*mir* or *obshchina*), which handled many minor local legal disputes, including those involving inheritance and property, under Russian customary law. For example, there are several accounts of persons being put to death for witchcraft in the Ukraine in the eighteenth century: in 1711 ten women were tried by ducking; in 1738 a landowner suspected of witchcraft was beaten and burned to death; a woman under torture admitted to turning herself into a goat or a dog and killing people by invoking spirits; in 1770 a Turk was dipped in tar and burned to death; a Uniate priest was suspected of spreading plague by sorcery and was buried alive. In all these cases it was popular fear, usually of epidemics associated in the popular mind with witchcraft, and not legal process, which led to the killings.[123]

This kind of witch-hunting, especially in rural areas, continued in the nineteenth century, in Russia as elsewhere in Europe.[124] Sometimes quasi-judicial assemblies at local levels could be involved – in the late eighteenth and early nineteenth century the above-mentioned *mir* and *obshchina*, the largely peasant communal units of administration, had judicial functions but employed procedures (e.g. the *sud bozhii* or 'judgment of God' in which the accused had to swear on an icon while being scrutinized closely for any twitch or change in demeanour which might be interpreted as divine condemnation) and concepts of crime which owed more to traditional rural practice than to the enacted law of the land. There are many cases of women being accused of *porcha* (*maleficium*), usually as a result of trying to influence their husbands by magic.[125] Charges of *porcha* in the 1820s–1840s could be referred upwards into the formal legal system as far as the courts of the *guberniia* (major province).

The legal historian Levenstim mentions many cases including the ducking of witches in the 1880s,[126] the burning of witches by peasants in 1879 (the local jury acquitted most of the perpetrators and sentenced the rest to a church penance) and 1889 (in this case on a spit with the consent of her son!), a witch beaten to death in 1894, and *kolduny* killed, sometimes for putting the Evil Eye on weddings, in 1879, 1880, 1888, 1895.[127] In 1880, in the Penza province alone three witches were killed.[128] And women were punished for witchcraft by beating in 1884 and 1886.[129] The Russian folklorist and ethnographer of the beginning of the twentieth century E.N. Eleonskaia was told by a seventy-five-year-old informant in the Mozhaisk area of Moscow province that the whole peasant commune *mir* once gathered together on the feast of Agrafena Kupal'nitsa (24 June) to kill a *prozhinshchitsa*, a witch who blighted rye crops at midnight or midday on that day. They stoned a cat which appeared at the crossroads and was thought to be the transformed witch, and immediately the woman suspected of being the witch fell ill and remained so until she died (twelve years later!).[130] The final absurd detail makes the story all too believable, but its importance lies in the fact that it should have been told at all. Much more recently, in 1997, a woman was killed and another woman and five children injured in an attack on an alleged witch in the village of Terekhovo near Kursk. The police officer in charge of the case remarked: 'You can go anywhere in Russia these days and witchcraft is a daily part of life'.[131]

But as in other periods of history and other countries, neither local hysteria, nor the strictures of the law, nor the preaching of priests, nor the efforts of educationists seem to have had much success in extinguishing the practice of popular magic and divination. These continued to exist under the Soviet regime, despite official hostility to anything which could be labelled superstition (including any organized religion, Freudian and Jungian psychology, genetics, cybernetics), and in the post-Soviet conditions of *laissez-faire*, ideological collapse and the influence of frivolous Western New Ageism, with the help of unscrupulous entrepreneurs, they are positively flourishing.

Notes

1. Valerie Flint in her *The Rise of Magic in Early Medieval Europe*, which gives a good overview of a very wide range of sources, goes as far as to claim that the medieval Church abandoned its opposition to magic and divination and began instead to make active use of them. This view, curiously advanced in an emotional New Age interpretation, is unsupported by serious evidence, and ignores the history of the topic in the Orthodox Churches, but there is sufficient confusion among Christian writers, and sufficient evidence of the magical interests of individual members of the clergy, at least to lend some slight colour to the idea.

2. For an old but still useful general survey see *ERE*, IV, s.v. *Divination (Christian)*; for more recent discussions see Barb, 'Survival of the Magic Arts'; Aune, 'Magic in Early Christianity'; Kieckhefer, *Magic in the Middle Ages*, pp. 36–42: 'Magic, Early Christianity, and the Graeco-Roman World'.

3. Kieckhefer, *Forbidden Rites*, p. 11.

4. For a translation of the text see *Edificatory Prose of Kievan Russia*, pp. 33–4, 81, 87–8.

5. Beneshevich, *Pamiatniki*, col. 4, art. 7.

6. Smirnov, *Materialy*, p. 10.

7. Ibid., p. 41.

8. Ibid., p. 65.

9. Ibid., pp. 45–7. Intent by a wife to murder her husband with *zelie* is one of the grounds for granting a man a divorce, according to the eleventh-century canon law code of Iaroslav, which resurfaces in many later collections of ecclesiastical law: see Sreznevskii, *Slovar'*, s.v. *zelie*.

10. See Fennell, *History of the Russian Church*, pp. 56, 58.

11. *Stoglav*, ch. 41, pp. 128, 142. Cf. the practice in the later sixteenth century of the *benandanti* of Friuli described in Ginzburg, *The Night Battles*, p. 163; and see Ch. 9.2.

12. For a good overview of this topic see Wilson, 'Witchcraft and Heresy'. On the development of the association from the time of the early Church with particular reference to Dualism and the Orthodox tradition see Yuri Stoyanov, 'The Magus as Heresiarch'. Kieckhefer has very useful things to say about 'The Inquistion' as a 'mythical entity of polemic literature' in 'The Office of Inquisition and Medieval Heresy'.

13. See Barb, 'The Survival of Magic Arts'; MacMullen, *Enemies of the Roman Order*, ch. 3 and 4; and a flurry of more recent pieces including: Castello, 'Cenni sulla repressione del reato di magia'; Trombley, *Hellenic Religion and Christianization*, ch. 1, iv, 'The Legislation against Sorcery'; Shlosser, 'Pagans into Magicians'; Greer, *Fear of Freedom*, esp. pp. 119–24; Montero, *Política y adivinación*.

14. See Luck, *Arcana mundi*, p. 256.

15. For the background to this incident see Perrie, *Pretenders and Popular Monarchism*, p. 15.

16. For a useful survey of this topic see Morton Smith, 'How Magic was Changed by the Triumph of Christianity'. Eve Levin, in her detailed study of Orthodox Slav attitudes to sex, states bluntly that Slav

Orthodox writers did not distinguish between witchcraft and paganism: Levin, *Sex and Society*, p. 42.

17. On this link see Ch. 9.

18. A useful list of cases was given by that curious connoisseur of esoterica Montague Summers in the introduction to his English translation of the *Malleus maleficarum*, London, 1928, pp. xi–xii.

19. Geitler, *Euchologium. Glagolski spomenik manastira Sinai brda*, f. 105v.

20. Dubler, *Abū Ḥāmīd*, p. 63.

21. Alexander, 'Incantations', p. 344, notes that the practice is as old as the Code of Hammurabi. See also Zguta, 'Ordeal by Water' for wider discussion of this practice among the Slavs.

22. *Sudebniki XV–XVI vekov*, p. 9.

23. *Sudebniki XV–XVI vekov*, pp. 354, 384.

24. Popov, *Sud i nakazaniia*, p. 130.

25. *Polnoe sobranie russkikh letopisei*, X, s.a.

26. See Butler, 'Foreign Impressions of Russian Law', p. 81, quoting Herberstein and Fletcher.

27. See Haney, *From Italy to Muscovy*, pp. 67–70.

28. At pp. 148–9 in the record of the trials published in Pokrovskii, *Sudnye spiski*.

29. Fennell, *The Correspondence between Prince A.M. Kurbsky and Tsar Ivan IV*, pp. 2–3, 68–9.

30. Skrynnikov, *Ivan the Terrible*, pp. 20, 163–5. The details of the events described are not firmly established and are partially derived from anecdotal stories.

31. For a good overview see Golikova, 'Organizatsiia politicheskogo syska v Rossii XVI–XVII vv.'

32. See the third edition of the Soviet encyclopedia, *Bol'shaia sovetskaia entsiklopediia*, s.v.

33. Eleonskaia, *Zagovor*, reprint pp. 100–1. For 'spells on the wind' see Ch. 2.3.2.

34. Quoted from *FRE*, III, col. 466a.

35. See Perrie, *Pretenders and Popular Monarchism*, pp. 15 and 28.

36. Tel'berg, *Ocherki politicheskogo suda*, p. 67.

37. Min'ko, *Sueveriia*, p. 27. Min'ko gives no detailed evidence for this claim, but lists a number of doctors who were in fact executed for sorcery.

38. Min'ko. *Sueveriia*, p. 23.

39. Kivelson, 'Patrolling the Boundaries', gives an interesting examination of cases of this kind, though even in these cases the accusation was often by a master against a servant.

40. Uspenskii, 'Tsar and Pretender', esp. pp. 273–6. For a good survey of the materials relating to Dmitrii and magic see Perrie, *Pretenders and Popular Monarchism*, pp. 55–6, 67–8, 76–7, 91–104, 112–13, 110, 242. For discussion of an alternative binary approach to cultural equivalence – 'witch'/'saint' – see Kieckhefer, 'The Holy and the Unholy'.

41. Thus in the *Chronograph of 1617*, *PLDR XVI–XVII*, pp. 328, 332. The first attested use of *tsygan* 'gypsy' is 1558 (Vasmer, *Ètimologicheskii slovar'*, s.v.) – the association with magic is interesting in view of the later reputation of gypsies as fortune-tellers in Russia.

42. Massa, *A Short History*, p. 148.

43. Danilov, *Drevnie rossiiskie stikhotvoreniia*, pp. 79, 81.

44. For the association of magpies and witches see pp. 80–1.

45. There are certainly records for witchcraft cases in the seventeenth century: see Bibliography for Novombergskii, Cherepnin, Zguta, Kivelson.

46. This important addition to the number of known witchcraft trials in Russia was published by Valerie A. Kivelson in 1991: see her 'Through the Prism of Witchcraft: Gender and Social Change in Seventeenth-Century Muscovy'.

47. Muchembled, 'Satanic Myths', p. 160. See also for England: Thomas, *Religion and the Decline of Magic*, index, s.v. *conspiracy*. Perhaps the most modern case involving both England and Russia is that of Aleister Crowley who offered, via Walter Duranty, the *New York Times* correspondent in Moscow, to provide the Soviet Union with a new magical religion to help extirpate the Orthodox Church. See Ryan, 'The Great Beast', p. 156.

48. Golikova, 'Organizatsiia politicheskogo syska v Rossii XVI–XVII vv.', p. 31.

49. Moscow, RGADA, fond 6, ed. khr. 3.

50. Longworth, *Alexis*, p. 199.

51. Moscow, RGADA, fond 6, ed. khr. 7. Fears of poisoning at court continued into the eighteenth century, when Peter the Great had his recently deceased physician Erskine (Areskin) opened up to see if he had been poisoned. Peter's scientific curiosity and peculiar sense of humour no doubt also played a role.

52. Longworth, *Alexis*, p. 221; Golikova, 'Organizatsiia politicheskogo syska v Rossii XVI–XVII vv.', p. 33.

53. Kotoshikhin, *O Rossii*, fols 171–2.

54. See Hughes, *Russia and the West*, pp. 80–8.

55. *Rozysknye dela o Fedore Shaklovitom i ego soobshchnikakh*, III, cols 1235–71.

56. See *Rossiiskoe zakonodatel'stvo X–XX vekov. 4. Zakonodatel'stvo perioda stanovleniia absoliutizma*, pp. 328–9.

57. Popov, *Sud i nakazaniia*, p. 370.

58. See Bobrovskii, *Voennoe pravo v Rossii pri Petre Velikom*, pp. 134–5, 144–5, 158–60. Bobrovskii concludes that the relevant articles of Peter's code are in fact derived from Swedish and German codes. As far as I can discover, subsequent Russian and Soviet legal historians have ignored Bobrovskii's findings on this point, although he is quoted extensively by Epifanov on other aspects of Peter's military law: Epifanov, 'Voinskii Ustav Petra Velikogo'. This was the main Soviet study of Peter's military law, and appearing as it did just after the Second World War and in the middle of the Stalin cult of personality, was mainly concerned to rebut bourgeois falsifications about foreign influences and credit Peter personally with creating a military code and practice which culminated in the victories of the Red Army under Stalin. He does not discuss articles 1 and 2. The several non-Russian historians who have discussed Peter's military law have been interested primarily in comparative law or administrative reform, and as far as I can discover have not dealt with this issue either.

59. For some discussion of the *Carolina* in English see Esmein, *A History of Continental Criminal Procedure*, p. 305 ff.

60. See Midelfort, *Witch Hunting in South Western Germany 1562–1684*, pp. 22–3 for some discussion of the effect of the *Carolina* in legal attitudes to witchcraft.

61. Voskresenskii, *Zakonodatel'nye akty Petra I*, p. 29. General Adam Weide was one of Peter's inner circle. He had been an officer of the Preobrazhenskii regiment and had been one of those who were sent abroad by Peter to study foreign military methods, and had arranged Peter's trip to England in 1698. He was much involved in the administrative reforms of Peter's reign, in particular the introduction of the collegial system based on the Swedish model (he had been a prisoner-of-war in Sweden), and the recruitment of foreign specialists, including experienced lawyers. In 1717 he was appointed Vice-President of the College of War under Prince Alexander Menshikov.

62. See Peterson, *Peter the Great's Administrative and Judicial Reforms*, p. 406. This book also deals with the *Voinskii artikul*, but there is no discussion of the witchcraft provisions.

63. *Pamiatniki russkogo prava*, 8, Moscow, 1961, p. 485.

64. From the time of Peter up to 1793 military service was for an indefinite period 'so long as one's health and strength allow', thereafter twenty-five years until this was reduced in 1834 to twenty: see Keep, *Soldiers of the Tsar*, pp. 156, 334.

65. Smilianskaia, '"Suevernaia" knizhitsa', p. 33.

66. And not only in Russia. Thomas (*Religion and the Decline of Magic*, p. 274) remarks of late medieval and early modern England: 'Friars and chaplains were invariably involved in the political conspiracies of the fifteenth century which made any use of magical aids. It is a striking feature of the sorcery cases recorded in the early sixteenth century that the participants so often included a priest'.

67. Speranskii, *Rukopisnye sborniki XVIII veka*, pp. 86–92.

68. Eleonskaia, *Zagovor*, reprint, p. 101.

69. For some discussion see Cracraft, *Church Reform*, pp. 238–43.

70. See Cracraft, *The Church Reform of Peter the Great*, esp. pp. 100–7.

71. Ibid., p. 191.

72. *PSZ*, VIII, No. 5761.

73. Smilianskaia, 'Doneseniia 1754 g.', p. 255.

74. *Polnoe sobranie zakonov*, I, no. 7450.

75. Smilianskaia, 'Doneseniia 1754 g.', p. 256, n. 9.

76. Semevskii, *Slovo i delo! 1700–1725*, pp. 37–42.

77. Shorokhov, *Korporativnoe zemlevladenie*, pp. 38–9.

78. *Zapiski . . . I.V. Lopukhina*, pp. 84–5.

79. Cyprian had himself been a magician and employer of devils – see p. 13.

80. *Opisanie dokumentov i del*, cols. 272–6.

81 Ibid., col. 346. One of the objects of Peter's Church reform of 1721 (the *Dukhovnyi reglament*) was to prevent such impostures and abuses of religion: for the English text see Cracraft, *For God and Peter the Great*, pp. 26–9, 37–8, 57, 106–7, 141.

82. *Polnoe sobranie postanovlenii*, I, no. 250, pp. 301–7.

83. *Opisanie dokumentov i del*, 3 (1723), cols. 11–13.

84. Ibid., 3, col. 175.

85. Ibid., 5 (1725), col. 361.

86. Ibid., 8 (1728), col. 612. The spell is published in Smilianskaia, 'Zagovory', p. 368. On Baba Iaga see Cherepanova, *Mifologicheskaia leksika*, pp. 99–109; Kondrat'eva, *Metamorfozy sobstvennogo imeni*, s.v.

87. *Opisanie dokumentov i del*, 8 (1728), cols 439–40.

88. Ibid., col. 105.

89. Ibid., 9 (1729), col. 346.

90. Ibid., col. 698.

91. Ibid., 10 (1730), cols 693–4, 1306–7.

92. Ibid., 11 (1731), col. 202.

93. Ibid., 12 (1732), col. 132.

94. Ibid., 14 (1734), col. 17. The case was not concluded until 1740.

95. Ibid., col. 529.

96. Ibid., 20 (1740), cols. 331–3.

97. Ibid., 26 (1746), col. 455.

98. Ibid., 34 (1754).

99. Ibid., col. 482.

100. Ibid., 39 (1759), col. 377.

101. Ibid., col. 220.

102. The accusation of making animal cries, associated with the hysterical *klikushi*, and considered to be a consequence of *porcha* (Evil Eye or other kinds of malefic magic), was common in witchcraft cases in the seventeenth century also: see Cherepnin, 'Iz istorii drevnerusskogo koldovstva XVII v.', pp. 95–6.

103. *Opisanie dokumentov i del*, 50 (1770), col. 413.

104. See Pokrovskii, 'Ispoved' altaiskogo krest'ianina'.

105. The spell is published in Smilianskaia, 'Zagovory', p. 364.

106. Loc. cit.

107. The spell is published in Smilianskaia, 'Zagovory', pp. 364–6, 600.

108. See Tedeschi, 'Inquisitorial Law', p. 85.

109. For an overview in English see de Madariaga, 'Penal Policy'.

110. The complicated case is summarized in Truvorov, 'Volkhvy i vorozhei', pp. 711–12.

111. Tel'berg, *Ocherki politicheskogo suda*, pp. 61–8 (esp. 67–80). This interpretation is supported by Golikova, 'Organizatsiia politicheskogo syska v Rossii XVI–XVII vv.', pp. 33–4.

112. 'Whispering over paper, herbs and drink' were among the magical practices listed as criminal offences under Catherine the Great in the later eighteenth century: see below.

113. Popov, 'Rozysk o Moisee Churine'.

114. See Vostokov, *Opisanie*, p. 551.

115. *PSZ*, VI, 3963; Cracraft, *Church Reform*, p. 292. The galley fleet, established by Peter the Great on Italian models and continuing in existence until the early years of the nineteenth century, was an important element in Russian sea power. It was administratively separate from the 'ship' navy (*Morskoi flot*, lit. 'sea fleet') and was largely manned by convicted criminals.

116. Beliaev, 'Bytovye ocherki'.

117. See *Rossiiskoe zakondatel'stvo X–XX vekov*, vol. 5: *Zakonodatel'stvo perioda rasstsveta absoliutizma*, Moscow, 1897, pp. 275, 316. An English law of 1736 makes it illegal to *pretend* to use witchcraft; the English *Fraudulent Mediums Act* of 1951 is similarly concerned with those who *fraudulently* claim to be mediums or to possess supernatural powers.

118. Smoke divination is very ancient, but not, so far as I can discover recorded elsewhere in Russian contexts, except for a very simple methods of marriage and weather divination – see Ch. 4.5.2. What is meant here is probably the practice of putting spells on weapons by means of fumigation, usually with smoke from some 'magic' herb.

119. *PSZ*, XX, No. 14392; XXI, No. 1539.

120. This was the *Polnoe sobranie zakonov rossiiskoi imperii*, published in 1830 and containing more than 30,000 laws arranged chronologically from 1649 to 1825.

121. *Ustav*, st. 30–31, izd. 1890. Popov, *Sud i nakazaniia*, p. 383.

122. Hartley, *Social History of the Russian Empire*, p. 111, also p. 124: 'Policing of the countryside remained largely outside the control of the state, and, as far as it existed at all, it was conducted by landowners among their serfs or by peasant communities themselves'.

123. Antonovich, *Koldovstvo*, pp. 18, 26; Alexander, *Bubonic Plague*, pp. 30, 107, 113.

124. For details of some cases see Worobec, 'Witchcraft Beliefs and Practices'.

125. See Minenko, *Russkaia krest'ianskaia obshchina*, pp. 151–3. Minenko also notes the significant fact that the accused were usually incomers to the area.

126. Levenstim, 'Sueverie', 1, pp. 157–219 (204–5).

127. Ibid., p. 181.

128. Ibid., p. 185.

129. Ibid., p. 201.

130. Eleonskaia, 'Zapisi obychaev i obriadov', p. 221.

131. Michael Specter, '"Sorcery" and a Murder in a Forgotten Village', *International Herald Tribune*, April 7, 1997, p. 2.

Fig. 1 Russian costumes including that of a fortune-teller (3).
(From Thomas Bankes, *A New . . . System of Universal Geography*, London, c. 1792)

Fig. 2   Russian New Year marriage divination with chickens.
(From a nineteenth-century Russian popular print)

Fig. 3   Russian New Year divination.
(From a nineteenth-century Russian popular print)

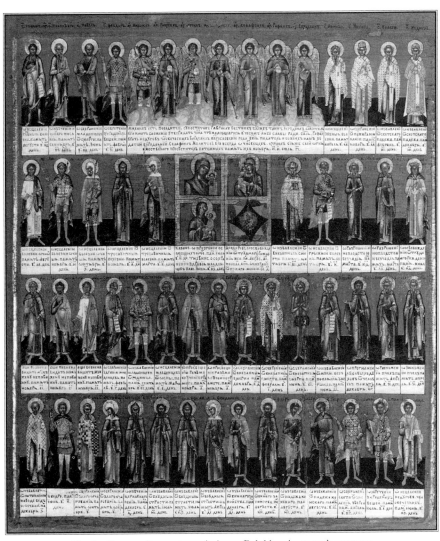

Fig. 4   Composite apotropaic icon. Palekh, nineteenth century.
(Courtesy of Christie's, London)

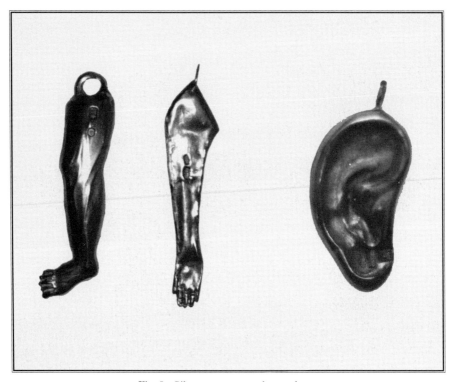

Fig. 5   Silver *ex-voto* arm, leg and ear.
(Elworthy Collection, Pitt Rivers Museum, Oxford)

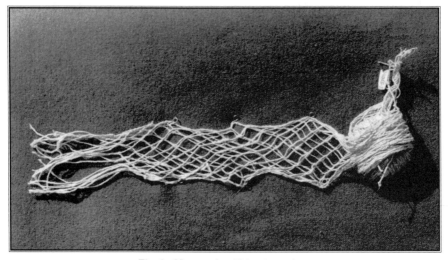

Fig. 6   Net amulet Vologda region.
(Ethnographic Museum, St Petersburg)

Fig. 7   Russian pectoral crosses for a woman (left) and a man.
(Elworthy Collection, Pitt Rivers Museum, Oxford)

Fig. 8   The wonder-working icon of the Virgin of Akhtyrka. Eighteenth century.
(Russian popular print)

Fig. 9 A *zmeevik* amulet, the so-called 'Chernigov *grivna*'. Eleventh century.
(State Historical Museum, Moscow)

Fig. 10 A composite pendant amulet
?Nineteenth century.
(Ethnographic Museum, St Petersburg)

Fig. 11   The *triasavitsy* (daughters of Herod, personifications of fevers) with St Sisinnius,
the four Evangelists and St Michael.
(Russian popular icon)

Fig. 12   'Herod's daughters': dolls representing *triasavitsy* (fever demons). Twentieth
century.
(Ethnographic Museum, St Petersburg)

Fig. 13 The 'Passport to Heaven' or letter to St Peter. Engraving by Bernard Picart, 1732.
(From *Cérémonies et coutumes religieuses de tous les peuples du monde*, Amsterdam, 1733)

Fig. 14   Printed text of the 'Passport to Heaven'. Eighteenth century.
(Dimsdale Collection. Courtesy of Mr Robert Dimsdale)

Fig. 15 'Circle of Solomon'. 1879.

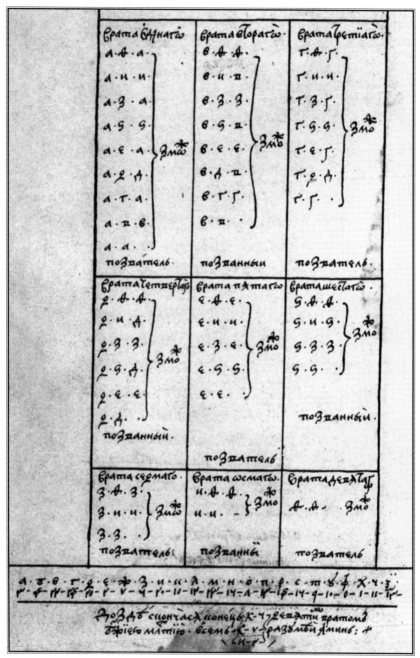

Fig. 16   Onomantic table from the Russian version of the pseudo-Aristotelian *Secretum secretorum*. Sixteenth century.

(Oxford, Bodleian Library, MS Laud Misc. 45, p. 48)

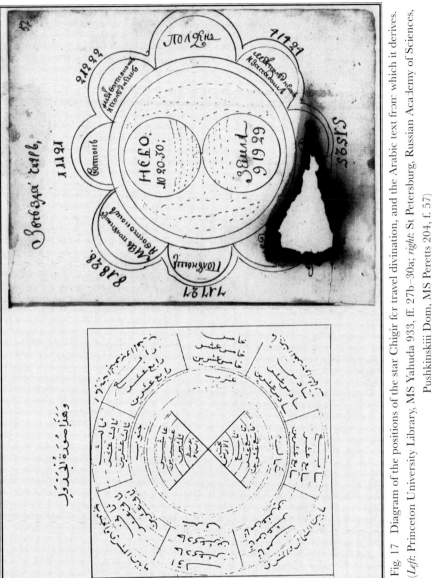

Fig. 17 Diagram of the positions of the star Chigir for travel divination, and the Arabic text from which it derives. (*Left*: Princeton University Library, MS Yahuda 933, ff. 27b–30a; *right*: St Petersburg, Russian Academy of Sciences, Pushkinskiĭ Dom, MS Peretts 204, f. 57)

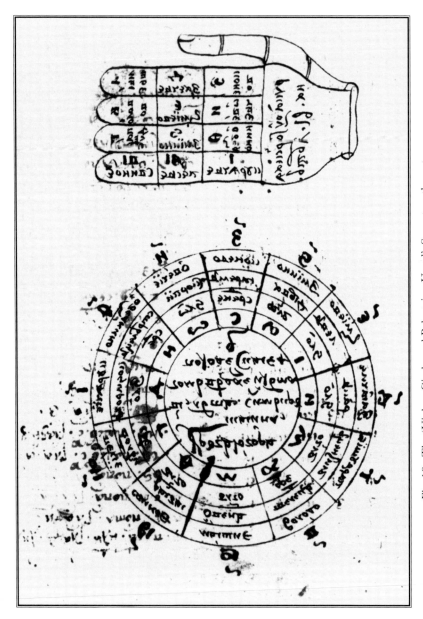

Fig. 18   The 'Uighur Circle and Polovtsian Hand'. Seventeenth century.
(Library of the Russian Academy of Sciences, St Petersburg, MS Arkh. C. 204, f. 170v.

LIST OF WORKS CITED

Abaev, V.I.: 'Obraz Viia v povesti N. V. Gogolia', *Russkii fol'klor. Materialy i issledovaniia*, III, Moscow–Leningrad, 1959, pp. 363–8.

Abagar na Filip Stanislavov, Rim, 1651, ed. B. Raikov, Sofia, 1979.

Abbott, G.F.: *Macedonian Folklore*, Cambridge, 1903.

Abraham, Lyndy: 'Arthur Dee, 1579–1651: A Life', *Cauda Pavonis*, n.s. 13, 2, 1994, pp. 1–14.

Abramov, I.: 'Chernigovskie malorossi. Byt i pesni naseleniia Glukhovskogo uezda Chernigovskoi gubernii', *Zhivaia starina*, 1905, p. 548ff.

Acta Ioannis, ed. T. Zahn, Erlangen, 1880 (repr. Hildesheim, 1975).

Addabbo, Anna Maria: 'Le formule magico-mediche dei ricettari tardo latini', *Atti e memorie della Colombaria*, LVIII, n.s. XLIV, 1993, pp. 133–51.

Adler, William: *Time Immemorial. Archaic History and its Sources in Christian Chronography from Julius Africanus to George Syncellus*, Dumbarton Oaks Papers XXVI, Washington DC, 1989.

Adon'eva, S.V. and Ovchinnikova, O.A.: *Traditsionnaia russkaia magiia v zapisiakh kontsa XX veka*, St Petersburg, 1993.

Afanas'ev, A.N.: 'Iazycheskie predaniia ob ostrove Buiane', *Vremennik Obshchestva istorii i drevnostei rossiiskikh*, 1851, kn. 9, pp. 1–24.

Afanas'ev, A.N.: *Narodnye russkie legendy*, Novosibirsk, 1990 (reprint of Moscow, 1859).

Afanas'ev, A.N.: *Narodnye russkie skazki*, 3 vols, Moscow, 1984–5 (reprint of 1855–64).

Afanas'ev, A.N.: *Poèticheskie vozzreniia slavian na prirodu*, 3 vols, Moscow, 1865–9.

Afanas'ev, A.N.: *Russkie zavetnye skazki*, Moscow, 1991 (reprint of Geneva, 1862).

Agapitos, Panagiotis A.: 'The Erotic Bath in the Byzantine Vernacular Romance *Kallimachos and Chrysorrhoe*', *Classica et Medievalia*, XLI, 1990, pp. 257–73.

Agapkina, T.A.: 'Slavianskie obriady i verovaniia, kasaiushchikhsia menstruatsii', in *Seks i èrotika v russkoi traditsionnoi kul'ture*, ed. A.L. Toporkov, Moscow, 1996, pp. 103–50.

Ainalov, D.: 'Ocherki i zametki po istorii drevne-russkogo iskusstva. V. Kolomenskii dvorets', *IORIaS*, 18, 3, 1913, pp. 103–19.

Aksakov, S.T.: *Chronicles of a Russian Family*, London, 1924 (original Russian published in 1856).

Aksenton, Iu. D.: 'Svedeniia o dragotsennykh kamniakh v Izbornike Sviatoslava 1073 g. i nekotorykh drugikh pamiatnikakh', in *Izbornik Sviatoslava 1073. Sbornik statei*, Moscow, 1977, pp. 280–92.

Albertus Magnus, being the approved, Verified, Sympathetic and Natural Egyptian Secrets; or White and Black Art for Man and Beast Translated from the German, ?New York, c. 1880.

Albertus Magnus [pseudo]: *The Book of Secrets of Albertus Magnus of the Virtues of Herbs, Stones, and certain Beasts, also a Book of the Marvels of the World*, ed. Michael R. Best and Frank H. Brightman, Oxford, 1973.

Al-Biruni: *Al-Biruni's Book on Pharmacy and Materia Medica*, ed. Hakim Mohammed Said, Karachi, 1973.

Alcock, A.: 'A Coptic Magical Text', *Bulletin of the American Society of Papyrologists*, XIX, 1982, pp. 97–103.

Aleksandriia. Roman ob Aleksandre Makedonskom po russkoi rukopisi XV veka, ed. M.N. Botvinnik, Ia. S. Lur'e, O.V Tvorogov, Moscow–Leningrad, 1965.

Aleksandryia, ed. U.V. Anichenka, Minsk, 1962.

Alekseev, M.P.: *Slovari inostrannykh iazykov v russkom azbukovnike XVII veka*, Leningrad, 1968.

Alexander, J.T.: *Bubonic Plague in Early Modern Russia*, Baltimore, 1980.

Alexander, Paul J.: 'The Diffusion of Byzantine Apocalypses in the Medieval West and the Beginnings of Joachimism', in *Prophecy and Millenarianism: Essays in Honour of Marjorie Reeves*, London, 1980, pp. 55–106.

Alexander, Paul J.: *The Byzantine Apocalyptic Tradition*, Berkeley and London, 1985.

Alexander, P.S.: 'Incantations and Books of Magic', in Emil Schurer, *The History of the Jewish People in the Age of Jesus Christ (175 B.C.–A.D. 135)*, revised and enlarged English version edited by Geza Vermes, Fergus Millar, Martin Goodman, III, 1, Edinburgh, 1986, pp. 342–79.

Almazov, A.I.: *Tainaia ispoved' v pravoslavnoi vostochnoi tserkvi*, Odessa, 1894.

Alpatov, M.V.: *Freski tserkvi Uspeniia na Volotovom Pole*, Moscow, 1977.

Al-Ṭabarī: *The History of al-Ṭabarī*, ed. Franz Rosenthal, I, New York, 1989.

Ancient Christian Magic: Coptic Texts of Ritual Power, ed. Marvin Meyer and Richard Smith, New York, 1994.

Andersen, J.: *The Witch on the Wall. Medieval Erotic Sculpture in the British Isles*, Copenhagen, 1971.

Anderson, F.I.: *German Book Illustration through 1500. Herbals*, New York, 1983.

Andreev, N.P.: *Russkii fol'klor*, Moscow–Leningrad, 1936.

Andreeva, M.A.: 'Politicheskii i obshchestvennyi èlement vizantiisko-slavianskikh gadatel'nykh knig', *Byzantinoslavica*, II, 1930, pp. 47–73, 395–415; III, 1931, pp. 430–61; IV, 1932, pp. 65–84.

Anichkov, E.V.: *Istoriia russkoi literatury*, Moscow, 1908.

Anikin, I.L.: 'K proiskhozhdeniiu pamiatnikov vrachebnoi pis'mennosti', *Sovetskoe zdravo-okhranenie*, 1986, 5, pp. 67–9.

Antologiia pedagogicheskoi mysli Drevnei Rusi i Russkogo gosudarstva XIV–XVII vv., ed. S. D. Babishin, B. N. Mitiurova, Moscow, 1985.

Antonova, V.I., and Mneva, N.E.: *Katalog drevnei russkoi zhivopisi*, 2 vols, Moscow, 1963.

Antonovich, V.B.: *Koldovstvo. Dokumenty protsessy izsledovanie*, St Petersburg, 1877.

Apian, Peter: *Instrumentbuch*, Ingolstadt, 1533.

Appleby, J.H.: 'Arthur Dee and Johannes Bánfi Hunyades: Further Information on their Alchemical and Professional Activities', *Ambix*, 24, 2, 1977, pp. 96–109.

Appleby, J.H.: 'Some of Arthur Dee's Associations before Visiting Russia Clarified, including Two Letters from Sir John Mayerne', *Ambix*, 26, 1, 1979, pp. 1–15.

Appleby, J.H.: *A Selective Index to Siberian, Far Eastern, and Central Asian Russian Materia Medica*, Research Publications of the Wellcome Unit, no. VIII, Oxford, 1987.

Apuleius: *Apulei Apologia, sive pro se magia liber*, ed. H.E. Butler and A.S. Owen, Oxford, 1914 (reprint Hildesheim, 1967).

Apuleius: *Metamorphoses*, ed. and trans. J.A. Hanson, 2 vols, Cambridge, Mass., 1989.

Apuleius: *The Works of Apuleius*, London, 1888.

Arber, Agnes: *Herbals*, Cambridge, 1986.

Arkhangelskii, A.S.: 'K izucheniiu drevne-russkoi literatury', *Zhurnal Ministerstva narodnogo prosveshcheniia*, 1888, July.

Arkhipov, A.A.: 'O proiskhozhdenii drevneslavianskoi tainopisi', *Sovetskoe slavianovedenie*, 1980, 6, pp. 79–81.

Arkhipov, A.A.: *Drevnerusskaia Kniga Proroka Daniila v perevode s drevneevreiskogo*, chast' 1, Institut russkogo iazyka AN SSSR, Predvaritel'nye publikatsii, CLI, Moscow, 1982, reprinted in *idem, Po tu storony Sambationa.*

Arkhipov, A.A.: *Iz istorii gebraizmov v russkom knizhnom iazyke XV–XVI vekov* (avtoreferat), Moscow, 1982, reprinted in *idem, Po tu storony Sambationa.*

Arkhipov, A.A.: *Po to storonu Sambationa. Etiudy o russko-evreiskikh kul'turnykh, iazykovykh i literaturnykh kontaktakh v X–XVI vekakh,* Monuments of Early Russian Literature 9, Oakland, Cal., 1995.

Armstrong, Terence: *Yermak's Campaign in Siberia,* Hakluyt Society, second ser. 146, London, 1975.

Arsenii: *Opisanie slavianskikh rukopisei biblioteki Sviato-troitskoi Sergievoi Lavry,* I, Moscow, 1878.

Artsikhovskii, A.V. and Ianin, V.L.: *Novgorodskie gramoty na bereste (iz raskopok 1962–1976),* Moscow, 1978.

Astakhova, A.: '"Sound Shaping" of East Slavic Zagovory', *Oral Tradition,* 7, 2, 1992, pp. 365–72.

Aune, David E.: 'The Apocalypse of John and Graeco-Roman Revelatory Magic', *New Testament Studies,* XXXIII, 1987, pp. 481–501.

Aune, David E.: 'Magic in Early Christianity', *Aufstieg und Niedergang der römischen Welt,* II, 23, Berlin New York, 1980, pp. 1507–57.

d'Auteroche, Chappe: *Voyage en Sibérie,* 4 vols, Paris, 1678.

Baehr, S.L.: '"Fortuna Redux": The Iconography of Happiness in Eighteenth-Century Russian Courtly Spectacles', in *Great Britain and Russia in the Eighteenth Century: Contacts and Comparisons,* ed. A.G. Cross, Newtonville, Mass., 1979, pp. 109–22.

Baehr, S.L.: 'The Masonic Component in Eighteenth-Century Russian Literature', *Russian Literature in the Age of Catherine the Great,* ed. A. Cross, Oxford, 1976, pp. 121–39.

Baehr, S.L.: *The Paradise Myth. Utopian Patterns in Early Secular Russian Literature and Culture,* Stanford, 1991.

Bagatti, B.: 'I Giudeo-cristiani e l'anello di Salomone', *Recherches de science religieuse,* LX, 1972, pp. 151–60.

Balaban, M.: 'Evrei-vrachi v Krakove i tragedii getto XV–XVII v.', *Evreiskaia starina,* 1912, 1, pp. 38–53.

Baldaev, D.S., Belko, V. K., Isupov, I.M.: *Slovar' tiuremno-lagerno-blatnogo zhargona,* Moscow, 1992.

Baldwin, Martha R.: 'Toads and Plague: Amulet Therapy in Seventeenth-Century Medicine', *Bulletin of the History of Medicine,* 67, 1993, pp. 227–47.

Balov, A.: 'Ocherk Poshekhon'ia. 3. Narodnye gadaniia', *Ètnograficheskoe obozrenie,* 39, 1898, 4, pp. 69–81.

Baranov, E.Z.: *Moskovskie legendy,* Moscow, 1993.

Barb, A.: 'Antaura, the Mermaid and the Devil's Grandmother', *Journal of the Warburg and Courtauld Institutes,* XXIX, 1966, pp. 1–24.

Barb, A.: 'Birds and Medical Magic', *Journal of the Warburg and Courtauld Institutes,* 13, 1950, pp. 316–22.

Barb, A.: 'Der Heilige und die Schlangen', *Mitteilungen der Anthropolog. Ges. in Wien,* 82, 1952, pp. 1–21.

Barb, A.: 'Mystery, Myth, and Magic', in *The Legacy of Egypt,* Oxford, 1971, pp. 142–7.

Barb, A.: 'The Survival of the Magic Arts', in Arnaldo Momigliano, ed., *The Conflict between Paganism and Christianity in the Fourth Century,* Oxford, 1963, pp. 110–25.

Barb, A.: 'Three Elusive Amulets', *Journal of the Warburg and Courtauld Institutes,* 27, 1964, pp. 1–22.

Barber, P: *Vampires, Burial, and Death: Folklore and Reality,* New Haven and London, 1988.

Baring, Maurice: *What I saw in Russia,* London, 1927.

Baron, Salo Wittmayer: *A Social and Religious History of the Jews. Late Middle Ages and Era of European Expansion 1200–1650. XVII. Byzantines, Mamelukes and Maghribians,* 2nd edn, New York, 1980.

Bartashevich, G.A.: *Magichnae slova. Vopyt dasledavannia svetapogliadnaŭ i mastatskaŭ asnovy zamoŭ*, Minsk, 1990.

Baxter, Rev. M.: *Louis Napoleon, The Destined Monarch of the World*, London, 1861.

Beaver-Bricken Espinola, Vera: 'Copper Icons in Daily Use in Old Russia', *Russian Copper Icons and Crosses from the Kunz Collection: Castings of Faith*, ed. R.E. Ahlborn and V. Beaver-Bricken Espinola, Washington, 1990, pp. 8–10.

Begunov, Iu. K.: *Koz'ma Prezviter v slavianskikh literaturakh*, Sofia, 1973.

Behringer, Wolfgang: *Witchcraft Persecutions in Bavaria: Popular Magic, Religious Zealotry and Reason of State in Early Modern Europe*, Cambridge, 1997 (translation of German edition *Hexenverfolgung in Bayern*, 1987)

Beichner, Paul E.: *The Medieval Representation of Music, Jubal or Tubalcain*, Notre Dame, 1954.

Bekkum, W.J. Van: 'Alexander the Great in Medieval Hebrew Literature', *Journal of the Warburg and Courtauld Institutes*, 49, 1986, pp. 218–26.

Beliaev, I.S.: 'Bytovye ocherki proshlogo. Volshebstvo i koldovstvo. Vorozhcia zemskii d'iachek Maksim Markov', *Istoricheskii vestnik*, 1905, 9, pp. 848–61.

Beliaev, I.S.: 'Bytovye ocherki proshlogo. Zhenskie chary', *Istoricheskii vestnik*, 1905, 8, pp. 485–99.

Belobrova, O.A.: 'K istorii knizhnoi miniatiury i narodnoi kartinki kontsa XVII pervoi poloviny XVIII veka', in *Narodnaia kartinka XVII–XIX vekov. Materialy i issledovaniia*, ed. M.A. Alekseeva, E.A. Mishina, St Petersburg, 1996, pp. 71–91.

Belobrova, O.A.: *Nikolai Spafarii. Èsteticheskie traktaty*, Leningrad, 1978.

Belova, O.V.: 'Edinorog v narodnykh predstavleniiakh i knizhnoi traditsii slavian', in *Zhivaia starina*, 1994, 4, pp. 11–15.

Belyi, Iu. A.: 'Ob istochnike izobrazheniia astronomicheskikh instrumentov v russkoi matematicheskoi rukopisi nachala XVII veka', *Istoriko-astronomicheskie issledovaniia*, XXV, 1982, pp. 181–5.

Beneshevich, V.N.: *Pamiatniki drevne-russkogo kanonicheskogo prava* (Russkaia istoricheskaia biblioteka, t. 6), St Petersburg, 1908.

Beneshevich, V.N.: *Drevneslavianskaia Kormchaia XIV titulov bez tolkovanii*, II, revised by Iu. K. Begunov, I.S. Chichurov, Ia. N. Shchapov, Sofia, 1987.

Berger, Albrecht: *Das Bad in der Byzantinischen Zeit*, Miscellanea Byzantina Monacensia 27, Munich, 1982.

Bernshtam, T.A.: 'Devushka-nevesta i predbrachnaia obriadnost' v Pomor'e v XIX–nachale XX v.', in *Russkii narodnyi svadebnyi obriad*, ed. K.V. Chistova, T.A. Bernshtam, Leningrad, 1978, pp. 48–71.

Berry L.E., and Crummey, R.O.: *Rude and Barbarous Kingdom. Russia in the Accounts of Sixteenth-Century English Voyagers*, Madison, etc., 1968.

Berynda, Pamvo: *Leksikon slavenorosskii*, Kiev, 1627.

Bethencourt, Francesco: 'Portugal: A Scrupulous Inquisition', in *Early Modern European Witchcraft. Centres and Peripheries*, ed. Bengt Ankarloo and Gustav Henningsen, Oxford, 1990, pp. 403–22.

Beza, Marcu: *Paganism in Rumanian Folklore*, London, 1928.

Billington, James H.: *The Icon and the Axe*, London, 1966.

Birnbaum, H.: 'On Some Evidence of Jewish Life and Anti-Jewish Sentiments in Medieval Russia', *Viator*, IV, 1973, pp. 225–55.

Bitel, Lisa M.: '*In visu noctis*: Dreams in European Hagiography and Histories, 450–900', *History of Religions*, 31, 1991, pp. 39–59.

Blankoff, J.: À propos du «dvoeverie» et des amulettes «zmeeviki», *Communications présentées par les slavisants de Belgique*, Brussels, 1973, pp. 67–84.

Blok, A.: 'Poèziia zagovorov i zaklinanii', in *Istoriia russkoi literatury*, ed. E.V. Anichkov, I, Moscow, 1908, pp. 81–108 (reprinted in *Sobranie sochinenii*, V, Moscow Leningrad, 1962).

Blum R. and Blum E.: *The Dangerous Hour: The Lore and Culture of Mystery and Crisis in Rural Greece*, London, 1970.

Bobrovskii, Ia.E.: *Mifologicheskii mir drevnikh kievlian*, Kiev, 1982.

Bobrovskii, P.O.: *Voennoe pravo v Rossii pri Petre Velikom*, vyp. 1, St Petersburg, 1882; vyp. 2, 1886.

Bocharov, G.N.: 'Russkie siuzhetno-ornamental'nye izdeliia s peregorodchatoi emal'iu', in *Srednevekovoe iskusstva. Rus'. Gruziia*, Moscow, 1978, pp. 237–50.

Boehr, Max von: *Dolls and Puppets*, New York, 1966.

Bogatyrev, Pierre: *Actes magiques, rites et croyances en Russie Subcarpathique*, Paris, 1929.

Bogdanov, K.A.: *Den'gi v fol'klore*, St Petersburg, 1995.

Bogoslovskii, M.: *Petr I*, I, Moscow, 1940.

Bokdam, Silviane: 'Les Mythes de l'origine de l'astrologie', in *Divination et controverse religieuse en France au XVI siècle*, Cahiers V.L. Saulnier, 4, Paris, 1987, pp. 57–72.

Bolonev, F.F.: *Narodnyi kalendar' semeiskikh Zabaikal'ia (vtoraia polovina XIX–nachalo XX v.)*, Novosibirsk, 1978.

Bolonev, F.F.: 'O nekotorykh arkhaicheskikh èlementakh v zagovorakh russkogo naseleniia Sibiri', in *Traditsionnye obriady i iskusstvo russkogo i korennykh narodov Sibiri*, ed. L.M. Rusakova, N.A. Minenko, Novosibirsk, 1987, pp. 66–78.

Bolte, Johannes: *Georg Wickrams Werke*, IV, Tübingen, 1903.

Bonner, Campbell: 'Demons of the Bath', in *Studies Presented to F.L. Griffith*, London, 1932, pp. 203–8.

Bonner, Campbell: *Studies in Magical Amulets*, Ann Arbor, 1950.

Bonner, Campbell: 'Two Studies in Syncretistic Amulets', *Proceedings of the American Philosophical Society*, 85, 5, 1942, pp. 466–71.

Boss, V.: *Milton and the Rise of Russian Satanism*, Toronto, 1991.

Boss, V.: *Newton and Russia: the Early Influence 1698–1796*, Cambridge, Mass., 1972

Bouché-Leclerq, A.: *Histoire de la divination dans l'antiquité*, I, Paris, 1879.

Boyer, Régis: *Le Monde du double: La magie chez les anciens Scandinaves*, Paris, 1986.

Bozoky, Edina: 'Mythic Mediation in Healing Incantations', in *Health, Disease and Healing in Medieval Culture*, ed. Sheila Campbell, Bert Hall, David Klausner, New York, 1992, pp. 84–92.

Brand, John: *Observations on Popular Antiquities*, 2nd edn, London, 1900.

Bratley, G.H.: *The Power of Gems and Charms*, London, 1907.

Brevant, Francis B.: 'The German *Volkskalender* of the Fifteenth Century', *Speculum*, 53, 2, 1988, pp. 312–42.

Brewer, E.C.: *A Dictionary of Miracles, Imitative, Realistic, and Dogmatic*, new edn, London, 1901.

Brewer, E.C.: *Dictionary of Phrase and Fable*, London, revised edn, n. d.

Briggs, Katharine: *A Dictionary of Fairies*, London, 1976.

Brock, S.P.: 'A Dispute of the Months and Some Related Syriac Texts', *Journal of Semitic Studies*, XXX, 2, 1985, pp. 181–211.

Bronshten, V.A.: 'Novyi vzgliad na istoriiu goroskopa Petra Velikogo', *Germenevtika drevnerusskoi literatury*, 7, ch. 2, pp. 441–53.

Bruce, Peter Henry: *Memoirs of Peter Henry Bruce*, London, 1782, reprinted London, 1970.

Das Buch als magisches und als Repräsentationsobjekt, ed. Peter Ganz, Wolfenbütteler Mittelalter-Studien, Bd 5, Wiesbaden, 1992.

Budge, E.A.W.: *Syrian Anatomy, Pathology and Therapeutics, or 'The Book of Medicines'*, London, 1913.

Bulanin, D.M.: *Perevody i poslaniia Maksima Greka*, Leningrad, 1984.

Bulgakovskii, D.G.: *Pinchuki. Ètnograficheskii sbornik. Pesni, zagadki, poslovitsy, primety, predrassudki, pover'ia, suever'ia i mestnyi slovar'* (=*Zapiski Imperatorskogo Russkogo geograficheskogo obshchestva po otdeleniiu ètnografii*, XIII, 3), St Petersburg, 1890.

Burnaby, Fred: *A Ride to Khiva*, London, 1876.

Burnett, Charles S.F.: 'The Eadwine Psalter and the Western Tradition of the Onomancy in Pseudo-Aristotle's *Secret of Secrets'*, *Archives d'histoire doctrinale et littéraire du moyen âge*, 1988, pp. 143–67.

Burnett, Charles S.F.: 'A Note on Two Astrological Fortune-Telling Tables', *Revue d'histoire des textes*, XVIII, 1988, pp. 257–62.

Burnett, Charles S.F.: 'An Unknown Latin Version of an Ancient Parapēgma: The Weather-forecasting Stars in the *Iudicia* of Pseudo-Ptolemy', in *Making Instruments Count: Essays on Historical Scientific Instruments Presented to Gerard L'Estrange Turner*, ed. R.G.W. Anderson, J.A. Bennett, W.F. Ryan, Aldershot, 1993, pp. 27–41.

Burnett, Charles S.F.: 'Arabic Divinatory Texts and Celtic Folklore: A Comment on the Theory and Practice of Scapulimancy in Western Europe', *Cambridge Medieval Celtic Studies*, 6, Winter 1983, pp. 31–42.

Burnett, Charles S.F.: 'Divination from Sheep's Shoulder Blades: A Reflection on Andalusian Society', in *Cultures in Contact in Medieval Spain: Historical and Literary Essays presented to L.P. Hartley*, ed. D. Hook and B. Taylor, London, 1990, pp. 29–45.

Burnett, P.P.: 'Russian Playing Card History From the Beginnings to 1917', *The Playing Card*, XIII, 4, 1985, pp. 97–113.

Burtsev, A.E.: *Obzor russkogo narodnogo byta severnogo kraia*, 3 vols, St Petersburg, 1902.

Buslaev, F.: *Istoricheskaia khristomatiia tserkovno-slavianskogo i drevnerusskogo iazykov*, Moscow, 1861.

Buslaev, F.: *Moi dosugi*, Moscow, 1886.

Butler, W.E.: 'Foreign Impressions of Russian Law to 1800: Some Reflections', *Russian Law: Historical and Political Perspectives*, ed. W.E. Butler, Leiden, 1977, pp. 65–92.

Bychkov, A.F.: *Opisanie slavianskikh i russkikh rukopisei Imp. Publichnoi biblioteki*, St Petersburg, 1878.

Cabrol, F., ed.: Dictionnaire d'archéologie chrétienne et de liturgie, Paris, 1907–53.

Caesarius of Heisterbach: *The Dialogue on Miracles* (1220–1235), transl. H. von E. Scott and C.C. Swinton Bland, London, 1929.

Cameron, A.: 'The History of the Image of Edessa: The Telling of a Story', in *Okeanos* (= *Harvard Ukrainian Studies*, VII), 1983, pp. 80–94.

Capane, Carolina: 'La magia a Bisanzio nel secolo XIV: Azione e reazione. Dal Registro de Patriarcato constantinopolitano (1315–1402)', *Jahrbuch der Oesterreichischen Byzantinistik*, XXIX, 1980, pp. 237–62.

Capp, Bernard: *Astrology and the Popular Press. English Almanacs 1500–1800*, London, 1979.

Carlson, Maria: *'No Religion Higher than Truth'; A History of the Theosophical Movement in Russia, 1875–1922*, Princeton, 1993.

Castello, Carlo: 'Cenni sulla repressione del reato di magia dagli inizi del principato fino a Constanzo II', in *Atti dell'Academia romanistica Constantiniana. VIII Convegno internazionale*, 1987, pp. 665–93.

Catholic Encyclopaedia, 17 vols, New York, 1907–18.

CCAG = *Corpus codicum astrologorum graecorum*.

Chambers, D.C.: *A Renaissance Cardinal and his Worldly Goods: Francesco Gonzaga (1444–83)*, Warburg Surveys and Texts 21, London, 1992.

Charmasson, T.: *Recherches sur une technique divinatoire; la géomancie dans l'occident médiéval*, Paris, 1980.

Chenakal, V.L.: 'Iakov Vilimovich Brius, russkii astronom nachala XVIII veka', *Astronomicheskii zhurnal*, 28, 1, 1951, pp. 1–14.

Cherepanova, O.A.: 'Nabliudeniia nad leksikoi Stoglava (Leksika, sviazannaia s poniatiiami dukhovnoi i kul'turnoi zhizni)', in *Russkaia istoricheskaia leksikologiia i leksikografiia*, vyp. 3, Leningrad, 1983, pp. 17–25.

Cherepanova, O.A.: 'Tipologiia i genezis nazvanii likhoradok-triasavits v russkikh narodnykh zagovorakh i zaklinaniiakh', in *Iazyk zhanrov russkogo fol'klora*, Petrozavodsk, 1977, pp. 44–57.

Cherepanova, O.A.: *Mifologicheskaia leksika russkogo severa*, Leningrad, 1983.

Cherepnin, L.V.: 'Iz istorii drevnerusskogo koldovstva XVII v.', *Ètnografiia*, VIII, 1929, 2, p. 86–109.

Chernetsov, A.V.: 'Ob odnom risunke Radzivillovskoi letopisi', *Sovetskaia arkheologiia*, 1977, 4, pp. 301–6.

Chernetsov, A.V.: 'K izucheniiu Radzivillovskoi letopisi', *Trudy Otdela drevnerusskoi literatury*, XXXVI, 1981, pp. 274–88.

Chernetsov, A.V.: 'Medieval Russian Pictorial Materials on Paganism and Superstitions', *Slavica Gandensia*, 7–8, 1981, pp. 99–112.

Chernetsov, A.V., *Zolochenye dveri XVI veka*, Moscow, 1992.

Chicherov, V.I.: 'Zimnii period russkogo narodnogo zemledel'cheskogo kalendaria XVI–XIX vekov' (=*Trudy Instituta étnografii im. N. N. Miklukho-Maklaia*, n.s., XL), Moscow, 1957.

Chikachev, A.G.: *Russkie na Indigirke*, Novosibirsk, 1990.

Chistiakov, M.: 'Narodnoe predanie o Briuse', *Russkaia starina*, 1871, IV, pp. 169–70.

Chistov, K.V.: *Russkie narodnye sotsial'no-utopicheskie legendy XVII–XIX vv.*, Moscow, 1967.

Cholova, Tsvetana: *Estestvenonauchnite znaniia v srednovekovna Bãlgariia*, Sofia, 1988.

Cholova, Tsvetana: 'La Cosmologie et les systèmes cosmographiques en Bulgarie médiévale', *Bulgarian Historical Review*, 1987, 2, pp. 33–46.

Chrysostom, John: *In kalendas*, in Migne, *Patrologia graeca*, 48.

Ch[ulkov]., M.: *Abevega ruskikh sueverii, idolopoklonnicheskikh zhertvoprinoshenii, svadebnykh prostonarodnykh obriadov, koldovstva, shemanstva, i proch.*, Moscow, 1786 (second edition of M. Chulkov, *Slovar' russkikh sueverii* below).

Chulkov, M.: *Slovar' russkikh sueverii, idolopoklonnicheskikh zhertvoprinoshenii, svadebnykh prostonarodnykh obriadov, koldovstva, shemanstva, i proch.*, Moscow, 1772.

Clark, J. Kent: *Goodwin Wharton*, Oxford, 1984.

Claussen, B., and Borchling C.: *Niederdeutsche Bibliographie. Gesamtverzeichnis der niederdeutschen Drucke bis zum Jahre 1800*, Neumünster, 1931–36, I, no. 475.

Cleminson, R: 'The Miracle *De juvene qui Christum negaverat* in the pseudo-Amphilochian *Vita Basilii* and its Slavonic Adaptations', *Parergon*, n.s. 8, 1992, pp. 1–15.

Cockayne, O.: *Leechdoms, Wortcunning, and Starcraft of Early England*, 3 vols, London, 1864–6.

Collins, Samuel: *The Present State of Russia*, London, 1671.

Consett, Thomas: *The Present State and Regulations of the Church of Russia*, 2 vols, London, 1729.

Coren, Stanley: *The Left-Hander Syndrome*, London, 1992.

Cormack, Robin: 'Miraculous Icons in Byzantium and their Powers', *Arte cristiana*, LXXVI, fasc. 724, 1988, pp. 57–60.

The Council in Trullo Revisited, ed. George Nedungeatt, Michael Featherstone, *Kanonika* 6, Rome, 1995.

Coxe, W.: *Travels in Poland, Russia, Sweden, and Denmark*, London, 1784 (edition seen: fifth edn, London, 1802).

Cracraft, J.: *The Church Reform of Peter the Great*, London, 1971.

Cracraft, J.: *For God and Peter the Great*, Boulder, 1982.

Cross, A.G.: *Anglo-Russica*, Oxford, 1993.

Cross, A.G.: 'The Bung College or British Monastery in Petrine Russia', *Study Group on Eighteenth-Century Russia Newsletter*, 12, 1984, pp. 14–24.

Cross, A.G.: *A Lady at the Court of Catherine the Great. The Journal of Baroness Elizabeth Dimsdale, 1781*, Cambridge, 1989.

Cross, A.G.: *Russia under Western Eyes, 1517–1825*, London, 1971.

Cross, A.G.: 'The Russian *Banya* in the Descriptions of Foreign Travellers and in Depictions of Foreign and Russian Artists', *Oxford Slavonic Papers*, n.s. 24, 1991, pp. 34–59.

Cross, J.F.: *A Brief Historical account of the Empire of Russia*, London, 1654, quoted in Cross: *Russia under Western Eyes, 1517–1825*, London, 1971, p. 88.

Crull, Jodocus: *The Antient and Present State of Russia*, London, 1698.

Cumont, F.: 'Les Présages lunaires de Virgile et les "selenodromia"', *Antiquité classique*, II, 2, 1933, pp. 259–70.

Dagron, G.: 'Sviashchennye obrazy i problema portretnogo obraza', in *Chudotvornaia ikona v Vizantii i Drevnei Rusi*, ed. A.M. Lidov, Moscow, 1996, pp. 19–43.

Dal', L.V.: 'Zametki o mednykh grivnakh XII veka', *Drevnosti. Trudy Moskovskogo arkheologicheskogo obshchestva*, I, 1, 1874.

Dal', V.: *O poveriiakh, sueveriiakh i predrassudkakh russkogo naroda*, 2nd edn, St Petersburg, 1880 (reprinted St Petersburg, 1996).

Dal', V.: *Poslovitsy russkogo naroda*, 3rd edn, IV, St Petersburg–Moscow, 1904.

Dal', V.: *Poslovitsy russkogo naroda*, Moscow, 1989 [reissue of 1957 edition].

Dal', V.: *Tolkovyi slovar' zhivogo velikorusskogo iazyka*, 2nd edn, Moscow–St Petersburg, 1880–82.

dall'Olmo, Umberto: 'Latin Terminology relating to Aurorae, Comets, Meteors and Novae', *Journal of the History of Astronomy*, 11, 1980, pp. 10–27.

Dan, J.: 'The Seventy Names of Metatron', *Proceedings of the Eighth World Congress of Jewish Studies*, Division C (1982), pp. 19–23.

Dando, Marcel: 'The Neutral Angels', *Archiv für das Studium der neueren Sprachen und Literaturen*, Bd 217, 2, 1980, pp. 259–76.

Danilov, K.: *Drevnie rossiiskie stikhotvoreniia, sobrannye Kirsheiu Danilovym*, Moscow–Leningrad, 1958.

Darkevich, V.P. and Putsko, V.G.: 'Proizvedeniia srednevekovoi metalloplastiki iz nakhodok v Staroi Riazani (1970–1978 gg.)', *Sovetskaia arkheologiia*, 1981, 3, pp. 218–31.

d'Auteroche, Chappe: *Voyage en Sibérie*, 4 vols, Paris, 1768.

Davidan, O.I.: 'Skarabei iz Staroi Ladogi', *Arkheologicheskii sbornik*, 29, 1988, pp. 112–16.

Defoe, Daniel: *A Journal of the Plague Year*, ed. L. Landa, London, 1969.

Delatte, A.: *Anecdota atheniensia. I. Textes grecs inédits relatifs à l'histoire des religions*, Liège–Paris, 1927.

Delatte, A.: *La Catoptromancie grecque et ses dérivés*, Liège–Paris, 1932.

Delatte, A.: 'Études sur la magie grecque', *Musée Belge. Revue de philologie classique*, XVIII, 1914, pp. 5–96.

Delatte, A.: *Herbarius: Recherches sur le cérémonial usité chez les anciens pour la cueillette des simples et des plantes magiques*, *Mémoires*, Classe des lettres, Académie royale de Belgique, 2 série, LIX, fasc. 4), Brussels, 1961.

Delatte, A.: 'Note sur les manuscrits astrologiques du Mont Athos', *Annuaire de l'Institut de philologie et d'histoire orientales et slaves*, 11, 1951, pp. 107–12.

Delatte, L.: 'Un Office byzantin d'exorcisme', *Mémoires*, Classe des lettres, Académie royale de Belgique, 2 série, t. LII, 1957.

Delatte A. and Derchain, Ph.: *Les Intailles magiques gréco-égyptiennes*, Paris, 1964.

Deletant, D.: 'The Sunday Legend', *Revue des études sud-est européennes*, XV, 3, 1977, pp. 431–51.

De Madariaga, Isabel: 'Freemasonry in Eighteenth-Century Russian Society', in *idem*, *Politics and Culture in Eighteenth-Century Russia*, London, 1998, pp. 150–67.

De Madariaga, Isabel: 'Penal Policy in the Age of Catherine II', in *idem*, *Politics and Culture in Eighteenth-Century Russia*, London, 1998, pp. 97–123.

De Madariaga, Isabel: *Politics and Culture in Eighteenth-Century Russia*, London, 1998.

De Madariaga, Isabel: *Russia in the Age of Catherine the Great*, London, 1981.

Demkova, N.S.: 'Drevnerusskie rukopisi v nekotorykh sobraniiakh FRG', *Trudy Otdela drevnerusskoi literatury*, XXXVII, 1983, pp. 371–81.

Demkova, N.S. and Droblenkova, N.F.: 'Povest' o ubogom cheloveke, kak ot diavola proizveden tsarem', *Trudy Otdela drevnerusskoi literatury*, XXI, 1965, pp. 252–8.

De Nigromancia of Roger Bacon, ed. and transl. A.-M. Macdonald, Gillette, NJ, 1988.

Dergacheva-Skop, E.I. and Romodanovskaia, E.K.: 'Sobranie rukopisnykh knig Gosudarsvennogo arkhiva Tiumenskoi oblasti v Tobol'ske', in *Arkheografiia i istochnikovedenie Sibiri*, Novosibirsk, 1975, pp. 64–143.

Der Nersessian, Sirarpie: 'La Légende d'Abgar d'après un rouleau illustré de la Bibliothèque Pierpont Morgan à New York', *Bulletin de l'Institut archéologique bulgare*, X, 1936, pp. 98–106.

Derzhavin, G.R.: *Sochinenia Derzhavina*, ed. Ia. Grot, St Petersburg, 1876.

De Santos Otero, Aurelio: *Die handschriftliche Überlieferung der altslavischen Apokryphen*, Bd. 1, Berlin, 1978, Bd. II, Berlin, 1981 (supplemented by Francis Thomson in *The Slavonic and East European Review*, 58 (1980), 2, pp. 256–68, and 63 (1985), 1, pp. 73–98.)

Dewey, Horace W.: 'Some Perceptions of Mental Disorder in Pre-Petrine Russia', *Medical History*, 31, 1987, pp. 84–99.

D'iachenko, G.: *Polnyi tserkovno-slavianskii slovar*, Moscow, 1900 (repr. Moscow, 1993).

Diels, Hermann: 'Beiträge zur Zuckungsliteratur des Okzidents und Orients', *Abhandlungen der Königlichen Preussischen Akademie der Wissenschaften*, 1907 and 1908.

Divination and Oracles, ed. Michael Loewe and Carmen Blacker, London, 1981.

Dmitriev, L.A.: *Zhitiinye povesti russkogo severa kak pamiatniki literatury XIII–XVII vv.*, Leningrad, 1973.

Dmitrieva, R.P.: *Skazanie o kniaziakh vladimirskikh*, Moscow–Leningrad, 1955.

Dobrianskii, F.: *Opisanie rukopisei Vilenskoi publichnoi biblioteki, tserkovno-slavianskikh i russkikh*, Vil'no, 1822.

Dobschütz, E. von: *Christusbilder: Untersuchungen zur christlichen Legende*, Leipzig, 1909.

Domostroi po spisku Imperatorskogo Obshchestva istorii i drevnostei rossiiskikh, Moscow, 1882 (reprinted in *Domostroi*, Bradda Rarity Reprints, no. 18, Letchworth, 1971).

The Domostroi. Rules for Russian Households in the Time of Ivan the Terrible, ed. and transl. Carolyn Johnston Pouncy, Ithaca and London, 1994.

Donaldson, Bess Allen: *The Wild Rue. A Study of Muhammadan Magic and Folklore in Iran*, London, 1938.

Drage, C.L.: *Russian Literature in the Eighteenth Century*, London, 1978.

Drage, C.L.: *Russian Word-Play Poetry fron Simeon Polotskii to Derzhavin*, London, 1993.

Dragomanov, M.: *Malorusskie narodnie predaniia i rasskazy*, Kiev, 1876.

Drexler, W.: 'Alter Beschworungsformeln', *Philologus*, 58, 1899, pp. 594–616.

Dubasov, I.I.: 'Ocherki Tambovskogo byta XVII i XVIII stoletii', *Istoricheskii vestnik*, 1894, 6, pp. 153–65.

Dubler, C.E.: *Abū Ḥāmid el Granadino y su Relación de viage por tierras eurasiáticas*, Madrid, 1953.

Dubov, I.V.: *I poklaniashesia idolu kamenu*, St Petersburg, 1995.

Dujčev, I.: 'Apocrypha Byzantino-slavica', in *idem*, *Medioevo byzantino-slavo*, Rome, 1971, pp. 323–7.

Duling, D.C.: 'The Testament of Solomon', in *The Old Testament Epigrapha*, ed. J.H. Charlesworth, London, 1983, I, pp. 935–87.

Duncan-Flowers, Maggie J., Maguire, Eunice Dauterman, and Maguire, Henry P.: *Art and Holy Powers in the Early Christian House*, Illinois Byzantine Studies II, Urbana and Chicago, 1989.

Dundes, Alan, ed.: *The Evil Eye. A Folklore Casebook*, New York and London, 1981.

Dunning, Chester S.L., ed.: *Jacques Margeret: The Russian Empire and Grand Duchy of Muscovy. A 17th-century Account by Jacques Margeret*, Pittsburgh, 1983. Annotated translation of Jacques Margeret, *Estat de l'Empire de Russie et Grande Duché de Moscovie*, Paris, 1607.

Dvornik, Francis: *Byzantine Missions among the Slavs. SS. Constantine-Cyril and Methodius*, New Brunswick, 1970.

Early Modern European Witchcraft. Centres and Peripheries, ed. Bengt Ankarloo and Gustav Henningsen, Oxford, 1990.

The Edificatory Prose of Kievan Rus', tr. William R. Veder, introd. William R. Veder and Anatolij Turilov, Harvard Library of Early Ukrainian Literature: English Translations, vol. 6, Cambridge, Mass., 1994.

Edwards, H. Sutherland: *The Russians at Home*, 2nd edn, London, 1861.

Efimenko, P.S.: *Materialy po ètnografii russkogo naseleniia Arkhangel'skoi gubernii*, Moscow, 1877.

Egeria: John Wilkinson, *Egeria's Travels to the Holy Land*, Warminster, 1981.

Eis, Gerhard: *Wahrsage texte des Spätmittelalters*, Berlin, 1956.

Eisenberger, E.J.: 'Die Wahrsagen aus dem Schulterblatt', *Internationales Archiv für Ethnographie*, 35, 1938, pp. 49–116.

Eisler, R.: 'Der Fisch als Sexualsymbol', *Imago*, 3, 1914, pp. 165–96.

Eleonskaia, A.S.: 'Gumanisticheskie motivy v «Otrazitel'nom pisanii» Efrosina', in *Novye cherty v russkoi literature i iskusstve XVII–nachalo XVIII v.*, Moscow, 1976, pp. 263–76.

Eleonskaia, E.N.: 'Gadanie pod Novyi god v Kozel'skom uezde', *Ètnograficheskoe obozrenie*, (1909) 1910, 2–3.

Eleonskaia, E.N.: *K izucheniiu zagovora i koldovstva v Rossii*, Shamordino, 1917 (reprinted in *idem*, *Skazka, zagovor i koldovstvo v Rossii*, Moscow, 1994, pp. 100–43).

Eleonskaia, E.N.: 'Otgoloski drevnikh verovanii v skazke', in *idem*, *Skazka, zagovor i koldovstvo v Rossii*, Moscow, 1994, pp. 23–32.

Eleonskaia, E.N.: *Sel'sko-khoziaistvennaia magiia* (= *Memuary ètnograficheskogo otdeleniia Obshchestva liubitelei estestvoznaniia, antropologii i ètnografii*, vyp. 3), Moscow, 1929 (this was never issued but was eventually published from a proof copy in *idem*, *Skazka, zagovor i koldovstvo v Rossii*, Moscow, 1994, pp. 144–78).

Eleonskaia, E.N.: *Skazka, zagovor i koldovstvo v Rossii*, Moscow, 1994 (revised edition of published and unpublished work written between 1905 and 1934).

Eleonskaia, E.N.: 'Zapisi obychaev i obriadov Moskovskoi gub. Mozhaiskogo y.', in *idem*, *Skazka, zagovor i koldovstvo v Rossii*, Moscow, 1994, pp. 193–230.

Elukin, J.M.: 'The Ordeal of Scripture: Functionalism and the Sortes Biblicae in the Middle Ages', *Exemplaria*, 5, i, 1993, pp. 135–60.

Elworthy, F.T.: *Horns of Honour, and other Studies in the By-ways of Archaeology*, London, 1900.

Elworthy, F.T.: *The Evil Eye. An Account of this Ancient and Widespread Superstition*, London, 1895.

Emmerson, R.K.: *Antichrist in the Middle Ages. A Study of Medieval Apocalypticism, Art, and Literature*, Manchester, 1981.

Encyclopaedia of Religion and Ethics, ed. J. Hastings, Edinburgh and New York, 1908–20.

Encyclopedia of Religion, ed. M. Eliade, New York and London, 1987.

Èntsiklopediia «Slova o Polku Igoreve», ed. O.V. Tvorogov *et al.*, 5 vols, St Petersburg, 1995.

Epifanov, P.P.: 'Voinskii Ustav Petra Velikogo', in *Petr Velikii: Sbornik statei*, ed. A.I. Andreev, Moscow–Leningrad, 1947, pp. 167–213.

ERE – Encyclopaedia of Religion and Ethics, ed. Hastings.

Eremin, I.P.: *Literatura drevnei Rusi*, Moscow–Leningrad, 1966.

Eremina, V.I.: 'Zagovornye kolybel'nye pesni', in *Fol'klor i ètnograficheskaia deistvitel'nost'*, St Petersburg, 1992, pp. 29–34.

Erffa, Hans Martin von: *Ikonologie der Genesis*, I, Munich, 1989, pp. 400–4.

Ermolov, A.: *Narodnaia sel'skokhoziaistvennaia mudrost' v poslovitsakh, pogovorkakh i primetakh. I. Vsenarodnyi mesiatseslov*, St Petersburg, 1901.

Erofeeva, N.N.: 'Son Tat'iany v smyslovoi strukture romana Pushkina "Evgenii Onegin"' in *Son – semioticheskoe okno*, XXVIe Vipperovskie chteniia, Moskva, 1993, Milan–Moscow, 1994, pp. 96–106.

Esipov, G.V.: 'Koldovstvo v 17om i 18om stoletii iz arkhivnykh del', *Drevniaia i novaia Rossiia. Illiustrirovannyi istorichesku sbornik*, 1878, pp. 61ff, 157ff, 234ff.

Esmein, A.: *A History of Continental Criminal Procedure, with Special Reference to France*, London, 1914.

Ètnokul'turnye protsessy v Karelii, Petrozavodsk, 1986.

Ètnosemiotika ritual'nykh predmetov, St Petersburg, 1993.

Evans, Norman: 'Doctor Timothy Willis and his Mission to Russia, 1599', *Oxford Slavonic Papers*, n.s. 2, 1969, pp. 40–61.

Faccani, Remo: 'Jan' Vyšatiče l'«anno dei maghi». (Episodi del conflitto tra la «nuova» e la «vecchia fede» nella Rus' dell'XI secolo)', in *Il battesimo delle Terre Russe: Bilancio di un millennio*, ed. Sante Graciotti, Florence, 1991, pp. 25–43.

Fahd, Toufic: *La Divination arabe*, Leiden, 1966.

Faraone, Christopher A.: 'The Agonistic Context of Early Greek Binding Spells', in *Magika Hiera. Ancient Greek Magic and Religion*, New York and Oxford, 1991, pp. 3–32.

Faraone, Christopher A.: 'The "Performative Future" in Three Hellenistic Incantations and Theocritus' Second Idyll', *Classical Philology*, 90, 1995, pp. 1–15.

Fasciculus geomanticus, Verona, 1687.

Fasmer [Vasmer], M: *Ètimologicheskii slovar' russkogo iazyka*, 2nd edn transl. and augmented by O.N. Trubachev, 4 vols, Moscow, 1964–73.

Fedotov, G.P.: *The Russian Religious Mind*, Cambridge, Mass., 1946.

Fennell, J.L.I.: *The Correspondence between Prince A. M. Kurbsky and Tsar Ivan IV of Russia 1564–1579*, Cambridge, 1955.

Fennell, J.L.I.: *A History of the Russian Church to 1448*, London, 1995.

Fennell, J.L.I.: *Kurbsky's History of Ivan IV*, Cambridge, 1965.

Festugière, A.J.: *La Révélation d'Hermès Trismégiste. I. L'Astrologie et les sciences occultes*, 3rd edn, Paris, 1950.

Feydit, Frédéric: *Amulettes de l'Arménie chrétienne*, Venice, 1986.

Fiensy, D.A.: 'Revelation of Ezra', in *The Old Testament Epigrapha*, ed. J.H. Charlesworth, London, 1983, I, pp. 601–4.

Figurovskii, N.A.: 'The Alchemist and Physician Arthur Dee', *Ambix*, 13, 1965, pp. 35–51.

Filosofskaia mysl' v Kieve, ed. V.D. Beloded *et al.*, Kiev, 1982.

Flier, Michael S.: 'Court Ceremony in an Age of Reform: Patriarch Nikon and the Palm Sunday Ritual', in *Religion and Culture in Early Modern Russia and Ukraine*, ed. by Samuel H. Baron and Nancy Shields Kollmann, DeKalb, 1997, pp. 73–95.

Flint, Valerie: *The Rise of Magic in Early Medieval Europe*, Oxford, 1991.

Florinskii, V.M.: *Russkie prostonarodnye travniki i lechebniki*, Kazan', 1879.

Flusser, David: '*Palaea historica*. An Unknown Source of Biblical Legends', *Scripta hierosolymitana*, XXII, Jerusalem, 1971, pp. 48–79.

Fonkich, B.L.: *Grechesko-russkie kul'turnye sviazi v XV–XVII vv. (grecheskie rukopisi v Rossii)*, Moscow, 1977.

Forbes, T.R.: *The Midwife and the Witch*, Newhaven and London, 1966.

Forbes, T.R.: 'Verbal Charms in British Folk Medicine', *Proceedings of the American Philosophical Society*, 115, 4, 1971, pp. 292–316.

Fortis, Alberto: *Viaggio in Dalmazia*, Venice, 1774 (English version, *Travels in Dalmatia*, London, 1778).

Franklin, S.: 'The Empire of the *Rhomaioi* as Viewed from Kievan Russia: Aspects of Byzantino-Russian Cultural Relations', *Byzantion*, LIII, 2, 1983, pp. 508–37.

Franklin, S.: 'Greek in Kievan Rus'' in *Homo Byzantinus. Papers in Honor of Alexander Kazhdan* (=*Dumbarton Oaks Papers*, vol. 46), 1992, pp. 69–81.

Franklin, Simon: 'The Reception of Byzantine Culture by the Slavs', *The 17th International Byzantine Congress. Major Papers*, New Rochelle, 1986, pp. 383–97.

Franko, I.: *Apokrifi i legendy z ukrains'kikh rukopisiv*, I–V, L'vov, 1896–1910.

Fraser, D.: 'The Heraldic Woman', in *The Many Faces of Primitive Art*, ed. D. Fraser, New Jersey, 1966, pp. 36–99.

Frazer, J.G.: *Folklore in the Old Testament*, London, 1918.

Frazer, J.G.: *The Golden Bough. A Study in Magic and Religion*, 3rd edn, 12 vols, London, 1907–15.

Frazer, J.G.: *The Golden Bough. A Study in Magic and Religion*, abridged edition, London, 1922.

Gager, John G.: *Curse Tablets and Binding Spells from the Ancient World*, New York and Oxford, 1992.

Ganulich, A.K.: 'Kollektsiia russkikh upriazhnykh bubentsov A.K. Ganulicha', *Pamiatniki kul'tury. Novye otkrytiia. 1985*, Moscow, 1987, pp. 438–41.

Gardiner, S.C.: *Foreign Loanwords in Russian 1550–1690*, Oxford, 1965.

Garrett, Susan R.: *The Demise of the Devil*, Minneapolis, 1989.

Gaster, M.: 'The Hebrew Version of the Secretum Secretorum. A Medieval Treatise ascribed to Aristotle', *Journal of the Royal Asiatic Society*, October 1907, pp. 879–912 and January and October 1908, pp. 111–62, 1065–84.

Gaster, M.: *Literatura populară romănă*, Bucharest, 1883, pp. 506–9.

Gaster, M.: 'Rumanian Popular Legends of the Lady Mary', *Folklore*, 1923, pp. 55–85.

Gaster, M.: *The Sword of Moses*, London, 1896.

Gaster, M.: 'The Twelve Dreams of Sehachi', *Journal of the Royal Asiatic Society*, 1900, pp. 624–35.

Gaster, M.: 'Two Thousand Years of a Charm against the Child-Stealing Witch', *Folk-lore*, 11, 1900, pp. 129–62.

Gaster, M.: 'Zur Quellenkunde deutschen Sagen und Mürchen', *Germania*, 1881, pp. 199–213.

Geitler, L.: *Euchologium. Glagolski spomenik manastira Sinai brda*, Zagreb, 1882.

Georgiev, Mincho: 'Osnovni cherti mediko-biologichno poznanie (IX–XIV v.)', *Istoricheski pregled*, 1988, kn. 7, pp. 50–62.

Gibbon, William Baker: 'Popular Star Names among the Slavonic-speaking Peoples', PhD dissertation, Pennsylvania University, 1956.

Giedion, Siegfried: *Mechanization Takes Command: A Contribution to Anonymous History*, New York, 1970 (first published 1948).

Gifford, Douglas J.: 'The Charm: A Contribution to Modern and Medieval Anthropology', *Romanica*, 6, 1973, pp. 43–58.

Ginzburg, Carlo: *The Night Battles. Witchcraft and Agrarian Cults in the Sixteenth and Seventeenth Centuries*, London, 1983 (translation of *I Benandanti*, 1966).

Girshberg, V.B.: '«Koz'l'rog» v Izbornike Sviatoslava', *Drevnerusskoe iskusstvo*, Moscow, 1972, pp. 81–9.

Gistarychny sloŭnik belaruskai movy, Minsk, 1982.

Glickman, Rose L.: 'The Peasant Woman as Healer', in *Russia's Women. Accommodation, Resistance, Transformation*, ed. Barbara Evans Clements, Barbara Alpern Engel, Christine D. Worobec, Berkeley, 1991, pp. 148–62.

Gnuse, Robert: *Dreams and Dream Reports in the Writings of Josephus*, Leiden, etc., 1996.

Gobert, E.G.: 'Le Pudendum magique et le problème des cauris', *Revue africaine*, XCV, nos 426–7, 1951, pp. 5–62.

Gogol', N.V.: *Sobranie khudozhestvennykh proizvedenii v piati tomakh*, 2nd edn., Moscow, 1960.

Golenchenko, G.Ia.: '"Kalendar"' Frantsiska Skoriny', in *Istoriia knigi v Belorussii*, Minsk, 1976, pp. 26–39.

Golikova, S.: 'Derevenskii koldun. Delo Agafona Usova', *Rodina*, 1993, 4, pp. 102–3.

Golikova, N.B.: 'Organizatsiia politicheskogo syska v Rossii XVI–XVII vv.' in *Gosudarstvennye uchrezhdeniia Rossii XVI–XVIII vv.*, pp. 11–36.

Golubinaia kniga. Russkie narodnye dukhovnye stikhi XI–XIX vekov, Moscow, 1991.

Goncharov, Ivan: *Oblomov*, transl. David Magarshak, Harmondsworth, 1954.

Goodenough, Erwin R.: *Jewish Symbols in the Greco-Roman Period*, 13 vols, New York, 1953–68.

Goodman, David: *Power and Penury. Government, Technology and Science in Philip II's Spain*, Cambridge, 1988.

Gordon, Benjamin: 'Oculus Fascinus', *Archives of Ophthalmology*, 17, pp. 290–319.

Gorelkina, O.D.: 'K voprosu o magicheskikh predstavleniiakh v Rossii XVIII v. (na materiale sledstvennykh protsessov po koldovstvu')', in *Nauchnyi ateizm, religiia i deistvitel'nost'*, Novosibirsk, 1987, pp. 289–305.

Gorfunkel', A.Kh.: 'Andrei Belobotskii – poèt i filosof kontsa XVII–nachala XVIII v.', *Trudy Otdela drevnerusskoi literatury*, XVIII, 1962, pp. 188–213.

Gorfunkel', A.Kh.: '«Velikaia nauka Raimunda Liulliia» i ee chitateli', *XVIII vek*, V, 1962, pp. 336–48.

Górska, Barbara: *Katalog kalendarzy XVII–XVIII w. w zbiorach Biblioteki Ossolineum*, Wrocław, etc., 1968.

Gougaud, Louis: 'La Prière dite de Charlemagne et les pièces apocryphes apparentées', *Revue d'histoire ecclésiastique*, XX, 1924, pp. 211–38.

Gradov, B.A., Kloss, B.M., and Koretskii, V.I.: 'K istorii arkhangel'skoi biblioteki D.M. Golitsyna', *Arkheograficheskii ezhegodnik*, 1978, pp. 238–53.

Graham, Hugh: 'A Brief Account of the Character and Brutal Rule of Vasil'evich, Tyrant of Muscovy (Albert Schlichting on Ivan Groznyi)', *Canadian-American Slavic Studies*, IX, 2, 1975, pp. 204–72.

Graham, Stephen: *Part of the Wonderful Scene*, London, 1964.

Graham, Stephen: *The Way of Martha and the Way of Mary*, New York, 1915.

Graham, Stephen: *Undiscovered Russia*, London, 1914.

Graham, Stephen: *With the Russian Pilgrims to Jerusalem*, London, 1913.

Grandjouan, J.-O.: *L'Astragale et le pari*, Paris, 1969.

Granger, Byrd Howell: *A Motif Index for Lost Mines and Treasures Applied to Redaction of Arizona Legends, and to Lost Mine and Treasure Legends Exterior to Arizona*, FF Communications no. 218, Helsinki, 1977.

Granstrem, E.E.: 'Grecheskii original otrechennoi knigi «Putnik»', *Trudy Otdela drevnerusskoi literatury*, 24, pp. 72–4.

Granstrem, E.E.: 'Otgolosok vizantiiskogo suyeveriia v drevnerusskoi pis'mennosti', *Issledovaniia po drevnei i novoi literature*, Leningrad, 1987, pp. 48–9.

Granstrem, E.E.: 'O proiskhozhdenii glagolicheskoi azbuki', *Trudy Otdela drevnerusskoi literatury*, 11, 1955, pp. 300–13.

Grattan, J.H.G. and Singer, Charles: *Anglo-Saxon Magic and Medicine*, Oxford, 1952.

Greenfield, Richard: 'Fallen into Outer Darkness. Later Byzantine Depictions and Conceptions of the Devil and the Demons', *Etnofoor*, V, 1/2, 1992, pp. 61–80.

Greenfield, Richard: 'St Sisinnios, the Archangel Michael and the Female Demon Gylou: The Typology of the Greek Literary Stories', *Byzantina*, 15, 1989, pp. 82–141.

Greenfield, Richard: 'Sorcery and Politics at the Byzantine Court in the Twelfth Century: Interpretations of History', in *The Making of Byzantine History. Studies Dedicated to Donald M. Nicol*, Aldershot, 1993, pp. 73–85.

Greenfield, Richard: *Traditions of Belief in Late Byzantine Demonology*, Amsterdam, 1988.

Greer, Rowan A.: *The Fear of Freedom. A Study of Miracles in the Roman Imperial Church*, Pennsylvania UP, 1989.

Grendon, Felix: 'The Anglo-Saxon Charms', *The Journal of American Folk-Lore*, XXII, 1909.

Grieve, M.: *A Modern Herbal*, London, 1931.

Grignaschi, M.: 'L'Origine et les métamorphoses du "Sirr al asrār"', *Archives d'histoire doctrinale et littéraire du moyen âge*, 43, 1976, pp. 7–112.

Grignaschi, M.: 'Remarques sur la formation et l'interprétation du *Sirr al-'asrār*, in *Pseudo-Aristotle, The Secret of Secrets*, pp. 3–33.

Grmek, M.D.: *Les Sciences dans les manuscrits slaves orientaux du moyen âge*, Conférences du Palais de la Découverte, série D, no. 66, Paris, 1959.

Gromyko, Andrei: *Memories*, London, 1989.

Gromyko, M.M.: *Trudovye traditsii russkikh krest'ian Sibiri (XVIII–pervaia polovina XIX v.)*, Novosibirsk, 1975.

Gromyko, M.M.: *Traditsionnye normy povedeniia i formy obshcheniia russkikh krest'ian XIX v.*, Moscow, 1986.

Gruber, Karl: *Südtiroler Heilgenhimmel. Namenpatrone in der heimischen Kunst*, Bozen, 1991.

Gruzdev, V.F.: 'Rukopisnye lechebniki v sobranii Pushkinskogo Doma', *Trudy Otdela drevnerusskoi literatury*, XXIX, 1974, pp. 343–8.

Gubernatis, Angelo De: *La Mythologie des plantes, ou les légendes du règne végétal*, Paris, 1878 (reprint Milan, 1976).

Gur'ianova, N.S.: 'Staroobriadcheskie sochinenia XIX v. o Petre I antikhriste', in *Sibirskoe istochnikovedenie i arkheografiia*, Novosibirsk, 1980, pp. 140–1.

Gur'ianova, N.S.: *Krest'ianskii antimonarkhicheskii protest v staroobriadcheskoi èskhatologicheskoi literature perioda pozdnego feodalizma*, Novosibirsk, 1988.

Guthrie, Matthew: manuscript *Noctes Rossicae, or Russian Evening Recreations*, BL Add. MS 14,390 (before 1795).

Haase, Felix: *Volksglaube und Brauchtum der Ostslaven*, Breslau, 1939.

Halkin, Fr.: *Bibliotheca hagiographica graeca*, III, 3rd edn, Brussels, 1957, pp. 69–79 (Nos 2401–4: *Sisinnius et Sisinnodorus fratres, cum Meletina sorore*).

Halkin, Fr.: *Novum auctarium Bibliothecae hagiographicae graecae*, Brussels, 1984, p. 259.

Hamel, J.: *England and Russia*, London, 1854.

Hand, Wayland D.: *Boundaries, Portals, and Other Magical Spots in Folklore*, Folklore Society, Katharine Briggs Lecture No. 2, London, 1983.

Handwörterbuch des deutschen Aberglaubens, ed. E. Hoffmann-Krayer, Hanns Bachtöld-Stäubli, 10 vols, Berlin, 1927–42.

Haney, Jack V.: *From Italy to Muscovy. The Life and Works of Maxim the Greek*, Munich, 1973.

Hansmann, Liselotte, and Kriss-Rettenbeck, Lenz: *Amulett und Talisman. Erscheinungsform und Geschichte*, Munich, 1966.

Harkins, P.W.: *St John Chrysostom: Baptismal Instructions*, London, 1963.

Hart, Laurie Kain: *Time, Religion, and Social Experience in Rural Greece*, Lanham, 1992.

Hartley, Janet M.: 'Russia in 1812. Part 1: The French Presence in the *Gubernii* of Smolensk and Mogilev', *Jahrbücher für Geschichte Osteuropas*, 38, 2, 1990, pp. 178–98.

Hartley, Janet M.: *A Social History of the Russian Empire 1650–1825*, London, 1999.

Hastrup, Kirsten: 'Iceland: Sorcerers and Paganism', in *Early Modern European Witchcraft. Centres and Peripheries*, ed. Bengt Ankarloo and Gustav Henningsen, Oxford, 1990, pp. 383–401.

Haxthausen, August von: *Studies on the Interior of Russia*, ed. S.F. Starr, Chicago and London, 1972.

Hazlitt, W.C.: *Dictionary of Faiths and Folklore: Beliefs, Superstitions and Popular Customs*, London, 1905 (reprinted 1995).

Heikkinen, Antero, and Kervinen, Timo: 'Finland: The Male Domination', in *Early Modern European Witchcraft. Centres and Peripheries*, ed. Bengt Ankarloo and Gustav Henningsen, Oxford, 1990, pp. 319–38.

Hellberg, E.F.: 'Kak v zerkale: gadanie i son Tat'iany', *Studia slavica finlandensia*, 6, 1989, pp. 1–19.

Henein, N.H. and Bianquis. T.: *La Magie par les Psaumes*, Bibliothèque d'études coptes, 12, Cairo, 1975.

Herberstein, Sigmund von: *Rerum Moscoviticarum commentarii*. English translation in *Notes upon Russia*, 2 vols, ed. R.H. Major, Hakluyt Society, 1851–2, and *Description of Moscow and Muscovy 1557*, ed. B. Picard, transl. J.B.C. Grundy, London, 1969.

Hercher, R. in *Philologus*, VIII, 1853, pp. 165–8.

Herrin, Judith: *The Formation of Christendom*, London, 1987.

Hildburgh, W.L.: 'Some Cairene Amulets for Houses and for Horses and Donkeys', *Man*, 1913, 1, pp. 2–3.

Hoffmann, Gerda: *Beiträge zur Lehre von der durch Zauber verursachten Krankheit und ihrer Behandlung in der Medizin des Mittelalters*, Inaugural-Dissertation zur Erlangung der Zahnärzlichen Doktorwürde an der Friedrich-Wilhelms-Universität zu Berlin, Leiden, 1933

Hoffmann, Heinz: 'Satorquadrat', in Pauly-Wissowa, *Realencyclopädie der Classischen Altertumswissenschaft*, Supplementband XV, Munich, 1970.

Hone, William: *The Every-Day Book and Table Book; or Everlasting Calendar of Popular Amusements*, London, 1826.

Horoško, Leüh: 'A Guide to Belorussian Mythology', *The Journal of Belorussian Studies*, I, 2, 1966, pp. 68–79.

Hübner, Wolfgang: *Die Begriffe 'Astrologie' und 'Astronomie', in der Antike. Wortgeschichte und Wissenschaftssystematik, mit einer Hypothese zum Terminus 'Quadrivium'*, Akademie der Wissenschaften und der Literatur, Mainz, Abhandlungen der Geistes- und Sozialwissenschaftlichen Klasse, 1989, Nr. 7, Mainz, 1990.

Hughes, Lindsey A.J.: *Russia and the West. The Life of a Seventeenth-Century Westernizer Prince Vasily Vasil'evich Golitsyn (1643–1714)*, Newtonville, 1984.

Hughes, Patrick: *Dictionary of Islam*, London, 1885, p. 136.

Hullkrantz, Åke: 'Divinationsformer: en klassifikation', in *Nordisk folktro Studiertillägnade Carl-Herman Tillhagen 17 Dec. 1976*, Nordisk museet, 1976, pp. 49–70.

Huttenbach, Henry R.: 'Muscovy's Calendar Controversy of 1491–1492', *Science and History. Studies in Honor of Edward Rosen* (=*Studia Copernicana*, XVI), 1978, pp. 187–203.

Hüttl-Worth, Gerta: *Die Bereichung des russischen Wortschatzes im XVIII. Jahrhundert*, Vienna, 1956.

Hüttl-Worth, Gerta: *Foreign Words in Russian. A Historical Sketch, 1550–1800*, Berkeley and Los Angeles, 1963.

Iatsimirskii, A.I.: 'K istorii lozhnykh molitv v iuzhno-slavianskoi pis'mennosti', *Izvestiia Otdeleniia russkogo iazyka i slovesnosti*, XVIII, 1913, 4, pp. 16–126.

Iatsimirskii, A.I.: 'Melkie teksty i zametki po starinnoi i russkoi literature', *Izvestiia Otdeleniia russkogo iazyka i slovesnosti*, 4, 1889, 2, pp. 423–75.

Iatsimirskii, A.I.: *Bibliograficheskii obzor apokrifov v iuzhnoslavianskoi i russkoi pis'mennosti.*Vyp. 1, *Apokrify vetkhozavetnye*, Petrograd, 1921.

Iatsimirskii, A.I.: *Slavianskie i russkie rukopisi rumynskikh bibliotek*, St Petersburg, 1905.

Iavorskii, Iu.A.: 'Karpatorusskoe pouchenie o snakh', *Karpatskii svet*, 1928, 8, pp. 282–5.

Iavorskii, Iu.A.: *Novye rukopisnye nakhodki v oblasti starinnoi karpatorusskoi pis'mennosti XVI–XVIII vekov*, Prague, 1931.

Ikonen und ostkirchliches Kultgerät aus Rhenischen Privatbesitz, Cologne, 1990.

Iliadou, D.S.: 'Ho Hagios Dēmētrios kai hoi Slavoi' in *Pepragmena tou 8 Diethnous Bizantinologikou Synedriou, Thessalonikē 1953*, 3 vols, Athens, 1958, III, pp. 128–40.

In-Ho L. Ryu: 'Moscow Freemasons and the Rosicrucian Order', in *The Eighteenth Century in Russia*, ed. J.G. Garrard, Oxford, 1973, pp. 198–232.

Iorga, N.: *Byzance après Byzance*, Bucharest, 1935.

Isaevich, Ia.D.: 'Redkaia inkunabula', *Al'manakh bibliofila*, Moscow, 1973, pp. 194–9.

Iskrin, Mikhail: 'Kto takoi Martyn Zadeka?', *Al'manakh bibliofila*, 2, 1975, pp. 169–76.

Istoriia estestvoznaniia v Rossii, ed. N.A. Figurovskii, 3 vols, Moscow, 1957–62.

Istrin, V.: *Aleksandriia russkikh khronografov*, Moscow, 1893.

Istrin, V.M.: 'Khronika Ioanna Malaly v slavianskom perevode', *Zapiski Akademii nauk po istoriko-filologicheskomy otdeleniiu*, ser. VIII, I, 1897, pp. 6, 3.

Istrin, V.M.: *Khronika Georga Amartola v drevnem slavianorusskom perevode*, I, Petrograd, 1920.

Iudin, A.V.: 'Ob imenakh zvezd-«pomoshchnits» v russkikh zagovorakh', in *Iazyk russ'kogo fol'klora*, ed. Z. Tarlanov, Petrozavodsk, 1992, pp. 66–71.

Iudin, A.V.: *Onomastikon russkikh zagovorov*, Moscow, 1977.

Iudin, V.: *Dni velichal'nye. Stranitsy narodnogo khristianskogo kalendaria*, Saratov, 1992.

Ivanits, Linda J.: *Russian Folk Belief*, New York and London, 1989.

Ivanova, A.A.: 'Gadaniia na zimnie sviatki', *Russkaia slovesnost'*, 1995, 1, pp. 3–7.

Ivanov, A.I.: *Literaturnoe nasledie Maksima Greka*, Leningrad, 1969.

Ivanov, E.P.: *Russkii narodnyi lubok*, Moscow, 1937.

Ivanov, P.V.: 'Narodnye rasskazy o ved'makh i upyriakh', *Sbornik Kharkovskogo istoriko-filologicheskogo obshchestva*, 3, 1891.

Ivanov, M.I.: 'Narodnye obychai, pover'ia i gadaniia. Gadaniia v noch' na Ivana Kupala', *Tverskaia starina*, 1912, 6, pp. 15–16.

Ivanov, V.V., and Toporov, V. N.: *Issledovaniia v oblasti slavianskikh drevnostei*, Moscow, 1974.

Izbornik, ed. L.A. Dmitriev and D.S. Likhachev, Moscow, 1969.

Izmirlieva, Valentina: 'The Aetiology of the Seventy-Two Diseases: Investigating a Byzantino-Slavic False Prayer', *Byzantino-Slavica*, 59, 1, 1998, pp. 181–95.

Jagič, V.: 'Opisi i izvodi iz nekoliko južnoslovinskih rukopisa. XVI. z Sredovječni liekovi, gatanja i vračanja', *Starine*, X, 1878, pp. 81–126.

James, M.R.: *The Apocryphal New Testament*, Oxford, 1924.

James, Richard: see Larin.

Jerusalem Pilgrimage 1099–1185, ed. by John Wilkinson with Joyce Hill and W.F. Ryan, Hakluyt Society, second series 167, London, 1988.

Jewish Encyclopedia, New York and London, 1907.

Johansen, Thomas: '"Now We've Got It". Danish Treasure Hunting Seen from a Structural Point of View', *Folklore*, 102, 2, 1991, pp. 220–34.

John of Salisbury. *Policraticus* (English partial text in Joseph B. Pike, *Frivolities of Courtiers and Footprints of Philosophers*, Minneapolis, 1938).

Johnstone, Penelope: 'Aconite and its Antidotes in Arabic Writings', *Journal for the History of Arabic Science*, vol. 1, no. 1 (1971), pp. 65–71.

Jones, Malcolm: 'Folklore Motifs in Late Medieval Art. III: Erotic Animal Imagery', *Folklore*, 102, 2, 1991, pp. 192–219.

Jones, W. Gareth: *Nikolay Novikov, Enlightener of Russia*, Cambridge, 1984.

Jones, William: *Finger-Ring Lore*, new edn, London, 1908.

Jubé, Jacques: *La Religion, les moeurs et les usages des Moscovites*, ed. Michel Mervaud, *Studies on Voltaire and the Enlightenment*, 294, Oxford, 1992.

Kachanovskii, V.V.: 'Molitva s apokrificheskimi chertami ot zlogo (vredonosnago) dozhdia' , *Izvestiia Otdeleniia russkogo iazyka i slovesnosti*, II, 4, 1897, pp. 608–10.

Kagan, M.D., Ponyrko, N.V., Rozhdestvenskaia, M.D.: 'Opisanie sbornikov XV v. knigopistsa Efrosina', *Trudy Otdela drevnerusskoi literatury*, 1980, pp. 3–300.

Kagan-Tarkovskaia, M.D.: 'Drevnerusskie vracheval'nye molitvy ot ukusa zmei', *Trudy Otdela drevnerusskoi literatury*, 46, 1993, pp. 287–93.

Kalendarno-obriadovaia poèziia sibiriakov, ed. F.F. Bolonev, M.N. Mel'nikov, Novosibirsk, 1981.

Kamentseva, E.I., Ustiugov, N.V., *Russkaia sfragistika i geral'dika*, Moscow, 1963.

Kantorovich, Ia.: *Srednevekovye protsessy o ved'makh*, St Petersburg, 1899 (reprint Moscow, 1990).

Karamzin, N.M.: *Istoriia gosudarstva rossiiskogo*, 12 vols, St Petersburg, 1816–29.

Karamzin, N.M.: *Natal'ia the Boyar's Daughter (1792)*, in *Russian Tales*, London, 1803.

Kargapol'tsev, S. Iu., and Bazhan, I.A.: 'Ob odnoi kategorii ukrashenii-amuletov rimskogo vremeni v

Vostochnoi Evrope', *Sovetskaia arkheologiia*, 1989, 3, pp. 163–70.

Karpov, A.: *Azbukovniki ili alfavity inostrannykh rechei*, Kazan', 1877.

Karskii, E.F.: *Belorusy* (III. Ocherki slovesnosti belorusskogo plemeni. 2. Staraia zapadnorusskaia pis'mennost'), Petrograd, 1921.

Kasten, Ll.A.: *Seudo Aristóteles Poridąt de las Poridades*, Madrid, 1957.

Kazanskaia istoriia, ed. V.P. Adrianova-Peretts, G.N. Moiseeva, Moscow–Leningrad, 1954.

Keep, J.L.H.: *Soldiers of the Tsar: Army and Society in Russia 1462–1874*, Oxford, 1985

Keil, G.: "Gart", "Herbarius", "Hortus". Anmerkungen zu den ältesten Kraüterbuch-inkunabeln', in *Gelêrter der arzenîe, ouch apotêker'. Beiträge zur Wissenschafts-geschichte. Festschrift für Willem F. Daems*, Würzburger medizinhistorische Forschungen, XXIV, 1982, pp. 589–635.

Keil, G.: 'Hortus Sanitatis, Gart der Gesundheit, Gaerde der Sunthede', in *Medieval Gardens*, Dumbarton Oaks Colloquium on the History of Landscape Architecture, IX, Washington, 1986, pp. 55–68.

Keil, G.: *Die deutsche Literatur des Mittelalters. Verfasserlexikon*, IV, 1, 1983, s. v. *Hortus sanitatis*.

Kelsiev, V.I.: *Sbornik pravitel'stvennykh svedenii o rasskolnikakh*, 4 vols, London, 1860–62.

Kemp, P.: *Healing Ritual. Studies in the Technique and Tradition of the Southern Slavs*, London, 1935.

Kerenskii, P.F.: 'Drevnerusskie otrechennye verovaniia i kalendar' Briusa', *Zhurnal Ministerstva narodnogo prosveshcheniia*, CLXXII, 1874, pp. 52–79.

Kharuzina, V.: 'Po povodu zametki P. Andre o novom ètnogroficheskom muzee v Antwerpene', *Ètnograficheskoe obozrenie*, LXXV, 1907, 4, pp. 91–103.

Khodzhiev, I · 'K voprosu o vostochnykh predshestvennikakh pskovskoi gadatel'noi knigi', in *Arkheologiiai istoriia Pskova i pskovskoi zemli*, Pskov, 1988, pp. 55–6.

Khrenov, L.S.: *Narodnye primety i kalendar'*, Moscow, 1991.

Khaldūn, Ibn: *The Muqaddimah. An Introduction to History*, transl. and ed. by Franz Rosenthal, New York, 1954.

Kieckhefer, R.: 'Avenging the Blood of Children: Anxiety Over Child Victims and the Origins of the European Witch Trials', in *The Devil, Heresy and Witchcraft in the Middle Ages: Essays in Honor of Jeffrey B. Russell*, Leiden, 1998, pp. 93–109.

Kieckhefer, Richard: *Forbidden Rites: A Necromancer's Manual of the Fifteenth Century*, Stroud, 1997.

Kieckhefer, Richard: 'The Holy and the Unholy: Sainthood, Witchcraft and Magic in Late Medieval Europe', *Journal of Medieval and Renaissance Studies*, 24, 3, 1994, pp. 355–85.

Kieckhefer, Richard: *Magic in the Middle Ages*, Cambridge, 1989.

Kieckhefer, Richard: 'The Office of Inquisition and Medieval Heresy: The Transition from Personal to Institutional Jurisdiction', *Journal of Ecclesiastical History*, 46, 1, 1995, pp. 36–61.

Kirchenhoffer, H.: *The Book of Fate*, London, 1822.

Kirilov, N.: 'Interes izucheniia narodnoi i tibetskoi meditsiny v Zabaikal'e', *Ètnograficheskoe obozrenie*, XIX, 1893, 4.

Kirkor, A.: 'Ètnograficheskie vzgliady na Vilenskuiu guberniu', *Ètnograficheskii sbornik*, III, 1858.

Kititsina, L.: 'Khleb. Iz materialov po narodnomu pitaniiu Kostromskogo kraia', *Trudy Kostromskogo nauchnogo obshchestva po izucheniiu mestnogo kraia*, XLI, Kostroma, 1927, pp. 98–9.

Kivelson, Valerie: 'Patrolling the Boundaries: Witchcraft Accusations and Household Strife in Seventeenth-Century Muscovy', *Harvard Ukrainian Studies*, 29, 1995, pp. 302–23.

Kivelson, Valerie: 'Political Sorcery in Sixteenth-Century Muscovy', in *Cultural Identity in Muscovy, 1359–1584*, ed. A.M. Kleimola and G. D. Lenhoff, Slavica, 1997, pp. 267–83.

Kivelson, Valerie: 'Through the Prism of Witchcraft: Gender and Social Change in Seventeenth-Century Muscovy', in *Russia's Women. Accommodation, Resistance, Transformation*, ed. Barbara Evans Clements, Barbara Alpern Engel, Christine D. Worobec, Berkeley, 1991, pp. 74–94.

Klaniczay, G.: 'Shamanistic Elements in Central European Witchcraft', in *Shamanism in Eurasia*, pt 2, Göttingen, 1984, pp. 404–22.

Klaniczay, G.: 'Witch-hunting in Hungary: Social or Cultural Tensions', *Acta ethnographica Acad. Sci. Hung.*, 37 (1–4), 1991/92, pp. 67–91.

Kleimola, Ann M.: *Justice in Medieval Russia: Muscovite Judgment Charters* (pravye gramoty) *of the Fifteenth and Sixteenth Centuries*, Transactions of the American Philosophical Society, n.s. 65, 6, Philadelphia, 1975.

Klein, L.S.: 'Pamiati iazycheskogo boga Roda', in *Iazychestvo vostochnykh slavian*, Leningrad, 1990, pp. 13–26.

Kliaus, V.L.: 'Serdtsa ptits i polovye organy zhivotnykh kak sredstva liubovnoi magii', in *Seks i èrotika v russkoi traditsionnoi kul'ture*, ed. A.L. Toporkov, Moscow, 1996, pp. 313–22.

Kliaus, V.L.: *Ukazatel' siuzhetov i siuzhetnykh situatsii zagovornykh tekstov vostochnykh i iuzhnykh slavian*, Moscow, 1977.

Kliaus, V.L.: 'Zagovory i magicheskie sredstva', in *Russkii èroticheskii fol'klor*, ed. A. Toporkov, Moscow, 1995, pp. 344–61.

Klibanov, A.I.: *Reformatsionnye dvizheniia v Rossii*, Moscow, 1960.

Klijn, A.F.J.: *Seth in Jewish, Christian and Gnostic Literature*, Supplements to Novum Testamentum XLVI, Leiden, 1977.

Klintberg, B.: *Svenska trollformler*, Stockholm, 1965.

Kobiak, N.A.: 'Indeks lozhnykh knig i drevnerusskii chitatel'', *Khristianstvo i tserkov' v Rossii feodal'nogo perioda*, Novosibirsk, 1989, pp. 352–63.

Kobiak, N.A.: 'Indeksy otrechennykh i zapreshchennykh knig v russkoi pis'mennosti', in *Drevnerusskaia literatura. Istochnikovedeniia*, Leningrad, 1984, pp. 45–54.

Koch, Fred C.: *The Volga Germans in Russia and the Americas from 1763 to the Present*, University Park, Penn. and London, 1977.

Kolchin, A.: 'Verovaniia krest'ian Tul'skoi gubernii', *Ètnograficheskoe obozrenie*, 42, 3, 1899, pp. 1–60.

Kolesova, V.V., ed.: *Domostroi*, Moscow, 1990.

Kondrat'eva, O.A.: 'Greben' v pogrebal'nom obriade (po materialom drevnerusskikh mogil'nikov X–XII vv.', in *Iazychestvo vostochnykh slavian*, Leningrad, 1990, pp. 37–42.

Kondrat'eva, O.A.: 'Krest'ianskie zoomorfnye metallicheskie grebni i drevnie traditsii v ikh izgotovlenii', *Pamiatniki kul'tury. Novye otkrytiia 1983*, Leningrad, 1985, pp. 452–8.

Kondrat'eva, T.N.: *Metamorfozy sobstvennogo imeni*, Kazan', 1983.

Kononov, N.N.: 'Iz oblasti astrologii. Obzor statei: Planetnika, Zvezdochtetsa, Koliadnika, Gromnika, Lunnika, Trepetnika, Tainaia tainykh, Lechebnika i pr. ruk. XVIII v. A.G. Pervukhina', *Drevnosti. Trudy slavianskoi komissii imp. Moskovskogo arkheologicheskogo obshchestva*, Moscow, 1907, IV, 1, pp. 16–53.

Konovalova, O.F.: 'Sravnenie kak literaturnyi priem v *Zhitii Stefana Permskogo*', *Sbornik statei po metodike prepodavaniia inostrannykh iazyk i filiologii*, Leningradskii tekhnologicheskii institut kholodil'noi promyshlennosti, I, Leningrad, 1963, pp. 117–38.

Korb, J.G.: *Diary of an Austrian Secretary of Legation at the Court of Czar Peter the Great*, London, 1863.

Koretskii, B.A. Gradov, B.M. Kloss, V.I.: 'K istorii arkhangel'skoi biblioteki D.M. Golitsyna', *Arkheograficheskii ezhegodnik*, 1978, pp. 238–53.

Korobka, N.I.: 'Kamen' na more i kamen' alatar' , *Zhivaia starina*, 1908, 4, p. 422.

Koshel', P.: *Istoriia nakazanii v Rossii*, Moscow, 1995.

Kosheleva, O.E. and Simonov, R.: 'Novoe o pervoi russkoi knige po teoreticheskoi geometrii XVII veka i ego avtore', *Kniga. Issledovaniia i materialy*, XLII, Moscow, 1981, pp. 63–73.

Kostomarov, N.I.: 'Ocherk domashnei zhizni i nravov velikorusskogo naroda v XVI i XVII stoletiiakh', *Sovremennik*, 83, 1860 (also published as book; 3rd edn 1887, reprinted 1992, another modified version 1993).

Kotansky, Roy: *Greek Magical Amulets. The Inscribed Gold, Silver, Copper, and Bronze Lamellae.* Part 1, *Published Texts of Known Provenance, Papyrologica Coloniensia*, XXII, 1, 1994.

Kotansky, Roy: 'Incantations and Prayers for Salvation on Inscribed Greek Amulets', in *Magika Hiera. Ancient Greek Magic and Religion*, New York and Oxford, 1991, pp. 107–37.

Kotermak, Iurii, of Drohobych, *Judicium prognosticon anni 1483 currentis Magistri Georgii Drohobicz de Russia almi studii bononiensis artium et medicinae doctoris*, Rome, 1483.

Kotoshikhin, Grigorii: *O Rossii v tsarstvovanie Alekseia Mikhailovicha*, ed. A.E. Pennington, Oxford, 1980.

Kovtun, L.S.: 'Planida furtuna schastnoe koleso (k istorii russkoi idiomatiki)', *Trudy Otdela drevnerusskoi literatury*, XXIV, 1969, pp. 327–30.

Kozyrev, N.: 'Svadebnye obriady i obychai v Ostrovskom uezde Pskovskoi gubernii', *Zhivaia starina*, 1912, 1, pp. 75–94.

Kramer, H. and Sprenger, J.: *Malleus maleficarum*, transl. Montague Summers, London, 1928 (reprint 1996).

Kretzenbacher, L.: 'Südost-Überlieferung zum Apokryphen "Traum Mariens"', *Sitzungsberichte zu Bayerische, Akademie der Wissenschaften. Philosophisch-historische Klasse*, 1975, 1.

Krianev, Iu.V. and Pavlova, T.P.: 'Dvoeverie na Rusi', in *Kak byla kreshchena Rus'*, Moscow, 1988, pp. 362–74.

Krinichnaia, N.A.: *Domashnyi dukh i sviatochnye gadaniia*, Petrozavodsk, 1993.

Krinichnaia, N.A.: *Lesnye navazhdeniia. Mifologicheskie rasskazy i pover'ia o dukhe khoziaina lesa*, Petrozavodsk, 1993.

Krinichnaia, N.A.: *Predaniia russkogo severa*, St Petersburg, 1991.

Krinichnaia, N.A.: *Russkaia narodnaia istoricheskaia proza: voprosy genezisa i struktury*, Leningrad, 1987.

Kriss, Rudolf, and Kriss-Heinrich, Hubert: *Peregrinatio neohellenika. Wallfahrtswanderungen im heutigen Griechenland und in Italien*, Vienna, 1955.

Kruger, Stephen F.: *Dreaming in the Middle Ages*, Cambridge, 1992.

Kruglov, G.: *Russkie obriadovye pesni*, Moscow, 1982.

Krumbacher, K.: *Geschichte der Byzantinische Litteratur, 527–1453*, 2nd edn (=*Handbuch d. klass. Altertums-Wissenschaft*, X, i), Münich, 1897.

Kuev, Kuio: *Azbuchnita molitva v slavianskite literaturi*, Sofia, 1974.

Kukushkina, M.V.: *Monastyrskie biblioteki russkogo severa: Ocherki po istorii knizhnoi kul'tury XVI–XVII vv.*, Leningrad, 1977.

Kulakovskii, S.: 'Sostav Skazaniia o chudesakh ikony bogomateri Rymlianini', in *Sbornik statei v chest' akademika Alekseia Ivanovicha Sobolevskogo*, Leningrad, 1928, pp. 470–5.

Kulikowski, Mark: *A Bibliography of Slavic Mythology*, Columbus, 1989.

Kurbskii, A.M.: *Istoriia o Velikom Kniaze Moskovskom*, St Petersburg, 1913.

Kurs znakharstva, narodnykh zagovorov, i raznykh poleznykh sovetov, Moscow, 1914.

Kuzakov, V.K.: 'O vospriiatii v XV v. na Rusi astronomicheskogo traktata «Shestokryl»', *Istoriko-astronomicheskie issledovaniia*, XII, Moscow, 1975, pp. 113–20.

Kuzakov, V.K.: *Ocherki razvitiia estestvennonnauchnykh i tekhnicheskikh predstavlenii na Rusi v X–XVII vv.*, Moscow, 1976.

Kuznetsov-Krasnoiarskii, I.: *Rafli. Pamiatniki starinoi russkoi pis'mennosti*, Tomsk, 1905 (review by S.K. K-v in *Ètnograficheskoe obozrenie*, 1905, 4, pp. 129–32).

Kuźnicka, Barbara: 'The Earliest Printed Herbals and Evolution of Pharmacy', *Organon*, XVI–XVII, Warsaw 1980–81, pp. 255–66.

Lakhtin, M.Iu.: 'Starinnye pamiatniki meditsinskoi pis'mennosti', *Zapiski Moskovskogo arkheologicheskogo instituta*, XVII, 1912.

Larin, B.A.: *Russko-angliiskii slovar'-dnevnik Richarda Dzhemsa 1618–1619*, Leningrad, 1959.

Larner, Christina: *Enemies of God*, London, 1981.

Lastoŭski, A.V.: *Gystoriia belaruskaĭ (kryŭskaĭ) knigi*, Koŭna, 1926

Laurent, V.: 'Amulettes byzantines et formulaires magiques', *Byzantinische Zeitschrift*, XXXVI, 1936, pp. 300–15.

Laurent, V.: *Les 'Mémoires' du Grand Ecclésiarque Sylvestre Syropoulos sur le concile de Florence (1438–1439)*, Paris, 1971.

Lawson, J.C.: *Modern Greek Folklore and Ancient Greek Religion. A Study in Survivals*, Cambridge, 1910.

Le Grand et le Petit Albert, intr. Bernard Husson, Paris, 1970.

Lea, Henry C.: *Superstition and Force*, 2nd edn, New York, 1870.

Lebedeva, A.A.: 'Material'nye komponenty, ikh kharakter i rol' v traditsionnom obriade russkikh starozhilov Tobol'skoi gubernii (XIX–nachalo XX v.)', in *Russkii narodnyi svadebnyi obriad*, ed. K.V. Chistova, T.A. Bernshtam, Leningrad, 1978, pp. 202–19.

Lebedeva, A.A.: 'Znachenie poiasa i polotentsa v russkikh semeino-bytovykh obychaiakh i obriadakh XIX–XX vv.', in *Russkie: semeinyi i obshchestvennyi byt*, Moscow, 1989, pp. 229–48.

Leeming, H.: 'Polish and Polish-Latin Medical Terms in Pre-Petrine Russian', *Slavonic and East European Review*, 42, 1963, pp. 89–109.

Leeming, H.: 'Polonisms in a Seventeenth-Century Ruthenian Text', *Slavonic and East European Review*, 46, 1968, pp. 282–314.

Leighton, Lauren G.: 'Gematria in "The Queen of Spades": A Decembrist Puzzle', *Slavic and East European Journal*, 21, 4, 1977, pp. 455–69.

Leighton, Lauren G.: 'Puškin and Freemasonry: "The Queen of Spades"', in *New Perspectives on Nineteenth-Century Russian Prose*, ed. George J. Gutsche and Lauren G. Leighton, Columbus, 1982, pp. 15–25.

Lemerle, P.: *Le Premier Humanisme byzantin*, Paris, 1971.

Lemerle, Paul: *Les Plus Anciens Récits des miracles de Saint Démétrius*, Paris, 1979–81.

Lepskaia, N.I.: 'K istorii slova *planeta*', in *Ètimologicheskie issledovaniia po russkomu iazyku*, vyp. 5, Moscow, 1966, pp. 49–59.

Les Lapidaires grecs, ed. R. Halleux, J. Schamp, Paris, 1985.

Levack, Brian P.: *The Witch Hunt in Early Modern Europe*, London, 1987.

Levenstim, A.A.: 'Sueverie v ego otnoshenie k ugolovnomu pravu', *Zhurnal Ministerstva iustitsii*, 1897, 1, pp. 157–219; 2, pp. 62–127 (also as *Aberglaube und Strafrecht*, Berlin, 1897).

Levin, Eve: 'Childbirth in Pre-Petrine Russia: Canon Law and Popular Traditions', in *Russia's Women. Accommodation, Resistance, Transformation*, ed. Barbara Evans Clements, Barbara Alpern Engel, Christine D. Worobec, Berkeley, 1991, pp. 44–59.

Levin, Eve: '*Dvoeverie* and Popular Religion', in *Seeking God. The Recovery of Religious Identity in Orthodox Russia, Ukraine and Georgia*, ed. Stephen K. Batalden, DeKalb, 1993, pp. 31–52.

Levin, Eve: *Sex and Society in the World of the Orthodox Slavs*, Ithaca, 1989.

Levin, Eve: 'Supplicatory Prayers as a Source for Popular Religious Culture In Muscovite Russia', in *Religion and Culture in Early Modern Russia and Ukraine*, edited by Samuel H. Baron and Nancy Shields Kollmann, DeKalb, 1997, pp. 96–114.

Lewis, G.L.: 'Eight Stars that Never Were', *Erdem*, 3, 3, pp. 809–18 and plates.

Lewis, Naphthali: *The Interpretation of Dreams and Portents*, Toronto and Sarasota, 1976.

Liber Rasis ad Almansorem, Venice, 1487.

Libro de ajedrez, dados y tablas de Alfonso X el Sabio, ed. Pilar García Morencos, Madrid, 1977.

Likhacheva, O.P.: 'K izucheniiu «Slova o tvari i o dni, rekomem nedelia»', *Trudy Otdela drevneruskoi literatury*, XXIV, 1969, pp. 68–71.

Linder, I.M.: *Shakhmaty na Rusi*, 2nd edn, Moscow, 1975.

Listova, T.A.: 'Nekotorye verovaniia russkikh krest'ian, sviazannye c khristianstvom', in *Arkheologiia i istoriia Pskova i pskovskoi zemli*, Pskov, 1988, pp. 26–9.

Listova, T.A.: «Nechistota» zhenshchiny (rodil'naia i mesiachnaia) v obychaiakh i predstavleniiakh russkogo naroda', in *Seks i èrotika v russkoi traditsionnoi kul'ture*, ed. A.L. Toporkov, Moscow, 1996, pp. 151–74.

Loginov, K.K.: *Material'naia kul'tura i proizvodstvenno-bytovaia magiia russkikh Zaonezh'ia*, St Petersburg, 1993.

Lokhteva, G.N.: 'Materialy Aptekarskogo prikaza vazhnyi istochnik po istorii meditsiny v Rossii XVII v.', in *Estestvennonauchnye znaniia v Drevnei Rusi*, Moscow, 1980, pp. 139–56.

Longo, Haisa Pessina: *Iurii Drogobich. Georgius de Russia, Rettore a Bologna nel XV secolo*, Bologna, 1988.

Longworth, Philip: *Alexis, Tsar of All the Russias*, London, 1984.

Loorits, Oskar: *Der Heilige Kassian und der Schaltjahrlegende*, FF Communications no 149, Helsinki, 1954.

Lotman, Iu.M.: *Roman A.S. Pushkina Evgenii Onegin'*, Leningrad, 1980.

Lotman, Ju.M. and Uspenskij, B.A.: 'New Aspects in the Study of Early Russian Culture', in Ju.M. Lotman and B.A. Uspenskij, *The Semeiotics of Russian Culture*, ed. Ann Shukman, Ann Arbor, 1984, pp. 36–52.

Lotman, Ju.M. and Uspenskij, B.A.: 'The Role of Dual Models of Russian Culture (up to the End of the Eighteenth Century)', in Ju.M. Lotman, B.A. Uspenskij, *The Semeiotics of Russian Culture*, Ann Arbor, 1984, pp. 3–35.

Lotman Iu. and Uspenskii, B.A.: 'K semioticheskoi tipologii russkoi kul'tury XVIII veka', in *Materialy nauchnoi konferentsii (1973). Khudozhesvennaia kul'tura XVIII veka*, Moscow, 1974, pp. 259–82.

Luck, Georg: *Arcana mundi. Magic and the Occult in the Greek and Roman Worlds*, Baltimore and London, 1985.

Ludolph, H.W.: *Grammatica Russica*, Oxford, 1696.

Lunt, H.G. and Taube, M.: 'Early East Slavonic Translations from Hebrew?', *Russian Linguistics*, 12, 1988, pp. 147–87.

Luppov, S.P.: *Kniga v Rossii v XVII veke*, Leningrad, 1970.

Lur'e, Ia.S.: *Russkie sovremenniki Vozrozhdeniia. Knigopisets Efrosin. D'iak Fedor Kuritsyn*, Leningrad, 1988.

Luria [Lur'je], Jakov S.: 'Unresolved Issues in the History of the Ideological Movements of the late Fifteenth Century', in *Medieval Russian Culture*, ed. Henrik Birnbaum and Michael S. Flier, California Slavic Studies XII, Berkeley, etc. 1984, pp. 150–71.

Lydus, Johannes: *Liber de ostentis et calendaria graeca omnia*, ed. C. Wachsmuth, Leipzig, 1887

Lyndoe, Edward: *Everybody's Book of Fate and Fortune*, London, 1935.

Lysenko, O.V., and Ostrovskii, A.B.: 'Logicheskie skhemy okkazional'nykh obriadov vyzyvaniia dozhdia belorusskogo Poles'ia', in *Iazychestvo vostochnykh slavian*, Leningrad, 1990, pp. 108–19.

MacKinnon, Ian: 'Drivers register 666 reasons for new numbers', *The Independent*, 2 February 1990, p. 1.

Maclean, Fitzroy: *To the Back of Beyond*, London, 1974.

MacMullen, R.: *Enemies of the Roman Order: Treason, Unrest and Alienation in the Empire*, Cambridge, Mass., 1966.

Madar, Maia; 'Estonia I: Werewolves and Poisoners', in *Early Modern European Witchcraft. Centres and Peripheries*, ed. Bengt Ankarloo and Gustav Henningsen, Oxford, 1990, pp. 257–72.

Magdalino, Paul: 'Church, Bath and *Diakonia* in Medieval Constantinople', in *Church and People in Byzantium*, Twentieth Spring Symposium of Byzantine Studies, Manchester, 1986, ed. Rosemary Morris, Birmingham, 1990, pp. 165–88.

Maguire, E.D., Maguire, H.P., and Duncan-Flowers, M.J.: *Art and Holy Powers in the Early Christian House*, Illinois Byzantine Studies II, Urbana and Chicago, 1989.

Maikov, L.N.: 'Velikorusskie zaklinaniia', *Zapiski Imp. Russkogo geograficheskogo obshchestva po otdeleniiu ètnografii*, II, 1869, pp. 417–580. (Reprinted St Petersburg Paris, 1992, with new pagination, postscript and notes by A.K. Baiburin.)

Maimonides: *Moses Maimonides' Glossary of Drug Names*, ed. Max Meyerhof, English transl. and ed. F. Rosner, Philadelphia, 1979.

Makarenko, Aleksei: *Sibirskii narodnyi kalendar' v ètnograficheskom otnoshenii* (= *Zapiski Imp. Russkogo geograficheskogo obshchestva po otdeleniiu ètnografii*, XXXVI), St Petersburg, 1913.

Makarov, N.A., and Chernetsov, A.V.: 'K izucheniiu kul'tovykh kamnei', *Sovetskaia arkheologiia*, 1988, 3, pp. 79–90.

Makarov, N.A.: 'Drevnerusskie amulety-toporiki', in *Arkheologiia i istoriia Pskova i pskovskoi zemli*, Pskov, 1988, pp. 30–2.

Makarov, N.A.: 'Magicheskie obriady pri sokrytii klada na Rusi', *Sovetskaia arkheologiia*, 1981, 4, pp. 261–4.

Makashina, T.S.: 'Sviatye Kosma i Damian v russkom fol'klore', *Zhivaia starina* , 1994, 3, pp. 18–21.

Makhnovets', O.I.: *Ukrains'ki pis'menniki. Bio-bibliografichnii slovnik*, I, Kiev, 1960.

Maksimov, S.V.: *Nechistaia, nevedomaia i krestnaia sila*, St Petersburg, 1903 (reprint in 2 vols, Moscow, 1993).

Mal'm, V.A.: 'Krestiki s èmal'iu', in *Slaviane i Rus'*, ed. E.I. Krupnov, Moscow, 1968, pp. 113–17.

Maloney, Clarence, ed.: *The Evil Eye*, New York, 1976.

Malov, A.: *Pis'ma k voinam*, St Petersburg, 1831.

Malyshev, V.I.: *Drevnerusskie rukopisi Pushkinskogo Doma*, Moscow Leningrad, 1965.

Mango, C.: 'The Legend of Leo the Wise', *Recueil des travaux de l'Académie serbe des sciences*, LXV, 1960, pp. 59–93.

Mansi, J.: *Sacrorum conciliorum: nova et amplissima collectio*, 54 vols, Graz, 1960–61 (reprint of 1901–27 edition).

Mansikka, V.J.: *Der Religion der Ostslaven*, Folklore Fellows Communications 43, Helsinki, 1967 (first published 1921).

Mansikka, V.J.: *Über russische Zauberformeln*, Annales Academiae Scientiarum Fennicae, ser. B, tom. 1, Helsinki, 1909.

Mansvetov, I.D.: *Vizantiiskii material dlia skazaniia o 12 triasavits*, Moscow, 1881.

Manzalaoui, M.A.: 'The Pseudo-Aristotelian *Kitāb Sirr al-Asrār*: Facts and Problems', *Oriens*, 24 (1970–71), pp. 147–257.

Manzalaoui, M.: 'Secretum Secretorum', in *Dictionary of the Middle Ages*, vol. 11, New York, 1988, p. 135.

Manzalaoui, M.A.: *Secretum secretorum. Nine English Versions*, Early English Text Society 276, Oxford, 1977.

Marana, Giovanni Paolo: *The Third Volume of Letters written by a Turkish Spy*, London, 1691.

Margeret, Jacques, *see* Dunning.

Markevich, N.A.: *Obychai, pover'ia, kukhnia i napitki malorossian*, Kiev, 1860 (reprinted in *Ukraintsi: narodni viruvannia, povir'ia, demonologiia*, Kiev, 1991).

Markov, E.L.: 'Derevenskii koldun', *Istoricheskii vestnik*, XXVIII, 1887, April, pp. 5–24.

Markus, R.A.: 'Augustine on Magic: A Neglected Semiotic Theory', *Revue des Études Augustiniennes*, 40, 1994, pp. 375–88.

Marqués-Rivière, J.: *Amulettes, talismans et pantacles dans les traditions orientales et occidentales*, Paris, 1938.

Massa, Isaac: *A Short History of the Beginnings and Origins of These Present Wars in Moscow under the Reign of Various Sovereigns down to the Year 1610*, trans. G. Edward Orchard, Toronto, 1982.

Materialy dlia istorii Moskovskogo vospitatel'nogo doma, I, 3, Moscow, 1883.

Mathers, S.L. Macgregor (ed.): *The Book of Sacred Magic of Abra-Melin the Sage*, London, 1897.

Mathers, S.L. Macgregor (ed.): *The Key of Solomon the King*, London, 1909.

Mathiesen, Robert: 'Magic in *Slavia Orthodoxa*: The Written Tradition', in *Byzantine Magic*, ed. Henry Maguire, Dumbarton Oaks, 1995, pp. 155–77.

Matveeva, R.P.: *Mifologicheskie rasskazy russkogo naseleniia vostochnoi Sibiri*, Novosibirsk, 1987.

Mazalova, N.E.: 'Zhiznennaia sila severnorusskogo «znaiushego»', *Zhivaia starina*, 4, 1994, pp. 26–8.

Mazo, Margarita: '"We don't summon Spring in the Summer". Traditional Music and Beliefs of the Contemporary Russian Village', in *Christianity and the Arts in Russia*, ed. William C. Brumfield and Milos M. Velimirovic, Cambridge, 1991, pp. 73–94.

McCartney, Eugene S.: 'Praise and Dispraise in Folklore', *Papers of the Michigan Academy of Science, Art, and Letters*, 28 (1943), pp. 567–93 (reprinted in Dundes, ed., *The Evil Eye*, pp. 9–38.)

McGinn, Bernard: *Antichrist: Two Thousand Years of the Human Fascination with Evil*, San Francisco, 1995.

McNeill, John T. and Gamer, Helena M.: *Medieval Handbooks of Penance*, New York, 1938 (reprint 1965).

Meaney, Audrey L.: *Anglo-Saxon Amulets and Curing Stones*, BAR British series 96, 1981.

Ménard, Philippe: 'La Baguette magique au moyen âge', *Mélanges de langue et de littérature médiévales offerts à Alice Plache*, Annales de la Faculté des lettres et sciences humaines de Nice, 48, 1984, pp. 339–46.

Merkulova, B. A.: *Ocherki po russkoi narodnoi nomenklature rastenii*, Moscow, 1967.

Merrifield, Ralph: *The Archaeology of Ritual and Magic*, London, 1987.

Meshcherskii, N.A.: *Istochniki i sostav slaviano-russkoi perevodnoi pis'mennosti IX–XV vekov*, Leningrad, 1978.

Meshcherskii, N.A.: *Istoriia iudeiskoi voiny Iosifa Flaviia v drevnerusskom perevode*, Moscow–Leningrad, 1958.

Metham, J.: *The Works of John Metham*, ed. H. Craig, Early English Text Society 132, London, 1916.

Michelis, Cesare G. De: *I nomi dell'avversario. Il 'Papa Anticristo' nella cultura russa*, Turin, 1989.

Midelfort, H.C. Erik: *Witch Hunting in Southwestern Germany 1562–1684*, Stanford, 1972.

Miller, David B.: 'The Lübeckers Bartholomäus Ghotan and Nicolaus Bülow in Novgorod and Moscow and the Problem of Early Western Influences on Russian Culture', *Viator*, LXXIX, 1978, pp. 395–412.

Miller, Patricia Cox: *Dreams in Late Antiquity*, Princeton, 1994.

Miller, Vs.: 'Assiriiskie zaklinaniia i russkie narodnye zagovory', *Russkaia mysl'*, Moscow, 1896, kn. 7, pp. 66–89.

Miloradovich, V.P.: 'Zhit'e-byt'e lubenskogo krestianina', *Kievskaia starina*, 1902, nos 4, 6, 10; 1903, nos 2, 3, 7–8; 1904, nos 5, 6 (reprinted in *Ukraintsi: narodni viruvannia, povir'ia, demonologiia*, Kiev, 1991, pp. 17–341).

Milton, John: *A Brief History of Muscovia*, London, 1682.

Minenko, N.A.: *Russkaia krest'ianskaia obshchina v Zapadnoi Sibiri XVIII–pervaia polovina XIX veka*, Novosibirsk, 1991.

Minenko, N.A.: *Russkaia krest'ianskaia sem'ia v Zapadnoi Sibiri (XVIII–pervoi poloviny XIX v.)*, Novosibirsk, 1979

Mincnok, E.V.: 'Podbliudnye gadaniia derevni Voilovo Kaluzhskoi oblasti', in *Russkii èroticheskii fol'klor*, ed. A. Toporkov, Moscow, 1995, pp. 235–42.

Minkh, A.N.: 'Narodnye obychai, obriady, sueveriia, i predrassudki krest'ian Saratovskoi gubernii', *Zapiski imperatorskogo Russkogo Geograficheskogo obshchestva po otdeleniiu ètnografii*, XIX, 2, 1890.

Min'ko, L.I.: 'Magical Curing: Its Sources and Character, and the Causes of its Prevalence?', *Soviet Anthropology and Archaeology*, XII, 1, Summer, 1973, pp. 3–33; XII, 2, Fall, 1973, pp. 34–60; XII, 3, Winter 1973–74, pp. 3–27 (first published in *Nauka i tekhnika*, 1971).

Min'ko, L.I.: *Sueveriia i primety*, Minsk, 1975.

Moeller, Walter O.: *The Mithraic Origin and Meanings of the ROTAS-SATOR Square*, Leiden, 1973.

Montero, Santiago: *Política y adivinación en el Bajo Imperio Romano: emeradores y haruspices (193 D.C.–408 D.C.)*, Collection Latomus 211, Brussels, 1991.

Mordovina, S.P., and Stanislavskii, A.L.: 'Gadatel'naia kniga XVII v. kholopa Pimena Kalinina', in *Istoriia russkogo iazyka. Pamiatniki XI–XVIII vv.*, Moscow, 1982, pp. 321–36.

Moscadi, L. Baldini, 'Murmur nella terminologia magica', *Studi italiani di filologia classica*, 48, 1976, pp. 254–62.

Moszyński, K.: *Kultura ludowa słowian. Cz. II, Kultura duchowa*, Krakow, 1934.

Motsia, A.P.: 'Nekotorye svedeniia o rasprostranenii khristianstva na iuge Rusi po dannym pogrebal'nogo obriada', in *Obriady i verovaniia drevnego naseleniia Ukrainy*, Kiev, 1990, pp. 114–33.

Mouterde, R.: 'Objets magiques. Recueil S. Ayvaz', *Mélanges de l'Université St Joseph*, XXV, 6, 1942–3, pp. 105–28.

Muchembled, Robert: 'Satanic Myths and Cultural Reality', in *Early Modern European Witchcraft. Centres and Peripheries*, ed. Bengt Ankarloo and Gustav Henningsen, Oxford, 1990, pp. 139–60.

Muller, A.V.: *The Spiritual Regulation of Peter the Great*, Seattle, 1972.

Munitiz, J. ed.: *Nikephoras Blemmydes: A Partial Account*, Leuven, 1988.

Murgoci, A.: 'The Evil Eye in Rumania and its Antidotes', *Folklore*, 34, 1923, pp. 357–62.

Murray, A.J.R.: *A History of Board Games other than Chess*, Oxford, 1952.

Na putiakh iz zemli permskoi v Sibir'. Ocherki ètnografii severnoural'skogo krest'ianstva, ed. V.A. Aleksandrov, Moscow, 1989.

Narodnaia kartinka XVII–XIX vekov. Materialy i issledovaniia, ed. M.A. Alekseeva, E.A. Mishina, St Petersburg, 1996.

Narodnyi prazdnik. Iz opyta raboty uchrezhdenii kul'tury oblasti, Vologda, 1991.

Năsturel, Petre: 'Autour du phylactère slavo-roumain de Budăneşti', *Recueil IV. Études et documents balkaniques et méditerranéens*, 13, Paris, 1987, pp. 52–5.

Naveh, J. and Shaked, Sh.: *Amulets and Magic Bowls. Aramaic Incantations of Late Antiquity*, Jerusalem and Leiden, 1985.

Naziratel, ed. V.S. Golyshenko, R.V. Bakhturina, I.S. Filippova, Moscow, 1973 (edition of the Old Russian sixteenth-century translation of Petrus de Crescentiis, *Opus ruralium commodorum* (*c*. 1305), probably from the Polish edition of 1549).

Nekrylova, A.F.: *Russkie narodnye gorodskie prazdniki, uveseleniia i zrelishcha*, Leningrad, 1984.

Nelli, R.: 'La Prière aux soixante-douze noms de Dieu', *Folklore* (Carcassonne), 8, 1950, pp. 70–4.

Neschastnyi Nikanor, ili prikliuchenie zhizni rossiiskogo dvorianina, St Petersburg, 1775 (pt. 1 only) and 1787–9.

Neugebauer, O.: *Greek Horoscopes*, Memoirs of the American Philosophical Society 48, Philadelphia, 1959.

Neugebauer, O.: 'Studies in Byzantine Astronomical Terminology', *Transactions of the American Philosophical Society*, n.s., 2, Philadelphia, 1960.

Nielsen, Inge: *Thermae et Balnea. The Architecture and Cultural History of Roman Public Baths*, Aarhus, 1990.

Nikephoras: *Breviarium*, ed. C. Mango, Dumbarton Oaks, Washington, 1990.

Nikiforov, A.: 'Russkie povesti, legendy i pover'ia o kartofele', *Izvestiia Obshchestva istorii, arkheologii i ètnografii pri Kazanskom universitete*, 32, 1 (republished as a pamphlet with new pagination, Kazan', 1922).

Nikiforovskii, N.Ia.: *Prostonarodnye primety i pover'ia, suevernye obriady i obychai, legendarnye skazaniia o litsakh i mestakh*, Vitebsk, 1897.

Nikitina, Iu.I.: 'Risunki-graffiti iz Sofii novgorodskoi', *Sovetskaia arkheologiia*, 1990, 3, pp. 220–32.

Nikitina, N.A.: 'K voprosu o russkikh koldunakh', *Sbornik Muzeia antropologii i ètnografii*, VII, Leningrad, 1928, pp. 229–325.

Nikolaeva, T.V.: *Drevnerusskaia melkaia plastika XI–XVI vekov*, Moscow, 1968.

Nikolaeva, T.V., and Chernetsov, A. V.: *Drevnerusskie amulety-zmeeviki*, Moscow, 1991.

Novaković, St.: 'Apokrifski zbornik našego vijeka', *Starine*, XVIII, 1886.

Novichkova, T.A.: *Russkii demonologicheskii slovar'*, St Petersburg, 1995.

Novombergskii, N.Ia.: *Koldovstvo v Moskovskoi Rusi XVII stoletiia*, St Petersburg, 1906 (= *Materialy po istorii meditsiny v Rossii*, t. 3, ch. 1).

Oberegi i zaklinaniia russkogo naroda, ed. M.I. and A.M. Peskov, Moscow, 1993.

Obolensky, D.: *The Byzantine Commonwealth*, London, 1971.

Obolensky, D.: 'Late Byzantine Culture and the Slavs. A Study in Acculturation', *XV Congrès international d'études byzantines, Athènes 1976. Rapports et co-rapports*, Athens, 1976, pp. 3–26.

Obolensky, D.: 'The Cult of St. Demetrius of Thessaloniki in the History of Byzantine-Slav Relations', *Balkan Studies*, XV, Thessaloniki, 1974, pp. 3–20.

The Occult in Russian and Soviet Culture, ed. Bernice Glatzer Rosenthal, Ithaca and London, 1997.

Odeberg, H.: *3 Enoch or the Hebrew Book of Enoch*, Cambridge, 1928.

Odin million 500,000 snov, Moscow, 1896.

Oinas, Felix J.: *Essays on Russian Folklore and Mythology*, Columbus, Ohio, 1985.

Oinas, Felix J.: 'Folklore and History', *Palaeoslavica*, 2, 1994, pp. 31–47.

Oinas, Felix J.: 'Heretics as Vampires and Demons in Russia', in *Essays on Russian Folklore and Mythology*, pp. 121–30.

Oinas, Felix J.: 'Legends of the Chuds and Pans', *Slavic and East European Journal*, 12, 1968, pp. 184–98 (reprinted in *idem, Studies in Finnic-Slavic Folklore Relations*, Folklore Fellows Communications no. 205, Helsinki, 1969).

Oinas, Felix J.: 'The Devil in Russian Folklore', in *Essays on Russian Folklore and Mythology*, pp. 97–102.

Olaus Magnus, *A Description of the Northern Peoples, 1555*, ed P.G. Foote, Hakluyt Society, 2nd series 150, 3 vols, London, 1996–8.

Olearius, Adam: *Voyages and Travells of the Ambassadors Sent by Frederick Duke of Holstein to the Great Duke of Muscovy and the King of Persia. . .*, London, 1669 (passages as reprinted in Basil Dmytryshyn, *Medieval Russia. A Source Book, 900–1700*, 2nd edn, Hinsdale, 1973, pp. 290–1).

Opie I., and Tatem, M.: *A Dictionary of Superstitions*, Oxford, 1989.

Opisanie dokumentov i del, khraniashchikhsia v arkhive sv. pr. Sinoda, 1 (1542–1721), St Petersburg, 1869.

Opisanie rukopisei sobraniia Chertkova, Novosibirsk, 1986.

Origen, *Contra Celsum*, ed. Henry Chadwick, 2nd rev. edn, Cambridge, 1965.

Orlov, A.S.: 'Amulety «zmeeviki» Istoricheskogo muzeia', *Otchet GIMa za 1916–1925*. Prilozhenie V, Moscow, 1926.

Ostrovskii, A.B.: 'Pravoslavnye nagrudnye kresty: simvolika i plastika', in *Traditsionnye verovaniia v sovremmennoi kul'ture ètnosa*, St Petersburg, 1993, pp. 123–39.

Ostrovskii, A.B.: 'Pravoslavnye nagrudnye kresty (zrimye cherty simvolov)', *Ètnograficheskie tetradi*, vyp. 8–9, 1995, pp. 54–73.

Ostrovskii, A.B.: 'Lechebno-magicheskii kompleks s ikonoi Bozhei Materi', in *Ètnosemiotika ritual'nykh predmetov*, St Petersburg, 1993, pp. 79–98.

Ovsiannikov, O.V., and Riabinin, E.A.: 'Srednevekovye gruntovye mogil'niki Terskogo berega', *Sovetskaia arkheologiia*, 1989, 2, pp. 201–11.

Palmer, Richard: '"In this our lightye and learned tyme": Italian Baths in the Era of the Renaissance', in *The Medical History of Waters and Spas*, ed. Roy Porter, London, 1990, pp. 14–22.

Pamiatniki literatury Drevnei Rusi. Nachalo russkoi literatury. XI–nachalo XII veka, Moscow, 1978.

Pamiatniki literatury Drevnei Rusi. Vtoraia polovina XV veka, Moscow, 1982.

Pamiatniki literatury Drevnei Rusi. Konets XV–pervaia polovina XVI veka, Moscow, 1984.

Pamiatniki literatury Drevnei Rusi. Konets XVI–nachalo XVII vekov, Moscow, 1987.

Pamiatniki literatury Drevnei Rusi. XVII vek, kn. 2, Moscow, 1989.

Pamiatniki russkoi kul'tury pervoi chetverti XVIII veka v sobranii Gos. ordena Lenina Ermitazha, Moscow–Leningrad, 1966.

Pamiatniki starinnoi russkoi literatury, izdannye G. Kushelev-Bezborodko, 4 vols, St Petersburg, 1862.

Panchenko, A.: 'Ètnograficheskie vzgliady na Vilenskuiu guberniu', *Ètnograficheskii sbornik*, III, 1858.

Panchenko, A.M.: *Russkaia kul'tura v kanun petrovskikh reform*, Leningrad, 1984.

Papyri graecae magicae, ed. K. Preisendanz, 1st edn, Leipzig, 1928–31, 2nd edn, 1973.

Parkinson, John: *A Tour of Russia, Siberia and the Crimea 1792–1794*, ed. W. Collier, London, 1971.

[Paul of Aleppo]: *The Travels of Macarius. Extracts from the Diary of the Travels of Macarius, Patriarch of Antioch . . . 1652–1660* (the English abridgement published by Laura Ridding, London, 1936).

Pavlov, A.S.: *Nomokanon pri Bol'shom trebnike*, Moscow, 1897.

Pennington, Anne E.: 'South Slavs in Malta', *Byzance et les Slavs. Études de civilisation. Mélanges Ivan Dujčev*, Paris, 1979, pp. 333–5.

Pera, Pia: *I Vecchi Credenti e l'Anticristo*, Genoa, 1992.

Peretts, V.N.: *Kukol'nyi teatr na Rusi*, St Petersburg, 1895.

Peretts, V.N.: 'Materialy k istorii apokrifa i legend. 1. K istorii Gromnika. Vvedenie, slavianskie i evreiskie teksty', *Zapiski Istoriko filologicheskogo fakulteta Imp. Sanktpeterburgskogo universiteta*, LIV, 1, 1899.

Peretts, V.N.: 'Materialy k istorii apokrifa i legendy. K istorii Lunnika', *Izvestiia Otdeleniia russkogo iazyka i slovesnosti*, 1901, pp. 1–126.

Peretts, V.N.: *Slovo o Polku Igorevym*, Kiev, 1926, pp. 238–46.

Perevezentseva, T.G., ed.: *Russkaia narodnaia igrushka*, n.p., n.d. (1990s).

Perkowski, Jan L.: *The Darkling. A Treatise on Slavic Vampirism*, Columbus, Ohio, 1989.

Perrie, Maureen: *The Image of Ivan the Terrible in Russian Folklore*, Cambridge, 1987.

Perrie, Maureen, *Pretenders and Popular Monarchism in Early Modern Russia: The False Tsars of the Time of Troubles*, Cambridge, 1995.

Perry, John: *The State of Russia under the Present Czar*, London, 1716 (reprinted London, 1967).

Perunov, M.N.: *Liubovnye, tselitel'nye i okhranitel'nye zagovory*, Novosibirsk, 1992.

Peterson, Claes: *Peter the Great's Administrative and Judicial Reforms: Swedish Antecedents and the Process of Reception*, Stockholm, 1979,

Peterson, Erik: 'ΕΙΣ ΘΕΟΣ', *Forschungen zur Religion und Litteratur des alten und neuen Testaments*, XXIV, 1926.

Picchio, R.: 'Chapter 13 of *Vita Constantini*: Its Text and Contextual Function', *Slavica Hierosolymitana*, 7, pp. 133–52.

Picchio, R.: 'A proposito della Slavia ortodossa e della communità linguistica slava ecclesiastica', *Ricerche slavistiche*, 11, 1963, pp. 105–27.

Pietersma, Albert: *The Apocryphon of Jannes and Jambres the Magicians*, Leiden, 1994.

Pigin, A.V.: *Iz istorii russkoi demonologii XVII veka: Povest' o besnovatoi zhene Solomonii*, St Petersburg, 1998.

Pigin, A.V.: 'Narodnaia mifologiia v severnorusskikh zhitiiakh', *Trudy Otdela drevnerusskoi literatury*, XLVIII, 1993, pp. 331–4.

Pingree, David: ed., *Picatrix. The Latin Version of the Ghāyat Al-Ḥakīm*, Studies of the Warburg Institute 39, London, 1986.

Pingree, David: *The Thousands of Abu Maʿshar*, Studies of the Warburg Institute 30, London, 1968.

Pinkerton, Robert: *Russia: or, Miscellaneous Observations on the Past and Present State of Russia*, London, 1833.

Plessner, M.: 'Hermes Trismegistus and Arab Science', *Studia islamica*, II, pp. 45–59.

Pliny, *Naturalis historia*, Loeb edn., London, 1938–62.

Ploss, H.; Bartels, M.; Bartels, P.: *Das Weib in der Natur- und Volkerkunde*, 11th edn, ed. F. von Reitzenstein, 3 vols, Berlin, 1927.

Pluzhnikov, V.P., and Simonov, R.A.: 'Goroskop Petra I', *Trudy Otdela drevnerusskoi literatury*, XLIII, 1990, pp. 82–100.

Pócs, Éva: *Fairies and Witches at the Boundary of South Eastern and Central Europe*, Folklore Fellows Communications, no. 243, Helsinki, 1989.

'Podlinnye reestry knigam vziatym, po vysochaishemu poveleniiu, iz palat H. I. Novikova v Moskovskuiu dukhovnuiu isvetskuiu tsenzuru', *Chteniia v imp. Obshchestve istorii i drevnosti rossiiskikh pri Moskovskom universitete*, 1871, 3, pp. 17–46.

Podobedova, O.I.: *Miniatiury russkikh istoricheskikh rukopisei. K istorii russkogo litsevogo letopisaniia*, Moscow, 1965.

Poèziia krest'ianskikh prazdnikov, ed. V.G. Bazanova, 2nd edn, Leningrad, 1970.

Pokrovskii, N.N.: 'Ispoved' altaiskogo krestianina', in *Pamiatniki kul'tury. Novye otkrytiia. Ezhegodnik 1978*, Leningrad, 1979, pp. 49–57.

Pokrovskii, N.N.: 'Narodnaia èskhatologicheskaia «gazeta» 1731 g.', in *Issledovaniia po drevnei i novoi literature*, Leningrad, 1987, pp. 290–7.

Pokrovskii, N.N.: 'Staroobriadchestvo vostoka strany kontsa XVII–serediny XIX vv.', in *La cultura spirituale russa*, Trento, 1992, pp. 179–209 (183–5).

Pokrovskii, N.N.: *Sudnye spiski Maksima Greka i Isaka Sobaki*, Moscow, 1971.

Pokrovskii, N.V.: *Siiskii ikonopisnyi podlinninik*, I, St Petersburg, 1895.

Pokrovskii, V.: *Istoricheskaia khrestomatiia*, 2nd edn, Moscow, 1897.

Polnoe sobranie postanovlenii i rasporiazhenii po vedomstvu pravoslavnogo ispovedaniia rossiiskoi imperii, 14 vols, St Petersburg, 1872–1916.

Polnyi pravoslavnyi bogoslovskii èntsiklopedicheskii slovar', St Petersburg, 1913.

Polnyi slovar' sibirskogo govora, Tomsk, 1992.

Polotskii, Simeon: *Orel rossiiskii*, Obshchestvo liubitelei drevnei pis'mennosti 133, 1915.

Pomerantseva, E.V.: *Mifologicheskie personazhi v russkom fol'klore*, Moscow, 1975.

Popov, Ardalion: *Sud i nakazaniia za prestupleniia protiv very i nravstvennosti po russkomu pravu*, Kazan', 1904.

Popov, G.: *Russkaia narodno-bytovaia meditsina: Po materialam ètnograficheskogo biuro kniazia V. N. Tenisheva*, St Petersburg, 1903.

Popov G.V. and Ryndina, A.V.: *Zhivopis' i prikladnoe iskusstvo Tveri XIV–XVI veka*, Moscow, 1979.

Popov, N.A.: 'Rozysk o Moisee Churine o volshebnykh ego pis'makh, proizvodivshiesia v Arkhangel'ske i Kholmogorakh v 1724 godu', *Chteniia v imp. Obshchestve istorii i drevnostei rossiiskikh pri Moskovskom universitete*, 1880, II, pp. 23–35.

Porfiriev, I.Ia.: 'Apokrificheskie molitvy po rukopisiam Solovetskoi biblioteki', *Trudy 4-ogo arkheologicheskogo s"ezda*, II, Kazan', 1891, pp. 1–24.

Porfir'ev, I.: *Apokrificheskie skazaniia o novozavetnykh litsakh i sobytiiakh*, St Petersburg, 1890.

Porfir'ev, I.: *Apokrificheskie skazaniia o vetkhozavetnykh litsakh i sobytiiakh*, Kazan', 1872.

Povest' o Kulikovskoi bitve. Iz letopisnogo svoda XVI veka, Leningrad, 1980.

Povest' o prikhozhenii Stefana Batoriia na grad Pskov, ed. V.I. Malyshev, Moscow–Leningrad, 1952.

Povest' o Zosime i Savvatii, ed. O.A. Kniazevskaia *et al.*, 2 vols, Moscow, 1986.

Poznanskii, N.: 'Sisinieva legenda-obereg i srodnye ei amulety i zagovory', *Zhivaia starina*, 1912, 1, pp. 95–116.

Poznanskii, N.: *Zagovory. Opyt izsledovaniia i razvitiia zagovornykh formul*, Petrograd, 1917 (repr. Moscow, 1995).

Drevnerusskaia pritcha, ed. N.I. Prokof'ev and L.I. Alekhina, Moscow, 1991.

Prokhorov, G.M.: 'K istorii liturgicheskoi poèzii: gimny i molitvy patriarkha Filofeia Kokkina', *Trudy Otdela drevnerusskoi literatury*, XXVII, 1972, pp. 120–49.

Prokhorov, G.M.: 'Knigi Kirilla Belozerskogo', *Trudy Otdela drevnerusskoi literatury*, XXXVI, 1981, pp. 50–68.

Prokhorov, Lev: *Volshebnoe zerkalo . . .*, Moscow, 1794 (SK, no. 8840).

Prokop'eva, N.N.: 'Zhenskaia rubakha v ritualakh zhiznennogo tsikla', in *Ètnosemiotika ritual'nykh predmetov*, St Petersburg, 1993, pp. 58–68.

Propp, V.Ia.: *Istoricheskie korni volshebnoi skazki*, Leningrad, 1986 (first published 1946).

Propp, V.Ia.: *Russkie agrarnye prazdniki*, Leningrad, 1963.

Pseudo-Albertus: *De secretis mulierum, item de virtutibus herbarum, lapidum et animalium*, Amsterdam, 1648, published together with pseudo-Michael Scott, *De secretis naturae*.

Pseudo-Aristotle: The Secret of Secrets: *Sources and Influences*, ed. W.F. Ryan and Charles B. Schmitt, Warburg Institute Surveys IX, London, 1982.

Pskovskie letopisi, ed. A.N. Nasonov, II, Moscow, 1955.

Puhvel, Martin: *The Crossroads in Folklore and Myth*, New York, 1989.

Pushkin, Aleksandr: *Eugene Onegin*, transl. and commentary by Vladimir Nabokov, 4 vols, New York, 1964.

Puteshestvie kitaiskogo poslannika k kalmytskomu Aiuke Khanu, s opisanie zemel' i obychaev rossiiskikh, St Petersburg, 1782.

Pyliaev, M.I.: *Dragotsennye kamni: ikh svoistva, mestonakhozhdeniia i potrebleniia*, 3rd edn, St Petersburg, 1896.

Pypin, A.: 'Issledovaniia dlia ob"iasneniia o lozhnykh knigakh', *Letopis' zaniatii Arkheograficheskoi kommissii*, 1, 1862.

Pypin, A.N.: 'Dlia istorii lozhnykh knig. (Trepetnik. Dni dobrye i zlye. Rafli.)', *Arkhiv istoricheskikh i prakticheskikh svedenii, otnosiashchikhsia do Rossii*, 1860–61, kn. 2, pp. 15–27.

Pypin, A.N.: *Lozhnye i otrechennye knigi russkoi stariny*, pt. 3 of *Pamiatniki starinnoi russkoi literatury, izdaniye G. Kushelev-Bezborodko*, St Petersburg, 1862.

Rabinovich, V.L.: *Alkhimiia kak fenomen srednevekovoi kul'tury*, Moscow, 1979.

Rabinovich, V.L.: *Obraz mira v zerkale alkhimii*, Moscow, 1981.

Radermacher, L.: *Griechische Quellen zur Faustsage*, Vienna–Leipzig, 1927 (= *Sitzungsberichte d. Akad. d. Wiss. in Wien*, Phil.-Hist Klasse 206. Bd. 4. Abh.).

Radojčić, N.: 'Srpski Abagar', *Ètnolog*, Ljubljana, LV, 1930–31.

Radojković, Bojana: *Filakteriji, enamluci, pripojasnice*, Belgrade, 1974.

Rainov, T.: *Nauka v Rossii XI–XVII vekov*, Moscow–Leningrad, 1940.

Ralston, W.R.S.: *Russian Folk-tales*, London, 1873.

Ralston, W.R.S.: *The Songs of the Russian People, as Illustrative of Slavonic Mythology and Russian Social Life*, 2nd edn, London, 1872 (reprinted New York, 1970).

Ramer, Samuel C.: 'Traditional Healers and Peasant Culture in Russia, 1861–1917', in *Peasant Economy, Culture, and Politics of European Russia 1800–1921*, ed. E. Kingston-Mann and T. Mixer, Princeton, 1991, pp. 207–34.

Riabinin, E.A.: 'Iazicheskie priveski-amulety drevnei Rusi', *Drevnosti slavian i Rusi*, Moscow, 1988, pp. 55–62.

Riabinin, E.A.: 'Zoomorfnye ukrasheniia drevnei Rusi X–XIV vv.', SAI (Arkheologiia SSSR, vyp. E1–60), 1981.

Richardson, W.: *Anecdotes of the Russian Empire*, London, 1784.

Riddle, John M.: *Marbode of Rennes' (1035–1123) De Lapidibus*, Wiesbaden, 1977.

Ritner, R.K.: *The Mechanics of Ancient Egyptian Magical Practice*, Studies in Ancient Oriental Civilization, no. 54, Chicago, 1993.

Da Roma alla Terza Roma: Studi e documenti. Series of conference papers published irregularly under various imprints from about 1983.

Romanov, E.R.: *Belorusskii sbornik*. (Vyp. 4. Zagovory, apokrifi i dukhovnye stikhi), Vitebsk, 1891.

Rondeau, Lady Jane: *Letters from a Lady who Resided some Years in Russia*, London, 1775.

Rorschach, Kimerly: *Drawings by Jean-Baptiste Le Prince for the Voyage en Sibérie*, Philadelphia, 1986.

Ross, D.J.A.: *Alexander Historiatus. A Guide to Medieval Illustrated Alexander Literature*, Warburg Institute Surveys, 1, London 1963.

Rossiiskoe zakonodatel'stvo X–XX vekov, Vol. 5 *Zakonodatel'stvo perioda rasstsveta absoliutizma*, Moscow, 1988–97.

Rossiiskoe zakonodatel'stvo X–XX vekov. Vol. 4 *Zakonodatel'stvo perioda stanovleniia absoliutizma*, Moscow, 1986.

Rovinskii, D.: *Russkie gravery i ikh proizvedeniia s 1564 g. do osnovaniia Akademii khudozhestv*, Moscow, 1890.

Rovinskii, D.: *Russkie narodnye kartinki*, 5 vols and Atlas (4 vols of plates), St Petersburg, 1881–4.

Rovinskii, D.: *Russkie narodnye kartinki*, 2 vols, St Petersburg, 1900.

Rowland, Robert: '"Fantasticall and Devilishe Persons": European Witch Beliefs in Comparative Perspective', in *Early Modern European Witchcraft. Centres and Peripheries*, ed. Bengt Ankarloo and Gustav Henningsen, Oxford, 1990, 161–90.

Rozanov, S.: 'Narodnye zagovory v tserkovnykh Trebnikakh', in *Sbornik statei v chest' akademika Alekseia Ivanovicha Sobolevskogo*, Leningrad, 1928, pp. 30–5.

Rozysknye dela o Fedore Shaklovitom i ego soobshchnikakh, III, St Petersburg, 1891.

Russell, J.: 'The Evil Eye in Early Byzantine Society. Archaeological Evidence from Anemurium in Isauria', *Jahrbuch der Österreichischen Byzantinistik* (XVI. Int. Byz. Kongress. Akten, 11/3), XXXII, 3, 1982, pp. 540–56.

The Russian Primary Chronicle, Laurentian Text, ed. and transl. Samuel H. Cross and Olgerd P. Sherbowitz-Wetzor, Cambridge, Mass., 1953.

Russkaia dramaturgiia poslednei chetverti XVII i nachala XVIII v., ed. O.A. Derzhavina, Moscow, 1972.

Russkaia èpicheskaia poèziia Sibiri i Dal'nego Vostoka, ed. A.P. Derevianko et al., Novosibirsk, 1991.

Russkaia svad'ba. Svadebnyi obriad na Verkhnei i Srednei Kokshen'ge i na Uftiuge (Tarnogskii raion Vologodskoi oblasti), ed. N.I. Kalmykova, D.M. Balashov, Iu.I. Marchenko, Moscow, 1985.

Russkie narodnye prazdniki i obriady, Petropavlosk na Kamchatke, 1992.

Russkii fol'klor. Bibliograficheskii ukazatel' 1881–1900, ed. T.G. Ivanova, Leningrad, 1990.

Russkii risovannyi lubok kontsa XVIII–nachala XX veka iz sobraniia Gos. Istoricheskii muzei, Moskva, Moscow, 1992.

Ryan, W.F.: 'Alchemy and the Virtues of Stones in Muscovy', in *Alchemy and Chemistry in the 16th and 17th Centuries*, ed. P. Rattansi and A. Clericuzio, Dordrecht, 1994, pp. 149–59.

Ryan, W.F.: 'Alchemy, Magic, Poisons and the Virtues of Stones in the Old Russian *Secretum Secretorum*', *Ambix*, 37, 1, 1990, pp. 46–64.

Ryan, W.F.: 'Aristotle and Pseudo-Aristotle in Kievan and Muscovite Russia', in *Pseudo-Aristotle in the Middle Ages: The Theology and Other Texts*, edited by Jill Kraye, W.F. Ryan and C.B. Schmitt, Warburg Institute Surveys and Texts XI, London, 1986, pp. 97–109.

Ryan, W.F.: 'Astronomical and Astrological Terminology in Old Russian Literature' (unpublished Oxford D. Phil. dissertation), 1969.

Ryan, W.F.: 'Astronomy in Church Slavonic: Linguistic Aspects of Cultural Transmission', in *The Formation of the Slavonic Literary Languages*, UCLA Slavic Studies 11, Columbus, 1985, pp. 53–60.

Ryan, W.F.: 'Bead Calculator', in *Tradescant's Rarities. Essays on the Foundation of the Ashmolean Museum*, ed. A. Macgregor, Oxford, 1983, p. 253.

Ryan, W.F.: 'Curious Star Names in Slavonic Literature', *Russian Linguistics*, 1, 1974, pp. 137–50.

Ryan, W.F.: 'Drevnerusskii perevod zhizneopisaniia Aristotelia Diogena Laertskogo', *Slavia*, XXXVII, 2 (1968), pp. 348–55.

Ryan, W.F.: 'The Great Beast in Russia: Aleister Crowley's Theatrical Tour to Moscow in 1913 and his Beastly Writings on Russia', in *Symbolism and After. Essays on Russian Poetry in Honour of Georgette Donchin*, Bristol, 1992, pp. 137–61.

Ryan, W.F.: 'John Tradescant's Russian Abacus', *Oxford Slavonic Papers*, new ser., V, 1972, pp. 83–8.

Ryan, W.F.: 'Magic and Divination: Old Russian Sources', in *The Occult in Russian and Soviet Culture*, q.v., pp. 35–58.

Ryan, W.F.: 'Navigation and the Modernization of Petrine Russia: Teachers, Textbooks, Terminology', in *Russia in the Age of the Enlightenment: Essays for Isabel de Madariaga*, Macmillan, London, 1989, pp. 75–105.

Ryan, W.F.: 'The Old Russian Version of the Pseudo-Aristotelian *Secretum secretorum*', *The Slavonic and East European Review*, 56, 2, 1978, pp. 242–60.

Ryan, W.F.: 'The Onomantic Table in the Old Russian *Secreta secretorum*', *Slavonic and East European Review*, XLIX, 1971, pp. 603–6.

Ryan, W.F.: 'The Oriental Duodenary Animal Cycle in Old Russian Manuscripts', *Oxford Slavonic Papers*, new ser., IV, 1971, pp. 12–20.

Ryan, W.F.: 'The *Passion of St Demetrius* and the *Secret of Secrets*. An Onomantic Interpolation', *Cyrillomethodianum*, VIII–IX, 1984–5 (1986), pp. 59–65.

Ryan, W.F.: 'Rathborne's *Surveyor* (1616/1625): the first Russian Translation from English?', *Oxford Slavonic Papers*, XI, 1964, pp. 1–7.

Ryan, W.F.: 'The *Secretum secretorum* and the Muscovite Autocracy', in *Pseudo-Aristotle*: The Secret of Secrets: *Sources and Influences*, pp. 114–23.

Ryan, W.F.: 'Solomon, SATOR, Acrostics and Leo the Wise in Russia', *Oxford Slavonic Papers*, n.s. XIX, 1986, pp. 46–61.

Ryan, W.F.: 'What was the *Volkhovnik*? New Light on a Banned Book', *The Slavonic and East European Review*, 68, 4, 1991, pp. 718–23.

Ryan, W.F.: 'The Witchcraft Hysteria in Early Modern Europe: Was Russia an Exception?', *The Slavonic and East European Review*, 76, 1, 1998, pp. 1–36.

Ryan, W.F., and Wigzell, Faith: 'Gullible Girls and Dreadful Dreams: Zhukovskii, Pushkin and Popular Divination', in *The Slavonic and East European Review*, 70, 4, 1992, pp. 647–69.

Rybakov, B.A.: 'Arkhitekturnaia matematika drevnerusskikh zodchikh', in *Iz istorii kul'tury Drevnei Rusi. Issledovaiia i zametki*, Moscow, 1984, pp. 82–104 (reprint of article in *Sovetskaia arkheologiia*, 1957, 1).

Rybakov, B.A.: *Iazychestvo drevnykh slavian*, Moscow, 1981.

Rybakov, B.A.: 'Iskusstvo drevnikh slavian', in *Istoriia russkogo iskusstva*, 13 vols, Moscow, 1953–64, I, pp. 39–92.

Rybakov, B.A.: 'Prikladnoe iskusstvo i skul'ptura', in *Istoriia kul'tury Drevnei Rusi*, Moscow–Leningrad, 1951, II, pp. 399–404.

Rybakov, B.A.: 'Sbyt produktsii gorodskikh remeslennikov v X–XIIIvv.', *Uchenye zapiski MGU*, 93, 1946, pp. 94–5.

Rybnikov, P.N.: *Pesni, sobrannye P. N. Rybnikovym*, 2nd edn, ed. A.E. Gruzinskii, Moscow, 1910 (reprint, Moscow, 1991).

Rybnikov, P.N.: *Pesni, sobrannye P.N. Rybnikovym*, ed. B.N. Putilov, Petrozavodsk, 1989–91.

Ryndina, A.V. and Popov, G.V.: *Zhivopis' i prikladnoe iskusstvo Tveri XIV–XVI veka*, Moscow, 1979.

Ryu, In-Ho L.: 'Moscow Freemasons and the Rosicrucian Order', in *The Eighteenth Century in Russia*, ed. J.G. Garrard, Oxford, 1973, pp. 198–232.

Saintyves, P.: *Pierres magiques: Bétyles, haches-amulettes, et pierres de foudre. Traditions savants et traditions populaires*, Paris, 1936 (reprint of article in vol. 2 of the *Corpus du folklore préhistorique*).

Sakharov, I.P.: *Skazaniia russkogo naroda. Russkoe narodnoe chernoknizhie. Russkie narodnye igry, zagadki, prislov'ia i pritchi*, St Petersburg, 1885 (reprint Moscow 1990).

Sakovich, A.G.: 'Moskovskaia narodnaia graviura vtoroi poloviny XIX veka', in *Narodnaia kartinka*

XVII–XIX vekov. Materialy i issledovaniia, St Petersburg, ed. M.A. Alekseeva, E.A. Mishina, St Petersburg, 1996, pp. 138–59.

Samodurova, Z.G.: 'K voprosu o kharaktere istochnikov estestvennonauchnykh znanii v Vizantii VII–XII vv.', *Vizantiiskii vremennik*, 53, 1992, pp. 62–70.

Savage-Smith, Emilie, and Smith, Marion B.: *Islamic Geomancy and a Thirteenth-Century Divinatory Device*, Malibu, 1980.

Savel'eva, E.A.: *Biblioteka Ia. V. Briusa*, Leningrad, 1989.

Saxo Grammaticus, Gesta Danorum, ed. A. Holder, Strassburg, 1886.

Saxo Grammaticus: The History of the Danes, ed. and transl. Peter Fisher, 2 vols, Cambridge, 1979.

Schäfer, Peter: 'Jewish Magic Literature in Late Antiquity and Early Middle Ages', *Journal of Jewish Studies*, XLI, 1, 1990, pp. 75–91.

Scheffer, Nathalie: 'Days of the Week in Russian Religious Art', *Gazette des beaux-arts*, 28, 1945, pp. 321–34.

Schiffmann, L.H., and Swartz, M.D.: *Hebrew and Aramaic Incantation Texts from the Cairo Genizah*, Sheffield, 1992.

Schire, T.: *Hebrew Amulets. Their Decipherment and Interpretation*, London, 1966.

Schlosser, Franziska E.: 'Pagans into Magicians', *Byzantinoslavica*, LII, 1991, pp. 49–53.

Schlumberger, G.: 'Amulettes byzantins anciens destinés à combattre les maléfices et maladies', *Revue des études grecques*, V, 1892, pp. 73–93.

Schmitt, Charles B.: 'Francesco Storella and the Last Printed Edition of the Latin *Secretum secretorum*', in *Pseudo-Aristotle*: The Secret of Secrets (see above), pp. 124–31.

Schmitz, H.J.: *Die Bussbücher und die Bussdisziplin der Kirche*, 2 vols, Mainz, 1883–6.

Schreiber, W.L.: *Die Kraüterbücher des XV. und XVI. Jahrhunderts*, Munich, 1924.

Schulze, W.A.: 'Wetter glocken im Rheinland', *Monatshefte für evangelische Kirchengeschichte des Rheinlandes*, 1982, pp. 345–51.

Schulze, W.A.: 'Wetterglocken und Dreikönigsglocken in Wurtemberg-Hohenzollern', *Blätter für würtemburgische Kirchengeschichte*, 1982, pp. 329–42.

Schwartz, James H., and Schwartz, Frances M.: 'Engraved Gems in the Collection of the American Numismatic Society: 1. Ancient Magic Amulets', *Museum Notes*, 24, 1979, pp. 149–97.

Schwillus, Harald: *Kleriker im Hexenprozeß. Geistliche als Opfer der Hexenprozesse des 16. und 17. Jahrhunderts in Deutschland*, Würzburg, 1992.

Scot, Reginald: *The Discovery of Witchcraft*, London, 1930 (edition of the 1584 *editio princeps*).

Scurlock, J.A.: 'Baby-snatching Demons, Restless Souls and the Dangers of Childbirth: Medico-Magical Means of Dealing with some of the Perils of Motherhood in Ancient Mesopotamia', *Incognita*, II, 2, 1991, pp. 135–83.

Seaman, Gerald: 'An Eighteenth-Century Russian Pocket-Book', *Slavonic and East European Review*, 60, 2, 1982, pp. 262–72.

Sedov, V.V.: 'Amulety kon'ki iz drevnerusskikh kurganov', in *Slaviane i Rus'*, Moscow, 1968, pp. 151–7.

Sedov, V.V.: 'Ob odnoi gruppe drevnerusskikh krestov', *Drevnosti slavian i Rusi*, Moscow, 1988, pp. 63–6.

Sedova, M.V.: 'Amulet iz drevnego Novgoroda', *Sovetskaia arkheologiia*, 1957, 4, pp. 166–7 and fig. 1.

Sedova, M.V.: 'O dvukh tipakh privesok ikonok severo-vostochnoi Rusi', in *Kul'tura srednevekovoi Rusi*, Leningrad, 1974, pp. 191–4.

Seks i èrotika v russkoi traditsionnoi kul'ture, ed. A.L. Toporkov, Moscow, 1996.

Seligmann, S.: *Der Bose Blick*, 2 vols, Berlin, 1910.

Seligmann, S.: *Die magischen Heil- und Schutzmittel aus der unbelebten Natur*, Stuttgart, 1927.

Seligmann, S.: 'Die Satorformel', *Hessische Blätter für Volkskunde*, XIII, 1914, pp. 154–83.

Seligmann, S.: *Die Zauberkraft des Auges und das Berufen*, Hamburg, 1922.

Semenov, P.P., *Travels in the Tian'-Shan' 1856–1857*, ed. C. Thomas, Hakluyt Society, 2nd ser. 189, 1998.

Semenova, L.N.: *Ocherki istorii byta i kul'turnoi zhizni Rossii. Pervaia polovina XVIII v.*, Leningrad, 1982.

Semenova-Tian-Shanskaia, O.P.: *Zhizn' Ivana* (=*Zapiski Imperatorskogo Geograficheskogo obshchestva po otdeleniiu ètnografii*, t. 39), St Petersburg, 1914.

Semevskii, M.I.: *Slovo i delo! 1700–1725*, 2nd edn, St Petersburg, 1884 (reprint Moscow, 1991).

Senderovich, S.: *Georgii pobedonosets v russkoi kul'ture*, Berne, 1994.

Seneca, *Naturales quaestiones*, Stuttgart, 1996.

Ševčenko, I.: 'The Greek Sources for the Inscription in Solomon's Chalice in the Vita Constantini', in *To Honor Roman Jakobson*, The Hague, 1967, III, pp. 1806–17.

Shanskii, N.M.: *Ètimologicheskii slovar' russkogo iazyka*, Moscow, 1963–.

Shapovalova, G.G. and Lavrent'eva, L.S.: *Traditsionnye obriady i obriadovoi fol'klor russkikh povolzh'ia*, Leningrad, 1985.

Shchapova, Iu.L.: 'Èlementy znanii po khimii neorganicheskikh soedinenii v Drevnei Rusi', in *Estestvennonauchnye znaniia v Drevnei Rusi*, Moscow, 1980, pp. 15–22.

Shchapova, Iu.L.: 'O khimii i tekhnologii stekla', in *Estestvennonauchnye predstavleniia Drevnei Rusi*, Moscow, 1978, pp. 74–81.

Shchapova, Iu.L.: *Steklo Kievskoi Rusi*, Moscow, 1972.

Shein, P.V.: *Materialy dlia izucheniia byta i iazyka russkago naseleniia severo-zapadnago kraia*, 3 vols, St Petersburg, 1887–92.

Shein, P.V.: *Velikoruss v svoikh pesniakh, obriadakh, obychaiakh, verovaniiakh, skazkakh, i legendakh i t. p.*, St Petersburg, 1898–90.

Shevelov, V.V.: 'Kul'tovye kamni v Kargopol'e', *Rossiiskaia arkheologiia*, 1992, 2, pp. 57–65.

Shipov, N.N.: 'Istoriia moei zhizni. Razskaz byvshago krepostnago krest'ianina Nikolaia Nikolaevicha Shipova, 1802–1862 g.', *Russkaia starina*, 31, 1881, pp. 138–9.

Shorokhov, L.P.: *Korporativno-votchinnoe zemlevladenie i monastyrskie krest'iane v Sibiri v XVII–XVIII vekakh*, Krasnoiarsk, 1983.

Shorter Encyclopedia of Islam, Leiden, 1961.

Shukman, Ann: *Literature and Semeiotics. A Study of the Writings of Iu. M. Lotman*, Amsterdam, 1977.

Shumov, K.E., Chernykh A.V.: 'Beremennost' i rody v traditsionnoi kul'ture russkogo naseleniia Prikam'e', in *Seks i èrotika v russkoi traditsionnoi kul'ture*, ed. A.L. Toporkov, Moscow, 1996, pp. 175–91.

Sibly: *The Popular Fortune Teller . . . by Sibly the Great Astrologer*, London, n.d. but twentieth century.

Siikala, A.-L.: *The Rite Technique of the Siberian Shaman*, Folklore Fellows Communications 220, Helsinki, 1978.

Simashkevich, M.V.: 'Ob obychae gadat' na knigakh Sviashchennogo pisaniia', *Podolskie èparkhial'nye vedomosti*, 1890, 22, pp. 457–65.

Simina, G. Ia.: 'Narodnye primety i pover'ia Pinezh'ia', *Russkii fol'klor*, XXI, 1981, pp. 99–114.

Simonov, R.A., Turilov, A.A., Chernetsov, A.V.: *Drevnerusskaia knizhnost'. (Estestvennonauchnye i sokrovennye znaniia v Rossii XVI v., sviazannye s Ivanom Rykovym)*, Moscow, 1994.

Simonov, R.A.: *Matematicheskaia mysl' Drevnei Rusi*, Moscow, 1977.

Simonov, R.A.: '"Nauka midicheskaia ot matematiki": traktat po vrachebnoi astrologii v russkom perevode XVII v.', in *Bukinisticheskaia torgovlia i istoriia knigi*, Moscow, 1990, pp. 29–43.

Simonov, R.A.: 'O metodologii i metodike izucheniya estestvennonauchnykh predstavlenii srednevekovoi Rusi', in *Estestvennonauchnye znaniia v Drevnei Rusi*, Moscow, 1980, pp. 4–11.

Simonov, R.A.: *Russkaia astrologicheskaia knizhnost' (XI–pervaia chetvert' XVIII veka)*. Moscow, 1998.

Simonov, R.A.: 'Russkie pridvornye «matematiki» XVI–XVII vekov', *Voprosy istorii*, 1986, 1, pp. 76–83.

SK = Svodnyi katalog, q.v.

Skeat, T.C.: 'An Early Medieval "Book of Fate": The Sortes XII Patriarchum. With a note on "Books of Fate" in general', *Medieval and Renaissance Studies*, III, 1954, pp. 41–54.

Skinner, Stephen: *Terrestrial Astrology. Divination by Geomancy*, London, 1980

Skripil', M.O.: 'Povest' o Savve Grudtsyne (teksty)', *Trudy Otdela drevnerusskoi literatury*, V, 1947, pp. 228–33.

Skrynnikov, R.G.: *Gosudarstvo i tserkov' na Rusi XIV–XVI vv. Podvizhniki russkoi tserkvi*, Novosibirsk, 1991.

Skrynnikov, R.G.: *Ivan the Terrible*, Gulf Breeze, FL, 1982 (transl. of *Ivan Groznyi*, Moscow, 1975)

Slavinets'kii, E.: *Leksikon latins'kii E. Slavinets'kogo. Leksikon sloveno-latins'kii E. Slavinets'kogo ta A. Korets'kogo-Satanovs'kogo*, ed. V.V. Nimchuk, Kiev, 1973.

Slovar' drevnerusskogo iazyka (XI–XIV vv), 10 vols, Moscow, 1988.

Slovar' knizhnikov i knizhnosti Drevnei Rusi, ed. D.S. Likhachev, D.M. Bulanin, *et al.*, Leningrad, 1987–.

Slovar' russkikh govorov Priamur'ia, ed. F.P. Filin, Moscow, 1983.

Slovar' russkogo iazyka XI–XVII vv., Moscow, 1975–.

Slovar' russkogo iazyka XVIII v., Leningrad, 1984–.

Slovar' sovremennogo russkogo literaturnogo iazyka, 1st edn, 17 vols, Moscow, 1948–65.

Smilianskaia, E.B.: 'Doneseniia 1754 g, v Sinod suzdal'skogo episkopa Porfiriia "Iakoby vo grade Suzdale koldovstvo i volshebstvo umnozhilos'" in *Khristianstvo i tserkov' v Rossii feodal'nogo perioda*, Novosibirsk, 1989, pp. 254–60.

Smilianskaia, E.B.: '"Suevernaia" knizhitsa pervoi poloviny XVIII veka', *Zhivaia starina*, 1994, 2, pp. 33–6.

Smilianskaia, E.B.: 'Zagovory iz rukopisnykh materialov XVIII veka', in *Russkii èroticheskii fol'klor*, ed. A. Toporkov, Moscow, 1995, pp. 362–70.

Smirnov, Iu.I.: 'Èpika Poles'ia (po zapisiam 1975 g.)', in *Slavianskii i balkanskii fol'klor*, Moscow, 1981, pp. 224–68.

Smirnov, S.I.: 'Materialy dlia istorii drevne-russkoi pokaiannoi distsipliny', *Chteniia v Obshchestve istorii i drevnostei rossiiskikh*, 242, kn. 3, 1912.

Smirnov, V.: 'Narodnye gadaniia v Kostromskom krae. Ocherk i teksty', *Trudy Kostromskogo nauchnogo obshchestva po izucheniiu mestnogo kraia*, XLI (Ètnograficheskii sbornik 4), Kostroma, 1927.

Smith, Morton: 'How Magic was Changed by the Triumph of Christianity', in *Graeco-Arabica. Papers of the First International Congress on Greek and Arabic Studies*, 3 vols, Athens, 1982–3, II, pp. 51–8.

Snegirev, I.M.: *Russkie prostonarodnye prazdniki i suevernye obriady*, I–IV, Moscow, 1837–9.

Sobolevskii, A.I.: *Perevodnaia literatura Moskovskoi Rusi XVI–XVII vv.*, St Petersburg, 1903.

Sokolov, Iu.M.: *Russkii fol'klor*, Moscow, 1941.

Sokolov, M.I.: 'Apokrificheskii material dlia ob"iasneniia amuletov, nazyvaemykh zmeevikami', *Zhurnal Ministerstva narodnogo prosveshcheniia*, CCLXII, 1889, June, pp. 339–68.

Sokolov, M.I.: 'Novyi material dlia ob"iasneniia amuletov, nazyvaemykh zmeevikami', *Drevnosti. Trudy slavianskoi kommissii Imperatorskogo arkheologicheskogo obshchestva*, 1, Moscow, 1895, pp. 134–202.

Sokolov, M.V.: *Ocherki istorii psichologicheskikh vozzreniia v Rossii v XI–XVIII vekakh*, Moscow, 1963.

Sokolova, V.K.: 'Predaniia o kladakh i ikh sviaz' s pover'iami', in *Fol'klor i ètnografiia*, Leningrad, 1970, pp. 169–80.

Sokolovy, B. and Iu.: *Skazki i pesni Belozerskogo kraia*, Moscow, 1915.

Soloukhin, Vladimir: *Searching for Icons in Russia*, London, 1971.

Solzhenitsyn, Alexander: *August 1914*, Harmondsworth, 1974.

Sonnik, goroskop, gadanie, Washington, 1977.

Sorlin, Irène: 'Femmes et sorciers. Note sur la permanence des rituels païens en Russie, XI–XIX siècle', *Travaux et mémoires de recherche d'histoire et civilisation de Byzance*, VIII, 1981, pp. 459–75.

Spasskii, I.G.: 'Proiskhozhdenie i istoriya russkikh schetov', *Istoriko-matematicheskie issledovaniia*, V, Moscow, 1965, pp. 269–420.

Spasskii, I.G.: 'Tri zmeevika s Ukrainy', *Srednevekovaia Rus'*, Moscow, 1976, pp. 358–62.

Speranskii, M.N.: *Russkaia ustnaia slovesnost'*, Moscow, 1917.

Speranskii, M.N.: *Iz istorii otrechennykh knig. 1. Gadaniia po Psaltiri*, Pamiatniki drevnei pis'mennosti, CXXIX, St Petersburg, 1899.

Speranskii, M.N.: *Iz istorii otrechennoi literatury. II. Trepetniki*, Pamiatniki drevnei pis'mennosti i iskusstva, CXXXI, St Petersburg, 1899.

Speranskii, M.N.: *Iz istorii otrechennykh knig. III. Lopatochnik*, Pamiatniki drevnei pis'mennosti, CXXXVI, St Petersburg, 1900.

Speranskii, M.N.: *Iz istorii otrechennykh knig. IV. Aristotelevy vrata ili Tainaia tainykh*, Pamiatniki drevnei pis'mennosti i iskusstva, CLXXI, St Petersburg, 1908.

Speranskii, M.N.: *Rukopisnye sborniki XVIII veka*, Moscow, 1963.

Sperber, D.: *Magic and Folklore in Rabbinic Literature*, Jerusalem, 1994.

Spier, J.: 'Medieval Byzantine Magical Amulets and their Tradition', *Journal of the Warburg and Courtauld Institutes*, 56, 1993, pp. 25–62.

Spitzer, Amitai I.: 'The Hebrew Translation of the *Sod ha-sodot* and its Place in the Transmission of the *Sirr al-asrār*', in *Pseudo-Aristotle, The Secret of Secrets*, pp. 34–54.

SRIa XI–XVII vv.= Slovar' russkogo iazyka XI–XVII vv., Moscow, 1975.

SRIa XVIII = Slovar' russkogo iazyka XVIII v., Leningrad, 1984.

Stara bălgarska literatura, ed. D. Petkanova, Sofia, 1981.

Stepanova, N.I.: *Chernaia magiia. Vorozhba. Koldovstvo*, Novosibirsk, 1994.

Stewart, Charles: *Demons and the Devil. Moral Imagination in Modern Greek Culture*, Princeton, 1991.

Le Stoglav ou les cent chapitres, transl. and ed. E. Duchesne, Paris, 1920.

Stoglav, ed. D.E. Kozhanchikova, St Petersburg, 1863 (reprinted Letchworth, 1971; for French translation and notes see Duchesne edition above.)

Stoyanov, Yuri: 'The Magus as Heresiarch in Medieval Orthodox Heresiology', forthcoming.

Stojanovi , L.: *Katalog narodne biblioteke u Beogradu IV. Rukopisi i stare shtampane kn'ige*, Belgrade, 1903.

Stone, G. ed.: *A Dictionarie of the Vulgar Russe Tongue, attributed to Mark Ridley*. Edited from the late sixteenth-century manuscripts and with an introduction. Bausteine zur slavischen Philologie und Kulturgeschichte, Reihe B: Editionen, Neue Folge, Band 8. Cologne etc, 1996.

Stone, M.E.: 'The History of the Forefathers, Adam and his Sons and Grandsons', *Journal of the Society of Armenian Studies*, 1, 1984, pp. 70–91.

Storms, G.: *Anglo-Saxon Magic*, The Hague, 1948.

Strack, H.L.: *Das Blut in Glauben und Aberglauben der Menschenheit*, Munich, 1900.

Strakhov, Aleksandr B.: *Kul't khleba u vostochnykh slavian. Opyt ètnolingvisticheskogo issledovaniia*, Munich, 1991.

Strakhov, Aleksandr B.: '"Kuvada" po staroobriadcheskoi rukopisi nachala XIX veka', *Palaeoslavica*, 1, 1993, pp. 101–10.

Strakhov, Aleksandr B.: 'Na sviatogo Nikolu . . .', *Palaeoslavica*, 2, 1994, pp. 49–83.

Strakhov, Aleksandr B.: 'Vostochnoslavianskoe *chur*: ot detskoi igry – k vzrosloi magii', *Palaeoslavica*, I, 1993, pp. 41–86.

Strakhov, Aleksandr B. and Heretz, L.R.: 'Disappearing Atlantis. From an Anthology of Polissian Folklore. I.', *Palaeoslavica*, I, 1993, pp. 161–81.

Strizhev, A.N.:*Kalendar' russkoi prirody*, Moscow, 1993.

Struys, Jean: *Les Voyages de Jean Struys en Muscovie . . .*, Amsterdam, 1681, appearing in English as Struys, J.: *The Voiages and travels of John Struys through Italy, Greece, Muscovy, Tartary, Media, Persia, East India, Japan and Other Countries in Europe, Africa and Asia*, London, 1684.

Sudebniki XV–XVI vekov, ed. B.D. Grekov, Moscow–Leningrad, 1952.

Sumarokov, A.S.: *Polnoe sobranie vsekh sochiinenii*, IV, Moscow, 1781.

Sumtsov, N.F.: *Kul'turnye perezhivaniia*, Kiev, 1890 (also in *Kievskaia starina*, 1889–90).

Sumtsov, N.F.: *Khleb v obriadakh i pesniakh*, Kharkov', 1885.

Sumtsov, N.F.: 'K ob"iasneniiu malorusskikh gadanii', *Kievskaia starina*, XXXIV, 1891, August, pp. 314–16.

Svenberg, Emmanuel: *Lunaria et zodiologia latina*, Göteborg, 1963.

Sveshnikova, T.N.: 'O nekotorykh tipakh zagovornykh formul', in *Malye formy fol'klora: Sbornik statei pamiati G.L. Permiakova*, ed. T.N. Sveshnikova, Moscow, 1995, pp. 121 9.

Sviatskii, D.O.: 'Skazanie of Chigire-zvezde i teleskopicheskie nabliudeniia Galileia', *Mirovedenie*, 17, 1 (60), 1928, pp. 1–6.

Svodnyi katalog russkoi knigi grazhdanskoi pechati XVIII veka, 5 vols, Moscow, 1962–7, supplement Moscow, 1975.

Swiderski, Richard M.: 'Clara the Fortune-Telling Chicken or Pop-Pavlovism in Chinatown', *Journal of Popular Culture*, VIII, 1, 1974, pp. 10–14.

Systerova, E.N. and Liakhova, E.A.: *Fol'klor Dal'nerech'ia*, Vladivostok, 1986.

Sytova, A. *et al.*: *The Lubok. Russian Folk Pictures 17th to 19th Centuries*, Leningrad, 1984.

Tailliez, F.: 'La Vierge dans la littérature populaire roumaine', in *Maria. Études sur la Sainte Vierge*, ed. Hubert du Manoir, 2, Paris, 1952, pp. 273–323.

Tannery, P.: 'Notice sur des fragments d'onomatomancie arithmétique', *Notice et extraits des mss.*, XXXI, 2, p. 248 (=*Mémoires scientifiques*, IX, p. 39) .

Tannery, P.: *Mémoires scientifiques*, IV, Toulouse–Paris, 1920, pp. 295–411 (Sciences exactes chez les Byzantins. Mémoire no. 14, 'Le Rabolion (traités de géomancie arabes, grecs, et latins)').

Tarasov, O. Iu.: *Ikona i blagochestie. Ocherki ikonnogo dela v imperatorskoi Rossii*, Moscow, 1995.

Taube, 'The "Poem on the Soul" in the Laodicean Epistle and the Literature of the Judaizers', *Harvard Ukrainian Studies*, 19, 1995, pp. 671–85.

Taube, M.: 'The Kievan Jew Zacharia and the Astronomical Works of the Judaizers', in ΙΟΥΔΑΙΚΗ ΑΡΧΑΙΟΛΟΓΙΑ *In Honor of Professor Moshe Altbauer*, Jews and Slavs, vol. 3, Jerusalem, 1995, pp. 169–98.

Taube, M.: 'Posleslovie k «Logicheskim terminam» Maimonida i eres' zhidovstvuiushchikhsia', in *In memoriam: Sbornik pamiati Ia. S. Lur'e*, St Petersburg, 1997, pp. 239–46.

Taube, M.: 'The Spiritual Circle in the Secret of Secrets and the Poem on the Soul', *Harvard Ukrainian Studies*, 18 (3–4), 1994, pp. 342–55.

Taube, M.: 'Solomon's Chalice, the Latin Scriptures and the Bogomils', *Slovo*, 37, 1987, pp. 161–9.

Tedeschi, John: 'Inquisitorial Law and the Witch', in *Early Modern European Witchcraft. Centres and Peripheries*, ed. Bengt Ankarloo and Gustav Henningsen, Oxford, 1990, pp. 83–118.

Tel'berg, G.G.: *Ocherki politicheskogo suda i politicheskikh prestyplenii v Moskovskom gosudarstve XVII veka* (=*Uchenye zapiski Imperatorskogo Moskovskogo universiteta. Otdel iuridicheskii*, vyp. 39), Moscow, 1912.

Tereshchenko, A.A.: *Byt russkogo naroda*, I–VII, Moscow, 1847-8.

Teteriatnikov, N.: 'Representations of St Nikita flogging the Devil', *Transactions of the Association of Russian American Scholars in U.S.A.*, 15, 1982, pp. 3-33.

Ternovskaia, O.A.: 'Bobochka v narodnoi demonologii slavian: "dusha-predok" i "demon"', in *Materialy k VI Mezhdunarodnomu kongressu po izucheniiu stran iugo-vostochnoi Evropy, Sofiia, 30.VIII.89–6.IX.89*, Moscow, 1989, pp. 151–61.

Thomas, D.L. and L.B.: *Kentucky Superstitions*, Princeton, 1920.

Thomas, Keith: *Religion and the Decline of Magic*, London, 1971.

Thompson, S.: *Motif-Index of Folk-Literature*, revised edn, 6 vols, Copenhagen, 1955–8.

Thomson, F.J.: '*Sensus* or *proprietas verborum* – Medieval Theories of Translation as Exemplified by Translation from Greek into Latin and Slavonic', *Symposium Methodianum. Beiträge der Internationalen Tagung in Regensburg (17. bis 24. April 1985) zum Gedenken der 1100. Todestag des Hl. Method*, Selecta Slavica 13, Neuried, 1988, pp. 675–91.

Thomson, F.J.: 'The Nature of the Reception of Christian Byzantine Culture in Russia in the Tenth to Thirteenth Centuries and its Implications for Russian Culture', *Slavica Gandensia*, 5, 1978, pp. 107–39.

Thomson, R. Campbell: *The Reports of the Magicians and Astrologers of Ninevah and Babylon*, II, London, 1900.

Thorndike, L.: *History of Magic and Experimental Science*, 8 vols, New York, 1934–58.

Thorndike, L.: *The Sphere of Sacrobosco and its Commentators*, Chicago, 1949.

Tikhomirov, M.N.: 'O dvenadtsati mongol'skikh mesiatsakh v starinnoi russkoi pis'mennosti', *Sovetskaia ètnografiia*, 1958, 3, pp. 21–7.

Tikhomirov, M.N.: *Russkaia kul'tura X–XVIII vekov*, Moscow, 1968.

Tikhonravov, N.S.: *Pamiatniki otrechennoi literatury*, I–II, Moscow, 1863 (III in *Sbornik Otdeleniia russkogo iazyka i slovesnosti*, 58, 4, 1894).

Timofeev, A.G.: *Istoriia telesnykh nakananii v russkom prave*, 2nd edn, St Petersburg, 1904.

Titts, A.A.: *Zagadki drevnerusskogo chertezha*, Moscow, 1978.

Tokarev, S.L.: *Religioznye verovaniia vostochnoslavianskikh narodov XIX-nachala XX veka*, Moscow–Leningrad, 1957.

Tolkovaia paleia 1477 goda, Obshchestvo liubitelei drevnei pis'mennosti, XCIII, 1892.

Tolstaia, S.M.: 'K sootnosheniia khristianskogo i narodnogo kalendaria u slavian: schet i otsenka dnei nedeli', in *Iazyki kul'tury i problemy perevodimosti*, ed. B.A. Uspenskii, Moscow, 1987, pp. 154–68.

Tolstoi, N.: 'Iz zametok po slavianskoi demonologii. I. Otkuda d'iavoly raznye', Σεμειωτική: *Materialy vsesoiuznogo simpoziuma po vtorichnym modeliruiushchim sistemam*, I (5), Tartu, 1974, pp. 27-32.

Tolstoi, N.I.: 'Iz zametok po slavianskoi demonologii. II. Kakov oblik d'iavol'skii', *Narodnaia graviura i fol'klor v Rossii XVII–XIX vv.* (K 150 – letie so dnia rozhdeniia D.A. Rovinskogo), Gosudarstvennyi muzei izobrazitel'nykh iskusstv im. A.S. Pushkina, Materialy nauchnoi konferentsii (1975), Moscow, 1976, pp. 288–319.

Tolstoi, N.I.: 'Narodnaia ètimologiia i struktura slavianskogo ritual'nogo teksta', *Slavianskoe iazykoznanie. X. Mezhdunarodnyi s"ezd slavistov. Doklady sovietskoi delegatsii*, Moscow, 1988, pp. 250–64 (reprinted in N.I. Tolstoi, *Iazyk i i narodnaia kul'tura*, Moscow, 1995).

Tolstoi, N.I.: 'Ne – ne "ne"', in N.I. Tolstoi, *Iazyk i narodnaia kul'tura. Ocherki po slavianskoi mifologii i ètnolingvistike*, Moscow, 1995, pp. 341–6 (first published 1971).

Tolstoi, N.I.: 'O prirode sviazei binarnykh protivopostavlenii tipa pravyi–levyi, muzhskoi–zhenskii', in *Iazyki kul'tury i problemy perevodimosti*, ed. B.A. Uspenskii, Moscow, 1987, pp. 169–83.

Tolstoi, N.I.: 'Opolzanie i opoiasivanie khrama', in N.I. Tolstoi, *Iazyk i narodnaia kul'tura. Ocherki po slavianskoi mifologii i ètnolingvistike*, Moscow, 1995, pp. 91–112 (first published 1987).

Tolstoi, N.I.: 'Russk. *chur* i *chush*', *International Journal of Slavic Linguistics and Poetics*, 31–2, 1985, pp. 431–7.

Tolstoi, N.I.: 'Set' (mrezha)', in N.I. Tolstoi, *Iazyk i narodnaia kul'tura. Ocherki po slavianskoi mifologii i ètnolingvistike*, Moscow, 1995, pp. 234–42 (first published 1988).

Tolstoi, N.I.: 'Shilikuny', in N.I. Tolstoi, *Iazyk i narodnaia kul'tura. Ocherki po slavianskoi mifologii i ètnolingvistike*, Moscow, 1995, pp. 270–9 (first published 1985).

Tolstoi, N.I.: 'Vyzyvanie dozhdia', in N.I. Tolstoi, *Iazyk i narodnaia kul'tura. Ocherki po slavianskoi mifologii i ètnolingvistike*, Moscow, 1995, pp. 78–90 (first published 1978).

Tomlin, R.S.O.: *Tabellae Sulis. Roman Inscribed Tablets of Tin and Lead from the Sacred Spring at Bath* (= Pt. 4, *The Curse Tablets*, of Barry Cunliffe, ed., *The Temple of Sulis Minerva at Bath, II: Finds from the Sacred Spring*), Oxford, 1988.

Tomov, Evtim: *Bulgarische Ikonen. Holzschnitt und Metallstiche*, Ramerding, 1989.

Toporkov, A.L.: «Perepekanie» detei v ritualakh i skazkakh vostochnykh slavian', in *Fol'klor i ètnograficheskaia deistvitel'nost'*, St Petersburg, 1992, pp. 114–18.

Townend, B.R.: 'The Narrative Charm with Reference to Toothache', *British Dental Journal*, LXXXV, 2, 1948, pp. 29–34.

Trachtenberg, Joshua: *Jewish Magic and Superstition. A Study in Folk Religion*, New York, 1939.

Traditsionnyi fol'klor vladimirskoi derevni (v zapisiakh 1963–1969), Moscow, 1972.

Trevor-Battye, Aubyn: *A Northern Highway of the Tsar*, London, 1898.

Trevor-Roper, H.: 'The European Witch Craze of the Sixteenth and Seventeenth Centuries', in *idem, Religion, the Reformation, and Social Change*, London, 1967 (2nd edn 1972).

Troianos, Spyros N.: 'Zauberei und Giftmischerei in mittelbyzantinischer Zeit', in *Fest und Alltag in Byzanz*, G. Prinzing, D. Simon, Munich, 1990, pp. 37–51.

Trombley, F.R.: *Hellenic Religion and Christianization c. 370–529*, Leiden, 1993.

Truvorov, A.N.: 'Volkhvy i vorozhei na Rusi, v kontse XVII veka', *Istoricheskii vestnik*, 1889, 6, pp. 701–15.

Tsonev, B.: *Opis na slavianskite r"kopisa v Sofiiskata narodna bibliotek*, II, Sofia, 1923.

Tubach, Frederic: *Index Exemplorum. A Handbook of Medieval Religious Tales*, FF Communications 204, Helsinki, 1969.

Tudorovskaia, E.A.: 'O vnepesennykh sviaziakh narodnoi obriadovoi pesni', in *Fol'klor i ètnografiia. Obriady i obriadovyi fol'klor*, Leningrad, 1974.

Turdeanu, Émile: *Apocryphes slaves et roumains de l'Ancien Testament*, Leiden, 1981.

Turgenev's Literary Reminiscences and Autobiographical Fragments, transl. D. Magarshack, London, 1958.

Turilov, A.A. and Chernetsov, A.V.: 'K kul'turno-istoricheskoi kharakteristike eresi "zhidovstvuiushchikh"', in *Germenevtika drevnerusskoi literatury. Sbornik 1: XI–XVI veka*, Moscow, 1989, pp. 407–29.

Turilov, A.A., and Chernetsov, A.V.: 'O perspektivakh izucheniia pis'mennykh istochnikov, otrazhaiushchikh narodnye verovaniia i obriady vostochnykh slavian', in *Arkheologiia i istoriia Pskova i Pskovskoi zemli*, Pskov, 1988, pp. 52–4.

Turilov, A.A. and Chernetsov, A.V.: 'Otrechennaia kniga Rafli', *Trudy Otdela drevnerusskoi literatury*, XL, 1985, pp. 260–344.

Ulozhenie: edition used: *Sobornoe Ulozhenie 1649*, ed. M.N. Tikhomirov, P. P. Epifanov, Moscow, 1961.

Unbegaun, B.O.: 'Cards and Card-Playing in Muscovite Russia', *The Slavonic and East European Review*, XLI, 1962–3, pp. 25–30.

Unbegaun, B.O.: 'La Religion des anciens slavs', in *Mana. Introduction à l'histoire des religions. II. Les Religions de l'Europe ancienne*, Paris, 1948, pp. 389–445.

Unbegaun, B.O.: 'Les Contemporains de Avvakum en présence des fossiles', *Revue des études slaves*, 38, 1960, pp. 207–9.

Unbegaun, B.O.: 'Les Slaves et la poudre à canon', *Revue des études slaves*, XL (= *Mélanges André Vaillant*), 1964, pp. 207–17.

'Up and Down the City Road', *The Independent*, 20 May 1989.

Usacheva, V.V.: 'Ritual'nyi obman v narodnoi meditsine', *Zhivaia starina*, 1996, 1, pp. 29–30.

Uspenskaia, A.V.: 'Nagrudnye i poiasnye priveski', *Trudy GIM*, 43, 1967, pp. 88–99.

Uspenskii, B.A.: see also Lotman.

Uspenskii, B.A.: 'Antipovedenie v kul'ture Drevnei Rusi', in *Problemy izucheniia kul'turnogo naslediia*, Moscow, 1985, pp. 326–36.

Uspenskii, B.A.: 'Dualisticheskii kharakter russkoi srednevekovoi kul'tury (na materiale "Khozheniia za tri moria" Afanasiia Nikitina)', in *Vtorichnye modeliruiushchie sistemy*, Tartu, 1979, pp. 59–63.

Uspenskii, B.A.: *Filologicheskie razyskaniia v oblasti slavianskikh drevnostei. (Relikty iazychestva v vostochnoslavianskom kul'te Nikolaia Mirlikiiskogo)*, Moscow, 1982.

Uspenskii, B.A.: 'Historia sub specie semioticae', in *Kul'turnoe nasledie Drevnei Rusi*, Moscow, 1976, pp. 286–92.

Uspenskii, B.A.: 'K simvolike vremeni u slavian: "chistie" i "nechistie" dni nedeli', in *Finitis duodecim lustris. Sbornik statei k 60 letiiu prof. Iu. M. Lotmana*, Tallin, 1982, pp. 70–5.

Uspenskii, B.A.: 'The Language Situation and Linguistic Consciousness in Muscovite Rus': The Perception of Church Slavic and Russian', in *Medieval Russian Culture*, ed. H. Birnbaum and M.S. Flier, California Slavic Studies 12, Berkeley etc., 1984, pp. 364–85.

Uspenskii, B.A.: 'Religiozno-mifologicheskii aspekt russkoi ekspressivnoi frazeologii. (Semantika russkogo mata v istoricheskom osveshchenii)', in *Semiotics and the History of Culture. In Honor of Jurij Lotman*, Columbus, Ohio, 1988, pp. 197–302.

Uspenskii [Uspensky], B.A.: 'Schism and Cultural Conflict in the Seventeenth Century', in *Seeking God. The Recovery of Religious Identity in Orthodox Russia, Ukraine and Georgia*, ed. Stephen Batalden, DeKalb, 1993, pp. 106–43.

Uspenskii, B.A.: *The Semiotics of the Russian Icon*, Lisse, 1976.

Uspenskii, B.A.: 'Tsar and Pretender: *Samozvančestvo* or Royal Imposture in Russia as a Cultural-Historical Phenomenon', in Ju.M. Lotman, B.A. Uspenskij, *The Semiotics of Russian Culture*, Ann Arbor, 1984, pp. 259–92.

Uspenskii, B.A., and Shishkin, A.B.: *Trediakovskii i iansenisty*, Paris, 1990 (separately published article from *Simvol*, 23, 1990).

Uspenskii, B.A.: 'Vospriiatie istorii v Drevnei Rusi i doktrina "Moskva Tretii-Rim"', in *Russkoe podvizhnichestvo*, Moscow, 1996, pp. 464–501.

Uspenskii, B.A.: '«Zavetnye skazki» A.N. Afanas'eva', in B.A. Uspenskii, *Izbrannye trudy. II. Iazyk i kul'tura*, 2nd edn, Moscow, 1996, pp. 162–84.

Uspensky (= Uspenskii), B.A.: 'Schism and Cultural Conflict in the Seventeenth Century', in *Seeking God: The Recovery of Religious Identity in Orthodox Russia, Ukraine and Georgia*, ed. Stephen Batalden, DeKalb, 1993, pp. 106–43.

Ustnoe poèticheskoe tvorchestvo russkogo naroda, Moscow, 1954.

Vahros, Igor: *Zur Geschichte und Folklor der grossrussischen Sauna*, FF Communications no. 197, Helsinki, 1966.

Vaillant, A.: *Le Livre des secrets d'Hénoch*, Paris, 1952.

Vaillant, A.: *Textes vieux-slaves*, Paris, 1968.

Van Bekkum, W.J.: 'Alexander the Great in Medieval Hebrew Literature', *Journal of the Warburg and Courtauld Institutes*, 49(1986), pp. 218–26.

Van den Baar, T.: 'On the SATOR Formula', in *Signs of Friendship. To Honour A.G.F. van Holk, Slavist, Linguist, Semiotician*, Amsterdam, 1984, pp. 307–16.

Vasilevich, U.A.: *Mify bats'ka shchyny*, Minsk, 1994.

Vasmer = Fasmer, M: *Ètimologicheskii slovar' russkogo iazyka*, 2nd edn transl. and enlarged by O.N. Trubachev, 4 vols, Moscow, 1964–73.

Vassiliev, A.: *Anecdota graeco-byzantina*, Moscow, 1893.

Veletskaia, N.N.: 'O genezise drevnerusskikh «zmeevikov»', *Drevnosti slavian i Rusi*, Moscow, 1988, pp. 206–10.

Vernadskii, G.V.: *Russkoe masonstvo v tsarstvovanie Ekateriny II*, Petrograd, 1917.

Versnel, H.S.: 'Some Reflections on the Relationship Magic – Religion', *Numen*, XXXVIII, 2, pp. 178–97.

Veselovskii, A.N.: 'Gadatel'nye knigi na Zapade i u nas', *Vestnik Evropy*, 1886, kn. 4.

Veselovskii, A.N.: 'Molitva sv. Sisinniia i Verzilovo kolo', *Zhurnal Ministerstva narodnogo prosveshcheniia*, CCXCIX, 1895, May, pp. 226–34.

Veselovskii, A.N.: 'Opyty po istorii razvitiia khristianskoi legendy, II', *Zhurnal Ministerstva narodnogo prosveshcheniia*, CLXXIII–CLXXV, 1876.

Veselovskii, A.N.: 'Razyskaniia v oblasti russkogo dukhovnogo stikha', *Sbornik Otdeleniia russjogo iazyka i slovesnosti*, XXXII, 4, p. 47.

Veselovskii, A.N.: 'Razyskaniia v oblasti russkogo dukhovnogo stikha. III. Alatyr' v mestnykh predaniiakh Palestiny i legendy o Grale', *Sbornik Otdeleniia russkogo iazyka i slovesnosti*, XXVIII, 2, 1881.

Veselovskii, A.N.: 'Razyskaniia v oblasti russkikh dukhovnykh stikhov. I. Grecheskii apokrif o sv. Feodore', *Zapiski Imp. Akademii nauk*, XXXVI, kn. 1, 1880.

Veselovskii, A.N.: 'Razyskaniia v oblasti russkikh dukhovnykh stikhakh. IV. Son o dereve v povesti grada Ierusalima i stikhe o golubinoi knige', *Zapiski Imp. Akademii nauk*, XL, kn. 2, 1882.

Veselovskii, A.N.: 'Zametki k istorii apokrifov', *Zhurnal Ministerstva narodnogo prosveshcheniia*, CCXLVC, 1886, June, pp. 293–7.

Vetuchov, A.: 'Zagovory, zaklinaniia, oberegi, i drugie vidy narodnogo vrachevaniia, osnovannye na vere v silu slova', *Russkii filologicheskii vestnik*, XLV, 1900, pp. 278–317.

Vickers, Brian: 'On the Goal of the Occult Sciences in the Renaissance', in *Die Renaissance im Blick der Nationen Europas*, ed. G. Kauffmann, Wiesbaden, 1991, pp. 51–93.

Vikan, G.: 'Art, Medicine, and Magic in Early Byzantium', *Dumbarton Oaks Papers*, 38, 1984, pp. 65–86.

Vikan, G.: 'How St Symeon made House Calls: The Role of Pilgrim Tokens in Effecting Miraculous Cures', *Eighth Annual Byzantine Studies Conference. Abstracts of Papers*, Chicago, 1982, p. 22.

Viktorov, A.E.: *Opisi rukopisnykh sobranii v knigokhranilishchakh severnoi Rossii*, St Petersburg, 1890.

Vilinbakhov, G.V.: *Gosudarstvennyi gerb Rossii: 500 let*, St Petersburg, 1997.

Vilinbakhov, G.V.: 'K istorii uchrezhdeniia ordena Andreia Pervozvannogo i evoliutsiia ego znaka', in *Kul'tura i isskusstva Petrovskogo vremeni*, Leningrad, 1977, pp. 144–54.

Vilinbakhov, V.B.: 'Taina ostrova Buiana (po sledam ischeznuvshei tsivilizatsii slavian iazychnykov XI–XII vv. na o. Rugen v Baltiiskom more)', *Nauka i religiia*, 1967, 9, pp. 52–5.

Vinogradov, N.: *Zagovory, oberegi, spasitel'nye molitvy*, St Petersburg, 1909 (originally published in *Zhivaia starina* for 1908).

Vinogradova, L.N.: 'Obshchee i spetsificheskoe v slavianskikh poveriiakh o ved'me', in *Obraz mira v slove i rituale*, Balkanskie chteniia, 1, Moscow, 1992, pp. 58–73.

Vinogradova, 'Seksual'nye sviazi cheloveka s demonicheskimi sushchestvami', in *Seks i èrotika v russkoi traditsionnoi kul'ture*, ed. A.L. Toporkov, Moscow, 1996, pp. 207–24.

Vinogradova, L.N. and Tolstaia, S.M.: 'Ritual'nye priglasheniia mifologicheskikh personazhei na rozhdestvenskii uzhin: formula i obriad', in *Malye formy fol'klora. Sbornik statei pamiati G. L. Permiakova*, ed T.N. Sveshnikova, Moscow, 1995, pp. 166–97.

Vinogradova, L.N. and Tolstaia, S.M.: 'Simvolicheskii iazyk veshchei: venik (metla) v slavianskikh obriadakh i verovaniiakh', in *Simvolicheskii iazyk traditsionnoi kul'tury*, Balkanskie chteniia, 2, Moscow, 1993, pp. 3–36.

Vladimirskii-Budanov, M.F.: 'Akty . . . Rumiantseva', *Chteniia v istoricheskom obshchestve Nestora Letopistsa*, 5, 3, 1891.

Vogel K.: 'Byzantine Science. XII. Superstition and Pseudo-Science', in *The Cambridge Medieval History*, Vol. IV *The Byzantine Empire*, Pt. II *Government, Church and Civilisation*, Cambridge, 1967, ch. XXVIII.

Vologodskii fol'klor, ed. I.V. Efremova, Vologda, 1975.

Voskresenskii, N.A.: *Zakonodatel'nye akty Petra I*, Moscow–Leningrad, 1945.

Vostokov, A.: *Opisanie russkikh i slovenskikh rukopisei Rumiantsovskogo muzeuma*, St Petersburg, 1842.

Vukanović, T.P.: 'Witchcraft in the Central Balkans. I. Characteristics of Witches', *Folklore*, 1989, 1, pp. 9–24.

Vukanović, T.P.: 'Witchcraft in the Central Balkans. II: Protection against Witches', *Folklore*, 100, 2, 1989, pp. 221–35.

Vysotskii, N.F.: *Narodnaia meditsina*, Moscow, 1911.

Vzdornov, G.: *Issledovaniia o Kievskoi Psaltiri*, Moscow, 1978.

Waite, A.E.: *The Book of Ceremonial Magic*, London, 1911.

Wallich, J.U.: *Religio Turcica, Mahometis vista, et Orientalis cum Occidentali antichristo comparatio*, Stade, 1659.

Walter, C.: 'The Intaglio of Solomon in the Benaki Museum and the Origins of the Iconography of the Warrior Saints', *Deltion tes christianikes archaiologikes Etaireias*, 4, 15 1989–90, pp. 33–42.

Walter, C.: 'The Portrait of Saint Parasceve', *Byzantinoslavica*, LVI, 3, 1995, pp. 753–7.

Walter, C.: 'The Thracian Horseman: Ancestor of Warrior Saints', *Byzantinische Forschungen*, XIV, 1, 1989, pp. 659–73.

Ward, Roy Bowen: 'Women in Roman Baths', *Harvard Theological Review*, 85, 2, 1992, pp. 125–47.

Warner, E.A.: *The Russian Folk Theatre*, The Hague–Paris, 1977.

Warner, E., and Kustovski, E.: *Russian Traditional Folksong*, Hull, 1990.

Watson, Gilbert: *Theriac and Mithridatium. A Study in Therapeutics*, London, 1966.

Waugh, D.C.: '*Azbuka znameni lits*: Egyptian Hieroglyphs in the Private Chancery Archive', *Oxford Slavonic Papers*, new series, X, 1977, pp. 46–50.

Waugh, D.C.: *The Great Turkes Defiance. On the History of the Apocryphal Correspondence of the Ottoman Sultan in its Muscovite and Russian Variants*, Columbus, 1978.

Webster, Hutton: *Rest Days. A Study in Early Law and Morality*, New York, 1916.

Weideger, Paula: *History's Mistress. A New Interpretation of a 19th-century Ethnographic Classic*, Harmondsworth, 1986 (a translated selection from Ploss and Bartels, *Das Weib*, q.v., first published by Ploss in 1885).

Weisser, Christoph: *Studien zum mittelalterlichen Krankheitslunar. Ein Beitrag zur Geschichte laienastrologischer Fachprosa*, Würzburger medizinhistorische Forschungen, Bd. 21, Pattensen (Han.), 1982.

Weyer, Johann: *De praestigiis daemonum* in the English version of the 1583 (sixth) edition: *Witches, Devils, and Doctors in the Renaissance*, ed. G. Mora *et al.*, transl. J. Shea, Binghampton, 1991.

Whiston, William: *The Genuine Works of Flavius Josephus*, London, 1806.

Wigzell, Faith: 'Dream Books and Lady Macbeth's Cat', *The Slavonic and East European Review*, 66, 4, 1988, pp. 625–30.

Wigzell, Faith: *Reading Russian Fortunes: Print Culture, Gender and Divination in Russia from 1765*, Cambridge, 1998.

Wigzell, Faith: 'Russians who find Comfort in their Dreams', *The Independent*, June 7, 1989.

Wikman, K. Rob. V.: 'Popular Divination. Some Remarks concerning its Structure and Function', *Transactions of the Westermark Society*, II, 1953, pp. 171–83.

Williams, Edward V.: *The Bells of Russia*, Princeton, 1985.

Wilmot, M. and C.: *The Russian Journals of Martha and Catherine Wilmot*, ed. the Marchioness of Londonderry and H.M. Hyde, London, 1934.

Wilson, Stephen: 'Witchcraft and Heresy', in *Orthodoxie et hérésie*, ed. Christiane d'Haussy, Paris, 1993, pp. 39–52.

Winkler, H.A.: *Salomo und die Karina. Eine orientalische Legende von der Bezwingung einer Kindbettdämonin durch einen heiligen Helden*, Veröffentlichungen des Orientalischen Seminars der Universität Tübingen, 4, Stuttgart, 1931.

Wolfe, L.A.: *Objects with Semitic Inscriptions 1100 B.C.–A.D. 700. Jewish, Early Christian and Byzantine Antiquities*. Auction XXIII, Hotel Bellerive au Lac, Zurich, 20 November 1989.

Woodhouse, C.M.: *Capodistria. The Founder of Greek Independence*, London, 1973.

Worobec, Christine D.: 'Witchcraft Beliefs and Practices in Prerevolutionary Russian and Ukrainian Villages', *The Russian Review*, 54, 1995, pp. 165–87.

Wright, A.R. and Liones, T.E.: *British Calendar Customs: England*, II, London, 1938.

Wright, Lawrence: *Clean and Decent. The Fascinating History of the Bathroom and Water Closet*, London, 1960.

Yule, Henry, and Burnell, A.C.: *Hobson-Jobson: The Anglo-Indian Dictionary*, Ware, 1996 (reprint of 2nd edn 1902, first published 1886).

Zabelin, I.: *Domashnii byt russkikh tsarei v XVI i XVII st.*, Moscow, 1990 reprint of t. 1, ch. 1 of *idem*, *Domashnii byt russkogo naroda v XVI i XVII st.*, 4th edn, Moscow, 1918.

Zabelin, I.: *Domashnii byt russkikh tsarits v XVI i XVII st.*, 2nd edn, Moscow, 1872; 3rd edn, Moscow, 1901.

Zabelin, M.E.: 'Sysknye dela o vorozheiakh i koldun'iakh pri tsare Mikhaile Fedoroviche', *Kometa*, 1851, pp. 469–92.

Zabylin, M.: *Russkii narod. Ego obychai, obriady, predaniia, sueveriia i poèziia*, Moscow, 1880 (reprint 1989).

Zakonodatel'nye akty russkogo gosudarstva vtoroi poloviny XV–pervoi poloviny XVII veka, Leningrad, 1986.

Zamaleev, A.F.: *Filosofskaia mysl' v srednevekovoi Rusi*, Leningrad, 1987.

Zapiski I. V. Lopukhina, London, 1860 (reprinted Moscow, 1990).

Zelenin, D.: 'Iz byta i poèzii krest'ian Novgorodskoi gubernii', *Zhivaia starina*, 1905, 1–2, pp. 1–76.

Zelenin, D.K.: *Izbrannye trudy. Ocherki russkoi mifologii: umershie neestvennoiu smert'iu i rusalki*, Moscow, 1995 (edited and annotated version of work first published in Petrograd in 1916).

Zelenin, D.: *Russische (ostslavische) Volkskunde*, Berlin and Leipzig, 1927.

Zelenin, D.K.: *Velikorusskie skazki Permskoi gubernii*, Moscow, 1991 (first published Petrograd, 1914, here with notes by T.G. Bereguleva-Dmitrieva).

Zguta, R.: 'Monastic Medicine in Kievan Rus' and Early Muscovy', in Henrik Birnbaum and Michael S. Flier, eds, *Medieval Russian Culture*, California Slavic Studies, XII, Berkeley etc., 1984, pp. 54–70.

Zguta, R.: 'The Ordeal by Water (Swimming of Witches) in the East Slavic World', *Slavic Review*, 36, 1977, pp. 220–30.

Zguta, R.: 'The Pagan Priests of Early Russia: Some New Insights', *Slavic Review*, XXXIII, 1974, pp. 259–66.

Zguta, R.: 'Witchcraft and Medicine in Pre-Petrine Russia', *The Russian Review*, XXXVII, 1978, pp. 438–48.

Zguta, R.: 'Witchcraft Trials in Seventeenth-Century Russia', *American Historical Review*, 82, 5, 1977, pp. 1187–1207.

Zhuravlev, A.F.: *Domashnyi skot v pover'iakh i magii vostochnykh slavian*, Moscow, 1994.

Zhurzhalina, N.P.: 'Datirovka drevnerusskikh privesok-amuletov', *Sovetskaia arkheologiia*, 1961, 2, pp. 122–40.

Zier, Mark: 'The Healing Power of the Hebrew Tongue: An Example from Late Thirteenth-Century England', in *Health, Disease and Healing in Medieval Culture*, ed. Sheila Campbell, Bert Hall, David Klausner, New York, 1992, pp. 103–18.

Zimin, M.M.: *Koverninskii krai (=Trudy Kostromskogo nauchnogo obshchestva po obucheniiu mestnogo kraia*, vyp. 17), Kostroma, 1920.

Zinov'eva, V.P.: 'Ukazatel' siuzhetov sibirskikh bylichek i byval'shchin', in *Lokal'nye osobennosti russkogo fol'klora Sibiri. Issledovaniia i publikatsii*, Novosibirsk, 1985.

Zmeev, L.F.: *Russkie vrachebniki*. Pamiatniki drevnei pis'mennosti, CXII, St Petersburg, 1895.

Zubov, V.P.: 'Neizvestnyi russkii perevod "Traktata o sfere" Ioanna de Sakrobosko', *Istoriko-astronomicheskie issledovaniia*, VIII, Moscow 1962, pp. 221–39.

Zubov, V.P.: 'Primechanie k «Nastavleniiu, kak cheloveku poznat' schislenie let» Kirika Novgorodtsa', *Istoriko-matematicheskie issledovaniia*, VI, Moscow, 1953, pp. 173–212.

Zubov, V.P.: 'Quelques notices sur les versions russes des écrits et commentaires lulliens', *Estudios lulianos*, II, 1, 1958, pp. 63–6.

Zvezdochtets: Russkaia fantastika XVII veka ed. Iu.M. Medvedeva, Biblioteka russkoi fantastiki, 2, Moscow, 1990.

INDEX

This index does not include routine references to Christianity, God, the Devil, Russia, the Ukraine, Belorussia, most geographical names and most works listed in the bibliography. Names of saints, their icons and feast days are grouped together